Bagster's Bible Handbook

Bagster's Bible Handbook

Introduction by Dr. Walter Elwell

FLEMING H. REVELL COMPANY
OLD TAPPAN, NEW JERSEY

Library of Congress Cataloging in Publication Data

Bagster's Comprehensive helps to Bible study.
    Bagster's Bible handbook.

    Originally published as: Bagster's Comprehensive
helps to Bible study.
    1. Bible—Handbooks, manuals, etc.   I. Samuel
Bagster and Sons.   II. Title.
BS417.B33   1983   220   82-21613
ISBN 0-8007-1334-6

CONTENTS

PREFACE

This volume is a classic. It was first issued near the end of the nineteenth century by the distinguished Bible publishers Samuel Bagster and Sons of London. Except for the Introduction, which is unique to this edition, this is an exact reproduction of the *Bagster's Comprehensive Helps to Bible Study*. It reflects the devout character and meticulous care for detail of the elder Samuel Bagster, who was twice presented in the court of the king in recognition of his craftmanship.

With the hope that this concise treasury of Bible helps will aid persons to know the Lord Jesus Christ, through the study of God's Word, we are pleased to make it available to the public once again.

THE PUBLISHERS

FOREWORD

God has spoken to us supremely in the Bible, but for many people it is a closed book. The reasons for this are many. Some do not want to know what it says. Others never seem to find the time. Yet others try, but fail to understand it and so give up. Doubtless, many other reasons could be found.

For those who have tried, but failed, there is hope. It could well be that the reason is not that the Bible is all that hard to follow, but that the terms used or ideas expressed are foreign to the reader. If these were cleared up, the light would begin to shine through.

This book is designed to do just that. It is an attempt to put together introductory information that will help a person to "see the forest"—and the trees—at the same time. There is overview, giving the broad perspective, and there are detailed collections of information, giving guidance in the particulars. This volume stresses in the very beginning the necessity for both intelligent and devout reading. To read without intelligence is to wander in the darkness; to read without devotion is to leave our souls unfed. Both aspects are stressed in this book of helps to Bible study.

After reading the introductory material, you might wish to begin with a quick run through the summary of the Bible as a whole in chapters VII–XVIII. Here there are excellent, brief surveys of the contents of each book, including the Apocrypha and the history of the time between the two Testaments. There is nothing here that should offend anyone who is concerned about what the Bible says, although not everyone needs to agree with precisely everything that is said, especially regarding authorship. For example, the section called "The Hexateuch" (Chapter VIII) espouses a theory called "the documentary hypothesis" that finds differing strands of traditions in the first six books of the Bible, called the Jahvistic source (J), the Elohistic source (E), the Book of Deuteronomy (D), and the Priestly code (P). Most evangelicals would reject this formulation, because it disallows Moses as the author of the Pentateuch. However, the allowance of this view does not, in the minds of the writers of this handbook, preclude the Bible's full inspiration and authority. This is clearly stated in Chapter I.7 where inspiration is extended to the whole of Scripture, including its factual statements. The Bible does not lead us astray.

Elsewhere, a traditional conservative position is taken, especially in the New Testament where all the documents are ascribed to the writers usually associated with them.

When the overview is digested, the reader could turn to a more detailed study of many individual items to be found in pages 159–229. Here there is chronology, prophecy, a harmony of the Gospels, parables, miracles, Old Testament quotes in the New Testament, proper names, an index of ideas, and more. All of this provides a rich resource that can be used for virtually a lifetime of study.

Interesting historical material can be found on pages 83–158, covering such subjects as feasts, ancient dress, Jewish manners and customs, arms, armor, music, disease, plants, animals, geography, and much more. Here, too, information is available that will enhance the reading of the Bible, making it more understandable. An additional benefit is added for those who desire it, in the form of brief introductions to both Hebrew and Greek, the languages in which almost all of the Bible was written.

Because Bible study advances so quickly, it is necessary to add a brief supplement to the section "Modern English Versions" (Chapter V), not because what is there is inaccurate, but because more translations are available now than when this study guide was first prepared. Continuing the list:

12. The Revised Standard Version (RSV)

In 1937 a committee was formed to revise the American Standard Version of 1901 "in the light of the results of modern scholarship . . . for use in public and private worship, and to be in the direction of the simple, classic English style of the King James Version." The New Testament appeared in 1946 and the Old Testament in 1952. The committee, under the chairmanship of Luther A. Weigle, consisted of many of the best biblical scholars of the day, mainly of a liberal persuasion.

The publication of this translation, which consisted of over a million copies, was celebrated in an estimated three thousand religious services attended by at least two million people. It was an event unparalleled in religious publishing history. However, a storm of protest greeted the RSV's appearance because of the Bible's seemingly liberal bent, such as translating *almah* in Isaiah 7:14 as "young woman" rather than "virgin," and printing the pronouns referring to Jesus in lowercase, which in the minds of some denied His Deity. This protest even reached the stage of public Bible burnings.

As a translation, the RSV may be said to have accomplished what the publishers intended. It is literal without being wooden, and up-to-date without being faddish. It reads well enough, even if a bit pedestrian in places. It contains questionable readings, for a conservative, at any rate, preferring in several places translations that cast a doubt upon the accuracy of the biblical text. On the whole, however, it is a translation that is easy to read and understand, which is the real test that ought to be applied.

13. The New English Bible (NEB)

An ecumenical committee was established in 1947, which was gradually enlarged until its work was completed in 1970 when the entire Bible was offered to the public. The committee consisted mainly of British scholars; their aim was to provide "English readers, whether familiar with the Bible or not, with a faithful rendering of the best available Greek text into the current speech of our own time, and a rendering which should harvest the gains of recent Biblical scholarship." Regarding the Old Testament, it was said that "the translators have endeavoured to avoid anachronisms and expressions reminiscent of foreign idioms. They have tried to keep their language as close to current usage in England as possible while avoiding words and phrases likely soon to become obsolete."

The translation is flowing, elegant, and quite clear. The aim to use current usage of England is a strength and a weakness. For Americans it is perhaps too "English" and hence not on their own linguistic level. It has been criticized for being paraphrastic and overly wordy in places. Its style has been praised and condemned alike, no doubt reflecting the particular feelings of the reviewer. The text used was eclectic and many of the readings are quite well taken.

14. The New American Standard Bible (NASB)

Under the guidance of the Lockman Foundation, a new translation was prepared by fifty-five evangelical scholars, with the New Testament appearing in 1960 and the Old Testament in 1971. It is not simply a revision of the American Standard Version (ASV) of 1901, but is basically a new translation following the principles used in the ASV. The text used is a critical one, in similar fashion as the ASV, and not the *Textus Receptus* that underlies the KJV. The Dead Sea Scrolls were allowed to influence the translation in the appropriate places, but not unduly. Subsequent editions of the NASB have corrected some of the earlier infelicities in the translation, following the Lockman Foundation's principle of updating when appropriate.

As a translation the NASB reads well enough, but it could hardly be called flowing. Its treatment of questions requiring a negative answer is distinctive, but its excessive use of italics is distracting. Its theological conservatism is seen in the retention of traditional theological language. It is literal to the point of severity in places. A distinct improvement on the ASV, the NASB is widely used, but will probably not become an American standard for Bibles.

15. The Living Bible (TLB)

Begun in 1954 by Kenneth N. Taylor and requiring seventeen years to complete, *The Living Bible* has become a widely used Bible alongside more traditional translations. It began to appear in 1962 as *The Living Letters;* in 1971 the entire Bible was published. It is one of the most controversial Bible projects of this century, being soundly condemned by some and highly praised by others. The crux of the difficulty lies in the fact that it is a paraphrase, rather than a translation. The defenders of *The Living Bible* point out that any rendering of a literary work from one language into another involves paraphrase, even when it is called a translation. In this regard TLB only does it more thoroughly and consistently. They also point to its manifest popularity, owing to its readability and the clarity of its ideas. Detractors of TLB argue that it wanders too far from the original texts, is often eccentric in its ideas, and lowers the dignity of God's Word by making it read like a comic book.

Objectivity considered, *The Living Bible* has both strengths and weaknesses. It is unclear in places, excessively paraphrastic, and inconsistent in its handling of given ideas. Odd neologisms also occur, such as "Ausia" being used to designate Asia Minor. It is also true that one would have a hard time guessing what the Greek or Hebrew text said by reading *The Living Bible.* However, it is excellent in places and does communicate in a way that no other twentieth-century Bible does. As a resource to be used for study, alongside a more literal translation, TLB is in a class by itself.

16. **The New International Version** (NIV)

A Committee on Bible Translation was formed in 1965 which consisted of fifteen scholars. This was enlarged in 1967 when the New York International Bible Society took over sponsorship of the project and Edwin A. Palmer became the executive secretary. The New Testament appeared in 1973 and the Old Testament in 1978. The first edition of the complete Bible was the largest—1.3 million copies—in printing history for an English Bible. More than 110 evangelical scholars eventually participated in the whole project, being drawn from most of the English-speaking world, not the United States alone.

Textually, in the Old Testament, "the Masoretic Text as published in the latest editions of *Biblia Hebraica* has generally been followed except where the Dead Sea Scrolls, the Septuagint and other versions, variant manuscript readings and internal evidence have led to corrections in the Masoretic text." For the New Testament a critical, eclectic text was used.

As a translation, the NIV is innovative without being extreme, traditional, without being stolid. It strives for, and achieves, a certain dignity befitting religious literature. It is highly accurate and easily understood, using basically modern English to convey its message. It has tried to steer a middle course between excessive literalism and wanton paraphrase, but it has been criticized for being overly conservative in its theological renderings and dull in places.

17. **The New King James Version** (NKJV)

Entirely the work of Thomas Nelson Publishers, the New King James New Testament appeared in 1979 and the Old Testament in 1982. More than 130 conservative scholars from a wide range of Protestant denominations collaborated in this project, with Arthur Farstad serving as the executive editor. The NKJV intends to be in the tradition of the KJV—being a translation, not a paraphrase. Its translators retain the KJV's theological words and cadences. Its goal is to unlock "for today's readers the spiritual treasures found especially in the Authorized Version of the Holy Scriptures." The text followed is not that of modern critical scholars, but a somewhat modernized *Textus Receptus.*

As a translation, the NKJV is an admirable production. It could hardly be called brilliant, but it is easy to read and quite accurate. For those who hold an unqualified allegiance to the KJV and its textual base, this Bible is almost all they could hope for. It does modernize the KJV and corrects most of its most obvious flaws. For those who are not so committed to the KJV, this new Bible will not have much appeal.

It is the sincere desire of those who make this handbook available to you that it be of help in your Christian life. If it makes even one section of the Bible easier to understand, then it has accomplished at least a part of its purpose. If, in the process, it opens your heart up to God, who is the ultimate source of the Scriptures, and draws you closer to Him, then it has supremely accomplished its purpose. For what is the purpose of anything but to draw us more fully into the presence of God, in whom "we live and move and have our being"?

Walter A. Elwell, PhD
Professor of Bible and Theology
Wheaton College Graduate School

Bagster's
Bible
Handbook

BIBLE HELPS.

INTRODUCTION.

Two things are essentially requisite if the reading of the Bible is to be really interesting and profitable to us. It should be studied both intelligently and devotionally.

1. **Intelligent Study.**—The first requisite must be emphasised, not because it is by any means the more important of the two, but because it is much the more likely to be overlooked by people who nevertheless value the Bible very highly. The neglect of this condition is the reason why many earnest readers fail to find the good they expect to derive from their use of the Sacred Scriptures.

There has come down to us in the Bible a collection of ancient literature consisting of different books, written by different hands, for different people, under different circumstances, and often with very different purposes.

This collection embraces a great variety of styles of composition in History, Biography, Poetry, Proverbs, Discourses, Letters, &c.

The Books are evidently coloured by the characters of the various writers—the diligent historian—the broad-minded statesman—the enthusiastic seer—the cultured scholar—the earnest evangelist.

It must be clear that for the appreciative study of such works it is necessary to discriminate between one book and another, to learn all we can about the history of each of them, to consider the circumstances under which they were written, and thus to try to understand, to get into sympathy with, to "put ourselves in the place" of the ancient people who received them. Then it is necessary to use common-sense to avoid the twisting of the plain meaning of words, the finding of types and figures where they were never intended, and—a most frequent mistake—the resorting to isolated texts for the support of doctrines regardless of their context and of the circumstances of their writers and of the readers for whom they were originally designed.

2. **Devout Reading.**—The second requisite—that of studying the Bible reverently, with the heart—is still more important. Such is the peculiar character of the Divine Revelation that the most unintelligent reading, accompanied by a humble, devotional spirit, cannot fail to receive some blessing, although it must be disappointed of the best results of that reading which is both devotional and intelligent; while the most scholarly and critical study without reverence is utterly useless, not only for spiritual advantage, but even for a simple understanding of the meaning of Scripture. Therefore our study of the Bible should be undertaken with an earnest prayer for the guidance of the Holy Spirit, by whom the book was originally inspired, as in the words of the Psalmist, "Open Thou mine eyes that I may behold the wondrous things out of Thy Law" (Ps. cxix. 18).

For Biblical information generally, **see** Hastings' *Dictionary of the Bible.*

CHAPTER I.

GENERAL CHARACTERISTICS OF THE BIBLE.

1. **Names and Titles.**—In the Old Testament we first meet with references to the expression, "Book of the Law," as the title of a recognised inspired collection of a portion of the Bible (*e.g.*, 2 Kings xxii. 8). After the return from the Captivity the word "Scripture" gradually emerges as a distinctive title; but inasmuch as this word came to be confined to those portions of the Old Testament which were not included in "The Law" and "The Prophets," and which were called in Greek "Hagiographa" or "Sacred Writings," a word meaning "The Reading" was employed for the whole collection. The Greek "*Graphé*," or "Scripture," however, is used in the New Testament to designate the Old Testament generally (*e.g.*, Mark xii. 10), and among the first Christian Fathers it seems still to have been used in that sense. It was also applied to the New Testament in the second century after Christ. "Scripture," then, is the earliest name for the whole Bible. The title "Bible" does not seem to have come into use until the fifth century of our era. It is derived from the Greek "*Biblia*" which means "Books." The Bible consists of "The Books;" it is a whole library in itself; it is pre-eminently *the* library, and it needs no more distinctive designation than that implied by the grand simplicity of its title. The word "Testament," signifying a "will," is a translation of a Greek word which has a second meaning, viz., a "covenant." There can be no doubt that this second meaning—not the one that now stands for the title of the two portions of our Bible—is the true one. The Jewish Scripture is "The Old Covenant;" the Christian Scripture is "The New Covenant."

2. **Historical Origin.**—The Old Testament consists of the Sacred Literature of the Jews. The New Testament was also written by men who

were Jews, either by birth or by adoption. In origin the Bible is a Semitic Book. Nearly all of it was written in the East, and the whole by men of an Eastern race. It is Oriental in tone and flavour throughout. This fact needs to be borne in mind when we attempt to translate its rich, bold imagery into the dull, prosaic, matter-of-fact language of the West. At the same time the Orientalism of the Bible is a distinct advantage in translation, and this on two accounts. In the first place, the Eastern style of thought is concrete and illustrative. Instead of presenting us with naked abstract ideas, it clothes its truths in the forms of tangible things. It speaks in parables, and we can often translate the parable where the subtle thought of a remote order of mind could not be conveyed in direct language, because the parable deals with things that are the same to the eye whatever words are used in describing them. This helps the Bible to become a book for all peoples and ages. Then, in the second place, while the West has passed through the greatest revolutions of habit and civilisation, the East is changeless. The manners and customs of Syria to-day are those of Canaan in the days of Abraham. The immobile East is a perennial commentary on the Bible. Here we have a providential fitness in the Bible to become a book intelligible in its smallest details to inquiring minds of all generations. Lastly, the Bible is an ancient book. The latest word of it was written some eighteen centuries ago. Therefore information on ancient history will help us to understand the book. But the everlasting freshness which lives in it, in spite of its archaic flavour, is one grand proof of its eternal truth and Divine authority. It is not a curious relic from the ruins of antiquity only fit to be kept under a glass case in a museum. It is the most modern book in its present-day interest and application to real life.

3. **Varied Structure.**—We can never complain of monotony in the Bible. Its pattern is richly variegated in shape and colour ; it is as different as possible from the dull uniformity of the Koran. There are characteristic differences of style among the writers. On the other hand, these very variations help to emphasize the wonderful unity of the Bible. It is not by accident that men have come to bind the several books into one volume. The Bible is essentially one. It is not one as a dead mass of sandstone is one, with every particle the exact counterpart of its fellow ; but it is one as the tree is one, though the roots do not visibly resemble the leaves. It has an organic unity ; it is one growth ; there is one spirit and life in it. This implies a higher unity than that of monotonous uniformity. It testifies to the presence of the One Spirit breathing through all the different authors, and slowly ripening one grand purpose of redemption throughout the long ages.

4. **Gradual Process.** —Revelation has been gradual and progressive. God did not make known to Abraham all that He revealed to St. Paul. The Divine self-manifestation given to the Jews is far exceeded by that bestowed on Christians. We have a historical revelation—one given at different times and by advancing stages. The neglect of this truth has led to great confusion in comparing Scripture with Scripture. Although the acorn is vitally identical with the oak, it would be absurd to limit our notion of the full-grown tree out of consideration for the seed from which it sprang, or to complain of a discord and contradiction in nature because the one was not identical in shape and size with the other. The difficulties rising out of the seeming inconsistency between various parts of the Bible, and the objections which have been urged against earlier portions of Scripture by viewing them in the full light of the New Testament, chiefly result from the great mistake of ignoring the progressive course of revelation. When this is recognised those difficulties assume a very different character.

5. **Literary Form.**—The Bible is a work of literature, not a manual of scientific theology. It is not composed in the cold, precise phraseology of science. It glows with life and fire. It abounds in metaphors. It was not written for theologians, but for all sorts and conditions of men. It is essentially a popular book. The profoundest thoughts which can ever engage the mind of a philosopher are in it, and it is far from being simple in the sense of shallowness. Nevertheless, it does not address itself to the learned classes, but to the people. Its language is colloquial and fluent. Therefore it must be read in a natural and popular sense. The immense benefits conferred by the spread of the Bible among all classes of people is a proof of the error of the Roman Catholic notion that it is a dangerous book, not to be entrusted in the hands of ordinary people for fear of its being misunderstood. In its main teaching the Bible is intelligible to all who will read it in the right spirit.

6. **Spiritual Character.**—We cannot fail to detect a wonderful elevation in the tone and spirit of the Bible throughout. Even when it treats of common everyday events it lifts them into a higher atmosphere. Although it is compelled to deal with the most painful instances of moral degradation, its handling of them is as pure as it is courageous. Occasionally it employs the keen weapon of sarcasm, but it is too serious to be flippant, and too sympathetic to be cynical. It tears off cloaks of hypocrisy and self-deception, but never so as to degrade the idea of humanity or induce despair of the future. It is the most heart-searching of books, and yet it is the most hopeful. It is always on the side of right ; to read it reverently is to put one's self under the influence of a power that makes for righteousness. Truthfulness is stamped on every page. These wonderful moral and spiritual characteristics of the Bible point to something far beyond its literary merits ; they are features of its superhuman relations as an inspired record of Divine revelation.

7. **Inspiration.**—The word *Revelation* stands for the act of God in making truth known to men, and then, in a secondary sense, for the truth itself which is thus made known ; *Inspiration* is the name of the special influence of the Holy Spirit under which the writers of the Bible worked. We speak of the revelation of God in the Bible, and of the inspiration of the writers of the Bible.

(1.) *The Scope of Inspiration.*—Some have attempted to limit this entirely to spiritual truths to the exclusion of facts of history, &c. But the revelation of God is largely made by means of these facts. It is as important for us to know the facts which embody Divine ideas as it is for us to have naked thoughts truly presented to us. Moreover, it is impossible to separate the facts and the ideas of revelation. They blend together—the ideas usually growing out of the facts even when they are not entirely enshrined within them. Jesus Christ expressly promised the aid of the Holy Spirit in helping the historical memory (John xiv. 26). On the other hand, the writers of the Bible were evidently free to use their several characteristic styles of diction, and to clothe their records in the phrases current in their times. There is no reason to suppose that they were inspired to know more than the revelations which they recorded. They were required to use all reasonable human means for ascertaining knowledge within their reach. As historians they quoted from previous authorities. Thus the Book of Jasher is cited in the Old Testament, and St. Luke tells us that he referred to eye-witnesses of the life of Christ in collecting materials for his Gospel (Luke i. 1-4).

(2.) *The Proof of Inspiration.*— Our Lord frequently appealed to the Old Testament as a book of Divine authority; and He promised to the chief writers of the New Testament the help of the Holy Spirit (John xiv. 26), and commissioned them with His own authority (Matt. xxviii. 18-20). Therefore when we first believe in Jesus Christ we are largely helped to believe in the inspiration of the Bible. Then revelation is often self-evidencing. The veil is lifted so that we may see truth with our own eyes. A discovery which we could never have reached by ourselves is brought to us, but after it has been thus once made known we can now recognise its truth. It is like the solution of an enigma when the key has been supplied. The highest truth convinces us of its own worth by its very elevation. But further confirmation has been added. To contemporaries miracles were sometimes given as "signs" attesting the authority of a Divine messenger. For us the great results of revelation in the history of Christendom afford the principal proofs of the reality of the revelation. This test has been supplied us by our Lord as the rule for judging between the true and the false prophet. "By their fruits ye shall know them" (Matt. vii. 15-18). See Paterson Smyth, *How God Inspired the Bible;* Lee, *The Inspiration of the Scriptures;* Rowe, *The Nature and Extent of Divine Inspiration;* Myers, *Catholic Thoughts on the Bible, &c.;* Briggs, *Biblical Study,* and *The Bible, the Church, and Reason;* Horton, *Revelation and the Bible;* Sanday, *Bampton Lectures, Inspiration.*

CHAPTER II.

ORIGINAL LANGUAGES.

THE original language of the Old Testament is Hebrew, with, in the later books of Jeremiah, Daniel, and Ezra, a sprinkling of Aramaic, while that of the New Testament is Greek.

1. **The Hebrew.** — Hebrew and Aramaic are branches of a family of languages spoken by tribes of the same stock occupying a region in South-Western Asia, including Aramæa, with Babylon and Nineveh in the north, Syria in the middle, and Arabia in the south—Aramaic being spoken in the first, Hebrew, with Phœnician, in the second, and Arabic, with Ethiopic, in the third—all of which go under the name of Semitic, as being languages of the Semitic race, or the descendants of Shem. These languages are all composed of words with triliteral roots, and are all of a type in keeping with the impassioned spirit and unbending temper of the tribes that spoke them.

As the great ancestor of the Jewish people came out of the north, the dialect he spoke must have been Aramaic; but by the time the speech of his descendants assumed a written form we find they had foregone the language of their first father, and adopted the language of Canaan, which was the primitive Hebrew. The Hebrew letters are written from right to left, so that the words are read backwards, and the book throughout in this manner, beginning at what to us looks like the end. The alphabet consists exclusively of consonants. In original Hebrew there were no indications of vowels. Points, written above and below the consonants, and called Massoretic, from the Massorah, a post-canonical revision of the text, were afterwards added, in order to preserve the original, or rather traditional, pronunciation of the words and sentences. So long as the Hebrew was a spoken language there was no need for these points; but after it was superseded by the Aramaic, acquired by the Jewish people during their captivity in Babylon, care was taken to preserve the original pronunciation, and points of the nature referred to were invented and adopted. The points are often a key to the sense and interpretation, both as accepted at the time and as established by subsequent exegesis. The care with which in this, as in other respects, the text has been transmitted is due to the prevailing belief that it was in its spoken as well as written form of Divine inspiration.

2. **The Greek.**— The language of the New Testament is not pure Greek. After the time of Alexander the Great, Greek was spread throughout the dominions of the Macedonian Empire as the language of literature and commerce. But it was somewhat modified by the influence of local manners, as well as by an infusion of foreign elements, and the result was known as the *Koinè dialectè* (*i.e.,* the common dialect). This was least corrupt at Alexandria; in the East, and when employed in the intercourse of traders, it was further modified. The New Testament is written in the Eastern, popular form of the dialect. What is lost in classical purity is to be balanced by the gain of simplicity. Composing in a foreign tongue, the authors of the New Testament do not construct long involved sentences such as we meet with in classic authors. Thus what they write is more easily translated, and more readily understood by people of various languages. The New Testament was written in this language, not because the authors did not know Aramaic (Acts xxii. 2), but because the Greek-speaking classes of the time were found to be more open to the teachings of Christianity than the merely Aramaic-speaking, and because Greek offered the readiest vehicle for the dissemination of a religion meant to reach all nations. Moreover, it should be observed, the Jews themselves had already become familiar with it as a sacred language by means of the Septuagint Version

3

of the Old Testament, in which it had been used to express the ideas and forms of thinking native to the race among whom the Christian gospel had originated. It is plain that the writers of the New Testament were intimately familiar with this version, and the Greek in which they write bears unmistakable traces of modes of thinking and expression cast like it in the mould of old Hebrew thought and feeling. Their Greek is a Greek instinct with, and expressive of, both Hebrew and Christian ideas. See Bagster's *Hebrew Old Testament, Practical Hebrew Grammar, Analytical Hebrew Lexicon;* Gesenius' *Hebrew and Chaldee Lexicon; Student's Critical New Testament; Analytical Greek Lexicon to the New Testament;* and *Greek Student's Manual;* also Davidson, *Hebrew Grammar and Syntax;* Winer, *Grammar of New Testament Greek;* Blass, *Grammar of the New Testament;* Thayer, Translation of Grimm's *Clavis;* The Bible Society's *Greek Testament* (edited by Nestlé)—the best and most accurate text; Westcott and Hort, *New Testament in the Original Greek;* and for a complete critical apparatus—Tischendorf, *Novum Testamentum Græce* (8th edit.).

CHAPTER III.

ANCIENT MANUSCRIPTS.

THE reverence of the Jews for their sacred Scriptures has led to scrupulous care in copying and preserving the text with the greatest possible accuracy, so that there is much more uniformity in the readings of the various Hebrew MSS. of the Old Testament than is usually to be found in the case of books that have been transmitted from antiquity. Accordingly, we may have more assurance in trusting to the correctness of the text than otherwise we should venture on when we considered the comparatively modern dates of all the MSS. that have been discovered hitherto. Most of the known Hebrew MSS. only include portions of the Old Testament, and but few of them are of earlier date than the tenth century A.D. Apparently the most ancient is one recently acquired by the British Museum, and this was written probably at the end of the eighth century or the beginning of the ninth. Therefore the comparative age of MSS. scarcely comes into account in the consideration of points of textual criticism connected with the Old Testament.

With the New Testament the case is very different. Here we meet with a great number of various readings—as many as 182,000 have been detected. This would be a very alarming statement if it stood alone. But when we look into it we see that it is chiefly owing to the existence of a very great number of MSS., most of which are of no critical value. Thus it is that many of the various readings can be rejected at once as dependent on no good authority. Then of the remainder a large number are purely verbal or orthographical, and have no effect on the sense of the passages in which they occur. Of *seven-eighths* of the words of the New Testament there can be no question, all copies agreeing in giving them. Criticism is at most concerned with the remaining eight. But here it has accomplished much. The great majority of questions concerning various readings have been settled by an indisputable balance of evidence,

and there is only *one-sixtieth* about which any real uncertainty can be felt. Even with this fraction the majority of the doubtful readings are not of the first importance.

The science of textual criticism, which is engaged in the settlement of the text where the readings are doubtful, is dependent on two kinds of evidence—*intrinsic* evidence, in which the inherent probability of the sense of a passage is considered, and *documentary* evidence, which draws upon three sources of information —(1) manuscripts, including MS. lectionaries, (2) versions, and (3) quotations in the Fathers.

There are more than 2000 known MSS. of the New Testament in whole or part. These are divided into two classes—*uncial* and *minuscule* (popularly known as *cursive*). In the uncial MSS. the letters are all capitals; the minuscule MSS. make use of a small current hand. The change of style in penmanship took place about the ninth century A.D. No minuscule MS. is to be found of earlier date than that century, and no full uncial after the tenth century. In the oldest MSS. the letters are square-shaped, of equal size throughout, with no distinction of thick and thin lines, and no accents, breathings, or punctuation marks. There are no divisions into chapters or verses; nor are the words divided, the whole running evenly on and joined together as one solid block of letters. Subsequently various devices were employed for chapter and sectional divisions; but the chapters as they now stand in our Bibles were marked out as late as the year 1248, or thereabouts, by Cardinal Hugo, and our verses by R. Stephens, who began by making them in the margin of his Greek Testament during a journey from Paris to Lyons in they ear 1551.

About the year 332 Constantine ordered Eusebius to have fifty easily legible complete copies of Scripture executed by skilful caligraphists for the churches of his new capital. Eusebius says they were "sumptuously prepared volumes" (Vit. Con. iv. 37). Earlier MSS. must have been much less pretentious and costly. It is not probable that any of the fifty have come into our hands, for the oldest extant MSS. do not exactly agree with Eusebius's arrangement of the Canon, and we need not be surprised that earlier MSS. have all perished. Probably the original autographs were written on flimsy papyrus (*see* 2 John 12), which would be soon worn out with frequent reading. Many subsequently written copies of the New Testament were destroyed in times of persecution—especially during the great Diocletian persecution. The oldest MSS. of the New Testament that we now possess date from the fourth century. These are fine works in good vellum, such as would not have been readily produced in the more ancient times before the Church had acquired wealth and influence.

It is customary to indicate the several uncial MSS. by the use of Roman, Greek, and Hebrew letters (*e.g.*, B, Δ, ℵ), using Arabic figures for the minuscule MSS. (*e.g.*, 3, 70, 537), and small Roman letters for Latin MSS. (*e.g.*, d, e, f). The same letter is sometimes employed for two or more MSS. of different parts of the New Testament. Thus D of the Gospels and Acts is a different book from D of St. Paul's Epistles. The latter is marked, for distinction, D$_2$. The manuscripts have undergone correction, or

4

mutilation, from various successive editors. The various readings thus inserted are indicated by textual critics by letters, numbers, or asterisks. Thus D^b, or D^2, or D^{**} would mean a correction of D by a second hand ; D^c, or D^3, or D^{***} one by a third ; and so on.

The following are the oldest and most important known manuscripts :—

B. Codex Vaticanus.—Fourth century. In the Vatican Library at Rome. A small quarto of thin delicate vellum, said to be made of the skins of antelopes, the writing in three columns of small uncials, which run on continuously with no breaks between the words, and no breathings or accents by the first hand, and very rare indications of punctuation. A photographic replica of this precious document is in the British Museum. Westcott and Hort attach the highest value to this MS. for the purity of its text. It contains most of the LXX. and the New Testament down to Heb. ix. 14, thus omitting the Pastoral Epistles, the Epistle to Philemon, and the Apocalypse. The Apocalypse has been added by a much later hand.

א. Codex Sinaiticus.—Fourth century. Discovered in 1844 at the Convent of St. Catherine, Mount Sinai, by Tischendorf, who picked out forty-three leaves of the LXX. from a basket of papers said to have been designed for lighting the oven fire. Under the influence of the Emperor of Russia, Tischendorf was permitted to carry the MS. away with him to St. Petersburg, where it is now preserved. This MS. is of beautiful vellum, and the writing is in four columns on each page. It has the same primitive characteristics as B, which it much resembles in its readings. Tischendorf held that it was written by four scribes in succession, and that the fourth was the same man as the writer of B. Hort did not accept this view, but it was supported by Scrivener. א contains great part of the LXX., all the New Testament, the Epistle of Barnabas, and a considerable fragment of the Epistle of Hermas. One peculiarity of it is that it places St. Paul's Epistles before the Acts of the Apostles.

A. Codex Alexandrinus.—Fifth century. Presented to Charles I. by Lucan, patriarch of Constantinople, and now in the British Museum, and exposed to view in the Manuscript Room of the King's Library. There are two columns to the page. This MS. contains the Old Testament and nearly the whole of the New Testament.

C. Codex Ephraemi Syri.—Fifth century. In the Royal Library at Paris. This is a palimpsest, i.e., a document from which the original writing had been erased and on which other matter had been inscribed. In the twelfth century the works of St. Ephraem were thus imposed on this copy of the New Testament. By a chemical process the original writing has been revived, and the MS. made available for textual criticism. It contains fragments of all the books of the New Testament except 2 Thessalonians and 2 John.

D. Codex Bezæ.—Sixth century. At Cambridge ; having been presented to the University in 1581 by Theodore Beza. It contains the old Latin version as well as the original Greek—the Greek on the left-hand page and the Latin on the right. It consists of the Gospels and Acts only. This MS. is exceedingly interesting on account of its striking peculiarities as well as its affinity to the text used by so ancient a father as Irenæus, who lived in the second century. It

furnishes many curious additions to the received texts. Scrivener says, "No known MS. contains so many bold and extensive interpolations"—as many as 600 have been traced in the Acts alone. Rendel Harris maintains that its Latin text is older than its Greek, and that the latter has been altered into conformity with the former. Resh holds that it represents the text of a scholar of about the year 140 which was since altered and corrupted.

E. Codex Basiliensis.—Eighth century. Now at Basle. This MS. is interesting, because it comes nearer to the generally received text than any of its contemporaries.

F. Codex Boreeli.—Ninth century. At Paris.

L. Codex Regii.—Eighth century. At Paris.

N. Codex Purpureus.—Sixth century. This is only a fragment of the Gospels on thinnest vellum, which is dyed purple. The letters are of silver, excepting those for "God" and "Christ," which are of gold.

Δ. Codex Sangallensis.—Ninth century. In the monastery of St. Gall, Switzerland, where probably it was written.

Among MSS. of the Epistles of St. Paul we may notice the following, in addition to B, א, A, which contain those epistles, together with other parts of the New Testament :—

D. Codex Claromontanus.—Sixth century. At Paris. This MS. contains the Greek original and the Latin version in parallel pages, without punctuation marks, breathings, or accents by the first hand. It has the Epistle to the Hebrews after that to Philemon.

E. Codex Sangermanensis, also known as Petropolitanus.—Ninth century. The greater part of St. Paul's writings are in this MS. ; but there are gaps.

F. Codex Augiensis.—Ninth century. At Cambridge. Like D, this manuscript gives the Latin version as well as the Greek text. It contains St. Paul's Epistles, but parts are missing. The Epistle to the Hebrews is not included.

G. Codex Boernerianus.—Ninth century. At Dresden.

H. Codex Coislinianus.—Sixth century. A very valuable MS., but now only fourteen leaves of it remain, of which twelve are in Paris and two at St. Petersburg.

In the attempt to settle the text where it is given variously in different MSS., a number of considerations have to be taken into account. It is evident that the rough and ready method of simply counting MSS. would be most unsatisfactory. The tendency is generally to give most weight to the oldest MSS. But this is not followed as a fixed rule. The older MS. of two that are under examination may have been copied from one that is not so old as the copy from which its junior has been taken ; or the older MS. may be manifestly more faulty, or derived from a more faulty source. Then several MSS. which are evidently all derived from a common parent MS. cannot together amount to more weight than that of the parent. But more important than these individual valuations is that which rises out of the sorting of texts given by MSS., versions, and Fathers into great classes or schools. It is found that certain groups of MSS. agree more or less closely in giving a certain style of text, and sometimes this is also traced in versions and in quotations by the Fathers. In this way four texts have been indicated.

These are named *The Syrian*, represented by A, &c., and coming nearest to the *Textus Receptus*, that on which our Authorised Version is founded ; *The Western*, represented by D, &c., and followed by the Old Latin and one of the Syrian versions ; *The Alexandrian*, partially represented by ℵ, C, &c. ; and *The Neutral*, represented by B, and largely by ℵ, &c., and regarded by the predominant critics as, on the whole, the purest. No one of these texts can be relied on exclusively. Unfortunately it would appear that corruptions crept into the text of the New Testament books early in the second century—long before the oldest and best extant MSS. were written. It is, therefore, by an elaborate comparison of data and the careful weighing of evidence in every case of a various reading that errors are eliminated. There can be no reasonable doubt that the labours of experts in this field have been richly rewarded by the production of most valuable results. Thus such a critical edition of the Greek Testament as Westcott and Hort's, or Tischendorf's, or that of the Revisers, is a vast improvement on the Greek Testaments of Erasmus and Stephens, from which the Authorised Version was made. Accordingly it is not only on account of its greater correctness of rendering, but also because of the more accurate readings of the Greek text on which it is found, that we may rely on the Revised Version as bringing us back more exactly to the original utterances of Scripture.

See Scrivener, *Introduction to the Criticism of the New Testament*, edited by Miller ; Hammond, Kenyon, Nestlé, Lake, on *Textual Criticism ;* Hort, *Introduction* to Westcott and Hort's Greek New Testament ; Gregory, *Prolegomena* to 8th edit. of Tischendorf's Greek New Testament.

CHAPTER IV.

ANCIENT VERSIONS OF THE ORIGINAL SCRIPTURES.

A.—Versions of the Old Testament.

1. The Septuagint.—This Greek version is the oldest known to us ; it was executed at Alexandria, in Egypt, by different translators at different periods, commencing in the time of the early Ptolemies, about 285 B.C. Such a translation was called for by the exigencies of the Jews themselves, particularly of those of the Dispersion, among whom Hebrew was fast becoming a dead language, and the later Greek their mother tongue. It is known also as the Greek or the Alexandrian Version ; while the name Septuagint, or LXX., was given to it on the ground of the tradition that it was the work of seventy, or rather seventy-two, Jews, who had been brought from Palestine for the purpose, and were fabled, according to one tradition, to have executed the whole in as many days, and, according to another, to have each done the whole in separation from the rest, with the result that the version of each was found to correspond miraculously word for word with that of all the others. The truth is, as is evident from the comparatively loose way in which, as a translation, it is in many parts done, that it was the work of Egyptian Jews, and not Palestinian ones, who would have gone about it with a more religious regard to the text. It began with the translation of the books of Moses, and was continued from time to time till about 130 B.C. by the translation of the rest, the whole being the achievement of several independent workmen, who executed their parts, some with greater, some with less, fidelity and success. Indeed, the character of the translation differs greatly in the different books. It is in some cases tolerably free ; in others, and these the majority, verbal to a painful degree ; and all alike betray the influence of the Hebrew originals. It swarms with such strong Hebraisms that a pure Greek could scarcely understand it. The version thus produced soon passed into general acceptance with the Greek-speaking Jews, even in Palestine itself ; and its general circulation, by their presence in the Greek cities, paved the way for the apprehension and spread of Christianity in the heathen world. The Septuagint was the Greek version current at the time of the planting of the Christian Church ; it was universally accepted by the Jews of the Dispersion as the text of Scripture ; and the numerous quotations that occur in the New Testament from the Old are, with rare exceptions, cited from it. After it had been adopted by the Christians, the Jews gave up the use of this version. But it has continued to be regarded as of more or less authority by Christian biblicists, and is to this day the accepted version of the Old Testament in the Greek Church.

2. Aquila's Version.—Aquila was a Greek, born at Sinope, in Pontus, who passed from Paganism to Judaism, by way, it is said, of Christianity, submitting even to the rite of circumcision, that he might enjoy all the privileges of the favoured race. His version, of which only part remains, was one of three Greek versions executed in the second century A.D. Its object was to supply a literal rendering of the Hebrew text for the benefit of those who were more familiar with Greek than the original, in opposition to the Septuagint, which had been appropriated by the Christians, and in the interests of Judaism. It is so literal as to be often in violation of the idiom, and even grammar, of the Greek language ; when the literal rendering is departed from it is in the translation of passages which seemed to countenance the Christian contention that Judaism was but a foreshadow and prediction of what had been fulfilled in Christ, and as such was destined to pass away.

3. Theodotion's Version.—Theodotion appears to have been a native of Ephesus, and an Ebionite, that is, a Judaising Christian ; and his version, which belongs also to the second century, was less a translation than a revision of the LXX., the result of which was the introduction of many of his emendations into the latter, and the substitution therein of his version of the Book of Daniel for the original one, which survives only in one MS. The polemic interest in which this revision was executed was similar to that of Aquila's version.

4. Symmachus' Version.—The version of Symmachus, who appears to have been an Ebionite of Samaria, was executed in the second century, subsequently to the preceding, and was a freer as well as a more intelligent rendering of the original, being probably intended to correct the

bad Greek of Aquila's work and the bad Hebrew of Theodotion's. It formed the third of the six versions given in Origen's Hexapla, the rest, also in Greek, being designated respectively fifth, sixth, and seventh.

5. **The Targums.**—These are translations, or rather paraphrases, of, with two or three exceptions, the several books of the Old Testament in Aramaic, which, from the period of the Captivity, had, both in Babylonia and Palestine, become the spoken language of the Jewish people in lieu of Hebrew. These renderings, of which only a comparatively few survive, were executed presumably in connection with the service of the Synagogue. They were accompanied with comments and instances in way of illustration. At first the Targums were delivered orally, and they were handed down for long from generation to generation through the medium of tradition, which did not improve them. The greatest uncertainty prevails regarding the origin and history of the written forms in which a few of them have been preserved. Onkelos, the author or editor of a Targum on the Pentateuch, which is, it seems, an excellent and honest piece of work, is said to have sat at the feet of Gamaliel together with the Apostle Paul; and Jonathan, the son of Uzziel, to whom we owe another on the historical and prophetical books, is made out to have been a disciple of the school of Hillel, who was born 120 B.C. In their present shape these Targums are not older than the end of the third century—that of the Song of Solomon is as late as the sixth century. They are mainly of value as an exhibition of the style of exegesis in popular acceptance among the Jews at the time and place of their composition, if not also of those committed to writing. The so-called Jerusalem Targum, and that of the pseudo-Jonathan, on the Pentateuch, are of quite a different stamp, and are surcharged with fanciful and allegorical legendary matter, such as is met with in the Talmud.

B.—Versions of both the Old and the New Testaments.

1. **The Peshitto.**—This is a Syriac version of the whole Bible, with the exception of 2 Peter, 2 and 3 John, and Jude, and the Apocalypse, executed by Judaic Christians for the use of the Syrian Church during the second century. Its title, which means *simple*, was given to it either because it aimed at being a literal translation, or more probably because it was intended for use among simple people, as a popular translation, a Syriac *Vulgate*. The Old Testament was translated directly from the Hebrew original, and is still of service in questions of exegesis, while the version of the New Testament is to this day of value in determining questions affecting the original text. The renderings of the Old Testament frequently agree with those of the Septuagint, although another translation into Syriac was afterwards executed in closer conformity with that version. Two copies of the Gospels in Syriac are pronounced by some scholars to be more ancient than the Peshitto—(1) the *Curetonian*, contained in a MS. brought by Archdeacon Tattam from Egypt and published by Cureton; (2) the *Sinaitic*, a still earlier text discovered by Mrs. Lewis at the Monastery of St. Catherine on Mount Sinai,

and published in 1894. Possibly these are two variant texts of an ancient version. The Gospels at least must have been translated into Syriac by about the first half of the second century. Tatian's *Diatessaron* is a Syriac harmony of the four Gospels written but a little after the middle of that century, and founded on a Syriac version. Other versions are much later—the *Jerusalem* in the fifth century, and the *Harclean* in the sixth.

2. **Old Latin Version.**—It was in North Africa, towards the end of the second century, that a beginning was made of the translation of the Scriptures into Latin, being rendered necessary by the rise and existence in that quarter of a Latin-speaking Church; but the attempt was both rude in execution and partial in extent. The Greek Septuagint, and not the Hebrew original, was the text translated. The translations were the fruit of merely individual and successive efforts, and the result was a compilation of very unequal merit.

3. **The Itala.**—This was not really a new version, as formerly supposed, but an attempt to correct the corrupt text of the old Latin version, which had assumed a variety of forms in different MSS. The revision was probably twofold, aiming at a better rendering of the Greek by comparison with the LXX., and also a smoother Latin style. St. Augustine speaks of this as the best Latin version in his time. It was compiled in North Italy, more or less under episcopal authority. It has been described as "a stepping-stone towards the Vulgate."

4. **The Vulgate.**—This version was executed by St. Jerome at intervals from 385 to 404 A.D., under the direction of Pope Damasus. It was called for by the great variety of texts that still prevailed in spite of the revision made by the authors of the *Itala* and the very corrupt character of most of them. As yet no Latin translation direct from the Hebrew existed. Jerome's work was first a revision of the Latin version made with reference to the LXX. and the Greek of the New Testament. Subsequently he made a new translation of the Old Testament from the Hebrew original—all except the Psalms, which we may suppose, from the familiar use of them in public worship, would not be acceptable in a new form. These, therefore, still stand in the Vulgate as a rendering of the Greek version. Jerome's version was vastly superior to its predecessor, and though it was at first received with suspicion, it rapidly grew in favour, so that for a thousand years it was the only Bible known to Western Christendom. Its common use led to its receiving the title *Vulgate*. At the end of the eighth century Alcuin revised the text of the Vulgate, which had got corrupt under the hand of careless scribes. This he did at the command of Charles the Great, who wished to provide a standard Bible in simple intelligible Latin. At the same time Theodulf, Bishop of Orleans, effected a revision which is preserved at Paris. The "Mazarin Bible"—so called because it was first noticed by bibliographers in the library of Cardinal Mazarin—is a printed copy of the Vulgate in two volumes, dated from 1452, and attributed to Gutenberg. The Council of Trent authoritatively established the Vulgate as the Bible of the Catholic Church, and Sixtus V. commenced a revision, which was superseded by one executed

by Clement VIII. In the year 1592 this Pope issued a Bull ordering every subsequent edition to be assimilated to that which he had produced. It is commonly known as the *Clementine Vulgate*, and is at this day the authorised Bible of the Roman Catholic Church. It is not a really critical edition.

For the LXX. see Bagster's *The Greek LXX., with an English Translation;* Swete, *The Old Testament in Greek according to the Septuagint;* Tischendorf, *Vetus Testamentum Græce.* For the Syriac see Bagster's *Syriac New Testament* and *Syriac Lexicon to the New Testament;* Mrs. Lewis, *The Four Gospels Translated from the Sinaitic Palimpsest;* Hamlyn Hill, *The Diatessaron of Tatian.* For the old Latin texts see Bishop Wordsworth, *Old Latin Biblical Texts.* For the Clementine Vulgate see Bagster's *Latin Bible;* and for a critical edition of the Vulgate New Testament, Bishop Wordsworth, *Novum Testamentum Latinum.*

CHAPTER V.

MODERN ENGLISH VERSIONS.

IN the fourth century Ufhilas, the apostle of the Goths, gave his countrymen of Eastern Europe a version of the Scriptures in their own tongue, and subsequently portions of the Bible were translated into the Anglo-Saxon and other languages. Nevertheless, for a thousand years the Vulgate was practically the only Bible of Western Christendom. Where the Latin tongue was superseded in the south by the more modern European languages that sprang from the fusion of Teutonic invaders with the native races, the Bible in that tongue could be no longer the book of the common people. In northern countries, of course, Latin was always a foreign language. Thus, in process of time, the Bible was lost to the people, and remained only as the text-book of learned schoolmen. The dawn of a new age of Christian history was marked by a recovery of the Bible as a book of the laity. In the light before the dawn, which appeared as early as the fourteenth century, this recovery was commenced by the appearance of Wycliffe's Bible.

1. **Wycliffe's Bible.**—The reformer commenced by a translation of the Apocalypse. This was followed by the Gospels, with a commentary, and then by the remaining books of the New Testament, a complete edition of which, with a new rendering of the Apocalypse, appeared about 1380. The translation of the Old Testament was undertaken by Wycliffe's friend, Nicholas of Hereford; but the work was broken off abruptly in the middle of Baruch, because the translator was summoned to London to answer for his heresies, and excommunicated in the year 1382. Nicholas then left England, and his task was completed, it is supposed, by Wycliffe, who was thus enabled to have the joy of seeing the Bible in the hands of his countrymen in their own tongue before he died in 1384. Wycliffe's Bible was made from the Latin Vulgate, not from the original. There was a quaint homeliness in the style of the language, and yet the translation was often so painfully literal as to be obscure. Technical terms were often translated; thus "high-priest" became "archbishop" throughout. In 1388 Wycliffe's Bible was revised by John

Purvey, and in this improved form it superseded the original version, and in spite of proscription by Convocation in 1408, was widely circulated among all classes. Appearing before the age of printing, Wycliffe's was a manuscript Bible. It was not printed until the year 1848.

The modern European versions of the Bible, especially those that belong to the period of the Reformation, arose out of other and cruder attempts of a popular cast, executed at a time when the languages themselves were only in process of formation. Those now in use are of a date coincident with the period when the languages of Europe took their present shape, and they appear in many cases to have contributed not a little to fix the final forms of them. This is especially true of the German and English versions, the former having been preceded by seventeen now in disuse, and the latter by that of John Wycliffe and other translations of parts of the Scriptures. These versions belong to the classics of their respective languages, a result doubtless due in great part to the influence of the truth and spirit of the original on the translators in the work of translation, and, through them, on the people themselves. They sprang from the conjunction of the Reformation and the Revival of Letters in the fifteenth century. The translation of such a book at such a time, when the appeal lay from the court of Rome to the court of conscience, could not fail to have a regulative effect on the language, as well as the manners, of the people, seeking, as the best of them were, for guidance from above.

2. **Luther's Version.** — This is deserving of notice, both for the man's sake whose work it was, the circumstances in which he achieved it, the spirit and manner of its execution, and the power it exercised on the life and thinking, as well as the language, of the German people. No greater man ever addressed himself to such a task, in no case was it undertaken and done against such odds, in no other version is there such a clear insight into and living sympathy with the spirit of the original, and no other had such an instantaneous, electric effect on a nation, breathing, as it were, new life into all the ramifications of their being. It was begun by Luther when virtually a prisoner in the Castle of Wartburg, and under protestation, as it seemed to him, of the prince of darkness himself, and finished among hindrances and obstructions, the New Testament in 1522, the Pentateuch in 1523, and the whole, the Apocrypha included, in 1534. It is instinct with the spirit of the original, and couched in a language which went direct to the heart of the mass of the German-speaking world. The translation is always made from a sympathetic appreciation of the sense, never from a merely blind adherence to the letter, and it is to this day virtually the version of all the Protestant nations of Northern Europe.

3. **Tyndale's Translation.**—This, though not the first attempt to translate the Bible into the English tongue, was the first that had any considerable influence on subsequent translations. Wycliffe's, which preceded it by nearly two hundred years, was based, not on the original, but on the Vulgate, and the language, though homely and idiomatic, was already, in Henry VIII.'s time, out of date. Tyndale's was the first that was moulded by a knowledge of the

original, while it was no less adapted to the intelligence of the humblest class. It was begun with a determination to "cause a boy that driveth the plough to know more of the Scriptures" than a divine "recounted for a learned man," and it was done so faithfully that to it we owe those qualities which have endeared the Authorised Version that sprang from it alike to learned and unlearned. It was the chosen work of the author's life, and he prosecuted it under the most formidable discouragements. He had to expatriate himself to achieve it, and the price was in the end the forfeiture by betrayal of his life. The New Testament was finished at Cologne, and printed partly there and partly at Worms in 1526; and though the first copies, when issued in England, were bought up and burned, much of our "authorised" version in use is word for word taken from it. The Pentateuch—which had to be twice done, the first version having perished in a shipwreck that Tyndale suffered on the coast of Holland—was published in 1530, the Book of Jonah three years later, and subsequently some Old Testament fragments. There has been much dispute on the question whether Tyndale translated directly from the Hebrew. He was in close contact with well-known Hebrew scholars; he was himself a man of scholarly habits, and was said to know Hebrew by a contemporary writer, Buschius; he asks his critics to correct his work after comparing it with the Hebrew; and his notes contain references to Hebrew words and grammar. All these facts point to a comparison with the Hebrew text, if not to a translation made entirely from the original. Copious notes accompanied Tyndale's Pentateuch, many of them sharply polemical against Romanism. In 1534 Tyndale issued a second edition of his New Testament with considerable improvements; other editions followed—a fact which shows that the book was read and sought after.

4. **Miles Coverdale's Translation.**—This is a version in English of the whole Bible, and the first issued under royal sanction, being dedicated to Henry VIII. It was done at the instance of Thomas Crumwell, and was brought out in the year 1535, having been printed abroad. Executed throughout as a task, and with an eye to the favour of the authorities in Church and State, it is far inferior both in spirit and faithfulness to Tyndale's version, and at times it displays a timid hesitancy unworthy of a manly faith in the truth. Neither was the author so well qualified in point of scholarship for the task committed to him, and his version was merely a translation from other versions, such as the Vulgate and Luther's, with such assistance as could be safely borrowed even from Tyndale's. The work can boast, however, of having been the object of persecution, some 2500 copies, printed in Paris, having, in spite of royal edicts, been seized by the Inquisition and doomed to be burnt.

5. **Matthew's Bible.**—This was Tyndale's version of the New Testament, and of the Old Testament from Joshua to II. Chronicles, together with Coverdale's version of the remainder of the Old Testament and the Apocrypha occasionally modified. The work was compiled by John Rogers, the first who suffered martyrdom under Mary, and published under the name of Thomas Matthew, to disarm suspicion and distrust. Its production was due to dissatisfaction with Coverdale's; and under the influence of Cranmer, "who liked it better than any translation hitherto made," its publication was authorised by the king in 1537, who was thus got to sanction what in connection with Tyndale's name he had formerly condemned. This translation, notwithstanding the superior scholarship it showed, proved too candid and bold to retain the footing it seemed to have won, especially as it was accompanied by alarming notes, and soon it had to make way for another that would give rise to less uneasiness among the privileged classes of the community. A sort of expurgated edition of Matthew's Bible, *i.e.*, one cleared of the dangerous tendency towards Protestantism, was produced in 1539 by an obscure scholar named Taverner. But this book did not meet the requirements of the age.

6. **Cranmer's, or the Great Bible.**—This translation was issued under authority in 1539, and continued to be the authorised version till 1568. It was called the "Great Bible," because it appeared in a large folio form for use in churches, and "Cranmer's," because of a long preface by the Archbishop prefixed to it in 1540. It professes to be a true translation after the Hebrew and Greek texts, the fruit of the labours of "divers excellent learned men, expert in the foresaid tongues," but it is at bottom Coverdale's version, or rather Matthew's; that is to say, Tyndale's, revised. The tone of the translation is moderate, as its issue under Cranmer's auspices might lead us to expect; and it is unaccompanied by notes of any kind, the reader having only marginal references to help him, and being counselled to accept the interpretations of such as are "godly learned in Christ." It appeared with an illustration on the title-page representing the king delivering the Word of God to his bishops on his right hand and his nobles on his left; the people are standing by and applauding the act. Some portions of the Great Bible still survive in the Book of Common Prayer. The Psalms arranged for the daily services of the Church are in that version.

7. **The Geneva Bible.**—This translation, on the basis of Tyndale's, was executed at Geneva by certain learned men dissatisfied with Cranmer's version, Coverdale among the number, who had fled there for refuge during the Marian persecution; and it was finished, the New Testament in 1557, and the Old Testament in 1560, the Apocrypha being left out in some copies. It was handier, and therefore cheaper, than Cranmer's; was the first to be printed in Roman type and to be divided into verses; and was accompanied with a Bible dictionary and notes in exposition; so that it became widely popular, and exercised a very great influence on the religious and civil history of the period. Its editors, imbued with the opinions of Calvin on theology and civil government, had given expression to them in their annotations; and the translation, with these helps to its exposition, became, and for a time, even in the face of the Authorised Version, continued to be, the Bible of the Puritans of England and of the covenanting Scots, both of whom drew their inspiration from it in the war they waged for the civic supremacy of the Sacred Book. It is this version of the Bible that is known as the *Breeches Bible*, from the

translation in it by the word "breeches" of that which in the Authorised Version is rendered "aprons" (Gen. iii. 7).

8. The Bishops' Bible.—This was a folio version, avowedly based on Cranmer's, executed by eight bishops of the Church, together with some deans and professors, each of whom was responsible for his own section, at the instance and under the supervision of Archbishop Parker, and issued, after great preparation and with great pomp, in 1568-72, in three portions, each preceded by a portrait, respectively, of Queen Elizabeth, the Earl of Leicester, and Lord Burleigh. Though got up in opposition to the Geneva Bible, it followed the division into verses there adopted, and further arranged the Books of the Old Testament into four groups, legal, historical, sapiential, and prophetic. It could not cope with the Geneva version, and being, moreover, too large and too costly, its circulation was limited and its life short. It is the only Bible in which passages are marked for omission in the public worship of the Church.

9. The Douay Bible.—This is an English version for the use of English Roman Catholics, based on the Vulgate, and executed, the New Testament at Rheims in 1582 and the Old Testament at Douay in 1609. It is characterised by not a few pedantries, and accompanied by notes of a dogmatic and polemic nature in justification of Roman Catholic beliefs and practices.

10. The Authorised Version.—This version was executed between the years 1607 and 1610, and was one of the chief fruits of a conference on ecclesiastical matters held at Hampton Court in 1604 under the presidency of James I. It was due to a widespread dissatisfaction with the versions in use, the Bishops' Bible being obnoxious to the Puritans, the Geneva to the king, and both to scholars. The movement for a revision began with the Puritans, and was backed by the king, to whom belongs the merit of having instituted the necessary proceedings and guided matters to a satisfactory result. The Bishops, in uneasy apprehension of the issue to themselves and their order, would fain have let things alone, but His Majesty had set his heart upon giving effect to the proposal, and the royal will was done ; so that the version which was the fruit of the decision was not undeservedly called *King James' Bible.* The translation was the work of forty-seven men, selected with marked fairness and discretion, partly from the Church supporters, partly from the Puritan body, and partly from the learned class ; and these were divided into three groups of two sections each, who, under instructions from the king, held their sittings for three years severally at Westminster, Cambridge, and Oxford. Each section had a separate portion of the Bible allotted to it, but the work of each was submitted to all the rest for approval, and then the whole was revised by a committee of six, who met for nine months in Stationers' Hall, London, and who received for their services from the Stationers' Company thirty pounds each, the rest of the work having been done for nothing, with only the uncertain prospect of some poor preferment in charity from the Church. The king's necessities were too great to enable him to do more than recommend the labours of the translators to the benevolent regard of others interested ; but he was careful to provide that neither Church nor State should

suffer damage from the enterprise, for he issued instructions to the translators to depart as little as possible from other received translations, especially the Bishops', and, above all, to sanction no innovation that would disturb the orthodoxy or peace of the Church. The translators were careful in the main to respect the rules laid down by the king, and the result was a translation that at length superseded every other, and that has since woven itself into the affections of the whole English-speaking people. The men who executed it evidently felt the influence of the same spirit that breathes in the original, and they produced a version that will remain to all time a monument of the simplicity, dignity, grace, and melody of the English language. Its very style has had a nobly educative effect on the national literature, and has contributed more than anything else to prevent it from degenerating into the merely frivolous or formal.

11. The Revised Version.—This is the result of repeated expressions of dissatisfaction with the Authorised Version, repeated attempts to amend it, and repeated calls for its revision on account of the faulty state of the original text it proceeded upon, the comparatively defective knowledge of the original languages on the part of the translators, and the proved presence of many inaccuracies, errors, and obscurities in the renderings. It originated in a resolution of the Convocation of the province of Canterbury in February 1870. The work of revision was committed to two companies, composed of men of tried Biblical scholarship representing various religious communities, the one to revise the Old Testament and the other the New. These companies commenced their sittings in the month of June 1870, and proceeded with their work in co-operation with two similar American companies, acting according to the same instructions with themselves. The principles and rules under which they worked were drawn up by a committee of Convocation, and these amounted in substance to this, that no change should be introduced except on good authority, none except such as the sense demanded, and all should be in a style agreeable to that of the Authorised Version. The New Testament was finished in November 1880, and the Old Testament in July 1884, both dating from the Jerusalem Chamber, Westminster. This Revised Version gives evidence of being the work of men well qualified as scholars for their task, and animated with an equally tender regard for both the original Scripture and the Authorised Version. It is certainly much more accurate in text and translation than the older version, but less pure and musical in its English. See Lovett, *The Printed English Bible,* as handbook ; Mombert, *English Versions of the Bible ;* Eadie, *The English Bible ;* *Annals of the Bible ;* and Weymouth, *The New Testament in Modern Speech.*

CHAPTER VI.

THE CANON OF SCRIPTURE.

THE word "canon," in its primary signification, meant a "straight rod ;" afterwards it came to stand for a "rule" or a "body of rules," *i.e.,* for that which keeps things straight. The application of this word to the contents of the Bible has been explained in two different ways. By some it is supposed to have been first used for the "rule" which determined what books should be enclosed in the list of sacred Scriptures, and then for the books thus selected; by others it has been taken for a designation of those books as themselves forming together the "rule" of faith. The latter interpretation seems to be most in accordance with the analogous use of the word in early times. Canonical Scriptures, then, are writings which have been accepted as authoritative in regulating belief and conduct. The title "canon" stands both for the catalogue of these books, and for the books themselves.

1. **The Old Testament Canon.**—*a. Its Formation.*—We meet in early times with references to the sacred book of the Law; but there is nothing to show that any other books of Scripture were drawn together into one sacred collection before the time of the Captivity. As yet, it would seem, psalms, prophecies, and histories were detached and scattered as separate works. Ezra is credited with having formed the first Jewish canon in conjunction with "the great synagogue" of 120 scribes. Himself a scribe and a priest, Ezra saw the immense importance of gathering his fellow-countrymen, on their return from exile, under the ægis of the ancient covenant. They had been banished for a persistent breach of this covenant; now they were forgiven and restored in penitence and renewed consecration, it was most necessary that they should have the guidance of the inspired writings in which the covenant is set forth and enforced. The foundation was laid by Ezra; according to a statement of the second book of Maccabees the construction of the canon was continued by Nehemiah, for there we read "how he, founding a library, gathered together the acts of the kings, and the prophets, and of David, and the epistles of the kings concerning the holy gifts" (2 Macc. ii. 13). The third and final step could not have been taken much later than the time of the Maccabees, when the Jews were oppressed by Antiochus. It has been said that this persecution was for the Old Testament what the persecution of Diocletian was for the New, *i.e.,* "it was the final crisis which stamped the sacred writings with their peculiar character." From about this time the Jewish Bible appears as one whole and complete work. Discussions were afterwards raised as to the right of certain books to retain their place in the canon—Proverbs on account of its supposed contradictions, Ecclesiastes because of its apparent scepticism, Canticles for its sensuous tone, Esther for its not containing the name of God. But none of these books were removed, and the Old Testament canon remained unchanged in the hands of the Jews in spite of question and criticism.

b. Its Contents.—The canon of the Old Testament embraced three great divisions—the Torah or Law, the Nebiim or Prophets, and the Kethûbîm or Psalms—so called because the Psalms stood first in the list. In the Greek version the third division was called *Hagiographa,* i.e., *sacred writings.* While this collection is known among us as the Old Testament, it is known among the Jews as the Tenak, from the consonants in this word being the initial ones of Torah, Nebiim, and Kethûbîm; or the Twenty-four, from the number, according to one computation, of the books in the canon. The sacred books were, as we find in Josephus, originally reckoned at twenty-two, and this number was made out, it is thought, by regarding Judges and Ruth, 1 and 2 Samuel, 1 and 2 Kings, 1 and 2 Chronicles, Ezra and Nehemiah, Jeremiah and Lamentations, with all the Minor Prophets, as respectively one. The division of the books into thirty-nine, as at present, is effected by separating Ruth from Judges, dividing Samuel, Kings, and Chronicles into two books each, detaching Nehemiah from Ezra, and breaking up the Minor Prophets into twelve, according to the number of the authors.

The recognised canon of the Old Testament Scriptures was the one accepted by the Palestinian Jews, and it was adopted from them by the Christian Church, under sanction of Christ (Matt. v. 17) and His apostles, by whom it was quoted as "holy" (Rom. i. 2), spoken of as "given by inspiration of God" (2 Tim. iii. 16), and uniformly treated as God's Word; although the Septuagint confounded canonical Scripture with uncanonical by adding post-canonical books to the canonical ones without any note of distinction. Some variations of the actual contents of the canon must be noticed. (1.) *The Sadducean.* It has been said that the Sadducees received only the books of Moses; but this assertion is devoid of authority. (2.) *The Samaritan.* The mixed population that broke off from the Jews in the time of Ezra and set up their own worship at Mount Gerizim, carried with them the Pentateuch, but no other books of the Hebrew Scriptures. Consequently their canon was restricted to the first five books. The Samaritan Pantateuch has a distinct value of its own on account of its independence of other versions. (3.) *The Alexandrian.* The Jewish colony in Egypt lost the rigorous exclusiveness of Judaism, and submitted to the influence of Greek culture. The effect of this change is seen in the production of such a book as the "Wisdom of Solomon." That work and other books of the "Apocrypha" were included in the Septuagint, the Bible of the Greek-speaking Jews of Egypt. Thus, while the Samaritan canon is much narrower than that of the Palestine Jews, the Alexandrian canon is wider and more comprehensive. (4.) *The Patristic Canon.* The use of the Septuagint by the Church Fathers led to a confusion between canonical and Apocryphal canons. St. Augustine, enumerating the books which are contained in "the whole canon of Scripture," includes the Apocryphal books without any clear marks of distinction. Most of the lists given by the Fathers include the book of Baruch, some of them exclude Esther; some give other books of the Apocrypha as Holy Scripture, and a larger number insert the names of these books in their lists, but expressly place them in a second rank. (5.) *The Roman Catholic Canon.* This was determined by the Council of Trent (1546), which pronounced the enlarged canon, including the Apocrypha, to be deserving of "equal veneration," and added a list of books to prevent the possibility of doubt. Later Romanists, however, have sought for means of escape from this decisive judgment. (6.) *The Canon of the Reformed Churches.* This is identical with the Hebrew canon, and is therefore based on the highest and most ancient authority. It excludes the Apocrypha from the list of books of authority in doctrine; but the Church of England commends the use of the Apocryphal books "for example of life in instruction of manners." On the authority of the Greek Fathers the Greek Church also adheres to the Hebrew canon. This is the canon of our English Bibles.

2. **The New Testament Canon.**—*a. Its Formation.*—The "Scriptures" of the early Church were the Jews' "Scriptures," the Old Testament. It was only in course of time and by degrees that the books of the New Testament were collected and used as a portion of the Bible, side by side with the venerated ancient writings of the Law and the Prophets. The apostolical writings were read with all the authority of the apostles who indited them. The Gospels were treasured for the sayings and doings of our Lord, which they recorded. But in the earliest ages the oral testimony of those who had seen Jesus Christ, and then the traditions derived from these witnesses, were so highly valued in the Church that the written records were only resorted to in the second place, and where the much-loved floating memories failed. The first step towards the formation of a canon was made in the second century, when the Gospels were separated from the mass of ancient literature that had gathered round the traditions of the story of Christ. Justin Martyr (about 155) refers to the Synoptic Gospels as "Memoirs" of the Lord Jesus. As early as 140 the heretic Marcion put forth, together with his mutilated version of St. Luke, which he called "The Gospel of Christ," an "Apostle" containing ten epistles of St. Paul. Then a list of books is found in the "Muratorian Fragment"—an anonymous document—in the West, and another in the Peshitto in the East. A little later the equivalence of New Testament with Old Testament writings is unmistakably recognised. Irenæus speaks of the Scriptures, without distinction of Old and New Testaments, as "perfect, inasmuch as they were uttered by the Word of God and His Spirit," and he compares the four Gospels to the four winds, saying, "There could not be more th»n four Gospels, or fewer." It would seem, however, that the Epistles were still kept in a separate volume, apart from the Gospels. Clement of Alexandria refers to "The Apostle" and to "The Gospel" as distinct, definite collections of Scriptures. Hitherto no complete canon of the whole of the New Testament appears as clearly accepted and generally recognised. The Gospels were so highly venerated that no other writings, not even the inspired Epistles of apostles, could be allowed to rank by their side. Thus there was first the "*Instrumentum Evangelicum*," containing the four Gospels, and secondly the "*Instrumentum Apostolicum*," containing the Acts of the Apostles, together with the Pauline and other Epistles. The first definite statement of the canon now generally received, put forth at a council of any authority, was issued from the third Council of Carthage in 397. This was not a General Council, but only a Synod of the African Church. Nevertheless, its decision was accepted throughout the West; and although some discussion arose on the Epistle to the Hebrews, from this date the New Testament stood as one book, admitting of no separation, addition, or diminution. The East was slower to give up the older habits in its treatment of the New Testament. The question of the canon was reopened at the time of the Reformation,

when the authority of Church councils and the decisions of antiquity were called in question by fearless private inquiry. To Protestants the value of the settlement of the canon is not derived from the authoritative decisions of councils, but from the appreciation of its contents by successive ages of Christians, as well as from a conviction of the authenticity and genuineness of writings that claim to come to us with the authority of apostolical authors.

b. Its Contents.—The special evidence in favour of the several books will come before us later on, when we are considering those books *seriatim*. Here our attention is confined to the position of the books in the canon.

The Peshitto Syriac list of books, which dates back to the second century, contains all the books of our New Testament except the Apocalypse, Jude, 2 Peter, and 2 and 3 John. This was the canon followed by the Eastern Church for some time after the decision of the Council of Carthage in the West. The value of its admissions is far greater than the fact that it omits some of the minor books. Here we have the Syrian Church, close to the very centre of primitive Christianity, and as early as the second century, bearing testimony to the bulk of our New Testament. The Old Latin Version, the Bible of the great African Church, contains all tne New Testament except Hebrews (which, however, was translated separately before Tertullian's time), 2 Peter, and perhaps James. Origen's list includes the four Gospels, the Pauline Epistles, the Apocalypse, 1 John, 1 Peter, and as not accepted by all, 2 and 3 John and 2 Peter; the Epistle to the Hebrews is discussed, and James and Jude elsewhere included. The historian Eusebius, who lived 300 years after Christ, makes an important statement. He divides the sacred writings into three classes. 1. *Universally recognised Scriptures*— the four Gospels, the Acts of the Apostles, the fourteen Pauline Epistles, 1 John and 1 Peter, and *perhaps* the Apocalypse. 2. *Scripture not universally recognised*—the Epistles of James, Jude, 2 and 3 John, and 2 Peter. 3. *Spurious writings*—the Acts of Paul, the Shepherd, the Apocalypse of Peter, the Epistle of Barnabas, the Didachè, and *perhaps* the Apocalypse of John.

When the question of the canon was reopened by the Reformers, Erasmus denied the apostolic origin, but not the canonicity, of Hebrews, 2 Peter, and the Apocalypse. Luther treated the whole question with the greatest freedom, slighting those books which did not appear to agree with his opinions; accordingly, he set Hebrews, Jude, James, and the Apocalypse at the conclusion of his version, and made more or less disparaging remarks about them. Calvin, on the other hand, though he threw some doubt on 2 Peter, accepted all the books in our New Testament. The English Bible includes the first and second lists of Eusebius, but rejects the third list. This corresponds with the New Testament accepted in both the Greek and Roman Churches, and now used in all the great Protestant Churches.

See Ryle, *The Canon of the Old Testament;* Buhl, *Canon of the Text of the Old Testament;* Charteris, *Canonicity* (for citations from the Fathers); Westcott, *Hist. of the Canon;* Reuss, *Hist. of the Canon;* Davidson, *The Canon of the Bible;* Moore, *New Test. in Christian Church.*

CHAPTER VII.

THE CONTENTS OF SCRIPTURE.

LEADING features and characteristic topics of each book may be stated as follows :—

A. THE OLD TESTAMENT.

1. THE HEXATEUCH.

(1.) Genesis.—The early history of mankind and the patriarchs.
(2.) Exodus.—The exodus and the moral law.
(3.) Leviticus.—The priestly law.
(4.) Numbers.—The social and political law.
(5.) Deuteronomy.—The prophetic law.
(6.) Joshua.—The conquest of Canaan.

2. THE NATIONAL HISTORY OF ISRAEL.

(1.) Judges.—The dark ages of Israel.
(2.) Ruth.—An idyll, with hope of better days.
(3.) Samuel.—Establishment of the kingdom.
(4.) Kings.—Political history of the kingdoms of Judah and Israel.
(5.) Chronicles.—Priestly history of the two kingdoms.
(6.) Ezra.—The priestly restoration after the Captivity.
(7.) Nehemiah.—The political restoration.
(8.) Esther.—A picture of the exile.

3. POETICAL BOOKS.

(1.) Job.—The drama of Providence.
(2.) The Psalms.—Hebrew lyrics and hymns of worship.
(3.) Canticles.—The Hebrew pastoral.
(4.) Lamentations.—Hebrew Elegies.

4. BOOKS OF WISDOM.

(1.) Proverbs.—Didactic practical wisdom.
(2.) Ecclesiastes.—Reflective practical wisdom.

5. THE FOUR GREAT PROPHETS.

(1.) Isaiah.—The evangelical prophet.
(2.) Jeremiah.—The prophet of sorrow.
(3.) Ezekiel.—The priestly prophet.
(4.) Daniel.—The apocalyptic prophet.

6. THE TWELVE MINOR PROPHETS.

(1.) Hosea.—The prophet of Divine love.
(2.) Joel.—The preacher of the locust judgment.
(3.) Amos.—The lay prophet and unconventional preacher of righteousness.
(4.) Obadiah.—The preacher of judgment upon Edom.
(5.) Jonah.—The foreign missionary.
(6.) Micah.—The rustic Isaiah and evangelical prophet.
(7.) Nahum.—The preacher of judgment upon Nineveh.
(8.) Habakkuk.—The preacher of judgment upon Babylon.
(9.) Zephaniah.—The herald of the day of wrath for the world and judgment upon Judah.
(10.) Haggai. — The prophet of the second temple.
(11.) Zechariah. — The preacher of the Messianic kingdom in opposition to the kingdoms of earth.
(12). Malachi.—The herald of the coming of the Lord.

B. THE NEW TESTAMENT.

1. THE FOUR GOSPELS.

(1.) The Synoptic Gospels—
    a. St. Matthew.—The Gospel for the Jews.
    b. St. Mark.—The Gospel for the Romans.
    c. St. Luke.—The Gospel for the Gentiles.
(2.) St. John.—The supplementary Gospel.

2. THE ACTS OF THE APOSTLES.

The history of the early spread of Christianity.

3. THE PAULINE EPISTLES.

(1.) Romans.—Justification by faith.
(2.) 1 and 2 Corinthians.—The power of the cross applied to conduct.
(3.) Galatians.—The law and the Gospel.
(4.) Ephesians.—The Church as the body of Christ.
(5.) Philippians. — The identification of the Christian with Christ.
(6.) Colossians.—The glory of Christ.
(7.) 1 and 2 Thessalonians.—Christian life in view of the second advent.
(8.) 1 and 2 Timothy and Titus.—Pastoral epistles.
(9.) Philemon.—Christianity in domestic life.

4. HEBREWS.

The superseding of the old covenant by the new.

5. THE GENERAL EPISTLES.

(1.) James—Practical Christianity.
(2.) 1 and 2 Peter.—Christian privileges and duties.
(3.) 1, 2, and 3 John.—The life of love.
(4.) Jude.—Dangers of apostasy.

6. THE REVELATION.

Coming judgments and the second advent.

Special commentaries for most of the books of the Bible will be mentioned at the close of each of the chapters dealing with those books When none such are recommended, the following works may be consulted : (1) Critical works— *The International Critical Commentary ; The Expositor's Greek Testament ;* (2) Commentaries for English readers—*The Cambridge Bible ; The Century Bible.*

CHAPTER VIII.

THE HEXATEUCH.

THIS name has been given to the first six books of the Old Testament—*i.e.,* the books known as the Pentateuch together with Joshua—on the ground that they constitute one work. In subject the book of Joshua is a direct continuation of what precedes ; the several materials out of which it is composed are of the same character ; and the style and method of handling these materials are also identical in the Pentateuch and Joshua. The first five books were early known as the Pentateuch. They were called by the Jews the "Five-fifths of the Torah," or Law ; and of this designation the word Pentateuch, applied to the collection in the Septuagint and the Vulgate, is the Greek translation or equivalent. The word "Torah," which means "oral instruction," is used in reference to the whole of the Mosaic revelation. The names by which the several divisions are known are of Greek origin, and were invented to give some idea of tne respective contents of the books, or of some striking portion of them, although among the Jews it is customary to designate them severally by the initial words. Thus Genesis is called Bereshith, that expression, meaning "In the Beginning," being its first word.

Origin and Construction.—Until recent times it was held both by Jews and by Christians, practically without question, that Moses was the author of the entire Pentateuch. But Carlstadt, in the sixteenth century, raised questions as to the Mosaic authorship; and Andreas Masius said, "The Pentateuch in its present form is the work of Ezra or another inspired man." In the seventeenth century Hobbes, in his "Leviathan," wrote, "The Pentateuch is a work *about* Moses, not *by* Moses, yet based on originals by the hand of Moses."

Spinoza even went the length of ascribing all the historical portions of the Bible, this included, to the pen of Ezra. But it was Jean Astruc, a Belgian physician, who in 1760 first laid down the lines along which criticism has since proceeded, by distinguishing between the portions in which the Divine Being is called Elohim, or God (E.V.), and Jehovah, or LORD (E.V.), and assigning these to different authors, calling the one the Elohist and the other the Jehovist. This distinction, supported by other characteristic differences, such as appeared in the language, &c., was applied by him only to Genesis, but it was subsequently extended to the three books that follow. These portions were at first supposed to have been pieced together in a loose, disconnected manner, according to a hypothesis called the "fragmentary"; but that hypothesis was at length superseded by another called the "supplementary," which saw in the Elohistic portion the primitive groundwork, and regarded the work of the Jehovist as of the nature of a supplement. Ere long this hypothesis also was superseded by another, viz., that the Jehovist did not "fill in" the Elohistic groundwork, "his narratives being originally independent; and it was not till long after their composition that they were welded by a redactor into a single whole with other documents, some earlier and some later than themselves."

Thus, according to this criticism, the Hexateuch was composed of three portions, the Elohistic, the Jehovistic, and the Deuteronomic, the author of which last was further alleged to have been the redactor of the whole, these three representing severally the priestly, the prophetic, and the popular religious points of view. The first portion is largely regulative of worship and priestly offices, and contains historical matter bearing upon the institution of these things. It has been also called the "priestly code."

Later criticism has considerably modified this assortment of the constituent parts of the Hexateuch. According to the view generally accepted by the advanced school of critics there are four principal elements: (1) that of the Jahvist—who uses the word *Jahveh* (Jehovah), and represents the prophetic age and spirit—referred to as J ; (2) the Elohistic writing, *i.e.*, that in which the word *Elohim* (God) is used—known as E, a combination of these two being recognised as JE ; (3) the work of the author of Deuteronomy—called D ; and (4) that of the compiler of the bulk of the priestly legislation in Leviticus and kindred contributions to other parts of the Hexateuch which are attributed in this scheme of criticism to the time of Ezra—called P after the "priestly code."

These views have now been substantially adopted by most of the professors of Old Testament studies in the two English universities of Oxford and Cambridge, and also by most of those in the Scotch universities. They are based on an analysis of the several books, and a comparison of the Hexateuch with the history of Israel. Thus it is maintained that the Levitical system was not known in the time of the Judges and Kings before the Captivity. In particular, it is urged that, while in the Hexateuch only one central place of worship is sanctioned, in the history before Josiah many places of sacrifice are allowed without rebuke, and even used by inspired prophets, *e.g.*, Elijah at Carmel; that while in the Levitical system the priests must be of the family of Aaron, and are sharply distinguished from other Levites, in Deuteronomy, and in the history, notably in Judges, Levites are treated as priests; and that, on the whole, the history exhibits a simpler religious worship than that of the Levitical law, the movement only becoming a progress if the elaborate ritual stands at the end and not at the beginning of the story of Israel.

On the other hand, the discoveries of the Egyptian Exploration Society, and all that has been deciphered from monuments throwing any light on the subject, tend to establish the historical truth of the narrative contained in the Hexateuch. The route of the exodus is confirmed by Professor Palmer and M. Naville. According to Mr. Reginald Stewart Poole, the most recent discoveries and interpretation of hieroglyphics distinctly favour the antiquity of the Pentateuch. Egyptian names are given more correctly in the Pentateuch than in the later histories, and the details are true to Egyptian life.

It was once asserted that the art of writing was not practised as early as the time of Moses ; but Professor Sayce has demonstrated with an abundance of evidence that this assertion was too hastily made, and was not in accordance with facts that have since come to light. There are extant inscriptions of much earlier dates. Then it is to be observed that the references to the law in Ezra always imply its antiquity, never treating it as a new composition. It cannot be supposed that a great religious awakening sprang from a sheer misrepresentation. The same may be said of the discovery of the law-book—probably Deuteronomy—in the reign of Josiah, which resulted in a great reformation (2 Kings xxii., xxiii.).

These are the principal lines of discussion ; but the controversy goes into elaborate details. Without attempting to pursue it further in this place, we may gather from it the following general conclusions :—

There must have been an ancient law among the priests. There is no reason to deny that this was in writing, or that it originated with Moses. It may well be that a law which a people could not yet live up to should lie in abeyance and be ignored by the nation. As much as this was implied by Josiah's reformation, when he discovered the book of the law and set to work to bring the national worship into harmony with it. But it seems to be clearly established that this underwent successive revisions. There is nothing derogatory of its Divine authority in supposing that so great an inspired authority as Ezra should have been commissioned to bring it up to the requirements of his age.

It is now generally agreed that the materials out of which the Hexateuch was composed were not written out afresh, as would have been the case with a modern history, but that, in accordance with the custom of ancient writers, they were taken over bodily. Thus we have a flood of light on points that formerly occasioned much perplexity. For example, there are two parallel accounts of the Creation, and two of the Flood. Since it is now made clear that these come from separate sources, it is uncritical to cite them as instances of contradictions in the Bible, as sceptical writers were accustomed to do. They should be regarded historically as representing different statements of the subjects they treat of taken from different standpoints. It is an immense advantage to study the old narratives thus discriminatingly. In this way many difficulties that have perplexed anxious readers will be removed.

Genesis.—*Its Title.*—This title is first found applied to the book in the Septuagint version, because it contains an account of the *genesis*, or beginning, of things, and especially of the history of the chosen people. It is called in Hebrew Bereshith (*i.e.*, In the Beginning), its first word, and, in the Talmud, the Book of Creation, or the Book of Abraham, Isaac, and Jacob. However criticism may discuss its formation, the book contains, beyond a doubt, documents of the most profound religious and historical interest.

It has two main divisions, the first (*a*) extending from the beginning to the call of Abraham (chaps. i.-xi.), and the second (*b*) from the call of Abraham to the settlement of the children of Israel in Egypt (chaps. xii.-l.); and it concerns itself mainly with the history of five patriarchs and their families—Adam and Noah, Abraham, Isaac, and Jacob.

Contents.—*a.* The Elohistic account of creation of the heavens and the earth with its inhabitants (chap. i. 1-25). Man made after God's image, and his rank in creation (26-31). God rests on and hallows the seventh day (chap. ii. 1-3). The Jehovistic account of creation (5-7). The garden of Eden planted, and man installed in it (8-17). A helpmeet created for him (18-23). The marriage relation grounded on it (24, 25). The tempter and his temptation (chap. iii. 1-5). The fall and its consequences (6-24). Cain and Abel (chap. iv. 1-8). The Divine judgment on Cain (9-15). The separation in the first family of the godless Cainites from the godly Sethites (16-26). Genealogy of the patriarchs in the line of Seth from Adam to Noah (chap. v.). The Sethites corrupt themselves by intermarriage with the Cainites (chap. vi. 1-4). The Lord resolves to destroy them all except Noah (5-13). Noah prepares an ark (14-22). Entry into the ark, and the Flood (chap. vii.). The Flood abates; Noah leaves the ark, and sacrifices; God accepts the sacrifice and takes away the curse, in mercy rejoicing against judgment (chap. viii.). The covenant of God with Noah and his posterity, who found separate families (chap. ix.).

Their dispersion over the earth (chap. x.). A combination against the Divine purpose of the dispersion of mankind, defeated by the confusion of tongues (chap. xi. 1-9). The line of Shem traced to Abram (10-32). *Note.*—In this division the consecration of the Sabbath (chap. ii. 1-3), the distinction between clean and unclean beasts (chap. vii. 2, *seq.*), and the commands to Noah (chap. ix. 1-7) point onwards to the ordinances of the Levitical era, while the statements as to Terah's offspring (chap. xi. 26-30) await their expansion in chapters xii. 5; xiii. 5, *seq.;* xix.; xxii. 20, *seq.;* and xxiv.

b. The call of Abram, his departure in faith, arrival in the land of promise, and sojourn in Egypt, with failure of his faith (chap. xii.). He returns to Canaan; Lot separates from him; God establishes the promise in him (chap. xiii.). Abram fights against Chedorlaomer, and rescues Lot; Melchizedek blesses him and receives tithes (chap. xiv.). Promise to Abram of an heir, and of the land to his seed, he believing it and receiving a sign (chap. xv.). Hagar becomes a mother, giving birth to Ishmael (chap. xvi.). God renews His covenant with Abraham, ordains circumcision as its sign, and promises him a son by Sarah (chap. xvii.). Three mysterious visitors appear who renew the promise to Sarah herself, and intimate the purpose of the Lord to destroy Sodom and Gomorrah, whereupon Abraham intercedes with Him (chap. xviii.). Two angels visit Lot in Sodom, and save Lot, but destroy Sodom and Gomorrah (chap. xix. 1-29). Lot's lapse into heathenism; his daughters give birth to Moab and Ammon (30-38). The Lord protects Sarah (chap. xx.). The heir is born and Ishmael cast out, but the Lord cares for him (chap. xxi. 1-21). Abraham makes a covenant with Abimelech, and calls on the Lord at Beersheba (22-34). Abraham's faith tried and perfected in the offering of Isaac (chap. xxii. 1-19). Nahor's family, with Rebekah in prospect (20-24). Sarah dies, and Abraham buys a burying-place for her in the land (chap. xxiii.). Eliezer goes to fetch a wife for Isaac from the daughters of Nahor; Rebekah accompanies him back, and becomes Isaac's wife (chap. xxiv.). Abraham's children by Keturah sent away from Isaac with gifts (chap. xxv. 1-6). Abraham dies and is buried in Machpelah (7-11). Ishmael's sons and Ishmael's death (12-18); Rebekah is blessed with two children; their birth and character (19-28). Esau sells his birthright to Jacob (29-34). The promise continued and guaranteed to Isaac (chap. xxvi. 1-25). The covenant of peace with Abimelech makes with him (26-33). Esau marries a daughter of Heth to the grief of his parents (34, 35). Esau is cheated of his father's blessing by Jacob, pleads unavailingly to be blessed also, and has to go with a mere earthly blessing, vowing the while vengeance on his brother (chap. xxvii. 1-41). Rebekah therefore sends Jacob off to Laban her brother, and persuades Isaac to consent, lest Jacob also should marry a daughter of Heth (42-46). Jacob departs for Laban, blessed and cautioned by his father, and Esau now chooses a daughter of Ishmael to wife (chap. xxviii. 1-9). Jacob dreams, and the Lord appears to him; he raises a memorial pillar and vows a vow (10-22). Jacob assists Rachel at the well, and is welcomed by Laban her father (chap. xxix. 1-15). Leah and Rachel (16, 17). Jacob loves Rachel and engages to serve seven years for her, but Leah is given him instead (18–26). He serves other seven years for Rachel (27–30). Jacob's children (chap. xxix. 31–xxx. 24). Jacob enriches himself at Laban's expense (25–43). He steals away from Laban, but is pursued and overtaken by Laban at Gilead (chap. xxx. 1–25). Mutual recriminations, and Laban relents and they make a covenant (26–55). Jacob is comforted by the appearance of God's host, and sends his family and flocks before him with presents to conciliate Esau (chap. xxxii. 1–23). He wrestles with the Unknown and prevails (24–32). Jacob meets Esau his brother, and they part in peace (chap. xxxiii. 1–16). He settles at Shechem in Canaan (17–20). Dinah's fall and Simeon and Levi's revenge, with Jacob's fear (chap. xxxiv.). Jacob at Bethel (chap. xxxv. 1–15). Rachel dies and is buried (16–20). Jacob's sons; Isaac's death and burial (21–29). Esau and his sons, the dukes of Edom (chap. xxxvi.). Jacob's partiality to Joseph (chap. xxxvii. 1–4). Joseph's dreams (5–9). His father rebukes him and his brothers envy him (10, 11). Joseph is sent forth to seek his brothers and is sold by them (12–28). Jacob deceived mourns for him as dead (29–35). Joseph under Potiphar (36). Judah's wicked conduct justifying the removal of the chosen seed into Egypt (chap. xxxviii.). Joseph in trust under Potiphar (chap. xxxix. 1–6). Falsely accused and in prison (7–23). Interpretations of the butler's and baker's dreams, which are fulfilled (chap. xl.). Joseph interprets Pharaoh's dream and is set over the land of Egypt (chap. xli. 1–46). The years of plenty and famine (47–57). Joseph's brethren, all except Benjamin, sent to Egypt for corn (chap. xlii. 1–13). Joseph sends them back for Benjamin, to try them (14–38). They return with Benjamin (chap. xliii.). Their troubles in trial of them (chap. xliv.). Joseph makes himself known and sends for his father (chap xlv.). Jacob goes down to Egypt with his family and settles in Goshen (chap. xlvi.). Jacob before Pharaoh (chap. xlvii. 1–12). Joseph buys up the land of Egypt for Pharaoh (13–26). Jacob makes Joseph promise to bury him beside his father (27–31). Jacob blesses Joseph in Ephraim and Manasseh (chap. xlviii.). Jacob blesses his other sons, assigning the pre-eminence to Judah (chap. xlix.). Jacob dies and is buried with his fathers (chap. l. 1–13). Joseph comforts his brethren, and gives orders concerning his bones, and dies (14–26).

Exodus.—The title of this book suggests its leading topic. "Exodus" means a "going out." The first part of the book describes the grand deliverance with which the national history of Israel opens. Genesis dealt with the early traditions of the race and with the personal and family biographies of the patriarchs. Exodus stands at the dawn of the history of the nation of Israel. It falls into two main divisions—(a) Historical (chaps. i.–xviii.), and (b) Legislative (chaps. xix.–xxxviii.).

Contents.—a. The History.—The Israelites increase in Egypt and suffer oppression, under which the Lord preserves them (chap. i.). Moses their deliverer is born and providentially cared for (chap. ii. 1–10). He avenges an act of oppression, and flees to Midian (11–22). The Lord calls to him from the midst of the bush that burned, yet remained unconsumed (chap. ii. 23 ;

iii.). The Lord, when Moses is reluctant to go, promises to be with him, and appoints his brother Aaron his spokesman (chap. iv. 1–17). Moses goes, must circumcise his children by the way, is joined by Aaron, and received by the elders of Israel (18–31). Moses appears before Pharaoh and is repulsed (chap. v. 1–4). Matters growing worse than before, the people complain, and Moses appeals to the Lord (5–23). Moses sent with a pledge from the Lord to the people (chap. vi. 1–9). He is sent again to Pharaoh (10–13). Moses' reluctance being once more overcome, he appears with Aaron before Pharaoh (14–30, and chap. vii. 1–13). The plagues : 1. The waters smitten that they stank (chap. vii. 14–25). 2. The frogs (chap. viii. 1–14). 3. The lice (15–19). 4. The flies (20–32). 5. The cattle-murrain (chap. ix. 1–7). 6. The boils (8–12). 7. The hail (13–35). 8. The locusts (chap. x. 1–20). 9. The darkness (21–29). The Lord threatens to slay all the first-born in Egypt both of man and cattle (chap. xi.). The Passover and the feast of unleavened bread are appointed (chap. xii. 1–28). 10. The first-born are slain, and that night the Israelites make their exodus out of Egypt (29–51). Sanctification of the first-born and solemn renewal of the feast of unleavened bread (chap. xiii. 1–16). The children of Israel under Divine direction make for the Red Sea (17–22). They are led through the Red Sea, while Pharaoh's host in pursuit of them are drowned (chap. xiv.). Thanksgiving song of Moses and Miriam (chap. xv. 1–21). By the waters of Marah and Elim (22–27). On entering the wilderness of sin the people murmur ; the Lord sends manna and quails (chap. xvi.). They murmur again at Rephidim, and the Lord gives water from the rock (chap. xvii. 1–7). Amalek attacks them and is overcome by the intercession of Moses (8–16). Jethro visits the camp and advises Moses to appoint judges (chap. xviii.).

b. The Legislation.—The Israelites being at Sinai, the Lord announces His covenant, and the people sanctify themselves (chap. xix.). The promulgation of the Ten Commandments (chap. xx. 1–17). The people are afraid (18–21). The altar of sacrifice to be henceforth the meeting-place between the Lord and the people (22–26). Laws instituted to regulate the social life of the people (chaps. xxi.–xxiii. 13). Israel to appear three times a year before the Lord (14–19). An angel is appointed to go before them ; him they must obey and not provoke (20–23). They must hold no fellowship with the Canaanites or their gods (24–33). Ratification is made of the covenant (chap. xxiv. 1–11). Moses called up into the Mount, where he remains forty days and forty nights (12–18). Free-will offerings are required of the people for the erection of a tabernacle of worship (chap. xxv. 1–9). The ark and the mercy-seat (10–22). The table of shewbread (23–30). The golden candlestick (31–40). The structure of the Tabernacle (chap. xxvi.). The altar of burnt-offering (chap. xxvii. 1–8). The fore-court (9–19). The holy oil (20, 21). The investiture and consecration of Aaron and his sons to the priesthood takes place (chaps. xxviii. and xxix.). The altar of incense and the service connected with it (chap. xxx. 1–10). Ransom money (11–16). The brazen laver (17–21). The holy anointing oil (22–33). Incense (34–38). Bezaleel and Oholiab are appointed to superintend and execute the work (chap. xxxi. 1–11). The Sabbath is enjoined again (12-17). The Lord gives Moses the two tables of stone (18). The people, while Moses is on the Mount, make a golden calf (chap. xxxii. 1-6). The Lord threatens them, but spares them at the intercession of Moses (7-14). Moses' zeal for the Lord in the camp (15-29). He intercedes for the people, yet the Lord punishes them (30-35). The Lord renews His promises, and offers to send His angel with them, instead of going in the midst of them any more Himself (chap. xxxiii. 1-6). Moses prays to the Lord, and He shows him His glory (7-23, and chap. xxxiv. 1-9). The people are to keep the covenant with the Lord and not play falsely with Him (10-28). The Lord gives the people new tables of the Law, and they see with awe the reflection of His glory in the face of Moses (29-35). Regulation regarding the times of work (chap. xxxv. 1-3). Offerings brought for the erection of the Tabernacle (4-29). Public appointment of Bezaleel and Oholiab to the work (30-35). The execution of the work (chap. xxxvi.). The contents of the Tabernacle (chap. xxxvii.). The altar of burnt-offering, the laver, and the forecourt (chap. xxxviii. 1-20). The material used (21-31). The priests' raiment (chap. xxxix. 1-31). The delivery of the finished work to Moses (32, 33). The Lord gives directions (chap. xl. 1-15). The Tabernacle is erected (16-33). The glory of the Lord fills it (34, 35). The cloud and the fire that rest on and accompany it (36-38).

Leviticus.—This book, which is designated in Hebrew Vayikra, from its first word, and by the Rabbis as the "Law of the Priests" and the "Law of the Offering," bears the title it holds in our Bibles because it chiefly contains the laws and ordinances appointed to regulate the services of the sanctuary conducted by a priesthood of the tribe of *Levi*. The narrative portion of it embraces a period of one year, commencing with the institution of the Tabernacle worship and terminating with the eve of the departure of the children of Israel from the wilderness of Sinai ; but it is nearly all legislative, the only narrative portions being the consecration of Aaron and his sons, the death of Nadab and Abihu and the stoning of the blasphemer. The legislation it contains is no longer from Mount Sinai, which the people were forbidden to approach, but from the Tabernacle in the midst of them, through which alone they were permitted to draw near to God. This legislation consists mainly of six divisions—the first, (a) respecting Sacrifices ; the second, (b) the Priests ; the third, (c) the Bodily Purity required of Israel in connection with worship ; and the fourth, (d) the Holiness required of Israel as the people of God ; the fifth, (e) the Feasts ; and sixth, (f) remaining Legislation.

Contents.—a. The Sacrifices.—General directions concerning the burnt-offering (chap. i.), the meat-offering (chap. ii.), the peace-offering (chap. iii.), the sin-offering for the priest and the people (chap. iv.), the trespass-offering (chap. v.). Directions for the priests in regard to these offerings (chaps. vi. and vii.).

b. The Priests.—The consecration and investiture of Aaron and his sons (chap. viii.). Assumption of the priestly office by them, with offerings for themselves and the people (chap.

ix. 1-23). Fire from the Lord to consume the burnt-offering (24). Judgment on Nadab and Abihu for offering strange fire (chap. x. 1-5). Injunctions to the priests (6-20).

c. Bodily Purity.—Animals clean and unclean, or that may or may not be eaten (chap. xi.). Purification after childbirth (chap. xii.). Regulations regarding leprosy (chaps. xiii. and xiv.). Other bodily defilements in men and women (chap. xv.). The yearly purification on the Day of Atonement (chap. xvi.).

d. Holiness.—Restrictions as to the offering and eating of blood as well as of a dead carcass (chap. xvii.). Moral duties of the Israelites (chaps. xviii.-xx.). Qualifications and special duties belonging to the priestly state (chaps. xxi. and xxii.).

e. The Feasts.—The Sabbath (chap. xxiii. 1-3). The Passover (4-8). The Feast of First-fruits (9-14). The Feast of Weeks (15-22). The Feast of Trumpets on New Year's Day (23-25). The Day of Atonement (26-32). The Feast of Tabernacles, or Booths (33, 34).

f. Remaining Legislation.—The golden candle-stick and the shewbread (chap. xxiv. 1-9). Law regarding blasphemy, and a blasphemer stoned (10-16). Compensation for crime (17-22). The Sabbath of the seventh year (chap. xxv. 1-7). The jubilee year (8-55). Promises and threats (chap. xxvi.). Vows (chap. xxvii.).

Numbers.—This title is a translation of the word "Arithmoi," a designation applied to the book by the LXX. in consideration of two "numberings" of the people, one at the beginning and the other at the close of the narrative. It embraces a period of thirty-eight years and three months, and continues the history from the eve of the departure of the camp of Israel out of the wilderness of Sinai to its arrival on "the plains of Moab by Jordan near Jericho," just prior to the conquest of the land of Canaan. It is divided into three epochs—(a) the Preparations for the March, (b) the March itself, and (c) the Preparations for the Conquest.

Contents.—a. Preparations for the March.—The census of the tribes, with a view to war (chap. i. 1-46). Exemption of the Levites (47-54). Disposition of the tribes in camping and marching (chap. ii.). Census of the Levites and their duties (chaps. iii. and iv.). The purification of the camp (chap. v. 1-4). The trespass-offering (5-10). The jealousy-ordeal (11-31). The Nazarite law (chap. vi. 1-21). The priestly benediction (22-27). Offerings of the chiefs of the tribes at the dedication of the Tabernacle (chap. vii.). The consecration of the Levites (chap. viii.). The Passover in the second year after the Exodus (chap. ix. 1-14). The pillar of cloud and fire over the Tabernacle (15-23). The use of the silver trumpets (chap. x. 1-10).

b. The March.—Movement of the camp out of the wilderness of Sinai (chap. x. 11-36). The murmuring and judgment at Taberah (chap. xi.). Sedition of Aaron and Miriam, and Miriam's leprosy (chap. xii.). The spies and their report of the land and its inhabitants (chap. xiii.). The refusal of the people to go forward, and the judgment of the Lord (chap. xiv. 1-39). Defeat by Amalek (40-45). Different sacrificial laws (chap. xv. 1-31). A Sabbath-breaker punished (32-36). The law of fringes (37-41). The rebellion of Korah, Dathan, and Abiram, and the murmuring of the people (chap xvi.). Confirmation of Aaron's authority by the budding of his rod (chap. xvii.). The service of the priests and Levites, and their revenues (chap. xviii.). The water of separation, or purification (chap. xix.).

c. *Preparations for the Conquest.*—Death of Miriam (chaps. xx. 1). Moses smites the rock at Meribah (2-13). Embassy to Edom (14-21). Death of Aaron (22-29). The Canaanites destroyed at Hormah ; the fiery serpents ; the conquest of the land of Sihon and Og (chap. xxi.). Balak, king of Moab, sends for Balaam to curse Israel (chap. xxii.). Balaam blesses instead of cursing (chap. xxiii.). Balaam prophesies the future of Israel (chap. xxiv.). Idolatry committed in Moab, and its punishment (chap. xxv.). A second enumeration of the people (chap. xxvi.). Decision on the inheritance of daughters (chap. xxvii. 1-11). Joshua appointed Moses' successor (12-23). Laws regarding offerings and festivals (chaps. xxviii. and xxix.). Laws regarding vows (chap. xxx.). The conquest of the Midianites (chap. xxxi.). Settlements allotted to the tribes of Reuben, Gad, and the half tribe of Manasseh east of the Jordan (chap. xxxii.). Successive encampments in the wilderness (chap. xxxiii. 1-49). The Canaanites to be rooted out (50-56). The boundaries of the Holy Land defined and those who are to divide it (chap. xxxiv.). The appointment of cities for the Levites and cities of refuge (chap. xxxv.). Directions respecting heiresses (chap. xxxvi. 1-12). A subscription forming the conclusion of the book (13).

Deuteronomy.—The title of this book, which signifies "the second law," is derived from the LXX., and was applied to it because it was regarded as in the main a re-statement and reinforcement of the Divine law previously proclaimed in the wilderness. It contains the farewell address of Moses to the people in the plains of Moab on the last month of their wanderings, and it winds up with his appointment of Joshua to be his successor, his song at the close of his pilgrimage, his benediction, and his death. It is written throughout in a solemn hortatory vein, and in the spirit of an inspired prophet rather than that of an unimpassioned lawgiver. The farewell address consists of three discourses—the first, (a) extending to chap. iv. 40 ; the second, (b) to chap. xxvi. 19 ; the third, (c) to chap. xxx. ; and (d) conclusion to chap. xxxiv.

Contents.—a. *First Discourse.*—Israel to occupy Canaan (chap. i. 1-21). This purpose hitherto frustrated by their lack of faith (22-46). The kings of the Amorites and of Bashan given into their hands as a pledge that the promise would be fulfilled (chaps. ii. and iii.). The observance of the covenant the condition of continuing in the land (chap. iv. 1-40). Three cities of refuge appointed east of the Jordan (41-43).

b. *Second Discourse.* — The law to be rehearsed (chap. iv. 44-49). The covenant at Horeb called to mind (chap. v. 1-5). The ten commandments, with the circumstances of their delivery and the lesson (6-33). A zealous observance and enforcement of the law of the Lord the condition of well-being (chap. vi.). For this end the Canaanites and their idolatries to be rooted out (chap. vii.). Israel to recall the past dealings of the Lord (chap. viii.). Israel

to look to the Lord and remember His judgments against them (chap. ix.). Divine mercy as shown in the past (chap. x.). God's judgments in their behalf and the promise implied in them (chap. xi. 1-17.) An exhortation to obedience (18-25). The blessing and the curse (26-32). All monuments of idolatry to be destroyed (chap. xii. 1-4). Israel to have but one place for religious offerings (5-28). Idolatrous snares to be shunned (29-32). All who entice to idolatry and the idolatrous cities to be destroyed (chap. xiii.). Idolatrous mourning practices forbidden (chap. xiv. 1, 2). Things clean and unclean (3-21). Tithes and their distribution (22-29). The year of release and its obligations (chap. xv.). The passover (chap. xvi. 1-8). The feast of weeks (9-12). The feast of tabernacles (13-17). Judges to do justice (18-20). Idolatry forbidden (21, 22, and chap. xvii. 1-7). The priests as judges (8-13). The law for the king (14-20) ; of the priests, Levites, and prophets (chap. xviii.). Cities of refuge to be established (chap. xix. 1-10). Landmarks and witnesses (11-21). Ordinances in regard to war (chap. xx.). Expiation of a murder by one unknown (chap. xxi. 1-9). The treatment of a captive taken to wife (10-14). The right of the first-born (15-17). The refractory son (18-21). The burial of one hanged (22, 23). Other laws touching domestic and social life (chaps. xxii.-xxvi.).

c. *Third Discourse.*—Stones to be erected on Mount Ebal inscribed with the words of the law (chap. xxvii. 1-8). The people to obey the voice of the Lord (9, 10). The people to assemble, half on Mount Gerizim and half on Mount Ebal (11-13). Curses to be pronounced (14-26). Blessings (chap. xxviii. 1-14). Curses (15-68). Exhortations to keep the covenant (chap. xxix.). God's mercy to the penitent (chap. xxx. 1-10). The commandment written on the heart to be obeyed (11-14). Life and death set forth in it (15-20).

d. *Conclusion.*—Moses delivers the law to the priests and encourages the people and Joshua (chap. xxxi.). Moses' song (chap. xxxii. 1-44). Moses to die and be buried outside the land of promise (45-52). The blessing of Moses, the man of God (chap. xxxiii.). Moses on the top of Pisgah (chap. xxxiv. 1-4). He dies (5-8). Joshua succeeds him (9). Moses' greatness as a prophet (10-12).

Joshua.—This book is so called because it contains the history of Israel under the guidance of Joshua, beginning with his appointment to the leadership and concluding with his death. The book covers a period of twenty-five years, and contains an account of, (a) the Invasion of Canaan, (b) the Conquest of it, (c) the Distribution by lot of the Land, and (d) Joshua's Farewell to the people, and his Death. Throughout the book Joshua is but the Lord's minister, and it is the Lord who at once prepares the way, and fights and provides, for Israel.

Contents.—a. *The Invasion.*—God encourages Joshua for his work (chap. i. 1-9). The people commanded to get ready (10-18). Spies are sent to Jericho, and their report (chap. ii.). The miraculous passage of the Jordan (chaps. iii. and iv.). The circumcision of Israel, the Passover at Gilgal, and the ceasing of the manna (chap. v. 1-12).

b. The Conquest.—Vision of the Captain of the Lord's host and miraculous fall of Jericho (chap. v. 13 to chap. vi. 1–27). Israel suffers defeat before Ai for a sin in the camp (chap. vii. 1–5). The Lord appealed to (6–9). The offence revealed and the expiation prescribed (10–15). The punishment by death of Achan and his family (16–26). The taking of Ai (chap. viii. 1–29). The blessing and cursing on Mounts Ebal and Gerizim (30–35). Confederacy against Israel (chap. ix. 1, 2). Crafty submission of the Gibeonites (3–27). Victory over the confederate kings of the south (chap. x.). Victory over the confederate kings of the north, with the occupation of the strong cities of the land (chap. xi.). List of the conquered kings (chap. xii.).

c. The Division of the Land.—Divine order to apportion the land, although only conquered in part (chap. xiii. 1–14). The portions on the east allotted to Reuben, Gad, and half Manasseh (15–33). In the camp at Gilgal; Caleb's portion and Judah's (chaps. xiv. and xv.). Joseph's portion, or Ephraim's and half Manasseh's (chaps. xvi. and xvii.). At Shiloh the Tabernacle is erected (chap. xviii. 1–10). Benjamin's portion assigned (11–28). The allotment of Simeon, Zebulun, Issachar, Asher, Naphtali, and Dan (chap. xix. 1–48). Inheritance given to Joshua (49–51). The cities of refuge appointed (chap. xx.). Forty-eight cities allotted to the Levites (chap. xxi.). The transjordanic tribes dismissed to their own portions (chap. xxii.).

d. Joshua's Farewell and Death.—Joshua's exhortation (chap. xxiii.). He renews the covenant at Shechem (chap. xxiv. 1–28). His death (29–33).

See Driver, *Introduction to the Literature of the Old Testament;* Bennett and Adeney, *Biblical Introduction.* For the critical view of the Hexateuch see also W. R. Smith, *The Old Testament in the Jewish Church;* Wellhausen, *History of Israel;* Kuenen, *The Hexateuch.* For the defence of the Mosaic authorship of the Pentateuch or its antiquity see Cave, *Inspiration of the Old Testament;* Bissell, *The Pentateuch;* Green, *Moses and the Prophets,* and *The Hebrew Feasts.* Also see Driver, Bennett on *Genesis;* Gray on *Numbers;* Driver on *Deuteronomy.*

CHAPTER IX.

THE NATIONAL HISTORY OF ISRAEL.

Judges.—This book is so called because it contains an account of certain signal deliverances which the Lord wrought out by the hands of men who were named "judges," when one tribe of Israel after another was threatened with extinction by the Canaanites who had been left in the land. These "judges" were of the character of heroes rather than magistrates, but they are justly named, as it was by them the Lord executed His judgments. There is mention by name of twelve in this book, though only six attain special distinction; and they are all rather tribal than national heroes, there being as yet no king in Israel to unite the tribes into one. The account covers the time from the death of Joshua to the birth of Samuel, and is not so much a history as a collection of narratives of events, some of which were contemporaneous. The text of the book, of which the body supplies the examples, is given in chap. ii. 14–23, and there are six cycles of revolt, chastisement, and deliverance recorded. The story is one throughout: the apostasy and consequent affliction of the people, their conversion, deliverance, and consequent state of peace ; and the object of the book is to show that, as often as Israel sins against the Lord, so often does she fall under the power of her enemies, and that, so soon as she returns to her allegiance, so soon will the Lord raise up a deliverer for her ; while, at the same time, from the emphasis repeatedly laid on the fact that there was no king in Israel, a reference is implied to the better state of things to be expected from the establishment of the kingdom. The book, in its present form, seems to belong to the prophetic period, but it is composed for the most part of older documents, which the compiler has arranged and edited. It consists of three parts—(*a*) an Introduction, (*b*) the Oppression of Israel by her enemies and the Divine Deliverance by the Judges, and (*c*) an Appendix.

Contents.—a. Introduction.—The Canaanites only partially rooted out (chap. i.). Israel rebuked and warned by the Lord (chap. ii. 1–5). Israel under Joshua, and after (6–13). The Lord's anger with Israel in their apostasy (14–23). The nations left to prove them (chap. iii. 1–7).

b. Israel in its Apostasy, Oppression, and Deliverance.—Oppressed by Chushan-rishathaim and delivered by Othniel (chap. iii. 8–11). Oppressed by Eglon and delivered by Ehud (12–30). Shamgar smites six hundred Philistines (31). Israel oppressed by Jabin of Hazor, and delivered by Barak at the call and with the help of Deborah ; the episode of Jael, the wife of Heber (chap. iv.). Deborah's triumph song (chap. v.). Israel, sore oppressed by Midian, cries to the Lord (chap. vi. 1–6). The Lord sends a prophet (7–10). The call to Gideon to deliver the people (11–24). Gideon destroys his father's altar to Baal, and sacrifices to the Lord (25–32). He collects an army (33–35). His fleece a sign (36–40). He reduces his army from twenty-two thousand to three hundred (chap. vii. 1–8). His dream (9–15). He routs the enemy (16–22). He pursues them as far as the Jordan with the help of Ephraim (23–25 and chap. viii. 1–3). The Jordan crossed and the enemy finally defeated ; the men of Succoth and Penuel punished (4–21). Gideon refuses a crown, but makes an ephod to the ruin of his family (22–35). Abimelech, with the help of the Shechemites, king by the murder of all his brothers save Jotham (chap. ix. 1–6). Jotham's parable and threat of a curse (7–21). The curse fulfilled (22–57). Tola and Jair judge Israel (chap. x. 1–5). Israel apostatizes and is oppressed by the Ammonites and the Philistines (6–15). Jephthah called to the leadership against Ammon (chap. xi. 1–11). His reply to the king of Ammon (12–28). His vow and victory (29–33). The vow fulfilled (34–40). The Ephraimites rise up against Jephthah and his Gileadites, but are smitten (chap. xii. 1–6). Jephthah's death (7). Ibzan, Elon, and Abdon judges after him (8–15). The Philistines oppress Israel forty years (chap.

xiii. 1). The annunciation by the angel, and the birth of Samson (2-25). Samson chooses a wife of the Philistines, and finds occasion at the marriage feast to smite the Philistines (chap. xiv.). Faithlessness of his wife and her parents avenged (chap. xv. 1-6). Delivered bound into the hands of the Philistines, he snaps his bonds and smites a thousand with an ass's jawbone (7-17). He recovers his strength miraculously when wearied (18-20). He escapes from Gaza (chap. xvi. 1-3). Delilah finds out his secret, and the Philistines overpower him (4-22). His strength returns, and he slays more of his enemies by his death than in his lifetime (23-30). His burial (31).

c. The Appendix. — The story of Micah's idolatry (chaps. xvii. and xviii.). The outrage at Gibeah (chaps. xix.-xxi.).

Ruth.—This book belongs to the period of the Judges, and it derives its name from the principal subject of it, the Moabitish widow of a Hebrew, who, by her fidelity to her mother-in-law, recommended herself to Boaz, an Israelite, and became his wife and the ancestress of David. The story it tells is in pleasing contrast with what we learn of the times in the book that precedes it, and it supplies what would otherwise have been a missing link in the genealogy of the great monarch of Israel. It was evidently written not before, but after, the period of David's ascendency and acknowledged supremacy as king; so that between the time of the events related and the date of the composition we have an interval of such length as to require the author to explain,-as he does, usages which had fallen obsolete when he wrote it (e.g., chap. iv. 7). Who the author was, it is impossible to say, though tradition ascribes it, as also the Book of Judges, to Samuel. The story is charmingly told, it is marked by great simplicity of narration and minute truthfulness of detail, and it gives a delightful picture of Jewish life in the olden times.

Contents.—Ruth leaves the land of Moab and comes with her mother-in-law, Naomi, to Bethlehem (chap. i.). For her fidelity to her mother-in-law and devotion to His worship, the Lord blesses her on the field of Boaz (chap. ii.). By Naomi's advice she makes suit to Boaz, and is married to him (chaps. iii. and iv. 17). She becomes the ancestress of David (18-22).

Samuel I. and II.—These two books originally formed one, as in the Hebrew MSS. they still do. They were first divided into two by the LXX., and this division was adhered to in the Vulgate and subsequent versions. In the LXX. and the Vulgate they were numbered with the books that follow, and entitled the First and Second Books of Kings, although in the Hebrew canon they are named "Samuel." Both designations are appropriate: the former, since the books relate the history of the rise and growth of the kingdom under Saul and David; and the latter, seeing that it was Samuel who anointed both of these kings, and who was, if not the author of the story, the spiritual father and founder of the monarchy. Hebrew tradition, founding on 1 Chronicles xxix. 29, ascribes the authorship to Samuel, only as far, of course, as to the account of his death. But we have no record of this tradition earlier than A.D. 500. The work itself does not claim to be written by Samuel. Still there are indications of a compa-

ratively early date for the writing of the book, though not of contemporary authorship. (1.) The Pentateuch law is ignored and Moses is rarely named. This agrees with what we have seen as to the neglect of the law in the early centuries of the national history of Israel (see p. 14). (2.) The style of the language agrees with that of Joel and Isaiah—the best style of the golden age of Hebrew prose. (3.) The writer refers to original authorities, such as the Book of Jasher or the Upright, and The Bow. (4.) There are lifelike features in the narrative, which lead to the conclusion that the book is not only founded on, but also contains almost intact accounts of contemporary date, and even of eye-witnesses of the transactions. The story embraces a period of a hundred and thirty years, and extends from the end of the time of the Judges to the close of the reign of David, the connecting link being found in the civil judgeship of Eli and Samuel. The object of the narrative is to exhibit the kingdom as it realised itself in view of a divine ideal; and the prominence given to the lives of Samuel and David would seem to be due to a design to portray the one as the type of the prophetic, and the other as the type of the kingly, character—the king's counsellor, in this case, selecting the king, and not, as was the rule afterwards, the king his counsellor.

Samuel I.—This book contains an account of the judgeship of Samuel and of the reign of Saul, and is divided into three sections, which give respectively accounts of (a) the Revival or Restoration of the theocracy by Samuel (chaps. i.-vii.), (b) the Reign of Saul from his election to his rejection (chaps. viii.-xv.), and (c) the Fall of Saul and the Election of David, with the Persecution thereafter of the latter by the former (chaps. xvi.-xxxi.).

Contents.—a. Hannah receives a son from the Lord, whom she calls Samuel, and gives him to the Lord agreeably to her vow (chap. i.). Her prophetic song of praise (chap. ii. 1-10). While Samuel ministers before Eli the priest, Eli's sons by their ungodliness bring woe from the Lord upon their father's house (11-36). The Lord appears to Samuel, and after announcing the fall of Eli's house, appoints him as His prophet to all Israel (chap. iii.). The judgment is fulfilled, and the ark carried off by the Philistines (chap. iv.). The Philistines tremble before the ark (chap. v.). They send back the ark with offerings, and leave it with the men of Beth-shemesh (chap. vi. 1-18). The ark has to be removed, and is set up in Kirjath-jearim (19-21 and chap. vii. 1). At the word of Samuel, Israel turns to the Lord and conquers the Philistines (2-14). Samuel judges Israel (15-17).

b. The elders of Israel will have a king, in spite of the warning words of Samuel (chap. viii.). The Lord gives them Saul for king, and Samuel anoints him (chaps. ix. and x. 1-16). Saul is chosen by lot, and after his victory over the Ammonites is installed at Gilgal (17-27; chap. xi. 1-15). Samuel's last address to the people (chap. xii.). Saul's first victories over the Philistines (chaps. xiii. and xiv. 1-46). His other victories (47, 48). His family (49-52). Saul disobeys the Lord in the matter of the Amalekites, and Samuel is sent to announce his rejection (chap. xv.).

c. Samuel goes at the bidding of the Lord to Bethlehem and anoints David king (chap. xvi. 1-13). The Spirit of the Lord departs from Saul, and an evil spirit from the Lord possesses him (14, 15). A charmer is sought out and David is sent for. David breaks the spell of the evil spirit by playing on a harp (16-23), slays Goliath, is promoted to honour by the king, and becomes the friend of Jonathan (chaps. xvii. and xviii. 1-5). The fame of David awakens the jealousy of Saul, and he seeks to make away with him (6-30). David flees to Samuel, and Saul follows him, and begins to prophesy (chap. xix.). Jonathan tries reconciliation, but David has to flee again (chap. xx.). He flees to Nob, and then to Gath (chap. xxi.). Driven from thence, he hides in the cave of Adullam, then in the land of Moab, and finally in the forest of Hareth (chap. xxii. 1-5). Saul's vengeance on the priestly city of Nob (6-23). Saul pursues David to Keilah, then to the wilderness of Ziph (chap. xxiii.); then to the wilderness of Engedi, where David might have slain Saul, but spares him (chap. xxiv.). Samuel dies (chap. xxv. 1). Nabal offends David, but Abigail appeases him (2-44). Saul comes into David's power again, and is spared a second time (chap. xxvi.). David escapes into the land of the Philistines, receives Ziklag as a dwelling-place, and fights against the enemies of Israel (chap. xxvii.). The Philistines gather against Saul at Gilboa, and he consults the witch of Endor (chap. xxviii.). While David is kept back from going up (chap. xxix.) and is fighting with the Amalekites (chap. xxx.), Saul contends with the Philistines, and kills himself, after the battle goes against him and three of his sons are slain (chap. xxxi.).

Samuel II.—This book contains a narrative of the Reign of David, and is divided into four sections, which give respectively account of (*a*) the reign at its commencement (chaps. i.-iv.), (*b*) the reign at the height of its power and glory (chaps. v.-ix.), (*c*) David's fall and restoration (chaps. x.-xx.), and (*d*) the close of the reign (chaps. xxi., xxii.), to which is added an appendix (chaps. xxiii., xxiv.).

Contents.—*a.* Lament of David over the death of Saul and Jonathan (chap. i.). David goes up in the direction of Hebron, and is there anointed king over Judah; while Abner raises Ishbosheth, Saul's son, to be king over the rest of Israel (chap. ii. 1-11). In the civil war that ensued, Abner retires (12-32). Abner gives up Ishbosheth and goes over with the rest of Israel to David, yet is murdered by Joab, to the great grief of the king (chap. iii.). Ishbosheth is also slain, but David avenges the murder on its perpetrators (chap. iv.).

b. David is anointed in Hebron king over all Israel (chap. v. 1-5). He takes the stronghold of Zion, and makes Jerusalem his capital city, after smiting the Philistines again twice over (6-25). David brings up the ark to Zion with expressions of rejoicing, and pitches a tent for it there (chap. vi.). He would build a temple for the Lord, but is forbidden, while the Lord promises He will establish his seed on the throne for ever (chap. vii.). He now subdues all his enemies round about, and establishes an administration for the execution of justice and judgment in his kingdom (chap. viii.). He shows kindness to the house of Saul (chap. ix.).

c. David goes forth against the children of Ammon, and defeats the Syrians who had been hired to help them (chap. x.). While Joab prosecutes the war and overthrows Ammon, David, who tarries at home, commits the double crime of adultery with Bathsheba, and the murder of Uriah, her husband (chap. xi.). Nathan by a parable convicts him of his guilt, and he repents, but the Lord in grave displeasure does not suffer his child to live (chap. xii. 1-18.). David's grief (19-23). Solomon is born (24, 25). Joab destroys Rabbah and all the Ammonitish cities (26-31). Ammon, David's son, for his outrage on his sister, Tamar, has to fall by the hand of Absalom, her brother (chap. xiii. 1-33). Absalom flees into exile (34-39). Ere long Absalom is brought back and is received by the king (chap. xiv.). Absalom revolts against his father, and forces him to flee from Jerusalem (chaps. xv. and xvi. 1-4). Shimei curses the king, and does him dishonour (5-14). Absalom enters Jerusalem as king, and by Ahithophel's counsel takes possession of his father's concubines (15-23). Ahithophel would have him go forth against his father, but Hushai dissuades him and warns David (chap. xvii. 1-23). Absalom takes the field, but his army is beaten, and himself slain (24-29, and chap. xviii. 1-18). David is told, and he mourns for Absalom (19-33, and chap. xix. 1-4). Joab remonstrates with him, and the king is brought back to Jerusalem by the men of Judah (5-40). A strife arises in consequence between Judah and Israel (41-43); upon which Sheba attempts a bootless revolt (chap. xx. 1-22). The kingdom is restored (23-26).

d. The land suffers for the sins of Saul, and his sons are given up to death by way of an atonement (chap. xxi. 1-14). David is delivered out of the hands of the Philistines (15-22). His song of praise to the Lord (chap. xxii.). The last words of David (chap. xxiii. 1-7). David's mighty men (8-39). The numbering of the people and the plague (chap. xxiv.).

Kings I. and II.—These books, like the two preceding, formed originally one, and appear as one in the Hebrew canon. The division into two was the work of the LXX., in which, as in the Vulgate, they are designated severally as the " Third and Fourth Books of Kings "—the books of Samuel being called the First and Second. They contain, as the title implies, the history of the nation under the kings, and the narrative covers a period from its establishment under David to the fall of the kingdom of Judah. It commences with the death of David and the accession of Solomon, and extends to the Babylonian exile. During this time the kingdom falls into two, named respectively Israel and Judah. For their sins both kingdoms go into captivity, first Israel and then Judah, more than a hundred and thirty years after. It is less a history of the kings themselves than of the theocracy, in which the prophets play a conspicuous and important *rôle*, since it is according as their words are listened to or disregarded that the national fortunes are determined. The author appears to have belonged to this class, but who he was is uncertain. The Talmud assigns the work to Jeremiah, but this is improbable. The author writes after the commencement of the Captivity, and from the place of it, but he draws from documents of an earlier date, and incorporates in his account narratives many of which look as if they proceeded from contemporaries. His object, which is didactic, is to show how Israel, on the one hand, because of her apostasy and persistent disregard of the prophet's word, fell into deeper and deeper guilt, till she became hopelessly demoralised, and had to be driven from her land ; and how Judah, on the other hand, though she too must go into captivity, might, if she repented and returned to the Lord, yet recover all her forfeited privileges.

Contents.—The history is divided into three parts and gives an account (*a*) of the Reign of Solomon, (*b*) of the Kingdoms of Israel and Judah till the fall of the former, and (*c*) of the Kingdom of Judah after the dispersion of Israel till the captivity at Babylon.

Kings I.—*a.* When David is failing with years, Adonijah attempts to seize the throne (chap. i. 1-10). David has Solomon anointed king (11-40). Adonijah flees for refuge to the altar, and is forgiven on doing homage to Solomon (41-53). David gives a charge to Solomon and dies (chap. ii. 1-11). Solomon establishes himself in the kingdom (12-46). He marries a daughter of Pharaoh (chap. iii. 1-3). He sacrifices at Gibeon, and asks to obtain from the Lord a wise and an understanding heart, and gives a proof of his wisdom (4-28). The glory of his reign is seen in the list of his princes and officers, the prosperity of the people, the extent of his dominion, and his fame for wisdom (chap. iv.). Solomon collects materials for a temple, and workmen (chap. v.). The temple is begun ; the plan of it, and its extent (chap. vi. 1-10). The Lord encourages Solomon in the work (11-13). The interior is described, and the sanctuary (14-36). It is finished (37, 38). Solomon builds a palace for himself, and Hiram is fetched from Tyre to build pillars and make vessels of brass (chap. vii.). The ark and the tabernacle with their vessels are brought into the temple (chap. viii. 1-11). Solomon's address to the people on this occasion, and his prayer in dedication (12-53). He blesses the people, offers sacrifices, and keeps a feast to the Lord, in which all Israel joins (54-66). The Lord reveals Himself, and gives Solomon a pledge that He has heard his prayer (chap. ix. 1-9). Hiram's reward (10-14). He leaves Solomon employed in the work (15-25). He builds a navy (26-28). The Queen of Sheba's visit (chap. x. 1-13). Solomon's riches and glory (14-29). Solomon is seduced by strange women to serve other gods (chap. xi. 1-8). The Lord threatens in consequence to rend all the kingdom except one tribe from his son, and meanwhile raises up adversaries to trouble him (9-40). The death of Solomon (41-43).

b. The ten tribes revolt from Rehoboam, the son of Solomon, and erect the kingdom of Israel under Jeroboam, who builds him cities and sets up an idolatrous worship in Bethel and Dan (chap. xii.). A prophet is sent to denounce judgment on Jeroboam, but he repents not (chap. xiii.). Ahijah denounces judgment on his house and kingdom (chap. xiv. 1-18). His death (19, 20). Rehoboam does evil, and Shishak from Egypt invades the land (21-28). Rehoboam dies (29-31). After Abijam, who succeeds him, and does evil, comes Asa, who does good, but allies himself with Syria against Israel (chap. xv. 1-24). Baasha exterminates the house of Jeroboam in Israel, and supplants it, but follows in its footsteps (25-34). The house of Baasha falls by the hand of Zimri, as Jehu had foretold (chap. xvi. 1-14). Omri succeeds Zimri, who burns himself (15-28). Ahab reigns and establishes the worship of Baal in Samaria (29-34). Elijah denounces against Ahab drought and famine (chap. xvii. 1). He retires to the brook Cherith, where ravens feed him (2-7). He retires to Zarephath, where a widow miraculously supports him (8-16). He restores her son (17-24). Elijah shows himself to Ahab, and proves that Jehovah, not Baal, is God, and slays the prophets of Baal (chap. xviii. 1-40). He prays, and the Lord sends rain (41-46). He flees from Jezebel, and prays that he may die, but is told to arise and eat (chap. xix. 1-8). He journeys to Horeb, but is recalled by the Lord, who appears to him, and sends him to anoint Hazael, Jehu, and Elisha (9-18). Elisha leaves all and follows him (19-21). Ahab makes a covenant with the king of Syria, whom he has twice defeated by the hand of the Lord ; the Lord is displeased with him and sends a prophet to denounce a judgment on him and his people (chap. xx.). Elijah denounces judgment on him for the murder of Naboth, but because he repents the punishment is deferred to his son's days (chap. xxi.). Ahab is seduced by lying prophets, in spite of the warning of Micaiah, to go up against Syria, and is slain (chap. xxii. 1-40). Jehoshaphat reigns well over Judah (41-50). Ahaziah succeeds Ahab, and does evil in Israel (51-53).

Kings II.—*a.* Ahaziah dies by the hand of the Lord according to the warning of Elijah, because he consulted Baal-zebub instead of the Lord (chap. i.). Elijah is translated to heaven, but leaves his mantle on Elisha, who is acknowledged his successor, which he proves himself to be (chap. ii.). Jehoram, who succeeds Ahaziah, overcomes Moab, as Elisha, seeing Jehoshaphat was with him, had predicted (chap. iii.). Elisha multiplies the widow's oil (chap. iv. 1-7). He is entertained by the Shunammite woman and gives her promise of a son (8-17). He raises her dead son to life (18-37). He works other wonders (38-44). Naaman comes to him and is healed of his leprosy (chap. v. 1-19). The leprosy cleaves to Gehazi, because he takes a reward of Naaman (20-27). Elisha makes iron swim (chap. vi. 1-7). He strikes with blindness the Syrians who had been sent to take him (8-23). Samaria is besieged by the Syrians and in famine, when the king sends to slay Elisha (24-33). The prophet promises plenty for the next day, and it is found in the morning that the Syrians have fled and left their stores behind them (chap. vii.). The Shunammite, who had left during the famine, gets back her land (chap. viii. 1-6). Elisha sorrowfully foresees Hazael will be king of Syria, and Hazael succeeds Ben-hadad (7-15). In Judah, Jehoram establishes the Baal worship and receives his due reward (16-24). Ahaziah, his son, serves Baal also (25-29). Jehu is anointed king of Israel (chap. ix. 1-26). Ahaziah and Jezebel are slain (27-37).

b. Jehu destroys Baal out of Israel (chap. x. 1-28), but not the calf-worship, for which the kingdom suffered at the hand of Hazael (29-36).

In Judah, Athaliah seeks to destroy the house of David, but Jehoash is preserved by Jehoiada and is made king (chap. xi.). He does well so long as Jehoiada lives, but afterwards ill, and his servants slay him (chap. xii.). In Israel, Jehoahaz sins, and suffers from Hazael, as Joash after him (chap. xiii. 1–13). Joash acknowledges Elisha a prophet of the Lord, and is promised victory over the Syrians (14–19). Elisha dies, and his bones prove quickening (20, 21). Hazael dies (22–25). In Judah, Amaziah rules righteously, but does not abolish the high places (chap. xiv. 1–4). Jehoash defeats and spoils him, Azariah succeeding him (5–22). Jeroboam II. succeeds Joash in Israel and restores its boundaries (23–29). In Judah, Azariah reigns well, but is smitten with leprosy, his son Jotham being regent, who succeeds him (chap. xv. 1–7). The family of Jehu extinct (8–12).

c. Shallum succeeds, but is slain by Menahem, under whom Israel becomes tributary to Assyria (13–22). Assyria oppresses Israel (23–31). In Judah, Jotham reigns righteously, only removes not the high places, for which the Lord prepares a scourge (32–38). Ahaz reigns wickedly, and calls in Tiglath-pileser, king of Assyria, against Syria (chap. xvi. 1–9). He introduces an altar from Damascus, and otherwise defiles the temple (10–20). In Israel, Hoshea revolts from Assyria and leagues with Egypt, and the king of Assyria makes an end of the kingdom of Israel (chap. xvii. 1–23). The Assyrian king colonises the land (24). Native idolatrous worship becomes rampant in Samaria (25–41).

d. In Judah, Hezekiah reigns, uprooting idolatry and restoring the worship of Jehovah, while Israel goes into captivity (chap. xviii. 1–12). Sennacherib defies Hezekiah (13–37). Isaiah, when appealed to, comforts Hezekiah (chap. xix. 1–7). Sennacherib renews his defiance, and Hezekiah prays to the Lord (8–19). Isaiah prophesies again (20–34). The Assyrian army is destroyed by the Lord (35–37).

Hezekiah is sick unto death, and prays the Lord; the Lord promises to add fifteen years to his life (chap. xx. 1–11). The king of Babylon sends congratulations through messengers, who are shown the treasures in Jerusalem (12, 13). Isaiah foretells the Babylonian captivity (14–21). Manasseh seduces Judah back to idolatry (chap. xxi. 1–9). The Lord delivers the people over into the hands of their enemies (10–18). Amon's wicked reign (19–26). Josiah restores the temple (chap. xxii. 1–7). He is shown the book of the law, and rends his clothes (8–11). He sends to the prophetess Huldah, who confirms his fear (12–20). He has the book read to the people, and renews the covenant (chap. xxiii. 1–3). He abolishes idolatry (4–20). He keeps the passover (21–23). Notwithstanding his zeal, the curse is not taken away (24–27). He is slain in battle (28–30). His successors become subject to Egypt (31–37). Jehoiakim and his successors fall under the power of Babylon and rebel (chap. xxiv.). Nebuchadnezzar lays siege to Jerusalem, and takes king Zedekiah captive, putting out his eyes (chap. xxv. 1–7). The city is defaced, its valuables carried off, and an end made of Judah (8–26). Jehoiachin is honoured in Babylon (27–30).

Chronicles I. and II.—These books originally formed one, having been first divided by the LXX. into two, and they are expressly continued in Ezra and Nehemiah, which are, moreover, written in the same style, from the same standpoint, and in the same interest, as if by one author. They are called Chronicles after the title "Chronica" given in the Vulgate, ascribed to Jerome, and agreeably to the Hebrew title, "Acts of the Days," *i.e.*, journals or annals; while in the LXX. they receive a name which implies that, in the regard of the Greek translators, they contain matters "left out" in the other historical books. The narrative runs parallel with that of the preceding historical books, especially that of Samuel and Kings; but, whereas the earlier history is written from a prophetic standpoint, this is written from a priestly, and it gives prominence throughout to the history of the kingdom of Judah, as the stay and support of the ritual of divine institution centred in Jerusalem. It forms, along with Ezra and Nehemiah, not so much a history of the nation as one of the church, an ecclesiastical history. The author was animated by religious zeal; and his object was to exhibit the purpose of providence with the nation as revealed in its past history, and to re-establish the people in the land on the lines indicated by this providential history. He seeks to recall the community to love for the sanctuary and zeal for the Lord and His service by reference to those passages in the life of David and his successors, which show how the fortunes of the nation depended on the possession or absence of this spirit. Hence, already in the genealogy, he dwells with preference on the kingdom of Judah and the priesthood of Levi; he neglects most of the history of Saul, and passes at once to that of David; he says nothing of the northern kingdom by itself, occupying himself exclusively with the southern remnant, and giving especial prominence to those chapters in which the kingdom and the priesthood are united in a common zeal for the temple and its worship, and for the institutions of the law generally.

Chronicles I.—*Contents.*—*a.* Genealogies from Adam to David, and thence to Elioenai and his sons (chaps. i.–iii.). Genealogies of the tribes, and more particularly that of Levi (chaps. iv.–vii.). Lists of those who settled in Jerusalem after the Exile (chaps. viii. and ix.).

b. The kingdom is founded in David, and lost to the family of Saul, which perishes (chap. x.). David is chosen king, and sets up his throne in Zion (chap. xi. 1–9). David's mighty men, and their names and exploits (10–47). Those who came to him at Ziklag and at Hebron, their skill, prowess, and helpfulness (chap. xii.). David comes for the ark, but fears to bring it to Zion (chap. xiii.). Hiram builds him a house of cedar; David triumphs over the Philistines, and is feared by surrounding nations (chap. xiv.). He brings up the ark to the city, with accompaniments of rejoicing, by the ministry of the Levites (chaps. xv., and xvi. 1–7). He indites a psalm of thanksgiving (8–36). He appoints ministers to wait on the ark (37–43). David would build a temple to the Lord, but reserves this honour for his son, in whom his kingdom is to be established (chap. xvii.). The Lord gives victories to David, and he dedicates his trophies to the Lord (chap. xviii.). David resents an affront done him by Ammon, and the Syrians make peace with him (chaps. xix., and xx. 1-3). He subdues the Philistines (4-8). He numbers the people, and displeases the Lord (chap. xxi. 1-7). He repents, and chooses pestilence for his punishment (8-15). He sees the people perish, and intercedes till the plague is stayed (16-30). He gets ready materials for the temple, and gives a charge to Solomon (chap. xxii.). He makes Solomon king, and increases the priesthood of the temple (chaps. xxiii. and xxiv.). He appoints and distributes the singers (chap. xxv.). He appoints the keepers of the gate and the treasures (chap. xxvi.). He appoints captains and princes (chap. xxvii.). He exhorts them and Solomon his son (chap. xxviii.). He sets an example to the people to offer willingly to the Lord (chap. xxix. 1-9). He blesses the Lord, sees Solomon king, and dies (10-30).

Chronicles II.—*Contents.*—Solomon accepted of the Lord for his offerings at Gibeon (chap. i. 1-6). He asks and obtains wisdom (7-12). His forces and great wealth (13-17). He sends to Tyre for workmen and labourers to build the temple (chap. ii.). He begins to build it on Mount Moriah (chap. iii. 1, 2). Its dimensions, structure, vessels, &c., described (3-17, and chap. iv.). As the votive offerings and the ark are introduced, the house is filled with a cloud (chap. v.). Solomon blesses the people, and praises the Lord (chap. vi. 1-11). He consecrates the house, and invokes the Divine presence and blessing (12-42). The Lord answers with fire, and fills the house with His glory (chap. vii. 1-3). Solomon sacrifices, and keeps the feast of seven days (4-11). The Lord appears and renews His covenant with the house of David (12-22). Solomon builds cities (chap. viii. 1-6). He makes the Canaanites tributary (7-10). He regulates the service of the temple, &c. (11-18). The Queen of Sheba visits him (chap. ix. 1-12). His wealth and dominion (13-28). He dies (29-31). Rehoboam succeeds him, and Israel revolts from Judah under Jeroboam (chap. x.). The theocracy is established in Rehoboam (chap. xi.). Rehoboam sins, and Shishak comes up against Jerusalem and spoils the temple (chap. xii.). Abijah succeeds him, and fights in the name of David and his priests against Jeroboam, and prevails (chap. xiii.). Asa succeeds him, and strengthens himself in the Lord, and prevails over his enemies (chap. xiv.). He and his people renew the covenant with the Lord, and make offerings in the temple (chap. xv.). He seeks aid from Syria, and not the Lord, against Baasha, and is rebuked (chap. xvi. 1-10). He dies, and is buried with honour (11-14). Jehoshaphat succeeds him, and waxes mighty because of his regard for the law of the Lord (chap. xvii.). He makes league with Ahab, but is for his piety preserved in the battle against the Syrians, while Ahab falls (chap. xviii.). Being rebuked for this unholy alliance, he appoints judges in the land to do justice, and Levites in Jerusalem over the people in all matters of the Lord (chap. xix.). The hosts of Moab and Ammon are destroyed before him by the Lord for his zeal in the worship of His house (chap. xx. 1-34). His ships are broken because he joined himself with the king of Israel (35-37). Jehoram succeeds him, but does wickedly, and dies miserably according to the word of Elijah (chap. xxi.). Ahaziah succeeds him, but does

wickedly, and is slain by a destruction from the Lord (chap. xxii. 1-9). All the house of David, except Joash, is destroyed by Athaliah (10-12). Jehoiada the priest and his Levites anoint Joash king and slay the usurper (chap. xxiii. 1-15). He restores the worship of God and the throne to the line of David (16-21). Joash is zealous for the house of the Lord all the days of Jehoiada (chap. xxiv. 1-16). Afterwards he forsakes the Lord, and is slain by his own servants (17-27). Amaziah succeeds him, and does right, but not perfectly, and is overthrown (chap. xxv.). Uzziah succeeds him and reigns well and prosperously, but usurps the priesthood and is smitten with leprosy (chap. xxvi.). Jotham succeeds him and reigns righteously and prospers (chap. xxvii.). Ahaz succeeds him, but serves Baal, and suffers disaster upon disaster (chap. xxviii.). Hezekiah succeeds him, and begins his reign with cleansing the house of the Lord by the hands of the priests and Levites, after which he makes offerings in the temple (chap. xxix.). He proclaims a passover, which is kept in Jerusalem amid demonstrations of zeal for the worship of the Lord (chap. xxx.). He makes regulations and provisions for the temple service, and the people joyfully respond with offerings (chap. xxxi.). Sennacherib invades Judah, but his army is destroyed and himself slain (chap. xxxii. 1-23). Hezekiah sins and humbles himself (24-26). His greatness and end (27-33). Manasseh succeeds him, but does wickedly, is taken captive and afterwards restored (chap. xxxiii. 1-20). Amon succeeds him, but does wickedly, and is slain (21-25). Josiah succeeds him, and is zealous for the house of the Lord (chap. xxxiv. 1-13). He reads in the book of the law, and learns with sorrow the predicted destruction of Jerusalem (14-33). He appoints a passover (chap. xxxv. 1-19). He goes against Pharaoh-necho, and is slain (20-27). His successors reign wickedly, and Jerusalem is destroyed (chap. xxxvi. 1-21). Cyrus issues a proclamation granting a right to the captives to return and to rebuild the temple (22-23).

Ezra.—This book is clearly a continuation of the Book of Chronicles, the closing paragraph of which it recites in its opening verses. It embraces a period of seventy-nine years—from 536 to 457 B.C., and records two successive returns of the people from captivity, the former in the reign of Cyrus, and the latter in that of Artaxerxes under Ezra. It is partly written in Aramaic.

The section vii. 27-ix. is written in the first person by Ezra himself, and chap. x. is also probably founded on his memoirs, although this chapter, like the earlier part of the book, is marked off from Ezra's composition by being written in the third person.

Though this and the succeeding book embrace a period of a hundred and twelve years, the narrative refers only to what happened in twenty of them, as the authors merely record what served their purpose in writing. That purpose was to give an account of the progress of the restored theocracy in Judah and Jerusalem, particularly in what related to the temple and the temple priesthood.

Contents.—Cyrus, at the command of the Lord, issues a proclamation to rebuild the temple (chap. i. 1-4). Sheshbazzar (Zerubbabel) and his company go up with gifts, and with vessels of gold and silver originally taken from the temple (5-11). The list of those who go up with their oblations (chap. ii.). The altar is restored and the offerings (chap. iii. 1-6). The foundation of the temple is laid amid expressions of joy and weeping (7-13). The work is opposed, and Artaxerxes is appealed to, who orders its suspension (chap. iv.). Haggai and Zechariah encourage the builders, and the work goes on in spite of the prohibition (chap. v.). Darius confirms the decree of Cyrus, and the work is finished (chap. vi. 1-15). The feast of dedication is kept, and also the passover, with joy (16-21). Ezra, whose pedigree from Aaron is given, goes up to Jerusalem with a company in the seventh year of Artaxerxes (chap. vii. 1-10). He bears a written commission from Artaxerxes, and blesses the Lord (11-28). The list of those who go up (chap. viii. 1-14). Ezra sends to Iddo for the priests and proclaims a fast (15-23). He charges them with the treasures which are deposited in the temple (24-36). He deplores the intermarriages with the heathen women that have arisen, and prays to the Lord with confession of the sin (chap. ix.). Ezra reforms the abuse, and the people repent and promise amendment (chap. x.).

Nehemiah.—This book, which is the last of the historical books, and which, after a break of twelve years, continues the narrative in Ezra, takes the part from the principal actor in the scenes which it describes. Nehemiah was a man of royal degree and in high favour, being king's cup-bearer at the court of Artaxerxes. The narrative embraces a period of thirty-two years —from 444 to 412 B.C. We have Nehemiah's own writings in extracts from his memoirs— those portions of the book which are written in the first person.

Contents.—Nehemiah hears at the Persian court of the sad state of Jerusalem, and mourns and prays with fasting (chap. i.). He receives a commission from Artaxerxes to rebuild the walls, and comes and encourages the work (chap. ii.). The names and order of the builders (chap. iii.). He goes on with the work, notwithstanding the scorn of his enemies (chap. iv. 1-6). He has his eye on their plottings (7-12). He arms the workers, and puts them on their guard (13-23). The people complain of the exactions of their brethren, and he makes the usurers promise a full restitution (chap. v. 1-13). He refers them to his own unselfish example (14-19). The work is finished (chap. vi.). He gives Hanani and Hananiah charge over Jerusalem (chap. vii. 1-4). The list of those who first came back from Babylon with their oblations (5-73). How Ezra read the law to the people, and they were comforted and instructed, and kept it (chap. viii.). The people do penance, fasting in sackcloth, with earth upon them, and read in the book of the law (chap. ix. 1-5). They make confession to the Lord, and covenant with the Lord (6-38). The names of those that sealed the covenant, to which the rest adhered (chap. x.). The distribution of the population, and a list of the chiefs (chap. xi.). The priests that came up at first (chap. xii. 1-9). The line of the high priests (10-21). Chief Levites of the time (22-26). The dedication of the wall (27-43). The offices of the temple priests and Levites (44-47). The people separate from the tribes mingled among them (chap. xiii. 1-3). Nehemiah returns to reform abuses which have set in (4-31).

Esther.—This book takes its name from the chief figure of the story contained in it—an orphan Jewess of the tribe of Benjamin, brought up under the fostering care of her cousin Mordecai, an officer at the court of Persia; chosen for the royal harem; and raised to be the consort of the king, Ahasuerus, who has been identified with Xerxes. It was the last of the books to be admitted into the Hebrew canon. The name of the author is not known. Held in high esteem by the Jewish people, it is read through in their synagogues at the feast of Purim, when the name of Haman is uttered with every expression of execration and contempt, such as hissing, stamping, and clenching the fist. The name of God is not once mentioned in the course of the book, but there is implied throughout a reference to an overruling Providence.

Contents.—Ahasuerus makes a feast and summons Vashti his queen to show her beauty to the people and princes (chap. i. 1-11). She refuses, and he is wroth, and by advice of his wise men the king resolves to give her royal estate to another, and decrees the subjection of all wives to their husbands' wishes (12-22). He collects the fairest of his kingdom into the house of the women, Esther, Mordecai's fosterchild, among the number (chap. ii. 1-14). She presents herself before him and is made queen (15-18). Mordecai sits at the king's gate, and both counsels Esther and saves the life of the king (19-23). Haman is advanced by the king, but not being honoured by Mordecai, he obtains his revenge in a decree to destroy all the Jews against a day which he fixes by *lots* (chap. iii.). Mordecai clothes himself in sackcloth and mourns (chap. iv. 1-3). The queen hears and is told the reason (4-9). She is persuaded to intercede with the king, but meanwhile ordains a fast of three days (10-17). She prepares a banquet for the king and Haman (chap. v. 1-8). Haman retires elated, but still mortified on account of Mordecai (9-13). He erects a gallows for Mordecai fifty cubits high (14). The king is providentially admonished of Mordecai's good services in saving his life, and is reminded how he has gone unrewarded (chap. vi. 1-4). He takes counsel with Haman, who advises him, and becomes the agent of Mordecai's honour (5-11). Haman's friends foresee his fall (12-14). Esther, at a second banquet, intercedes with the king for her people, and accuses Haman to his face (chap. vii. 1-6). The king dooms him to the gallows prepared for Mordecai (7-10). Mordecai, the Jew, is appointed to Haman's office (chap. viii. 1, 2). Esther pleads with the king for the reversal of his decree against her people (3-6). This he cannot reverse, but he empowers the Jews to avenge themselves on their enemies (7-14). The Jews everywhere rejoice, and the people fear them (15-17). They avenge themselves on the day fixed for their own extermination, slaying 75,000 in all of their enemies (chap. ix. 1-16). They rest and make the day a day of feasting and gladness, sending portions to one another (17-19). Mordecai sends letters ordaining, while Esther confirms, the two days' festival of *Purim*, or lots (20-32). The greatness of Ahasuerus, and Mordecai who stands next him, and is held in high honour among the Jews, seeking their good (chap. x.).

See Thatcher, *Judges and Ruth;* A. R. S. Kennedy, 1 *and* 2 *Samuel;* Skinner, 1 *and* 2 *Kings* (Century Bible); Ryle, *Ezra and Nehemiah* (Cambridge Bible); Farrar, 1 *and* 2 *Kings;* Bennett, 1 *and* 2 *Chronicles;* and Adeney, *Ezra, Nehemiah, and Esther* (Expositor's Bible).

CHAPTER X.

THE POETICAL BOOKS.

Hebrew Poetry.—Hebrew life and history supply no motive for epic poetry, and the Hebrew character has no faculty for dramatic poetry ; so that the literature, as a consequence, contains no epic poem, and no properly dramatic composition. The poetry is, therefore, either lyric or gnomic, *i.e.*, subjectively emotional or sententiously didactic; the former belonging to the active or stirring, and the latter to the reflective or quiet, periods of Hebrew history. The lyric we find in the Psalms, the Song of Solomon, and the Lamentations of Jeremiah, and the gnomic in the books of Proverbs and Ecclesiastes, while the book of Job, which is only dramatic in form, is partly lyric and partly gnomic.

Hebrew rhythm consists not, as with us, in a rise and fall of accent, a melody of the sound, but in a certain so-called parallelism of clauses, a melody of the sense. By the word parallelism is understood an arrangement of two or more sentences side by side. This is done in three ways. There may be a *synonymous*, an *antithetic*, or a *synthetic* parallelism, according as there is a sameness, a contrast, or a further expression of the thought.

(1.) The simplest and by far the most common form of parallelism is the *synonymous*. Here the same thought is repeated with a change of language, *e.g.*, Psalm xvi. 6 :—

"The lines are fallen unto me in pleasant places ; Yea, I have a goodly heritage."

(2.) In the *antithetic* form of parallelism, a truth is given first positively and then negatively, or two opposite states are put in contrast, *e.g.*, Psalm i. 6 :—

" For the Lord knoweth the way of the righteous : But the way of the ungodly shall perish."

(3.) *Synthetic* parallelism carries the thought of the first clause further and expands it, adding new meanings, explaining the contents, or deducing consequences, *e.g.*, Isaiah l. 5, 6 :—

"The Lord hath opened mine ear, And I was not rebellious, nor turned away back. I gave my back to the smiters, And my cheeks to them that plucked off the hair : I hid not my face from shame and spitting."

The verse requires at least two members, which must by such parallelism be knit into unity ; and the distich or couplet is, in general, to be regarded as its ground-form, although there are some verses which have three (Ps. vii. 6), four (Ps. v. 10), five (Ps. xi. 4), and even six (Song of Solomon iv. 8) members.

The Hebrew elegy has a peculiar meter of its own. The lines are exceptionally long ; and each line is broken into two unequal parts, the first part being about as long as an average line of Hebrew poetry, and the second shorter. This metre is found in Amos v. 2 ; Isa. xiv. 4 *ff.*; Lam. i., ii., iii., iv., &c. As an illustration take the verse :—

" Her princes are become like harts—that find no pasture, And they are gone without strength—before the pursuer " (Lam. i. 6).

Job.—This book belongs to the "Wisdom" poetry of Israel. But it is written in a dramatic form, and even as literature claims a first place among the masterpieces of the poets of all ages.

1. *Date and Authorship.*—The book of Job was for long believed to be one of the oldest books in the world, and to have had its origin among a patriarchal people, such as the Arabs ; but it is now pretty confidently referred to a Jewish author of the age of Jeremiah or later. The character of the book bespeaks a knowledge and experience peculiarly Jewish. The problem, at once in the statement and the solution of it, points to a Jewish origin, although in the treatment there is an overstepping of the limits both of properly Jewish life and Jewish ideas.

2. *Subject and Problem.*—The book may be regarded as a sublime drama of God's providence and man's suffering. It is based on a narrative of unparalleled calamities. But it consists for the most part of dialogue, poetic and passionate, vehement in denunciation, keen in satire, sublime in its higher thoughts. The several characters are true to their individual differences throughout. Job is a righteous man sorely tried, not infallibly patient, but unflinchingly faithful to God, who nevertheless needs to be rebuked for his pride, while he is honoured and rewarded by God for his fidelity. The three friends represent the conventional notion of their age—that suffering is a sure sign of sin. But they have their several *rôles*. Eliphaz is the prophet of visions and oracles ; Bildad is the sage, the pedant of ancient lore, the rabbi of his day, who bases his statements on the dicta of venerable authorities ; Zophar is neither a prophet nor a sage, but a common respectable person, yet bigoted and dogmatic. Elihu, on the other hand, is a young man in whose mind a new light is breaking. He is far superior in intelligence and in heart to the "three comforters."

The problem of the book is complex. The primary object seems to be to show that God can win and man can give disinterested devotion. Thus Satan is answered when he asks scornfully, "Doth Job serve God for naught ?" Job's fidelity is a lesson to Satan, and the record of it is a lesson to all cynical disbelievers in truly disinterested service of God, and an encouragement of all attempts to live the higher life in spite of loss and suffering. Here a secondary purpose emerges. The popular notion that suffering is only the punishment of sin has to be refuted, and it is refuted most passionately. But no full explanation of the meaning of adversity is offered. On the contrary, the attempt to solve the mystery is regarded as beyond the scope of human thought. Nevertheless through all God can be trusted, and in the vision of God the soul of the sufferer finds its rest. Moreover, one end of the affliction of the servant of God is discovered in the purging of the vision of God. Thus at the last Job exclaims, "Now mine eye seeth Thee."

There are three views given of the character of human sufferings; the first, that of Job's three friends, that they are punitive and corrective; the second, that of the Prologue, that they are probative; and the third, that revealed by the Almighty, that they are part of a system of things, the secret and scope of which no one knows anything of but Himself, being understood only by Him "whose way is in the deep, whose path is in the great waters, and whose footsteps are not known." This last is the view which Job in the end accepts, and which is by implication the author's also. Traces of this sentiment pervade the book, and it is more or less familiar to all the speakers; but it was matter of mere hearsay till the Lord Himself opened Job's own eyes, as Job himself felt assured He would at length do (chap. xix. 25, *et seq.*). The object of the appearance of the Almighty to Job in the end, according to Ruskin, "is to convince Job of his nothingness; and so when the Deity Himself has willed to end the temptation, and accomplish in Job that for which it was sent, He does not vouchsafe to reason with him, still less does He overwhelm him with terror or confound him by laying open before his eyes the book of his iniquities. He opens before him only the arch of the day-spring and the fountains of the deep, and amidst the covert of the reeds, and on the heaving waves, He bids him watch the kings of the children of pride: 'Behold now Behemoth, which I made with thee.'"

3. *Contents.*—The book consists of five parts : (*a*) the Prologue (chaps. i., ii.), (*b*) a series of Discussions divided into three cycles, all except the last of four speeches each (chaps. iii.-xiv., xv.-xxi., and xxii.-xxxi.); (*c*) that in which Elihu expostulates (chaps. xxxii.-xxxvii.); (*d*) that in which the Almighty appears (chaps. xxxviii.-xlii. 1-6); and the Epilogue (chap. xlii. 7-17).

a. *The Prologue.*—Job's prosperity and godly character (chap. i. 1-5). To try him, Satan is allowed to bereave him of all he has, and his children too, but he repines not (6-22). Next smitten with a loathsome malady, he bows to the affliction as of the Lord (chap. ii. 1-10). His three friends come to console him, and sit with him in silence (11-13).

b. *The Discussions. First Cycle.*—Job breaks out into sinful repining; he curses the day of his birth, wishes for death, and wonders what God can mean by his wretchedness (chap. iii.). Eliphaz now breaks silence and expostulates with him, and asks where the comfort is with which he used to comfort others in the like case (chap. iv. 1-5). Eliphaz relates his experience of an awful vision (6-21). Job should accept trouble as the fruit of sin and not despise the chastening of the Almighty, who in that case would deliver him (chap. v.). Job justifies his impatience by appeal to the weight of his troubles, and chides his friends that, instead of showing him kindness, they only load him with reproaches (chap. vi.). Job magnifies his despair, and wonders why God so set Himself against such a being as he, who is nothing, and to come to nothing (chap. vii.). Bildad now breaks in, and

questions Job's innocence from what has befallen him (chap. viii. 1-7). God is just, he argues, and neither casts off the perfect, or rather the penitent man, nor upholds the evil-doer (8-22). Job admits this, but, while he prays God to show him His reasons, pleads that God is too great for him to contend with or come to terms with, and though he can justify himself before man, he cannot with Him (chap. ix.). Yet he wonders that God should so deal with him, wishes he had never been born, and prays for a little respite before he goes whence he shall not return (chap. x.) Zophar wonders that Job should ask an explanation of the Almighty, as presuming it possible to understand Him (chap. xi. 1-11), but bids him repent, and all will yet be well (12-20). Job twits his friends with their assumption, and shows that he has observed the ways of the Lord more wisely than they have (chap. xii.). Job owns the hand of God in his sufferings as much as his friends do, and appeals from them to Him (chap. xiii.). He prays God to consider his frailty and mortality, and spare him (chap. xiv.). *Second Cycle.*—Eliphaz charges Job with impiety in excusing himself, and appeals to the experience of the wise as telling against his innocence (chap. xv.). Job appeals with tears from the judgment of his friends to God, whose arrows are in him to witness for him (chap. xvi.). He appeals to God to witness for him while he lives, otherwise he has none to stand up for him, and his candle must go out in darkness (chap. xvii.). Bildad would have Job to consider the sorrows that overtake the wicked, insinuating that such have fallen upon him (chap. xviii.). Notwithstanding the hand of the Lord seems against him, Job feels He is with him, and will ere long appear to vindicate him (chap. xix.). Zophar shows how the triumph of the wicked is short (chap. xx.). Job shows that the dispensations of Providence are a deep beyond his friend's fathoming (chap. xxi.). *Third Cycle.* —Eliphaz enumerates certain sins Job must have committed that he is reduced to such a pass, and exhorts him to find his portion in the Almighty (chap. xxii.). Job turns away from Eliphaz to God: might he yet establish his innocence before Him ere he dies (chap. xxiii.). He shows how wrong it is to maintain that all suffering is the punishment of sin, since evil-doers of all sorts enjoy good (chap. xxiv.). Bildad ends the colloquy by repeating the words of Eliphaz: How can puny man match himself with his Maker? (chap. xxv.). Job needs not be told how great God is, and how little we know of Him (chap. xxvi.). Yet he is sure of his integrity, and that the wicked will perish (chap. xxvii.). He knows the value, but God only knows the place, of wisdom, and that man's wisdom is to fear Him (chap. xxviii.). He yearns for the time when by the favour of God he was a blessing to many and held in honour (chap. xxix.). He complains that the vilest despise him now, and that God has no pity on him (chap. xxx.). Yet he knows his innocence, and would be weighed in an even balance (chap. xxxi.).

c. *Elihu interposes with his solution.*—This he does, because Job justified himself, and his friends were silenced (chap. xxxii.). He charges Job with presumption, and would have him see the gracious meaning of God's dispensations (chap. xxxiii.). He vindicates God's righteousness (chap. xxxiv.). He rebukes Job for thinking God would condescend to answer him, especially when he makes his appeal in such an arrogant vein (chap. xxxv.). He pleads God is righteous, and will have all men to magnify Him (chap. xxxvi.). He shows how great and terrible is God's majesty (chap. xxxvii.).

d. *The Lord appears to Job.*—He asks him how he presumes to contend with Him, and challenges him to explain the many secrets of His power and wisdom as displayed in nature (chaps. xxxviii. and xxxix.). Job lays his hand on his mouth ashamed (chap. xl. 1–5). The Lord shows His power in His works (6–24 and chap. xli.). Job now sees God in it all, and humbles himself (chap. xlii. 1–6).

e. *The Epilogue.*—The Lord is angry with Job's friends, who yet are accepted through the intercession of Job (chap. xlii. 7–10). Job's prosperity is restored twofold (11–17).

Psalms.—This designation was first given to the collection by the LXX., as containing songs intended to be sung with instrumental accompaniments. The Jewish name is "Tihillim," Praises, or "Tephilloth," Prayers (Ps. lxxii. 20), the proper name for an individual Psalm being "Mizmor," of which "Psalm" is the translation. They are all lyrical, and appear to have been collected for liturgical purposes. Their range is co-extensive with nearly all divine truth, and this is presented in lights that have proved inspiring to the Church in all periods of her history. They have been pronounced to contain "the truest emblem ever given of a man's moral progress and warfare here below," to record "the faithful struggle of an earnest human soul towards what is good and best—struggle often baffled, sore baffled, down as into entire wreck : yet a struggle never ended ; ever, with tears, repentance, true unconquerable purpose, begun anew."

The collection, which is of very varied authorship, has been divided into five Books : the first containing Ps. i.–xli.; the second, Ps. xlii.–lxxii.; the third, Ps. lxxiii.–lxxxix.; the fourth, Ps. xc.–cvi.; and the fifth, Ps. cvii.–cl.

Seventy-three psalms bear the inscription "To David ;" but we cannot be sure that all of these psalms were written by the poet-king, and it may be that psalms written in the spirit of David would receive the title. Most of them are in the earlier part of the psalter, viz., thirty-seven in Book I., eighteen in Book II., one in Book III., two in Book IV., fifteen in Book V. The psalms ascribed to Asaph and the sons of Korah are found only in Books II. and III. Asaph was a Levite, and one of the leaders of David's choir (see 1 Chron. vi. 39). The psalms which bear his name are twelve, viz., l. and lxxiii.–lxxxiii. The sons of Korah were also Levites engaged in temple-singing (see 2 Chron. xx. 19). Twelve psalms are ascribed to them, viz., xlii.–xlix., lxxxiv., lxxxv., lxxxvii., lxxxviii. It is probable that the "sons of Korah" were not the authors of the psalms which bear their name, but that the name signifies that the psalms were designed to be sung by the sons of Korah. Books II. and III. are distinguished from the rest of the psalter by the more common use of the word *Elohim* (God), in preference to the word *Jehovah* (Lord). Most of the psalms in Books IV. and V. are anonymous. Some psalms belong to the times of Solomon, of

Jehoshaphat, and of Hezekiah. The Captivity produced its own melancholy psalmody—*e.g.*, Psalm cii. The return from the Exile was marked by a great outburst of psalmody.

Contents.—Book I. Ps. i. is introductory to the whole Psalter, and sums up the assured lesson of the psalms generally, viz., that only good can befall the righteous, and only evil the wicked. Ps. ii. warns all men and nations who plot against the Lord and His King that they are only plotting their own ruin. Ps. iii. is a morning hymn ascribed to David, and expresses his exulting assurance that the Lord will hear and help him out of deepest distresses. Ps. iv., an evening hymn, contains a pleading of the godly man, as the man of God's choice, with the ungodly, not to turn his glory into shame, and to offer sacrifices of righteousness. Ps. v. is a prayer of the godly man to God, Who hates the wicked, to reveal His displeasure with them and His good pleasure in the righteous. Ps. vi. is the first of the seven so-called "penitential psalms,"[1] in which the Psalmist prays the Lord to ease him of the soul-and-body-afflicting sorrows wherewith his enemies encompass him, and bids the troubler be gone, and, by implication, the sorrow he causes him, as the Lord *has* heard him. Ps. vii. contains an appeal of the righteous man to the righteous God to avenge him of those who seek to crush him, or to bring the wickedness of the wicked to a speedy end and establish the righteous. Ps. viii., while it adores the glory of God in the heavens, also celebrates the praises of God in the babe and suckling, and wonders at the honour and dominion He has bestowed on this creature grown into a man. Ps. ix. is an outburst of thanksgiving to God by the Psalmist for scattering and destroying his enemies, to the rebuke of the wicked, and the joy of all God-fearing men. Ps. x. asks why God hides Himself, seeing that the wicked prevail and boast themselves against Him, yet acknowledges that He sees it all, and will, as He has done, come forth to judge between the oppressed and the oppressor. Ps. xi. contains the answer of the Psalmist to his enemies, who boast his refuge is gone, telling how his refuge is the Lord, who will yet shower ruin on the wicked and show favour to the righteous. Ps. xii. complains that, as proof of prevailing ungodliness, men no longer speak sincerely to one another, and declares that it is vain for the false tongue to boast, as only the Lord's words, which are pure, will in the end hold good. Ps. xiii. is the persecuted soul passing from despair, through supplication, to the actual, well-nigh ecstatic enjoyment of God's salvation. Ps. xiv. represents God as looking down upon a world, all, except a few faithful men, become godless, seeing they not only do no good themselves, but consume those who do good, and accusing the world of ignorance of His righteous judgments. Ps. xv. depicts the character to which, if a man attain, it shall become a dwelling-place wherein he shall never be moved—the character of the man who alone shall dwell in God's holy hill. Ps. xvi. expresses the Psalmist's satisfaction in God, and his anticipation of an abiding joy at length in His presence. Ps. xvii. is a prayer of the Psalmist to God, his trust, to be kept from his enemies, the men of the world, whose portion is in this

[1] The others are Ps. xxxii., xxxviii., li., cii., cxxx., and cxliii.

life, and who have no hope, as he has, in a better. Ps. xviii. is a grand hymn of praise to God, and trust in Him, for the wonderful deliverances He has wrought, and continues to work, for David and his seed after him (see 2 Sam. xxii.). Ps. xix. celebrates the testimony of the heavens, and especially of the sun, to the glory of God, and the value that attaches before all to the fear of God in the heart of man, and the law of God inscribed in the book of revelation. Ps. xx. is a prayer of the people for the king, that the Lord would hear his petitions and grant him victory in the battle he fights under the Lord's banner. Ps. xxi. is a hymn of thanksgiving for the victory prayed for, and an expression of assurance that God will yet grant the king greater victories. Ps. xxii. is a loud and prolonged cry to God for help on the part of one who in the deepest abasement, and surrounded by enemies, ready to take his life, feels as a man forsaken of God, Who he yet knows is not far off, and will interpose to save him, for the glory of His own name, and to the conversion of all nations—a situation that realised itself to the full in the sorrows of the Crucified and the glory to God in His deliverance out of them. Ps. xxiii. is connected with the preceding, and expresses with calm assurance the belief that God never forsakes His own, but cares for them as a shepherd does for his flock, and not the less but the more when danger threatens them. Ps. xxiv. is a characterisation of the man who shall ascend God's holy hill, followed by a characterisation of Him who has been exultingly installed on Zion King of Glory. Ps. xxv. is a prayer by one who trusts in God, that He would, for His own name's sake, teach him and guide him, as well as redeem Israel out of all his troubles. Ps. xxvi. is a prayer to God by one who would take rank with the upright, that He would search and see how he hates the conduct and company of wicked men. Ps. xxvii. expresses the Psalmist's confidence in God in the midst of trouble, and his longing to see the goodness and beauty of the Lord in the land of the living. Ps. xxviii. is a prayer of the Psalmist to God, as the Salvation and Shepherd of Israel, to save him from the wicked, and to judge them. Ps. xxix. is a call to see the glory and hear the voice of God in the thunder, observing how He shakes the earth, but Himself remains unshaken, and continues the King and strength of His people. Ps. xxx. is a thanksgiving of the Psalmist to God for preserving his life to praise Him, after he has, by the hiding of God's countenance, been brought nigh to the gates of death. Ps. xxxi. is a psalm of trust in God as a deliverer, and a prayer from the depths to Him to have mercy, and both silence the wicked and encourage the upright. Ps. xxxii. is the second of the penitential psalms, and celebrates the blessedness of forgiveness, consequent on the confession of sin, as an experience containing a lesson of warning and instruction to others. Ps. xxxiii. is a call on the righteous to praise the Lord as the one sovereign Power and Ruler in heaven and on earth, and to trust in Him as doing all He does, and saying all He says, in very faithfulness. Ps. xxxiv. is a song of praise to God, and a call to praise Him for His favour and deliverance to them that seek Him by the way of righteousness indicated in it. Ps. xxxv. is a call of the Psalmist to God to arm Himself in

his defence, and confound those who are rejoicing in his misfortunes and expectant of his ruin. Ps. xxxvi. expresses the revulsion of godly abhorrence with which the Psalmist turns from the godless conduct of the wicked to the righteous and gracious ways of God. Ps. xxxvii. is a call to trust in the Lord notwithstanding the prosperity of the wicked, seeing their end is to be cut off, and only the righteous shall be established. Ps. xxxviii. is the third of the penitential psalms, in which the Psalmist, after describing the depth and loneliness of his sufferings, bodily and mental, sends up his cry to God as the One who alone can help and deliver him. Ps. xxxix. is the plaint of one who, feeling his chastisement is of the Lord, turns away from man to his Maker to have pity on his frailty and spare him. Ps. xl. is a prayer of the Psalmist to God, from the midst of the troubles in which he has involved himself, to deliver him from them and confound his enemies. He praises God for past deliverances, in which God has taught him that what is required of him, and what will prove the rock of his confidence, is not sacrifice, but obedience to the divine will. Ps. xli. is a prayer of the Psalmist to God to have pity on him for His name's sake, seeing his friends show no pity, preceded by a declaration of the blessedness that belongs to those who consider their neighbours' distresses.

Book II.—Ps. xlii. represents a soul comforting itself with hope in God, in circumstances of trouble so overwhelming as to provoke its enemies to load it with cruel reproaches as if God had cast it off. Ps. xliii. bespeaks the same circumstances as the last, but is more explicit as to the source of the soul's distress and what will conquer its depression. Ps. xliv. is a complaint to God on the part of His people, that He should seem to have forgotten them when they have not forgotten Him, a prayer that He who had wrought deliverances for them in the past would interpose for them now. Ps. xlv. is a marriage-song composed on the occasion of the nuptials of a royal bridegroom and bride, described in terms which have led the Church to identify the bridegroom with her Head, and the bride with herself as His wife and the mother of His children. Ps. xlvi. is a sublime expression of calm confidence in God as the security of His people in times of trouble, conceived after the experience of a signal divine deliverance for the Church, in whose midst He dwells. Ps. xlvii. is a hymn of triumph, in which the Psalmist calls upon all nations to praise the Lord as the declared God of the whole earth. Ps. xlviii. is a song in praise of Zion as the city in which God has made Himself known as the refuge of His people against their enemies. Ps. xlix. celebrates the different fortunes of the wise man and the fool, of those who trust in God and those who trust in wealth—who are described as void of understanding and like the beasts that perish. Ps. l. is a call to the whole world to witness how God judges His people, how the only sacrifice He will be found to accept even of them, is the sacrifice of thanksgiving for His benefits and obedience to His will. Ps. li. is a prayer, conceived in deepest penitence, for remission of confessed sin and for regeneration of heart, offered in the assurance that the sacrifices of God are a broken spirit, and that He is glorified by nothing so much as the gratitude of a forgiven man, and the sacrifices to which that gratitude may prompt him. Ps. lii. contrasts the fate of the man who fortifies himself in his wickedness by his wealth with that of the man whose boast is the mercy of God. Ps. liii. repeats Ps. xiv., with a variation in vers. 5 and 6, adapted possibly to a slight change of circumstances. Ps. liv. is a prayer of the Psalmist to God to judge, for His name's sake, between his enemies and him by their destruction, accompanied with thanksgiving for the deliverance as if already achieved. Ps. lv. is a broken, passionate prayer to God, in which the Psalmist, in bitter experience of the wickedness and treachery of those about him, first longs that he may escape from them, and then, since he cannot escape, entreats that death may suddenly seize them, quieting himself down in the end with the thought that, after all, he has no reason, as a righteous man, to be so moved. Ps. lvi. is a plaint to God on the part of one who, in the midst of his enemies, trusts in Him, and who feels his indebtedness to Him. Ps. lvii. is like the last, written in circumstances of trouble, and full of trust in God, whose mercy it celebrates. Ps. lviii. is an appeal to God to vindicate His righteousness against the injustice in high places, which is deaf when it should hear, and dumb when it should speak. Ps. lix. is a prayer of the Psalmist to God to avenge him on adversaries who continually seek his ruin, accompanied with praise to God as his refuge in trouble. Ps. lx. is a cry of the people to God, as their one confidence, to retrieve the losses they have suffered, and make good His promises. Ps. lxi. is a prayer of the king, on the ground of past mercies, to God to be his stay and protection, so that he may live to praise His name and perform his vows to Him in His tabernacle. Ps. lxii. is an expression of confidence in God, and a call to trust in Him as against those who delight in lies and trust in oppression. Ps. lxiii. has been pronounced to contain " the spirit and soul of the whole book," and expresses an ardent longing for communion with God as the sole fountain of life, and for separation from those who are given over to deceit and wickedness. Ps. lxiv. is a cry to God against the devices of the wicked, which it describes, and a prediction that God will so confound them that all men shall fear Him. Ps. lxv. is a hymn of praise to God for His mercy and goodness, as shown in His presence with His people, in His power to control the tumult of the seas and the nations, and in the blessings of harvest. Ps. lxvi. is a call to the whole earth to praise the Lord for the redemption of Israel, and an engagement of the Psalmist to pay his vows, with a summons to all to listen to God's mercies to him. Ps. lxvii. is the expression of a longing that God would so show His favour unto Israel that all nations may know His name and join in His praise. Ps. lxviii. is a magnificent hymn in praise of the Lord, because, after a succession of victories on behalf of His people, He finally establishes His throne on Zion amidst songs of triumph, to the discomfiture of His enemies and the joy of the whole earth. Ps. lxix. is the cry of a righteous man, whose soul is pining away under the reproaches of ungodly men, and a prayer that God will show mercy to His people by the exclusion of the wicked from His kingdom. Ps. lxx. is a repetition, with slight variations, of Ps. xl. 14

seq. Ps. lxxi. is the prayer of an old man for deliverance out of the hands of his enemies, in terms borrowed largely from other psalms, such as Ps. xxii., xxxi., xxxv., and xl. Ps. lxxii. is, like Ps. ii., xx., xxi., and xlv., a "royal psalm," and is a prayer of the king for the spirit of justice, that he may judge the people, and especially the poor, with judgment, with a celebration of the issue, which it is foreseen will one day prove world-wide and everlasting.

Book III.—Ps. lxxiii. expresses the misgivings of a good man in regard to the Divine government of the world, when he beholds the prosperity of the wicked and the affliction of the righteous, and it shows how he reassures himself and regains his faith at sight of the sudden and terrible end of his enemies. Ps. lxxiv. is a call to God to stay and avenge the desecration of His sanctuary, by appeal to the jealous regard He has all along shown for the honour of His name and the salvation of His people. Ps. lxxv. is a song of praise to God as judge, and as sure in His own set time to vindicate His justice in judging between the righteous and the wicked. Ps. lxxvi. is a song of praise to God as achieving the salvation of His people in a way that strikes terror into the heart even of kings and princes. Ps. lxxvii. exhibits a soul in trouble reassuring itself by the thought of the many wonders God had wrought for His own in the days of old. Ps. lxxviii. is a historical psalm conceived with a view to expound the meaning of God's dealings at different periods with the nation, and warn the existing generation of the danger of not walking in His ways. Ps. lxxix. is a lament over the occupation of Jerusalem by an enemy, and the ruin and carnage with which he has filled its streets, with a call to God to avenge the blood of His servants, that the heathen may fear His name. Ps. lxxx. is an appeal to God, in a time of trouble and reproach, to have regard to the Church He has Himself planted, and guard it from desecration and devastation, so as to revive His own that they may be a praise to Him. Ps. lxxxi. is a festive hymn calling upon the people, agreeably to His own appointment, to rejoice in the Lord for His redeeming mercy, and to mingle fear with their rejoicing, lest by their disloyalty they should displease Him, as their fathers had done. Ps. lxxxii. is a warning to judges who pervert justice, that they, though they think not, are themselves under a Judge who will judge them, and whose judgment cannot fail. Ps. lxxxiii. is a call to God to arise and vindicate Himself, as in days of old, by confounding the counsel and scattering the forces of a formidable combination intent on the ruin of His Church. Ps. lxxxiv. expresses a deep, ardent longing for the communion of saints, from which the writer is for the time excluded, but which he hopes to enjoy again. Ps. lxxxv. is a prayer that God may take away from His people the tokens of His anger by turning their hearts towards Him, preceded by an acknowledgment of His mercy in reversing their captivity. Ps. lxxxvi. is a prayer to God for help from trouble, from Whom alone it can be looked for, as a God full of compassion and gracious. Ps. lxxxvii. is a hymn in praise of Zion as the city of God, and as one day to be the source of new spiritual life to a company of people gathered together out of all nations. Ps. lxxxviii. exhibits a soul in deep distress, having lost the vision of God, but still cherishing faith and crying to God for deliverance. Ps. lxxxix. is a pleading with God, who has established His throne in David, to remember His covenant and revisit His people.

Book IV.—Ps. xc. is a meditation on the Eternal as the Creator and the Destroyer of all generations of mankind, yet as the portion and secure dwelling-place of those who apply their hearts to wisdom, and as establishing the works of their hands. Ps. xci. celebrates the watchful care of the Almighty over those who trust in Him, and their perfect peace, and it represents Him as promising such all safety and honour. Ps. xcii. is a song in praise of the loving-kindness and faithfulness of God to the righteous, as revealed in ways which the brutish man and the fool cannot understand. Ps. xciii. celebrates the majesty of the Lord as from of old ruling the world and fulfilling His word, unmoved by whatever may seem to lift up its head against Him. Ps. xciv. is an appeal to God to avenge oppression and frustrate the vain thoughts of the wicked, conceived in the quiet assurance that all their schemes are doomed to defeat. Ps. xcv. has been called the "invitation psalm;" it contains a call to worship the God of the whole earth as the Shepherd of His people, coupled with a caution to give heed unto His word. Ps. xcvi. is an exultant call to the whole earth to worship the Lord, in prophetic anticipation of the time when He shall appear to judge the world with righteousness. Ps. xcvii. is a call to the righteous to rejoice in consideration of the sure signs of God's approach, which may be seen in the revelation of His judgment before the eyes of all nations. Ps. xcviii. is in the strain of Ps. xcvi., and a summons to all, even the inferior creation, to rejoice over the approaching advent of the Lord to judgment. Ps. xcix. is, like the preceding, a call to praise and exalt the Lord as executing righteousness and judgment in Jacob. Ps. c. is a call to all people to rejoice in and worship the Lord as the everlasting Father and Shepherd of His people. Ps. ci. expresses the resolve of a man in authority, by God's help, to allow no wicked thought to enter his heart, and no wicked person to stand in his presence. Ps. cii. is the cry to God of a good man, who is alternately depressed and elated, according as he looks, on the one hand, to the present, and on the other hand, to the future, fortunes of the Church. Ps. ciii. is a hymn in which the Psalmist, under a sense of the depth and extent of the Divine compassion, calls upon all everywhere to bless God's holy name. Ps. civ. is a psalm in praise of the great and gracious works and ways of the Lord, as these appear in the broad field of nature in subordination to the necessities of His creatures. Ps. cv. is a call to praise the Lord for His faithfulness in keeping His covenant with Israel, with an admonition to keep His laws. Ps. cvi. is one of a series of "hallelujah psalms," in which the forbearance of the Lord with Israel is especially magnified, and His favour is regarded as a token of His gracious purpose.

Book V.—Ps. cvii. is a call to thank the Lord for His mercy in hearing the cries of the distressed to Him for deliverance, and setting them free, or giving them enlargement. Ps. cviii. is composed of Ps. lvii. 5–11 and Ps. lx. 6–12, adapted to some new occasion. Ps. cix. contains a succession of imprecations on the head of the wicked, on the part of one who is the object of their cruel hatred for his fear of the Lord and his regard for His law. Ps. cx. is the fruit of an inspired conviction on the part of the Psalmist that his king, as he is the anointed, so he will be the acknowledged king and priest of all nations, to be superseded by no other for ever. Ps. cxi. is a celebration in public of the greatness, grace, righteousness, and faithfulness of God in His works, and of the benefit of fearing Him. Ps. cxii. expatiates on the character and blessedness of the upright. Ps. cxiii. is the first of the "Hallel," i.e., a series, extending to Ps. cxviii., of hymns sung at the great feasts; it is a song of praise to the Lord for His greatness and condescension. Ps. cxiv. celebrates the submissiveness with which the brute powers of nature subserved God's purpose from the day when, choosing Israel as His sanctuary, the Lord led the people out of Egypt. Ps. cxv. is a call to all classes of the people to trust in the Lord for having vindicated His godhead over all the gods of the heathen. Ps. cxvi. is a psalm in which the author, after signifying his unspeakable gratitude to God for His mercies to him, makes open proclamation of his obligation and determination henceforth to serve Him. Ps. cxvii. is a call to all peoples to praise Israel's God. Ps. cxviii. is a song of rejoicing and triumph in the wonderful dispensations of the Lord to His people, and a thanksgiving to Him for His mercies. Ps. cxix. is the longest of the psalms, and is divided into twenty-two stanzas (the number of the letters in the Hebrew alphabet), each consisting of eight verses of two members, and each verse beginning with the same letter; the first eight, e.g., beginning with aleph, the second with beth, &c. Its one theme is the law of the Lord, and it has been pronounced "the most precious of all the psalms in its overflowing and glorious passion of love for that law." Ps. cxx. is the first of fifteen sequent "songs of degrees," "goings up," or "ascents," presumptively so called as having been sung by the companies of pilgrims as they "went up" to the annual feasts at Jerusalem; and it expresses the latent satisfaction the pilgrim felt, in view of the peace he expected to enjoy in God's worship, at his separation from a neighbourhood where he was constantly subjected to, and stung by, the reproaches of ungodly men, among whom it was as ill with him as if he lived among a savage tribe. Ps. cxxi. is the call of the believing soul to the faint-hearted one to trust in the ever-watchful care of the Keeper of Israel, who made heaven and earth. Ps. cxxii. expresses the joy of the pilgrim in Jerusalem, its worship and its memories, and his satisfaction in her good. Ps. cxxiii. is the upward trustful glance of a soul to Him who sitteth in the heavens as the only refuge from worldly men. Ps. cxxiv. is a call to Israel, since but for the Lord their enemies would have proved too many for them, to bless His name for His marvellous deliverances out of their hands. Ps. cxxv. celebrates the everlasting security of those who trust in the Lord, while it indicates the several portions of those who do good and those who work iniquity. Ps. cxxvi. is an expression of the wonder and joy of the captive over his miraculous deliverance from bondage, and a prayer from amid tears, which the new situation provokes, for the complete restoration of Israel.

Ps. cxxvii. is an expression of how vain is every enterprise, whether personal or social, without the Divine sanction and co-operation, and how strong the man is who regards his children as a heritage from the Lord. Ps. cxxviii. celebrates the, especially domestic, felicity of the man that fears the Lord. Ps. cxxix. is a call to Israel to consider how, though afflicted from her youth up, the Lord has interposed to deliver her and confound her enemies. Ps. cxxx. is a cry from the depths for forgiving mercy on the basis of faith in God's Word, and a call to Israel to hope in Him for redemption from its iniquities. Ps. cxxxi. represents a soul humbling itself before God as a little child, and bidding others hope in Him with a like humility. Ps. cxxxii. is a prayer to God to remember David's zeal for Him, and the promises He made to David and his seed after him. Ps. cxxxiii. celebrates the blessedness of true unity, comparing it to a holy all-sanctifying oil, and an all-refreshing dew. Ps. cxxxiv. is a greeting addressed to the priests entering the temple in the evening, and a greeting to those leaving it. Ps. cxxxv. is an exhortation to those who minister in the temple to praise the Lord for His grace shown to Israel, and His wonderful doings in their behalf. Ps. cxxxvi. is a thanksgiving hymn to the Lord as the creator of the heavens and the redeemer of His people. Ps. cxxxvii. is a patriotic hymn expressive of devotion to Jerusalem, and of resentment against those who sought her destruction. Ps. cxxxviii. is a thanksgiving to God for His faithfulness to His word, a prediction of the recognition by kings of His glory as the God of the lowly, and an expression of utmost confidence in Him. Ps. cxxxix. is the fruit of a profound insight into, and is a lofty expression of a believing sense of, the omniscience and omnipresence of God in His character of the Holy One, who will have no fellowship with what is unholy. Ps. cxl. is a prayer for protection from the words and snares of the ungodly, and that their evil wishes may take effect on themselves. Ps. cxli. is in the main a prayer to be kept from evil and any partnership in it, and that evil may befall the wicked. Ps. cxlii. is the cry of a lonely man to God as his only refuge in trouble, that the righteous, seeing his deliverance, may rejoice and take courage. Ps. cxliii. is the last of the penitential psalms; it is the earnest appeal of one in trouble to his God to deliver him and lead him into the land of the upright, where he would fain dwell. Ps. cxliv. is a prayer to God on the part of one who feels his own limitations, to rescue him out of alien hands and to bring back the golden age of the world. Ps. cxlv. is a hymn of praise to God for His unsearchable greatness and the boundlessness of His grace. Ps. cxlvi. is the first of a series of "hallelujah psalms," which extends to the close of the Psalter; it is a call to trust, not in man, but in the Lord alone, in consideration at once of the attributes of His grace and the eternity of His kingdom. Ps. cxlvii. enumerates and celebrates the gracious acts of the Lord in favour of His people. Ps. cxlviii. is a magnificent anthem, in which the heavens and the earth, and the hosts of them, are called on to praise and magnify the God of Israel. Ps. cxlix. is a call to Israel to rejoice in God her king, and to go forth in His name to execute vengeance on the nations. Ps. cl. is the doxology of the whole Psalter, in which all beings in all places are called to celebrate the name of the Lord with all instruments of music.

The Proverbs.—The Hebrew title of this book is the "Mishlé," i.e., the maxims, "of Solomon." Together with Job, Ecclesiastes, and certain Psalms, it constitutes the "Chokhmah," or "Wisdom" literature of the Hebrews. Though ascribed to Solomon, these maxims are obviously not all of his composition, or even of his collection, being of very varied authorship, and the vintage of the observation and experience of many wise men at different periods of Jewish history.

1. *The Subject and Scope of the Book.*—The subject of the book is wisdom as it affects moral conduct, and this as the fruit of reflection on experience in the light of God's truth. The principles inculcated are largely ethical, resting, however, on a religious basis, and they concern the individual, not as a citizen of any particular community, but as a member of the human race. The rules laid down have respect neither to the observances required by the Law, nor to the privileges and promises dwelt on by the Prophets, but only to that moral and religious life which is the affair of every man and every society of men. Here Israel as a nation retires into the background, and man as man comes to the front, but it is man in the light of the religion of Israel, and as fulfilling his destiny in the fear of Israel's God. The issues of life and death are the same as in the covenant with Moses, and the condition in both cases is the observance or non-observance of God's commandments. There is no change in the principle, but in the expansion of it, and that amounts to the laying of the foundation of a kingdom of God which shall include all nations. Here the bonds of Jewish exclusiveness are burst, and a catholic religion virtually founded.

2. *Date and Authorship.*—The proverb belongs to the latest development of Jewish thought, and is the conception of a class of men who are in the book itself designated "the Wise," in contradistinction, as would appear, to the priest and the prophet (Jer. xviii. 18). These men were persons of a devout, considerate turn of mind, who had the interests of the community at heart, and had constituted themselves the guardians of its morals, specially of those of the young and the inexperienced in the ways of the world. They occupied pretty much the same standing as the philosophic class in Greece, only the problems they busied themselves with were not speculative, but spiritual, i.e., such as bore upon the interests of life. This class belonged necessarily to the latest period of Jewish history, when the Jewish commonwealth was breaking up, and the Jews, by mingling with other nations, were beginning to see the narrow limits within which they were restricting the ancient creed. Their teachings are all professedly the teachings of reflection; and reflection sets in only after history has supplied the data on which it works.

3. *Divisions.*—The book consists of several distinct parts:—(a.) The title and a general preface, in statement of its purpose and ground principle (chap. i. 1-7). (b.) A series of introductory discourses in recommendation of true wisdom (chaps. i. 8-ix. 18). (c.) The proverbs called of Solomon (chaps. x.-xxii. 16). (d.) The words of the wise in two collections (chaps. xxii. 17-xxiv.

22, and chap. xxiv. 23-34). (*e.*) The proverbs of Solomon which the men of Hezekiah collected or copied out (chaps. xxv.-xxix.). (*f.*) The words of Agur and King Lemuel (chap. xxx. and chap. xxxi. 1-9). (*g.*) The praise of a virtuous housewife and mother (chap. xxxi. 10-31).

4. *Contents.—a.* Chap. i. 1-7 explains that the collection was put together to instruct the young and inexperienced in wisdom, and to sharpen the intelligence, widen the sympathies, and fortify the character of such as love wisdom.

b. Chaps. i.-ix. contain no fewer than fifteen separate series of pleadings, representations, or remonstrances in favour of wisdom. The first, contained in chap. i. 7-19, is a caution to consort not with sinners. The second, in chap. i. 20-33, is a warning to those who make light of wisdom's words. The third, in chap. ii., sets forth the advantages of the acquisition of wisdom. The fourth, in chap. iii. 1-18, indicates the happiness of the man who is devoted to wisdom. The fifth, in chap. iii. 19-26, pleads that the ways of wisdom are sure, seeing that on it the heavens and the earth are established. The sixth, in chap. iii. 27-35, is an exhortation to do all the good we can to our neighbours and beware of the ways of wicked men. The seventh, in chaps. iv., v. 1-6, enumerates the advices and cautions a wise father had given his son. The eighth, in chap. v. 7-23, is a warning to eschew the house of the strange woman. The ninth, in chap. vi. 1-5, contains an exhortation to one who has become surety for a neighbour. The tenth, in chap. vi. 6-11, contains a warning against indolence. The eleventh, in chap. vi. 12-19, enumerates certain signs of a worthless character, and seven things hateful to the Lord. The twelfth, in chap. vi. 20-35, is an exhortation to respect the law of father and mother. The thirteenth, in chap. vii., pleads with the young man to give his affections to wisdom, and not to the strange woman, whose arts are depicted, and her power to ruin. The fourteenth, in chap. viii., introduces wisdom herself as appealing in all thoroughfares to the sons of men, and pleading with them to listen to her as a counsellor to whom not only kings have respect when they rule righteously, but whom even the Lord Himself regarded when He made and established the heavens and the earth. The fifteenth, in chap. ix., represents wisdom as a housewife who has made every provision for her guests, and an instructress of such as respect her.

c. Chaps. x.-xxii. 16 constitute the original nucleus of the collection, and contain 374 proverbs, which are of miscellaneous character, and generally arranged in no visible order. They are for most part in antithetical distichs.

d. Chaps. xxii. 17-xxiv. 34 contain proverbs sometimes in one verse, sometimes in two or three, and even more, while many of the verses consist of three or four members.

e. Chaps. xxv.-xxix. open with a statement that the proverbs which follow were collected by "men of Hezekiah." These chapters contain proverbs of a more ancient date than many of the rest, which may be distinguished by their concreteness and simplicity, and usually contain a comparison, as chap. xxv. 26, 28.

f. Chaps. xxx., and xxxi. 1-9, contain sayings of two Emirs of North Arabia, whose religious knowledge and faith proclaim them to have been of Jewish birth.

g. Chap. xxxi. 10-31. This depicts the virtuous and capable wife and mother.

Ecclesiastes.—This title, which we receive through the Vulgate, is the translation into Greek by the LXX. of the Hebrew title "Koheleth," a word which is, agreeably to Jewish tradition, rendered "preacher," but meant originally "gatherer, or summoner, together," and means here one who, personifying Wisdom (for the word is feminine, as that for wisdom is), gathers men together to listen to her verdict.

1. *Date and Authorship.*—This book was for long accepted as the production of Solomon, written in his old age, and intended as a warning to others against sundry delusions of which he had himself been the victim; but it is now, from internal evidence, and by almost universal consent, allowed to be the work of one who wrote as late as 400 B.C.—though in the name of Solomon, and dramatically personifying the famous king. The most striking evidences for this conclusion are—first, the testimony of the author, that he "*was* king in Jerusalem" (chap. i. 12), which Solomon to the day of his death never ceased to be; secondly, the political circumstances in which the book was written, as seen in chaps. iv. 13-16; v. 8; viii. 1 *seq.;* and thirdly, the post-exilian language. It evidently belongs to the period when the reflective spirit prevailed.

2. *Aim and Object.*—The standpoint of the author is a religious one, the data on which he rests are given in experience, and his object is to expose the vanity of every source of satisfaction which is not founded on the fear, and has not respect to the commandments, of God. Nor is this a new discovery, for the doctrine is one which constitutes the very ground-principle of the Jewish faith, to which the Jewish people had ever and anon to be called back. It is exactly what Moses meant when, recognising the essentially spiritual nature of man, he resolved religion into loyalty to God's law, into doing, and continuing to do, God's will. Man is so constituted that he cannot find satisfaction in anything short of the active discharge of his duties as a man, made by, made after, and made for God; and it is to this conclusion the experience of the author of Ecclesiastes leads up. Even the observations and maxims of wisdom alone are nothing, only the practice of wisdom avails; and only that wisdom is worthy of study which can be turned to practical account. The preacher arrives at this result, however, not by appeal to the authority of Moses, but by reference to a succession of experiences in confirmation of the vanity of every other course. And if, as he finds, vanity is to be written over the whole field of human experience, he is well assured, and careful to maintain, that this is not the fault of the system of things, but due to the folly of man (chap. vii. 29). Man is ever trying to find some way to happiness apart from the plain one prescribed by the law of his being and the limits of his life. He will have something other, and be something other, than is possible under that law and within those limits. All this is vain.

3. *Contents.*—Man has no profit in his labour here (chap. i. 1-3). The earth with the elements is ever moving; man looks wearily on, then goes, and never more returns (chap. i. 4-11). Know-

ledge is vain, for it cannot alter things, and only increases sorrow (chap. i. 12-18). Pleasure is vain, and all the labour spent on the production and accumulation of the means of it (chap. ii. 1-11). Wisdom is as vain as folly, for though it is better, in the end it fares no better (12-17). The fruit of labour is vain, as it may fall into the hands of a fool, or one who has no right to it (18-23). To seek enjoyment is vain, for it is the gift of God, and not the fruit of striving (24-26). It is vain for a man to strive to transcend his limits, which are fixed, and within which alone it is well with him (chap. iii. 1-15). It is vain to look for justice here, seeing at the last man has no pre-eminence over the beasts, so that he must seek his portion in his own work or nowhere (16-22). The life of man on earth is vain, for those in power as well as those under oppression have no comforter (chap. iv. 1-3). Labour from envy, or avarice, or selfishness is vain (4-12). For an upstart, however wise, to supplant an old king, however foolish, is vain (13-16). Formalism and superstition in religion are vain, and reverence is to be shown towards God in worshipping Him, praying to Him, and paying vows to Him (chap. v. 1-7). Oppression is vain (8, 9). Riches are vain, and sometimes worse than vain (10-17). Everything is vain, except for a man to enjoy the good of his labour so far as he is capable, and under such limits as God wills (18-20). For a man to have good given him and not to be allowed to enjoy it, is vanity (chap. vi.). The maxims of wisdom are proofs of the vanity of life (chap. vii. 1-6). Wisdom is vain, except as preserving the life of him that hath it (7-14). It is a folly and a snare to be righteous or wise overmuch (15-26). Wise men are rare, and wise women rarer (27, 28). All this vanity has its root not in the use but the abuse of the reason God has given to man (29). It is a vanity that the righteous do right and are forgotten, and that the wicked do wrong and are remembered (chap. viii. 1-14). Man, being in this plight, has nothing for it but to do and enjoy his own work, and cease to puzzle himself over the work of God (15-17). All beyond is darkness (chap. ix. 1-10). Reward and honour are not according to desert in this life (11-18). Wisdom is often outweighed by a little folly (chap. x. 1-3). We must be patient under rulers who have power to work harm (4-18). Let a man do and enjoy good from his youth up while he may, and not vainly vex himself about the consequences, so be that his life is of a quality to stand the test of the judgment (chap. xi.). The Creator is to be remembered in youth ere the evil days come which sum up the vanity (chap. xii. 1-8). The grand conclusion —perhaps added by a later writer—is that the only life worth living is one of devotion to God and obedience to His commandments, for no earthly rewards, but in view of a future judgment (9-14).

The Song of Solomon, or the Book of Canticles. —This book is called in Hebrew the Song of Songs, a title which is translated in the Vulgate into Canticum Canticorum. Some have regarded it as a collection of separate poems; but the more general opinion is, that it is one work in the form of a dramatic idyl, two or three leading characters taking part, and the "Daughters of Jerusalem" appearing as a sort of chorus. The greatest diversity of opinion has been entertained on the question of the meaning of this book. The Targum shows that the later Jews regarded it as an allegory of the history of Israel. The first indication of its being treated allegorically among Christians is seen in the Alexandrian Father Origen, a writer who also allegorised other books of Scripture to an extent never followed in the present day. His allegorical treatment of the Song of Solomon, however, was generally accepted in the Church, though not without protest, Theodore of Mopsuestria contending for the literal sense of the poem. Thus it came to be understood as a representation of the love of Christ for His Church, or for the individual soul. In the present day grave doubts as to the correctness of this view have been expressed. It has been pointed out that the poem itself gives no hint of an allegorical signification, a silence which is contrary to the analogy of all known allegories. The chapter headings in our Bible, which are constructed in accordance with this method of interpretation, are quite late additions, not part of the original text. The Bible itself does not anywhere suggest an allegorical interpretation of the Song of Solomon. Our Lord and His disciples never even mention or quote the book. Therefore those who allegorise it have only the precedent of the Fathers to appeal to, not the authority of Christ or Scripture. Under these circumstances it is a grave question whether the attempt to read a deep spiritual meaning in the book should be encouraged. The erotic form of religion which is thereby engendered is not in harmony with the robust teaching of the New Testament.

Even those who still retain the allegorical interpretation of the Song of Solomon must admit that the words of the poem have also literal meanings. According to some, in its literal sense the work celebrates the nuptials of Solomon with a bride of simple, rustic manners. According to the more generally accepted view, the Shulammite is a maiden whom Solomon tries to win, but who has a shepherd lover to whom she remains faithful in spite of all the blandishments of the court. Thus the book celebrates the glory of fidelity to true love, and the beauty of simple, country manners in contrast to the luxury of court life and the degenerate habits of polygamy. If this is a correct interpretation it is manifest that Solomon could not have written the book, although it belongs to a time soon after his reign. The author was probably a member of the northern kingdom of Israel, and his aim appears to have been in part to present a contrast between the morals of the south and those of the north, in justification possibly of the separation.

Contents.—Chaps. i.-ii. 7 represent the Shulammite in the royal palace, where the ladies of the court hold a colloquy with her, to prepare her for the visit of the king, who, when he appears, has no attractions for her compared with those of her far-away lover. Chaps. ii. 8-iii. 5 represent her as telling of her lover and his love, her cruel separation from him, and her dream about him. Chaps. iii. 6-v. 1 represent Solomon entering Jerusalem in state and as expressing his admiration for the maiden, which is overborne by a passionate appeal from the north, to which alone the maiden responds. Chaps. v. 2-viii. 4 represent the maiden as relating a dream, the

34

ladies of the court sympathising with her, and the suit of the king as unavailing. Chap. viii. 5-14 records the victory and the return of the maiden.

See Lowth, *The Sacred Poetry of the Hebrews;* A. B. Davidson, *The Book of Job* (Cambridge Bible); and Peake (Century Bible); Davison and Witton Davies, *The Psalms* (Century Bible); Delitzsch, *The Psalms and Proverbs;* Cheyne, *Job and Solomon;* Plumptre, *Ecclesiastes* (Cambridge Bible); Bradley, *Lectures on Ecclesiastes;* Ginsburg, *The Song of Songs;* Adeney, *Canticles and Lamentations* (Expositor's Bible).

CHAPTER XI.

THE FOUR GREAT PROPHETS.

PROPHECY, in one sense, is co-extensive with revelation, and the name of prophet is often given in the Scriptures to men, such especially as Moses, who were not prophets in the technical sense (see THE PROPHETS). Prophecy proper begins with the institution of the theocracy in a civic form, and the office of the prophet is to admonish the people in regard to their duties and privileges as members of the theocratic state. At first the prophets appear as the advisers of the civil ruler, they counselling the course of action and he giving it effect; but by-and-by the latter rebels, and an antagonism arises, which becomes more and more pronounced as the history proceeds. This we see as early as the days of Elijah and Elisha. The earlier prophets left no written prophecies behind them, the times being stormy, and the crisis calling for something to be done rather than said. The written prophecies belong to a later period. Most of them were spoken before they were committed to writing. To understand a prophecy aright, it is necessary to know the time in which it was delivered; and the question of date is therefore of more importance in connection with it than in connection with the poetical books just considered.

The written prophecies have been classified according to the time of their composition, agreeably to one system of grouping, as prior to, contemporaneous with, or subsequent to, Isaiah; or agreeably to another and better, as prophecies of the northern prophets, such as Amos and Hosea; those of the Assyrian period, such as Isaiah and Micah; those of the Chaldean period, such as Jeremiah and Ezekiel; and those of the latest prophets, such as Haggai and Malachi. But a review of the books as they stand in our Bible gives us first the Greater Prophets, and secondly the Minor Prophets. It should be understood that this arrangement is determined by the length of the books, not by the comparative rank of the writers. The minor prophets are not to be regarded as necessarily less important persons than the greater prophets. Amos may have been a grander man than Ezekiel—yet Amos is classed with the minor and Ezekiel with the greater prophets. This simply means that we have less of the writings of Amos preserved than of those of Ezekiel—and so of the other minor prophets.

Isaiah.—Isaiah the son of Amoz prophesied in the reigns of Uzziah, Jotham, Ahaz, and Hezekiah, kings of Judah. He flourished between the years 740 and 701 B.C., was a citizen of Jerusalem, and a man apparently of considerable account in the city. He was married and had a family, the members of which, as well as himself, had names given to them which were symbolical of the condition and prospects of the kingdom of Judah at the time, his own name meaning Jehovah the Salvation; his sons' names being—Immanuel, God with us; Shearjashub, a remnant shall return or be converted; and Maher-shalal-hash-baz, spoil speedeth, prey hasteneth. In this last name the prophet expresses his sense of impending national calamity, while the others reflect his faith and his hope, how, nevertheless, in the end God would be found to stand by His people, and they by Him.

1. *The Period of Isaiah.* — Everything is outwardly going well with both the northern and the southern kingdoms when the prophet's eye discovers the signs of coming judgment; and before the end of his ministry the kingdom of the north has fallen, and that of the south is only saved from a similar fate by the intervention of Providence—the conquest of Samaria being in 722 B.C., and the defeat of Sennacherib's siege of Jerusalem in 701. Assyria was the dominant heathen power of the period, and it was bent, in its lust of empire, on subjugating all the neighbouring nations. Isaiah foresaw that, for their unfaithfulness, the Jewish people, along with others, would fall a prey to its ravages, and that no combination with the rest on their part would save them from the fate in store for them, yet that the Lord would not altogether forsake His people, and that a remnant should return and rebuild Zion. It was nothing to him that the northern kingdom had fallen, or that he saw Assyria gathering its hosts to encompass and destroy Jerusalem; for the nearer and more formidable the advance of the enemy was, the stronger and more assured grew his faith that God was with His people, and would interpose to save the remnant of His chosen flock. Isaiah lived to see the fulfilment of his words in the total collapse of the designs of Assyria against the holy city.

2. *Authorship of the Later Prophecies.*—In the twenty-seven concluding chapters of the book we are amid events which happened one hundred and fifty years after Isaiah's death, when Babylon, having succeeded to the power and rôle of Assyria, is in turn overthrown by Cyrus to the release from captivity of the chosen people. The question naturally arises, Is this the work of the son of Amoz and contemporary of Hezekiah? If so, we must conceive of the prophet projecting himself into the period of the Captivity, describing it as present in elaborate details, and comforting the exiles of that remote age with the prospect of restoration to the home of their fathers—and all this many generations before the trouble had come upon the nation, and even before the Babylonian power had risen into importance. Only a disbeliever in Divine inspiration can deny that such a feat of prophecy is possible. If a prophet can foretell the future at all, it is unreasonable to stumble at the claim to foresee it with an unusual copiousness. Nevertheless it has been pointed out that in all other cases the Hebrew

prophets chiefly concerned themselves with the present condition of the world. Their references to the remote future were few, and principally devoted to the grand Messianic Hope. It was not their function to turn aside from the sins and needs of contemporaries, and write as if they belonged to a distant future, filling their pages with details of that future and ignoring the circumstances of their day. Though they did predict, their chief work was not prediction, but preaching in the name of God with regard to the sins and troubles around them. If Isaiah wrote the portion in question, he would be more than predicting the future. He would be ignoring the present, and writing as though he were in the midst of the future time and for the benefit of that time. This would be quite possible as a miracle, for all things are possible with God. But it shows no unbelief in God to say that it is contrary to the custom of prophecy, contrary to the analogy of other prophecies. Besides this consideration, it is urged that the author of the later portion is not a man of the same temper as the author of the earlier; there is more "copiousness, pathos, and unction" about him, but "less fire, energy, and concentration," than in his predecessor; while his inspiration is founded on a deeper spiritual insight, and his hopes and expectations built upon a different view of the method of salvation. This, as is alleged, appears in the substitution for the original ideal of a conquering prince of the new ideal of a suffering Saviour, bearing and bearing away the sins of the nation. On such considerations among others the hypothesis of a second Isaiah—or even a third or more—is founded. Some of the prophecies which belong to the later Isaiah appear among those of the earlier, such, it is alleged, as those contained in chaps. xiii. 2–xiv. 23, xxiv.–xxvii., xxxiv., and xxxv. On the other hand, those who maintain the unity of the book of Isaiah, point to the unanimity of Jews and Christians down to quite recent times. Undoubtedly it is difficult to understand how so great a work as the later chapters constitute could have been contributed by prophets not a vestige of whose existence has been preserved in history or tradition. It cannot be denied that this is one of the richest and most exalted portions of the whole Bible. It matters comparatively little whether we know the name of the man who wrote each part of it, since we know the Divine Author from whom it sprang.

3. *Divisions of the Book.*—These are into two main divisions, the first of which has been divided into (a) the Prelude (chap. i.); (b) Prophecies of the calamities to come upon Judah (chaps. ii.–v.); (c) the Call of Isaiah (chap. vi.); (d) Prophecies concerning Immanuel as the consolation of Israel under Assyrian oppression (chaps. vii.–xii.); (e) concerning the fate of Babylon (chaps. xiii.–xiv. 27); (f) the Burdens (chaps. xiv. 28–xxii.); (g) Desolation coming on Tyre (chap. xxiii.); (h) concerning the early days of Return (chaps. xxiv.–xxvii.); (i) the Woes (chaps. xxviii.–xxxiii.); (j) concerning Edom and Israel (chaps. xxxiv. xxxv.); (k) concerning Sennacherib (chaps. xxxvi.–xxxix.). The second has been divided into three sections concerning (a) the true God of Israel and the false gods of Babylon (chaps. xl.–xlviii.); (b) the servant of the Lord (chaps. xlix.–lvii.); (c) Israel after the flesh and Israel after the spirit (chaps. lviii.–lxvi.).

4. *Contents.*—First Division—(a.) Chap. i. describes the spiritual condition of the people, to whom the prophet prophesies, urging them to penitence, if they would escape God's judgments. (b.) Chaps. ii.–iv. predict the downfall of the false, and the erection of the true, glory of Israel, as this last appears achieving itself in the way of judgment. Chap. v. denounces a sevenfold woe from the Lord on the nation for their abuse of His gifts, the iniquity of their ways, and their neglect of His vineyard. (c.) Chap. vi. gives an account of Isaiah's vision of the Divine glory, his consecration to his office, and the burden of his commission. (d.) In chap. vii. Ahaz is cautioned not to league himself with Assyria against the kings of Syria and Israel, and receives a sign in the promised birth of Immanuel. In chaps. viii.–ix. 1–7 Isaiah predicts the triumph of Assyria over Syria and Israel within two years, but that Immanuel will be found to be the defence of Judah. Chaps. ix. 8–x. 4 describe how Israel sins against the Lord more and more, and how the Divine judgments fall correspondingly heavier and heavier. Chaps. x. 5–xii. represent Assyria as a mere rod in the hand of the Lord to chastise His people, and predict the re-establishment of the throne of David in Jerusalem with rejoicing, when God's judgments have done their work. (e.) Chaps. xiii.–xiv. 27 represent the Lord as mustering His hosts against the pride of the Chaldee, Assyria's successor, and His ransomed as singing a song of triumph over the fallen foe. (f.) Chap. xiv. 28–32 cautions Philistia not to exult over the affliction that has come upon the house of Judah. Chaps. xv. and xvi. picture in pitiful terms the desolation with which the Lord is about to lay low the pride of Moab. Chap. xvii. denounces the judgments of God on the Syro-Israelitish spoilers of the land of Judah, excepting a small remnant. Chap. xviii. represents the prophet as calling upon Ethiopia to witness how the Lord has broken the power of Assyria, and Ethiopia as doing homage to him. Chap. xix. predicts the judgments of the Lord on Egypt, and the conversion in consequence of both it and Assyria to the Lord. Chap. xx. represents Isaiah warning the nation against trust in Egypt and Ethiopia by a symbolical action in exhibition of their shameful subjugation to the power of Assyria. Chap. xxi. 1–10 represents Isaiah as, for the comfort of Judah, foreseeing with horror and describing the terrible fate of Babylon. Vers. 11–17 contain the judgment on Edom and Arabia. Chap. xxii. 1–14 represents the prophet as lamenting that Jerusalem in her false confidence is blind to the judgments of the Lord, and as threatening greater for this blindness. Vers. 15–25 announce the fall of Shebna, the treasurer and the head of the disorder, with the appointment of a successor, who in his pride of office shall also in turn come to grief. (g.) Chap. xxiii. predicts the desolation to come on Tyre, her after-revival, and the lapsing of her wealth to the service of the Lord. (h.) Chap. xxiv. pictures the judgments to come on the inhabitants of the earth as preliminary to the glorious establishment of God's kingdom. Chap. xxv. forecasts the time when the salvation of Zion shall be accomplished in the sight of all nations. Chap. xxvi. is a call to trust in the Lord and wait for Him as working salvation by judgment, and as raising His slain ones to life again. Chap.

xxvii. represents the Lord's judgment-work done, and the Lord as gathering together and keeping watch over His chosen. (*i.*) Chap. xxviii. foresees the doom which the men of Ephraim, compared to drunkards, are bringing down on their heads by their infatuation, and warns the men of Jerusalem that they too will come under the same scourge, if they with like infatuation make lies their refuge instead of the God with whom alone they should keep covenant, but whose ways they neither see nor understand. Chap. xxix. promises to Jerusalem—the lion of the Lord —unexpected deliverance out of threatened destruction, but such a deliverance as shall astonish the nation and give it a rude awakening out of its spiritual delusions. Chap. xxx. is a warning to the people, to put no trust in Egypt or any other world power, but to wait for the Lord, who will, without any action even on their part, break Assyria in pieces. Chap. xxxi. is a call to turn from trust in Egypt to trust in the Lord, and see the judgment of the Lord on Assyria. Chap. xxxii. foretells the reign of Immanuel after a season of trouble on the women who are at ease in Zion. Chap. xxxiii. describes the dismay with which the Lord by His judgments will paralyse the nations and the ungodly, while it portrays the character and the stronghold of those who will stand secure in the midst of them. (*j.*) Chap. xxxiv. calls upon the nations to mark God's indignation against them, and especially His judgments on the land of Edom. Chap. xxxv. describes in anticipation the joy and blessedness of the time which shall succeed the day of the Lord's vengeance. (*k.*) Chap. xxxvi. relates how the Assyrian army threatens vengeance on Jerusalem, and how the matter is reported to Hezekiah. Chap. xxxvii. relates how Hezekiah in his distress both consults Isaiah and lays the matter before the Lord, and how, as Isaiah predicted, the Assyrians are smitten by the angel of the Lord. Chap. xxxviii. relates how the Lord prolongs Hezekiah's life, and records Hezekiah's song of thanksgiving. Chap. xxxix. relates how Hezekiah makes a display of his treasures to the messengers of the king of Babylon, and how Isaiah predicts therefrom the Babylonish captivity.

Second Division.—(*a.*) Chap. xl. is a message of comfort to the people in view of the approaching advent of the Lord, whose greatness of power and unfathomableness of wisdom the prophet goes on to magnify. Chap. xli. is a challenge of the Lord to the nations, and a call to His people to judge between Him and the gods opposed to Him. Chap. xlii. calls attention to the servant of the Lord, his proper function and mode of action, while it rebukes Israel as such for not understanding and resting in God's salvation-workings in their behalf. Chap. xliii. is an appeal of the Lord to the people to witness that He is their Saviour, and a pledge to work still greater wonders for them, notwithstanding all their sins and shortcomings. Chap. xliv. is a call of the Lord to Israel to note how by His doings for them He is persuading the nations of the vanity of their idolatries, and how by restoring them, through Cyrus especially, He is showing that He alone of all the gods is able to fulfil His word. Chap. xlv. challenges Israel to regard Cyrus as God's servant, seeing that by him God is bringing about their salvation, and thereby the salvation of the ends of the earth. Chap. xlvi.

bids Israel consider how omnipotent their God is, and how helpless the idols of Babylon. Chap. xlvii. is an outburst of exultation over the humiliation of Babylon under the hand of the Lord. Chap. xlviii. summons Israel to acknowledge the hand of the Lord in their deliverance, and warns them not to imitate the hard-heartedness of their fathers. (*b.*) Chap. xlix. introduces the prophet of chap. xlviii. 16 as, in the name of the true Israel, bidding away all mistrust and staying himself in the Lord his God, whose purposes will not fail. Chap. l. makes the prophet charge Israel's captivity to their own sin, and counsels them to accept the fact in the spirit in which it is accepted by him, and they will not be confounded. Chap. li. is a pleading with them to consider and see how the Lord is with them, and how the cup of affliction given them is passing into the hands of their oppressors. Chap. lii. is a call to rejoice, and a picture of rejoicing, over the return of Israel from captivity. Chap. liii. exhibits the servant of the Lord as suffering and sorrow-stricken unto death for the sins of the people, and as thereby making intercession for them. Chap. liv. calls upon Zion to rejoice that the day of the Lord's anger is past and her heritage established. Chap. lv. is an exhortation to Israel to accept the proffered salvation and continue loyal to Him who redeems her by righteousness. Chap. lvi. ensures the proffered salvation to those only who have regard to justice, but to all of them, and describes those who teach otherwise as blind guides and mere self-seekers. Chap. lvii. rejects all who have forsaken the covenant of the Lord and accepts only the humble ones who respect it. (*c.*) Chap. lviii. is the repudiation of all worship that is not, and the approval of worship that is, associated with the practice of justice and mercy. Chap. lix. refers the miseries of the people to their sins, and promises salvation only to such as turn from them. Chap. lx. is a description of the glory that shall shine forth and the honour that shall come upon Zion after her restoration, when the Lord shall be her light. Chap. lxi. contains the message from the Lord by the prophet to the afflicted in Zion, and enumerates the consequent blessings. Chap. lxii. expresses the divine eagerness with which the prophet waits for the emancipation of Zion. Chap. lxiii. pictures the Lord as returning from His work of judgment on Edom, which He has thus visited for love to His people. Chap. lxiv. is a supplication to the Lord with confession of sin and a pleading with the Lord to show mercy. Chap. lxv. gives the Lord's answer, how He had called His people and they did not respond to Him, but that, for all that, His promises would be fulfilled on the faithful. Chap. lxvi. describes the homage God respects and the character of those whose worship shall be accepted in Zion.

Jeremiah.—The author of the prophecies of this book was the son of Hilkiah, a priest, and a native of the priestly city of Anathoth, situated three miles north of Jerusalem. He was early called to the prophetic office (chap. i. 6), and he began his career as a prophet in his native place. This he soon left, to prosecute his calling in Jerusalem; and here, in the exercise of it, he spent the greater part of his life. His ministry commenced seventy years after the close of

Isaiah's, and extended from the thirteenth year of Josiah's reign to the eleventh of Zedekiah's, *i.e.*, from 626 to 586 B.C., thus embracing a period of forty years. It was a lifelong protest against the iniquity and folly of his countrymen, and conceived in bitter foreboding of the hopeless ruin they were bringing down upon their heads. He had no wife or child to care for ; his one care was his country, and his country ill requited him for his zeal in its behalf. Though, from his connections, a man of some account in the city, his constant rebukes and warnings brought him into disfavour with the people ; his friends "dealt treacherously" with him ; his enemies made him the "daily" butt of their "reproach and derision;" and more than once plots were laid against his life, and even steps taken to carry them into execution. But the path they were pursuing he saw led only and wholly to ruin ; the vision of this filled and saddened his heart, and he could not, and would not, hold his peace. Naturally a quiet, and even timid, man, he became outspoken and fearless, but it was the corruption of the time that roused him, and the ruin which was coming upon all he loved. The more the corruption increased, the louder became his denunciation, and the fiercer the hatred of the people to him on that account. It was not only on religious grounds, but also on political, that he suffered at the hands of his countrymen, for he stood against them in their preference of an alliance with Egypt to submission to Babylon, foreseeing that it was in connection with the latter the Divine purpose was to work itself out. He lived to see the issue of his pre lictions in the captivity of the people, though he did not go into captivity himself, the conqueror having shown favour to him and allowed him to remain as he had wished. He appears to have been afterwards forced to go down into Egypt, and to have ended his life in that country. His contemporaries were Zephaniah, Habakkuk, Ezekiel, and Daniel. He is the author, it is thought, of some of the Psalms.

1. *His Prophecies.*—The burden of these may be summed up in one word : to witness to the nation that, except in jud ment, there was no deliverance possible for it—that salvation could come to it only in that way. Only through dissolution and death could the emancipation and restoration of Israel ever be achieved. This was what Jeremiah insisted on throughout to the close of his ministry ; yet with only one immediate result, that the worthless, by withstanding his word, brought on their ruin the sooner, while the better-disposed found in the fulfilment of it wherewith to comfort themselves in the day of their calamity. But this winnowing of the worthless from the worthy was not for nothing ; it prepared the way and laid the foundation for after-developments of the purposes of the Eternal (see THE PROPHETS : THEIR MISSION AND MESSAGE).

2. *Their arrangement.*—This, so far as there is method in it, is not according to the order of time, but with regard to the subject-matter. In the succession of the prophecies we see the national corruption waxing worse and worse, and the judgment approaching with a less and less questionable certainty ; but from time to time the delivery of these prophecies is intermixed with assurances that the dispensation is

a necessary step towards the fulfilment of God's gracious purposes. With the advent of the catastrophe in the captivity of the nation and the destruction of the city, the prophet's work is done, and the narrative of it closes, so that what follows is of the nature of supplement or appendix. The book divides itself into four sections : (*a.*) The Introduction in chap. i. (*b.*) Prophecies relating to home events in chaps. ii.–xlv. (*c.*) Prophecies relating to other nations in chaps. xlvi.–li. (*d.*) Supplement in chap. lii.

3. *Contents.*—(*a.*) Chap. i. contains the prophet's call, his twofold vision, and the Lord's command and encouragement. (*b.*) Chap. ii. reminds Israel of her covenant with the Lord, rebukes her for unfaithfulness, and threatens her with judgment. Chap. iii. declares that Israel has forfeited her privileges, but promises forgiveness and restoration, if she will yet repent with confession of her sins. Chap. iv. is a call to prepare for the coming judgment, with a description of it and its accompanying horrors and calamities. Chap. v. charges all with iniquity and threatens all with judgment. Chap. vi. is a despairing proclamation of a judgment that will fill every one with anguish, and a no less despairing lamentation over the obduracy of all classes of the people. Chap. vii. declares that what God requires is a moral regeneration, and that no mere sacrifices will save the people. Chaps. viii. and ix. contain the lament of the prophet over the people after reflection on the impending troubles. Chap. x. describes the folly of idolatry, forecasts the coming woe, and deprecates the Lord's anger. Chap. xi. is a denunciation of judgment, which is resented by the people. Chap. xii. deprecates the prosperity of the wicked, dreads sorer experiences, but comforts with future prospects. Chap. xiii. forebodes evil by symbols of a rotten girdle and bottles filled with wine, and pleads with Judah while regarding her as incurable. Chap. xiv. contains a succession of pleadings on behalf of the people. Chap. xv. contains further appeals and replies, preceded by a description of the impending woes. Chap. xvi. counsels the prophet to an ascetic course, and threatens a judgment so thorough that even the heathen will recognise it. Chap. xvii. denounces the certain judgment of God against sin, and pledges the Divine favour to such as are faithful and conform to God's law. Chap. xviii. draws a lesson from the work of the potter, and contains a prayer of the prophet for retribution on his enemies. Chap. xix. 1–13 denounces judgment under the symbol of a broken bottle. Chaps. xix. 14–xx. 6 denounce judgment on Pashur, who had put Jeremiah in the stocks. Chap. xx. 7–18 represents the prophet as appealing to the Lord, and breaking out into a passion of grief. Chap. xxi. contains the prophet's answer to Zedekiah, who had consulted with him on Nebuchadnezzar's declaration of war, and his advice to king and people. Chap. xxii. continues the prophet's exhortation, is a lament for Jehoahaz, and a denunciation of judgment against Jehoiakim and Coniah, or Jehoiachin, for their iniquity. Chap. xxiii. pronounces woe on, and administers rebuke to, the false shepherds, while it promises a better time, when righteousness shall prevail. Chap. xxiv. contains the vision of the two baskets of figs. Chap. xxv. foretells the captivity and the

desolation that is to come on all nations. Chap. xxvi. relates how Jeremiah was for his faithfulness impeached by the priests and prophets, but acquitted by the princes and people. Chap. xxvii. warns the neighbouring nations and Zedekiah, with the priests and people. Chap. xxviii. relates how Hananiah prophesied falsely, was rebuked by Jeremiah, and punished by the Lord. Chap. xxix. relates how Jeremiah writes to the captives in Babylon not to trust the false prophets among them, seeing the word of the Lord is gone forth against them. Chap. xxx. promises return from captivity and the restoration of Jerusalem. Chap. xxxi. promises a penitent return and a restoration with a new covenant. Chap. xxxii. relates how the Lord instructs Jeremiah to purchase a field, and how Jeremiah asks and receives of the Lord an explanation. Chap. xxxiii. renews the promise of return and restoration. Chap. xxxiv. complains of the treatment of the Hebrew servants, and predicts the burning of the city and the captivity of the king. Chap. xxxv. contrasts the conduct of the Rechabites with that of the men of Judah, approving of the former and reprobating the latter. Chap. xxxvi. relates how Jeremiah, by command of the Lord, has his prophecies written in a roll to be read in the ears of the people, how the king reads it, and has it burnt, and how the prophet has it re-written. Chap. xxxvii. relates how Jeremiah foretells the return of the Chaldeans, who had laid siege to the city and had been compelled to raise it ; how he is imprisoned on suspicion, but afterwards released by Zedekiah. Chap. xxxviii. relates how Zedekiah consents to Jeremiah's being put in a dungeon, but how the prophet is rescued by Ebed-Melech, and again consulted by the king. Chap. xxxix. relates the capture of the city by the king of Babylon, and the fates respectively of Zedekiah, Jeremiah, and Ebed-Melech. Chap. xl. relates how Jeremiah remains in the land, how Gedaliah proceeds to govern it, and is vainly warned of a plot against his life. Chap. xli. relates how Ishmael murders Gedaliah and carries off captives, whom Johanan rescues, preparing to flee with them into Egypt. Chap. xlii. relates how Jeremiah is consulted, and how he finds the will of the Lord to be that they should remain. Chap. xliii. relates how Johanan and all the people go down to Egypt, taking Jeremiah along with them, and how Jeremiah predicts the fall of Egypt. Chap. xliv. relates how Jeremiah rebukes and warns the Jews that have gone into Egypt, and how he finds them as obstinate as the rest, and ends with a threat of yet further punishment. Chap. xlv. is a word of comfort and reproof from Jeremiah to Baruch, his scribe. (c.) Chap. xlvi. contains prophecies first and second against Egypt. Chap. xlvii. prophesies against Philistia. Chap. xlviii. is a prophecy against and a lament over Moab, ending with a promise of restoration even to that heathen nation. Chap. xlix. contains prophecies regarding Ammon, Edom, Damascus, Kedar, Hazor, and Elam, ending again with a promise of restoration. Chap. l. contains a prophecy regarding Babylon, a threat of punishment to her for her pride, and a promise of restoration to Israel, while Babylon's doom is enlarged on. Chap. li. bids Israel leave Babylon to her fate, and further amplifies the description of her doom. (d.) Chap. lii. gives an account of the capture of the city

and the severities thereafter, with an enumeration of the captives to Babylon, and a last notice of Jehoiachin.

Lamentations.—This title is from the Vulgate, and is a translation of the designation "Threnoi" given to the book in the Septuagint, the Hebrew name of it being "Echah," meaning How, as that is the word with which several of the laments begin. It is one of the poetical books, and accordingly it is not classed with the prophets in the Hebrew Bible, being preceded by Canticles and Ruth, and followed by Ecclesiastes and Esther ; but it is placed in our Bibles after Jeremiah, because it has been ascribed to him, although it does not itself claim to be written by the prophet. It seems to have been written shortly after the fall of the city and in the sight of its ruins. The subject-matter is connected with what is related in Jer. xxxix. and lii., and is a lament over the desolation of the land, the exile of the people, the destruction of the temple, the fall of the kingdom of Judah, and other miseries that distressed the prophet. The book is composed of five laments connected together by the subject-matter and the spirit that inspires them. Each is divided according to the number of letters in the Hebrew alphabet, the twenty-two verses in chaps. i., ii., iv. respectively beginning with the successive letters, chap. iii. having three verses to each letter, and chap. v. not having the letters in alphabetical order. *Contents.*—Chap. i. dwells upon the solitude and misery of the city. Chap ii. describes the ruin that has overtaken her, and acknowledges that she has brought it on by her sin. Chap. iii. complains of the bitterness of the sorrow, but regards the hand that inflicts it as merciful. Chap. iv. admits that the sufferings experienced are consequent on sin. Chap. v. details anew the miseries endured, and prays for deliverance.

Ezekiel.—1. The author of this book was a native of Jerusalem, and, like Jeremiah, of priestly descent, a member of a family of aristocratic standing in the city. When, as would appear, about twenty-five years of age, and after he had seen some service as a priest, he was carried away captive to Babylon along with Jehoiachin and other noble Jews in 597 B.C., and before the destruction of Jerusalem (2 Kings xxiv. 15). He must have been a witness of the plundering of the temple by Nebuchadnezzar, as recorded in 2 Kings xxiv. 13, and his prophecies give evidence of a familiar acquaintance with its structure (chap. viii. 5-16, &c.). His place of banishment was Tel-Abib, on the banks of the river Chebar, about 200 miles north of Babylon. Here he settled with his family, and here he established himself as the prophet of the Captivity, his house being the *rendezvous* of all who mourned over the dispersion and sought for the restoration of Israel (chaps. viii. 1 ; xi. 25 ; xiv. 1, &c.). It was in the fifth year of his exile that the call came to him to assume the prophetic office, and this function he continued to discharge in behalf of the Captivity for at least twenty-two years, the latest date in his book being 570 B.C.

2. In his capacity as prophet of the Captivity, Ezekiel had two duties to discharge : the first was to announce to the captives the destruction of Jerusalem, and therewith the ruin of

the throne of David; and the second was to comfort them and stir them up with the prospect of a new Temple and a new Jerusalem better and more glorious than those that had been destroyed. Towards the fulfilment of this prospect both the captivity of the people and the destruction of the city were necessary, as otherwise they could not be brought to see how they had broken the covenant of the Lord with them, and how He would not fulfil His part so long as they refused to fulfil theirs. He therefore urged repentance as a *sine qua non* to the fulfilment of the promise of a day of better things. And how effectively he wrought on the minds of the exiles is evident, for from being worshippers of strange gods we find them zealous only for Jehovah, and from being regardless of God's law they appear as studious of its statutes and intent on the fulfilment of them.

3. The announcement of the destruction of Jerusalem by Ezekiel appears to have preceded the event, and is presumed to be connected with a similar prediction by Jeremiah, between whom and the former in his exile a communication was kept up. It was not till after this event that Ezekiel saw his visions of the future, while in the interval he occupied himself with the judgments that must first come on the surrounding nations, as a necessary preliminary to the salvation of Israel. Ezekiel's prophecies, accordingly, corresponding as they do in arrangement with the order in which they were uttered, are divisible, after the introduction (chaps. i.-iii. 21), into three groups: (*a*) Those concerning the judgment of God on Jerusalem (chaps. iii. 22-xxiv.); (*b*) those concerning the judgments of God on the heathen (chaps. xxv.-xxxii.); and (*c*) those announcing the future glory of the people of Israel (chaps. xxxiii.-xlviii.).

4. Ezekiel appears in his prophecies as a man of great force of faculty and unbending firmness of purpose, while his fervour of spirit is coupled with the utmost clearness and discretion of intelligence, so that he never suffers his feelings to override his reason.

Contents.—Introduction. Chap. i. records the call of the prophet, and his vision of the cherubim and of the glory of the Lord. Chap. ii. introduces the prophet as receiving his commission, and as having a roll given to him to eat, in which are written "lamentations, mourning, and woe." Chap. iii. introduces the Lord as encouraging the prophet, and as appointing him to be His watchman over Israel.

a. Prophecies concerning the judgment of God on Jerusalem.—Chap. iv. predicts symbolically the siege of the city, and the Captivity, with its results and its purpose. Chap. v. predicts symbolically the nature of the judgments, and gives the reason for them. Chap. vi. shows that God's judgments are to punish the people for, and save them from, their idolatries. Chap. vii. describes how utter and complete will be the judgment. Chaps. viii.-xi. predict the rejection of the nation for its idolatries. Chaps. xii.-xix. give a detailed account of the sins of the age. Chaps. xx.-xxiii. explain the purpose of the Lord in the judgment, and specify the sins that led to it. Chap. xxiv. sets forth the destruction of the city, and the inexpressibleness of the sorrow.

b. Prophecies concerning the judgment of God on other nations.—Chap. xxv. 1-7 prophesies against Ammon. Vers. 8-14 prophesy against Moab and Edom. Vers. 15-17 prophesy against the Philistines. Chaps. xxvi.-xxviii. 19 prophesy against Tyre. Vers. 20-24 prophesy against Sidon. Vers. 25, 26 contain a promise of the restoration of Judah. Chaps. xxix.-xxxii. prophesy against Egypt.

c. Prophecies affecting the future of Israel.—Chap. xxxiii. represents the prophet as a watchman to warn the people, and calls upon the people to repent, seeing the judgment has come. Chap. xxxiv. pronounces a woe to the shepherds that care not for the flock, and witnesses to one who will care for it. Chap. xxxv. prophesies against Edom for its usurpation of Israel. Chap. xxxvi. is a promise on the part of the Lord to sanctify and restore Israel. Chap. xxxvii. pictures the revival and gathering again into one of all Israel under the figures of the resurrection of a field of dry bones and the union into one of two sticks. Chaps. xxxviii. and xxxix. describe the mustering of the hostile armies of Gog from the land of Magog, and their disastrous defeat as that of the last enemy that shall come up against Israel. Chaps. xl.-xlviii. describe in detail the final arrangements connected with the reorganised theocracy, such as the structure, size, and equipments of the temple, the regulations regarding the sacrifices and the festivals, and the distribution of the land among the twelve tribes.

Daniel.—Of the reputed author of this book, which bears his name, we know nothing except what the book itself tells us and what Ezekiel (chaps. xiv. 14, 18, 20, and xxviii. 3) confirms regarding his character as an exemplar in both wisdom of intelligence and uprightness of life. From the book itself we learn that he was of noble birth, and that, while but a youth, he was carried away to Babylon, together with others of his class, in the third year of Jehoiakim (605 B.C.), and about eight years before his contemporary, Ezekiel. Being of fine physique and rare endowment, he was selected, with three others of kindred quality, to be trained for office in the court of the king; and for this purpose he underwent a three years' discipline in all the wisdom of the land under the chief of the eunuchs, with the result that, when at length he and his companions were introduced into the royal presence, they were found to be superior "in wisdom and understanding" to "all the magicians and enchanters of all the realm." The proof Daniel thus early gave of his capability was verified as often afterwards as it was put to the test; and in the exercise of his wonderful gifts he rose step by step to the highest official positions, first in the Babylonian and then in the Persian empire. It was less, however, by his native ability than by his fear of the Lord that he attained this elevation, and because the Lord intrusted him with a knowledge of secrets which He made known to no other. Thus as an interpreter of dreams, in which those secrets were shadowed forth, he commended himself and the God he feared to Nebuchadnezzar first, and then to Cyrus.

1. *Date of Authorship.*—The Book of Daniel was accepted by the Jewish people and by the early Christians. Until modern times the only person to throw doubt on it was the anti-Christian writer Porphyry (about 305 A.D.). But recently

it has been again asserted that the book was not written till the third century before Christ, or even as late as the persecution of Antiochus Epiphanes (168 or 167 B.C.). The principal reasons that have been brought forward in favour of the late date of the book are — (1) its place in the Hebrew Bible with the Hagiographa, not with the prophets; (2) the silence of Jesus the son of Sirach (writing about 200 B.C.), who gives a list of the other prophets; (3) peculiarities of language, e.g., the use of many Persian words, Greek names of musical instruments; western Aramaic, such as was spoken in Palestine, but not in Babylon; the late form of the Hebrew text; (4) difficulties in harmonising certain points in the narrative with history; (5) the suitability of the book to the circumstances of the oppression of the Jews by Antiochus Epiphanes. Against the late date now proposed, and in favour of the traditional association of the book with the name of Daniel, several interesting archæological facts have been brought forward quite recently. The discoveries of Babylonian antiquities and the decipherment of the ancient brick libraries have brought to light the manners and customs of, Babylon, which are found to agree in a remarkable way with the pictures so graphically portrayed in the Book of Daniel. Until these discoveries were made it was said that there was no room for Belshazzar in history—his name not being met with except in this book. But now the name has been discovered in inscriptions as *Belshar-usur*, the son of Nabonidas, the last king of Babylon. The historical character of Daniel himself cannot well be questioned, and these modern discoveries tend to authenticate the narrative of the book that bears his name, although it can scarcely be maintained that they dispose of the weighty arguments in favour of a late date for the composition of the work.

2. *Divisions of the Book.*—The Book of Daniel is written partly in Hebrew and partly in Aramaic, the introduction being in Hebrew. The divisions are two—first (*a*) historical (chaps. i.-vi.), and second (*b*) prophetic, composed of a succession of apocalyptic visions.

3. *Contents.*—a. Chap. i. tells how Daniel and his companions, under training of the chief of the eunuchs, and fed, at their own request, on pulse and water, grew into supremely capable and attractive young men, and were found such by the king. Chap. ii. relates how Daniel saved himself, his companions, and all the wise men of Babylon by the Lord's revealing to him the matter and meaning of the king's dream, and so with his companions was appointed to posts of authority in the kingdom. Chap. iii. shows how, for refusing to worship an image set up by the king, Shadrach, Meshach, and Abednego were cast into a fiery furnace, miraculously delivered therefrom by the Most High God, and thereafter promoted to honour in the province of Babylon. Chap. iv. relates how Nebuchadnezzar dreams again, how Daniel interprets the dream, how it comes to pass, and how the king learns to humble himself before the God of Daniel. Chap. v. relates how Daniel interprets to Belshazzar the handwriting on his palace wall, and how the interpretation is fulfilled that night in the overthrow of the city and the occupation of it by Darius the Mede. Chap. vi. relates how Darius is induced to pass a decree

which Daniel could not keep, and how Daniel for breach of it is thrown into a lion's den, but saved by his God, while his persecutors are doomed to the lions, and have none to deliver them.

b. Chap. vii. gives Daniel's first dream-vision, in the first year of Belshazzar's reign, describing the four world-powers under the image of four beasts. Chap. viii. gives his second vision, in Belshazzar's third year, relating to the ram and the he-goat. Chap. ix. records his supplication with confession to the Lord, and the visit of Gabriel to him to announce to him the term of the days. Chaps. x. and xi. give his third vision, in the third year of Cyrus, of the four Persian kings, and of Alexander with his successors, on to the subjugation of Syria as a preliminary to Messiah's kingdom. Chap xii. predicts the resurrection of just and unjust, and gives Daniel's last vision of the man on the waters of the time-river.

See G. A. Smith, *The Book of Isaiah* (Expositor's Bible); Whitehouse, *Isaiah* (Century Bible); Bennett, *Jeremiah* (Expositor's Bible); Davidson, *Ezekiel* (Cambridge Bible); Driver, *Daniel* (Cambridge Bible).

CHAPTER XII.

THE MINOR PROPHETS.

THE Minor Prophets form in the Hebrew canon one whole, and go collectively under the name of the Book of the Twelve Prophets. They cover a period of four hundred years, from the ninth to the fifth century before Christ, but they are not arranged in the order of the time of their production, as will appear from the following account of them separately.

Hosea.—The author of this book, a native of the northern kingdom of Israel, and a contemporary of Isaiah, prophesied to the people under Jeroboam II. and his degenerate successors down to Hoshea, the last of the kings of Israel, from before 746 B.C. to 735-4 B.C., or perhaps to 722 B.C. At the commencement of his ministry, while Jeroboam II. was king, the internal condition and external relations of the community, still governed as it was with some respect for the law of the Lord, seemed fairly prosperous; but all the while there were corrupting influences at work, and these began to assert themselves with the death of the king. The root of the evil lay in the free scope the people had had to indulge their idolatrous proclivities, which had only been suppressed, not destroyed, and in the encouragement those propensities received at the hands of the priests, who would profit more as the ministers of Baal than as the ministers of Jehovah. All fear of the Lord and regard for His word died out of the hearts of the people, all forms of immorality began to prevail, and the national vigour to decay; and when trouble came, there was no longer recourse to the Almighty Protector, but to alliance with certain world-powers, such as Assyria and Egypt All this was painfully evident to the prophet's mind, and for long he strove to avert it. Under Jeroboam he was witnessing continually against the sin of the people, and calling them to repent and return to the Lord, who would yet receive them (chaps. i.-iii.) ; but when, after this, he saw, in their more and more rampant degeneracy, that his warning words were without effect, he ceased to plead with the people, and began to denounce on them Divine judgment as the only remedy adequate to work their repentance (chaps. iv.-xiv.). His book accordingly divides itself into two parts ; in the first (a) Israel, who is represented as an unfaithful wife, is invited to return to Jehovah her husband (chaps. i.-iii.), and in the second (b) is the announcement of the Divine judgment and its issue (chaps iv.-xiv.).

Contents.—a. Chap. i. relates how the prophet, at the command of the Lord, takes a wife, who proves unfaithful, and who bears children to him in her unfaithfulness, in order that thereby he may symbolise the relationship in which Israel stands to Jehovah. Chap. ii. is an exhortation to Israel to forsake her adulteries and return to the Lord, who will betroth her anew. Chap. iii. describes symbolically how the Lord will ransom and woo back His faithless bride.

b. Chap. iv. describes the gross immorality of the people as encouraged by the priests. Chap. v. describes the guilt and the punishment, from which last there is no escape except in repentance. Chap. vi. shows how evanescent is Israel's repentance as compared with her obstinate sinfulness. Chap. vii. shows the depth of Israel's depravity and the outward signs of her decay. Chap. viii. announces the imminence of the judgment and its causes. Chap. ix. gives a picture of the calamity which Israel has all along been drawing down on her head. Chap. x. gives examples of Israel's guilt and punishment. Chap. xi. shows how the Lord has all along pursued Israel with His love, and how Israel has requited it. Chaps. xii.-xiv. record the issue of the Divine judgments.

Joel.—Of the author of this book we know nothing, except that he belonged to the region of Judah, and lived probably in Jerusalem, and was perhaps a priest. His book testifies, too, that he was a man of tender feeling, warm enthusiasm, and glowing imagination, and that he possessed a gift, unsurpassed by any other Old Testament writer, of clear, vivid, and eloquent expression. We are as much in the dark about the time and circumstances of his life as we are about his personal history, seeing there are no data given in the book by which we can certainly identify its composition with any single event as occurring at the time in the national history. We can only conclude, as there is no mention in it of Assyria or Babylon, and none of the internal controversies which exercise the other prophets from Amos to the Captivity, such as that between the worship of Jehovah and idolatry, that it was not written within the period when the latter prophesied, but must have been written either before or after. The manner and purity of the style, and certain vague allusions to early events, as in chap. iii. 7-11, would seem to point to the former conclusion, and the book was accordingly referred to the time of Joash, a date somewhere between 837 and 797 B.C. On the other hand, recent criticism assigns it to a period

later than the Captivity, the purity of the style alleged in evidence of the former view being accounted for as in great part "the fruit of literary culture." The grounds adduced in favour of the post-exilian theory are—first, the mention in chap. iii. 1, 2, of the Captivity, the dispersion of the people, and the allotment of their land to others ; secondly, that there is no mention of a king in the land, only " of sheikhs and priests ; " and thirdly, that the character of the worship prevalent at the time (chaps. i. 9 ; ii. 14) is, in the regard of recent criticism, of post-exilian origin. But be this as it may, the book is written on the great broad lines of all Hebrew prophecy, and reads us the same great moral lesson which all the other prophetic books do, that from the judgments of God there is no outlet for the sinner except in repentance, and that in repentance lies the pledge of deliverance from all evil and the enjoyment of all good.

1. *Divisions.*—The occasion of the warning of the prophet in this book is the visitation on the land of a plague of locust-swarms, and the occurrence of an all-withering drought ; and as this warning, from chap. ii. 18, showed signs of proving effectual, the prophet gave the reins to his imagination in picturing the blessed time sure to follow. Thus the book divides itself into two sections at chap. ii. 18, the former (a) being a description of the present calamity and a call to repentance and prayer ; and the latter (b) being a promise from the Lord, who has heard the prayer of His people, that He will, on the ground of its sincerity, henceforth shed only blessing on them, and reserve all His fury for, and ere long pour it out upon, those that rise up against them.

2. *Contents.—a.* Chap. i. delineates the two plagues of the locusts and the drought, and calls upon the people to humble themselves before the Lord. Chap. ii. 1-17 represents these plagues as forecasts of greater, as calls to repentance, and as effective for this end.

b. Chap. ii. 18-27 promises to recompense the people abundantly for all they have suffered. Vers. 28-32 promise an outpouring of the Spirit, and threaten collateral judgments. Chap. iii. continues the threat of judgment and the promise of blessing.

Amos.—The author of this prophecy represents himself as originally a poor shepherd of Tekoa in Judah, a place ten miles south of Jerusalem, and as a cultivator of sycamore-fruit. Without connection with the prophetic class, and without preparation for the prophetic office (chap. vii. 14, 15), he was moved by the Spirit of God to raise his voice against idolatry, as the source of the corruption he sorrowfully saw abounding around him. Accordingly he went to Bethel, the centre of the calf-worship, there to announce the judgment of God which such an idolatrous practice was drawing down on the whole nation. This was in the reigns of Uzziah and Jeroboam II., and probably about the year 763 B.C., when there was an eclipse of the sun (see Amos viii. 7).

From 2 Kings xiv. 8-14, it appears Judah was at the time dependent on Israel, the affairs of the latter being in a prosperous way, and those of the former in a state of prostration (see chap. ix. 11). Nevertheless it was the kingdom of Israel that was on the downward road, and not

Judah, for there the fallen tabernacle of David would be raised again. To announce this to Israel, which had grown secure from prosperity under Jeroboam II., was the object of the mission of this prophet; the earthquake (mentioned in chap. i. 1) occurring two years after his mission to Jeroboam—like the plague of locusts with the prophet Joel—was a warning of the judgment the Lord was preparing for His people and those of the nations that did not fear Him; and the prophet's word, both spoken and written, was to provoke the people to give heed and repent of their doings.

1. *Divisions and Style of the Book.*—The book has been divided into two sections—the first (*a*) containing denunciations of the Divine displeasure against idol-worship, especially in the northern kingdom, the course of the judgment as described by the prophet being poetically likened to a thunderstorm rolling over the surrounding nations, touching Judah in its progress, and finally settling upon Israel (chaps. i.-vi.); and the second (*b*) containing symbolical visions of the overthrow of Israel and the promise of a restoration (chaps. vii.-ix.). All this is given in a style at once clear, vigorous, and graphic, and the illustrations with which the book abounds are such as we might expect from one who was born and bred in the country.

2. *Contents.*—*a.* Chaps. i. and ii. threaten judgment on Syria, Philistia, Tyre, Edom, Ammon, Moab, Judah, and Israel, on the two last for the base contempt of their covenant mercies. Chap. iii. states the reason for the judgment on Israel, and describes it. Chap. iv. relates how, all other chastisement having failed, the Lord will try more severe measures. Chaps. v. and vi. announce the overthrow of the kingdom of Israel.

b. Chap. vii. gives the visions of the locusts, of the devouring fire, and of the plumb-line, and the opposition to the prophet at Bethel. Chap. viii. gives the vision of a basket of ripe fruit, rebukes the oppression of the poor, and threatens a spiritual famine in the land. Chap. ix. threatens desolation and promises restoration.

Obadiah.—Of the author of this book we know absolutely nothing, and he cannot be identified with anybody of the same name, which was a common one among the Jewish people, as the corresponding one Abdallah is among the Arabs. There is also some uncertainty in fixing the time when he wrote, but the weight of evidence from internal sources goes to show that it must have been shortly after the destruction of Jerusalem, 586 B.C. That calamity is the only one which adequately tallies with the description given by the prophet, and it would appear it was one in bringing about which the Edomites, the objects of his denunciation, had borne a share, and over which they had given expression to boastful exultation. These people, as is known, were the descendants of Esau, and, as they had all along shown an unfriendly feeling to their brethren of Israel, so now it must have given them no small satisfaction to see and assist in their prostration under the power of Babylon. It was to comfort the Jews in exile, who were naturally smarting under this disgrace, that the prophecy was written; and its burden is to assure them that the disgrace is only for a time, and that a decree has gone forth from the Lord which, while it promises salvation to them, will effect the ruin of Edom and all opposed to them—a prophecy, as regards Edom, finally fulfilled in 135 B.C., under John Hyrcanus. The book is divided into two sections, the first predicting the destruction of Edom (vers. 1–16), and the second the restoration of Israel (vers. 17–21).

Jonah.—The subject and commonly assumed author of this book is evidently the same as the prophet mentioned in 2 Kings xiv. 25 as a native of Gath-hepher, in the tribe of Zebulun, who belonged, therefore, to the northern kingdom, and prophesied in the reign of Jeroboam II., *i.e.*, at the close of the ninth century B.C. According to this passage and the book before us, his mission as a prophet was twofold—first, to direct Jeroboam to restore the ancient border of the kingdom; and, second, to preach, at the bidding of the Lord, repentance to the people of Nineveh. It is of Jonah in connection with the latter mission that this book treats, and the meaning and purpose of it has been represented as follows : —In the time of the prophet it was clear that Divine judgment was coming upon the kingdom of Israel, and it was already revealed that Assyria, of which Nineveh was the capital, was the agent by which this judgment was to be wrought out. But in the proportion that any heathen nation happened to be called to this work, in that very proportion was it thought by the Jew to bring itself under the ban of Jehovah. It was forgotten that the mercy which the Jew hoped for would be extended to the heathen, and there was no thought of anything but the Divine judgment they were provoking on their own heads by their treatment of Jehovah's chosen. Of this uncharitable view Jonah and his contemporaries had to be undeceived. Hence the purpose for which he was sent to Nineveh was not simply to effect the conversion of her people, but to teach, from the result, that the Lord has pity on the heathen as well as the Jews, and would forgive them too on repentance. Thus the story of the prophet is to be viewed symbolically, and as itself a prophecy ; and hence this book, though in form purely historical, has been assigned a place not among the historical but among the prophetic books of the Old Testament.

There are many who doubt the historical reality of the story of Jonah. It may be, though there is no indication of this, that the whole is an allegory in historical form. On the other hand, the language is simple, and the style that of a matter-of-fact historian. The geographical and historical allusions agree with what is known from other authorities.

Contents.—The book has been divided into four sections—first, Jonah's disobedience and his punishment (chap. i. 1–16); second, his prayer and consequent deliverance (chaps. i. 17–ii. 10) ; third, his preaching to the Ninevites, and their consequent repentance (chap. iii.) ; and fourth, his displeasure that the threatened judgment is not executed, and God's rebuke of him (chap. iv.).

Micah.—The author of this book was a native of Moresheth, a small town in the south-west of Judæa near Gath, and a contemporary of Isaiah, Hosea, and Amos, being probably the youngest of the group. His name is a contracted form of Micaiah, which means, "Who is like Jehovah?" and it appears, according to the fashion of the times (see ISAIAH), to have been given to him or adopted by him as a sign to the people of Israel. His prophecies are in the same vein as those of Isaiah, and both numerous and close are the coincidences which have been traced between them. A greater sternness of temper is at first sight apparent, and a greater severity of tone pervades his prophecies, but from time to time a deep tenderness of heart reveals itself (chap. i. 10), and his pleading is as urgent as any wherewith an inspired messenger of heaven has sought to reconcile the sinner to God (chap. vi. 8). Chap. vii. 8-20 is referred to as "one of the sweetest passages of prophetic writing." Micah's style is clear, vivid, concise, and poetic. His prophecies predict the destruction of the northern kingdom and its capital Samaria (chap. i. 6-8), the destruction of Jerusalem (chaps. iii. 12; vii. 13), the Captivity (chap. iv. 10), the Return (chaps. iv. 1-8; vii. 11), the establishment of the theocracy in Zion (chap. iv. 8), and the ruler to come out of Bethlehem (chap. v. 2).

1. *Divisions of the Book.*—It has been divided into three sections—(*a*) chaps. i.-iii.; (*b*) chaps. iv. and v.; and (*c*) chaps. vi. and vii.

2. *Contents.*—*a*. Chap. i. contains a threatening of judgment on Samaria and Jerusalem, and the prophet's lament over it. Chap. ii. refers the cause, while it describes the punishment, to the sins of the princes and rulers. Chap. iii. describes the cruel conduct of these men, foretells the fate of the false prophets, and refers again to the national sin and judgment.

b. Chap. iv. predicts the return of prosperity to Zion. Chap. v. predicts the birth and rule of the Messiah, with the abolition of war and idolatry.

c. Chaps. vi. and vii. state the case between the Lord and His people.

Nahum.—The author of this prophecy was a native of a place called Elkosh, which some identify with a village on the banks of the Tigris, and others, who are more probably correct, with a place in the region of Galilee. The date of the book must come after the destruction of Thebes, *i.e.*, later than 664 B.C., and probably near the time of the overthrow of Nineveh in 607 B.C. The object of Nahum's mission was to comfort the Jew in the near presence of so formidable a foe as Assyria, and to announce the destruction of that overbearing power, and especially of its capital city Nineveh. The style of the prophet is as classical as that of Isaiah, and is not inferior to his in force and originality of thought, clearness of expression, and purity of diction. His prophecy is divisible into three strophes, which are coincident with the chapters.

Contents.—Chap. i. announces the Divine purpose to inflict judgment on the Assyrian oppressor of His people. Chap. ii. anticipates the glad tidings of the conquest, sack, and destruction of Nineveh. Chap. iii. represents the guilt of the city and depicts its inevitable ruin.

Habakkuk.—Of the author of this book we know nothing, except that he was of the Levitical class, and appears to have had duties in connection with the liturgical service of the temple; neither have we any certain knowledge of the time when he lived, except that he prophesied before the arrival of the Chaldæans in the land

to execute judgment on Judah. Though Jewish tradition refers the time when he lived to the last days of the reign of Manasseh, and many eminent critics agree with this view, the weight of internal evidence would seem to point to the reign of Jehoiakim as the date in question, somewhere between the years 608-598 B.C. Habakkuk's prophecy belongs, both in substance and form, to the classic period of Hebrew literature, and is written in a style which has been described as being "for grandeur and sublimity of conception, for vigour and fervour of expression, for gorgeousness of imagery, and for melody of language, among the first productions of that literature." The spirit of the prophecy is one, viz., faith in the righteous ways of the Lord; but the burden is twofold: to denounce the judgments of God on the land for the violence and wrong that prevail in it, as about to be inflicted by the hand of a power still more violent and unjust in its ways; and to comfort the generation of the righteous with the assurance of a time when this very rod of God's wrath shall, in the pride of its power, be broken in pieces, and the Lord be revealed as seated in His holy temple.

1. *Divisions of the Book.*—The book is in two parts, the first (*a*) containing the twofold denunciation of judgment (chaps. i. and ii.), and the second (*b*) the prophet's prayer for its fulfilment (chap. iii.).

2. *Contents.*—*a*. Chap. i. bewails the general corruption abroad among the people, and predicts the speedy vengeance of the Lord by the hand of the Chaldæans. Chap. ii. predicts the judgment of the Lord in turn on the despoiling Chaldæans.

b. Chap. iii. forecasts, in lyric strain, from the memories of the past, the coming judgment on the ungodly, and gives utterance to the assurance of faith with which the righteous will regard it.

Zephaniah.—Of this prophet we know only that he was well-born, probably of royal descent, and that he prophesied in the reign of Josiah, from 639 to 608 B.C., in the brief interval between the decline and predicted fall of Nineveh and the advance of Babylon. In the time of Josiah, though the administration of justice according to the law and the worship of Jehovah had been revived, yet both were only hypocritically observed, and idolatrous practices were still prosecuted in secret. It was the perception of this that stirred the godly soul of the prophet to warn the people of the consequences and persuade them to repentance. Yet, though the king united himself with the prophet to reform the people, both combined availed nothing to stem, or even check, the prevailing ungodliness. Rather did the wickedness increase, and the people ripen for the judgment, which already impended in the growing power and grasping spirit of Babylon. This judgment accordingly the prophet has in his eye; and while Habakkuk makes known the course and upshot of it, Zephaniah lays bare the cause, which he finds in the moral corruption of the people. Yet is his prophecy also a word of comfort to the pious, for neither can he, any more than the rest of the prophets, help seeing the meaning of all this in the dispensations of the Lord with His people. It is as clear to him as to them that the Lord is to achieve their salvation by judgment.

1. *Divisions of the Book.*—There are three sections—the first (*a*) embracing chap. i. ; the second (*b*) embracing chaps. ii.-iii. 8 ; and the third (*c*) contained in chap. iii. 9-20.

2. *Contents.*—(*a.*) Chap. i. predicts the judgment that is to come upon all the world, and especially the despisers of God in Judah and Jerusalem. (*b.*) Chaps. ii.-iii. 8 contain an exhortation to repentance in view of this judgment. (*c.*) Chap. iii. 9-20 promises the conversion of the nations in consequence of the glorification of Israel.

Haggai.—The author of this book is the first of the prophets of the Restoration, that is, of Jerusalem and the Temple after the Captivity, Zechariah, his contemporary, being the second, and Malachi, a hundred years after, the third. He appears to have been one of the captives who returned from Babylon under Zerubbabel and Joshua ; and, inspired by the tradition, if not the recollection, of what the city and its temple had been, he seems to have come up with the others to Jerusalem, animated by a special zeal for rebuilding in a style worthy of the best days. The foundation-stone of the temple was laid in 535 B.C., and from various causes of a discouraging nature, the work of building went on but slowly till about 520 B.C., when, signs of the Divine displeasure having appeared on account of the laggard spirit in which it was prosecuted by the people, Haggai was inspired to lift up his protesting voice and rouse their patriotism. His appeal made a deep impression, and proved successful, for in four years the work was finished, and the temple dedicated to the worship of Jehovah as of old, 515 B.C. The style of Haggai is prosaic, but his diction is, on the whole, pure and clear. Together with Zechariah, he is mentioned in Ezra v. 1 as having had to do with encouraging the building of the temple.

1. *Divisions of the Book.*—There are four separate prophetic utterances, at intervals indicated with more than usual precision, each delivered also with more than usual effect.

2. *Contents.*—Chap. i. reproaches the people for their neglect in restoring the temple, and intimates the success of the appeal. Chap. ii. 1-9 is an encouragement, a month after the zealous resumption of the work, to go on, despite the disparaging remarks of the old men who had seen the former temple. Vers. 10-19 contain, after two more months, a further encouragement to go on, from consideration of the consequences of neglect on the one hand, and perseverance on the other. Vers. 20-23, delivered the same day as the last, give encouragement to Zerubbabel.

Zechariah.—The prophet whose name this book bears was the contemporary and colleague of Haggai, and the circumstances, therefore, in which he prophesied are the same as those related in connection with that prophet. He was of priestly descent, a man of influence and a leader among those who returned from captivity under Zerubbabel. He began his prophetic office two months after Haggai, and he continued to prophesy at first for two years, contributing not a little by his inspired wisdom to encourage the temple-builders at their work and ensure its completion. Like Haggai, he appears to have had

a great deal to do with the reorganisation of the temple worship and the reconstruction of the psalter ; and tradition says that both were members of the Great Synagogue. Zechariah seems to have been born and bred in Babylon ; and the fact that his prophecies are cast and coloured pretty much like those conceived there, such as Ezekiel's, goes to justify the supposition. The book has been divided into two great sections (*a* and *b*), but the authenticity of the latter, beginning with chap. ix., has been much debated. With the commencement of that chapter there is a sudden change, not only in the style of the prophesying, but also in the subject and character of the prophecies ; and the reader is no longer among scenes in which the writer himself moved and acted, so that many conclude that what follows must be the composition of a different author, and belong to a different crisis of Jewish history.

Contents.—*a.* Chaps. i.-vi. 8 contain, after an introductory call to repentance (chap. i. 1-6), a series of eight visions—the first, of a band of angelic horsemen in a myrtle grove (7-17) ; the second, of the four horns destroyed by the four carpenters (18-21); the third, of the vision of the man sent out to measure the limits of the city (chap. ii.) ; the fourth, of the acquittal of Joshua and his typical installation to the high-priesthood (chap. iii.) ; the fifth, of the golden candlestick, with its miraculous supply of oil (chap. iv.) ; the sixth, of the flying roll (chap. v. 1-4) ; the seventh, of the woman in the midst of the ephah (5-11) ; and the eighth, of the four chariots of God's wrath issuing from between two brazen mountains (chap. vi. 1-8). Chap. vi. 9-15 gives an account of the symbolical crowning of Joshua. Chaps. vii. and viii. contain the decision regarding the observance of the fasts that had been instituted in connection with the capture and destruction of Jerusalem.

b. Chaps. ix. and x. predict the destruction of the surrounding nations, and the safety and triumph under their king of the Jewish people. Chap. xi. concerns the rejection of the shepherd. Chaps. xii.-xiv. describe the final victory of Israel.

Malachi. — Of the author of this book nothing is known, and as the name, which means Messenger of Jehovah, does not occur anywhere else in the Old Testament, it has been regarded and accepted in some versions of the Bible, and by several critics, as an appellative or official title, as is surmised, of Ezra, Nehemiah, or some other person. Whether Malachi be the name of a real person or not, his prophecies refer to abuses which did not begin to make their appearance till fifty years after the restoration of the temple ; and it must have been some considerable time after that before they assumed the dimensions in which the prophet here denounces them. These abuses appear to have come to a head in the interval between the first and second visits of Nehemiah to Jerusalem, and it is probable, from his description of the people agreeing with that of Neh. xiii. 6 *seq.*, that it was on the occasion of this second visit that this "last of the prophets" uttered his warning words, about 420 B.C. Not only do we miss the old prophetic fire, but an impression is given as if the prophetic office were ended. He sums up all he has to say by referring his hearers back to the law of the Lord, as that to which all the prophets before him had borne witness, and finishes by a prediction of the time, now not far off, when the first of his line—Elijah—should revive and usher in the judgment which is to precede the final redemption and the reconciliation of "the fathers to the children and the children to the fathers."

1. *Divisions of the Book.*—The prophecy is one, but the sections are three :—(*a*) chaps i. 6–ii. 9 ; (*b*) chap. ii. 10–16 ; and (*c*) chaps. ii. 17–iv., the whole preceded by an Introduction, chap. i. 1–5.

2. *Contents.*—The Introduction reminds the people of the special regard the Lord has for them. (*a.*) Chap. i. 6–14 rebukes the priests for their profanation of the Lord's name, their pollution of His altar, and their hireling spirit, in consideration of which God threatens to cast them off and accept the homage of the Gentiles. Chap. ii. 1–9 rebukes the priests for their want of reverence of God's name and regard for His law. (*b.*) Chap. ii. 10–16 rebukes both priest and people for their intermarriages with idolatrous aliens. (*c.*) Chaps. ii. 17–iv., while rebuking the people for their sceptical morality and their scoffing spirit, reassert the certain approach of God's judgment, with the promise to all who obey His voice and wait for His salvation.

See Farrar, *The Minor Prophets;* Cheyne, *Hosea and Micah;* Perowne, *Obadiah and Jonah, Haggai, Zechariah, and Malachi* (Camb. Bible) ; Horton, and Driver, *The Minor Prophets* (Century Bible); Harper, *Amos and Hosea;* Geo. A. Smith, *The Twelve Prophets.*

CHAPTER XIII

THE APOCRYPHA.

THE name "Apocrypha" is given to a collection of books which we first find inserted in the Septuagint version of the Scriptures, and the composition of which dates from the period following the Captivity to the Christian era, if not later. Though the work of Jews, these books have no place in the Hebrew canon, which closes with the book of Malachi, and they are consequently not accepted by the Jews as of canonical authority. The Hebrew canon was made to terminate when the voice of prophecy ceased ; but the Alexandrian Bible was extended so as to include as well the voice of wisdom, which is more pervasive and has a wider scope than the spirit of prophecy ; only the wisdom enforced is always the wisdom inculcated in the canonical books, which is uniformly practical and religious —*i.e.*, based on the fear of God and the duty of observing all His commandments. "To the Alexandrian," as Prof. A. B. Davidson remarks, "the varied Jewish literature of the post-prophetic times was precious as well as the books that were more ancient ; and he carefully gathered the scattered fragments of his national thought, as far as they were known, within the compass of the canon." To this class of literature the name Apocrypha, literally "hidden writing," was given, to distinguish it from what was accepted as canonical—*i.e.*, regarded as determinative in matters, not of private thinking, but of public doctrine or confession ; a name which, as we have seen, is synonymous with non-canonical writing.

Of this literature there are in the English version fourteen books, and these have been inserted in it between the Old Testament and the New, arranged in the following order :—(1) I. Esdras ; (2) II. Esdras ; (3) Tobit ; (4) Judith ; (5) The Additions to the Book of Esther ; (6) The Wisdom of Solomon ; (7) The Wisdom of Jesus, the Son of Sirach, or Ecclesiasticus ; (8) Baruch ; (9) The Song of the Three Holy Children ; (10) The History of Susanna ; (11) The History of the Destruction of Bel and the Dragon ; (12) The Prayer of Manasseh, King of Judah ; (13–14) The Two Books of Maccabees. These books occur in a different order in the Septuagint, I. Esdras coming before Ezra, Tobit and Judith after Nehemiah, the Prayer of Manasseh after the Psalms, the Wisdom of Solomon and Ecclesiasticus after the Canticles, and Baruch after Jeremiah ; and they were introduced into the English version by Miles Coverdale in 1535, and retained in the authorised version of 1611, though now hardly, if ever, printed along with it. They are divisible into native-historical, as I. Maccabees ; quasi-historical, of a hortatory nature, as Judith ; fabulously historical, as Bel and the Dragon ; prophetical, of a hortatory nature, as Baruch or II. Esdras ; and philosophical, or rather gnomic, as Ecclesiasticus.

a. Historical value.—These books differ widely in historical value. Some of them, *e.g.*, I. and II. Maccabees, are sober narratives of important national events ; others are tales of private life ; others again full of idle and wildly superstitious trifles. But even these latter books throw light on the period in which they were written. The same may be said of those valuable books which set forth the wisdom-teaching of the Jews. All these works were written after the Dispersion from different centres of Jewish life and in different moments of its history ; and they show us what was the state of the Jewish people, and what were their thoughts and feelings, in those centres and at those moments. Thus from Tobit, written at Babylon in the Persian period, we get a glimpse of the inner and outer condition of the exiles there as affected by their surroundings ; from Ecclesiasticus, written in Palestine, we learn how it was with those who remained at home as affected by theirs ; and from the Wisdom of Solomon, written in Egypt, we see something of the effect which Greek philosophy had on Jewish modes of thinking. From each of these centres proceeded influences which contributed either positively or negatively to affect even Christian ideas, and to fashion these into shapes which they would not otherwise have assumed. Already we see influences at work which subsequently gave birth and form to two great tendencies that, in a more or less developed state, confronted Christianity in Judæa at its first appearance in history ; these were Phariseism and Sadduceeism, the former of purely native growth, and rigidly Jewish, and the latter of foreign derivation, and breathing a more or less ethnic spirit.

b. Theological interest.—In dogmatic teaching, the books of the Apocrypha never presume to stand on the same level with the canonical ones, but they always refer to those books and the writers of them as possessed of an authority to which no others can lay any claim. They look back to the times when the Hebrew Scriptures were written as times of special Divine favour and manifestation and to the men who flourished in them as of a stamp the like of which it were presumptuous to hope to see again. All the prophets occupy in their regard a standing of special eminence, and of Moses, in particular, they speak in terms such as they employ for no other man.

The Divine Being is conceived of in them in the main as in the canonical books, but the idea of God, while sometimes more limited, is also more metaphysical and less anthropomorphic than we find in the Old Testament. In creating the world God is sometimes represented as having only given life and form to matter independently existent. In governing it He appears as guided by a wisdom and love which are supreme in His nature. There is frequent mention of good and bad angels of a spiritual nature, yet capable of assuming a human shape, and often occupied as ministers in the government of the world—Satan among the chief of the bad ones, in particular, and Asmodæus, who had power to take away life, but who could be exorcised by the burning of a substance the smell of which sufficed to scare him. The human being is, in his spiritual part, which is recognised as distinct from his corporeal, of the same nature as his Maker, and, because endowed with reason and amenable to moral law, he has authority over all his Maker's works. Considerations of self-interest are, however, the chief inducements presented to persuade this moral being to act rightly, and weightier duties are too often sacrificed to calculations of temporary advantage. Under a self-interested theory of morals, there grew up a system of rewards and punishments, which extended itself into the future, and took shape in a heaven of conscious happiness and in a hell of conscious woe. Though strangely enough there is no mention of the Messiah in these books, there is the distinct hope of a kingdom corresponding to the Messianic, in which the dispersed should return to Zion, and Zion itself become the rallying-point for the converts of all nations.

In all this we remark a clear development of Jewish ideas, but it is not of such as are radical to the Jewish faith, and it pursues "a path which, if followed, would," as Lange observes, "lead away from, and not to, the manger of Bethlehem." Even in the best books a considerable moral degeneracy may be discerned : the old idea of righteousness is merged and lost in that of mercy, and a mercy which limits itself, too, to mere acts of charity—an indication that the authors had no longer their feet fast on the great foundation-principle of the Jewish faith, that righteousness is the one basis on which the whole world of spiritual beings rests.

1. **I. Esdras.**—In the LXX. this book is placed before our Ezra, which is there called II. Esdras. The Vulgate, reckoning Ezra and Nehemiah as I. and II. Esdras, describes this book as III. Esdras. The object of the writer appears to have been to compile from various sources a history of the rebuilding of the temple and the restoration of the appointed service in it from the period before its destruction, when the legal cultus ceased ; but the contents are ill arranged, and agree in the main with what we read already in certain chapters of 2 Chronicles, Ezra, and Nehemiah. The only original portions of the book are chaps. iii.-v. 6, containing an interesting discussion on what is the strongest of all things, and deciding in favour of "Truth." It is of uncertain authorship and date, though it was most probably written in the first or second century B.C. It was held in considerable account by Josephus, and is often quoted by him.

2. **II. Esdras.**—This book appears in the Vulgate as IV. Esdras. It was anciently known as the "Apocalypse of Ezra." Its object is to encourage the Jews suffering from heathen oppression by the prospect of speedy deliverance, under which their oppressors would be judged, and they themselves would enjoy all the promised blessings of the Messianic kingdom. This prospect is presented in a series of seven visions, of which the scene is laid in Babylon, and the time thirty years after the destruction of the city. The text is evidently of Jewish authorship, but probably it was written in Greek, and the book is by a growing consensus of opinion assigned to a date somewhere between A.D. 81 and 96. Chaps. i., ii., and xv., xvi., are late additions, the former of doubtful date, but the latter now generally assigned to about A.D. 260-268.

3. **The Book of Tobit.**—This is an extremely delightful, and even artistic delineation, according to ancient legend, of the life and vicissitudes of a pious Israelitish family in the Assyrian captivity. It consisted of Tobit himself, Anna his wife, and Tobias his son, all of whom are held up to honour for their strict observance of the law of the Lord, and their deeds of charity to those who love it. The spirit which breathes in it is that of genuine piety, and much of it is summed up in chap. iv. 21, where it is written, "Fear not, my son, that we have been made poor ; for thou hast much wealth, if thou fear God, and depart from all sin, and do that which is pleasing in His sight." Special prominence is given in this book to the ministry of angels, both good and bad—among the former Raphael, and among the latter Asmodæus, already referred to. The author of the book was a Jew, who wrote in the East, as the style of his imagery would indicate. The greatest diversity of opinion has prevailed as to the date of this book—some placing it as early as the seventh century B.C. (!), others as late as the second A.D. It is now generally assigned to the first or second century B.C.

4. **The Book of Judith.**—The subject of this book is the victory of the Jews over Holofernes, the captain of an invading Assyrian army, by the help of the heroic conduct of a wealthy, beautiful, and pious Jewish widow of the name of Judith. She enters the camp of the invader as his army lies outside her native place, Bethulia, with only a single maid as attendant, wins the confidence of the chief, persuades him to drink while alone with him in his tent till he is brutally intoxicated, and then cuts off his head with his own sword, making good her escape with it back to her countrymen. Having suspended this trophy from the walls, the townspeople make a feint of attacking the Assyrian camp at daybreak, with the result that the enemy are seized with confusion, and pursued in utter rout by the Jews as far as Damascus. This evidently fictitious story presents us

with a type of ferocious heroism and magnificent patriotism on the part of a woman. It was originally written in Aramaic ; it is of unknown authorship, and its date is uncertain, but the spirit that breathes in it would seem to point to the age of the Maccabees.

5. The Additions to the Book of Esther.—These are additions to the story of Esther and Mordecai, and are seven in number. They were intended to supplement that story, and are found skilfully interpolated in their proper places in the Septuagint version. The first gives an account of a dream of Mordecai, which serves as an introduction, and anticipates the principal events of the story. The second, inserted between the 14th and 15th verses of Esther iii., gives the decree of Haman dooming the Jews to death and their property to confiscation. The third, which succeeds chap. iv., contains the prayers of Esther and Mordecai to the Lord to avert the threatened disaster. The fourth and the fifth are annexed to the third, and explain how Esther succeeded in presenting herself before the king. The sixth is the edict of the king superseding that of Haman, and is placed after the 13th verse of chap. viii., where the edict is mentioned. And the seventh, intended to conclude the narrative, contains another dream of Mordecai, and intimates the institution of the feast of Purim. The authors of these additions were probably Alexandrian Jews. Those of least worth are the edicts of the Persian king, but the prayers breathe a pious spirit.

6. The Wisdom of Solomon.—This is the most beautiful of the Apocryphal books, and it is written in a style which shows a thorough knowledge of Greek. The author was probably an Alexandrian Jew of the close of the second century B.C., who was familiar with Greek philosophy, and who, in opposition to the errors of heathenism, especially its idolatry, sought to recommend the superiority of the wisdom which proceeds from the fear of God, the observance of His laws, and the knowledge of His way of salvation. The book belongs to the Jewish literature of the *chokmah*, or wisdom, type, and thus it follows in the tradition of Job and Proverbs. This literature can scarcely be called philosophic ; it is too disjointed and popular. But the Hebrew mind was not metaphysical, and among the Jews the genuine wisdom and practical ethics here set forth take the place of philosophy among the Greeks. Wisdom is somewhat personified in Proverbs, and more so in the Book of Wisdom. Still, the author does not regard it as an actual person. The doctrine of the immortality of the soul is distinctly taught, but in a Greek way, without any reference to the resurrection. The book falls into two main divisions—chaps. i.-ix. being gnomic and hortatory, and chaps. x.-xix. furnish historical examples. Archdeacon Farrar agrees with Kuenen in dating it about A.D. 40. But this view is not generally accepted, most writers fixing a date near 100 B.C. The book appears to be known to some of the writers of the New Testament.

7. The Wisdom of Jesus, the Son of Sirach, or Ecclesiasticus.—This book contains a body of wise maxims, or apothegms, in imitation, as regards matter as well as form, of the Proverbs of

Solomon, and an appendix on the men who were disciples of wisdom. Its general aim, as has been said, is "to represent wisdom as the source of all virtue and blessedness, and by warnings, admonitions, and promises to encourage in the pursuit of it." All wisdom originates in God and dwells in Him. Wisdom is the first-born of His creatures. Practical wisdom is to fear God and obey Him. Virtue is rewarded in this world and vice punished. Rites and observances are enjoined because they come down from the ancients, almsgiving and prayer as meritorious works. The author was Jesus, son of Sirach, or Sira, of Jerusalem (chap. l. 27), who was perhaps (chap. l. 1-26) a contemporary of the High Priest Simon the Just (310-291 B.C.), and his book was written in Hebrew, and extant as such in Jerome's time, though it comes down to us only in Greek. This Greek translation is given out as the work of the author's grandson, who is said to have executed it in Egypt about the middle of the third century B.C. Schürer believes the work to have been completed at the beginning and translated towards the close of the second century B.C.

8. The Book of Baruch.—This is a body of additions to the prophecies of Jeremiah, which, though not genuine historically, yet exhibit a piety and a zeal nurtured by the word and spirit of the Old Testament. It contains a penitential prayer of the depressed people in the time of the Captivity, a prayer for deliverance from merited punishment, an exhortation to Israel to seek for wisdom to direct them in the law of the Lord, words of comfort from Zion to her captive children and to Jerusalem, and the so-called Epistle of Jeremiah, which is said to have been addressed to the captives when carried away to Babylon, to caution them against the horror and folly of idolatry. The date and authorship of the work are uncertain, though it is in part ascribed by Ewald to the period of "dangerous rising against the Persians"—in the fourth century B.C. It consists of two parts—(1) chaps. i.-iii. 8, after a historical preface giving a confession and prayer for Israel in the Captivity ; (2) chaps. iii. 9-v. 9, consisting of admonitions and encouragements. The former was probably originally written in Hebrew, the latter in Greek. To the Book of Baruch is appended the "Epistle of Jeremy," probably written about 100 B.C.

9. The Song of the Three Holy Children.—This is a hymn in which the three friends of Daniel are represented as having sung the praises of God in the fiery furnace, and in which their miraculous deliverance is poetically delineated. It was originally written in Hebrew, but it is unmistakably spurious, being wholly unadapted to the circumstances in which it professes to have been composed, as well as in different parts glaringly inconsistent with itself.

10. **The History of Susanna.**—This is a story conceived to glorify Daniel in his character of judge, and it appears to have been written in Greek, though probably on the basis of an old Hebrew story. It appears to have an anti-Sadducean tendency.

11. **The History of Bel and the Dragon.**—This,

48

like the last, is a pretended addition to the Book of Daniel. It relates how Daniel persuaded Cyrus of the vanity of idol-worship, and it was evidently composed in declaration of the absurdity of the practice.

12. The Prayer of Manasseh.—A prayer of this monarch was on record in the histories of the kings of Israel, but it perished along with them; and this composition is an attempt to compensate for the loss of it. It is so manifestly ungenuine that even the Council of Trent excluded it from the canon of Scripture. It appears to be the expression of the inner remorse of a penitent sinner.

13. The First Book of Maccabees.—This is a narrative, at once connected, detailed, and graphic, of the heroic struggle which the five sons of Mattathias the priest maintained for thirty-three years, from 175 to 135 B.C., against the power of the kings of Syria. It is written from the standpoint of orthodox, rigidly legal Judaism; it was probably composed at the close of the reign of John Hyrcanus (135–107 B.C.), and it contains an authentic account of the events narrated. The author's aim is partly to prove the fulfilment of the prophecies of Daniel (Dan. xi.), and partly to supply a gap in an important period of Jewish history. The original was written in Aramaic, but the book comes down to us in the form of an excellent Greek translation.

14. The Second Book of Maccabees.—This book gives an account of Jewish history from about the year 175 to 160 B.C., and is preceded by two letters from the ecclesiastical authorities in Jerusalem to the Jews in Egypt to induce the latter to regard the temple at Zion as the centre of religious service, and to invite their presence at the feast of the dedication. The narrative portion describes the great persecution under Antiochus Epiphanes, and the fortunes and triumph of Judas. This description is interwoven with legendary matter, and is far from reliable. The so-called Third and Fourth Books of Maccabees are late compositions, and they were not even received into the Vulgate.

In addition to the Apocryphal writings enumerated above, mention may also be made, from the respect paid them in the early Church, of the Book of Enoch, the Sibylline Oracles, the Apocalypse of Baruch, the Psalms of Solomon, the Assumption of Moses, the Ascension of Isaiah, the Book of Jubilees, the Testaments of the Twelve Patriarchs, and the Pirke Aboth.

1. The Book of Enoch.—This book, which consists of 108 chaps., and is quoted in Jude, vers. 14, 15, first came to the general knowledge of the learned about the beginning of the present century. It professes to be a series of revelations made in heaven and elsewhere to the patriarch Enoch, and written down by him for the benefit of posterity. These revelations are of an apocalyptic character, and pretend to unveil the secrets of the world of nature as well as the world of spirit, and to penetrate into the future of things both here and hereafter. The body of the book, for it is extensively interpolated, belongs to the second century B.C., is of diverse authorship, and was written in Aramaic.

2. The Sibylline Oracles.—These are books partly of Jewish, partly of Christian origin, which profess to give from certain heathen Sibylline sources oracles which express quasi-Biblical truths, coloured by the experience and times of their authors. They derive their name from being imitations of the utterances of the Sibyls, heathen prophetesses, generally of extreme age, who "represented the voice of God in nature," and whose words gave evidence of unusual visionary power.

3. The Apocalypse of Baruch.—This is of Syriac origin, and purports to be from the pen of Baruch, who speaks throughout in the first person. It professes to foresee, among other things, the destruction of Jerusalem by the Romans, but it was evidently written after the event.

4. The Psalms of Solomon.—These are eighteen psalms of Palestinian origin, and they are valuable for the light they shed on the political attitude of the Jews in the time of our Lord, if, as appears from certain indications in the psalms themselves, they were composed soon after the taking of Jerusalem by Pompey (63 B.C.). They are written from the standpoint of the Pharisees. Their theme is the vengeance of the Lord on behalf of His people for the wrongs they suffered at the hands of the invader, who had been appointed merely to scourge the rulers for their usurpations, but had gone beyond his commission in tyrannising over the Jews. They appear to have been originally composed in Hebrew.

5. The Assumption of Moses.—Only fragments of this book were known until the year 1861, when a palimpsest of a large portion of it discovered in the Ambrosian Library at Milan was published by the librarian. It purports to be a prophetic forecast by Moses, addressed to Joshua, of Jewish history down to the times of Herod the Great, who is personally described with the exactness of a historical account. It is presumed, therefore, that the writing belongs to about the beginning of our era, and that it is the book which records the strife between the archangel Michael and Satan over the body of Moses, referred to in the Epistle of Jude (ver. 9).

6. The Ascension or Martyrdom of Isaiah.—This book gives an unconnected account of the martyrdom of Isaiah, and a vision vouchsafed him in the reign of Hezekiah. It appears to be the book to which we owe the tradition, referred to in Heb. xi. 37, that Isaiah was sawn asunder, for at ver. 14 of it we read, "But Isaiah, while he was being sawn, did not cry nor weep, but his mouth spoke with the Holy Spirit until he was cut in two pieces." It is of recent discovery, and is partly of Christian and partly of Jewish authorship.

7. The Book of Jubilees.—This is a Haggadean commentary, in the usual Jewish style, on Genesis and the first part of Exodus, as far as the institution of the Passover, "being a free reproduction, under the profession of a revelation to Moses by an 'angel of the presence' on Sinai, of the matter of these narratives, with enlargements, interpolations, and interpretations peculiar to the Judaism of the later times." It was originally written in Hebrew, probably about the first century A.D. The author, in his narratives, takes as the basis of his reckoning the jubilee period of forty-nine years, which again resolves itself into seven year-weeks of seven years each, and then, in fixing the date of any event, he determines the exact month of the exact year of the exact year-week of the exact jubilee period in which it occurred; and from this circumstance the book derives its name.

8. The Testaments of the Twelve Patriarchs.— This professes to be the utterances of the twelve sons of Jacob, in which each gives an account of his life, such as embraces particulars not found in the Scriptures, while also exhorting his descendants. The book, however, is manifestly a Christian work, and probably it was written before the middle of the second century A.D. It is valuable as an indication of the ideas of Jewish Christians, and also for its testimony to New Testament books.

9. The Pirke Aboth.—The Pirke Aboth—*i.e.*, sayings of the fathers—is a Jewish collection of aphorisms after the manner of Jesus the Son of Sirach, by some sixty doctors learned in the law, whose names are given, each being represented as supplying two or more maxims characteristic of his teaching, and constituting the staple of it. These maxims are of a utilitarian character, connected, most of them, however, with religion, and inculcating the importance of familiarity with the precepts of the law.

See Speaker's Commentary, *Apocrypha;* Deane, *Pseudepigrapha;* Charles, *The Book of Enoch, The Book of Jubilees, The Apocalypse of Baruch;* Ryle and James, *The Psalms of Solomon.*

CHAPTER XIV.

JEWISH HISTORY BETWEEN THE OLD AND THE NEW TESTAMENT PERIODS.

THIS comparatively neglected period is one of great importance in the development of Judaism, and notice of it is called for here to account for the changed condition in which we find both the Jewish people and their religion at the commencement of the New Testament age. The period was one of great change in the world at large. It witnessed no less than the rise and fall of the Persian empire, the extension into the East of Greek civilisation, and the ascendency of the Roman power over the great body of the nations. The Jews in the New Testament are in many important respects a changed people from what they appear in the Old, and this change was mainly brought about by the relations into which they were thrown with the other powers of the world. Except under the discipline to which in these relations they were subjected, they never would have realised, as they then did, the purpose of Heaven in their separation, never have conceived of themselves as the ministers of the true religion to other nations. This was one fruit of the dispensation which threw them into the most singular and trying situations; what were the others, and how were they produced?

From the date of the return from the Captivity the Jews are no longer divided tribes, but one people; no longer prone to idolatry, but rigid monotheists; and no longer jealous of their political independence, but content if only let alone in their religious creed and their forms of worship. The preservation and the practice of the religion of their fathers is their one calling, and the spread and final triumph of that religion, with what is involved in it, their one hope. Except in the early part of this period, they have no longer a prophet among them indeed, but they have prophetic books; and these they collect and study as the very oracles of God, and as they had not done when the books were first committed to their keeping. Scribes busy themselves with copying these books, and synagogues in which they are read, and which are resorted to more than the temple, are everywhere erected. But by degrees the oral word of tradition is raised to the level of the written, and ere long to a superiority over it, as affording the key by which it is to be read. In this way the Jewish religion is subverted, but an occasion is afforded for the rise and development of the Christian faith, which springs directly out of its primitive root. The Jews had sought that at second hand which could only be had from the fountain-head, and the function of Christianity was to call them back to this original source, so that the Divine Author of it could say: "Had ye known Moses, ye would have known Me, for he wrote of Me" (John v. 46).

Two great events operated in the production of the changes referred to—the merging of Babylonia in the Persian empire under Cyrus, and the subjugation of Persia in turn by Alexander the Great. And the epochs which these two events inaugurated in Jewish history are known respectively as (A) the Persian Period (536-333 B.C.), and (B) the Grecian Period (333-167 B.C.).

A.—THE PERSIAN PERIOD.

1. Cyrus and his Successors.—The connection of the Jews with Persia began with the reign of Cyrus, and the first fruit of it was their liberation from the captivity of Babylon, which Cyrus had conquered (538 B.C.); their restoration—42,000 of them, it is alleged—to their own land, principally about Jerusalem; and the re-establishment of their religion in the rebuilding of the temple, which was finished 515 B.C. Cyrus may have had political reasons for this friendliness, but his conduct was received in good part by the Jewish race. He was looked upon as their benefactor, and regarded as "anointed" by the Lord for their deliverance from the Babylonian yoke. What they had seen in Babylon had effectually cured them of their affection for idol-worship. Formerly it was supposed that Cyrus was a believer in One Supreme God. But recently it has been proved, from the deciphering of a small clay cylinder now in the British Museum, that he was a worshipper of the old heathen idols of his ancestry. Nevertheless, he was enlightened and large-minded, and the Jews could not help regarding their patron as an ally, and they might hope, under his patronage, to work out their destiny as they could not do on more independent terms. They now felt no call on them to battle for political free-

dom, under Cyrus they had all the freedom they needed to fulfil the mission they were to accomplish; and it almost seemed as if the Messiah they looked for had appeared in the Persian king. Accordingly, they now began to be conscious of their priestly mission, and to regard themselves as the peculiar people of God. They were at Jerusalem for religious ends, and their fate was independent of all secular changes. This was the true idea of their destiny, and they became for the first time conscious of it under the Persian rule.

The successors of Cyrus continued to show the same friendly feeling to the Jewish people that he had shown, and this policy was attended with the same benign effects on their history and the development of their religious life. It was one of these successors, perhaps the ill-fated Xerxes, who, as we read in Esther, averted the meditated destruction of the race throughout his empire, and in commemoration of whose interposition the Jews observe the Feast of Purim to this day. It was only when the religion of the Persian again became offensive, and only with the introduction into it of rites of a lascivious or immoral nature, that the Jew began to regard his protector with distrust and finally repugnance, and to be subjected, in consequence, to persecution and affront. Having refused to accept a high-priest at the dictation of the Persian monarch, the Jewish people had imposed upon their temple-service the most oppressive burdens, and had to witness their Holy of Holies desecrated by profane acts. But by this time the Persian empire was near its own dissolution, and the generation following witnessed its downfall before the arms of Alexander the Great. The Persian supremacy had lasted for two hundred years, but it had accomplished its purpose. Under its influence Judaism had attained a substantive existence and assumed a definite shape; it was now necessary it should have scope for development in a wider area, and this was accorded to it by the conquests of the Macedonian king. It had received all the help it could from the religion and countenance of the Parsee; it was now to find an auxiliary, as well as a foil, in the philosophy, literature, and language of Greece.

2. **The Samaritan Schism.**—To the Persian period, however, belong other developments than those just indicated, and these must first be traced. It is to it we must refer the rise of the Samaritan Schism, the existence of which prolonged itself to the days of Christ and later. The Samaritans appear to have consisted of remnants of the northern kingdom of Israel and foreign colonists introduced in place of the captives carried away by the Assyrian king. These colonists naturally brought along with them their native idol-worship, and this gradually engrafted itself on Jewish observances, so that there arose a people claiming the standing and privilege of the Jew, but credited with, if not actually indulging in, practices henceforth wholly alien to Jewish feeling and faith. The Jews who returned from the Captivity regarded them in consequence with aversion, though they were no worse than they themselves had been prior to that event; and they refused to accept their proffered assistance in rebuilding the walls and temple of Jerusalem. This refusal was meant to signify that they disowned them; and the latter, so interpreting it, took their revenge by erecting a temple and instituting a rival temple-service of their own. The spot they chose for this purpose was Mount Gerizim; and they justified their selection by reference to events mentioned in the Pentateuch as investing it with a special sacredness, and by maintaining that it was here Adam had built his first altar, Abraham had brought his son Isaac to offer in sacrifice, and Jacob had seen his vision on his way to Padan-Aram, an evidence that heaven lay right overhead. The contention which grew out of this matter between the Jews and the Samaritans was a fierce and obstinate one, but, in the end, it was the occasion of good results. The latter had taken their stand on the exclusive Divine authority of the Pentateuch, and this provoked the former to consider whether the other sacred books were not of equal validity and deserving of kindred respect. The investigation led to a conclusion in the affirmative, and to the institution of Judaism proper, which grounded itself henceforward on the obligation to observe all that is required in the whole compass of these books. From this time forward the Jew was distinguished for the respect he paid to all these writings, and for his presumed fulfilment to the letter of the observances they required. The Samaritans, on the other hand, not only limited their sacred Scripture to the Pentateuch, but they kept it as good as a sealed book; and hence Christ, speaking as a Jew, could say to the Samaritan woman at the well—"Ye worship ye know not what: we know what we worship: for salvation is of the Jews" (John iv. 22).

3. **The Synagogue.**—The institution of the Synagogue, though traceable to Jewish practices in the Exile, belongs to this period, and is connected with the awakened interest in the sacred books; one main purpose of its institution being to afford an opportunity to the Jew everywhere of becoming, as he was bound to be, familiar with what they taught. High as the Temple and its service still stood in the esteem of every Jew, it was now extensively felt to be of secondary importance to the Synagogue and its service. With the erection and extension of the latter the people were being slowly trained into a truer sense of the nature of religious worship, and gradually made to feel that to know the will of God and do it was a more genuine act of homage to Him than the offering of sacrifices upon an altar or the observance of any merely religious rite (see SYNAGOGUE). Under such training the issue between the Jew and the Samaritan became of less and less consequence; but the Jew, and not the Samaritan, was on the pathway which led direct to the final worship of God in spirit and in truth. If he came short of the goal, it was because he prided himself more on privilege than on service, more on possessing the oracles of God than on observing their requirements. It was assurance enough to him of the Divine favour to be the privileged custodian of the Divine Word, and in this assurance he flattered himself into a delusive peace, and a still more delusive hope.

4. **The Great Synagogue.**—The Great Synagogue, or Assembly, as it is called, is another of the institutions that belong to this period, and one which appears to have contributed not

a little towards the development of the Jewish faith and life. The date of its origin and the character of its composition is matter of uncertainty, but it was only of temporary duration, and it was dispensed with as unnecessary after it had fulfilled the purpose for which it was instituted. That purpose appears to have been to carry on and complete the work begun by Ezra, and to give final form to the creed and worship of the Jewish Church. A Jewish tradition says—"Moses received the law from Sinai; he transmitted it to Joshua, Joshua to the elders, the elders to the prophets, and the prophets to the men of the Great Assembly, who added thereto these words : 'Be circumspect in judgment, make many disciples, and set a hedge about the law.'" To them is ascribed the final settlement and arrangement of the Jewish Scriptures, the introduction of a new alphabet of square letters, the regulation of the Synagogue worship, and the adoption of sundry liturgical forms, as well as the establishment of the Feast of Purim. They also probably instituted the "schools" for the learned study of the Scriptures, the teachers of which were afterwards known under the name of the "scribes," and the pupils the "disciples of the wise." These schools were accounted of such authority as at length to override that of the law itself. Under their teachings Judaism acquired that rigidity of form which an organism assumes when the life has gone from it.

Such are some of the changed aspects of Jewish life which developed in the Persian period ; and it has even been surmised, not without reason, that certain phases of Jewish belief and practice were directly affected by Persian influence, and in some cases derived from a Persian source. Attention has been called to the partial similarity between the ultimate faith of the Jew and the Zoroastrian Persian faith in regard to the ideas of God and the antagonism between good and evil : it is legitimate to infer that the practice of the Persian, with whom the ritual of the temple and the services of the priest were of comparatively insignificant account, might have contributed in some slight degree to reconcile the Jew to the simple worship of the Synagogue. That excessive refinement, too, which prevailed among the stricter Jews in regard to things clean and unclean would seem to have been also influenced by Persian sentiments. The ceremonial of the Parsee is full of warnings and directions in regard to things and actions in themselves innocuous, as fraught in the hands of the evil genius with spiritual and moral contamination. One thing is certain, that ideas occur in the Apocryphal books of the Jews which bear the stamp of the Persian theosophy, and this appears more especially in the doctrine there accepted of angels and demons. Although the Jewish doctrine of angels made its appearance long before the Persian period, and the familiar title, "The Lord of Hosts," suggests the idea of spiritual servants of God in the heavenly regions, it was through their Persian protectors that the Jews first became familiar with the notion of varied orders of spirits both good and evil, who appear to have been originally regarded as the souls of men sent forth from the habitations of bliss or woe in the other world to bless or to curse.

B.—THE GRECIAN PERIOD.

At the commencement of this period the Jewish national character may be regarded as fully, or as good as fully, formed, and as having acquired a coherence that would rather intensify than relax in conflict with the forces which were now brought into the field. The moral principle of religion constituted the core of Jewish life ; and it was the faith of the Jew in this which was to be put to the test in the new circumstances. The result went to show that on this basis alone a religion could be reared, adapted to every grade of human life, and capable of entering into harmony with all the elements of human culture. On this basis both Jew and Greek were for the first time emancipated, or at any rate taught how they could be emancipated, into true spiritual freedom.

1. **The Macedonian Empire.**—In the course of the fourth century B.C. the Persian empire was overwhelmed and swallowed up by the world-wide conquests of Alexander the Great, and thus Syria and Palestine passed into the hands of a new master. Then the influence of Greece began to be felt in the East ; and though at first viewed with distrust, ultimately this new power was welcomed in the land of Judæa with friendly feelings. When the conqueror laid siege to Tyre and Gaza in 332 B.C., a deputation was sent to him from Jerusalem to offer him homage in the name of the Jewish nation ; and there is a tradition that he visited the holy city in person, and did homage to the high priest as the representative on earth of the God of heaven. Be that as it may, his treatment of the Jewish people was of a friendly and generous nature, and their gratitude showed itself in the respect which they afterwards cherished for his memory. Some of them even entered the lists of his army as he marched southward to the conquest of Egypt ; and we know, from the numbers of them that flocked to Alexandria (331 B.C.), what affection they had for the city that bore the great conqueror's name, and which he had founded in that country to be the metropolis of his empire.

It is notorious that the Grecian empire which Alexander sought to establish in the East broke up into fragments immediately after his death, in the strife which arose for supremacy among his generals. Two new powers, however, sprang up out of the ruins—the Ptolemies in Egypt and the Seleucidæ in Syria ; but both of them were by this time more or less imbued with ideas and aims which emanated from Greece, so that they were instrumental in extending Greek civilisation. In the time of the first Ptolemy the ruling class in Egypt was Grecian, and it was his successor who collected the literature of Greece in the library of Alexandria, and in whose reign the Septuagint version of the Hebrew Scriptures was begun (see ANCIENT VERSIONS). Between the Ptolemies and the Syrian monarchs the relations were hostile, and a strife arose in which the land of Judæa and its people suffered greatly. The Ptolemies respected the people, and left them in a moderate enjoyment of their freedom, as Alexander had done, but the land was laid waste by the crossing and re-crossing of the belligerent armies, and many of its inhabitants were forced to go into exile or perish. Thus Ptolemy I. three times took possession of it by the sword, and three times surrendered it under similar compulsion. It was not till 280 B.C. that Ptolemy II. established his rule for any lengthened period. In this way, however, the Jews in Palestine were brought into close contact with Greek civilisation ; and the founding of Greek cities, which was the form in which at this time Greek life incorporated itself, was seen all round their borders; although it must be confessed the Jews here were little, if at all, affected by Greek ideas through the neighbourhood of these cities, however much they may have been by certain Greek manners and customs, political institutions and styles of art. How the civilisation of Greece affected and was affected by the Jewish religion itself must be sought for in other quarters.

2. Spread of Greek Civilisation.

—It was in the Greek cities, and especially in Alexandria, to which, partly out of necessity and partly in the spirit of enterprise, they had recourse, that the Jews first felt the influence of Greek civilisation, and first emerged, by means of it, into secular world-history, while it was in Judæa that the Jewish religion preserved itself freest from all foreign adulterations. The Jews in Palestine adhered more strictly to the Jewish creed and practice than the Jews in Egypt, the latter giving evidence more than once of a greater laxity of religious observance. Nevertheless inheriting a moral character which was a tightly-woven tissue of the toughest fibre, they here gave proof of energy of intense quality, and recommended themselves to their fellow-citizens by their worth both intellectual and moral. Here they were taken into the councils of the king, and encouraged to contribute their quota to the general movement of civilisation then in progress. Some of them acquired a familiarity with Greek philosophy, and essayed a philosophic statement of Hebrew wisdom. Others had learned to express their thoughts in the Greek language, and these Jews addressed themselves to the task of supplying a demand for a translation of the Hebrew Scriptures into Greek. Thus they elevated Greek forms of thought and expression into vehicles for the communication of the truths of revelation, and prepared a medium for the reception and dissemination of the Gospel of Christ. To the Jews of Palestine we stand indebted for our knowledge of the Jewish faith in its strictness and purity ; but we have the Alexandrian Jews to thank for having first brought that faith, and Christianity which grew out of it, within the cognisance of other races, at a crisis, too, when, if left to itself, the world would have lapsed into a ruin from which nothing could have saved it. Nevertheless under the fourth Ptolemy the Alexandrian Jews fell in the regard of both prince and people. Their worldly prosperity, added to their religious exclusiveness and superciliousness, appears to have brought on this fate.

With the Jews of Palestine, however, it fared no better. It had been well with them indeed so long as they were subject to Egypt, but a change of masters brought a change of fortune. In the year 198 B.C. Syria regained the dominion over Judæa, and then troubles came thick and fast. Syria was more imbued with the Greek spirit than Egypt ; and a strong party, affected by the same spirit, sprang up in Jerusalem bent on Hellenising the Jewish creed. A war of the Syrian monarch with the expanding power of Rome, and the exactions demanded of the Jewish people to pay the costs, alone prevented the ascendency of this party. The aggressive spirit being thus checked, the more zealous Jews remained for a time passive ; but by-and-by a crisis arrived, and the whole nation rose in open revolt. The Hellenising party continued still active amongst them ; but it was the conduct of Antiochus Epiphanes, the Syrian monarch, that brought matters to a head. He had been disappointed in his designs to subvert the Jewish religion, and he gave vent to his rage by laying waste Judæa and Jerusalem itself (168 B.C.). This was one of the first acts of a series of tyrannies under which the Jewish spirit lay smouldering, ready even on the slightest occasion, in any quarter and at any moment, to flame forth. At length an occasion offered itself in the erection of a heathen altar at Modein, a small village eighteen miles north-west of Jerusalem, and the refusal of Mattathias the priest to offer a sacrifice thereon to the Syrian gods at the command of a Syrian embassy. And not only did he refuse to do so himself, but he slew with his own hand the Jew who came forward to do it for him, and then fell upon the Syrian emissary who had required the act ; after which, having quickly demolished the altar that had been erected to the dishonour of Jehovah, he rushed with his sons into the depths of an adjoining wilderness, calling upon all to follow him who had any regard for the covenant of the Lord. He soon gathered round him a goodly band, who did not scruple to defend their ancestral faith by the power of the sword. They sallied forth from time to time in formidable gangs, threw down the altars of the false gods, circumcised the uncircumcised children, and set themselves to effect a general clearance of heathenism out of the land. Thus began what is known as the "War of the Maccabees," and the issue to the Jew was the achievement of an independence which he had not enjoyed for four hundred years.

3. The Maccabees.

—This revolt against the insolence of Syria which had so grand an issue derived its name from *Judas Maccabæus*, one, probably the third, of the five sons of Mattathias, who had been appointed by his father to succeed him in the military leadership. And this Judas was worthy to give name to the movement, and to be elected its head, for he was a man of chivalric temper, great energy, firm determination, dauntless courage, and powerful physique. The men that followed him were the elect of his countrymen, and all of kindred faith and valour with himself. With them he encountered and overthrew successive musters of the hosts of Syria sent to crush him, and ere long he erected his standard on the walls of Jerusalem itself. Here, having purified the altar which had been desecrated, he dedicated it anew to Jehovah (165 B.C.); and the "Feast of Dedication," afterwards instituted, was a witness among the Jews to the event (John x. 22). For a time thereafter it seemed as if Judas and his little band would carry all before them, and that he might live to see his country relieved for ever of the Syrian yoke. But this was not to be ; for the Syrians gathered again in numbers against him, and though dissuaded from encountering them, he preferred to accept the challenge rather than dishonour himself by retreat. The result was that his little army was overpowered and himself surrounded and slain (160 B.C.). His brothers Jonathan and Simon saw him fall, and, rushing into the thick of the fray, snatched up his dead body and carried it off and buried it in Modein. The lamentation over him in Judæa was deep and universal; and it was just, for the story, as often as related, strikes a chord of sympathy in every true-hearted man and woman all the world over. The struggle indeed went on after his death, but it soon ceased to be a strife for the supremacy of the faith, and became less in the interests of the community than in those of the Asmonæan house. Thus the secular character which the conflict assumed became more and more pronounced.

Jonathan, the youngest brother of Judas, now succeeded by election to the leadership of the Maccabees, and a more hopeless enterprise than the one which this office required of him hardly ever fell to any man's lot. Fortunately a civil strife arose in Syria, and each party sought to buy up Jonathan's support. Jonathan, who was a politic man and ambitious, accepted the proffers of the strongest; and though still politically dependent on Syria, under him as high-priest Judæa became independent religiously. He did not, however, long retain his office, for he was betrayed into the hands of the rival Syrian party and put to death (143 B.C.). It was reserved for *Simon*, his brother, now an old man, but a wise one, who succeeded him, to consummate the supremacy of the Maccabees, called, from the family name, the *Asmonæan dynasty*, as hereditary high-priests, and finally to shake off the Syrian yoke. The divisions which still continued in Syria aided him in this enterprise, and he was gained over to side with the party that prevailed by promises which secured the independence for which he and his brothers had fought and bled. By provision of express treaty sundry strongholds in Judæa were handed over to be garrisoned by Jewish soldiers, and the national independence confirmed in 143 B.C. It was a great day for Judæa, and reckoned the commencement of a new era in its history. Simon had "made peace in the land, and Israel rejoiced with great joy; for every man sat under his vine and his fig tree, and there was none to fray them, neither was there any left in the land to fight against them" (1 Macc. xiv. 11–13). Nevertheless it was no more his fortune to meet death in the way of nature than it had been his brothers', for he was cruelly assassinated after a reign of eight years, and was succeeded by his son John Hyrcanus (135 B.C.).

Though *John Hyrcanus* had his troubles at first with Syria, he was soon able to reassert his independence, and even to make his influence felt beyond the borders of Judæa proper by laying waste Samaria and compelling the Idumæans (of whom came the family of Herod) to accept the Jewish faith at the point of the sword. Under him the Jewish people enjoyed a degree of prosperity which they had not experienced since the days of Solomon, although the splendour of his reign was marred by internal dissension. This was a strife between the parties of the Sadducees and Pharisees—who at this time were rising into prominence, and were already so violent that he felt driven to side with the

former against the latter. His end was more happy than that of the Maccabees who preceded him, for he died in peace (106 B.C.).

Aristobulus I., who followed John Hyrcanus, was the first of the Asmonæan family to assume the title of king, but he was worthy neither of this title nor of the family name, for he had forsworn that zeal for Judaism which had raised the Asmonæan to the throne, and had become a pronounced Helleniser. He was obnoxious to the Pharisees, and he died a painful death, full of gloom and horror at the guilt of his mother's and his brother's murder (105 B.C.).

Alexander Jannæus, his brother, succeeded him (105 B.C.), and his reign of twenty-six years was one not only of foreign strife, but of internal dissension. He led, or affected, a dissolute life, and took the side of the Sadducees against the Pharisees, agreeably to the example set by John Hyrcanus. He felt a special scorn for the latter party, and on one occasion gave expression to it in an act which he knew would be offensive to them, and which roused the popular rage against him: he poured the water of a sacred oblation in the temple on the ground, instead of, as he was required to do, on the altar. The rage of those present knew no bounds, and they began to pelt the king and the high-priest with citrons and other soft fruits with which they were provided, it being the Feast of Tabernacles. Such an insult was more than the king could be expected to stand, so he called in his mercenary troops, which were at hand, and as many as six thousand of the worshippers were sabred to death by them within the precincts of the temple. This was the beginning of a strife that continued all through his reign. On one occasion eight hundred Pharisees, who had fled for refuge to the fortress of Bethorne, were crucified in one day by the orders of this royal butcher. The Pharisees kept up their feeling of enmity against him to the last, and his death was an occasion of open rejoicing among them, and even of annual celebration for years afterwards.

On the death of Alexander the reins of government were assumed by *Salome Alexandra*, his queen (79 B.C.), who reversed the policy of her husband, and admitted the Pharisees to her councils, as her chief advisers. The result was a reaction which took the form of retaliation for the injuries of the past. The Sadducees, who had been the persecuting party, now became the persecuted, and the harsh measures that were adopted against them stirred up an opposition which divided the state. *Aristobulus*, the younger of the queen's two sons, headed this opposition; while *Hyrcanus*, the elder, took the queen's side, and was made high-priest. By-and-by this reaction assumed the form of open revolt, of which the hot-blooded Aristobulus was the prime instigator and leader. Thus a struggle arose between the two brothers for supremacy, which ended only with the interference of Rome, and the subjection of the nation to the Roman yoke.

At the beginning of the strife Hyrcanus had the worst of it, and he was even driven to capitulate, and to surrender all his rights. Encouraged by support, however, from Idumæa and Arabia, he was induced to take up arms again, and this time for once with success. One day, as his army lay round Jerusalem investing the temple-mount, occupied by his brother, an old man, Onias by name, noted for the efficacy of his prayers, was pressed into the besieger's service, and required to pray in his behalf. The old man, being urged, consented; and these were the terms of his prayer, which breathed a charity worthy of the Gospel of Christ :—"O God, King of the whole world, since these that stand with me are Thy people, and those that are besieged are Thy priests, I beseech thee that Thou wilt neither hearken to the prayers of those against these nor of these against those." It was a prayer which in every syllable, as well as in the whole tone of it, condemned the spirit of those who pressed him to offer it; and the words were no sooner uttered than the by-standers took up stones and stoned Onias to death. It thus appears that both parties were engaged in an internecine war, and, in the general frenzy, the peace-maker's pleadings could not be heard. The arms of Rome, however, were in the close neighbourhood, and the interposition of this dangerous foreign power, apparently on the call of the besieged in the temple-mount, put an end to the strife. Pompey, to whom the call was addressed, advanced to the rescue; but on a nearer approach he saw it his policy to take the side of Hyrcanus and carry on the siege. The besieged made a stout stand for their independence, and the siege lasted three months. At length the entrenchments were stormed, but the assailants encountered resistance to the death. Not till twelve thousand had fallen by the sword could the Romans claim the victory; nevertheless, when achieved, it was complete. The event occurred in 63 B.C.

4. **The Dispersion.**—Long before the time of Christ the Jews of the Dispersion were scattered far and wide in greater or smaller independent communities over many lands, and at the advent of Christianity they formed the great majority of the race. Very few of those who had been led at different times into captivity or had emigrated voluntarily returned to settle again in the land of their fathers. Located for the most part in the great cities, they enjoyed more scope for the development of their native energy, as traders particularly, than within the narrow limits of Palestine. In such cities as Alexandria and Antioch, where they had settled, protected by special privileges, they formed a large proportion of the inhabitants, and constituted an element of important account in the civic life. Thus dispersed, the Jews nevertheless continued still Jews, and were in religious belief and practice the same as if they had remained in Palestine. They felt they were of the same stock, stood on the same ground, cherished the same memories, grew up under the same institutions, and anticipated the same future. They had a common centre of worship in Jerusalem, which they upheld by their offerings, and they made pilgrimages thither annually in great numbers at the high festivals. But the root-principle of their life was their respect for moral law, and this drew on them the regard of men of other nations. The Jews faith in their religion, with the hope that inspired them, induced many of other creeds to embrace it; and these at the beginning of the Christian era were, under the name of *Proselytes*, reckoned at thousands of thousands, if not even millions.

Among this class, not excluding the Jews of the Dispersion themselves, Christianity found its earliest converts, and through them it won its way into the hearts of their heathen neighbours (see JEWISH SECTS AND PARTIES).

5. **Herod.**—In concluding this account of the history of the Jews between the close of the Old and the beginning of the New Testament periods, little needs to be said of the Roman domination, because, though it affected the relation of parties in the state, it had but slight influence on the character of the Jewish people at large as we find this at the commencement of the Christian era. The history was for a time mainly a strife between two rival families—the old Asmonæan family of Maccabæan descent, and a new Idumæan family represented by Herod—for the civic supremacy; and this was associated with a strife between the Sadducees and the Pharisees. At length the Pharisaic party, who supported the Idumæan claimant, prevailed; and Herod, who, though Idumæan by descent, was nominally a Jew by religion, became ruler of Judæa. On his accession, while recognising the Sanhedrin as an authority in the state, Herod made away with forty-five of its members, who were his zealous opponents, raised minions of his own to important public offices, and subjected the high-priesthood, which had previously been independent, to secular, that is, state control. Thus the Sadducees were driven from power, and had no longer any influence on affairs, except as a thorn in the side of their old enemies the Pharisees, with whom they kept up a constant wrangle, on matters henceforth of a kind, however, more theoretical than practical. To the Pharisaic party Herod showed a special favour, because, on principle, they did not take part in any merely secular quarrels, but confined their attention to matters spiritual. From all interference in the latter Herod scrupulously abstained, and the Pharisees were pleased. Not so the general populace. They disliked the humiliation of being again subjected, after the Maccabæan triumphs, to a foreign yoke, especially that of Rome, and they looked on Herod as king merely by Roman favour. The Asmonæan dynasty still stood high in popular estimation, and Herod, aware of this, and in dread of what it might lead to, removed first one and then another, and finally all, of the survivors of it, out of his path. His strength lay in cultivating friendship with Rome, and he ingratiated himself with the Emperor by sedulously developing the material resources of the province. He even had respect to the prestige of the Jewish faith, and devoted years to attempting the restoration of the Temple to something of its pristine glory. But just at the moment when his schemes were approaching completion his mind was disturbed by suspicions against two of his own children, whom he unjustly accused of designs against himself, and caused to be strangled. This crime was afterwards openly laid to his charge, and the bitter remorse which he experienced when he learned that his suspicions were unfounded aggravated a serious illness, with which he struggled hard, but to which he at last succumbed. His death took place in the year 4 B.C., the same year which marks the probable date of the Nativity, and its occurrence coincides with the beginning of the New Testament story.

During all these years the religious thought of the Jews revolved round two poles—regard for the law of the Lord, and the hope of a better future on the basis of its observance; and their zeal for the one was in hope of the other. This hope dates from the utterances of the old prophets of Israel, but in course of time it underwent marked modifications, so that the Messianic ideas of the later times differed materially from those of the earlier. The earlier hope chiefly centred in the fortunes of the nation; the later hope expanded through the teachings of the prophets into the idea of a kingdom of God which was to embrace the whole world. The whole was translated into a sphere apart from and above the present system of things, in which the powers of good wage such an unequal warfare with the powers of evil. It was to be inaugurated by a king expressly "anointed" of God to lay its foundations and gather in its elect. Such, in general terms, was the Messianic hope which grew up among the Jewish people prior to the New Testament times: it was one extensively cherished by the pious Jew at the advent of Christianity; and it was as the realisation of this hope that the Jew was persuaded to believe in the claims and promises of JESUS CHRIST. See Grætz, *History of the Jews;* Hunter, *After the Exile;* Drummond, *The Jewish Messiah.*

CHAPTER XV.

THE FOUR GOSPELS.

The name.—The word Gospel means "good news," and is the Anglo-Saxon equivalent of the Greek word Evangelion, which is employed in the New Testament to denote the announcement by Christ and His apostles of the near advent of the universal kingdom of God. It is here attached to the narratives which give an account of the character, life, and teaching of Him by whom that kingdom was established. We are not aware when the name was first applied to these narratives, but it is the designation by which they are commonly known as early as the third century.

The Four Gospels and the Four Evangelists.—The first three Gospels are distinguished from the fourth by the epithet " Synoptic," which is applied to them because they are summaries of the chief events, and all go over the same ground, in the history, while the author of the fourth follows lines of his own. Thus, while the former confine themselves almost exclusively to what took place in Galilee until Christ's last visit to Jerusalem, the latter gives prominence to His ministry in Judæa, and alone records His successive journeys to the Jewish capital, reporting, in the sixth chapter, only one of the discourses Christ delivered in the northern province. The former consist mainly of narrative, while the object of the latter is dogmatic, as well as probably supplementary, *i.e.*, to supply narrative deficiencies in the three earlier works. The interest of St. John's account centres in the person of Christ, that of the others in His Gospel. All the same the four accounts are in substantial agreement. and only view the same history from different standpoints. This diversity was noted in ancient symbolism by representing, agreeably to the imagery in Ezekiel, chap. i., Matthew as attended by a man, Mark by a lion, Luke by an ox, and John by an eagle; and criticism goes to justify to some extent the appropriateness of these symbols. For Matthew represents Christ as of the race of man, Mark as of royal dignity, Luke as of priestly connection and the Saviour of sinners, and John as the incarnation of the *Logos*, or the Divinity in flesh. In early Christian art the four evangelists were symbolised by four scrolls, or, in allusion to the streams of Paradise, by four rivers flowing down from a height, on which stood a cross and a lamb, as the heaven-filled fountain-heads whence the knowledge of Christ crucified flows to all parts of the world.

I. *The historical character of the documents.*— The authority of the Gospels has ever rested on the belief of their apostolic origin—*i.e.*, that they were written either by apostles or by "apostolical men,*" men of the age of the apostles, in whom the apostles had full confidence, who were amply qualified to write as well-informed contemporaries, and who did honestly record what they knew to have happened. This fact has recently been much contested, and the theory insisted on, that the Gospels are, partly the intentional, partly the unintentional, inventions of a later age, even as late as the latter half of the second century. The question professes to be one for impartial scientific criticism. But as it is handled by those who reject the Gospels, it does not come before us free from bias. On the contrary, we meet with evidences of a very strong bias, in a decisive refusal to admit any narrative of a miracle as historically authentic. Accordingly the question at issue has resolved itself into one of the possibility or impossibility of a miracle, *i.e.*, of an event happening otherwise than agreeably to the known processes of nature. Those who believe in its impossibility can never be persuaded of the validity of the narratives, while those who see no reason to doubt its possibility may well hold the proof of the apostolic authority of the accounts amply valid. On the other hand, it may be admitted that the record of miracles in itself may naturally raise a prejudice against a narrative on the ground of their improbability. Thus the "Life of St. Antony," ascribed to St. Athanasius, is rejected by many because of the absurd marvels which it contains. But then this is at best the story of a quaint hermit, not the picture of a second Christ. The miracles of Christ must be viewed in connection with the nature, life, and work of Christ. So regarded they may be seen to be perfectly consistent with His superhuman character. It may even be said that while there is a probability against miracles in the abstract, there is a probability in favour of Christ working miracles, because His divine nature prepares us to expect them. Thus the story is consistent throughout. At all events, as a set-off against any difficulties suggested in the Gospel narrative by the presence of miracles, we may take the portrait of Christ there given. Such a portrait speaks for its own truthfulness; and this conclusion is fortified by the fact that the documents concerned breathe a spirit and depict a character the very conception of which, not to mention the portrayal, is explicable only on the presupposition of their historical truth. The ages that followed, quite as much as the contemporary age itself, were simply incapable of the invention of such a character as that of Christ; so that, explain away the facts as we may, we have still to account for the miracle of the origin of the conception of the inimitable story of Jesus of Nazareth. We possess that story in our four Gospels. How are we to account for it? It is easier to do this by saying that it is true, than by saying that the early Church invented in its imagination so wonderful a character and so unique a life as the character and life of Jesus Christ. Christ stands behind the Gospels, and He is immeasurably greater than the Gospel writers. These men must have recorded true facts, because they were incapable of inventing what they wrote.

The external evidence for the antiquity and historical truth of the four Gospels is of a very high order. Irenæus, who was in touch with Asia Minor, Gaul, and Rome, and who knew Polycarp the disciple of John, not only acknowledged them, but venerated them so highly as to assign various reasons why he thought they must be just four, neither more nor less. The discovery of Tatian's *Diatessaron* places it beyond a doubt that this work was formed out of our Gospels, and goes to confirm the belief that Justin Martyr used them, for Tatian was a disciple of his. Justin refers to our Gospels as "Memoirs of the Apostles," because he is writing for persons outside the Church who did not know the Christian books. Although he states some things that are not in the four Gospels, whenever he ascribes anything to the "Memoirs," that saying is to be found more or less exactly in the Gospels. "The Shepherd of Hermas" appears to have a number of mystical allusions to the quadruple composition of the Gospels. The newly discovered "Sinaitic" Syriac Gospels is a proof that the four were very early translated into that language. Thus recent discoveries combine to establish the great antiquity of the Gospels. The books referred to date from the middle of the second century A.D. and earlier. Hippolytus, who wrote at the beginning of the next century, is a witness that some at least of the Gospels were known to Gnostics as early as the year 125, and commented on by these heretics. There are several passages in the Apostolic fathers that read like echoes of one or other of the Gospels. After this it is needless to cite writers of the end of the second and beginning of the third centuries—*e.g.*, Clement of Alexandria, Origen, and Tertullian, who quote and discuss all the four Gospels very frequently. But it may be added, that Tertullian is a witness to a Latin version of the Gospels, which therefore must have been extant in North Africa before the end of the second century.

2. *The synoptic problem.*—The close and peculiar connection of Matthew, Mark, and Luke, has given rise to "the synoptic problem," *i.e.*, the problem how to account for the striking resemblances between the Gospels side by side with their equally striking divergences. (1.) They are formed on a common plan, not giving a full biography of Christ, but select incidents, in some cases with many months intervening, and yet, to a considerable extent, giving the same incidents. (2.) They present us with the same groups of scenes, even when these are not his-

torically connected, in close succession, *e.g.*, the three incidents of the paralytic, the call of Levi, and John's disciples fasting, closely following one another in each of the synoptics (Matt. ix. 1–17; Mark ii. 1–23; Luke v. 18–39); similarly, the loaves and fishes, St. Peter's confession, and the Transfiguration (Matt. xv. 32–xvii. 23; Mark viii. 1–ix. 29; Luke ix.–x. 42); and again, the narrative of the murder of John the Baptist introduced in two Gospels *incidentally* to explain Herod's alarm (Matt. xiv. 1–12; Mark vi. 14–29). (3.) They contain many passages agreeing closely in words, down to the use of connecting particles (*e.g.*, identical sentences in the following passages, Matt. xxi. 33–44; Mark xii. 1–11; Luke xx. 9–18. Also in Matt. ix. 1–8; Mark ii. 1–12; Luke v. 17–26). Then we have identical variations from the LXX. in quoting the Old Testament (*e.g.*, Matt. iii. 3; Mark i. 3). It is impossible to pursue this comparison to any length without coming to the conclusion, that there must be some connection between the synoptics. Many theories of that connection have been started. By some, the Gospels are thought to have been derived from a common source or common sources; by others, they are held to be mutually dependent. If there was any common source, the question arises whether this was oral or written. The closeness of verbal resemblance, however, makes it very difficult to be satisfied with the theory of a common oral tradition. What is called "the triple tradition," consisting in those parts of the synoptics that are found in all three Gospels, has been regarded as representative of the primitive source. But it is found that this is virtually identical with a large part of Mark, and further, that the remainder of Mark—*i.e.*, its narratives, not its actual phrases—with the exception of but two or three incidents, is all found either in Matthew or in Luke. Accordingly, the majority of critics have now come to the conclusion that Mark is the primitive Gospel and largely the basis of the other two. But next, there are portions of Matthew and Luke which agree together, although they are not found in Mark. Therefore some other source common to the first and third Gospels must be postulated. Now the earliest writer to give any account of the Gospels is Papias, who lived in the first half of the second century. This writer mentions Mark's work, and also tells us that Matthew wrote the *Logia*, or Oracles, in the Hebrew tongue. Seeing that the common matter in Matthew and Luke which is not also in Mark consists chiefly of discourses, it is inferred that very probably both Gospels make use of Matthew's *Logia*. Thus we are brought to the two works named by Papias—Mark and the *Logia*—as the sources of the common elements in the synoptics. There are some who think that Mark knew and used the *Logia*, though to a much smaller extent than the other synoptic writers. Further, it has been pointed out, that some of the most curious and apparently meaningless variations between the synoptics may be accounted for on the hypothesis that they represent different translations of the same Aramaic words. This agrees with Papias' statement about the original form of St. Matthew's work, since by "Hebrew" he probably meant "Aramaic." These two sources may account for most of the material found in the two first Gospels. Luke must have used other sources also, especially for what is called his *pericope, i.e.*, the section ix. 51–xviii. 14, most of which is peculiar to the third Gospel. His own introductory statement implies that he had a variety of sources (Luke i. 2).

The Gospel according to St. Matthew: 1. *Its titular author.*—St. Matthew (chap. ix. 9) is also called Levi, the son of Alphæus, in Mark ii. 14 (see Luke v. 27), and is described as a publican, one whose business it was to collect the Roman custom on goods crossing the Sea of Tiberias, but who rose and left the receipt of custom on the simple call of Christ, and afterwards became one of His twelve apostles. We know nothing for certain of his after history, except what may in a general way be deduced from the tenor of this Gospel. From the structure, or drift, of it, it has been inferred that he was at first the apostle of Christianity to the Jews, probably in Palestine, and afterwards, in consequence of their rejection of his testimony, the witness of its truth to other nations, tradition says in Ethiopia, India, and Parthia, in which last country he is further said to have suffered martyrdom for the faith. He is generally represented in Christian art as an old man, with a large flowing beard, and often as occupied in writing his Gospel with an angel standing by his side.

2. *Original language.*—According to the unanimous testimony of the earliest writers in the Christian Church who refer to the subject, Matthew wrote his Gospel in Hebrew, *i.e.*, in Aramaic, the current language of Palestine. On the other hand, it is pretty generally agreed that our Gospel as it stands in Greek is not a translation from the Hebrew, but an original composition in Greek. Did Matthew write two Gospels? or were the ancient writers mistaken in supposing the Gospel was written in Hebrew? or lastly, was the Hebrew Gospel of which they wrote not genuine? Another piece of information throws some light on these questions. Later Church writers refer to and quote from a "Gospel according to the Hebrews," a book which was not accepted by the general Church, but used by Judaising sects. Some fragments of this Gospel remain, and they do not coincide with our Gospel. Yet we cannot suppose it likely that this book, rejected by the Church, only possessed by heretics and now lost, was the true work of the apostle; whilst our Gospel, which is a great and evidently inspired book, is only a second-hand imitation! Perhaps the Church tradition that Matthew wrote in Hebrew grew out of the knowledge that a Hebrew Gospel existed. This view is supported by the fact that none of the earliest writers referred to state that they themselves had ever seen the Hebrew original. It is quite possible that uncritical men who had only heard by report of a Hebrew Gospel, in many respects like St. Matthew's Gospel, should have imagined that this was the original work of the Apostle to the Hebrews. On the other hand, it is more probable that there is good foundation for the widespread and very ancient opinion that Matthew wrote in Hebrew. We have seen that the *Logia*, to which Papias refers, appears to be one of the principal sources of our Gospel. Thus it is called the "Gospel according to St. Matthew," owing to the fact that it contains Matthew's *Logia*.

3. *Genuineness.*—Irenæus quotes from our Gospel as Matthew's. Justin Martyr, who wrote only forty years after the death of John, frequently quotes from our Gospel. His quotations have been referred by some to another source—perhaps some document now lost—because they are not accurate. But Justin Martyr's quotations from the Septuagint are just as loose as his quotations from Matthew. When books were produced in the form of cumbrous rolls, and when verbal accuracy was not much considered, quotations from memory may have been frequently given without a reference to the authority cited. As the inaccuracy which would thus arise *is* seen with Justin's use of the Septuagint, there is no reason to be surprised at finding it also in his use of Matthew. Then the beautiful little Epistle to Diognetus—about the same date—appears to quote Matthew; so does Hegesippus. The later writers, Tertullian, Clement, and Origen, undoubtedly knew our Gospel. Henceforth the general acceptance of the book is unquestionable.

4. *Date.*—According to Irenæus, Matthew wrote his Gospel when Peter and Paul were founding the Church at Rome—a very confusing statement, as the Church at Rome most have been founded before either of these Apostles had visited the city. But the form of the predictions in chap. xxiv., which describe the doom of Jerusalem in close connection with the general judgment, without any indication that these events were not to occur at the same time, is at once an indication of the genuineness of the narrative, and of the fact that it was composed before the destruction of Jerusalem, *i.e.*, before A.D. 70.

5. *Aim.*—The aim of this Gospel is to show that the Messiah promised in the Old Testament has appeared as Jesus of Nazareth—in a form, however, which led to His rejection by the Jews, and their consequent rejection by Him, to the eventual emancipation and salvation of the Gentile nations (chap. xxviii. 19, 20). To this end it directs more attention to the fulfilment of prophecy than is seen in the other Gospels.

6. *Characteristics.*—The arrangement is often not chronological, but topical, while the matter which we more particularly owe to it embraces the Sermon on the Mount (chaps. v.–vii.), Christ's charge to His apostles (chap. x.), most of the parables in chap. xiii., that of the unmerciful servant (chap. xviii.), and some in chaps. xxi.–xxviii.

7. *Contents.*—Jesus Christ is descended from Abraham by way of David, and is miraculously conceived and born (chap. i.). The Magi are divinely directed to the place of His birth; Joseph takes Mary and the young child down to Egypt; Herod slaughters the babes of Bethlehem; on Herod's death Jesus is brought back to Nazareth in Galilee (chap. ii.). His forerunner appears to prepare His way, and baptizes Him amid signs from heaven of His Messiahship and Divine Sonship (chap. iii.). He is tempted by suggestions of the devil, which He must resist if He would fulfil His Messianic mission, and He foils the tempter by the Word of God. He retires to Capernaum, where He begins His ministry and calls His first disciples (chap. iv.). He delivers the Sermon on the Mount, and lays down the laws on which He is to found His kingdom (chaps. v.–vii.). Among other miracles,

He cures a leper, the son of the centurion, and Peter's wife's mother; He calls an admiring scribe to give proof of his faith by following Him, stills a tempest on the lake, and casts demons out of the demoniacs of Gadara into the swine (chap. viii.). He heals a paralytic; calls Matthew the publican; justifies His consorting with publicans and sinners, and His disciples for not fasting; heals the woman with the issue of blood; raises the daughter of the ruler to life; opens the eyes of two blind men; casts a demon out of a mute; and goes about teaching, and preaching, and healing all manner of diseases (chap. ix.). He chooses twelve apostles, and charges them (chap. x.). He sends an answer to a message from John, and bears witness of him, and the treatment that both John and He Himself were receiving at the hands of their generation; He upbraids the cities which had seen His works for their impenitence, but comforts Himself with the thought of those whom His Father had given to Him, and whom He invites to come to Him (chap. xi.). He justifies His disciples for plucking the ears of corn on the Sabbath when hungry, and incurs the displeasure of the Pharisees by an act of healing on that day, so that He withdraws to another place; He rebuts the charge of casting out demons by the prince of the demons, and imputes the disposition of His accusers to speak evil to the evil in their own hearts (chap. xii.). He teaches the multitude concerning the kingdom of heaven by the parables of the sower, the good seed and the tares, the mustard-seed, the leaven, the hid treasure, the goodly pearl, and the drag-net; He appears as a prophet among His own people, but they lend a deaf ear to Him, to their own loss (chap. xiii.). He hears of the fate of John, and retires into the desert on the other side of the lake, followed by the multitudes, on whom He has compassion, and whom He miraculously feeds; His disciples return by ship without Him, and are in danger from the waves, when He appears walking on the sea, to their great fear at first, but to the final appeasement of the storm and of their own agitation; when He lands, the sick flock to Him in crowds, and He heals them (chap. xiv.). The Pharisees charge His disciples with transgressing the tradition of the elders in regard to eating with unwashen hands, and He charges them with thereby transgressing the commands of God; He explains afterwards to the multitude the law of defilement, and His indifference to the offence which He has given to the Pharisees; He retires towards Tyre and Sidon, and heals the daughter of a Canaanitish woman, who prevails with Him by the greatness of her faith; He returns to Galilee, where the multitudes follow Him, and are healed and fed by Him (chap. xv.). When challenged to give the Pharisees and Sadducees a sign, He refuses, for their spiritual blindness, except that He points to the sign or signs sure to follow their rejection of Himself; He takes occasion afterwards to caution His disciples to beware of the false teaching of both these parties; at Cæsarea Philippi Simon Peter confesses the divinity of Christ, which he is virtually told is the corner-stone of the new gospel, but he is cautioned to have a care lest the cross, which is too visibly looming ahead, should seem inconsistent with his confession (chap. xvi.). Christ is transfigured before Peter, James, and John, and soon attended, amid signs from heaven, by Moses and Elijah; He shows His disciples that Elijah had appeared in John, and that, as the Scribes had done by John, so they would do by Him; He casts out a demon after His disciples have failed, and He ascribes their inability to the weakness of their faith; He tells them again, to their sorrow, that He must go to Jerusalem, and suffer at the hands of the authorities; He consents to pay the Temple tribute, and Peter is told he will find the money in the first fish caught by him (chap. xvii.). Christ present a little child as a pattern to His disciples, and cautions them against causing any such to stumble, as it is not His Father's will that one of these should be lost; He explains certain doctrines, especially the doctrine of forgiveness (chap. xviii.). He expounds His doctrine in regard to marriage and celibacy, blesses little children, and promises all to those that forsake all for His sake (chap. xix.). He expounds, by the parable of the labourers in the vineyard, the doctrine of rewards in His kingdom, and reminds the disciples of the reward that awaits Him; He rebukes the ambition of the sons of Zebedee, and gives sight to two blind men on His way up to Jerusalem for the last time (chap. xx.). He makes His triumphal entry into the city, but, after casting the traders out of the Temple, soon quits it again for Bethany; He returns in the morning, denouncing a fruitless fig-tree by the way; after silencing the chief priests, who challenge His authority, He speaks, for their admonition and warning, the parables of the two sons of the vinedresser and the wicked husbandmen (chap. xxi.). He speaks also the parable of the marriage-feast of the king's son; He silences the Herodians, the Sadducees, and the Pharisees, in the matters respectively of tribute to Cæsar, the resurrection, and the commandments of the law (chap. xxii.). He denounces the hypocrisy of the Scribes and Pharisees, and predicts the judgments coming upon Jerusalem (chap. xxiii.). He predicts the coming of the kingdom of God and His second advent (chap. xxiv.). He speaks the parables of the ten virgins and the talents; He announces the judgment of the nations according to their conduct to the least of His brethren (chap. xxv.). The rulers resolve to take His life; He is anointed by Mary in Bethany; Judas covenants to betray Him for thirty pieces of silver; Jesus institutes the Last Supper, predicts the fall of Peter, experiences an agony of suffering in the garden, is betrayed by Judas, is accused with contumely before Caiaphas, and denied by Peter (chap. xxvi.). He is delivered up to Pilate, Judas meanwhile relenting and giving back the money; Jesus is sentenced to be crucified; after being mocked and insulted, He is led out to Calvary and crucified between two robbers, after which His body is taken down from the cross and buried in Joseph's tomb (chap. xxvii.). He rises on the third day, and announces Himself as risen to Mary Magdalene and the other Mary, who had gone early to the sepulchre; He presents Himself to the eleven on a mountain, and commissions them to go and baptize and teach all nations, promising to be ever with them (chap. xxviii.).

The Gospel according to St. Mark: 1. *its author.* —The author of this Gospel is the John Mark spoken of in the Acts, and who accompanied first Paul and then Barnabas in their missionary journeys among the Gentiles (Acts xii. 12 et seq.; xiii. 5). He was the son of Mary, Barnabas' sister, apparently a woman of some standing, and of high repute among those that ministered to Christ, and at whose house in Jerusalem the apostles used frequently to assemble after the death and resurrection of their Master. He appears, from 1 Pet. v. 13, to have been a convert or spiritual child of St. Peter, who there calls him Mark, my son; and we learn from early Christian writers, that his Gospel is based on what he learnt from that apostle. It is certainly written from the standpoint of the apostle who first clearly recognised the divinity of Christ (Matt. xvi. 16); and it is an expanded narrative of the facts in Christ's life emphasised in St. Peter's own preaching, e.g., in his speech at the house of Cornelius at Cæsarea (Acts. x. 36–41). According to ecclesiastical tradition St. Mark went as a missionary to Egypt and other parts of Africa, where he suffered martyrdom for Christ in A.D. 62 or 66. He is regarded by tradition as the founder of the Koptic Church, and his body is said to have been buried in Venice, of which city he is the patron saint, and where the famous cathedral is dedicated to him. He is represented in Christian art usually as a man in the prime of life, accompanied by a winged lion, holding in his left hand his Gospel, and in his right a pen.

2. *Genuineness.*—Papias, who lived in the first half of the second century, tells us that " Mark, the interpreter of Peter, wrote exactly whatever he remembered, though he recorded it not in the order in which it was spoken or done by the Lord." Justin Martyr and Irenæus both quote from our Gospel. Tatian, Clement, and Tertullian also bear witness to it. There is some question, however, as to the genuineness of the concluding verses (xvi. 9–20).

3. *Date.*—The Gospel was, according to Irenæus, composed by Mark after the death of Peter and Paul. It was probably written after the year 62, when Mark appears only as a relative of Barnabas (see Col. iv. 10), and before the destruction of Jerusalem, and is alleged to have had its origin in Rome. Its original language, however, was Greek. There is no authority for a Roman Catholic tradition that it was written in Latin.

4. *Aim.*—The special aim of this Gospel seems to be to present what Christ did in such a light as to lead up to a belief in His Divine Sonship. It shows us the Son of Man proving Himself to be the Son of God by the signs and wonders which He works. The book was written for Gentile Christians, and not for Jews, and hence little stress is laid on references to Old Testament fulfilments, or to those forms of antagonism to Christianity which had a merely Jewish root.

5. *Characteristics.*—It gives more than any other of the Gospels the simple historical sequence of events in the public ministry of Christ, to which it limits itself, and it best supplies a basis for a harmony of these documents. It is mainly a narrative of the doings of Christ, and gives only a few of His parables and discourses, and those mostly in brief. The story never lags, but moves on by rapid steps; it abounds in graphic touches, and contributes minute traits, such as some vigilant eye-witness must have observed, while special notice is frequently taken of features expressive of the human nature of Christ.

6. *Contents.*—John preaches repentance, and prepares the people for Christ; Christ is baptized by John, and thereafter tempted in the wilderness; He appears in Galilee, and collects disciples; He casts out demons, heals the sick, and cleanses lepers, so that the fame of Him goes abroad (chap. i.). In Capernaum, He heals a paralytic, and reveals a power to forgive sins; He calls Levi, and justifies His eating with publicans and sinners, and also His disciples' plucking of the ears of corn on the Sabbath day (chap. ii.). He heals a man with a withered hand on the Sabbath day, and stirs up the hatred of the Pharisees against Himself; multitudes follow Him from all parts, and He calls the twelve aside to a mountain; His friends are uneasy about Him, and His enemies speak evil of Him; He owns only a spiritual kinship (chap. iii.). He speaks and explains the parable of the sower, while He justifies His teaching by parable; He speaks other parables; He and His disciples are overtaken by a storm on the lake, which He stills (chap. iv.). In the country of the Gerasenes, He casts the demons out of the demoniac into the swine; He heals the woman with the issue of blood, and restores the daughter of Jairus (chap. v.). His own townsfolk reject Him; He sends forth the twelve two and two; Herod hears of Jesus, and supposes Him to be John the Baptist, whom he has beheaded, risen from the dead; Jesus retires to a desert place with His disciples, but is followed by multitudes, whom He miraculously feeds: He appears to His disciples in a storm on the lake and stills it; people bring their sick from all parts to Him at Gennesaret (chap. vi.). The Pharisees accuse His disciples of eating with unwashen hands, and so transgressing the traditions of the elders, while He accuses them of transgressing the commandments of God by their traditions; He explains the law of defilement to the multitude; the Syrophœnician woman prevails on Him to heal her daughter; He heals a deaf mute (chap. vii.). He miraculously feeds a multitude a second time; the Pharisees require a sign, but none can be given; He cautions His disciples against the leaven of the Pharisees and the Herodians, and rebukes them for their dulness of understanding; He heals a blind man; He sets the cross before His disciples after they have confessed Him to be the Christ (chap. viii.). He is transfigured in the presence of Peter, James, and John, and explains the coming of Elijah; His disciples fail to cast out an evil spirit from a deaf and dumb child, and He rebukes them for their defective faith; He predicts His sufferings, and rebukes the ambition of His disciples by setting before them a little child for their model; they must be careful to cultivate a spirit of self-sacrifice (chap. ix.). He expounds the marriage-law; He blesses little children; a rich youth, who would fain follow Him, turns sorrowfully away when he learns what the conditions are; Christ bids His disciples note how hard it is for a rich man to enter the Kingdom, but assures those who forsake all to follow Him of the gain they will make by the exchange; He takes His disciples aside and forewarns them of what is about to happen to Him; the sons of Zebedee show an

ambitious spirit and are rebuked, while they are reminded that the greatest in His kingdom are the most self-sacrificing ; near Jericho, He heals blind Bartimæus (chap. x.). He enters Jerusalem in triumph ; He retires to Bethany, and on His return on the morrow denounces the fruitless fig-tree ; He expels the traffickers from the Temple ; He counsels His disciples to have faith ; He silences the Pharisees, who challenge the authority He exercises (chap. xi.). He speaks the parable of the wicked husbandmen ; He silences the Herodians, the Sadducees, and the Pharisees in the matters respectively of tribute to Cæsar, the resurrection, and the commandments of the law ; He exposes the hypocrisy of the Scribes ; He honours the widow for her mite (chap. xii.). He foretells the judgments that must come on the land before His reappearing ; He bids His disciples watch (chap. xiii.). The chief priests consort to take and kill Him; Mary anoints Him and is justified ; Judas undertakes to deliver Him up ; His disciples make ready the passover, and He institutes the Last Supper ; He foretells the desertion of His disciples ; He is sorrowful unto death in the garden ; He is betrayed ; He is forsaken by His disciples ; He is followed by a young man, who, when apprehended, leaves his cloak, and escapes naked ; He is led before the high-priest, tried, and condemned to death ; Peter denies Him (chap. xiv.). He is taken before Pilate, and delivered to be crucified ; they array Him in mock symbols of royalty, and crucify Him at Golgotha between two robbers ; at the ninth hour He calls upon God and gives up the ghost, amid signs from heaven, the women that followed Him looking on from afar ; He is buried in Joseph's tomb (chap. xv.). On the third day Mary Magdalene and another Mary come to anoint Him, and are told by a young man arrayed in white that He is risen ; He appears to Mary Magdalene and others, then to the eleven as they sit at meat ; He bids them preach His Gospel everywhere, and promises them power to work signs ; He ascends to heaven, and they go forth preaching everywhere, confirming the Word by signs (chap. xvi.).

The Gospel according to St. Luke: 1. *Its author.* —The author of this Gospel, whose full name was Lucanus, is, by the unanimous voice of tradition, identified with the "beloved physician" and "fellow-labourer" of St. Paul mentioned in Col. iv. 14 ; 2 Tim. iv. 11 ; and Philem. 24. He was by birth a Greek (Col. iv. 11 *et seq.*), a native of Antioch in Syria, and probably a Jewish proselyte before he became a convert, possibly under the] preaching of Paul, to the faith of Christ. He appears to have joined Paul on the second journey of the apostle to Troas, and to have been frequently afterwards in his company (Acts xvi. 10 ; xx. 5 ; xxi. 18 ; xxiv. 23 ; xxvii. 1–28). Of his history after the death of Paul we know nothing ; only tradition says that he died a martyr, and Jerome, that his body was buried in Constantinople. A dubious ecclesiastical tradition says he was a painter, as well as a physician, and even ascribes certain pictures to his pencil. On this account he is the patron saint of artists, and is usually represented in Christian art with an ox lying near him, and sometimes with painting materials, or in the act of painting the Virgin with the Child. Some expositors affect to see the artist, as they do

the physician, in certain graphic touches of his narrative.

2. *Genuineness.*—In addition to the unquestioning testimony of antiquity, one point is of special interest. The heretic Marcion, who wrote about A.D. 138, found the Gospel in general use, adopted it, and mutilated it to suit his own purpose. The Pauline spirit of the work speaks for its authorship. It is evidently written by the author of the "Acts." Irenæus, Origen, Tertullian, Tatian, and probably also Justin Martyr, bear witness to it.

3. *Date.*—St. Luke's Gospel can be proved to have been in use and familiarly known about A.D. 120. Probably it was written after the destruction of Jerusalem and about A.D. 80, it is not known where.

4. *Origin.*—This Gospel, as the opening verses show, originated in a desire to supply, from authentic sources familiar to the author, an accurate and narrative account of those events in connection with the life and ministry of Jesus Christ, the assured belief in which constituted the foundation-stone of the Church. This, the author tells us, "it seemed good" to him to do, notwithstanding the prior existence of other narratives, relying on "eye-witnesses and ministers of the Word ;" and he justifies the act on the ground that he has taken special pains to verify the whole story for himself, so that his account is to be regarded as confirmatory of the others in circulation in the Church. Though the matter of the narrative here given by St. Luke is derived from sources within his own immediate cognisance, there is good ground to believe that the account had the sanction of the Apostle Paul, and it actually corresponds in some points verbally with his version (compare Luke xxii. 19, 20, with 1 Cor. xi. 23–25). The Christ of Luke, at any rate, is emphatically the Christ of Paul —*i.e.*, the wide-reaching Saviour of the world ; the passages in this Gospel which do not occur in the others representing Him more specially in this light.

5. *Aim.*—St. Luke's Gospel is written, in the first instance, to confirm the faith of Theophilus, a native, it is thought, of Italy, and probably of Rome, and a man of some social position, in whose spiritual edification and Christian steadfastness, as in all likelihood a convert of his own, he took especial interest ; and its aim is to represent the Gospel of Christ as destined to bless all mankind, and Jesus as the Saviour at once of Jew and Gentile.

6. *Characteristics.*—This Gospel brings out the grace of God in Jesus Christ with great force and beauty. It especially illustrates the opposition of our Lord to Pharisaism in His willingness to receive sinners. It also shows the breadth of the Divine grace in extending to all classes, and an appreciation of what is good in all the poorer, humbler, and despised Samaritans and Gentiles, as well as Jewish publicans. The arrangement is only partially chronological, certain facts and discourses being grouped more according to the matter than the order of time. The literary style is better than that of the other Gospels, as befits the writing of an educated, professional man. This Gospel and the Acts of the Apostles approach more nearly to the "classic" Greek than the other New Testament narratives.

7. *Contents.*—The preface (chap. i. 1–4). An

angel appears to Zacharias, and promises his wife Elizabeth shall conceive a son, to be called John; an angel appears to Mary, and promises her a Son by the power of the Holy Ghost, to be called Jesus; Mary visits Elizabeth, and magnifies the Lord, when Elizabeth addresses her, inspired by the Holy Ghost; John is born, and his father prophesies; when grown up he retires to the wilderness (5–80). Joseph goes up to Bethlehem from Nazareth to be enrolled with Mary, when the promised Child is born; shepherds watching their flocks by night are supernaturally apprised of the event, and go to worship the Child; the Child is circumcised, and afterwards presented in the Temple; Simon recognises Him, and prophesies regarding Him; Anna, a prophetess too, gives thanks; Jesus visits Jerusalem with His parents when a boy of twelve, and gives signs of His sense of a higher parentage (chap. ii.). John appears preaching in the wilderness of Judæa the baptism of repentance, threatening some, and admonishing others; he refers the people to a greater One about to appear and baptize with the Holy Ghost and fire: Jesus is baptized by John amid signs from heaven in recognition of His being the Christ; His human descent from Adam is given (chap. iii.). Jesus is tempted of the devil, and proves that the devil has no power over Him; He returns to Galilee, and reveals His power; He announces Himself in Nazareth, but His claims are rejected and His life threatened; He casts out an evil spirit from a demoniac in Capernaum, and the fame of His power spreads abroad; He heals Peter's wife's mother and other sick, then goes forth to preach in all the synagogues of Galilee (chap. iv.). He reveals His Divine power to Simon Peter, and encourages him to follow Him, unworthy though Peter feels himself to be; He heals a leper, great multitudes crowd about Him, and He retires into the desert to pray; He heals a paralytic in vindication of His power to forgive sins; He justifies His eating with publicans and sinners, and His disciples in not fasting while He is with them (chap. v.). He justifies His disciples in plucking the ears of corn, and Himself in healing the withered hand on the Sabbath day, exciting thereby the wrath of His enemies; He prays all night, chooses the twelve, and heals all that come to Him; He shows, as in Matthew, chaps. v.–vii., who are blessed, and lays down some of the laws of His kingdom (chap. vi.). In Capernaum, He heals the servant of the centurion, and admires the faith of the latter; He raises from the dead the son of the widow of Nain; He satisfies the inquiries of John as to His Messiahship; He bears witness to John and against the treatment both He and His forerunner received at the hands of their generation; He sits down to meat, by invitation, in the house of Simon the Pharisee, and commends to his regard the conduct of the woman, a sinner, who had washed, and kissed, and anointed His feet (chap. vii.). He goes preaching in the cities, accompanied by the twelve and certain ministering women; He speaks and explains the parable of the sower, and otherwise teaches the people; He shows who His true kinsfolk henceforth are, when His mother and brethren would interfere with Him, He stills the storm on the lake; He casts the evil spirits out of the demoniac into the swine, and the people of the place beg Him to depart from them; He heals the woman with the issue of blood, and raises the daughter of Jairus (chap. viii.). He empowers and sends forth the twelve; Herod seeks to see Him; He feeds the multitude in the desert; Peter confesses Him to be the Christ, but is told that He whom he has confessed must suffer, and that they who follow Him must go the same road; He goes up into a mountain to pray, and is transfigured before Peter, James, and John; He casts out a demon which His disciples had not faith enough to do; He speaks of His sufferings, but His disciples do not understand; He rebukes their ambition, and recommends a little child to their regard as for Himself; He rebukes their undue jealousy and zeal for His honour; who so would follow Him, must give up and forsake all (chap. ix.). He appoints seventy evangelists, and sends them with instructions; the seventy return, exulting over the success of their mission, but are cautioned not to make that a ground of rejoicing; He rejoices in spirit, and thanks His Father that He has given it to simple-hearted souls to receive the mysteries of His kingdom; He bids the lawyer, who would learn of Him the way to eternal life, go and practise mercy, such as the Samaritan showed to the man whom the thieves had plundered and maltreated; He is entertained by Martha, but prefers Mary's homage to Martha's service (chap. x.). His disciples would know how to pray, and He teaches and encourages them; He casts out a demon, refutes the charge of His doing so by the prince of the demons, and shows that His action proves that the kingdom of God is come; He depreciates mere earthly relationships, and recognises only such as are spiritual; when asked for a sign, He points to Himself as a sign such as was not vouchsafed to Nineveh in Jonah, or to the Queen of Sheba in Solomon; He offers Himself as a light, but requires the single eye; being invited, He sits down to meat with unwashen hands in the house of a Pharisee, and takes occasion, when challenged, to rebuke the Pharisees for their attention to the outward to the neglect of the inward, the state of which alone either purifies or defiles; He denounces the Scribes and Pharisees (chap. xi.). He bids His disciples beware of the hypocrisy of the Pharisees, cast away all fear and care, and confide in and confess Him; He cautions them against covetousness, and exhorts them, from the case oft he rich husbandman, not to depend on earthly stores alone; they must forego all worldly anxiety, have faith in God, and be ready against the day of His second coming; He foresees the alienations He is causing in the world, and longs for the time when the pain of the process will be over; He bids the multitude read the signs of the time, and prepare especially against the judgment that surely is coming upon them (chap. xii.). He refers to certain judgments as constituting a call on the whole nation to repent; He compares the Jewish nation to a fig-tree left standing in the vineyard to see if any care of the husbandman may render it fruit-bearing; He cures a woman of an eighteen years' infirmity on the Sabbath, and justifies the act; He likens the kingdom of God to mustard-seed and leaven; He exhorts all who will to strive to enter into His kingdom, and promises admission to all who thus strive; He is prepared to go up to Jerusalem without fear of Herod, knowing well what awaits Him there (chap. xiii.). He heals a dropsical patient on the Sabbath, and justifies the act ; He discountenances the strife for precedence at feasts, and would have, not the rich, but the poor invited to them ; He speaks the parable of the great supper ; He requires all to reckon well the cost of becoming a disciple (chap. xiv.). He justifies His interest in sinners by the parables of the lost sheep, the lost piece of money, and the lost son, and represents their recovery as matter of rejoicing (chap. xv.). He speaks the parable of the unjust steward, as showing how much wiser the children of the world are than the children of light; He reproves the Pharisees, who scoff at His teaching ; He delivers the parable of the rich man and Lazarus (chap. xvi.). He pronounces a woe against those who offend any of His little ones, and lays down the law of forgiveness ; He exhorts to faith, and rebukes the passion for rewards ; He cures ten lepers on his way to Jerusalem, but only one, and he a Samaritan, returns to give thanks ; He foretells that the coming of His kingdom is not to be with observation, also His own return to the earth and the day of judgment (chap. xvii.). He bids them learn a lesson from the importunate widow, and tells the parable of the Pharisee and the publican ; a young ruler accosts Him, and would have eternal life, but sorrowfully turns away when he learns the price he must pay to obtain it ; Christ takes occasion to show the danger of riches, and the reward in store for those who forsake all for the kingdom of God ; He takes the twelve aside to forewarn them of His sufferings, but they do not understand what He says to them ; He gives sight to a blind beggar by the way (chap. xviii.). He calls Zaccheus the publican to Him, stays at his house, and welcomes him into His kingdom ; He delivers the parable of the pounds ; He enters Jerusalem in triumph ; He weeps over the city, as He foresees the judgments coming upon it ; He cleanses the Temple, and His teaching attracts the people, but provokes the Scribes against Him (chap. xix.). The chief priests challenge His authority, but He declines to answer them; He delivers the parable of the wicked husbandman ; He replies to the Pharisees, the Herodians, and the Sadducees in regard to tribute to Cæsar and the resurrection ; He bids His disciples beware of the Scribes (chap. xx.). He commends the widow with her mite ; He predicts the judgment to come on Jerusalem (chap. xxi.). The chief priests seek to put Him to death ; Judas agrees to betray Him ; He celebrates the passover and the Last Supper ; He rebukes the ambition of His disciples, while He appoints to them a kingdom ; He predicts the trial and fall of Peter ; He warns the disciples that trouble is at hand ; He suffers an agony in the garden ; Judas betrays Him and Peter denies Him ; He is mocked and insulted by those who hold Him ; He appears before the Sanhedrin, and is pronounced self-condemned (chap. xxii.). He is brought and accused before Pilate ; Pilate sends Him to Herod, who sends Him back ; Pilate hands Him over to be crucified ; Simon of Cyrene bears His cross ; He bids those who weep for Him weep rather for themselves and their children ; He is crucified between two robbers, one of whom rails on Him, while the other believes ; He gives up the ghost, the cen-turion glorifying God, the multitude returning smiting on their breasts, and the women standing afar off ; He is buried in Joseph's tomb (chap. xxiii.). The women visit the tomb on the third day and are told He is risen, as He said ; they tell the disciples, and Peter runs to the grave and finds He is not there ; Jesus overtakes two of them going to Emmaus, and reveals Himself to them ; He appears afterwards in their midst, and eats before them; He bids them wait for the promise of the Father ; He ascends up to heaven (chap. xxiv.).

The Gospel according to St. John: 1. *Its author*.—Originally, like his father Zebedee, a fisherman on the Galilæan Lake, he became first a disciple of John the Baptist, and then a follower, one of the earliest, of Jesus Christ. He was perhaps the youngest of Christ's disciples, a youth of an ardent, affectionate nature ; and he appears from the first to have won the special love and confidence of his Lord and Master, being at length specially designated as that disciple "whom Jesus loved." He was one of the three who were privileged to be present on occasions on which more than usual manifestations were vouchsafed of the Lord's glory ; and it was to his keeping, when He was dying, that the Lord committed His sorrowing mother, as to the one of the twelve that would stand to her in her Son's stead, and was the likest of them all to Himself. After his Master's death, St. John appears to have lived principally at Jerusalem, probably till the death of Mary, and afterwards to have taken up his residence at Ephesus, somewhere about the year A.D. 67, and after the death of St. Paul. Of this city he became virtually bishop, an office which he appears to have held, under various forms of persecution, till his death, which is vaguely conjectured to have taken place somewhere between A.D. 89 and 120. He lived to see the rise of the Gnostic heresy, which sought to resolve the facts of the gospel into the mere symbols of a philosophical system ; and he died protesting against it as a denial of the incarnation which he had witnessed in the person of his Master. His Gospel, bearing witness against this heresy, was almost, if not quite, his last legacy to the Church. In Christian art he is represented either as writing his Gospel, or as bearing a chalice from which a poison once given to him to drink seems to issue in the form of a serpent. He is also sometimes represented in a cauldron of boiling oil, into which, it was said, he had been thrown, and from which he was supposed to have escaped unhurt.

2. *Genuineness.*—The negative critics have made a special attack upon this Gospel, and have attempted to show that it was not known till the second half of the second century after Christ. It is impossible here to enter into the elaborate arguments on either side of the question. But it is a remarkable fact that, step by step, the opponents of the genuineness of the Gospel have had to give ground, and confess an earlier date for the appearance of the Gospel. In the first place, the discovery of the writings of Hippolytus shows that the Gospel was known to Gnostic heretics by at least as early a date as 125. Then Bishop Lightfoot's vindication of the Ignatian Letters puts it back another ten years, for these letters are soaked

through and through with the leading ideas of the fourth Gospel. Moreover, it has been shown that Justin Martyr frequently alludes to the peculiar ideas of this Gospel. The author of the Epistle to Diognetus, who lived about the time of Justin, evidently moulds his writing on the thoughts of John. There can be no reasonable doubt that the same man wrote the Gospel and the First Epistle of John; and Polycarp, in his Epistle to the Philippians, quotes from the latter. The Epistle of the Churches of Lyons and Vienna, in the reign of Marcus Aurelius, quotes John xvi. 2. The recent discovery of the *Diatessaron* is a strong confirmation of the antiquity and early acceptance of this Gospel, for here it appears in a harmony composed of all four Gospels. The so-called Gospel of Peter, another recent discovery, seems to confirm the fourth Gospel. But, after all, the sublime character of the work is its best witness.

3. *Date.*—This Gospel would appear to have been written at Ephesus, at the instance, as Jerome alleges, of the bishops of the Asiatic churches, with a view to confirm the faith of the Church in the divinity of Christ, of which St. John was the special witness. Its date must be long after the writing of the other Gospels, and towards the end of the first century. It is one of the latest books of the New Testament. There is a growing tendency among scholars who do not hold that St. John wrote the Gospel with his own hand, to admit that the apostle supplied the materials for it.

4. *Object or aim.*—According to the author himself, the aim he had in writing his Gospel was, that its readers "might believe that Jesus was the Christ, the Son of God, and that believing they might have life through His name." His object is to show that in Jesus Christ the eternal Word became flesh, in order that we might become partakers of the Divine life revealed in Him, which, however, the evangelist is all along careful to show no one can become who prefers the darkness to the light. This Gospel has been from of old defined as the spiritual Gospel, because it pre-eminently unveils the hidden spiritual principle, or the Divine nature of the person of Christ. But its great design is to bear witness to the Son of God as having come in the flesh, at once to the full divinity and the full humanity of the incarnation.

5. *Characteristics.*—St. John's Gospel presupposes the existence and prior circulation of the three Synoptics; and whereas the scene of their narratives is mostly laid in Galilee, the scene of his is chiefly in Judæa, recording as it does no fewer than seven visits of our Lord to the capital in the course of His ministry. The style of the Gospel is peculiar; it strongly accentuates words, such as "light," "life," and "truth," which occur in the others but rarely, and without the specialty of meaning and the frequency peculiar to this Gospel. Private conversations of Jesus Christ with individual visitors, and His training of the Apostles and discussions with the Jews, here take the place which the Synoptics devote to public discourses. This fact goes a long way to account for the difference of style between our Lord's speech in this Gospel and that in the earlier Gospels. There are fewer incidents, but those that are narrated are given with exceptional fulness of detail and exactness.

The geographical and time notes are peculiarly minute.

6. *Contents.*—The eternal Word has appeared as the light of men in the person of Jesus; John the Baptist testifies that the Son of God is come in Him, and points to Him as the Lamb of God; two of John's disciples follow Jesus, are persuaded of His Messiahship, and bring others to the same belief (chap. i.). Jesus turns water into wine at a marriage feast in Cana of Galilee, and asserts Himself as free henceforth from all merely human obligation; after which, however, He goes down with His kinsfolk to Capernaum; He goes up at passover-time to Jerusalem, drives the traffickers out of the Temple, and enigmatically refers those who challenge His authority to His power to rebuild the Temple which they are desecrating and destroying; many believe, but He trusts Himself to no man (chap. ii.). Nicodemus, believing in His Divine mission, privately visits, and would fain learn of Him, but cannot apprehend what Jesus means when He requires of him, as of every unspiritual man, that he must be born again; still less when He goes on to speak of the lifting up of the Son of Man, or the change to come on Himself. (Here the explanation is inserted by the evangelist (vers. 16-21) that while the purpose of God's love in Christ is salvation, the result may be condemnation.) John the Baptist testifies anew to Christ as the only-begotten Son of God (chap. iii.). Jesus goes from Judæa to Galilee by way of Samaria, and talks with the woman at Jacob's well; He offers living water, and announces a worship corresponding to the nature of God Who is spirit; He declares to the Samaritan woman that He is the Christ; the woman publishes the fact, and many of the Samaritans confess their faith in Him; Jesus rejoices in the event, but saddens as He forecasts what must happen before the ingathering of the fruit, while He sympathises with the reapers; He is now received in Galilee; He heals the nobleman's son at Capernaum (chap. iv.). Jesus goes up to Jerusalem, and on the Sabbath day, at the pool of Bethesda, heals the impotent man, who at His bidding takes up his bed and walks; the Jews persecute Him because He broke the Sabbath-law and called God His Father; Jesus justifies Himself by the example of His Father, in whose name and by whose power He will yet do greater works, in the resurrection of men and the final judgment; He appeals to the testimony of His works; He charges the Jews with incapacity to receive the testimony of God in their own Scriptures, and claims the witness of Moses (chap. v). He feeds the five thousand on the other side of the Sea of Galilee, and gives proof of his Messiahship, so that the multitude would take Him by force and make Him king; He retires to a mountain, but joins His disciples as they cross over to Capernaum, appearing to them walking on the waves and stilling a storm that had arisen; the multitudes follow Him, but He rebukes them for their carnal temper and their indifference to the spiritual benefits which He urges them to seek after; those who seek after such benefits are exhorted to believe on Him whom God has sent; others require a sign, and He points to Himself as the bread of life, and explains, what to the majority appears a hard saying, that it is only by participation in His life, which must be personally appropriated, that

they can share in His benefits; after this, many draw back, and the few that remain are led to anticipate a further sifting (chap. vi.). Jesus arrives suddenly in Jerusalem while the Feast of Tabernacles is being celebrated, though He has concealed His purpose from His relations; He explains the nature of His doctrine as Divine revelation, and that only those who know God by an endeavour to do God's will can know Him; when the Pharisees seek to take Him, He warns them that they would seek Him earnestly some day and would not be able to find Him; in the last day of the feast He announces Himself as the fountain of living water (chap. vii.). A woman taken in adultery is brought before Him, and her accusers put to shame; He announces Himself as the Light of the world; He vindicates the validity of His testimony of Himself; He foretells the subsequent relations of the Jews to Him; He lays down the law of true freedom; He shows the Jews that they are not Abraham's children, but the children of another; He claims to have existed before Abraham, and they take up stones to stone Him (chap. viii.). He heals on the Sabbath day a man born blind; the Sanhedrin attempt to corrupt and alarm the man; Christ converses with him; He accuses His enemies of wilful blindness (chap. ix.). He depicts a good shepherd by a parable; He is the good shepherd and the door of the sheep; He has other sheep not of the Jewish fold; He gives a proof of His Messiahship; He declares His oneness with the Father, and defends His words from the Old Testament Scripture (chap. x.). A report comes to Him that Lazarus is sick, and Jesus replies to the messengers that his sickness is not unto death; Jesus, knowing he was dead, goes to awake him, against the counsel of His disciples; He converses with Martha and Mary; He weeps at the grave; knowing He could raise the dead, He thanks His Father, and bids Lazarus come forth; the Sanhedrin takes steps against Him; He retires to Ephraim with His disciples (chap. xi.). Jesus is anointed by Mary in Bethany, and He vindicates the act, as done against His burial; He enters Jerusalem in triumph, and the Pharisees look on with apprehensions; certain Greeks seek to see Him; He foresees the hour is at hand when He will be glorified; He impresses on the people the responsibility of listening or not listening to Him (chap. xii.). He washes His disciples' feet at supper, and overcomes the reluctance of Peter; He explains the meaning of the act, and warns them of the presence of a traitor; He indicates Judas to John, upon which Judas rises from the supper-table and goes out; Jesus feels that His hour is come; He gives a new commandment, the spirit of which His disciples are to see exemplified in His death; He predicts the denial of Peter (chap. xiii.). While at the table, He comforts His disciples, in view of His departure, with the assurance that He is going to the Father, and coming back again to them to be with them in a more intimate relationship than they had yet enjoyed; He promises to them His Spirit, and leaves with them His legacy of peace (chap. xiv.). After rising from table, He encourages them further with the thought of the closer relationship in which He was henceforth to stand to them, and the more direct dependence on His Spirit which in that relation they would enjoy, employing for illustration the parable of the

vine and the branches; He lays down the law of love; He further promises the Spirit as their Helper (chap. xv.). He explains the expediency of His going, and the profit it would bring to them; he assures them that the sorrow which is coming will erelong be a source of joy to them; they should have the love of His Father (chap. xvi.). He now lifts up His eyes to heaven, and prays the Father to glorify Him, and sanctify them and all that are His (chap. xvii.). He retires into a garden, into which Judas follows Him to betray Him; He is led before Annas, father-in-law of Caiaphas, the high-priest; John accompanies Him into the court, but Peter remains in the porch, and disowns his Master; interrogated by Annas as to His teaching, He replies that His teaching was open to all the world, and no secret; Peter meanwhile denies Him the third time; Jesus is led bound to Caiaphas, and from him to Pilate; Pilate interrogates Him, and would fain release Him (chap. xviii.). Pilate brings Him forth arrayed as a king, which He had professed to be before Pilate, and would have the people acknowledge Him, but they cry out, Crucify Him, saying they have no king but Cæsar; Pilate delivers Him to be crucified; He is crucified, with a title over the cross written by Pilate, JESUS OF NAZARETH, THE KING OF THE JEWS; the soldiers part His garments among them; Jesus sees His mother among the women around His cross, and bids her behold in John a son, and John in her a mother; shortly after, He gives up the ghost; His side is pierced; He is buried in Joseph's tomb (chap. xix.). On the early morning of the third day, Mary Magdalene visits the grave and finds it empty; Peter and John find her report true; as Mary stands by weeping, Jesus appears to her; Mary tells the disciples that she has seen Him; that day Jesus appears in the midst of His disciples, all except Thomas; Thomas, too, sees and believes (chap. xx.). Jesus appears in Galilee to seven of His disciples at the Sea of Tiberias, and reveals Himself by a miracle; He eats bread with the disciples; He interrogates and gives a charge to Simon Peter; the evangelist concludes his narrative with the declaration that what he has told gives us no adequate conception of the greatness of Jesus (chap. xxi.).

For the New Testament as a whole see Salmon, *Introd. to the New Test.*; Marcus Dods, *Introd. to the New Test.*; Jülicher, *Introduction New Test.*; Weiss, *A Manual of Introd. to the New Test.*; Godet, *Introd. to the New Test.*; Bennett and Adeney, *Biblical Introduction.* For the Gospels see Stanton, *The Gospels as Historical Documents;* Ezra Abbot, Peabody, Lightfoot, Sanday, and Drummond, on *John;* Watkins, *Modern Criticism of St. John.* For Commentaries on the Gospels see *The Expositor's Greek Testament;* Westcott, *St. John; The Cambridge Bible; The Century Bible; The Commentary for Schools* (Cassell).

CHAPTER XVI.

THE ACTS OF THE APOSTLES.

THE Acts of the Apostles, *Acta Apostolorum,* do not give an account of the apostolic ministry of all the apostles, but in the main only of two—

of St. Peter, and especially of St. Paul ; and the narrative forms a continuation of the third Gospel, St. Luke, while under the influence of St. Paul, being the author of both (see p. 61). It professes to have been composed by the writer of one of the Gospels, and that St. Luke is to be understood is inferred from the fact that it is dedicated to the same person as his Gospel (chap. i. 1-3). It is written, moreover, in the same style of language and from the same standpoint, and it takes up the story where St. Luke's Gospel narrative leaves off. The narrative of the Acts finishes with the imprisonment of St. Paul in Rome (A.D. 62); and it would almost seem as if the purpose of the author in the two accounts had been to sketch the progress of the Gospel from its rise in the cradle of Judæa to its throne in the heart of the heathen world, the planting of it in both being under the sign of the cross, which Christ had taught His disciples to regard as the principle of its triumph. In the one account we have Christ making offer of His Gospel to the Jews, and, in prospect of its rejection by them, commissioning His disciples to carry it to the heathen nations ; and in the other we see the rejection of it by the Jews pronounced, and St. Paul, a witness of it, in bonds in the capital of the pagan world. The crucifixion of the Master, recorded in the one, culminates in His resurrection from the dead and His ascension to heaven ; the imprisonment of St. Paul in Rome, recorded in the other, is in assurance of the triumph of the faith. The latter narrative embraces a period of about thirty years, and it divides itself into two sections—the first (a) extending to the end of chap. xii., and the second (b) finishing the story.

Contents.—(a.) Jesus, after His resurrection, charges His disciples to wait in Jerusalem for the promise of the Father. bids them thereafter bear witness to Him from Jerusalem as a centre to the utmost nations, and then is taken up from them under cover of a cloud, with assurances that He would come back again as He had gone away ; they wait in an upper chamber in Jerusalem for the promise of the Spirit, and select by lot a successor to Judas in the person of Matthias (chap. i.). The Spirit is poured out with accompanying signs, and the first Christian Church is founded in Jerusalem, with a glowing enthusiasm of brotherly love (chap. ii.). Peter heals a lame man at a gate of the Temple, and explains to the multitude that it was a sign to them of the resurrection from the dead of Him whom they had crucified, that they might believe (chap. iii.). Peter and John are arrested and summoned before the Sanhedrin, and they refer them to the miracle as a sign that He whom they had crucified was alive again, and was making offer to them of the one salvation from sin ; being dismissed with a warning, they return to their brethren, who, by the report they bring, are filled with greater boldness in the faith and greater self-sacrificing love to one another, each parting with all he has, and laying it for the common good at the apostles' feet (chap. iv.). Ananias and Sapphira, professing to give up all, and keeping back part, are struck dead ; upon which great fear comes upon the whole Church, and all feel a holy earnestness ; the apostles wax bolder, and work more miracles, to the increase of the Church ; they are put in prison by the Sanhedrin, but an

angel opens the prison door, and they are bid go and preach in the Temple ; they are thence brought before the council, and admonished, but plead they must obey God, and preach repentance to the people ; Gamaliel advises the Sanhedrin to let them alone, and await the issue ; the apostles being scourged, are let go, and wax bolder still (chap. v.). The apostles are released from the charge of the poor, and give themselves wholly to the ministry of the Word, to the greater increase and edification of the Church ; Stephen, one of those appointed to care for the poor, is brought before the Sanhedrin on a charge of blasphemy against Moses and against God (chap. vi.). Stephen defends himself, and turns the Jews' charge against them upon themselves, denouncing them as having all through their history persecuted and slain the prophets sent them, as they had done to Christ ; upon which they load him with execrations, and thereafter hurl him out of the city and stone him to death ; Saul stands by, consenting to the act (chap. vii.). A great persecution follows, and the disciples are scattered abroad, all except the apostles ; Philip goes down to Samaria, and many in Samaria receive the Word and are baptized, Simon Magus being one of them ; Peter and John follow him in the power of the Holy Ghost ; Simon thinks this power can be purchased with money, is convicted of his wickedness, and prays that they would intercede for him that he may be forgiven ; Philip comes upon a eunuch of Ethiopia on his way to Jerusalem, reading the Scriptures at Isaiah liii., and shows him that the prophecy is fulfilled in Jesus, so that he believes and is baptized (chap. viii.). Saul goes on a persecuting mission to Damascus, and is arrested on the way near the city, and struck blind by a great light and converted to Christ ; Ananias, a disciple, is sent to restore his sight, and baptize him ; the Jews lay wait for him in Damascus, but he escapes ; he goes up to Jerusalem to join the disciples, but preaches so boldly as to be in such danger of his life that he has to be sent to Tarsus ; the Church has peace and multiplies ; Peter heals Æneas at Lydda, and being sent for, goes to Joppa, and restores Dorcas to life (chap. ix.). Cornelius, a devout centurion, and a Gentile, is told in a vision to send for Peter ; Peter sees a vision sent to correct a prejudice against obeying this call natural to him as a Jew ; Peter goes with certain disciples, and as he preaches to Cornelius and his company, the Holy Ghost descends on them and they are baptized (chap. x.). Peter goes up to Jerusalem, and, being challenged, justifies the admission of Gentile believers to the Church ; a Gentile church is founded in Antioch, which is ministered to by Barnabas and Saul, and where the disciples were first called Christians ; the disciples here send relief to the famine-distressed brethren in Judæa by the hands of Barnabas and Saul (chap. xi.). James is put to death by Herod Agrippa, and Peter is cast into prison, but delivered by an angel ; Herod accepts Divine honours, and is smitten with judgment ; meanwhile the Word of God prevails (chap. xii.). (b.) Barnabas and Saul return to Antioch along with Mark, where they are set apart to minister among the Gentiles ; they visit Cyprus, where Saul, now called Paul, smites Elymas with blindness, because he withstands them ; Mark returns to Jerusalem, and they come to Antioch of Pisidia, where Paul preaches in the synagogue the resurrection of Jesus; this message is received as glad tidings by the Gentiles, but rejected by the Jews, who persecute the missionaries (chap. xiii.). They go to Iconium and make disciples, but are driven thence also by the unbelieving Jews; at Lystra, Paul heals a cripple, and the heathen people would offer sacrifices to them as to gods; some foreign Jews stir up the people against them, so that they stone them; after this they return to Antioch, establishing and confirming churches by the way (chap. xiv.). Paul and Barnabas go up to Jerusalem to obtain the consent of the apostles and elders to the admission of the Gentiles without circumcision; the consent is obtained, and a decree issued requiring the observance of certain general laws, and sent forth in the form of an epistle by the hands of Paul and Barnabas and others; Barnabas separates from Paul, who chooses Silas for companion; Paul strengthens the churches of Syria and Cilicia (chap. xv.). In Lystra Paul circumcises Timothy, and takes him with him; he is called to visit Macedonia, and sets sail from Troas to Philippi; Lydia and her household are baptized; Paul casts out a spirit of divination from a maiden who brought gain to her masters by soothsaying, and he and Silas, after being beaten with rods, are cast by the authorities into prison; the prison doors are opened, and the prisoners' bands loosed, in circumstances which lead to the conversion of the jailor; the magistrates learn that they are Romans, and beg them to leave the city (chap. xvi.). They go to Thessalonica, and Paul preaches Christ in the synagogue, but while many believe, the Jews raise a tumult against them, so that they have to leave; they pass on to Beroea, where they make converts, but are persecuted out of the place by Jews from Thessalonica; Paul goes to Athens, leaving Silas and Timothy to follow; Paul encounters Stoics and Epicureans; and on the Areopagus preaches repentance and the resurrection, while he rebukes the idolatry of the city; his preaching is not without fruit (chap. xvii.). Paul proceeds to Corinth, where he stays, working with Aquila and Priscilla, and preaching in the synagogue on the Sabbaths; the Jews oppose, and he turns to the Gentiles, remaining in the city a year and a half; the Jews bring Paul before Gallio, the pro-consul, but Gallio, refusing to hear the case, dismisses him; Paul goes up to Jerusalem by way of Cenchreae, Ephesus, and Caesarea, and returns to Antioch; Apollos, an Alexandrian, a man mighty in the Scriptures, is won over to the faith, and sent to Corinth (chap. xviii.). Paul goes to Ephesus; he instructs and baptizes twelve disciples of John; he preaches first in the synagogue, and then in the school of one Tyrannus; Paul expels evil spirits, and persuades many to give up sorcery; the word prevails; the silversmiths raise a tumult against Paul and his fellow-labourers as spoiling their craft, but the disturbance is quieted by a speech of the town-clerk (chap. xix.). Paul goes to Macedonia and Achaia, returning to Troas; here he preaches till midnight; he restores Eutychus, who, overcome with sleep, had fallen down from the third storey; Paul goes by Assos to Miletus, and returns to Ephesus on his way to Jerusalem; he bids farewell to the elders at Ephesus, and they

part with him sorrowfully (chap. xx.). He lands at Tyre, where he is warned not to go up to Jerusalem; passing on to Caesarea, he is warned by a prophet from Judaea not to go, as the Jews there will deliver him to the Gentiles; he is determined to go up, though entreated to stay; he arrives, and visits the church, giving an account of the progress of the gospel; he is persuaded to pay a Jewish vow that he may conciliate the Jews; when he appears in the Temple, the Jews drag him forth and seek to kill him; the military interfere, and convey him to the castle, the crowd shouting, Away with him; he obtains permission from the captain to speak to the people (chap. xxi.). He bespeaks their favour by the narrative of his conversion, but when he comes to his mission to the Gentiles, they stop their ears and call for his death; the chief captain has him bound with a view to scourge him, but abstains when he learns that he is a Roman citizen (chap. xxii.). The chief captain has the Sanhedrin summoned together to hear him, but commands his soldiers to convey him back to the castle, lest he should be torn in pieces; forty men make a vow to kill him, and the chief captain, hearing of it, has him sent off under a guard to Caesarea, to Felix the governor, who detains him till his accusers come (chap. xxiii.). In five days a deputation arrives from the Sanhedrin, accompanied by Tertullus, an orator, who makes formal accusation; Felix hears Paul's defence, but defers judgment till he is better informed; he treats Paul courteously, and has private interviews with him, but comes to no decision, and hands him over to Festus, his successor (chap. xxiv.). The Jews accuse Paul to Festus, and would have him tried in Jerusalem, but he summons them before him at Caesarea; Paul defends himself, refuses to be tried in Jerusalem, and appeals to Caesar; Festus informs King Agrippa of Paul and his case; Agrippa wishes to hear Paul, and Paul is brought (chap. xxv.). Paul relates the story of his conversion, and preaches Christ as the fulfilment of the Jewish Scriptures; Festus regards him as a fanatic, but Agrippa is half inclined to believe him, and would have set him free if he had not appealed to Caesar (chap. xxvi.). Paul is shipped for Rome, and is treated with great indulgence by the way; he is shipwrecked, but saved, as are all on shipboard with him, agreeably to a promise given him from the Lord (chap. xxvii.). Cast on the island of Melita, he is treated kindly by the barbarians; they are fain to worship him as a god when they see how a viper which fastens on his hand does not harm him; he heals many sick on the island, and is sent away with friendly tokens; he arrives at Rome, a convoy of brethren going out to meet him; he has an abode by himself, with the soldier that guards him; he calls together the chief Jews in the city, and explains the occasion of his being in Rome; they are desirous of hearing him further; on a given day he reasons with them from morning to night out of their own Scriptures, to persuade them to the faith of Christ, some believing, and some disbelieving; he stays in Rome two whole years, and testifies boldly of the kingdom of God (chap. xxviii.).

See Hachett, *Commentary on Acts;* Bartlet, *Acts* (Century Bible); Plumtre, *Commentary for Schools, Acts;* Ramsay, *The Church in the Roman Empire.*

CHAPTER XVII.

THE PAULINE EPISTLES.

1. *Their Author.*—St. Paul, originally called Saul, was born in Tarsus, the capital of Cilicia, of parents who were Jews, apparently of a strict type, but he had the rights of Roman citzenship. He was sent when young to Jerusalem, where he studied at the feet of a great Jewish doctor, Gamaliel, and wrought at the trade of a tent-maker. Here he became zealous for the law, and distinguished himself by his enmity against those Jews who had apostatised from the faith of their fathers. He went about persecuting the Christians everywhere, and dragging them before the Sanhedrin, that they might be put to death, till, on the road near Damascus, whither he was bound, under commission from the Sanhedrin, in the work of persecution, he was arrested in his course, and suddenly converted, by a revelation of the glorified Christ Himself, into a disciple and preacher of the faith he had been seeking to crush (A.D. 35). The Book of the Acts records this narrative, as well as that of his missionary activity in the cause of Christ, and carries on his history till his appearance as a prisoner in Rome, in response to his appeal to answer to Cæsar the charges made against him. All through his career, as occasion required, he was ever and anon writing letters to the churches he had founded; and, in concern for their welfare, he wrote, from his imprisonment at Rome (A.D. 62), probably four epistles—those, namely, to the Ephesians, the Colossians, Philemon, and the Philippians, certainly the last. He appears to have been allowed (A.D. 63) a short furlough, which he used in visiting some of the churches; and on his return, in A.D. 65, he wrote letters to Timothy and Titus, as bearers of a commission from him to the churches respectively in Ephesus and Crete. There is a tradition that he visited Spain sometime during this period, according to a wish he had to carry the gospel-message to the western limits of the empire; but whether he did so or not, it was in the city of Rome his career was cut short, yet as he writes to Timothy, not till he had fulfilled his ministry (2 Tim. iv. 7). St. Paul is represented in Christian art with a sword, in symbol of his martyrdom; and an open book, in symbol of the new truth of which he was the apostle. He is generally painted as a man of short stature, with a bald forehead and a bushy grey beard; while the events of his life treated by the arts are chiefly his conversion, his baptism, his smiting Elymas blind, his shaking the viper off his hand into the fire, and his martyrdom.

2. *Their general purport.*—The general purport of these epistles is to teach that salvation is not possible by the works of the law, but is the free gift of God by and in Jesus Christ; and that every man, Jew as well as Gentile, is equally in need of, as he is equally welcome to this salvation, which is represented as experienced by faith in Christ crucified leading to death with Christ, rising again with Christ, and living with Christ in the inner life. This is the burden of the epistles, as it is the sum of St. Paul's gospel, and it is the exact opposite of the Pharisaic creed in which he had been brought up; his antagonism to that creed now not only enabled him to define better the character of the new faith, but to become to all nations the apostle of it as a religion deriving its inspiration direct from Christ, and alone adequate to the exigency of Jew and Gentile alike, seeing "all had sinned and come short of the glory of God." Both had failed to work out their own righteousness, and both were equally dependent on the righteousness of God in Christ.

3. *Their form.*—The style of these letters shows a man of an eager and impetuous temper, who, on that account, as well as through the fulness of his matter, is impatient of dialectic restraint. The theme is a pressing one, and the writer is too intent to gain his end to study his steps. In his hurry to carry his thought forward he sometimes forgets what he has been saying, and passes on to another point, more urgent perhaps, leaving the original sentence unfinished; while in his eagerness to express himself he is often careless of the coherence of his thought. He has no time to adjust himself to any formulæ: he must make his way at any expense. All forms are alike to him, and he will use any or use none, if only he can thereby gain his point. In his zeal for the issue, he becomes a Jew to the Jew, and a Greek to the Greek, and all things to all men, if so be he may win some. He appears in these epistles as a man who has a work to do, and who in the doing of it casts aside every weight.

A. *The Great Doctrinal Epistles.*

We have first a group of the four great epistles, the genuineness of which is not doubted by any critics of weight. These are Romans, 1 and 2 Corinthians, and Galatians. They have been called the "quadrilateral of Christianity," and they contain in themselves enough to establish the main truths of Christianity. They were written about the same time. There is more vigour in them than in any of the other epistles, and they have several points in common.

The Epistle to the Romans: 1. *The Church at Rome.*—This Church appears to have consisted partly of Jews and Jewish proselytes, but chiefly of Gentiles, who by the time the epistle was written, were formed into a regularly organised community. It is not known when or by whom this community was founded, but it would appear that Aquila and Priscilla, with whom Paul consorted at Corinth (Acts xviii.), were among the most conspicuous and zealous members. Possibly the Church was founded by pilgrims from Pentecost. It certainly was planted neither by Paul nor by Peter. Nevertheless St. Paul had been brought into very close relationship with it through those persons of whom he had been the spiritual teacher, so that he might well feel himself responsible for its welfare, and bound to see that its members were grounded and settled in the faith. It was of especial moment, too, that this Church, which was planted in the very centre of the Pagan world, should clearly and fully comprehend the Christian gospel; and there were urgent reasons why, seeing he could not visit the Church in person, Paul should communicate with it by letter. There were two errors of fundamental importance against which

I. CORINTHIANS.

it was necessary he should at once caution the Church at Rome, and it was to correct these errors that he wrote his epistle. It had come to his ears that the Jewish Christians, on the one hand, challenged the equal rights of the Gentiles, as such, to the privileges of the gospel; and that the Gentile Christians, on the other, regarded the rejection of the Jews as their final exclusion from God's kingdom; and he wrote this epistle partly to show that the one had no more right to the grace of God than the other, and that this grace contemplates the final conversion of the Jew as well as the Gentile.

2. *The date and place of the Composition of the Epistle.*—This, though it holds the first rank among the epistles of St. Paul, was not the first written, but the sixth, and was preceded by the two to the Thessalonians, that to the Galatians, and the two to the Corinthians. It was written at Corinth in the year A.D. 58, on the occasion of St. Paul's second visit to that city, and on the eve of his going up to Jerusalem with the proceeds of a collection made in Macedonia and Achaia (chap. xv. 25); and it appears to have been conveyed to the Church at Rome by Phœbe, a deaconess of the Church at Cenchreæ, a port of Corinth (chap. xvi. 1).

3. *The theme and the significance of the Epistle.*—The great theme of this epistle is, Righteousness a free gift of God, and Faith in Jesus Christ as the one way of salvation for all mankind, Jew as well as Gentile; and the significance of it is this, that it contains, if not the whole teaching of its author, that essential part of it which presents and emphasises the all-sufficiency of this faith.

4. *Its divisions.*—These are three: the first (a) (chaps. i.–viii.) showing how Jews and Gentiles possess by faith in Christ the only and perfect means of attaining salvation; the second (b) (chaps. ix.–xi.) showing how the Jew, though he has failed of attaining salvation, because he could not reconcile himself to the way, will one day be persuaded to believe, and by his conversion become a power in persuading others; and the third (c) (chaps. xii.–xvi.) showing the power of faith to sanctify the life in all its relations.

5. *Contents.*—a. Paul, in his capacity of apostle, salutes the Church as called to saintship, and wishes them grace (chap. i. 1–7); he expresses his affection for them and longing to visit them (8–15); he states the theme of the epistle, that righteousness is of God for Jew and Gentile alike and by faith (16, 17). No man can otherwise attain to this righteousness, since all are guilty before God and under condemnation (chaps. i. 18–iii. 20). Man ever attains to this righteousness only by faith, as appears in Abraham's justification (chaps. iii. 21–iv. 25). By this means, faith in Christ namely, man attains a blissful sense of acceptance with God (chap. v. 1–11). This acceptance in Christ is as universal as guilt and condemnation in Adam (12–21). This grace does not weaken, but it strengthens the obligations of righteousness, while it frees from the fetters of law (chaps. vi.–vii. 1–6). Yet is the law itself good, and only the occasion of evil by the operation of an evil principle which is hostile to man's better will (7–25). This contradiction can be removed only through Christ, whose spirit gives freedom, a sense of adoption, and the assurance of future glory (chap. viii.).

b. It is sad to think that the Jew has rejected this way of salvation (chap. ix. 1–5). Yet the promise was never to all the race, only to a select seed (6–13). This purpose of God is not to be challenged by us (14–19). The Jew has not attained to salvation because, as foreshadowed, he has not sought it aright (chap. x. 1–21). Yet is his rejection not final; it has paved the way for the admission of the Gentiles, through whom he too will be brought to Christ (chap. xi.).

c. St. Paul exhorts to holiness of life and charity in general, while he recommends obedience to rulers (chaps. xii. and xiii.) He exhorts to consideration for weaker brethren (chaps. xiv.–xv. 13). He explains his motive in writing this letter, and expresses his intention of visiting Rome (14–33). He sends greetings, and concludes with a benediction and a doxology (chap. xvi.).

I. **Corinthians: 1. *The Church at Corinth.*—**This Church was founded by St. Paul during the year and a half which he spent in the city in the course of his second missionary journey (Acts xviii.), and it consisted partly of Jewish, but mainly of Gentile converts, who, with one or two exceptions, were of the humbler class of citizens (chap. i. 26 seq.), the more cultivated classes holding aloof, and either treating it with scorn or setting it at nought. Not the less was this obscure community of deep interest to him who had planted it, and the apostle was careful to see that, when circumstances required him to go elsewhere, some one worthy to succeed him should be sent to carry on the work he had begun. Unhappily, however, Apollos, the substitute sent, was a more eloquent man than his master; and though he preached the same gospel, he presented it in a form which, while it might edify some, only dazzled others, and diverted their minds from the simplicity of the truth. The result was, that some preferred Apollos and others Paul; and a controversy arose to the disparagement of both, the weakening of their influence, and the damage of the gospel. This was a great grief to St. Paul, which was deepened still more by the presence of other elements of discord, in the rise of a Petrine party and a Christ party, both equally hostile to himself, and both bent on undermining his authority as an apostle. The Petrine party was probably intent on mixing up Jewish elements with Christianity, and the Christ party no less intent on discarding apostolic authority and human instrumentality altogether, being out of sympathy with and in antagonism to the other three, the Pauline, Apollonian, and Petrine sections. Such was the state of schism in the Church at Corinth when St. Paul wrote this epistle; the epistle itself will show what other evils required correction when it was written, and prompted the writing of it.

2. *The date and place of the Composition of the Epistle.*—The epistle was written at Ephesus towards the end of his nearly three years' stay in that city, a little before Easter, in A.D. 57 (chap. xvi. 8), after he had despatched Timothy to Corinth, and after he had himself resolved to journey through Macedonia and Achaia before going up to Jerusalem. Probably it was the third written of St. Paul's epistles, being preceded by I. and II. Thessalonians.

3. *Its occasion and object.*—The occasion of writ-

ing the epistle was—(1) the receipt of the tidings that had reached the apostle through "those of the household of Chloe" regarding the divisions in the Church; (2) the information he had received of a grievous case of immorality, as well as other faults in both faith and practice; and (3) the receipt of certain questions affecting practice referred to him for solution by the Church itself. The object of the epistle was fourfold : (1) to testify against the party divisions that had arisen, and to vindicate the writer's own authority; (2) to clear the Church of the impurities that had crept into it; (3) to counsel and direct the Church in the matters submitted to the apostle for decision; and (4) to instruct it in other matters in regard to which it seemed necessary and useful that he should set it right.

4. *Contents.*—Paul, as an apostle, salutes the Church, as called to saintship, and gives thanks for their growth in grace (chap. i. 1-9); he enlarges on their party divisions, and vindicates his own mode of teaching, intimating Timothy's mission to them, and his own intended visit (chaps. i. 10-iv. 21); he deals with the case of immorality, and censures the indifference of the Church in the matter, referring to a former epistle in regard to keeping company with fornicators (chap. v.); he condemns the practice of litigation before heathen tribunals, and reverts to the plague-spot of unchastity (chap. vi.); he answers the inquiries of the Church about marriage, and about the celibacy of virgins and widows (chap. vii.); he treats of eating things sacrificed to idols, and of Christian freedom generally (chap. viii.); he shows how he waived his own right and performed his duties (chap. ix.); he returns to the subject of meats offered to idols (chap. x.); he censures and corrects certain disorders in the assemblies of the Church, particularly in respect of the behaviour of women and the celebration of the Lord's Supper (chap. xi.); then follow the sections respecting the exercise of spiritual gifts, including the magnificent panegyric of charity (chaps. xii.-xiv.); he next expounds and defends the doctrine of the resurrection (chap. xv.); he gives directions concerning collections, writes of his own movements, commends Timothy and others, conveys greetings, and concludes with a salutation and benediction (chap. xvi.).

II. Corinthians: 1. *The place and date of the Composition of the Epistle.*—This epistle was written in the same year as the first epistle, but from Macedonia, whither the apostle had gone to meet Titus, whom he had sent to Corinth to ascertain and report to him the state of matters in the Corinthian Church before he himself visited it.

2. *Its occasion and object.*—The occasion of writing this epistle arose from the reports which first Timothy and then Titus had brought to St. Paul regarding the effect of the previous epistle on the dispositions and relations of the Corinthian Church; and one object of writing it was to regain their confidence as an apostle of the Lord, so that, when he appeared among them in person, it might not be in the spirit of chastisement, but for edification in love; his main purpose being to re-establish among them his apostolic character and reputation, which the Petrine party especially had sought to undermine.

3. *Its general character and divisions.*—It breathes a spirit, on the one hand, of thankful-

ness, and, on the other, of indignation : of thankfulness that the admonitions of the first epistle had produced the desired effect; and of indignation at those who still sought to question the authority of an apostle whose ministry had been so sealed and sanctioned by the Spirit's work. Erasmus compares its course to that of "a river which sometimes flows in a gentle stream, sometimes rushes down as a torrent bearing all before it, sometimes spreads out like a placid lake, sometimes loses itself, as it were, in the sand, and breaks out in its fulness at some unexpected place." It has been divided into three sections— the first (*a*), in which St. Paul sets forth his apostolic character and course of life, and his feeling in regard to the effect of the previous epistle (chaps. i.-vii.); the second (*b*), in which he gives directions about the collection for the poor saints in Judæa (chaps. viii., ix.); and the third (*c*), in which he vindicates his apostolic authority as against the Petrine party (chaps. x.-xiii.).

4. *Contents.*—(*a*) Paul gives thanks for the general state of the Church (chap. i. 1-14); he speaks of the visit he had promised, and his reason for putting it off (cuaps. i. 15-ii. 2); he refers to his former letter and his plans (chap. ii. 3-17); he refers to the fruits of his ministry, and ascribes the effect to God (chap. iii. 1-5); he exalts his ministry, and justifies his plain speaking (6-18); he dwells on the spirit and nature of his own labours (chap. iv.), of his own hopes (chap. v.), and of his own sufferings (chap. vi. 1-10); he protests his affection for the Corinthians, and dissuades them from intimacy with unbelievers (11-18); he further declares his views and feelings towards them (chap. vii.); (*b*) he exhorts them to liberality, and commends Titus to them (chaps. viii., ix.); (*c*)—perhaps an earlier epistle by St. Paul—his apostolic authority (chap. x.); he asserts his apostolic dignity (chap. xi. 1-7); he illustrates his forbearance (8-20); he dwells on his apostolic labours (21-33); he refers to revelations, but glories in his infirmities (chap. xii. 1-11); he refers again to the nature of his dealings with his converts (12-21); he concludes with warnings, greetings, and a doxology (chap. xiii.).

Galatians: 1. *The Churches in Galatia.*—Under the influence of Bishop Lightfoot's arguments, it had come to be generally supposed that the Galatians to whom St. Paul addressed his epistle were the Celtic people in the north of Asia Minor, the descendants of some vanquished hordes of invading Galatæ, or Gauls, who had come over, for marauding purposes, from Europe by way of the Hellespont, in the middle of the third century B.C., and were subject to Rome from 189 B.C., till the country was formed into a Roman province under Augustus in 25 B.C. But this province was much larger than the territory occupied by the emigrants, extending as far south as the towns of Antioch, Iconium, Derbe, and Lystra; and Professor Ramsay has adduced a mass of evidence to show that the name "Galatians" is given to St. Paul's correspondents in the more comprehensive sense, so that probably the epistle is addressed to the Churches which he founded during his first missionary journey, an account of which is given in Acts xiv. The epistle itself tells with what enthusiasm the Galatians listened to his words, and with what devotion they regarded his person. During the visit he paid to Galatia in the course of his third missionary journey, it would appear, he saw signs that the Judaising emissaries were, as usual, on his track, and he warned the Churches to be on their guard against them. He had hardly left, however, when he heard, to his sorrow, that these Judaisers were at work, and had persuaded the Churches to doubt, not only his apostolic authority, but even the truth of his teaching. He had taught them that for justification before God nothing more was necessary than to believe in the grace of God in Christ; but these intruders had persuaded them that they must also submit to circumcision. Many had suffered themselves to be deluded, and had submitted to this rite, especially in order that they might thereby escape the persecutions to which they were subjected by the Jews, while some of the rest had both spurned this yoke and given loose reins to their spiritual freedom.

2. *The date and place of the composition of the Epistle.*—On these points the greatest diversity of opinion prevails. The general opinion has been that the epistle was written in Ephesus some time between the years A.D. 54–57, and prior to the first Epistle to the Corinthians. But Bishop Lightfoot assigns good reasons for believing it was written from Macedonia or Achaia in the winter or spring of 57–58, and for interposing it between the second to the Corinthians and the Epistle to the Romans. He points out the remarkable resemblance between this epistle and that to the Romans, of the argument of which this is a sort of first rough draught; and he shows how improbable it is that a long interval of time could divide the two, and that epistles in some respect so different as those to the Corinthians should come between them.

3. *The object and character of the Epistle.*—It was to heal the mischiefs caused by his Judaising enemies that St. Paul wrote this epistle; in which, with holy zeal, he, on the one hand, defended his apostolic authority and the truth of his doctrine, and, on the other, repudiated the false spiritual freedom that had asserted itself, and showed how the man who was spiritually free would walk in the Spirit, and no longer fulfil the lusts of the flesh. Thus this is a true didactic epistle, being an assertion, on the one hand, of freedom from the law and justification by faith, and, on the other, of the fulfilment of the law by the power of the Spirit. Both these topics are presented and handled here as in no other epistle; the main theme of the apostle throughout is the apostasy of the Galatian Churches in their denial of his apostolic authority, and their repudiation of the doctrine of grace. "The sustained severity of this epistle," says Bishop Lightfoot, "is an equally characteristic feature with its unity of purpose. The Galatians are not addressed as the 'saints in Christ,' 'the faithful brethren.' The apostle has no congratulations, no word of praise for this apostate Church. . . . For this once only the pervading type of his epistles is abandoned, in the omission of the opening thanksgiving. The argument is interrupted every now and then by an outburst of indignant remonstrance. He is dealing with a thoughtless, half-barbarous people. They have erred like children, and must

be chastised like children. Rebuke may prevail where reason will be powerless." This epistle was Martin Luther's especial favourite; and well it might be, for it corroborated the great revelation first made to him by the pious monk, as he struggled blindly after spiritual light and freedom, "a man is not saved by singing masses, but by the grace of God,"—"a much more credible hypothesis," echoes Carlyle.

4. *Divisions.*—The epistle is divisible into three sections of two chapters each—the first (*a*) (chaps. i., ii.) being a vindication of Paul's claim to the apostleship; the second (*b*) (chaps. iii., iv.) a vindication of his doctrine; and the third (*c*) (chaps. v., vi.) hortatory or practical.

5. *Contents.*—(*a.*) Paul salutes the Churches as an apostle divinely appointed (chap. i. 1–5); he rebukes them for their departure from his gospel (6–10) he affirms that his gospel was revealed to him by God, and shows how otherwise he could not have received it (11–24); he shows further how he owed nothing to the other apostles, and had even rebuked Peter for compromising the gospel and substituting law for grace (chap. ii. 1–21). (*b.*) He remonstrates with the Galatians for having gone back to seek justification by works, after accepting salvation by faith, and shows that Abraham, whose children they would fain be, was justified by faith, and that the law could not justify (chap. iii. 1–12). Christ, he pleads, had freed from the curse of the law, and so fulfilled the promise made to Abraham prior to the law (13–18); the law, he argues, had been given to prepare for and lead up to the gospel (19–29); the law, he argues further, is for minors, and not men of full age, to which state, he says, the Galatians are bent on returning; after which he appeals to their former affection for him, and reprobates the conduct of those who would mislead them (chap. iv. 1–20); the law, he shows, bears witness against itself in the story of Hagar and Sarah viewed typically, the child of promise being the heir, to whom the son of the bondwoman must give way (21–31). (*c.*) Paul exhorts the Galatians to hold fast the freedom from the bondage of law which his gospel gives and which the false teachers are endangering, and beware lest this freedom degenerate into licentiousness (chap. v. 1–26); he exhorts to forbearance, friendly feeling, and liberality (chap. vi. 1–10); he cautions once more against the Judaisers, and appeals to his sufferings as proof of his sincerity (11–18).

B. *Epistles of the Captivity.*

Ephesians: 1. *The Churches addressed.*—Though, as it now appears in our New Testaments, this epistle is addressed to "the saints which are at Ephesus," there are good grounds for believing that the expression "at Ephesus" was not in the original text, but that it was inserted afterwards on the assumption that Ephesus was meant, for the expression is wanting in some of the oldest MSS. The epistle is referred to without challenge by Marcion, an early heresiarch, under the name of an Epistle to the Laodiceans; it does not contain, as St. Paul's usual manner of writing leads us to expect, any reference to the Church in question, or any greetings to individual members; and it appears from chap. iii. 2 of the epistle itself, "that its writer was personally unknown to those to whom he wrote, and that they, on their part, knew of him and of his work rather by the information of others than by actual experience," which was not the case with the Ephesians. Ephesus, as specially intended, being set aside, two other theories have been invented bearing upon its destination. The first and more probable one is that it is a circular letter, meant not for Ephesus alone, but for a number of Churches over a wider or narrower area in Asia Minor, or rather, perhaps, to be copied out afresh for each Church with the name of the Church filled in, so that the copy we have was really directed to Ephesus by the copyist; and the second is, that it is the epistle referred to in Col. iv. 16, and that it was not meant to be an epistle to the Church of Laodicea, but an "epistle to the Gentile converts, as such, in the first place of Laodicea, and, in the second place, of Colossæ."

2. *Genuineness of the Epistle.*—Though not unquestioned by some critics, this epistle stands on good evidence as a work of St. Paul. Not to mention doubtful allusions in Ignatius and Polycarp, Tertullian, Clement, and Origen testify to it. The only reasons for throwing doubts on the epistle have been derived from internal criticism. (1.) The style is said to be feeble. But the quiet subject did not call for the passionate language of the earlier epistles. Paul was now an old man, and in the calm of forced seclusion. (2.) It is said to contain references to Gnostic errors. True; but it has no allusions to the elaborate Gnostic systems of later days. Gnostic ideas are as early as Simon Magus. The spirit and thought of the epistle are worthy of the apostle throughout.

3. *Date and place of composition.*—This epistle appears to have been the earliest written during St. Paul's first imprisonment in Rome (A.D. 61–63). It dates from near the same time as the Epistle to the Colossians, as is evident not merely from the fact that Tychicus was the bearer of both (comp. chap. vi. 21 with Col. iv. 7), but also from the close affinity between them both in matter and style. The identity in style appears in the length and intricacy of the sentences; and the similarity of theme will appear if we compare chap. i. 10 with Col. i. 20; chap. i. 21 with Col. i. 16 and 20; chap. ii. 5 with Col. ii. 13; and chap. iv. 22 *seq.* with Col. iii. 8 *seq.*

4. *Occasion and object.*—The occasion of writing this letter was the opportunity that offered in the mission of Tychicus and Onesimus to the Church at Colossæ; and the object is to show that the Gentiles had a standing in Christ as well as the Jews; that their call into the Church was no mere accident, that it was the eternal purpose of God to gather all into oneness, or one body, in Christ, and that except in this oneness the fulness of Christ would not be revealed. Thus the epistle sets before us, as has been said, St. Paul's doctrine of the Church, the Church in its unity, "the completion of an edifice whose foundations had been laid in a past eternity, and which was to stand for ever."

5. *Contents.*—Paul salutes saints of the Gentiles in Christ Jesus, and refers the grace they have received to the eternal purpose of God to make them sharers in His salvation (chap. i. 1–14). He expresses his anxiety that they may realise the import of their calling and life in Christ (15–23). They had been raised by grace from a state of spiritual death to a state of spiritual life in the risen Christ, and were no longer "aliens, but of the household of God," united into one fellowship " for a habitation of God through the Spirit" (chap. ii.). It was for vindicating their privileges he was that day in bonds, and he begs them not to faint at his sufferings for their sake (chap. iii. 1–13). He prays for the continued indwelling of Christ in their hearts by faith (14–19). He ascribes praise to the Father in whose glory all terminates (20, 21). He urges them to use their diverse spiritual gifts for the edification of the one body whose head is Christ (chap. iv. 1–16). They must abandon their former principles and practices, and follow those which they have learned of Christ (17–24). This change must show itself in certain Christian virtues (25–32). They must imitate Christ, study purity, walk in the light, and shame the darkness (chap. v. 1–14). He enforces other virtues and exercises (15–21). He exhorts wives and husbands (22–32). He exhorts children and parents (chap. vi. 1–4). He exhorts masters and servants (5–9). He shows the secret of their strength, who their enemies are, and what the weapons of their warfare (10–20). He refers them to Tychicus, and wishes them peace (21–24).

Philippians : 1. *The Church at Philippi.*—This Church was the first planted by St. Paul, under Divine guidance, on the soil of Europe (about A.D. 52), Silas, with Luke and Timothy, being his associates in the work (Acts xvi.). The city, though founded by Philip of Macedon, was at this time a colony of Rome, having been so constituted by Augustus Cæsar, and its inhabitants were Roman citizens, jealous of their rights. The Jews appear to have formed a small portion of the community; they had not even a synagogue, but only a "place of prayer" beyond the confines of the city by the river side. It was to them, however, that St. Paul made his first appeal, and among those who worshipped with them he here won his first convert to Christ. This was Lydia, an Asiatic, a dealer in purple, whom, together with her household, he baptized into the Christian faith. Other conversions among the Gentiles soon followed, special mention being made of a Greek divining girl and the Roman jailor with his family, both of whom had seen evidences of the Divine power which accompanied the apostle's word. Such were the first fruits of St. Paul's ministry in Europe, and an earnest of its final conquest to Christ. Between the Church which grew out of these beginnings and its founder there subsisted all along a mutual affectionate regard, and the present epistle bears witness to the fact. He never ceased to care for their welfare, and they alone of all the Churches showed their affection for him by contributing to his support. They never entertained any doubt of his apostolic authority, nor questioned any doctrine that they had heard from his lips. The enemy had as yet sown no tares among them, and St. Paul saluted them as his "joy and crown" (chap. iv. 1).

2. *Genuineness of the Epistle.*—This cannot be reasonably doubted. The epistle bears the impress of the character of the apostle. There is nothing in it to suggest a motive for a forgery.

Clement of Rome—who may have known Paul —appears to allude to the epistle. Ignatius quite early in the second century refers to it. The epistle of the Churches of Lyons and Vienne (A.D. 177) quotes from it, and other writers equally early appear to allude to it.

3. *Date and place of composition.*—This epistle was written at Rome some time during St. Paul's imprisonment there, the only question being whether it was at the commencement or the close—that is, before or after the Epistles to the Colossians, Ephesians, and Philemon, all of which were written or despatched at or about the same time. The general opinion of scholars has been that it was written after these, but Bishop Lightfoot questioned this conclusion, and adduced strong reasons for assigning to it a prior date. His chief arguments are that in style and tone, as well as in the more prominent ideas, it bears a closer resemblance to St. Paul's earlier letters than his later ; and he quotes a number of passages to show how it resembles the Epistle to the Romans more closely than any other (comp. chap. i. 10 with Rom. ii. 18 ; chap. ii. 8-11 with Rom. xiv. 9-11 ; chap. ii. 2-4 with Rom. xii. 16-19 ; chap. iii. 4, 5, with Rom. xi. 1 ; chap. iii. 9 with Rom. x. 3 and ix. 31, 32, &c.) ; while, on the other hand, in the Epistles to the Colossians and Ephesians St. Paul has to grapple with errors which had not yet arisen when this epistle was written, so that he has to deal with a maturer development of Christian thought in those epistles.

4. *Occasion and character.*—The occasion for writing this letter was to acknowledge a message and a gift which the Philippians sent the apostle by the hands of Epaphroditus ; and one main object of it was to testify his joy over their manifestation of affection, to stir up in them the like gladness of heart, and to make his own joy more complete. It is the least dogmatic of all St. Paul's epistles, deals with no special phase of error, and presents in the most direct form a simple statement of Christian truth, such as the apostle was in the habit of expounding to minds unbiassed. Though he has no occasion specially to combat any error in doctrine, he cannot be blind to the rise in the Church of a spirit of rivalry, and he sets before them by way of example the self-sacrificing lowliness of Christ, and urges the cultivation of loyalty to everything noble and good.

5. *Contents.*—Paul sends a salutation to the Church, in which Timothy joins him (chap. i. 1, 2). He shows how much he has their spiritual state at heart, and how he prays for their growth in grace (3-11). He rejoices in his bonds as tending to the furtherance of the gospel, and is prepared to endure all for Christ's sake (12-26). He exhorts the Philippians to stand fast in the same spirit, and learn to deny themselves even as Christ did (chaps. i. 27-ii. 11). They must work out their salvation that they may approve themselves as the children of God (12-17). He purposes to visit them, but meanwhile sends Timothy to them, and Epaphroditus, who had fallen ill in ministering to his wants (18-30). He digresses to warn them against the Judaisers (chap. iii. 1-14), and against the Antinomians (chaps. iii. 15-iv. 1). He prays them to be of the same mind in the Lord, mentioning certain names (2, 3). He bids them rejoice, dismiss all anxiety, and aim at all noble things (4-9). He acknowledges their gifts as a token of their love, and wishes them every spiritual blessing in Christ (10-20). He sends salutations and his farewell benediction (21-23).

Colossians : 1. *The Church at Colossæ.*—This Church was not directly founded by St. Paul himself, but by Epaphras—who was a native of Colossæ, and who had been a convert, disciple, and delegate of his—probably about the time of the apostle's three years' sojourn in Ephesus (A.D. 54 or 55-57) ; and it appears to have been the least considerable of all the Churches to which he indited an epistle. The place, which was in Phrygia, and the ruins of which are hardly recognisable to-day, was by no means so important as Laodicea and Hierapolis, cities in the same valley, some twelve or fifteen miles to the west and north-west of it, where Christian Churches were also established ; and St. Paul does not seem to have even visited it. It was nevertheless a Pauline Church, because planted by an esteemed fellow-labourer of the apostle, and one in whose prosperity, therefore, St. Paul took a special interest, the more that he had heard of mischievous influences operating in the midst of it, such as threatened to frustrate the work of grace and to imperil its spiritual future (comp. chap. ii. 8, 16, and 20 seq.).

2. *Genuineness.*—Doubts have been raised by some as to the genuineness of this epistle on account of its reference to Gnostic heresies, and on account of its style being unlike that of St. Paul's earlier epistles. Even the negative critics have recently conceded that the epistle contains a nucleus undoubtedly written by St. Paul. But this concession should lead to the giving up of all question to the most sceptical, for the epistle holds together as one composition. It is no patchwork. Church writers from the middle of the second century refer to it as St. Paul's.

3. *Date and place of composition.*—This epistle was written in Rome, and probably about the year 63, and sent to Colossæ, together with the Epistles to the Ephesians and Philemon, by the hands of Tychicus, who was probably a native of Ephesus, and Onesimus, a converted runaway Colossian slave (see PHILEMON).

4. *Occasion and object.*—The occasion of St. Paul's writing the epistle was the report which he had received from Epaphras—who had come, as appears, all the way from Colossæ to Rome to consult him—concerning the condition of the Colossian Church and the dangers that threatened it ; and the object he had in writing it was to confirm its members in the faith they had received, and to guard them against certain errors in doctrine and practice which had appeared among them, and which, if indulged in, would be sure to corrupt and subvert the Church. There are two special errors, apparently in part of Jewish and in part of Gnostic derivation, against the anti-Christian character of which the Colossian Church is here warned—the first a doctrinal one, that the fleshly nature of man is not adequate vehicle for the reception and revelation of the Divine nature ; and the second, a practical one, deducible from it, that for the redemption of the spirit we must have recourse to direct mortification and purification of the flesh. The doctrine, as given from the first in the creed of the

Church, which St. Paul opposes to the former of these errors, is that all Divine fulness is literally incarnated in Christ; while the practical truth, as given from the first in the being of the Church, which he opposes to the latter error, is that our redemption from evil, and our victory over it, are achieved by fellowship with this Christ in His death and in His risen life. This is a twin epistle with the Epistle to the Ephesians. The two were written at about the same time; they resemble one another in thought, temper, and style; but while the letter to the Ephesians expounds the doctrine of the Church, this epistle sets forth the glory of Christ as chief theme.

5. *Contents.*—Paul salutes the Church, is grateful for their present attainments, and prays for their further advancement in the faith of Christ (chap. i. 1-12). He exalts Christ as Redeemer, as Head of the visible and invisible—*i.e.,* the natural and spiritual—universe, and His reconciling work (13-20). This Christ is their reconciler, and Paul as His minister is anxious to present them perfect in Him (chaps. i. 21-ii. 3). He charges them to abide in the truth which they had received (4-8). This truth was that all Divine fulness is in Christ, that the circumcision He requires is spiritual, that he has abolished the law of ordinances, and that He has triumphed over all spiritual powers (9-15). They must therefore forego mere ritual practices, and the worship of inferior beings, and identify themselves with Christ in His death and resurrection (chaps. ii. 16-iii. 4). Paul exhorts them to die with Christ by putting off certain vices, and to rise with Him by putting on certain graces (5-17). He exhorts wives and husbands, children and parents, servants and masters (chaps. iii. 18-iv. 1). He enforces prayer and thanksgiving, and a certain behaviour towards the unconverted (2-6). He sends salutations, and bids them farewell (7-18).

C. *Early Epistles.*

I. Thessalonians: 1. *The Church in Thessalonica.*—This Church was founded by St. Paul after his compulsory departure from Philippi, Silas and Timothy being his companions in the work, and it was therefore the second planted by him within the confines of Europe. From Acts xvii. 2-10 we learn that he began his work, as usual elsewhere, in the Jewish synagogue, where he preached on three successive Sabbaths, and, by proving from the Scriptures that Jesus was the promised Messiah, persuaded both Jews and proselytes, and some honourable women, to accept the faith of Christ. His success in the gospel awoke the jealousy and hostility of the rest of the Jews, who stirred up the Roman populace against him, so that on the fourth week of his sojourn he had to leave his mission unfinished, and betake himself to Berœa under cover of night. Fain would he have returned to complete his work, for the field was an important one, the place being a busy trading city on the great highway between Rome and the East, but he had to content himself for the time with sending Timothy to see how it fared with the infant community, and bring him back a report. It was a very young Church, and it was to be feared, as proved to be the case, that its members had but the crudest conceptions of

what they were to expect by believing in Christ. Moreover, there would appear to have been among them a number of converts from paganism, and there was a fear lest they in particular might have but imperfectly apprehended the meaning of the Christian faith.

2. *The date and place of composition of the Epistle.*—This epistle was written from Corinth pretty early, it appears, in the period of the apostle's year and a half stay in that city, a few months after the planting of the Thessalonian Church, *i.e.,* somewhere towards the end of the year 52 or the beginning of 53. It was the first written of St. Paul's epistles, and shares with St. James the claim to be the first written book of the New Testament.

3. *Occasion, object, and general character.*—The occasion for writing this epistle was the return of Timothy to Corinth with the report that he had been sent to bring back regarding the state of the Thessalonian Church, about which St. Paul was naturally so tenderly anxious; and his object in writing it was to express his joy at the "good tidings" he had heard of their "faith and charity," to exhort them to continue steadfast in their adherence to the gospel, and to set them right on certain matters in which it appeared they still required instruction, as well as to comfort them under their discouragements. They must beware of lapsing into the heathen vices of sensuality and covetousness, must not neglect the duties of their earthly calling in the enthusiasm which the expectation of the return of the Lord to judgment had awakened, nor be concerned about those who had fallen asleep, as though they would not be sharers in the blessings of the advent. This epistle is simpler in style than those written later; it is addressed to a Church under persecution by the Jews, and not, as afterwards, by the Judaising Christians; it is conspicuous for the absence of the ordinary doctrinal element, the word "justification" not once occurring in it; and it is inspired with a sense of the near advent of the Lord, for which the fear is that the Thessalonians may not be ready. The epistle may be divided into two sections—narrative (*a*) (chaps. i.-iii.) and hortatory (*b*) (chaps. iv., v.), the former being especially valuable because of the picture it gives us of the apostle himself.

4. *Contents.*—(*a.*) Paul salutes the Church, is grateful for their soundness in the faith, and magnifies the grace of God in their conversion and their exemplary behaviour in the gospel (chap. i.). He reminds them of his life and ministry among them (chap. ii. 1-12). He is grateful for the spirit in which they had received his message, and for their steadfastness under persecution (13-16). He has longed to see them, has sent Timothy to inquire after them, and has been consoled by his report (chaps. ii. 17-iii. 10). He utters a prayer in their behalf (11-13). (*b.*) He urges them to aim after godliness and abstain from impurity and covetousness (chap. iv. 1-8), to increase in brotherly love (9, 10), to live diligently and honestly (11, 12). He comforts them concerning the brethren that are dead, and exhorts them to be ready against the coming of the Lord (chaps. iv. 13-v. 11). They must live aright, and fulfil their social duties (12-15). He enjoins other duties, prays for them, and sends his salutations and benediction (16-28).

II. Thessalonians: 1. *The Epistle: its date and the place of its composition.*—It was written apparently from Corinth, in the year 53, a few months after the first epistle, and it is the second written of the Pauline epistles.

2. *Occasion, object, and general character.*— The occasion for writing this further epistle was a report which had come to the apostle's ears that the doctrine which he taught, particularly that respecting the coming of the Lord, had been misapprehended or misrepresented; and his object in writing it was to correct the false impressions produced, and to caution the Church against certain men who had either falsified his teaching or forged a letter in his name. The Christians must not neglect their ordinary avocations, as though the day of the Lord were close at hand; that day would not come till the powers of evil had wrought their worst, and the cup of their iniquity was full. The epistle is, in style, spirit, and structure, much like the first, only the tone is sharper and more imperious, as though it dealt with those who required such treatment. It is the first really dogmatic epistle of St. Paul, and it unfolds his doctrine of the last days, as well as teaches the right relation of the Christian to earthly things, and especially to his calling in the world. It is divided, after the salutation, into three portions—(*a*) introductory, (*b*) dogmatic, and (*c*) hortatory.

3. *Contents.*—(*a.*) Paul thanks God for the Church's growth in faith and love, praises them for their endurance under persecution, comforts them with the recompense in prospect at the Lord's coming, and protests his own desire for their perfection in the Christian life (chap. i.). (*b.*) He refutes the notion that the day of the Lord is at hand by reference to the signs which must first appear, especially in the manifestation of Antichrist (chap. ii. 1–12). (*c.*) He urges them to hold fast by the truth they have been taught, solicits their prayers in his behalf, warns them against unsteadiness and idleness, and concludes with a salutation and a benediction (chaps. ii. 13–iii. 18).

D. *Pastoral Epistles.*

The Pastoral Epistles are three in number— viz., I. Timothy, II. Timothy, and Titus. They are so called because they bear upon pastoral duties. They all belong to the same period, towards the close of St. Paul's life. If the apostle had been released from imprisonment for a time and then imprisoned a second time, the epistles date from the interval between his release from his first imprisonment in Rome and his death—an interval during which he had paid a brief visit to the Churches he had founded in the East.

Genuineness. — The only doubts thrown on these epistles in early times came from Gnostics, whose ideas are condemned in them. Those who reject the epistles now rest their case less on any weakness of testimony than on the internal character of the writings. (1.) But private letters may be naturally in a more broken style than public ones. (2.) The historical references which do not seem to fit in with the narrative of St. Paul's life in the "Acts" would have been avoided by a forger, and the difficulty about them disappears if we accept the hypothesis of a second imprisonment. (3.) The reference to Gnostic errors is general, and agrees with the early form of Gnosticism. (4.) Episcopacy is not developed as it was developed during the first half of the second century, and the Church government is of an early, though not of the earliest, type.

I. Timothy: 1. *To whom addressed.*—Timothy, to whom this epistle was addressed, appears to have been a native of Lystra, and is first mentioned in Acts xvi. 1 *seq.*, on the occasion of St. Paul's second visit to the district. His mother was a Jewess, and his father a Greek; together with his mother and grandmother he had been converted to Christ by St. Paul himself (chap. i. 2), probably on the apostle's first visit to Lystra. Being related to both the Gentile and the Jewish sections of the Church, and possessed of qualities which endeared him to both, St. Paul early associated him with himself in his missionary work, having first circumcised him, to remove any prejudice that might exist against him on the part of the Jews. He appears to have conceived a warm affection for St. Paul as his spiritual father, to have henceforward attached himself to him as his attendant, and to have been of great service to him in his work. He was sent by the apostle more than once as his deputy to distant churches; he followed St. Paul to Rome, and was with him during his imprisonment; after the apostle's death he settled in Ephesus, where, according to tradition, he held the office of bishop, and in the end suffered martyrdom for Christ.

2. *The occasion and object of the Epistle.*—The occasion for writing this epistle was St. Paul's having just left the Ephesian Church in charge of Timothy, and the consideration of the advantage it might be to him if he possessed some written instruction from the apostle to guide him in the management of its affairs. The writer's object, therefore, was to direct Timothy in the discharge of his ecclesiastical duties both of doctrine and of good order. He must be rigorous in discountenancing certain heresies then prevailing, and have respect to certain directions in appointing to offices in the Church, in the selection of widows, and in the punishment of offenders.

3. *Contents.*—Paul salutes and greets Timothy (chap. i. 1, 2). He explains why he left him in Ephesus, and describes the false teachers (3–7). He explains the use of the law and its agreement with the gospel (8–11). He refers to his own conversion, and exhorts Timothy (12–20). He exhorts to prayer for all men, referring to the universality of the gospel (chap. ii. 1–7). He speaks of the part to be taken by men in public prayer, which leads him to speak of the proper place and subjection of women (8–15). He lays down precepts respecting bishops and deacons (chap. iii. 1–13). He states the object and purport of these directions (14–16). He writes of false teachers about to appear, and gives directions in regard to them (chap. iv. 1–11). He gives general exhortations (12–16). He gives general directions regarding the government of the Church (chap. v.). He gives exhortations to slaves and masters (chap. vi. 1, 2). He exhorts to sound doctrine, godliness with contentment, and other virtues (3–10). He charges the man

of God (11-16), and the rich (17-19), and Timothy by name (20, 21).

II. Timothy: 1. *The destination and date of the Epistle.*—Everything confirms the opinion that the destination of this epistle was Ephesus, the same as that of the first, and that it was probably the last written of all St. Paul's epistles.

2. *Its occasion and object.*—The occasion of writing this epistle was a feeling on the part of the apostle that his end was approaching, and the direct motive was a desire that Timothy should come to Rome, and bring John Mark with him; while the object of writing it was to invite them to come with all speed, and meanwhile to convey the apostle's final fatherly counsel and exhortations to Timothy, in case, when he came to Rome, it should be out of St. Paul's power to do so.

3. *Contents.*—Paul greets Timothy (chap. i. 1, 2). He declares his love towards him and his anxiety to see him, while he praises his faith and that of his mother and grandmother (3-5). He exhorts him to steadfastness by reference to the character of the gospel and his own example (6-14). He refers to examples of desertion and of fidelity (15-18). He exhorts Timothy from these examples (chap. ii.). He warns him of evil days as not only coming, but actually come, in the presence of insincere and ungodly men (chap. iii. 1-9). He contrasts Timothy's training and steadfastness with theirs (10-17). He solemnly exhorts him to attend to the duties of his ministry, in view of the defection of many, and his own departure near at hand (chap. iv. 1-8). He urges him to come quickly, refers to his own state as well as that of others, and sends greetings (9-22).

Titus: 1. *To whom addressed.*—Of Titus, to whom this epistle is addressed, we know nothing, except what we learn of him in Galatians, II. Corinthians, II. Timothy, and this epistle, for he is not once mentioned by name in the Acts of the Apostles. From these sources we conclude that he was a Greek by birth, and a convert of St. Paul, that he accompanied Paul and Barnabas to the first council at Jerusalem (Acts xv.), and that he was one of those Gentile Christians on whose behalf the council issued its decree exempting such from the obligation to observe the Mosaic law. From the date of this event he appears to have been a constant companion of St. Paul, and to have been from time to time sent by him on missions of importance to the infant Churches (comp. 2 Cor. vii. 6-13; viii. 6; xii. 18). Titus was with the apostle during his imprisonment at Rome, and seems, together with Timothy, to have accompanied him after his release in the brief visit he paid to the Churches in the East. In the course of this visit, St. Paul would appear to have turned aside to see how it fared with the Christians in the island of Crete, and, when he departed, to have left Titus behind him to finish the work he had begun in organising the Churches. After completing the task, he would seem, as requested, to have rejoined the apostle, and to have remained with him till his death; after which, tradition says, he returned to Crete, where he finished his course as bishop of its churches.

2. *The occasion and object of the Epistle.*—The occasion for writing this epistle was the isolated position of Titus at Crete, left there to help the Churches, and therefore needing the apostle's counsels, and its object was to counsel, instruct, and encourage Titus in the task imposed on him, so that he might discharge it in the temper and spirit of the apostle, and duly represent him in his teaching and procedure.

3. *Contents.*—Paul salutes Titus (chap. i. 1-4). He explains that he left him in Crete to appoint elders in the cities, and describes the kind of persons to be selected for the office (5-9). He describes the character of the adversaries with whom he has to deal (10-16). He directs Titus how to exhort the different classes in the membership of the Church, and how to comport himself (chaps. ii.-iii. 11). He concludes with various directions and salutations (12-15).

E. A Personal Epistle.

Philemon: 1. *The person addressed.*—Philemon was an inhabitant of Colossæ, who had been converted to Christianity by St. Paul, probably during the time of his sojourn in Ephesus, and who was afterwards a prominent and zealous member of the Colossian Church, being characterised by St. Paul as a "fellow-labourer" in the gospel. His wife Apphia, and Archippus, another member of his household, were also zealous for the faith; and his house was a place of resort for Christian communion and worship in Colossæ.

2. *The Epistle: the date and place of writing.*—It was written at Rome about the year 63, and was sent to Philemon by the hands of Tychicus, the bearer of the epistle to the Church at Colossæ.

3. *Its occasion, object, and general character.*—The occasion of writing it was the return to Philemon of Onesimus, a slave, who had deserted his service, gone off with some of his property, and taken refuge in Rome, but who had been converted by St. Paul, and who was now a freedman of Christ, much loved of the apostle, and even a comfort to him in his bonds; and the object St. Paul had in writing was to recommend Onesimus to his master as now "a brother beloved," and to urge Philemon to receive him in the Lord as he would his own self. The letter is distinguished among the epistles of St. Paul as being a strictly personal one, but for all that it is not one of the least precious, and is well worthy of a place among the Christian scriptures. No epistle is more instinct with the Christian spirit, or affords us a nobler example of the Christian charity of the great apostle. He identifies himself, says Luther, in substance, with the poor slave in pleading with his master, even as Christ identifies Himself with us in pleading with His Father.

4. *Contents.* — Paul, with Timothy, salutes Philemon and his household, and wishes them grace (vers. 1-3). He expresses his thankfulness for Philemon's faith in Christ and services to the saints (4-7). He intercedes for Onesimus, as now true to his name, which means "helpful," although he may have been otherwise previously (8-21). He bespeaks a lodging against his own coming (22). He sends salutations and his benediction (23-25).

Hebrews: 1. *To whom addressed.* — Of the Hebrews, to whom this epistle was addressed, we know nothing, except what we gather from the work itself. Evidently they were Christians of Jewish descent, and of some standing. But in consequence of persecution at the hands of their Jewish brethren—amounting, it would appear, to threatened excommunication from the Jewish Church—they were in danger of making shipwreck of their faith in Christ, and had need of the exhortation to hold fast their confidence steadfast to the end. There is some reason to presume, from the characterisations it contains, that the epistle was not a general one; but that it was addressed to a special community, though where it seems impossible with any certainty to determine. Except Italy (chap. xiii. 24), there is no mention of any locality from the beginning to the end of the epistle; and the reference to it leaves us uncertain whether it was written to or from Italy. Jerusalem, Rome, Antioch, Alexandria, have been severally fixed upon as the likely seat of the community in question. Probably, however, as Bishop Wescott argues, the Hebrews here addressed resided somewhere in Palestine, but not at the capital.

2. *The occasion, object, and argument of the Epistle.*—The occasion of writing it was the pressure of persecutlon, of a nature tantamount to a challenge to renounce the cross of Christ, and which it was feared these Hebrews would too readily do, to the extent even of denying it altogether, and so, to their own ruin, crucifying the Son of God afresh—the alternative being either crucifixion *with* Christ, or the crucifixion *of* Christ. Therefore the object of writing it was to exhort and encourage them to endure whatever persecution and reproach they might have to face, as being pre-appointed to test and prove their divine sonship, and as the invariable, inevitable allotment of all believing men, of all the children of the Father in heaven. Its object was hortatory (chap. xiii. 22); and its Jewish-Christian readers were exhorted not to give up their faith in Christ and their hope in His promise, as if, in entertaining this faith and hope, they might forfeit their interest in the benefits of the covenant of God with their fathers. For the new covenant in Christ gave them all that the old covenant offered, so that with it they had in actual possession what the old covenant only guaranteed, and that in mere type and promise. The old covenant was abolished, or rather merged, in the new; and if the glory of the new was as yet unrevealed, the greatness of the Founder and His work were pledges sufficient that His Church, like Himself, would enter into its glory when its sufferings were complete like His. Let them hold fast, therefore, by their faith, and not hope the less, but the more, that they had to suffer for it. Their suffering for it was the test and triumph of their faith in it. And they were called to suffer "without the gate," like their Lord before them. To be rejected of their brethren for Christ's sake was the very "reproach of Christ" which they were called to face when they embraced His gospel. The argument on which the author bases his contention that the Christian dispensation surpasses and supersedes the Jewish is threefold, and is founded on the threefold superiority of the Head of the former over the heads of the latter, that Jesus is superior—first, to angels (chaps. i.-ii.); secondly, to Moses (chaps. iii.-iv. 13); and thirdly, to the high priest of the Jewish dispensation (chaps. iv. 14-xii. 29).

3. *Its authorship.*—The question of the authorship of this epistle has been long a puzzle with critics, and it is to this day uncertain who wrote it. On one point only are all trustworthy critics agreed—namely, that it was not written by St. Paul. The reasons for this conclusion appear to be three—first, that by many early Christian writers it is not classed among St. Paul's epistles, but is ascribed by some to Barnabas; secondly, that it is not written in St. Paul's style; and thirdly, that though the truths taught are the same, they are presented in this epistle in lights and relations different from those in which they are presented in the Pauline writings, the dominating, pervading idea in it being quite peculiarly the Priesthood of the Son. The claims of Barnabas are urged by some modern critics, while others are inclined to accept the opinion of Luther, founded on Acts xviii. 24, that the epistle was the work of Apollos. Nevertheless the epistle may still be reckoned Pauline in a secondary sense. Though not written by St. Paul, and though composed in a style of language and reasoned out on lines different from the style and method of the apostle, it advocates an essentially Pauline Christian truth. It is a true support of St. Paul's great doctrine of faith; and it seems to have been written by a disciple of that apostle, or at least by a Christian teacher of the Pauline school of thought, rather than by one of the stamp of James, Peter, or John.

4. *Contents.* — God has revealed Himself through His Son, who is placed above the angels (chap. i. 1-4). He is proved to be in name and dignity above the angels (5-14). Earnest heed, therefore, to be given to His words (chap. ii. 1-4). The world to come is subject to the Son, who was made perfect by suffering (5-18). Jesus has greater glory than Moses, seeing He is the Son over the house of God, while Moses was but a servant within it (chap. iii. 1-6). They who hold fast their faith in Him enter into God's rest, which Israel failed to do under Moses (chaps. iii. 7-iv. 13). Jesus is a sympathising high-priest— a priest, as called of God, and sympathising, as taken from among men (chaps. iv. 14-v. 10). The Hebrews are rebuked for their shortcoming, and warned against falling away (chaps. v. 11-vi. 20). Jesus is an high-priest after the order of Melchisedec; what that involves (chap. vii.). Jesus is a ministering priest of the true tabernacle, which the Lord pitched and not man, *i.e.*, the heavens (chap. viii. 1-6). The old covenant and the new contrasted (7-13). The Levitical and the Melchisedec ministries contrasted (chap. ix. 1-14). The Melchisedec ministry and the new covenant together (chaps. ix. 15-x. 18). The Hebrews are exhorted to avail themselves of the privileges of the new covenant (19-25). If they apostatise, there will be no hope for them (26-31). If they maintain their faith, it will carry them through (32-39). Instances are given of the triumph of faith, and its acceptability with God (chap. xi.). The Hebrews are encouraged to endure by Christ's example (chap. xii. 1-13). They are exhorted to peace and holiness (14-17). The two economies are contrasted, so as to strengthen their faith (18-29). General exhortations follow, and salutations (chap. xiii.).

See Bennett, and Adeney, *Biblical Introduction;* Lewin, *Life and Epistles of St. Paul;* Conybeare and Howson, *Life and Epistles of St. Paul;* Ramsay, *St. Paul the Traveller, &c.;*

Weizsäcker, *The Apostolic Age;* Bartlet, *The Apostolic Age.* For Commentaries see *Expositor's Greek Testament, Critical Commentary; Century Bible* on all the epistles; also Liddon, Vaughan, on *Romans;* Edwards, Stanley, Robertson (exposition), on *Corinthians;* Lightfoot, on *Galatians, Philippians, Colossians, Philemon;* Armitage, Robinson, on *Ephesians;* Jowett, Ellicott, on *Thessalonians;* Ellicott, on *The Pastoral Epistles;* Davidson, Westcott, Delitzsch, Vaughan, on *Hebrews.*

CHAPTER XVIII.

THE CATHOLIC EPISTLES AND THE REVELATION.

THE Catholic epistles are James, I. Peter, II. Peter, I. John, II. John, III. John, and Jude. The epithet "Catholic" was originally applied to I. John and I. Peter, in the sense of "encyclical"—*i.e.,* addressed not to any Church in particular, but to several communities; and it was afterwards applied to the rest, to distinguish them from the epistles of St. Paul.

James: 1. *To whom addressed.*—This epistle is addressed to Christians of Jewish descent, who, in accepting Christianity, had not renounced Judaism, the condition of whom had become familiar to the writer from his residence in Jerusalem, the centre of the Jewish worship, and the resort, for that purpose, of Jews from all quarters of the world. Indeed, most of the Christians with whom he had directly to deal were of this class, —nay, he may even be said to have been one of them himself, and he was therefore well acquainted with their state and circumstances. He addresses them as one who looks upon Judaism as the basis of Christianity, and as on the moral side leading up to it; and, in doing so, he admonishes them of certain principles and duties to which they were bound even as righteous men, not to say Christians.

2. *The author.*—The author of this epistle was, there is reason to believe, not James the son of Zebedee, but James, the brother of the Lord. He is spoken of as such in Matt. xiii. 55 and Mark vi. 3, and is identified by Paul as the James who presided over the mother-church of Jerusalem (Gal. i. 19; ii. 9, 12). That he was a prominent member of the community in question is plain from Acts xii. 17; xv. 13; xxi. 18; and the honour in which he was held would seem to have been due to the jealousy with which he guarded its rights as the Church of the circumcision. When the question arose as to the footing on which the Gentiles should be admitted into the Church, it was he who proposed the decree which bound them to do at least homage to the Jewish law by observing certain of its requirements. He was surnamed "the Just,' and was held in honour even by his unbelieving brethren. The more bigoted among them procured his condemnation, so that he was stoned to death; but the execution of the sentence caused great indignation among the people of Jerusalem. His death took place probably about A.D. 62.

3. *Genuineness.*—The historian Eusebius placed this epistle with those which were not universally accepted. But it is found in the ancient Syriac version, and was perhaps referred to by Clement of Rome, the Shepherd of Hermas, and

Irenæus. Luther objected to the epistle on doctrinal grounds, because it appeared to be contrary to St. Paul's doctrine of justification by faith. But a larger view will show that there is room in the wide range of Christian truth for the teachings of both James and Paul. The epistle is quite in harmony with the known character and teaching of James.

4. *Date.*—This must be assigned either to a very early or to a very late date—before the divisions on the question of observing the law or after it. Many Archaic touches concur to favour the earlier date. Probably, then, this must be considered the first written book of the New Testament, and must be assigned to the decade A.D. 40-50.

5. *Its occasion, object, and general character.*—If we accept the earliest date assigned to it, the occasion of St. James' writing this epistle was very likely his election to the position of chief ruling elder of the mother-church, an appointment which might, under the Spirit, seem to him to impose upon him the duty of addressing a word of counsel to his brethren elsewhere. It may be that the pride of rich Christians and the sufferings of persecuted Christians furnished special inducements for sending counsels to a Jewish Church in which these things were seen. The author's object in writing was to train the conscience of his readers up to the Christian standpoint and standard of duty, and to exhort and comfort them in view of the persecution to which, as Christians, they might be exposed. The sphere in which the epistle moves is that of Christian morality, and its standard of ethics is that given in the Sermon on the Mount, to which accordingly there is reference in chaps. i. 2, 4, 5, 9, 20; ii. 13, 14; iii. 17, 18; iv. 4, 10, 11; v. 2, 10, 12. A parallel has been drawn between its teaching and that of John the Baptist (comp. chap. i. 22, 27 with Matt. iii. 8; chap. ii. 15, 16 with Luke iii. 11; chap. ii. 19, 20 with Matt. iii. 9; and chap. v. 1-6 with Matt. iii. 10-12).

6. *Contents.*—The epistle treats of the purpose of trial and temptation (chap. i. 1-4); of the source and means of obtaining wisdom and steadfastness (5-8); of riches as perishable (9-11); of enduring and of yielding to temptation (12-15); of the source of all good gifts (16-18); of anger and meekness (19-21); of doers of the Word and mere hearers (22-25); of true and false religion (26, 27); of respect of persons as contrary to the law of love (chap. ii. 1-13); of faith that is dead without works (14-26); of the tongue as an organ of good and evil (chap. iii. 1-12); of the wisdom which is and which is not from above (13-18); of the spirit of the world and the spirit of God (chap. iv. 1-7); of humility before God (8-10); of evil-speaking (11, 12); of man proposing (13-17); the rich are warned (chap. v. 1-6); the poor are comforted (7-11); of swearing (12); of affliction and sickness (13-15); of confession (16); of prayer and converting the sinner (17-20).

1 Peter: 1. *To whom addressed.*—This epistle is addressed to the Churches in the districts of Asia Minor mentioned in chap. i. 1, and especially those members of them who were of Jewish origin. These Churches appear to have been all directly or indirectly founded by St. Paul, although the seed of the gospel may have been

78

first introduced by those Jews who, as we read in Acts ii. 10, came up from thence to Jerusalem, and witnessed the events of the day of Pentecost, in connection with which St. Peter took so prominent a part, and might be represented to be the chief actor. Thus it might naturally happen that his name would be regarded with honour among the Jewish Christians in those parts, and that he himself might be led to take a paternal interest in their affairs.

2. *Genuineness.*—This epistle was quoted by Polycarp and recognised by Papias early in the second century ; later, it was repeatedly quoted by Irenæus, Clement of Alexandria, Origen, and Tertullian. The internal notices of names, places, and conditions of church life all bespeak its genuineness. So does its character of spiritual riches.

3. *The author, date, and place of composition.*— "Peter" is the Greek equivalent of the Syriac appellative "Cephas," meaning a stone or a rock, with which Christ saluted Simon when He first met him. He made good his right to this title by that confession of his which is the rock on which Christianity is grounded and rooted (Matt. xvi. 16), himself being the first "living stone" in the temple ; by his being deemed worthy to be charged with the keys of the kingdom of heaven (ib. 19) ; by his being entrusted especially with the pastorate of the lambs of Christ's flock (John xxi. 15-17) ; by his being the first to declare, and that in Jerusalem itself, the Messiahship of the crucified Jesus (Acts ii. 14-36) ; and by his being the first to acknowledge the equal right of the Gentiles to a share in the inheritance of Israel (Acts x.). He is the principal figure in the history of the early Christian Church, but is soon eclipsed by the overpowering presence and zeal of St. Paul. He disappears after the first Council of Jerusalem, and the only other mention we have of him is in Gal. ii. 11-14, till he comes before the Church as the author of this and the subsequent epistles. He figures conspicuously, indeed, in ecclesiastical tradition and legend, but from this source little that is trustworthy can be gathered beyond the fact perhaps that he finished his career by martyrdom in the city of Rome. This epistle appears to have been written from Babylon, which has very questionably been identified by some with Rome ; and is referred to the date when St. Paul wrote his epistles to Timothy, on the ground that the state of things described in it corresponds exactly with that described in them. It must be allowed, however, that it is difficult to determine the time, place, and circumstances in which the epistle was written.

4. *Its occasion, object, and character.*—The occasion for writing this epistle was the report which Silvanus had brought the apostle of the fiery persecution with which the Churches addressed were being threatened by the civil power, and of the outrages they were suffering on account of the odium of the Christian name, associated as it was with evil-doing, specially disloyalty and revolution (chap. iii. 16) ; and his object in writing it was to comfort and fortify the Church in view of the impending fiery trial, to enforce on its members the duties—personal, social, and domestic—of their Christian calling as the best answer to the charges of their accusers, to prove to them how completely

their discharge of these depended on a spiritual apprehension of Christ and His work. The Churches addressed are especially comforted and encouraged by the hope of the coming of the Lord, which is represented as not far off. The character of the epistle corresponds with that of the writer as revealed in the Gospels and the Acts, being "ardent, impassioned, practical, and unspeculative," and showing a mind "which held with a fine Hebraic vehemence of faith the great facts and principles of Christianity, but could not, like the more subtle and logical Paul, give them a systematic expression."

5. *Contents.*—Peter salutes the sojourners of the Dispersion (chap. i. 1, 2). He gives thanks for the living hope into which they have been begotten (3-5). He rejoices with them over the issue of the present trial of their faith (6-9). He magnifies the salvation they enjoy as an object of interest to the prophets and angels (10-12). He exhorts them therefore to patience, obedience, holiness, and mutual love (13-25). He exhorts them to perfection, viewing them (*a*) as new-born babes, and (*b*) as God's spiritual temple and priesthood (chap. ii. 1-10). He exhorts them to act worthily of their profession, so as to win the favour of others (11, 12). He exhorts them to be subject to every ordinance of man for the Lord's sake (13-17). He exhorts servants (18-25). He exhorts wives and husbands (chap. iii. 1-7). He exhorts to mutual forbearance and love (8-12). He exhorts them how to act under persecution, instancing the example of Christ (13-22). They must imitate His suffering and the purity which that implies (chap. iv. 1-6). He exhorts them to certain personal and social duties, in view of the approaching end (chaps. iv. 7-v. 11). He commends Silvanus, and sends salutations (12-14).

II. Peter: 1. *Genuineness.*—This epistle has been regarded with more doubt than any other book of the New Testament. In the time of Eusebius it was reckoned among the disputed books, and references to it cannot be definitely fixed upon before Origen, in the third century, though the so-called second epistle of Clement of Rome, the Shepherd of Hermas, Justin Martyr, Melito of Sardis, Irenæus, and Theophilus have been thought by some to allude to it. II. Peter ii. 1-19 is so like Jude 3-16 that one of the passages must have been taken from the other, and that in Jude appears to be the original. This epistle is less Jewish in tone than I. Peter, and is not like it in style, and the people addressed seem to be different from those addressed in the first epistle, being established Christians, not the scattered Dispersion, though they are described as the same (chap. iii. 1). But the epistle might be genuine, and little known in the early Church, because not much in circulation, and perhaps even lost sight of for a time. Origen seems to have reckoned it as scripture, and if so he probably received it as such from an earlier age. It has been suggested that perhaps Silvanus helped the fisherman apostle with the earlier work, and St. Mark, or some other friend, with the later one, and that so the variations in style may be accounted for. The Churches may have grown in power and changed in character during the interval between the writing of the two epistles ; and thus, while the first refers to external enemies, the second treats of internal dangers. Hence a necessary change of tone. Further, it may be asked, why should not St. Peter have quoted from St. Jude? The epistle was received as in the Canon at the Council of Laodicea (A.D. 372), and the Council of Carthage (A.D. 397).

2. *To whom addressed.*—This epistle professes to be addressed to some at least of those to whom the former epistle was sent (chap. iii. 1), only they are described in more general terms than those to whom that was written (chap. i. 1), so as to include all who bore the Christian name.

3. *Its occasion, object, and general character.*—The occasion for writing this epistle was the appearance in the Church of certain fatal forms of error, both doctrinal and practical, and the purpose in writing was a desire to confirm the Christians in the faith they had received. The object throughout is twofold, and is given in chap. iii. 17, 18—first, that the readers might believe, lest, being led away with the error of the wicked, they should fall from their steadfastness; and second, that they might grow in grace and the knowledge of their Lord and Saviour; this last being the final aim of the whole, as the one means of fellowship with God (chap. i. 3, 4), of escape from the pollutions of the world (chap. ii. 20), and of access into the divine kingdom (chap. i. 11). The doctrinal errors against which they were warned were (*a*) the denial of the power, and (*b*) the denial of the coming of the Lord as judge; and the practical errors were offences against the way of righteousness (chap. ii.). The similarity between the second chapter of this epistle and the epistle of St. Jude strikes every reader, and a hypothesis in explanation has been hazarded, that Peter had seen Jude's letter, had felt appalled at the revelation, and deemed it his duty to caution the Churches he had already written to against the evils described, adopting St. Jude's terms in doing so. Compare the epistle of the latter with his question and the answer in John xiv. 22-24.

4. *Contents.*—Peter salutes those who have like faith with himself in the righteousness of their God and Saviour (chap. i. 1, 2). He exhorts them to growth and fruitfulness in the knowledge of Christ (3-11). He lays down the grounds on which this knowledge rests, in the testimony of apostles and the word of prophecy (12-21). He describes the erroneous teachers who were about to arise, their unholy practices, and the destruction sure to come upon them as of old (chap. ii.). He refutes the scoffers who deny Christ's coming (chap. iii. 1-10). He exhorts believers in view of the Lord's coming (11-18).

I. John: 1. *To whom addressed.*—The epistle is believed to have been originally addressed to the Churches of Asia Minor, of which Ephesus was the centre; and this on the ground at once of universal ecclesiastical tradition, and of the clear reference contained in it to heresies, such as the Docetic and the Cerinthian, which are known to have prevailed about the time in that quarter. Only the Churches are not addressed as infected with the heresies in question, but rather as, by their faith, in possession of what was proof against them.

2. *In what sense an epistle.*—It wants the form, but it has all the other qualities of an epistle: it is addressed by the writer to his readers as to those in whom he feels a deep personal interest, of whose condition he has an intimate knowledge, and to whom he has something special to say. It is properly a pastoral epistle.

3. *The author, date, and place of composition.*—The writer of this epistle is the same as the author of the fourth Gospel, as is evident from the close correspondence between the two works in both thought and expression; and this conclusion is confirmed by the unanimous voice of antiquity. The epistle refers to the Gospel, and presupposes it as already familiar to and still fresh in the minds of its readers, while being present throughout to the thought of the writer. It is quoted by Polycarp. Eusebius says that Papias made use of testimonies from this epistle. It must have been written towards the end of the author's life, somewhere during the last decade of the first century; and some think that Ephesus, others that Patmos, was the place of its composition.

4. *Its occasion, object, and general character.*—The occasion for writing this epistle was the appearance of Antichrist within the bounds of the Church, in the form of a denial that God had manifested Himself in the flesh, as declared in the Gospel, and confirmed by Christian experience; and the object of writing it was to emphasise the fact, that eternal life had appeared in Christ, and had overflowed from Him to His people, as was evident from their walk in the light, both as regards God and one another, and their separation from a world sitting in darkness and denying that the light is come, and is present; the final aim being to bear witness, not against the darkness, but for the light. St. John addresses himself throughout to believers (chap. v. 13), and he writes to remind them of what it is they have believed—to explicate, so to say, what is implicit in their faith, Christ being no longer viewed as the Jewish Messiah, but as the Saviour of the world, as indeed He is also in the author's Gospel. In this epistle, as a rule, the world is conceived of as anti-Christian, and the severance between it and the Church as total and final, so that it is not from its declared hostility she has any cause to feel afraid. The great enemy she has reason to dread is an internal one, seeking to introduce the world-spirit into her midst; but even in presence of such a foe those who are and abide in Christ will nowise be dismayed, or even disturbed.

5. *Contents.*—Introduction—eternal life revealed with a view to fellowship in it (chap. i. 1-4). God is light, and a fellowship with Him a fellowship in light (5-10). Sin disappears with the knowledge of Christ, or by being in Him; and he is in Him who walks as He walked (chap. ii. 1-6). The divine light manifests itself in love (7-11). The love of the world incompatible with the love of God, which alone endureth (12-17). Antichrist is defined, and believers are exhorted to abide in Christ (18-29). The children of God distinguished from the children of the devil (chap. iii. 1-12). Love the sign of having passed from death unto life (13-24). The rival spirits of truth and error (chap. iv. 1-6). The principle of the Christian life, love in God and in us (7-21). The power of this love (chap. v. 1-12). Christian confidence and assurance (13-21).

II. John: 1. *To whom addressed.*—The phrase rendered "elect lady" may be translated, "elect Kyria," or "lady Eklecte," and applied thus or in the usual form to some Christian nation; but the transition to the plural "ye" (ver. 6), the warning against receiving false teachers, the reference to an "elect sister" which sends greeting, &c., point to the conclusion that a Church is here addressed.

2. *The author and date of the epistle.*—The "elder" who writes it is evidently the author of the third epistle, as appears from the similarity of the thought and language; and the title he assumes is expressive of his office of overseer in the Churches he was personally connected with. But the question has been raised, Was this man the Apostle John? The two epistles agree in thought with the first Epistle of St. John; but they differ from it in style and language. They are placed by Eusebius in the list of books not universally received. This, however, may well be accounted for by their private character, so that they may not have been generally known in the early Church. If, as some think, they were written by the "presbyter John," who, as Papias tells us, was a disciple of the Apostle John, living at Ephesus, they might well reflect the apostle's teachings. The question does not affect the canonicity of the epistles, any more than the question whether Paul or Apollos, or any unknown author, wrote the Epistle to the Hebrews touches the canonicity of that work. This is not a question of authenticity. For the writer does not say whether he is the apostle or not. He merely calls himself "presbyter," or "elder." Nevertheless, Clement of Alexandria speaks of I. John as "the larger" epistle, implying that he knew at least one other epistle of the apostle's. The very simplicity of the title, and the calm authority of the writing, suggest an author higher in position that a mere "presbyter John," and agree better with the venerable apostle of that name. The epistle gives no indication of date or place of composition, but it is presumed to have been written about the same time and from the same quarter as the first epistle of St. John.

3. *Its object.*—The object of writing this epistle was to give warning against countenancing certain teachers who, by denying that Christ was come in the flesh, were subverting the first article of the Christian faith, and to exhort the Church addressed to eschew all such, and look to it that they continue faithful and fail not of their reward.

4. *Contents.*—A salutation (1–3); counsel and warning (4–11); conclusion (12, 13).

III. John: 1. *To whom addressed.*—This epistle is addressed to Gaius, who appears to have been one of the writer's converts, a man of good estate and generous disposition, and a native of the Ephesian district of Asia Minor.

2. *Its object.*—The object in writing the epistle was to bespeak the welcome and hospitality of Gaius to certain brethren who were on an evangelistic mission in his neighbourhood, and who, though they bore letters of commendation from the writer, had been refused the right hand of fellowship by the local ecclesiastical authorities, at the instigation of Diotrephes, who is censured as having acted from ambitious, unfriendly motives. The epistle affords a significant glimpse into the condition of things in the early Church.

3. *Contents.*—The salutation (ver. 1). The writer rejoices in the report he has received of Gaius, and wishes him prosperity and health (2–4). He commends to his hospitality brethren from a distance (5–8). He condemns the conduct of Diotrephes (9, 10). He commends Demetrius, who, it would seem, bore the letter (11, 12). The conclusion (13, 14).

Jude: 1. *To whom addressed.*—The epistle bears an address which includes, as its admonitions apply to, all who are sanctified in God, and called and guarded in Christ, but it was evidently intended for some circumscribed circle of such. The Judaic spirit in which it is written, and the reference in it to sayings and traditions familiar only to Jews, would seem to point to some circle of Jewish Christians, localised probably in one of the trading centres of heathenism. Clearly they were Christian communities, in the midst of whom a libertine spirit had arisen, which practically, in mere pride and wantonness, denied, and even derided, to their own ruin and that of the faith they professed, the authority and law of the Lord and Master.

2. *The author, date, and place of composition.* —Jude, or Judas, the author of this epistle, is by very general consent believed to have been the brother of St. James, who wrote the first catholic epistle, and connected, therefore, by birth with the family of our Lord. Except that, like others of the Lord's brethren, he was slow to believe at first in His Divine mission, we know nothing more of St. Jude than we may construe from the epistle, and in it he appears as a zealous believer and a defender of faith in Jesus as the only Lord. It is not possible to determine with any certainty the time when, or the place where, the epistle was written.

3. *Its occasion, object, and general purport.*— The occasion of writing this epistle was the appearance in the Churches addressed of the antinomian libertinism already referred to; and the object of writing it was to exhort the Churches to continue steadfast in the faith of all God's saints, and to assure them by appeal to the fate of the unbelieving in former times, of the judgment written in heaven against, and sure to overtake, all the children of disobedience. St. Jude alludes to two apocryphal books—"The Assumption of Moses" and the "Book of Enoch."

4. *Contents.*—Jude addresses and salutes the saints in Christ (vers. 1, 2). He explains the occasion and object of his writing (3, 4). He warns them by examples of Divine judgment on the disobedient (5–7). He characterises the evil-doers against whom he warns, and represents them as walking in the footsteps of Cain, Balaam, and Korah (8–11). He describes them in figures and images (12, 13). He refers to Enoch as predicting the coming of the Lord with His saints to inflict judgment on the ungodly (14–16). He recalls the warning of the apostles about mockers, sensual and schismatic, of the last time (17–19). Those addressed must build themselves up in faith, prayer, and love (20, 21). He advises them how to deal with the erring, and to keep themselves unspotted (22, 23). He gives praise to God as able to preserve them and present them before Himself without blemish (24, 25).

REVELATION.

Revelation: 1. *The name.*—The word "Revelation" is the Latin equivalent of the Greek word "Apocalypse," by which this book is designated in the original; and, so applied, it means an "unveiling," specially of the future, and that as regards the fortunes of the Church in her relation to the powers of the world. The book to which the name is given is therefore prophetic, but it is prophetic in a more or less darkly symbolic form, a form hence called apocalyptic. This epithet "apocalyptic" is applied to a large body of literature, originally Jewish, eventually Christian, after a model which dates from the days of Ezekiel and Daniel, or more properly from the second century B.C. It was the form Jewish prophecy assumed at a time when the Jewish Church seemed in peril of extermination from the hostile powers of the world, specially of Syria and Rome, and the uniform refrain of the prophecy was—The Lord will soon work out deliverance for His people by the coming Messiah. All these apocalypses were on the same plan, all breathed the same spirit, and all employed the same kind of mysterious, generally grotesque, imagery. They all profess to have been written by some ancient seer, such as Enoch, or Moses, or Ezra; and they represent their seer as, in his own person, foreseeing and foreshadowing history as it has taken place, and as exhorting the generations to come to wait patiently for the Messiah's kingdom (see APOCRYPHA). A literature of the same kind continued to be produced in early Christian times, with this difference, however, that, whereas the Jewish apocalypses look for *a* Messiah to come, the Christian apocalypses look for *the* Messiah to return. Of these, one is ascribed to St. Paul, and another to St. Peter; but the only one that can be reckoned genuine, is that which has been admitted into the Christian canon under the name of John.

2. *Its author and his standpoint.*—The author four times over calls himself John (chaps. i. 1, 4, 9 ; xxii. 8), but without any special designation by which to identify him; on which account, as well as for other reasons, it has become a question with critics, Which John—John the apostle, surnamed the Divine; or another John; or some one who assumed the apostle's name, after the fashion of the other apocalyptic writers? The testimony of antiquity, which extends back almost to apostolic times, is unanimous in ascribing it to the Apostle John, and with this agrees the internal evidence of the book itself. Three points of evidence may suffice in proof : first, the author describes himself as having testified of Christ, and having seen what he testifies (chap. i. 2), in terms similar to those which we meet with in John i. 14 ; xix. 35 ; and in I. John i. 1 *seq.;* secondly, he represents himself (chap. i. 9) as having been banished to Patmos for the word of God and the testimony of Jesus, and this fate antiquity testifies happened to no other than the Apostle John ; and thirdly, only one who was an apostle could have written as the author does in chaps. ii. and iii. to the seven Churches of Asia Minor, such power having been given to no other so to bind and loose in the kingdom of heaven. It is true there are diversities between the style of the Apocalypse and the other writings of St. John, which make it hard to believe in their common authorship, but there are, at the same time, striking similarities in thought and expression which give evidence of a profound affinity between them ; and no one can say how far the diversities referred to may not be due to the different state of mind suggested by the changed circumstances in which the author was placed, and by the subject that occupied him. The standpoint of the author is the standpoint of St. John, of a man who was born a Jew, but is now a Christian, with whom the old distinction between Jew and Gentile is lost in the common Christian faith, especially in view of the one great absorbing antagonism of Christ and Antichrist, and whose love to the one reveals itself in a proportionate hatred and abhorrence of the other.

3. *The date and place of composition.*—Ancient tradition assigns the years A.D. 95, 96, as the date at which the Apocalypse was written ; but modern criticism assigns to it an earlier date than the traditional one, and has gone the length of fixing on the time between the summer of 68 and the spring of 69, during, *i.e.,* the emperorship of Galba, the whole composition being regarded as referring back to the persecution of the Church by the Empire in the year 64, and pointing forward to the appearance of Antichrist himself in the person of Nero risen from the dead. In support of the conclusion that it was written before A.D. 70, appeal is made to chap. xi., which assumes that both Jerusalem and its temple are still standing. Debatable as the date of the composition may be, there has never been any doubt that it was written from Asia Minor, though it is uncertain whether the record of the revelation was indited in the place of its reception (chap. i. 9). According to a recent theory, it was based on older Jewish Apocalyptic writings.

4. *Its occasion and object.*—The occasion of writing the Apocalypse was the occurrence of a fierce and bloody persecution of the Christians either at the hands of the civil power of imperial Rome or from the Jews, and which threatened to wax worse and worse ; and the object in writing it was to confirm and strengthen the Church in its faith and patience by a series of visions which, while they pictured the formidable character of the powers arrayed against her, assured her that the Lord was on her side, and would soon appear for her deliverance and their discomfiture, the principal image in the visions vouchsafed her being that of the Lamb slain from the foundation of the world seated henceforth on the throne of the universe, as a pledge that all His slain ones would one day share in His glory.

5. *Language.*—The language has been defined as that of one who thinks in Hebrew but writes in Greek, and who, if he departs, as in chap. i. 4, 5, from the Greek idiom, does so not from ignorance, but to give a certain impressiveness and solemnity to his words.

6. *Theories of interpretation.*—Three leading systems of interpretation have prevailed in regard to the prophecies of this book, known severally as the Præterist view, the Historical, and the Futurist. The Præterist view is that the prophecies are all, or nearly all, fulfilled already ; the Historical view is that the field embraced is the history of the struggle between the Church and the world to the end of time, part of which is past and part future ; and the Futurist view is that the whole is still to be fulfilled, and refers to events that are to happen on the eve of the second advent. The first is the view which finds most favour among modern critics. This view has the recommendation that it is sanctioned by historical exegesis, the only sound basis of interpretation, and that it does not exclude the other interpretations which see in after events other and even still more striking fulfilments. Thus, according to many modern scholars, the key to the interpretation, as well as the date of the composition of the book, is to be found in chaps. xiii. and xviii.; and the beast is taken for the Roman Empire, the seven heads for seven emperors, the woman for the city of Rome, and the ten horns for imperial governors; also, the Emperor is Antichrist, the worship of whom is in direct antagonism to the worship of Christ. Professor Milligan advocates yet a fourth theory of interpretation. According to this view we are not to look for any definite, successive historical events in the symbolical pictures of this book, but they are to be taken in an ideal way as representing the continuous struggle of the powers of evil with the kingdom of Christ. Perhaps the most instructive lessons may be learnt from the Revelation when it is interpreted in this way. Certainly this is the most simple method of interpretation.

7. *Contents.*—General introduction (chap. i. 1-3). Address to the seven Churches (4-8). Introductory vision (9-20). The seven epistles (chaps. ii., iii.). The book of the future is sealed with seven seals, which are opened one after the other by the Lamb (chaps. iv., v.). A plague follows the opening of each seal (chap. vi.). Before the opening of the seventh seal, the Church is sealed from harm at the hands of her enemies (chap. vii.). When the seventh seal is first opened, seven angels appear, each with a trumpet, at the sound of each of which the earth is visited with plagues (chaps. viii., ix.). The angel standing on the sea and the land gives a little book which is eaten (chap. x.). The final judgment begins with the fall of Jerusalem (chap. xi.). A vision is vouchsafed of how the Church is preserved against her enemies (chap. xii.). The imperial power, with its accomplices, as embodying the hostility of the world, is described, and its destruction foreshadowed (chaps. xiii., xiv.). The final issue of the judgment is preceded by the appearance of seven angels, who pour out on the earth seven vials of wrath (chaps. xv., xvi.). The final doom of "Babylon," with its great ones and their agents, followed by the imprisonment of Satan for a time, is described, (chaps. xvii.-xx. 3). The millennium reign (4-6). Satan is released, and goes forth once more to deceive the nations, but is finally overthrown (7-15). The glory of the heavenly Jerusalem of the future is described (chaps. xxi.-xxii. 5). Conclusion (6-21).

See *Critical Commentary* and *Century Bible* for nearly all these books; also Mayor, on *The Epistle of St. James;* Plumptre (Camb. Bible) on *I. and II. Peter;* Westcott, on *I., II., and III. John;* Simcox (Camb. Bible), Milligan, on *Apocalypse;* Russell, *The Parousia.*

CHAPTER XIX.

THE JEWS AND RELATED PEOPLES.

1. **The Jews: their Race.**—*a. General characteristics.*—The Jews belong to the same race as the Assyrians, the Chaldæans, the Syrians, the Phœnicians, the Arabs, and the Edomites, all of whom go under the common name of Semitic, or Semite, as believed to have been all alike descendants of Shem. These are all marked by common features, such as appear in their language, their literature, their modes of thinking, social organisation, moral character, and religious practices. Their language is poor in inflection, has very few compound verbs and substantives, has next to no power of expressing abstract ideas, and is of simple primitive structure or syntax. Their literature has neither the breadth nor the flow of that of Greece or Rome, but it is instinct with a passion which lays hold of the very depths of being, and appeals to the ends of the earth. In their modes of thinking they are taken up with concrete realities instead of abstractions, and hence they have contributed little to science or philosophy, much as they have to faith. Their social order is patriarchal, with a leaning to a despotism which in certain of them, such as the Jews and Arabs, goes higher and higher till it reaches God, called therefore by Jude "the only Despot" (ver. 4).

b. Special characteristics.—It is among the Jewish people that this faith of the Semitic race culminates, and it is on the foundation thus laid among them that the religion rests which has become the faith of Christendom, and which is summarised by St. Paul as a faith in "one God, and one mediator between God and man, the man Christ Jesus" (1 Tim. ii. 5). Their rule in conduct is more or less determined by a moral standard, and by them more than by any other race has the moral principle, or the law of the conscience, been evolved in humanity as the sovereign law of life. Their religious belief, too, has an ethical basis, and this naturally resolves itself at length into a faith in one God, the Sole Ruler in heaven and on earth, and the law of Whose government is truth and righteousness. But it is not only by their high, rigid, ethical monotheism that the Jews are distinguished from the rest of their race; they are no less distinguished for the tenacity with which they have held by the faith and hope of their fathers; so that, though scattered up and down among the nations, they alone to this day maintain their integrity, and refuse to merge and lose themselves among the other tribes of the earth.

2. **The Related Peoples.**—Of these there were two classes: (*a*) those of the same race, and (*b*) those of different races. Of the former class the more remote were the ASSYRIANS, the CHALDÆANS, the SYRIANS, the PHŒNICIANS, and the ARABS; and the more nearly akin were the EDOMITES, the MOABITES, the AMMONITES, and the MIDIANITES; while those of different races were the EGYPTIANS, the HITTITES, the PERSIANS, the GREEKS, the ROMANS, and the SCYTHIANS.

a. Peoples of the same race as the Jews.—(1.) THE ASSYRIANS were Semites, a fact made apparent by their language as inscribed, and their physical features as engraved, on their monuments, together with the language and features of their descendants on the mountains near Mosul. They occupied a fertile country, of which Nineveh was the capital, and Rehoboth, Calah, and Resen chief cities, being bounded by Armenia on the north, Media on the east, Babylonia on the south, and the watershed of the Euphrates on the west. They reached a high stage of civilisation, as is evident from the witness of history and the ruins that remain of their cities, the monuments of their skill in engineering, and the sculptures indicative of their military prowess. Their origin is lost in the midst of antiquity, while their authentic history covers a period of five centuries, a result which was due less to the inherent strength of the empire than to the energy of its despots. The empire consisted of a congeries of tribes but ill compacted together, each of whom would seem to have contributed a god to the national pantheon.

(2.) THE CHALDÆANS or BABYLONIANS, so far as they were Semites, were of the same family as the Assyrians, but of an inferior physique, and occupied the flat fertile country, called Shinar, about the lower course of the Euphrates, the four chief cities being Babylon, Erech, Accad, and Calneh. They were amalgamated with the Accadian races, a dark, thick-lipped, short people, allied to the Mongols of Central Asia. The Babylonians were of the Aramaic branch of the Semitic stock, and the Assyrians, who were an offshoot from them, gradually gained an ascendancy over them. They worshipped a variety of divinities—Bel, the chief god ; Merodach, who is the son of Ea, the god of the Abyss (see Jer. li. 44), but who is sometimes confounded with Bel ; Istar, "the lady of battles," and the Babylonian Venus ; Samas, the sun-god, and other astronomical beings. Corrupt as the Babylonians were in morals, their religion reveals a sense of sin. The vast libraries of clay tablets that are being exhumed and decyphered show that they had attained to a high state of civilisation. Their palaces were well built, with pillars, and arches, and glazed and fluted bricks ; and they contained many beautiful objects, such as alabaster boxes, bronze statuettes, glass vases, ivories inwrought with gold ; many of these objects, however, may have been obtained from the Phœnicians. They practised cremation. and believed that at death the soul went to "the land of the silver sky."

(3.) THE SYRIANS or ARAMÆANS were clearly of Semitic origin, as we may see from their language, of which monuments remain in the Syriac versions of the Scriptures (see the PESHITTO). They occupied an ill-defined region to the north-east of Palestine, of which the capital was Damascus, and which extended north as far as Mount Taurus, east as far as the Tigris (thus including Babylonia), and south as far as Arabia. The language they spoke was called Aramaic from Aram, the Hebrew name of the highland district. That spoken in the west was also called Syriac, and that to the east Chaldee, the former being the language of Palestine in the time of Christ and that of Christ Himself. So long as they were independent they did not form a single state, and only when they became subject to, or connected with, other powers did they show anything like political unity.

(4.) THE PHŒNICIANS occupied a narrow strip of territory, of which the chief cities were Tyre and Sidon, on the eastern shore of the Mediterranean, bounded on the north and east by Syria and on the south by Judæa. They were unmistakably of Semitic descent. This is proved from what we know of their language, and confirmed by comparison with the Jews, whom they resembled in many respects, especially in their aptitude for trade, as well as their indomitable perseverance. Their religion was a kind of Nature-worship, in which the male and female principles obtained special recognition, and their commercial intercourse with other nations seduced them farther from the tendency to a monotheistic belief, to the detriment not only of themselves, but of the western nations.

(5.) THE ARABS are Semites, partly, it is said, through Joktan, a grandson of Shem, and partly through Ishmael, the son of Abraham. The Joktanite Arabs occupied the south and southwest of Arabia, while the Ishmaelites wandered further north. A few of the Arabs led a settled, but most of them a nomadic life ; and they consisted of independent tribes, often at deadly feud with one another.

(6.) THE EDOMITES were derived from Esau, and therefore regarded as the most closely related of all the Semites to the children of Israel. They inhabited a strip of wild, mountainous, yet not unluxuriant country, one hundred miles long by twenty miles broad, which extended from the south of Palestine to the Gulf of Akaba, and was known as Edom, and afterwards as Idumæa. They early showed a bitter hostility to their Israelitish kindred, and frequently joined with their enemies in attempting to crush them, but they were at length subdued and incorporated among them. Though they were a people of considerable importance, governed by dukes or kings, some of their ancestors appear to have lived in caverns of the mountains, and each tribe seems to have had its own god till compelled to do homage to the God of Israel.

(7.) THE MOABITES were closely akin to the Jews, being descendants of Lot, and they inhabited and cultivated a mountainous country east of the lower parts of Jordan and the Dead Sea. They stood in varied political relations to their kinsfolk, and eventually took sides with their adversaries, so as to expose themselves to judgment at the hands of God. The race is now extinct, or merged and lost among the tribes of Arabia. The famous *Moabite stone,* now in the British Museum, is a witness that in the ninth century B.C. their language was almost identical with that of the Hebrew people.

(8.) THE AMMONITES, being similarly descended from Lot, were cousins of the Moabites, to whom they stood otherwise in closest relation, and they inhabited a country bordering on the Syrian desert, and lying to the north of Moab between the rivers Arnon and Jabbok. They were a continual thorn in the side of the Jews, and had to be again and again coerced into submission. They were worshippers of a god akin to Moloch, and the Jews were forbidden by Nehemiah to intermarry with them.

(9.) THE MIDIANITES were an Arab race of Abrahamic descent by Keturah, and dwelt in a country extending from the Plains of Moab to the north of Arabia Felix. Though Moses married the daughter of Jethro, one of their sheiks, they proved troublesome to their neighbours the children of Israel, till Gideon scattered and subdued them. They were worshippers of Baal, and commerce with them was often injurious to the people of Israel. The name "Midianite," however, was sometimes extended to the whole Arab race.

b. Related peoples of different races.—(1.) THE EGYPTIANS of antiquity were partly of Asiatic and partly of African origin, probably with an infusion of blood from the Semitic family ; and they formed in various ways a most important link in the chain of world-history.

Egypt, the daughter of the Nile, as it has been called, was the seat of one of the oldest civilisations of the world, and that civilisation was already old before Egypt came into connection with the history of the Hebrew people. It touches Jewish history at four points : the time of the Patriarchs ; the age of the bondage and the exodus ; the days of Solomon and the later kings ; and the period of the upgrowth of the Jewish colony at Alexandria and the founding of the Alexandrian philosophy under Philo. When Abraham visited Egypt the three pyramids of Ghizeh had been already built, and the land had witnessed the rise and the fall of two empires, the empire, namely, of Lower Egypt, whose capital was Memphis, and that of Upper Egypt, whose capital was the hundred-gated Thebes of Homer. It was Menes who laid the foundation of the former, though at what age of the world no one knows, as the earliest records of Egypt supply no dates, the course of its history being indicated solely by the succession of the dynasties that ruled it. Of these history makes mention of no fewer than thirty, such was the frequency of revolution to which it was subject, and more than half of these had fallen before Abraham set foot on the soil of Egypt.

The dominant race in northern Egypt when Abraham entered it were the Hyksôs, or Shepherd Kings, a tribe of Semite origin, and their capital city was Tanis, or Zoan. They had long before invaded the land, driven into it probably by pressure from the north and east, and despite the struggles, oft-repeated, of the native princes to regain the ascendancy, had not only been able to maintain their ground, but to govern the subject people with a firm hand, which they did, it would appear, by adopting their religious creed and modes of living. This accordingly was the race still in power, in the north at least, when Jacob and his sons went down to settle in it, and it was a king of this race that allocated to them for dwelling-place the eastern frontier pasture-land of Goshen. And so long as this race continued to hold sway, so long was it well with them and their descendants, but with a change of dynasty their sorrows began, and with the accession of a "king that knew not Joseph."

The native Theban power, which still kept its ground in the south, had risen up, and though not without a hard and protracted struggle, through five generations it is said, not only driven them from the seat of power, but compelled them to evacuate the territory of which they had usurped the dominion. It was the princes of the 17th dynasty who carried this struggle on, but it was Ahmes, the founder of the 18th, that about 1590 B.C. brought it to a termination, and had also the merit of establishing for the

first time a native monarchy with sovereign power over the whole of Egypt. This dynasty proved the most potent that had ruled the land, for it not only united all classes, and both the regions, Upper and Lower, under one head, but it raised Egypt to the rank of one of the ruling powers of the world. Under Thothmes III., the greatest monarch of this dynasty, who reigned from about 1500 B.C. to 1450 B.C., nearly the whole of Western Asia with the island of Cyprus was brought under tribute, and Egypt became the rival of the great empires that had already risen and established themselves on the bank of the Euphrates and Tigris. This monarch, however, as did the others of his house, ruled Egypt with a high hand, for, excepting the priesthood and the military, on whom his power depended, the people under him were as hewers of wood and drawers of water. Nothing wonderful, therefore, is it that the alien Israelites living on the soil should have fared no better, and that they were weary of an oppression by which their lives were made "bitter" to them.

The monarchs of the 18th dynasty ruled the country with a rod of iron, and it would seem the Israelites had no resource but to submit to the yoke and murmur in silence. But the dynasty that succeeded, though no less tyrannical, showed a weaker hand, and the subject race began to entertain the thought of winning their freedom. The achievement of this was the thought that possessed the soul of Moses, and it was by his hand that God brought out for them the needed deliverance. The tyrants of the 19th dynasty, from whom they suffered most, were Seti I. and Ramses II., and it was they, who more than any, by compelling them to do slave work, "made their lives bitter with hard bondage." Being weaker as rulers than their predecessors, they had more reason to fear, and they thought to keep down insurrection by added oppression. Ramses, however, who died in 1281 B.C. after a reign of sixty-seven years and in whose reign Moses was born, was not the last of the oppressors of Israel in Egypt—the distinction belongs to a son of his and his successor Menaptah II. This was the Pharaoh whose heart God had hardened not to let Israel go, and in spite of whose obstinacy Israel under God made good their escape out of the house of their bondage. This Pharaoh could not with all his obstinacy conceal the native cowardliness of his heart, and the Israelites prepared to leave, though they might not have dared to defy the ukase of a Thothmes III., or even of a Ramses II. At last, accordingly, Meneptah let Israel go : he neither joined in the pursuit nor perished in the waters; and the monuments bear witness to his having lived and reigned after Israel had fled.

Of the subsequent connection of Egypt with Israel, in which relation alone we have anything to do with it here, little need be said. From the date of the fall of the 19th dynasty the power of Egypt began to decline, and it was only on the accession of the 22nd that, under Shishak I., that it showed signs of revival, and made itself felt for a time among the neighbouring nations. Shishak indeed was strong enough to cope even with Solomon (1 Kings xi. 40) ; he also made war against Rehoboam his son and captured Jerusalem (1 Kings xiv. 15, 16) ; but Assyria afterwards began to press hard upon Egypt, and though the Jewish king sought succour in Egypt against the common foe, the two nations found eventually that they were leaning on a "broken reed," and that Assyria first and Babylonia afterwards were too much for both of them. Nevertheless in the days of Jeremiah the Jews found in Egypt a city of refuge against the oppression of the latter power. In course of time the Jewish colony in Egypt became the most numerous and important branch of the "Dispersion."

The scripture name for Egypt is Mizraim, or the land of the two Mazors, meaning Upper Egypt and Lower, though the name Mazor is sometimes applied to the whole of it. The word Mazor denotes "fortification," and the name was originally given to Lower Egypt from the line of forts, called also the wall of *Shur*, which had been erected to defend it from invasion on the east, its weak side against aggression. Egypt was also called the "Land of the Sun, of the Flood, and of the Sycamore," while the native name was *Kam*, or Black, from the colour of the soil. Pharaoh was the common name of its kings, just as Sultan is of the ruler of Turkey, and Shah of the ruler of Persia. These Pharaohs, according to Professor Sayce, were, or professed to be, kings of the two lands, and wore the separate crowns of Upper and Lower Egypt. *Pathros*, "the land of the south" (Isa. xi. 11), was distinct from Mazor. It was only the united monarchy that held them together, and its inhabitants were called Pathrusins. *Caphtor* was the coast-land of the Delta, which was more thickly peopled by Phœnician colonists (Caphtorim) than the mother country itself.

The supreme deity was the sun, named at his rising "Ra," with the symbol of the hawk, and in his setting called "Tum." Many of the gods were merely animals, such as the sacred bull Apis; many of them had human forms with animal heads, such as the god Anubis. Nevertheless, the Egyptian sacred book, "The Ritual of the Dead," contains higher moral teaching than any other ancient pagan work. In the myth of Osiris there seems to be an unconscious prophecy of the resurrection, together with a solemn, soul-stirring vision of judgment. Down in the dim under-world the soul of the departed is tried before Osiris, the god of the dead, and his forty-two assessors, by being weighed in a pair of scales against "Truth" as the counterweight, while Thoth, the writing-god, stands by to enter the result on his tablet.

(2.) THE HITTITES were formerly confused with the small tribes of Canaan; but recent discoveries have shown that they formed a powerful empire in the days of the patriarchs. Long before the rise of the Assyrian, Babylonian, and Persian monarchies they held sway over much of the territory subsequently conquered by those powers. Their dominion extended as far as the borders of Egypt in the south-west, eastward to Mesopotamia, and northward above the limits of Syria, and beyond the Taurus Mountains. Traces of the great Hittite empire have been discovered in inscriptions scattered over Asia Minor. There appear to have been at least two capitals —a northern one at Carchemish on the Euphrates, and a southern one at Kadesh on the Orontes. From the name of one of their cities in the south of Canaan, Kirjath-Sepher—which means "Book Town"—taken in connection with the Hittite inscriptions, it has been inferred that the Hittites were a literary people, or, at all events, that

they were acquainted with the art of writing, and perhaps generally advanced in civilisation far beyond the condition of the nomadic patriarchs who led their flocks up and down in their territory, like the Bedouin of to-day, who maintain their simple, primitive life outside the culture of the towns. The Hittites were sufficiently powerful to engage in serious military expeditions and to force alliances with the Egyptians, who describe them on their stone monuments under the name of *Khetai*. The Assyrians have also preserved records of the same power. They were probably not allied to the Canaanite races, but were a Mongolian race from the highlands of Central Asia; therefore their empire appears as the outcome of the first of those westward migrations of Asiatic peoples which were afterwards seen in such a movement as that of the invasion of the Roman empire by the Huns.

(3.) THE PERSIANS belonged to the Aryan stock; and, indeed, Iran, meaning Aryan, was the original name of the country which they occupied, and which lay between the Caspian and the Persian Gulf. They were related rather to the Western than to the Eastern world, and it is from them that continuous history takes its start. In the extreme East life had remained stationary: it was in Persia it began to take a forward step. When we first meet them they are polytheistic and idolatrous. Thus, according to a clay cylinder now preserved in the British Museum, Cyrus, the conqueror of Babylon and the liberator of the Jews, was a devout worshipper of the pagan gods. But subsequently these people adopted the purer spiritual worship of Zoroastrianism, which originated on the confines of India. This is essentially dualistic—consisting of a principle of light, or good, and a principle of darkness, or evil. These were thought of as two personal beings, eternally separate and antagonistic, called Ormuzd and Ahriman — the one the author of all good, whom the Persians honoured and loved, and the other the author of all evil, whom they feared and hated. Man they thought of as related to both, and his duty to adore the one and disown the other as master. The influence of the Persian religion on the later development of the religion of Israel has been much over-estimated. Its essential dualism is at the very antipodes of the unflinching Hebrew faith in the supremacy of Jehovah over evil as well as over good. It is only in secondary matters that some influence may be suspected. Thus, the Persians believed in angels and archangels, meaning thereby grades of powers of good and evil; and among the Jews the belief in these, as well as in other spiritual worlds generally, is more marked after their intimacy with the Persian creed.

(4.) THE GREEKS were pure Aryans, and in early times they occupied the country in the south-east of Europe still known as Greece, and composed partly of islands and partly of a continent indented by bays in numberless shapes. The "Isles" of Greece appear to have been vaguely known in early times. Joel tells us that the Syrians sold children of Judah as slaves to the Greeks (Joel iii. 6). In the Book of Daniel Greece appears on the stage of the great world-empires (*e.g.*, Dan. viii. 21). Here we have a reference to the Macedonian empire of Alexander and his successors, which included Palestine and the Jews in its sweep of conquest. The odious Syro-Grecian dominion that called out the patriotic heroism of the Maccabees, was the outcome of this conquest of the East by Greece. It succeeded the Persian supremacy, but it fell to pieces before the onslaught of the iron legions of Rome. Macedon, however, was not purely Greek, and the political relation of the Greeks to the Jews, resulting from the establishment of the Macedonian empire, were less important than the intellectual consequences of the contact of Greek culture with Hebrew life and thought. All over Western Asia, Greek civilisation spread among the educated classes. In the time of our Lord, Greek was the language of universal literature. This is why the New Testament, though written on the whole by Jews, was nevertheless composed in the Greek language. The "Hellenists," i.e., Greek-speaking Jews of Grecian habits, constituted a large part of the Dispersion. At Alexandria, in particular, Judaism seemed to be overcome by the intellectual charms of Greece. Philo the Jew was Greek in thought, and he made it his business to convert the Hebrew Scriptures into allegories of Greek philosophy. Apollos was trained in this school of teaching, and the Gospel of St. John, and the Epistles to the Colossians and the Hebrews, bear traces of its influence. At Athens and at Corinth, in particular, St. Paul came into contact with popular Greek philosophy. Greek thought was essentially naturalistic. It discerned the beauty of nature, but except in the case of the great tragic writers, Æschylus and Sophocles, it was strangely blind to moral evil. Keen in intellect, the Greeks were scornfully sceptical of the spiritual truth which is the life of the Hebrew faith. And yet the searching questions of Socrates and the soaring speculations of Plato, as well as the lofty ethics of the Stoics, were like the law among the Jews—schoolmasters to bring men to Christ.

(5.) THE ROMANS were of a race allied to the Greeks, but of a different temperament. The genius of Greece was intellectual and artistic; its noblest feats were the creation of the Iliad and the Parthenon. The genius of Rome was practical and political; its highest achievements were the conquest and rule of the whole known world, so that the Mediterranean Sea became a Roman lake. Great in conquest, the Romans were greater in government. In the East they succeeded old empires built up by the sword, and only held together by the sword. But they introduced law and maintained their dominion by a wise administrative policy. Unlike the old brutal conquerors they were not the mere lords of subject slaves; they became the orderly rulers of well-organised provinces. They allowed large liberty of individual conduct, and even cherished the national religions of the people they conquered, introducing the strange gods of Egypt and Gaul to the cosmopolitan Pantheon at Rome. But they were merciless in suppressing dangerous indications of local patriotism, and they drained the provinces of tribute to satiate the idle population of the imperial city with vicious enjoyments. They appear in their worst light at their contact with the Jews. In the year 65 B.C., Syria, including Palestine, became a Roman province. The next year (64 B.C.) the ruthless Pompey marched an army into Judæa, took Jeru-

salem, and then, to the horror and rage of the Jews, violated the sanctity of the Temple by insolently bursting into the Holy of Holies, which he was astonished to find empty. The turbulent Jews were not attractive, and the province was handed over to a succession of the most cruel and dissolute procurators, who simply goaded the high-spirited people into insurrection. At Rome, on the other hand, Jewish proselytising was fashionable among the ladies of the upper classes. Moreover, the cosmopolitan spirit of the Roman empire tended to counteract the jealous exclusiveness of Judaism and to prepare the way for the world-wide religion of our Lord, "in whom is neither Jew nor Gentile, bond or free, but all are one."

(6.) THE SCYTHIANS.—The Scythians were a people of various tribes, which occupied a region of indefinite extent to the north and north-east of the Caspian Sea. Their relations as regards race are matter of mere conjecture, but they appear to have been of Tartar habits, and to have led a nomadic life, subsisting on the milk and flesh of horses, which constituted their chief wealth, and even, it is said, on human blood. At all events, they were regarded as a people at the lowest stage of physical and moral character, and wholly outside the pale of civilised life. They are nevertheless referred to by St. Paul, in Col. iii. 11, as not beyond the pale of Christian grace, and as capable of membership in the new humanity of which the head is Christ, whose gospel the apostle regards as by itself effective to the redemption of all the tribes of the earth.

See Bagster's *Records of the Past;* Maspero, *The Dawn of Civilisation in Egypt and Chaldœa;* Sayce, *Ancient Empires of the East,* and *The Hittites;* Rawlinson, *The Five Great Monarchies;* M'Curdy, *History, Prophecy, and the Monuments;* Max Duncker, *History of Antiquity;* Mahaffy, *Greek Life and Thought;* Mommsen, *The Provinces of the Roman Empire.*

CHAPTER XX.

JEWISH AND OTHER SECTS AND PARTIES MENTIONED IN SCRIPTURE.

1. The Nazirites.—A Nazirite, so called from "nazar," to separate, was one of either sex consecrated by a vow to the service of God in some special interest or with som special purpose, generally for a definite perio but sometimes for life. During the continuance of the vow, the Nazirite bound himself to abstain, not only from strong drink, but from every product of the vine, was forbidden to approach a dead body, and required not to cut the hair of his head, the long hair being the sign by which he professed his consecration. This vow was a religious one, such as even conferred a priestly sacredness on the person, the subject of it "all the days of his separation being holy to the Lord," and only released by offerings and sacrifices at the door of the Tabernacle (see Num. vi. 1-21). The obligation to keep the vow lasted usually for thirty days, sometimes for sixty, and even a hundred, and in one case for seven years, which had to be thrice repeated. Of Nazirites for life Scripture mentions only three—Samson (Judges xiii. 7), Samuel (1 Sam. i. 11), and John the Baptist (Luke i. 15), the designation being ap-

plied only to the first of the three; and in all these cases the vow was made by their parents for them before their birth.

The institution of Naziritism among the Jews appears to have been of early date; and Nazirites, according to Ewald, were numerous in early times, and afterwards in the more critical periods of Jewish history, especially in the two centuries or so which preceded the fall of Jerusalem. Various interpretations have been given of the Nazirite vow; but the one which seems to be best supported is that which regards it as an act of self-sacrifice, or an expression and assertion of the right of any and every man to offer himself in sacrifice or consecration in any service which God may require of him.

2. **The Rechabites.**—The Rechabites were of the tribe of the Kenites, a people of Arab origin and confirmed Bedouin habits, who attached themselves to the children of Israel in their wanderings, and entered Palestine along with them, having embraced the Israelitish faith. They derived their name from Rechab, a chief probably of one of the clans of this tribe, and the father or ancestor of Jehonadab, who was, so to speak, their lawgiver. Like the Nazirites, they were bound to abstain from all strong drink, and to maintain also the nomadic habits which their fathers practised in the wilderness, by neither building houses, nor sowing seed, nor planting vineyards or having any, and by dwelling all their days in tents. These rules they appear to have all along rigorously observed, so much so that, when, years after Jehonadab's death, they had to take refuge from the Chaldæan invasion within Jerusalem, they could not be tempted to break one of them, in consequence of which the word of the Lord came to Jeremiah, saying: "Jonadab, the son of Rechab, shall not want a man to stand before me for ever" (see Jer. xxxv.).

3. **The Samaritans.**—For an account of the Samaritans see chap. xiv. p. 51.

4. **The Casidins.**—The title "Chasidim," meaning the pious, was applied to the strict Jew after the Captivity to distinguish him from such as were more lax in their religious observances. The Casidins were those who were zealous for the purity and integrity of the national life and religion, and especially opposed to every innovation calculated in any way to have an enervating or corrupting influence upon these interests. The Hellenising spirit was specially offensive to them, and it was with pent-up indignation they witnessed the insolent attempts of Antiochus Epiphanes to introduce Grecian rites and erect pagan altars on the soil of Judæa. When, accordingly, Mattathias, the father of the Maccabbees raised the standard of revolt, they joined him to a man, and constituted the bone and sinew of the Maccabæan struggle. In this struggle they lost their distinctive name, but they reappeared in the form of *Pharisee*.

5. **The Pharisees.**—The Pharisees and Sadducees did not constitute distinct religious sects. They both belonged to the national religious community, and they should rather be regarded as parties within that community. The Pharisees were a party scrupulously exact in their interpretation and observance of the Jewish law, regarding it as the one canon appointed to regulate the life of the Jewish community in every department; and they were the representatives of that legal tendency which gave character to the development of Judaism proper during the period which elapsed between the date of the Captivity and the advent of Christianity (see JEWISH LEGALISM).

(1.) *Their origin.*—It was their zeal for the observance of the letter of the law to the full in every relation of life which distinguished them from the rest of the Jewish people; and the name they bore, which means "Separated," or "Separatist," was given them in mockery by their opponents, because of the attitude of isolation from the rest of the nation which, out of respect to this principle, they were compelled to assume at the epoch of their origin. That epoch was the period of the Maccabæan struggle. It appears to have been some time between the years 162 and 105 B.C. that they took up this ground; the occasion of their doing so was the discovery that the Maccabæan chiefs were aiming at more than that religious liberty which had been, as they understood, the single object of the revolt in which the rest of the nation had joined them. It appeared that these chiefs were now fighting for their own interests and not for God's—for the erection of a worldly kingdom, that would be the death of the theocracy, which it was the purpose of Providence they should establish; and from that moment the Pharisees stood aloof from the political party. They took up at first separate ground, though, in the end, they carried the great body of the nation along with them.

(2.) *Legalism.*—The law on which the Pharisees insisted was in the form laid down by the Scribes; and this included not only the written law, but the oral law, as being the traditionally-given Divine interpretation, when it was in reality only the clerical or ecclesiastical exposition and development, of the written law. This oral or traditional law they therefore not only held to be as binding as the written, seeing it was the key to it, but they considered it more criminal to question the authority of the former than that of the latter. It was only as expounded and applied by this oral law that the written law was to be interpreted and put in practice (see *Scribes*, chap. xiv. p. 50). He maintained that the law which the Jew was to observe was that which had been developed in the hands of the Scribes, and in doing so he laid down a principle which is the distinctive article of orthodox Judaism on the matter to this day.

(3.) *Religious opinions.*—The dogmatic views of the Pharisees were as distinctive of Judaism as their legal opinions, and it is in maintaining these views that they are more especially contrasted with the Sadducees in the New Testament. They believed (a) in a future retribution in the form of a resurrection of the righteous to everlasting life, and the consignment of the wicked to future punishment; (b) in the existence of purely spiritual, *i.e.*, incorporeal beings (see Acts xxiii. 8) such as angels; and (c) in the direct dependence of every event, and even moral action, on the co-operation of God in His providence, and this in perfect consistency with the doctrine of moral freedom and responsibility in man.

(4.) _Politics._—The political creed of the Pharisees was as distinctively Judaic as their theological, and it may be summed up as requiring the observance of one simple rule—to abstain from politics altogether, except in so far as they affected the religious life and interests of the nation. All that they sought for was perfect religious freedom, a free theocracy; and they were passively content with any government that conceded to them this privilege, content with their own _imperium_ in any _imperio._ Their separate standing in the community and their very name they owed, as we have seen, to their refusal to countenance the attempts of the later Maccabees to make a secular power of the Jewish religion. As they could not seek for political power themselves without damage to the sacred interests entrusted to them, so, if only they were left free in their religious life, they must not quarrel with any power that might win political ascendancy over them. "In no other way could the sacred, _i.e._, the clerical, character of the theocracy be maintained." Such was one side of the political creed of the Pharisees, and one which may be credited to the account of Judaism generally. But it also presented another side. The Pharisees clung most tenaciously to the Messianic hopes of their nation. They shared and promoted the national hatred to the Roman dominion and the rule of the Herods. In this respect they appeared as patriots, and seemed to contrast favourably with the worldly, temporising Sadducees, who were only too ready to sacrifice national rights for a peaceful possession of office. The Pharisees were the popular and democratic party. Although they submitted on principle to foreign rule, and duly paid tribute-money as well as tithes, they never quite reconciled themselves to the situation; and they were at length not unwillingly induced to side with the nation at large when roused from time to time to rebel against such domination. Had they at such moments kept as true to their political creed as they did to their legal and their theological standpoint, it might seem that a different fortune would have been the fate of the Jewish people; but, in general, they had full provocation for their resistance, because the powers of this world did not leave them alone, as indeed they have never yet left any in their attempts to realise on earth God's kingdom—a result which, however, may be due quite as much to arrogance on the one side as on the other.

Such are the principles of Pharisaism in the broadest sense, and they are the same as those held by the orthodox Jews generally. How, then, can they be reckoned as a party, and how do they appear in history as a fraction, often a small one, of the Jewish nation? The answer to this is twofold: first, they were at their origin a party, seeing they took up ground different from the mass of the people at a great crisis of their history; and secondly, in course of time the broader position which they at first took up became narrowed, in consequence of the undue importance they began to attach to externals in matters of religion. They had degenerated into mere formalists, which is the character they wear in the New Testament; and the stress they laid upon forms tempted them into an attitude of greater and greater singularity, so that their numbers became reduced at one time to not over six thousand. Thus the distinction between them and the rest of the community came to be limited chiefly to the observance or non-observance of the laws relating to cleanness and uncleanness, and they separated themselves from all who were not as strict in the observance of these rules as they were. They alone were the people of the Lord; all the rest were _Am-haaretz—i.e.,_ people of the land—and little or no better than heathen. It was in making this claim, and on the ground on which they made it, that they incurred the indignation and exposed themselves to the condemnation of Christ.

Though the Pharisees were thus repudiated by Christ, they were the party of the Jews that were held in highest regard by the body of the nation. "Amid all the changes of government under Romans and Herodians," remarks Schürer, "the Pharisees maintained their spiritual hegemony. Consistency with principle was on their side, and this consistency procured them the spiritual supremacy. . . . It was just because their requirements stretched so far, and because they recognised as true Israelites only those who observed them in their full strictness, that they made so imposing an impression on the multitude, who saw in these exemplary saints their own ideal and their legitimate leaders."

6. The Sadducees: (1.) _Their origin._—The Sadducees were originally members of the priesthood that constituted the governing nobility of the Jewish nation, holding in it the highest official positions; and they derived their name, it is now generally believed, from Zadok, an ancestor of the high-priestly family of Jerusalem, who is mentioned in 1 Kings ii. 35 and in Ezek. xliv. 15. They first came into prominence as a party in opposition to the Pharisees; and they are, in a rough way, definable by the antagonistic attitude which they assumed throughout their history to this sect. When Pharisaism arose, they were the party in power, and, by self-interest, concerned in upholding the policy against which Pharisaism at its origin was the protest. Originally they were the high officials of the Asmonæan dynasty, which would fain have established itself on the secularisation of the Jewish faith, and the chief promoters of that movement which sought to reduce Judaism to a mere state religion, and against which the Pharisees held out. And the respect which they thus showed for the secular interests of the nation over the religious or spiritual characterised their views and actions throughout all their history; all these were limited by an implied reference merely to the present life. They were the secularists of the Jewish faith, and would have prostituted that faith to merely secular purposes.

(2.) _Politics._—It is not, however, as representing any particular system or school of opinions that the Sadducees came first into view, but as a class in a certain social position. They were the historical aristocracy, or high-priestly class of the Jewish people; all men of wealth, and accustomed to occupy offices of influence in the community. They were jealous of their standing and authority in the state, and held by the old order of things against all innovation. Hence they represented, so to speak, the Tory or Conservative party among the Jews, just as the Pharisees did the High Church party. Though in small favour with the common people, they may have had their supporters in this class, and some may have sympathised with their opinions who scorned their aristocratic pretensions. However, it is their aristocratic attitude which primarily characterises them; and we have now to see what other attitudes they were driven to assume, mainly in consequence of the antagonistic position taken up by the Pharisees.

(3.) *Treatment of the Law.*—In opposition to the Pharisees, they acknowledged the obligation of only the written law, and refused to accept the authority of the Scribes and the tradition of the fathers in interpretation of its meaning and applications. It was for long believed that they admitted the authority of the Pentateuch only; but there is evidence to prove that this is a mistake, and that they regarded nearly all the written word as equally binding. The great point of difference here between them and the Pharisees lay in their rejection of the Pharisaic regard for the verdict of tradition. In some respects they were more severe, in others more lax, than the Pharisees in the legal sanctions or penalties by which they enforced the law, and they even surpassed the Pharisees sometimes in the rigour of their ceremonial requirements. In punishing crime they were more severe than their rivals, just because they interpreted the law more literally, so that they earned the ugly name of "Condemners." It was the Sadducees who insisted on the literal application of the *lex talionis*, "eye for eye," "tooth for tooth" (Deut. xix. 21). The Pharisees allowed a money compensation. But the Sadducees never swerved from the attitude they had taken up in the matter of the teaching of tradition. They do not appear to have denied that the Scribes were correct in the account they gave of its verdict; they only repudiated its binding authority over them, and in doing so they occupied a standpoint which might recommend them to many, the party, namely, of the older orthodoxy.

(4.) *Religious opinions.*—The dogmatic views which the Sadducees held were opposed to those of the Pharisees, as already stated in the previous section; and they were grounded on their rejection of traditional teaching, just as their legal views were. They denied, in opposition to that party (*a*), the immortality of the soul, and the doctrines of future retribution and the resurrection; (*b*) the existence of spirits, such as angels; and (*c*) the dependence of the free will of man on the Divine will, or its co-operation. In maintaining these positions, particularly the two first, they occupied strictly Old Testament ground—for, except in Daniel, there is little if any express mention in the Old Testament either of the resurrection of the body or of a state of rewards and punishments for the individual in the future world; only their doing so was from no wish merely to hold by what was old, or even scriptural, but because these views were in accord with the main article of their creed, which attached importance only to what had a bearing on this present life, *i.e.*, to that which in modern times goes under the name of secularism. For it is to be remembered that the Sadducees were originally and throughout a political party, and that they strove all along for ascendancy in the state as the representatives of the principle which sought the secularisation of the Jewish religion. This virtually meant, in the regard of the religious class, its Paganisation or its Hellenisation.

(5.) *History.*—The fortunes of the Sadducees as a political party in the state were very various. As the aristocracy they had originally all the power that the circumstances of the state admitted of, but as the representatives of the Hellenising tendency they were regarded with distrust, and more or less excluded from power, by the earlier Maccabæan chiefs; and it was not till the time of John Hyrcanus that they regained their ground, and became again the ruling party in Judæa. With the assumption of power by Salome, a reaction set in in favour of the Pharisees, but it was more on the religious side of things than the political, and the Sadducees were still able to maintain their influence in the state even to Herod's time and under him, despite his proscription of so many of their number on his accession to power (see chap. xiv. p. 55).

Evidence that the Sadducees were in the end, as they were certainly at their origin, merely a political party, and had no other hold on the Jewish mind, is to be found in the fact that history makes no mention whatever of them after the fall of the Jewish nation. The moment it ceases they disappear and fade away from human memory, a circumstance which accounts for the mistaken views that prevailed so long respecting their position and character. Their creed had no hold on any but themselves, and it had no value for themselves except as vindicating their political position.

7. **The Essenes.**—The Essenes were a religious communistic fraternity of the monastic order which grew up on the soil of Judæa some two centuries or so before Christ, and which had establishments in different parts of the country when Christ was on earth. We have the fullest accounts in Josephus, as well as in Philo and Pliny, respecting the character of the community, their manner of living, their religious observances, and their theological opinions, while the greatest obscurity prevails as regards their origin and the very meaning of their name. The first mention we have of them in Josephus is during the Maccabæan period, in 150 B.C., and the only plausible theory of their name is the one which traces it to a Hebrew root signifying "pious;" while the conclusion, presumably indicative of their origin, as vaguely summed up by Schürer, is (1) "that Essenism is first and mainly of Jewish formation, and (2) that in its non-Jewish features it has most affinity with the Pythagorean tendency of the Greeks."

(1.) *The community.*—This was probably not very large at any time, and, when Josephus wrote, it numbered only four thousand members. They were distributed in different parts of the land, and had establishments in the neighbourhood of towns, as well as in the depths of the desert by the Dead Sea. Each establishment was under the same system of rules, which were very strict, and was presided over by a master, to whom the members were bound to yield implicit obedience. The probation for admission to the order extended over three years, and at the commencement of it the novice was presented with a white dress, an apron, and a pick-axe, the badges by which the order was distinguished—the first, in symbol of purity; the second, in symbol of defence from impurity; and the third, to be at hand to dig a hole in the ground, and remove any impurity out of sight. Initiation into the order was by admission to eat of the common meal, and by a sort of oath of imprecation, lest one should fail in sincerity with the brethren, or betray any secret of the society to the uninitiated. Within the community the members had all things in common, and no man deemed anything he possessed or might earn as his own. Everything was the property of the community, and the needs of all were relieved, under management, of course, out of the common store. Each member had his own occupation, but in their association together they were all subject to a common rule. They all ate at one table, washed before sitting down, and began their meals, as well as their daily work, with prayer. Agriculture was the chief occupation, but they prosecuted also useful crafts ; only they were forbidden to make or produce anything harmful, such as weapons of war, swords, spears, &c., and expressly debarred from trade, as tending to encourage a spirit of covetousness.

(2.) *Moral principles.*—These inculcated extreme moderation in the gratification of every natural desire, abstinence from merely sensual indulgence, freedom from all emotional as well as animal excitement, and chastity of affection, with extreme modesty of behaviour. The desires of each were limited by his necessities, and they avoided everything like luxurious living. In their dress and food they were simple to a degree ; they contented themselves with the same dish in moderation every day, and they wore the same garment day by day till they could wear it no longer.

(3.) *Manners and customs.*—They had no slaves, but were all freemen serving one another ; they made and accepted simple statements without oath ; they forbade anointing with oil, as savouring of luxury ; they bathed themselves in cold water before meals, and after contact with anything, or with any one reckoned unclean ; they always wore a white dress ; they were especially modest in their demeanour ; but few of them married ; they offered no animal sacrifices ; and their meals consisted of food which, that it might be clean, was prepared for them by a priest, and at both sitting down to them and rising from them they gave God thanks. Owing to a statement of Jerome it has been often asserted that they neither ate meat nor drank wine. The assertion of the Latin father, however, was founded on an error ; the language of Josephus—who is Jerome's admitted authority—about the moderation of the Essenes in food and drink, points to the opposite conclusion.

(4.) *Religious opinions and practices.*—They held the same views as the Pharisees in regard to the providence of God as ordaining and regulating everything, and they had the same veneration for the law of Moses. High as their reverence was for this law, their reverence for the lawgiver was still higher, and the name of Moses was in their esteem next in sacredness to that of God Himself. They read and expounded the Scriptures in their diets of worship, and they had, it is said, a leaning towards allegorical interpretations. They were strict to the very letter, if not beyond it, in the observance of the Sabbath law ; and Jewish to the bone in everything except in their refusal to offer animal sacrifices in the Temple, in consequence of which they placed themselves outside the pale of the rest of the Jewish community. They had, moreover,

a strange un-Jewish regard, savouring almost of Baal-worship, for the sun as a symbol of the brightness which they imagined to invest the Divine majesty, and of that purity the recovery of which was the final aim of all the discipline to which they subjected themselves. They had their esoteric books and rites too ; and they studied the one and observed the other, in order to achieve more completely the purification they sought for. By this means they thought they brought themselves in closer *rapport* with the Divine fountain of all purity.

8. **The Zealots.**—The Zealots were a fanatical Jewish party which arose in Judæa at the commencement of the Roman procuratorship there, just after the deposition of Archilaus, through the action of the people who had complained to the emperor of his tyrannous conduct. This substitution by the imperial power of a Roman governor for a native prince, however well-meant and however acceptable it was to the Sadducæan section of the nation, was far from palatable to the great body of the people. From the first they never took kindly to the supremacy of any foreign power, and they always had a special dislike to the ascendancy of Rome. They had suffered beyond endurance from the house of Herod, the government of which had recommended itself to their Roman patrons ; and now, it seemed, that having got rid of that subordinate tyranny, they were to be directly subject to the parent tyrant-power. Their condition was becoming desperate, and they were ready to kindle up into open revolt. The doctrine of the Zealot sect which arose at this time was specially calculated to encourage this temper ; and it seized hold of and stirred the nation to its very depths. This was the denial of the right of any power to rule over the people of God's election, and the preachers of it called upon the nation to resist any such claim to the death as an insult to the nation's God. The first preachers of this doctrine were an extreme section of the Pharisees, although the doctrine itself may seem to be in contravention of the first principle from which Pharisaism took its start. The inconsistency, however, is only apparent ; for the Pharisees, though content on principle with the sovereignty of any foreign power that conceded to them religious freedom, were pledged to be the very first to resist any and every power that did not concede that right. They had installed themselves as the guardians of the religious interest, and they were the very people to call the rest to arms against any and every tampering with that interest. Moreover, the Pharisees saw in the appointment of a Roman procurator an accession of the Sadducees to greater power in the state, and against the dominance of that party they were bound by every motive to wage war to the death. Clearly it was out of zeal for the religious principles dear to the Pharisees that the Zealots called upon the people to resist the claim of the Romans to lord it over them.

9. **The Galilæans.**—The Galilæans, so far as they were a party, rose in northern Palestine, and they appear to have taken up the same ground in Galilee as the Zealots in Judæa. They were followers of one Judas of Galilee, who headed a rebellion against that assessment with a view to taxing the people, which took place under

Cyrenius, the first Roman procurator of the province, in A.D. 6, and were a source of trouble to the Roman power for many a day. They were daunted by nothing in the assertion of their rights, while they were reckless of the rights of others. In their fanaticism they overran the length and breadth of the country, introducing disorder and confusion wherever they went. The excesses they indulged in provoked a fierce revenge, and contributed more than anything to induce the Romans to vow the extermination of the whole nation. The name Galilæan became so opprobrious that it was employed by the enemies of Christ, and applied to our Lord to create a prejudice against Him in the minds of the Roman party (Matt. xxvi. 69).

10. **The Assassins.**—The Assassins (Sicarii), who derived their name from a poniard (*sica*) which they carried concealed in the folds of their dress, were an organised band of fanatics originating in the Galilæan rebellion, who played a violent part in the last desperate struggle of the nation for liberty. They appear to have been provided with a list of all the enemies of the cause who had been judged worthy of death, and to have gone about in quest of any such in order to despatch them privately. They would frequent the great festivals, spot their victim, seize an opportunity, and then, after inflicting a mortal wound on him, escape unseen among the crowd. They did not always ply their calling, however, in this underhand fashion, for they would sometimes muster together and appear in open war against the Romans, under a fanatical conception of that people as the enemies of their country and its God. They are mentioned in Acts xxi. 38.—See R. V.; A. V. has "murderers."

11. **The Herodians.**—The Herodians were supporters of the dynasty of the family of the Herods and their civil policy, whose greatest care was to preserve the public quiet, and avoid all occasions of offence to the Romans. They were content with the sway of a native prince under the protection of Rome, and apprehended nothing but evil to the state from a change of the political situation. They regarded the teaching of Christ as of a revolutionary character, and strove hard to convict Him of seeking to establish a kingdom that would be subversive of Cæsar's, the more so that they saw He despised them as merely self-seeking politicians. Neither Herod nor Cæsar, He saw, were anything to them; they only cared for the comfortable status they held under the arrangement between those potentates; and they had no more regard for God than they had for either of them; hence the admonition He addressed to them when challenged as to His political intentions : "Render to Cæsar the things that are Cæsar's, and to God the things that are God's " (Mark xii. 17).

12. **The Publicans.**—The Publicans whom we read of in the New Testament were not a sect or a party, but a class of the Jewish people, and were specially odious to the rest of the community as the collectors of the taxes imposed upon the nation, mostly at the instance of their foreign oppressors the Romans. The revenues of the province, or a district of it, were the property of some rich Roman citizen, or body of citizens, who stipulated to pay a certain sum into the Roman treasury (the *publicum*, whence the name *publicani*) for the right of collecting them, and who had agents in the province to employ natives to make the actual collection. These natives were not merely servants of the agent of the district ; they were the farmers of the tax, paying him so much for the right of collecting it, and making as much more as they could by extortion at the hands of the people. Thus the people paid for the privilege of being ruled and lorded over by a foreign race, not merely the sum which the imperial treasury required for its support, but as much more as would handsomely recompense those who undertook the burden of the collection. It was a nefarious system, and a source of oppression most galling to the subjects of it. To the Jewish race it must have been extremely so, and the agents connected with it were objects of detestation, more especially to the pious section of the community. For in their regard these agents were not the mere tools of a foreign oppressor ; they were traitors to their country and apostates from the faith of their fathers, worthy to be classed, as indeed they were, with heathen (Matt. xviii. 17), sinners (Matt. ix. 11), and harlots (Matt. xxi. 31). It was not unnatural that the relation of Christ to this class should have given offence to those who had such good ground for so regarding them. Dante, echoing the sentiment of Christendom, teaches that no man can sink lower in the moral scale than in betraying for money the highest that has been vouchsafed to him. The detestation with which Christendom was wont to regard the memory of Judas on this account may enable us to understand in some measure the feeling with which the pious Jew would regard the Publican.

13. **The Scribes.**—The Scribes were a non-priestly class, devoted first to multiplying copies of the law, and then to the study and exposition of it. They grew up in Judæa by the side of the priesthood during the Grecian period of Jewish history, and rose to a position of importance and influence in the community after the achievement of national independence under the Maccabees. During the Maccabæan struggle, and the period preceding it, the Law, as given by God for their guidance, had acquired a new religious value and significance in the minds of the people, and accordingly the students and interpreters of it began to rise more and more in the public esteem. The priests, to whom the Law had been committed, and who should have taught the people, had grown more intent on the maintenance of their own social status and political influence than the discharge of their spiritual office, and so they were gradually losing all hold of the people, who ere long looked no more to them, but to the Scribes, as their spiritual instructors. Henceforth the people, who had been taught to regard the Law as the directory of their life, regarded the Scribe and not the priest as its authoritative expounder. The public acknowledgment of the binding authority of the Law as sovereign in the whole domain of life dates from the days of Ezra (Neh. viii., ix.), and Ezra, who bound the people to keep it, was a priest ; but the priests that succeeded him were less zealous in directing the people in the fulfilment of the obligation, and

so the spiritual power passed for ever out of their hands.

The Scribes, who, in the days of Christ, were in the full possession of this spiritual power over the people, are known in the New Testament by several names. Of these *Scribes, i.e.*, writers, or men learned in what is written, is the translation of one; *Lawyers, i.e.*, men learned in law, or jurists, of another; and *Teachers of the Law*, of a third; while *Sopherim* is the designation they bear in Jewish literature. The name *Rabbi, i.e.*, my master, is found in the New Testament as the appellation of honour by which they were addressed; but it nowhere occurs, as in subsequent times, in the sense of a title. It gave rise, however, to the term *Rabbinism*, which, along with *Scribism*, has in modern times been invented to denote the peculiar principles and methods of the class, although Scribism denotes properly the earlier and stricter, and Rabbinism the later and freer, or looser, development of the system.

The Scribes were held in the greatest esteem by the people, and the highest places of honour were conceded to them. Their disciples were taught to regard them, and did regard them, as deserving of a reverence superior to that paid to father or mother; the spiritual parent being reckoned as much above the natural parent as the spirit and its interests are above the flesh and its interests. We are reminded of those Italian artists who carried this principle still farther, and not merely paid a higher regard to master than parent, but even abandoned the parental name and adopted one after the master. As far as it went, however, the honour paid to the Scribes was not in excess of the sense of gratitude by which their pupils were bound to them; the very zeal with which they devoted themselves to their pupils' benefit was worthy of this homage, for they preferred to work with their own hands for their support rather than make any profit out of the pupils. It was only after some time that they could be prevailed on to take any reward, and only their successors who, in subordinating the office to the reward and the honour it brought them, exposed themselves to the reproach of Christ as animated by a spirit of covetousness and a wish for display (Mark xii. 40, and Matt. xxiii. 5).

Scribism, though at first centralised in Jerusalem, soon extended its operations to other parts, and already in the days of Christ we recognise its presence in the province of Galilee, as we afterwards do among the Jews of the Dispersion, such as those of Babylon, to whom we owe that great repository of Rabbinical lore, the Babylonian Talmud. It is identified more with Pharisaism than with Sadducæism; for though there were Sadducees learned in the Law, it was the Pharisaic party that accepted it to the full, and were its practical interpreters.

Scribism proper had to do mainly, if not solely, with the Law as such, and the office of the Scribe in connection with it was (1) to develop the Law, (2) to teach it, and (3) to administer it practically.

(1.) *The development of the Law.*—This consisted in the amplification and specialisation of the original code, agreeably to the principles on which it was based, so that a complete readymade directory might be at hand for the guidance of the conscience in every variety of emergency that might arise. This process of elaborating and extending the Law went on for centuries, and the results of it were long handed down by tradition in the memory. The fruit of such a process was the institution of a most complex system of law; and the whole grew out of the labour of the Scribes acting in concert, and coming to conclusions after the most searching inquiry, keen discussion, and solemn deliberation. Thus were the Scribes the makers of the Law, as they afterwards became the arbiters of its verdict in disputed cases.

(2.) *The teaching of the Law.*—This was the chief duty of the Scribes, and it was their business to instruct in the knowledge of the Law as many capable youths as they could collect about them. The task both of teaching and of learning was toilsome to a degree; the subject was most complex, and in most cases the lesson had to be committed verbally to memory. It was only by endless repetitions that the teacher could convey the instruction, although the process might be made more interesting and lively by ingenuity on his part, and ingenuousness as well as smartness on the pupil's. This was secured by a mutual catechetical method at a certain stage in the discipline, when the master would propound cases for the decision of the pupil, and the pupil in turn draw out the learning of the master by questioning him. Nevertheless the task imposed upon the pupil was a very severe one: he must retain in his memory every word and syllable as it was committed to him by his teacher, and he must never teach to others anything but what he had been literally taught himself. This teaching went on in the days of Christ partly in schools attached to the synagogues and partly in the porches of the temple, the master being seated on an elevated chair, and the pupils on the ground round about him (Luke ii. 46; Acts xxii. 3).

(3.) *The administration of the Law.*—It was a further duty of the Scribes to judge in the courts of justice, and though they were not called on in every case to pass sentence, they were the immediate judges in important cases, and the ultimate judges in all.

Thus the function of the Scribe was mainly confined to the development, teaching, and administration of the Law, and it did not properly extend to the unfolding and enforcement of the doctrine of the rest of the Scriptures. But this, too, had to be studied as well as the Law, and it was the subject of a varied and elaborate interpretation. The Scribes also were custodians of the letter of the whole Scripture; and to their labours we owe not only the state of the text, but also other works which have contributed to preserve it in its purity and integrity.

The Halachah.—This word denotes properly that which is "customary," and was the name given by the Rabbis to the Law, as developed by the decision of the Scribes, on the basis of inferential reasoning or established custom. It was taken to be of higher authority than the written Law, although it was never held valid until it was sanctioned by a majority of the doctors.

The Haggadah.—This term, which means literally "legend," is the Rabbinical name for the system of professedly traditional, mostly fanciful, amplifications of the historical and didactic, as distinct from the legal, portions of the Jewish scripture, of which there is such store in Jewish apocalyptic literature, the Targums and the Talmuds. It is not an exposition as the Halachah is, but a reconstruing and remodelling of both history and dogma according to the views and theories of later times, in which the utmost liberty is taken with the original accounts. The Jews seem to have thought that they were bound to the letter of the Law, but that any amount of licence was allowed them in the treatment of history and dogma. Unlike the strict Halachah, however, the Haggadah does not profess to be authoritative. It is a popular literature, a collection of the most fantastic tales, a vast tangled forest of wild imagination. In it the fancy of ages found vent. No general literature being cultivated among the Jews, the poet and the novelist had the only scope for the exercise of their talents in commentaries on the Sacred Scriptures, which were commentaries only in name.

14. **The Proselytes.**—The Proselytes were converts to the Jewish faith from other races or nations, and were often designated in Scripture by the name of "strangers." They were originally received into the Jewish community on submission to the rite of circumcision, and bound to the observance of certain laws and institutions, such as the Sabbath and particular feast-days, in return for which they enjoyed certain valued privileges, though with drawbacks to remind them of their inferiority, and even subjection, to the born Jew. In the days of the monarchy some of them attained to positions of high eminence in the state, and others were content with the lowest rank in the community, if only they were reckoned among its members. This class became very numerous after the Dispersion, as the Jews came more into contact with people of other nations, and it was reckoned at hundreds of thousands, if not millions. The Proselytes appear to have been attracted to the Jewish faith by the character of its worship and the study of its sacred books. They were admitted into different grades of privilege according to the extent of their conformity to the Jewish law. They worshipped with the Jews in their synagogues, went up with them to the feasts at Jerusalem, and were admitted, according to their standing, to the services of the Temple. Some, who had accepted the ceremonial law, and were called " Proselytes of Righteousness," were admitted into the inner court; while others, who had accepted only the moral law, and were called " Proselytes of the Gate," were admitted only into the outer court. The membership of the former was by circumcision, baptism, and sacrifices; that of the latter by conformity to the seven "Precepts of Noah," *i.e.*, precepts directed against idolatry, profanity, murder, uncleanness, theft, rebellion, and eating blood. Recently, however, the " Proselytes of the Gate " have been regarded as no more than foreign residents, who were simply permitted to live among the Jews on the conditions laid down. The true Proselytes were zealous not only in the observance, but in the propagation, of the Jewish faith, and it was among them Christianity at the beginning found its readiest and most zealous converts.

15. **The Hellenists.**—The term Hellenist is applied to two different classes of people. It denotes either a Greek proselyte to Judaism, or a Christian of Greek as distinct from one of Jewish descent (Acts vi. 1 ; ix. 29); but it also denotes a Jew who has become Grecianised by contact with Greek civilisation, and learned to employ the Greek language to the exclusion of Aramaic. At first a Hellenist in this sense was a Jew who would fain have seen Jewish thought and life more or less transformed in spirit as well as fashion after a Greek pattern ; but when that idea was no longer to be entertained, in consequence of the expressed stern refusal of the Jewish people in the Maccabæan struggle to sink their nationality in the presence of any other, the term came to denote a Jew who was open to learn as much from the civilisation of the Greek as was consistent with the maintenance of the principles of his own religion in their integrity. The great centre in which this tendency, giving rise to a new phase of Jewish character and faith, began to develop was Alexandria, and the fruits of a Grecian quality which it produced were more pronounced in this city than in almost any other centre of the Dispersion. For not only were the Jewish scriptures here translated into Greek, but the Jewish mind here began to acquire quite a new expressiveness, and learned to assimilate forms of thought and action to which it was presumed to be alien. Here it was that Hellenism took its rise, and that the Jew proved, notwithstanding his professed exclusiveness, how wide an affinity the religion of his fathers had with those other forms of life which the Greek had developed for the good of humanity. It was the merit of the Hellenist that he recognised this affinity, and that he became the medium of broadening the Jewish faith and preparing the way for the Christian religion which was to baptize all nations.

16. **The Epicureans.**—The Epicureans derived their name from Epicurus (342-270 B.C.), a refined, gentle, kindly philosopher, who would have scorned the low use to which his principles were prostituted by his later followers. They held that the chief end of man was happiness, that the business of philosophy was to guide him in the pursuit of it, and that it was only by experience one could learn what would lead to it and what would not. They scouted the idea of reason as regulative of thought, and conscience as regulative of conduct, and maintained that our senses were our only guides in both. In a word, they denied that God had implanted in man an absolute rational and moral principle, and maintained that he had no other clue to the goal of his being but his experience in life, while the distinction of right and wrong was only a distinction of what was found to be conducive to happiness and what was not. Epicurus, however, was far from inviting his followers to pursue the pleasure of the moment. He taught that present pain must be borne for the sake of future pleasure, that calm, enduring pleasures were preferable to exciting ones, that it is more important to escape pain than to win pleasure, and therefore that a life of simple habits and few wants was the happiest life. The Epicureans had no faith in or fear of a Divine Being above man any more than of a Divine principle within man ; they held that the gods dwelt in unalterable bliss, unconcerned with human affairs, and taking no part in the government of the universe ; and they

94

scorned the idea of another world with its awards, and concerned themselves only with this world, which, however, in their hands, was no longer a kosmos, but a chaos. This was the favourite philosophy of the educated classes throughout the Roman world at the advent of Christ, and the prevalence of it must be reckoned one of the most signal signs of the times, in evidence of the widespread spiritual death that prevailed in that crisis of the world's history, and in justification of the zeal of the early disciples of Christ in the propagation of the Christian gospel.

17. **The Stoics** were the disciples of Zeno, and derived their name from the *stoa*, or portico, in Athens, where their master taught and founded the school in 280 B.C. The doctrines of this school were completely antagonistic to those of Epicurus, and among the disciples of it are to be reckoned some of the noblest spirits of the heathen world immediately before and after the advent of Christ. These appear to have been attracted to it by the character of its moral teachings, which was of a very high order indeed. Indeed, no higher moral system is anywhere to be found outside the influence of the inspired teachings of the Bible.

(1.) *Theology.*—The Stoic was a pantheist in the theological part of his creed. He believed in one all-pervading God. In his conception of the universe the world is God's body, God the world's soul. The world has no independent existence; but the presence of God in it makes it one vast living creature. All things are harmonised in an essential unity. What looks to us most evil really contributes to the good of the whole.

(2.) *Morals.*—Yet the optimism and pantheism of this system does not allow of easy morals. On the contrary, the Stoic cultivated a stern and lofty conception of human life and duty. "*Follow nature*" was his maxim. But this did not mean "yield to blind appetite." It meant, "live in harmony with nature, *i.e.*, with the great, universal order;" or, to put it another way, "*follow thine own rational nature so far as it remains in its own simplicity, and is not distorted or corrupted by art.*" He differed from the Epicurean in regard to pleasure, which he held to be a remission of the moral energy of the soul, while real happiness was to be found in the exercise of that energy. He did not go so far as the Cynics in despising all material good, and he held that, other things being equal, the wise man would prefer health, wealth, &c., to their opposites. But he did not hold those things to be in themselves positively good; they were only desirable because they helped the exercise of moral energy. He considered, too, that though pain might well be avoided for a similar reason, it was not an evil in itself. Every personal aim was to be rejected; every external end to be looked upon as alien to the highest purpose. The wise man was to live only for moral purpose, and this moral purpose was to be to conform himself to the order of the universe by following his rational nature.

(3.) *Influence.*—Stoicism could never be popular. Its austerity left it as the heritage of strong, lofty natures only. It had no pity for the weak. In this respect it was the opposite of the gospel of the Saviour, Who would not "crush the bruised reed, or quench the smoking flax." In the few select natures capable of living in its fine bracing atmosphere it produced a grand, manly, moral tone, which contrasts strongly with the weak self-indulgence of many who regard themselves as Christians. But, at the same time, it developed a spirit of hard and scornful pride. The Stoic was the Pagan Pharisee. Moreover, Stoicism broke down where it was most needed. It permitted suicide in the extreme case in which life appeared to be no longer worth living. Greek in its origin, Stoicism found its most congenial soil in the hardy Roman character. Indeed it won many adherents among the Romans, and was in vigorous life at Rome when Christianity appeared in the world.

18. **The Magi.**—The Magi, to whom the "wise men" who were guided by the star to the manger at Bethlehem (Matt. ii.) are understood to have belonged, were a priestly caste of Median or Persian origin, and of similar standing among the eastern nations to the Druids among the western, constituting, as they did, the "learned" class. They were held in high honour as priests and diviners, and were entrusted with the education of princes among the Persians especially; no enterprise of any importance was undertaken without their official advice. It was believed in those parts that all things were arranged and guided by an overruling providence, and that it was given to this class to know, as to no other, the secret purposes of the Deity, and even to prevail on Him to interpose in cases in which His worshippers needed His help. They were believers in the stars, as connected somehow with the destiny of mortals, and it was by the study of the heavens, as well as other natural phenomena, that they construed the purpose of God on earth. The first notice we have of them in Scripture is in connection with the Chaldæans, and the book of Daniel introduces them to us as the recognised diviners at the Babylonian court. The Jews, during the Captivity, appear to have taken to them with friendly feelings, as a class with whose religious beliefs they had much in common, and the sentiment seems to have been reciprocated cordially on their part. It was natural, therefore, that they should have been led to interest themselves in the fortunes of the Jewish people, and they may even have been induced to study Jewish history in the Hebrew sacred books. On the return of the Jews from Captivity, Judæa might well become an object of peculiar interest to them, and the star in the sky, when it appeared over Bethlehem, a sure omen that the day of the promised Messiah had at length dawned.

19. **The Gnostics.**—The Gnostics were heretics, consisting of various sects, that began to appear as early as the days of the Apostles, and that sought, agreeably to the philosophic opinions which they severally embraced, to extract an esoteric meaning out of the letter of Scripture, and the facts especially of Christianity, such as only those of superior speculative insight could appreciate. They set a higher value on knowledge (Gr. *gnosis*, whence their name) than faith. Thus their understanding of Christianity was speculative and not spiritual, and their knowledge of it the result of thinking and not of life. The Gnostics elaborated strange systems of the

unseen universe, peopling the vast interval between the infinite God and the finite material creation with emanating and descending series of existences. They made much of these celestial "genealogies" (Titus iii. 9) and doctrines of "angels" (Col. ii. 18). There is an implied reference to the Gnostic heretics in the writings of John and the later epistles of Paul. As far as can be gathered from his epistles, the Gnostics of St. Paul's time betray no acquaintance with the more elaborate systems which did not appear till the second century. They are rather to be associated with Jewish mystical speculations. The Cerinthians, referred to at p. 80, are presumed to have been a Gnostic sect. Simon Magus is also said to have proclaimed a system of Gnostic doctrine.

20. The Docetæ.—These were Gnostics who professed Christianity, but who, on account of their belief in the eternal antagonism of flesh and spirit, denied the reality of the Incarnation, and maintained that Christ was a man only in appearance and not in fact. His fleshly nature was either a mere illusion, or if real, His humanity was either not impregnated with the Spirit or not compacted of ordinary flesh and blood. Thus, in its relation to the person of Christ, did Gnosticism assume two phases, according as it denied, on the one hand, the divinity, or, on the other, the humanity, of Christ.

21. The Nicolaitans.—The Nicolaitans, who are mentioned only in Rev. ii. 6, 15, were a sect of heretics that arose in the Apostolic Church, in regard to the origin and character of whom the opinions of critics have been very various. That opinion, however, is probably the correct one which regards them as a party of professing Christians of Gentile descent, who refused to be bound by the decree of the Council of Jerusalem (Acts xv. 20, 29), which required them to abstain from "meats offered to idols," and from "fornication," or rather from the former as certain to tempt them to commit the latter, and follow in "the way of Balaam." They continued to take part in heathen festivals, and thus contributed to break down the distinction between the Church and the world, as well as to introduce the practices of heathenism into the worship of the Church. Thus perhaps we may identify them with the "followers of the way of Baal" referred to in 2 Peter ii. 15 and in Jude 11.

See Schürer, *History of the Jewish People in the Time of Christ;* Stapfer, *Palestine in the Time of Christ;* Zeller, *Stoics, Epicureans, and Sceptics;* and *A History of Ecclecticism in Greek Philosophy.*

CHAPTER XXI.

THE TABERNACLE AND THE TEMPLE.

A. THE TABERNACLE.

I. Its Origin, Names, and History.—*a.* ORIGIN. —The earliest sacred places of worship mentioned in Scripture are the local altars which were scattered about the country. The patriarchs in their wanderings erected altars at their places of temporary abode, especially whenever some new revelation from heaven had been received (Gen. xii. 7, 8; xiii. 18). These altars were in the open air, not covered by any temple, nor surrounded by any enclosure. They were usually built on the tops of hills, and we meet with them in the later history of Israel under the name of "High Places." It was also customary in early times to set up memorial stones on the sites of events of peculiar religious interest—such as the stone which Jacob planted at Bethel (Gen. xxviii. 18, 19). We meet with no reference in early Hebrew history either to a Tabernacle or to a Temple. But this question is mixed up with that of the origin and history of the Hexateuch (see chap. viii.).

b. NAMES.—The name Tabernacle means Tent. The first word used for this structure is "*Mish-cân*"—meaning "*Dwelling*" (Ex. xxv. 9); and it suggests the idea that the new erection had to be a dwelling-place for God. Another name is *Ohel*, which simply means "*Tent.*" The more exact designation is "*Tent of Meeting.*" This phrase does not mean *Tent of the Congregation,* as it is rendered in the English Authorised Version of the Bible—*i.e.,* the tent where the people meet together; but it means the *Tent where God meets His people,* as is plainly shown by Ex. xxix. 42–46. The tabernacle is also called " the tent of the testimony" (Num. ix. 15), and "the tabernacle of witness" (Num. xvii. 7; xviii. 2).

c. HISTORY.—According to the narrative in the Hexateuch, the Tabernacle was made in the wilderness under the direction of two inspired men, Bezaleel and Oholiab, from the voluntary offerings of the people (Ex. xxv.). It accompanied the nation in its wanderings, and was set up in the midst of the camp at every resting-place. In Canaan it was still moved from place to place during the unsettled time that followed the partial conquest of the land, until it was set up at Shiloh (Josh. xviii. 1), and then it remained there during the dark days of the history of the Judges. After the removal of the ark in the days of Eli (1 Sam. iv. 4), the Tabernacle, which had already been degraded by the immoral conduct of the priests, fell into neglect. In the days of Saul we find it at Nob, a city in the tribe of Benjamin, not far from Jerusalem (1 Sam. xxi. 1-6). The massacre of the priests and the flight of Abiathar left it without a priesthood. In the days of David we meet with it at Gibeon (1 Chron. xvi. 39). The construction of a new Tabernacle for the ark at Jerusalem left the old Tabernacle in a secondary place. But the two continued in existence till the building of Solomon's Temple.

II. The Structure with its Materials.—The *Tabernacle* formed a parallelogram 30 cubits long and 10 cubits broad, and, when erected, stood with its sides looking north and south, and its ends east and west. The sides and the western extremity were constructed of boards raised on end, sunk in sockets, and connected by more or less horizontal bars; while the extremity, which looked east and formed the entrance, was guarded by pillars and hangings. The interior was lined with curtains; the roof was of skins; and the flooring was the naked earth. The holy of holies occupied the western section, and formed one-third of the structure, being separated from the rest by a vail supported by pillars. The whole was surrounded by a court 100 cubits long and 50 cubits broad, the entrance being at the east end, the Tabernacle being well to the west of the enclosure, and the altar of burnt-offerings and the brazen laver in a line between.

a. THE FRAMEWORK.—(1.) The *Sockets* into which the ends, or *Tenons*, of the upright boards were sunk were 100 in number, and were all of silver.

(2.) The upright *Boards* were 10 cubits long, which was the height therefore of the Tabernacle, and 1½ cubits broad, and were 48 in number, being all of wood overlaid with gold.

(3.) The connecting transverse *Bars* were of shittim wood, covered with gold, and arranged in rows of five.

(4.) The *Pillars* were nine in number, four overlaid with gold, and resting on silver sockets, supporting the vail that separated the holy of holies from the holy place, and five similar ones resting on brazen sockets, and forming with their hangings the door of the sanctuary.

b. THE CURTAINS AND THE VAILS.—There were two curtain linings, the Cherub Curtains and the Goat's Hair Curtains—

(1.) The *Cherub Curtains* constituted the "Tabernacle" proper, and covered the whole interior, ceiling as well as sides—the groundwork being pure white linen inwoven all over with blue, purple, and scarlet, and figures of cherubim.

(2.) The *Goat's Hair Curtains* constituted the "Tent" of the Tabernacle, and extended along the roof and side walls to the floor, between these and the cherub curtains.

(3.) The *Inner Vail* was of the same material as the cherub curtains, and was covered with the same symbolic figures, but with a preponderance of blue, suggestive, as it is thought, of heaven; to which, as the proper chamber of Jehovah, it symbolised the entrance.

(4.) The *First* or *Outer Vail*, forming the door of the Tabernacle, was the same as the inner, only there were no figures of cherubim woven in it. None but the priests could enter by it; and it therefore symbolised the priestly lineage and purity required of all who can be admitted to minister at God's altar, or at whose hands Heaven will accept any spiritual service.

c. THE COVERINGS.—There were two Coverings forming the roof, an inner of *Rams' skins*, and an outer of *Badgers'* or perhaps *Seals' skins*, both being tanned and dyed—the inner red, and the outer, which was the stronger, blue.

III. The Several Parts of the Tabernacle and their Contents, with their Uses.—The Tabernacle consisted of (*a*) the Outer Court, and the Tent of Meeting or Tabernacle proper, which was divided into two parts, (*b*) the Holy Place, and (*c*) the Holy of Holies.

a. The COURT, as already defined, was included within sixty pillars, presumably of wood overlaid with brass, and topped with silver, and supporting rods, overlaid with silver, from which were suspended hangings of fine white linen inwoven with blue, and purple, and scarlet; the whole, as the sanctuary of worship, forming the court, or, with its divisions, the courts, of the house of the Lord. This court was open to all

to worship in, only no one could tread it who was not in the religious temper of which the surroundings were the symbol. It contained (1) the great *Brazen Altar* for the Burnt-offerings near the entrance, and (2) the *Laver*, further in towards the entrance of the Holy Place.

(1.) The *Brazen Altar*, which was 5 cubits square and 3 cubits high, stood in the centre between the entrance and the Tabernacle. It consisted of a framework of wood, overlaid with brass, and hollow—perhaps to be filled with earth—with a platform grating at half height all round for the priests to stand on, and projections like horns at the four corners; all the utensils connected with it were of brass. This was the altar of burnt-offerings, and it was chiefly used for the offerings of self-consecration, voluntarily brought by the people and wholly consumed by fire. The fat and some of the internal organs of animals offered as sacrifices for sin were also burnt on this altar, and the blood poured out at the foot of it.

(2.) *The Laver*, which was constructed of brass, of the polish in part of a mirror, stood between the brazen altar and the door of the Tabernacle, and served to wash part of the victims in, as well as the hands and feet of the priests, preparatory to offering sacrifice, or entering the Tabernacle. The washing symbolised the purity of heart that is required of all who minister in God's house or at His altar.

b. The HOLY PLACE, as already defined, occupied two-thirds of the Tabernacle, and was accessible to no one but the priests. It contained the *Table of Shewbread* on one side, the *Golden Candlestick* on the other side, and the *Golden Altar*, or *Altar of Incense*, between them, and facing the entrance to the Holy of Holies.

(1.) The *Table of Shewbread* stood on the north side, and was of wood overlaid with gold, being 2 cubits long, 1 broad, and 1½ high. On it stood an offering to the Lord of two piles of six loaves each of unleavened bread, renewed weekly, with frankincense, perhaps, in early times, also offerings of wine, all on plates or in vessels of pure gold. The twelve loaves, with the wine, symbolised primarily the offerings of the twelve tribes for the maintenance of the ministers of the sanctuary, in grateful acknowledgment of the divine bounty in the gifts of providence and grace. The title *Shewbread* is literally *Bread of the Presence*. This name has been interpreted in two senses. It has been taken as bread which symbolised the presence of God, bread in which God was mystically present, suggesting that the soul is nourished by God, as the body by the bread. It has also been taken as bread set in the presence of God, as a thank-offering to the Giver of every good and perfect gift. This second meaning is the simpler, and the one which agrees best with Old Testament ideas.

(2.) The *Golden Candlestick* stood on the south side, and was, with its utensils, of pure gold, wrought of a mass of a single talent (about 1500 oz.). It consisted of a vase and shaft with six branches, three on each side, the shaft being composed of a succession of floral, oblate, and oblong forms, the branches bulging out each into three almond-shaped bowls, and the whole seven surmounted with knobs, each with receptacles for the lamps. The oil used for the lamps was of the olive, pressed out by beating in a mortar, and the lamps, as there were no windows, must have burned continually day and night. The seven may have symbolised completeness, the oil the Spirit of God, the lamps its illuminating radiance, and their continual burning that the light of the Spirit would never die out.

(3.) The *Golden Altar* stood towards the entrance to the Holy of Holies, in a line with the ark inside, with only the vail intervening, and was of wood overlaid with gold, having four horns at the corners like the brazen altar. It was called the *Altar of Incense*, as only incense was offered on it, and that by the high-priest, morning and evening. The incense was of a special composition, after a divine prescription, and consecrated exclusively for the purpose; the fire which consumed it was brought from the altar of sacrifice, and the fragr ance produced penetrated to the very Holy of Holies. The whole symbolised the intercession, heard and accepted in heaven, of the great High-Priest, on the ground at once of His Divine human merits, and His propitiatory sacrifice.

c. The HOLY OF HOLIES, situated as already defined, was square, measuring 10 cubits in length, in breadth, and in height, and comprised the central and most sacred spot within the whole enclosure, to which all the rest was subordinate. Here were preserved and protected in sacred seclusion the most significant symbols of the whole worship. These were the Ark with its contents, the Mercy-seat, the Cherubim, and the Shekinah.

(1.) The *Ark* was a chest of acacia wood overlaid and lined with gold, 2½ cubits long, and 1½ in breadth and height. It stood on four feet, with rings at the ends for the poles on which it was borne aloft when there was occasion to remove it. It contained the "Two Tables of Stone," inscribed with the Ten Commandments, insistence on which constituted the vital point of the religion of Moses; "The Golden Pot with the Manna," kept as a symbol of the miraculous way in which God provided for His people in their wilderness journey; and "Aaron's rod, that budded," as a token of the rights of Aaron's family.

(2.) The *Mercy-seat*, the rendering of a word which means "covering," constituted the lid of the ark, and was of pure gold. It obviously symbolised the covering of sin in the act of forgiveness, but this on the ground of a sacrifice in propitiation, as it was sprinkled by the High-Priest on the great day of atonement with the blood of the victims slain and offered on the altar. It may be regarded as typical, therefore, of forgiveness on the ground of the accepted satisfaction of Christ.

(3.) The two *Cherubim*, which were symbolic forms of gold, stood at each end of the mercy-seat with expanded wings, facing each other, and, as it were, hovering pensively over it in mystic down-turned gaze. According to some, these stood for the Divine powers and attributes; by others they have been thought to symbolise the awe-struck interest with which the angelic world regards that ineffable divine compassion which to us is revealed in the mystery of the Cross.

(4.) The *Shekinah* was a supernatural radiancy or glory issuing from the mercy-seat and reflected from the cherubim, and was a symbol of the presence of the Deity enthroned on the mercy-seat; yet in a form which was little more than a token and a type of that more real presence which was first manifested in the life and death of Christ. It was symbolic of the Divine nature as Light, and especially as the Light of Life, in which alone is the gracious presence of God with His chosen people upon earth.

B. THE TEMPLE.

The Temple was constructed on the same plan, and to serve the same purposes, as the Tabernacle; but the materials were more durable and costly, and the style more elaborate and ornate. The arrangement, the sacred contents, the service, and the priestly ministrants were the same; but the accessories were grander and the effect more imposing. The treasures of wealth it contained became the envy of the surrounding nations, and the magnificence of it was the pride, as the restoration is the prayer, of the whole Hebrew people. There were three structures successively erected in Jerusalem : Solomon's Temple, built 1012, or, according to another reckoning, 975 B.C., and destroyed by Nebuchadnezzar 586 B.C.; Zerubbabel's, built about 516, and pillaged and desecrated by Antiochus Epiphanes 167 B.C.; and Herod's, on the ruins of the former, begun in 16 B.C., finished A.D. 29, and destroyed by the army of Titus A.D. 70. These were all erected on Mount Moriah, that being the spot where Abraham is said to have gone to offer up Isaac, and where David raised an altar to the Lord after taking the city from the Jebusites, on the very site of which ever after the Temple altar stood.

a. *Solomon's Temple.*—This is the Jewish temple *par excellence;* and the idea of its erection is due to David, who was not permitted to carry out his purpose, however, that honour being reserved for his son (2 Sam. vii.), although he himself went on making arrangements and collecting materials. The erection was begun in the fourth year of Solomon's reign, and finished towards the close of the eleventh year, Hiram, king of Tyre, supplying the craftsmen, the stones, and the cedar wood, and Solomon himself paying all the cost and providing many of the labourers (see 1 Kings vi. *seq.;* 2 Chron. ii. *seq.*). The Temple proper, Sanctuary, or *Naos*, was after the fashion of the Tabernacle, but the dimensions were double, and there were additions to it, in the shape of chambers on part of the roof and round three sides, for the accommodation of the priests, as well as a system of internal supports, not required in the original structure. All these are supposed to have been after a style suggested by models familiar to the Phœnician craftsmen who were engaged on the building. The sanctuary occupied the summit of the mountain; the courts of the Israelites were round the three sides on platforms below; the courts of the women—i.e., to which women had access—were on corresponding platforms still lower down; and the whole rose like a pyramid from a plateau, which formed at length the court of the Gentiles, and beyond which no one not a Jew was permitted to pass.

b. *Zerubbabel's Temple.*—This is the temple which, on the return from the Captivity, was built by decree of Cyrus under Ezra and Nehemiah (Ezra iii. and vi.), and which, though on a larger scale, was in a style much less sumptuous than Solomon's. Both material and workmanship were of far inferior value, and the comparison was suggestive of feelings of a saddening, if not a chilling, nature in the heart of many a pious Jew, as he recalled the glory of the former structure. The Jews refused the help of the Samaritans in its erection, and in retaliation and rivalry the latter reared a temple of their own on Mount Gerizim.

c. Herod's Temple.—This is the temple which was founded by Herod the Great, to conciliate the Jews, which superseded Zerubbabel's, and which, though, so far as the sanctuary was concerned, similar to that second temple in dimension as well as arrangement, was in outward appearance on a style of magnificence that surpassed both its predecessors. The whole was enclosed by two walls—an inner, in the shape of a parallelogram, of great strength, and adorned with porches and imposing gateways, and an outer of a square shape, and with embellished porticoes in a style superior to those attached to any other temple of the ancient world, the dimensions of the external one being 400 cubits each way. The outer wall was so strong on the east and the north sides as to form part of the defences of the city, and some of the gateways of the southern wall are still standing. But the most magnificent architectural features of this temple were the cloisters which were added to the outer court, those on the west, north, and east being composed of double rows of Corinthian columns supporting flat roofs, the most imposing of all being "the Royal Porch," which overhung the southern wall, and which, supported by 162 columns in four rows, formed the principal entrance to the temple. Seen from a distance, as it faced the east, the whole must have presented an impressive spectacle, the outer court with its structure forming one terrace, the inner with its structure forming a second, and the temple itself rising serenely above them both. In reality the whole stood at five levels, the first being the court of the Gentiles; the second, eight feet higher, that of the women; the third, ten feet higher still, that of Israel; the fourth, three feet more, that of the priests; and the fifth, the floor of the temple proper, which was eight feet above this, and consequently twenty-nine feet higher than the first. See Atwater, *History and Significance of the Sacred Tabernacle;* Edersheim, *The Temple;* Keil, *Biblical Archæology.*

CHAPTER XXII.

THE PRIESTHOOD AND THE TEMPLE WORSHIP.

Priesthood : *Definition.* — By priesthood is meant the office of a priest, or the priestly order ; and a priest is one consecrated to minister in matters pertaining to God, one appointed to a ministry through which spiritual as well as other help and guidance are ordained to be sought and secured from above. The institution of a class of men set apart to this office, wherever it exists, witnesses to a sense of the need of such mediation, and to a faith in the fact of it, or, in other words, is both a confession of the sin of man and a recognition of the grace of God, as well as an assent on the part of the worshipper to the reception of the latter on God's own terms. The existence of such an institution among the Jews at any rate implies this much ; and if this no longer exists within the Christian community, it is because the dividing wall between priest and people has been broken down, and each man has by Christ been admitted into the inner sanctuary and himself consecrated a priest, while Christ is revealed as the one High-Priest.

1. **The High-Priest.**—He was the chief of the Jewish priests ; and the dignity was hereditary from Aaron, in the line of Eleazar, his son. The holder of the office was distinguished from the common priesthood (*a*) by the manner of his consecration, and by certain specialities, (*b*) of requirement, (*c*) of function, (*d*) of dress, and (*e*) of civic status.

a. Consecration.—Besides a prior consecration after the manner of an ordinary priest, there was a further consecration by a solemn pouring of oil upon the head, as representing the whole person, so that the act symbolised complete dedication. This anointing oil, called holy, was of the composition prescribed in Exod. xxx. 22-25 ; and from his consecration with it, the high-priest is sometimes called by pre-eminence "the anointed priest," and even "the anointed one."

b. Requirements.—The high-priest must have been of legitimate birth, and without personal blemish ; he could only marry a virgin, but she might be chosen from among any one of the tribes of Israel. He was required to abstain from everything which might cause defilement, and prohibited from touching even the dead body of a parent, as well as from joining in acts expressive of mourning, such as rending his garments, or being present at the obsequies of the dead.

c. Functions.—Besides being qualified to discharge any priestly office, which, however, he did only on Sabbath days, new moons, and high festival occasions, the high-priest was the only priest permitted to enter the Holy of Holies, and that but once a year, on the day of atonement, when, arrayed in white linen, he sprinkled the blood of the sin-offering on the mercy-seat, and burnt incense within the vail (Lev. xvi.); and only he could consult the Urim and Thummim. It was also his duty to superintend and administer all that belonged to the services of the sanctuary. The "manslayer" who was pronounced innocent of wilful murder, and who had taken shelter in a city of refuge, where he found a sanctuary protecting him from the attack of the avenger of blood, was not to be allowed to leave till the death of the high-priest, when the cause of quarrel was supposed to come to an end.

d. Dress.—This, besides what was common to him with the rest of the priests, consisted of (1) the Breastplate, (2) the Ephod, (3) the Robe of the Ephod, and (4) the Mitre (Exod. xxviii.). (1.) The Breastplate, called also the breastplate of judgment, *i.e.*, of acceptance with God, was square, of gold, blue, purple, scarlet, and fine-twined linen, cunningly wrought, and set with twelve different kinds of stones in three rows of four, each with one of the names of the children of Israel engraved on it. It was fastened at the top by chains of gold to two onyx stones on the shoulders, and beneath by a lace of blue to rings in the ephod above the girdle. The mysterious oracle of Urim and Thummim was connected with this breastplate, the response being given, according to some, by certain changes in the appearance of it, or vouchsafed, according to others, only to him who wore it, the wearer being endowed with the oracular power. (2.) The Ephod was a richly and emblematically embroidered vestment of two parts, one covering the breast and supporting the breastplate, and the other covering the back. These were clasped to the shoulders by two onyx stones, on which were engraved the names of the tribes, six on each; and the whole was bound round the waist by a "curious girdle" of gold, blue, purple, scarlet, and fine-twined linen. (3.) The Robe of the Ephod was all of blue, and worn immediately under the ephod, though longer than it, but without sleeves, and with only slits for the arms. The opening through which the head was inserted had a border of woven work, and the skirt was trimmed with pomegranates, in blue, red, and crimson, between which were suspended bells of gold, the former, according to Josephus, being symbolic of lightning, and the latter of thunder, and probably intended to intimate to the people outside, by the sound which they made as he walked, the particular moment when the high-priest happened to enter into or retire from the sanctuary. (4.) The Mitre was a towering, somewhat conical headpiece, which in later times was surmounted by a conical crown of gold. A gold plate was fastened with blue lace in front, with the words HOLINESS TO THE LORD engraved upon it. This plate is said to have dated from the days of Moses, and to have survived the destruction of Jerusalem down to the sixth century of our era, after which history loses all trace of it.

e. Civic status.—Besides being chief of the priests, as also of the temple and its worship, the high-priest, though in the eye of the law on the same level as a common Israelite, was, under Jehovah, the spiritual head of the whole nation, and, in the later history, its political head also. The political headship of the high-priesthood dates from after the Exile, and extends from the commencement of the Greek era down to the days of Herod. The high-priests of the Asmonæan line were princes as well as priests, their authority being hereditary and for life, and only restricted by that of the Sanhedrin and by the will of the Greek suzerains. It was only after the Roman government gained the ascendancy that the office ceased to be for life and hereditary, although its holders still continued to wield great power in the state, and were always chosen out of a few privileged families, who, from their connection with the high-priesthood, constituted the most influential section of the Jewish aristocracy. History hands down to us the names of no fewer than twenty-eight of this class who held office during the Herodian period; and this fact justifies the conclusion, that occasionally there must have existed at the same time in the community several who had held the office, though they had now retired from it. These would appear to have retained no small influence over affairs after their retirement, as is evident from the appeal made to Annas, who was one of them, in connection with the accusation of Christ (John

xviii. 13); and they were still called high-priests, as it would seem even the members of their families sometimes were.

2. **The Priests.**—The priests were the descendants of Aaron, and, according to the Levitical law, they possessed, in virtue of this descent, the exclusive right of offering to God the sacrifices of the people, at first in the Tabernacle and then in the Temple of Jerusalem.

a. Qualifications.—A priest must have been able to prove his descent from Aaron, and he was bound to observe certain rules in regard to marriage, with a view to preserve the purity of the priestly stock, and guard the sanctity of the priestly order. He must have been free from all physical defects, for if not, he was debarred from officiating. These disqualifying defects are enumerated in Lev. xxi. 16-23; they were afterwards reckoned, by the subtle casuistry of the Jewish rabbis, to amount to 142. The priest must not touch the body of a dead person, or attend the obsequies of any one except a blood relation.

b. Consecration.—This consisted of three steps—(1) the washing of the body with pure water; (2) investiture with the priestly garments; and (3) a series of sacrifices, accompanied by certain symbolic acts significant of the priestly rank and function (Exod. xxix. and Lev. viii.).

c. The dress.—The material of the dress, which was worn by the priest only in the Temple, whether on duty or off, was all of linen, and it consisted of—(1) short breeches drawn over the hips and thighs; (2) a white, tight-fitting cassock, with a diamond pattern on it, of one woven piece, which reached nearly to the feet, and which was gathered round the body with a symbolically ornamented girdle; and (3) a turban or cap of a cup-shaped form. Besides these, all priests would appear to have also worn the ephod in later times, though at first this was confined to the high-priest, and they always went barefoot when engaged in the service.

d. Priestly courses.—The priests were so numerous that they could not all officiate at once, so that an arrangement had to be made whereby they might do so in regular rotation. Accordingly the whole body of the order was divided into twenty-four families, or courses of service, each of which was to serve in turn for a week—an arrangement which, though it is traced back to the time of David (1 Chron. xxiv. 7-18), appears to have first consolidated itself after the return from the Captivity. The twenty-four divisions were broken up into more or fewer subordinate ones, each, both principal and subordinate, under a "head," who is sometimes designated an "elder." These divisions, though of equal standing in the services of the sanctuary, were of unequal rank in the state, those from which the high-priests were drawn naturally acquiring at length greater influence and importance than the rest, to the ruin, as it happened, not only of the order, but of the commonwealth itself.

e. Emoluments.—Before the Exile the revenues of the priests would appear to have been at once slender and uncertain, and to have been derived exclusively from the small fraction which fell to their share of the offerings made to Jehovah. But with the return from the Captivity these increased to an enormous extent, and this was due to the increase of political power which the new order of things put into the hands of the priesthood. The priestly function from this time became the sovereign one of the state, and more and more of the offerings of the people and the wealth of the community was dedicated to its maintenance, in a dignity and an efficiency proportionate to the importance now assigned to it. Henceforward, if not earlier, the priests acquired a right to a larger share of, and a choicer selection from, the offerings, as well as a power to levy tithes of the whole people, and to lay claim for the service of the Lord to the first-born of men and cattle. (1.) Of the sacrifices they now received the whole of the sin-offerings and the trespass-offerings, and nearly all of the meal-offerings, though of the thank-offerings they received only two parts—the breast and the right shoulder—and of the burnt-offerings little more than the skins, which, however, were a source of no small revenue. (2.) But by far the greater portion of their revenue was derived from dues that were paid irrespectively of the sacrifices altogether, viewed in the light of taxes for the support of the Temple-service and its ministers. These were levied partly in the form of tithes, partly upon the produce of the soil, and partly upon the offspring of cattle. (3.) In addition to imposts on these, there fell to the priests votive-offerings, or the ransom of them, things specially willed away to their benefit, and certain indemnities, as for property unlawfully appropriated, and that could not be restored to its rightful owner. (4.) There were also imposts for their benefit intended to defray the expenses connected with public worship, the chief of which was the half-shekel tax, which every male Israelite of twenty years old and upwards was required to pay every year in the month Adar. All these and other imposts, added to the free-will offerings of the people, naturally contributed to increase the wealth and enhance the importance of the priestly order to an extent of which it is hardly possible to form any adequate conception.

3. **The Levites.**—In the dark and irregular days of the early settlement in Canaan "Priest" and "Levite" were synonymous terms; and it was not till after the centralisation of all worship in Jerusalem that the system laid down in the law was generally carried out. According to the law the Levite held an office subordinate to the priest, only the latter being permitted to minister at the altar, or even to cross the threshold of the sanctuary; while the duty of the former was limited to keeping watch over the Temple, slaying the victims, and making other preparations for the services which the priests alone conducted. In this order the musicians and doorkeepers of the Temple were by-and-by numbered, and the whole class was divided into courses like the priests proper. When not on duty in the Temple, they appear, like the majority of the priests, to have lived scattered up and down among the towns and villages of Judæa.

4. **Temple Functionaries and their Rank.**—Among the functionaries of the Temple, there was, first of all, the *High-Priest*, whose office has been already described above. Next to him stood the *Segan*, who was long supposed to have been the substitute of the high-priest, whose duty it was to act for him, should he happen, from defilement or otherwise, to be unable to take part in the service himself, but he is now believed to have been the functionary designated in the New Testament and elsewhere as the Captain of the Temple (see Acts iv. 1; v. 24, 26). It was his duty to superintend the arrangements for preserving order in and around the Temple, and to him were subordinate other officers who had duties of the same nature, and who went under the same name, he being styled the Chief Captain. Next to him ranked the *Presidents* of the courses of service, already referred to; but the rank they held had reference to their standing as priests, and not to any authority they might have in connection with the Temple worship.

Besides these functionaries there were others, who had respectively to do with (1) the Property, (2) the Police, and (3) the Religious Services of the Temple. (1.) Those who had charge of the Property were the *Treasurers* of the Temple; this property consisted of numerous sacred vessels of gold and silver, the rich vestments of the priests, the flour, wine, oil, and frankincense for the offerings, and large sums of money which belonged partly to the Temple itself and partly to private individuals who had deposited it there for safety. The Treasurers administered as well as guarded the property, and belonged mostly to the Levite class, although the principal ones and their chief were of the priestly order, the last being one of the most distinguished of the Temple officials. (2.) The duty of the Police, which did not extend into the sanctuary, was to see that the Temple regulations were observed, to open and shut the gates, and to keep guard day and night at all the barriers and approaches. This body consisted of Levites, arranged into twenty-four wards, under four captains, and posted on the east, west, north, and south sides of the Temple (1 Chron. xxvi. 12-18). (3.) In connection with the services of the Temple, there were several classes of officials whose duties respectively were such as providing the required offerings, preparing the shewbread or the frankincense, taking charge of the priests' garments, calling the officials to their duty or the people to prayers. Among these may be reckoned the *Musicians*, whose duty it was to accompany certain services, such as the offering of the daily burnt-offerings, with singing and playing of stringed instruments—the cymbal, the psalter, and the harp. *Reed-pipes* were introduced into the choral service on high festival occasions, such as the Passover, and also *trumpets*, which were blown by priests in connection with certain parts of the service, and from the roof of the Temple at dawn on Sabbath morning. Besides the functionaries above-mentioned were the *Nethinim*, whose services were of a menial kind, although of their precise nature we have no definite account.

5. **The Daily Temple Service.** — While the entire priesthood took part in the services on the occasion of the great annual festivals, the daily service was conducted by the twenty-four courses of priests, each course serving a week in succession, and commencing its duties by offering the Sabbath-evening sacrifice and replacing the shewbread on the tables. Corresponding to this division of the priests in connection with

the daily service there was a similar division of the Levites and the people, the former ministering, and the latter "standing by," during the service ; only the former required to be present in the Temple, while the latter were not required to attend except by deputy, provided, while the service lasted, they held solemn assembly, by prayer and reading the Law, in the synagogues. For the service the priests were required to be Levitically clean. In the service, they wore their official dress as a symbol of this purity ; during the term of it they were prohibited from drinking wine or anything intoxicating, and they had to bathe every day before engaging in it. The sacrifices which were offered were of two classes, public and private, the former being offered in the name and at the expense of the whole people, and the latter, which were partly voluntary and partly compulsory, in the name and at the expense of individuals. These again might be classified under three heads : (a) *burnt-offerings*, expressive of entire self-dedication, of which the whole was consumed on the altar ; (b) *sin-offerings* and *trespass-offerings*, for the purpose of expiation, of which only the fat was burnt, and the flesh was the portion of the priests ; (c) the *peace-* or *thank-offerings*, which were of an eucharistic nature, and of which, in like manner, only the fat was burnt, and the flesh was consumed by the offerer and his friends in festive celebration. Besides the regular sacrifices there were the *meal-offerings* and the *drink-offerings;* these were not sacrificial offerings, but only accompaniments of such sacrifices. The sacrifices were offered on the *altar of burnt-offering* (see TABERNACLE), the fire of which had to be kept continually burning by night as well as by day. The victims were slaughtered, flayed, and prepared for sacrifice in the open air to the north, within an enclosure which no one save the priests, except on special occasions, was permitted to enter. The most important part of the regular service of the sanctuary was the burnt-offering, which was made on behalf of the whole people at first every morning, a meal-offering being all that was made in the evening, till, at length, as the priestly service grew more important, a burnt-offering and a meal-offering, with a drink-offering, were offered both evening and morning ; and these morning and evening sacrifices continued to be offered in the Temple till the very eve of its destruction by the Romans, when the beleaguered people found there was not another victim to offer left within the precincts of the city, after which, from that day to this, they have wholly ceased. The priests were required to offer incense before the morning and after the evening sacrifices. They also had the charge of the lamps of the Temple.

See Ewald, *Antiquities of Israel;* Schultz, Bennett, *Old Testament Theology;* A. Edersheim, *The Temple;* E. W. Edersheim, *The Rites and Worship of the Jews.*

CHAPTER XXIII.

THE SYNAGOGUE.

1. **Its Origin and Object.**—The Synagogue was a Jewish institution of post-exilian origin, traces of which appear as early as the Maccabæan period,

and the origin of which dates possibly from the time of Ezra. It was primarily established, not so much for purposes of worship as for religious instruction, and to keep alive in the minds of the people a knowledge of the Law. The rules which regulated it required the people of a district to meet together twice every Sabbath for this purpose ; and so religiously did the Jewish people learn to regard the requirement, that the observance of it is a characteristic feature of Judaism to the present day. The study of the Law was henceforth their supreme duty, and the Synagogue was instituted both to instruct them in it and to remind them of the purpose of their separate existence and the consequent obligations.

2. **Its Rulers and Officials.**—In places where the population was wholly or mainly Jewish, the Synagogue was subject to the civil authorities ; in other cases it had an independent organisation of its own, the authority being in the hands of men called the *Elders of the Congregation.* These had all power to bind and loose, *i.e.*, to determine for their district what was unlawful ("binding"), and what lawful ("loosing") ; and being appointed to guard the purity of its membership, they could pronounce sentence of expulsion, and, in obstinate cases, even final excommunication, from the Jewish community and its privileges. Besides these elders, who had the general direction of the affairs of the congregation, there were three sets of officials attached to each Synagogue, not one of whom, however, had anything to do with the conduct of the service, the carrying out of that being the duty of the members. The first of these officials was the *Ruler of the Synagogue*, who had charge of the order of the service as well as the general concerns of the Synagogue, and in larger Synagogues was usually one of the elders, and perhaps stood alone as a solitary rabbi in smaller ones. It was part of his duty to call upon any one to read the Scriptures, pray, or address the congregation, to prevent all unseemly behaviour, and to look after the building. The *Reader* who conducted the worship does not always appear to have been one regularly appointed officer ; but probably this was the case in the larger synagogues. Then there were the *Receivers and Distributors of alms*—of the former of whom there were at least two, and of the latter three, attached to every congregation. And, lastly, there was the *Minister*, or servant, an officer whose business was to take charge of the sacred rolls used in the service, to punish offenders, and instruct the children in reading.

3. **The Building and its Furniture.**—The Synagogues were of various dimensions and styles of architecture, and were erected often outside the towns, and near streams, if possible, for purposes of ablution. In Galilee, as remains there testify, they generally lay north and south, and were entered on the south by a large central door and two small side-doors, the interior being sometimes divided into three and even five aisles by rows of columns. Every town, and even village, in Palestine had at least one Synagogue ; while in the cities there were several, sometimes distinguished from each other by a special emblem, as the olive or the vine. The furniture

of the Synagogue consisted of a recess for the sacred books, which were wrapped in linen and deposited in a case ; an elevated platform, from which to read the Law or address the congregation ; and a set of trombones and trumpets, to be blown on days of special solemnity.

4. The Order of Divine Service.

The distinguished and senior members of the congregation occupied the front seats, and it is thought men and women sat apart. The presence of ten was necessary to constitute an assembly for worship, and the chief parts of the service were the recitation of the *shema*, the prayer, the reading of the law, the reading of the prophets, and the benediction of the priest, to which in time were added a translation of the passages read, and a homily thereon for the edification of the congregation. The *shema*, so called from its first word, signifying "hear," consisted of Deut. vi. 3–9; xi. 13–21 ; Num. xv. 37–41. The *prayer*, which was after a prescribed form, was offered standing in front of the chest containing the scrolls of the law, and uttered by any one of the congregation whom the ruler might call upon, the body of the people joining in by responses from time to time. The *scriptures* of both the law and the prophets were read in a standing attitude by any one who might be called upon, although the precedence of doing so fell to one of priestly rank, if any such happened to be present. The law was so arranged that it was read through once every three years ; and the reading of it was followed by the reading of a selection from one of the other sacred books, only the reader was free to select any passage that the circumstances might suggest to him. Translation was added, because to many the original had become a dead letter, and exposition, that the hearers might better understand the sense of the words and their practical application. The translation into the vulgar dialect was done by an officer called the *meturgeman*, i.e., dragoman, interpreter, who rose up after the reading of each verse or triplet of verses, and gave orally, in Aramæan, the sense of the original, to which he sometimes added expositions. This practice led to the formation of the Targums (see p. 7). The *preacher* might be any member of the congregation distinguished for his learning or wisdom. He usually sat when delivering his discourse. The *blessing* at the end of the service was pronounced by a priest or consecrated person, and responded to by the people.

See Schürer, *History of the Jewish People in the Time of Christ;* Morison, *The Jews under Roman Rule.*

CHAPTER XXIV.

THE PROPHETS: THEIR MISSION AND MESSAGE.

NOTHING is more peculiarly characteristic of the religion and history of Israel than the mission of the prophets and the exercise of their unique gifts. Greece is famous for its poets, philosophers, and artists ; Rome for its soldiers, statesmen, and legislators ; Israel for its prophets. The prophet was not simply, nor was he chiefly, a seer of the future. He was a messenger of Jehovah, a man inspired by God to see his Lord's will, and sent forth to declare it. But while the true prophet of God was all this, a multitude of professional prophets existed—people who were trained to exercise prophetic functions, and who practised them as a profession—exciting themselves with music and wild dances. They were the dervishes of the Jews. Many of these men were not divinely inspired, and some of them prophesied contrary to the mind and will of God. It is important to observe the distinction between the two classes of men. Sometimes they are directly opposed to one another—the true prophets denouncing the professional prophets, and the latter persecuting the former. In course of time the professional order of prophets lost every spark of Divine inspiration, and every trace of a special mission. Then it became a mere echo of popular cries, and a base organ for the flattery of king and court. The true prophets, on the contrary, were too often "in opposition." They were driven to take up a post of antagonism to popular habits and royal wishes. Sometimes, Cassandra-like, they only earned hatred for their faithful warnings. But they always endeavoured to keep before the nation the high ideal of its true life. Their avocation was public and largely political. They performed the function in the state which the leader-writer of the modern newspaper, at his best, aims at exercising, i.e., they were the critics and censors of public policy. At the same time they took note of private morals. This was on the ground of a theocratic government. God was the true King of Israel, and the prophets constituted His ministry. Austere and sublime, they stood out as the national conscience incarnate, as the voice of God pleading with His people. This lofty vocation was not confined to men. It was seen in women—anticipated by Deborah in a very early age (Judg. iv., v.), and fulfilled also by Huldah at a later date (2 Kings xxii. 14).

The prophets, whose special function it was to interpret from time to time the meaning of Jehovah's dealings with the nation, may be distributed into five different classes, according to the part they played in the history of the theocracy, each one affirming a principle and taking a step in advance of his predecessor, as well as defining more clearly the ultimate destiny of the nation, and the final purpose of God in its election. These classes may be named after their conspicuous and representative members : that of (1) the Nebiim, (2) Elijah, (3) Amos, (4) Isaiah, and (5) Jeremiah.

1. The Nebiim, i.e., Prophets.

This class first appeared in the history of Israel about the time of Samuel, when the nation was threatened with extinction piecemeal at the hands of the Philistines, who had waged internecine war with its tribes under the Judges. Their mission at this particular juncture—for the prophetic function varied as the national crisis did—was to call the nation, as yet divided into a number of separate, independent clans, to a sense of its unity as a people chosen of Jehovah, to see it welded compactly into one under a single chief or king like other nations, and to rouse it to withstand as one man all attempts to enslave or crush it on the part of its enemies. To this office they were called by a heaven-inspired, irresistible impulse ; and their appeal was responded to by all the tribes of Israel as a summons from Jehovah to unite together; so that, whatever divisions might afterwards arise among the people, thenceforth they never ceased to regard themselves as one nation. And as these "Nebiim" had been the creators of the nation as a corporate unity, so they continued to act as the conservators of the national feeling and life. By degrees the prophetic order became an established institution in Israel, its members living together in societies, appearing in companies, and wearing a distinctive dress. They were united in colleges, were known as the "sons of the prophets," and were found grouped round the leading sanctuaries, such as those of Bethel and Gilgal. As thus invested with the care of the nation, they were charged with the guardianship of the national morality, and they dared in some cases to rebuke the kings if, even in their private conduct, they acted contrary to the law of righteousness, which the prophets deemed the bond of the national existence. The function they assumed was not the execution of the Law—that was the duty of the priests—but the exhortation of the people as citizens, or members of the theocracy, to observe its moral precepts; otherwise judgment from the Lord would surely overtake them as a nation. This was the ideal of their office, but it was one which, in course of time, became weaker and weaker in the prophetic consciousness. The recognition and institution of the order by the state proved unfavourable to the faithful discharge of its functions, and it was content at length to acquiesce where it should have rebuked and protested. By this temporising policy the official prophets gradually lost weight, and their unfaithfulness provoked others to assume the function which they now ceased to exercise. Sometimes the remonstrance came from a member of their own order; sometimes from one who, though "neither a prophet nor a prophet's son," felt directly called of God to do what they neglected to do, and so save the nation. Foremost among these reformers was Elijah the Tishbite, and to this class also belonged all the sixteen prophets whose writings are preserved among the canonical books of the Hebrew scriptures. None of them belonged to the established order, or, if any did, they rose above it, and placed themselves in opposition to it, while all of them professed themselves prophets of the God of Israel. Among these, for the first time, "the prophet stands more and more out as the typical organ of revelation, the type of the man who is Jehovah's intimate, sharing His secrets (Amos iii. 7; Jer. xxiii. 22), and ministering to Israel the gracious guidance which distinguishes it from all other nations (Amos ii. 11; Hos. xii. 10, 13), and also the sentences of awful judgment by which Jehovah rebukes rebellion (Hos. vi. 5)."

2. Elijah.—A new crisis had arrived in the history of the nation, and the prophetic order was either blind to the fact or indisposed to grapple with it. This was the institution by Ahab in Samaria, in compliment to Jezebel his wife, or rather to the Tyrian people with whom he was in league, of the worship of Baal by the side of the worship of Jehovah. This outrage roused the holy soul of Elijah, and he rose up against it in stern, resolute protest as a dishonour to the God of Israel. He felt that he had a call from the Lord to do so, and he obeyed the call,

though he knew not of another who would say yea to his message. The old "Nebiim," with no higher call, had aroused the nation to assert itself against a foreign power; it was for Elijah to arouse it to declare itself against a foreign god. Under them the Israelites had come to regard themselves as the people of Jehovah; they must be further taught by him that Jehovah would not own them unless they gave to Him an undivided allegiance. Such was Elijah's message from the Lord to the nation; and though he was not permitted the satisfaction of seeing the people accept it, he left his mantle on another who found an agent by whose hand the idolatry referred to was stamped out of Israel. This agent was Jehu, the son of Nimshi, whom Elisha, Elijah's successor, persuaded to go up against both the house of Ahab and the god Baal, and who did his work so thoroughly that not a member of the one nor a worshipper of the other was left in the land behind him. The final result was, that in later days formal and outspoken idolatry was no longer encouraged in state policy, the idolatry with which the prophets afterwards charged the nation being implied rather than expressed, and the worship being on the whole offered ostensibly to Jehovah, even when really to other gods. In this crusade against the worship of Baal, Elisha carried the schools of the prophets along with him so that they thenceforth stood out to a man against the false god, and prophesied, if they prophesied at all, only in the name of the God of Israel.

3. Amos.—Under the old prophets and Elijah, the Israelites had been taught to regard themselves as one people, and Jehovah as their God, but they had not learned to know on what terms this could be. A hundred years had come and gone, and though Jehovah had been admonishing them of the purpose of their election, they had failed to listen, had even fallen away from Him spiritually; they had exposed themselves to His anger, and there was none to deliver them out of His hands. There were now two kingdoms—Judah and Israel. Both were apostate, but the most guilty was the northern kingdom, Israel. This state of things Amos was the first to perceive, and he was the first to warn the people of the fate that was hanging over them. His warning must have pierced the ears of the dullest, for his words were: "The virgin of Israel is fallen; she shall rise no more; there is no one to raise her up" (Amos v. 2). A shepherd on the edge of the wilderness by the Dead Sea, he had not been unobservant of the dealings of the Lord with the nation at large, and had learned to regard Him as the God of Hosts no less than the God of Israel. The prophet saw Israel's God as the Lord of Hosts arraying Himself against His people (Amos iii. 13-15), and Assyria as the power He was about to employ in executing His judgments upon them. He would have the nation, therefore, look upon this power as Jehovah's instrument in the chastisement of their sins, and not the less but the rather to regard Him as the God of their fathers that He was meting out to them the needed judgment (Amos iii. 2). It was in vain for them to imagine that this judgment was coming upon them because they had been remiss in their worship of Jehovah, and that it might yet be averted by redoubling their offerings and sacrifices upon

His altars. They must know that the only propitiation that would appease Him was a return to the ways of righteousness; and that the ruin which was hanging over them was intended to be a lesson to the generations to come that His favour could be purchased with no less an offering. The great mistake lay in the supposition that the favour of God was secure to the chosen people independently of their own conduct and character. They had to learn that God would treat them according to their behaviour. If this behaviour continued evil in the sight of Heaven, the once chosen people would be cut off and cast aside. Even while God condescended to visit them it must be in fearful chastisements. The nation having fallen from its high mission, must suffer under the Divine displeasure.

4. **Isaiah.**—What properly constituted the new era of prophecy introduced by Amos was the discovery that the nation had offended Jehovah, and was incapable of amendment; that, therefore, Jehovah had decreed its dissolution; and that this dissolution was necessary before it could be restored; the nation must fall in order that Jehovah, the God of Israel, may out of the ruins raise up another that would be more to His praise. Amos first, and Hosea after him, both recognised in the impending ruin the Divine purpose of reconstruction, but neither of them gave any indication of where the materials were to be found out of which the new structure was to be built. This was reserved for Isaiah, the prophet of Judah. Isaiah saw that, if the nation was to be restored, the nation itself must supply both the materials and the motive; and he found the materials in a faithful remnant, and the motive in their faith and hope in Israel's God. He recognised the nation as more than the casket in which Jehovah had deposited the jewel of His law; he recognised it as consisting in part of those who prized this jewel as above all price, and would not part with it. He knew such, and his faith and hope were in them. He saw that on them, when led by the Great Messiah, depended the future of the theocracy, and that it was by them assured. The spiritual chain, he saw, was not broken, and could not be broken, because it was in Jehovah's hands. For him, it was by the children of the spirit, as distinct from the children of the flesh, that Jehovah's purposes were destined to be accomplished. Thus is Isaiah the revealer of two new truths in regard to the development of the Divine kingdom: first, that in the process there is no rupture of continuity,—that, to use Christ's words, salvation is still of the Jews; and, second, that its course is henceforth along spiritual lines—not only after the flesh, but after the spirit. And thus his vision of the future of the Divine kingdom came to overstep the limits which would confine it within the realm of Israel, and to represent it as destined to extend its sovereignty over all the nations of the earth. A golden future is now before Israel, and the source and centre of that future are to be expected in the shoot from the root of Jesse—the Christ of God.

5. **Jeremiah.**—Hebrew prophecy had still to take a further step before it could reach its culminating point, and Jeremiah was the prophet honoured to originate this movement. Isaiah looked for a national revival, and saw in the faithful remnant the nucleus round which it would take shape. Jeremiah had no faith in any reformation short of a reformation of the individual, and that could only be effected by a change of heart. Wellhausen rightly remarks, "Instead of the nation only, the heart and the individual conviction were to him the subject of religion. On the ruins of Jerusalem he gazed into the future filled with joyful hope, sure of this, that Jehovah would one day pardon sin and renew the relation which had been broken off—though on the basis of another covenant than that laid down in the law; and the basis of the new covenant he announced to be this: ' I will put My law in their inward parts, and write it in their hearts; and will be their God, and they shall be My people. And they shall teach no more every man his neighbour, and every man his brother, saying, Know the Lord; for they shall know Me, from the least of them to the greatest of them, saith the Lord ' " (Jer. xxxi. 33, 34). For Jeremiah, assured of his own personal salvation, knew that this was independent of the relation of Jehovah to the nation, and was entirely dependent on the relation of Jehovah to himself. And as it was with him, so he was satisfied it would be with others; only a personal relationship with Jehovah would hold good. Thus would the individual soul be brought into direct communication with the fountain of Divine wisdom, and be no longer dependent on a merely prophetic word; and thus would the impatient prayer of Moses find at length its quiet fulfilment: "Would God that all the Lord's people were prophets, and that the Lord would put His Spirit upon them" (Num. xi. 29).

Summary.—Thus did Hebrew prophecy fulfil its mission, and such were the five steps by which it reached this goal. It taught, first, by the Nebiim, that Israel must regard itself as one nation; secondly, by Elijah, that it must have Jehovah alone for its God; thirdly, by Amos, that as a nation it was not necessarily God's chosen, but that the favour of God depended on righteousness of conduct; fourthly, by Isaiah, that it existed for the preservation of a holy seed, which should flourish in the golden age of a promised Messiah of the house of David; and finally, by Jeremiah, that though the nation ceased to exist in political independence and unity, religion primarily concerned the individual, and was an affair of the conscience. Thus does Hebrew prophecy reach its highest point when it leads up to Christianity, the first requirement of which is a regeneration of the heart (John iii. 3), and the great promise of which is the outpouring of a spirit that "will guide into all truth" (John xvi. 13). There were true prophets, indeed, during and after the Captivity. But these messengers of God did not advance materially upon the position reached by Jeremiah.

See J. R. Smith, *Prophets of Israel;* Davidson, *Old Testament Prophecy;* Riehm, *Messianic Prophecy;* Briggs, *Messianic Prophecy.*

CHAPTER XXV.

THE JEWISH THEOCRACY.

Definition.—A theocracy is literally a state governed in the name of God, and the term has been applied, by Josephus originally, to the

Jewish state, because—though it might be given in a lower sense to the surrounding nations whose gods also were conceived of as their kings—Jehovah was acknowledged to be the author of the Jewish national constitution and the fountain of its law, and respect for these was felt to be matter of religious obligation. As was natural, accordingly, the interpreters of the law were the ministers of religion, and all the acts of the state were ratified by priestly sanction. The administration of the law was committed at first to officers of a more secular order, and it was only later that this power passed entirely into the hands of the priests, so that the government became hierarchic as well as theocratic. This theocratic order of things was administered in succession (1) by Judges, (2) by Kings, and (3) by the Priesthood.

1. The Judges as Rulers.—The foundation of Jewish theocratic legislation was laid by Moses, and its regulations were first carried out in the name of God by the administration of judges both during the founder's lifetime and after his decease. These judges were, for the most part, the heads of clans or families, each of whom in times of peace administered justice among his clansmen, and in times of war acted as their military head. In judging their several tribes these functionaries had frequent occasion to refer the matter to Jehovah, and this was done by recourse to the sanctuary and the priests. Thus were the tribes taught to look upon themselves as acting under Jehovah's instructions, and, in going forth against their enemies, as fighting the battles of the Lord. In the field, however, they proved unable to hold their own against their adversaries, and it was deemed politic, if they were to maintain their integrity among the nations, that they should array themselves under a single chief; by their election of a king they took rank among the nationalities of the earth, though to the detriment of their religious life. To Samuel, the seer, belongs the merit of having selected Saul, the son of Kish, as the man under whom they would unite, and of having called him to the leadership of their several hosts. By this time, owing to their union with the Canaanites, the nation advanced from the pastoral to the agricultural stage of civilisation.

2. The Kings, and the Monarchy.—With the election of a king, the judges, much as some of them had perverted justice, did not all at once cease to be its administrators; while the king was at first little more than a military commander-in-chief. The kings, like the judges, ruled in the name of Jehovah; and hence one of the first acts of David when he became king was to make his metropolis the religious as well as the political centre of the nation, by transferring to it the ark of the covenant of the Lord. David, however, like his predecessor, was more a man of war than a civil ruler, and it was only with Solomon his son that the monarchy was able to absorb into it and wield all the powers of the state. International politics and war were not Solomon's *forte;* and he devoted himself to matters of internal administration, so that his name afterwards became the synonym for a wise ruler and judge. His administration, however, was less distinguished for justice than for worldly policy, and the injustice in which it issued led, in the next reign, to the final rupture of the kingdom. By his passion for state magnificence he enriched one section of the nation at the expense, by exaction, of the other and greater; so that, when the government passed into his son's hands, the latter threw off the yoke as intolerable; while by the splendour of the Temple which he erected in the capital he gave an *éclat* to the Jerusalem priesthood, and thus paved the way for its assuming the sovereign authority of the state. The rupture of the monarchy, indeed, into the kingdom of the north, or Israel, and the kingdom of the south, or Judah, was not its dissolution; but in course of time the kings in both sections proved less careful of the honour of Jehovah and the good of the people than of their own pleasure, and so it fared in the end with both of the kingdoms, that first Israel, then Judah, were delivered over to their enemies as a judgment from the Lord. The chief injustice under which both perished was injustice in high quarters, for the kings, instead of living for the people, made the people live for them, and many of their exactions on their subjects were due to a worldly rivalry with other sovereigns. Indeed, what wrecked the monarchy, as it did the Jewish theocracy generally, was *first*, the desertion of the true God in imitation of the idolatry of heathen neighbours; and *second*, the vain ambition to establish a worldly kingdom that would be the envy of surrounding nations, as if Jehovah's purpose in choosing Israel was merely to show to other nations how much more He could do for His people than their gods could do for them.

3. The Priests as Rulers, and the Hierarchy.—The hierarchical government of the Jews dates from the re-establishment of the theocracy in Jerusalem by Ezra and Nehemiah, on the return from the Captivity, and the effect of its institution was to place the civil power of the state in the hands of the priests, and make them princes of the realm as well as the ministers of religion. The head of this hierarchy, or hierocracy, as it has been called, was the high-priest, and his peers were originally the members of his own family, the old Jerusalem priests of the house of Zadok, while a sharp distinction was observed between the descendants of Aaron and the common Levites. The special office to which the priesthood was called was the revival and conservation of the religious life of the people as prescribed in the book of the law, or the Pentateuch, and in this the priests were assisted by the Scribes, who so far were their zealous coadjutors, although under their sway greater stress was laid upon ceremonial than moral purity, as well as a respect for the services of the Temple. Nevertheless, the good effect of their government, or rather of what went on under it, especially in the synagogues, by the hands of the Scribes, was seen in the deepening and increase of personal piety among all ranks—as expressed in certain of the Psalms, in the greater interest that was now taken in the study of the law and the dealings of God with the nation, and in the clearer and firmer hold on the minds of the people of the purpose of God in their election, together with a larger view of Divine truth and of the workings of Providence. Had the hierarchy confined itself to this office, and been content to rest satisfied with such results, it would have gone well both with it and with the nation under it. But its members were now princes as well as priests, and the vices to which in the former relation they were subject soon began to show themselves among the order. In this relation it seemed as if they, like the kings before them, thought the nation existed for their personal ambition, and they soon began to evince a spirit of rivalry out of all keeping with concern for Jehovah's honour and the nation's good. But this strife for their own honour and aggrandisement was suicidal, and in course of time the power they wielded passed into other and alien hands. The foreign power proved tyrannical; and the nation grew restive and rebellious, till the struggle that followed terminated in the destruction of the Jewish state. This catastrophe did not happen, however, till the theocratic ideal had revealed itself as capable only of spiritual fulfilment, and had given promise of its realisation in the kingdom of God, now established in the life, death, and resurrection of Jesus Christ.

Thus did the theocracy not fail of its purpose, though the successive attempts under the judges, the kings, and the priests to nationalise it ended in defeat. The kingdom of God, which succeeded, was the fruit of the seed which was sown and matured under these successive administrations. Hard and formal as the Jewish religion became under the hierarchy, it was, as has been remarked, the necessary shell to protect the kernel, which might otherwise have been lost.

4. The Sanhedrin: (1.) *History.*—This Sanhedrin (Gr. *Synedrion*) was a council (originally municipal) which held its sittings at Jerusalem, and claimed sovereign authority and jurisdiction over the whole Jewish people. There is no notice of its existence prior to the Grecian period of Jewish history (see chap. xiv. p. 52), although it probably had its origin in the previous age. It originally bore the name of *gerousia, i.e.,* senate, and there is mention of it under this and other titles in 1 and 2 Maccabees. It was an aristocratic, not a democratic body, under the presidency of the high-priest. Its authority was limited from time to time, and it ceased to exist with the fall of Jerusalem (A.D. 70).

(2.) *Composition.*—The Sanhedrin, at its first institution, appears to have been a body representative of the nobility, that is, the high-priestly class, of the Jewish people, and it was therefore probably composed exclusively of members of the priesthood; but, if so, in course of time other elements were introduced, as the learned and the lay class rose into political importance, so that in the days of Christ we find it composed of Scribes, with their Pharisaic leanings, and laymen of age and experience (elders), as well as priests, whose sympathies were with the Sadducæan sect, the Pharisaic element becoming eventually the predominant one. It consisted of seventy-one members, inclusive of the president, and these held office for a term of years, if not for life. They were required to be all Jews by birth, were elected to membership either by the suffrages of the court itself, or, as in later times, by appointment of the Roman governor, and they were formally installed by the imposition of hands.

(3.) *Jurisdiction.*—Though it assumed authority, and asserted it, over the entire domain of Judaism (Acts ix. 2), the Sanhedrin, in the days of Christ, had no civil authority beyond the confines of Judæa proper; its authority did not extend even as far as Galilee, as is evident from its having no judicial authority over our Lord so long as He remained in that province. It took cognisance of all questions affecting the judicial interpretation and administration of the Mosaic law, and all inferior judges were bound, on pain of death, to acquiesce in its decisions. In the New Testament, Jesus is brought up before it on a charge of blasphemy (Matt. xxvi. 65; John xix. 7), Peter and John on a charge of being false prophets and deceivers of the people (Acts iv. and v.), and Paul on a charge of transgressing the law of Moses (Acts xxiii.). Under the Roman rule, it had independent authority in matters of police; it could order arrests by means of its own officers, and dispose of all offences against the law, except such as involved forfeiture of life, in which case the judgment, before it could take effect, had to be ratified by the civil power. Even a Roman citizen might render himself amenable to its authority, and in certain cases, such as by an act of intrusion into the inner court of the Temple, expose himself to a capital sentence, though this verdict might not be confirmed by the Roman governor.

(4.) *Judicial procedure.*—The members of the court sat in a semicircle, in order that they might see each other, the president, or Nasi, as he was called, being seated in the centre, while two clerks stood in front, one on his right hand and another on his left, to record, the one the votes for acquittal, and the other the votes for condemnation. In front, moreover, there sat three rows of the disciples of the learned men, or "the wise," as they were called. The prisoner had to present himself in a humble attitude, and dressed in black. In the case of a capital charge, the reasons for acquittal were first received, then those for conviction, and no one who had spoken in favour of the accused was allowed to vote for his condemnation, though the converse was permissible. The students were allowed to plead in the accused's behalf, but not otherwise, except in capital cases. For a sentence of acquittal a majority of one was enough, while for condemnation there required to be a majority of two. The former sentence could be pronounced on the day of the trial, the latter not till the day after. Thus our Lord was illegally condemned in having sentence of death passed against Him a few hours after being arrested.

(4). *Place of meeting.*—This appears to have been on the Temple-mount, at the western side of the enclosing wall. The meeting once held in the palace of the high-priest (Mark xiv. 53 *seq.*) is accounted for by its being night, when the gates of the enclosure would be shut.

See Schürer, *History of the Jews in the Time of Christ;* Stapfer, *Palestine in the Time of Christ;* Edersheim, *Life and Times of Jesus the Messiah.*

CHAPTER XXVI.

THE JEWISH FESTIVALS.

1. **The Sabbath.**—The Sabbath as a day of *rest* and special sanctity among the days of the week appears to have been of early institution, but

it is first mentioned as a day "holy to the Lord" in connection with the gathering of the manna in the wilderness (Exod. xvi. 23); and the publication of the command requiring its observance goes no further back than the delivery of the Law from Mount Sinai (Exod. xx. 10). Originally observed in recognition of God's "rest" from His work as Creator, it was now enjoined as commemorative of the "rest" which He had given His people from the bondage of Egypt, and its observance was required as an acknowledgment of the covenant that was thereupon established between God and the people to all generations. The entire day was to be given up in consecration to the Lord alone, not only as the Creator of the heavens and the earth, but as the Redeemer of Israel; and the observance of it was one of the distinctive badges of membership in the Jewish community. No law was held by the strict Jew to be more religiously binding, or was eventually so scrupulously hedged round with guards against every seeming violation.

2. The New Moon.—This was a holy day observed on the first of the lunar month, in connection with which there were offerings of special sacrifices, with trumpet accompaniments (Num. x. 10; xxviii. 11-15), and, latterly, a general suspension of work, public worship in the Temple, and assemblies of the people for religious instruction (1 Sam. xx. 5, 6, 29; 2 Kings iv. 23; Amos viii. 5).

3. The Passover, or Feast of Unleavened Bread. —This was the first and greatest of the three annual feasts instituted by Moses, and its celebration began on the fourteenth day of the month Nisan, or Abib (about March), the anniversary of the exodus from Egypt, and lasted eight days. Only unleavened bread was used during its observance, and a lamb one year old, known as the *paschal lamb*, or a kid, free from all blemish, was roasted whole, and eaten with bitter herbs in every household on the eve of the festival, the members partaking of it dressed in a travelling garb and in a standing attitude, like their ancestors on the eve of their departure from Egypt (Exod. xii. 1-51). After the Israelites settled in the land of Canaan, the celebration of this feast was connected with the ancient harvest festival, and, on its occurrence, the first ripe sheaf of the year was brought to the priest, to be waved by him before the Lord in thank-offering. Among other changes in its celebration, cups of red wine were afterwards added to the meal, and handed round in succession at specified intervals. The first and last days of the feast were days of solemn religious assembly.

4. Pentecost.—This festival was the second of the great Jewish feasts, and was so called because it was held on the "fiftieth" day after the second day of the Passover. It was also called "the feast of the harvest, the first fruits of labour" (Exod. xxiii. 16), "the feast of weeks" (Num. xxviii. 26), and "the day of first fruits." The fifty days, of which it was the last, represented the period of the grain-harvest—the sheaf of the Passover denoting the commencement, and the offering of two loaves at the Pentecost denoting the termination. These loaves were to be of native wheat and leavened;

and the offering of them constituted the distinguishing rite of the feast, which was accompanied, moreover, with sacrifices peculiar to itself (Lev. xxiii.). It was of a more freely festive character, and of more general celebration, than the Passover, although in observing it the people were likewise reminded of their deliverance from Egypt, and their obligation to keep the law of their Deliverer. It is regarded by the Jews as commemorative of the giving of the Law on Mount Sinai, and it is said to have been the custom among them at one time to spend the eve of the festival in thanksgiving to Jehovah for this gift.

5. The Feast of Trumpets.—This was the feast of the new moon, which fell on the first of the seventh month, or Tizri (about September), and it differed from the ordinary festivals of its class in being the seven days of holy convocation, a "day" of the blowing of trumpets, and in being accompanied by additional sacrifices (Num. xxix. 1-6);—the other *days of holy convocation* being two at the Passover, one at Pentecost, one on the Day of Atonement, and two at the Feast of Tabernacles. The meaning of this festival has been variously interpreted, but the common opinion is that it was the new year's day festival; the first of Tizri, on which it was celebrated, being reckoned the first day of the civil year, as this month was the month of ingathering of the year's harvest, and of ploughing and sowing for the next year.

6. The Day of Atonement.—This was a national fast rather than a festival, and the only one commanded in the Mosaic Law (see for the manner of its celebration Lev. xvi., xxiii. 26-32; Num. xxix. 7-11). Held on the tenth day of the month Tizri, and five days before the Feast of Tabernacles, it was the great day of humiliation before Jehovah on account of sin, and its observance as such was required of all the people on pain of being cut off from the congregation of Israel. This was the only occasion on which it was permitted to the high-priest to enter the Holy of Holies. He went accompanied with the offering of sacrifices for himself and the people, among which were two goats, of which the one was slain for Jehovah, and the other, after the high-priest had confessed over it all the sins of the people, was led into the wilderness and there let loose, hence, as some think, called the "scapegoat." It is now generally considered, however, that the word "scapegoat" is a mistranslation of the Hebrew original, and that the goat was sent out to "Azazel," a demon of the wilderness.

7. The Feast of Tabernacles.—This festival began on the fifteenth of the month Tizri, and lasted seven days, followed by a day of holy convocation. It was instituted principally in memory of the wandering tent-life which the children of Israel led in the wilderness. Like the festivals of the Passover and Pentecost, it had also an agricultural reference, and was held in celebration of the close of the harvest of the fruits, of wine and oil as well as corn, in consequence of which it was called also the *Feast of the Ingathering* (Exod. xxiii. 16). The feast was observed by the people dwelling in arbours made of branches of pine, olive, myrtle, and palm trees, and erected on the roofs of the houses and in the courts and streets (Neh. viii. 15, 16). There were also special sacrifices in connection with the celebration, and every seventh year the Law was read to the people at this feast. It was the festival *par excellence*, and was celebrated with more rejoicing than any other. Its observance was accompanied with music and dancing, with the blowing of the trumpets twenty-one times each day, with the drawing of water from the well of Siloam, and, in Jerusalem, with an illumination of the court of the women in the evening, which lit up the whole city. From the manner of its celebration it has been regarded as an acknowledgment of the equality of all ranks of the people before God, and their common indebtedness to Him for the bounties of the harvest.

8. The Feast of Dedication.—This festival is only once mentioned in Scripture, viz., in John x. 22. Its institution is recorded in 1 Macc. iv. 52–59. It was commemorative of the purification of the Temple after its profanation by the Syrians, and of the rebuilding of the altar by Judas Maccabæus in 164 B.C. It lasted eight days, commencing on the twenty-fifth of the month Chisleu (about December), and was observed with demonstrations of great rejoicing, every house being illuminated.

9. The Feast of Purim, or Lots.—This was an annual festival in commemoration of the preservation of the Jews from the threatened wholesale massacre of the race in Persia at the instigation of Haman, and which was so called because it was by casting lots that Haman decided on the day that would be most auspicious for the execution of this purpose (see Esther, p. 25). It lasted two days, being observed on the fourteenth and fifteenth of the month Adar (about February).

10. The Sabbatical Year.—According to laws prescribed in the Pentateuch (Exod. xxiii. 10 *seq.*; Lev. xxv. 2–7; Deut. xv. 1–11; xxxi. 10–13), every seventh year, beginning with the end of the harvest time, was to be a Sabbatical year, during which the land, as well as the vineyards and oliveyards, was to be left at "rest," partly for the benefit of the poor and the cattle, and partly as a recognition that the land was the Lord's, and also perhaps for the benefit of future produce—the rotation of crops being unknown; a release or a respite was to be granted to all debtors; and at the Feast of Tabernacles the Law was to be read before all the people.

11. The Year of Jubilee.—The Jewish law (Lev. xxv.) required that every fiftieth year the land which in the interval had passed out of its original owner's hands should be restored to him, that all who within that time had been forced to sell themselves into slavery should be released from bondage, and, if we are to accept an unsupported assertion of Josephus, that the claims of all creditors against debtors should be remitted. The year on which this was required was called the Year of Jubilee, because its commencement was announced by the sound of the "yobel," a kind of horn. This law does not appear to have been ever rigorously observed by the Jewish people.

See Schultz, Bennett, Davidson, on *Old Testament Theology*.

CHAPTER XXVII.

THE LAWS OF THE JEWS, AND THEIR ADMINISTRATION.

THE laws to be enumerated here are not the moral but the statute laws of the Jews, and these under the threefold division of Civil, Criminal, and Ceremonial.

A. THE LAWS.

I. THE CIVIL LAW is divisible into two kinds —(a) as regards Persons, and (b) as regards Things.

a. **As regards Persons:** 1. *Parents and children.* — The authority of parents, especially fathers, over the children was very great, while children were required to pay their parents all respect; and the penalty of death could, on complaint of the parent, be enforced by the elders of the congregation on any child that cursed father or mother (Lev. xx. 9; Deut. xxi. 18–21). Even he who "set lightly by father or mother" was cursed (Deut. xxvii. 16). Though the education of the children naturally devolved chiefly on the mother, the father was bound to instruct them in the statutes of the Lord (Deut. vi. 1, 7, 20; xi. 19). The elder son had an authority over his juniors (1 Sam. xx. 29), and he had a double share of the inheritance left by his father (Deut. xxi. 15–17). For the rights of daughters see Num. xxvii. 6–8; xxx. 3–5.

2. *Husband and wife.*—This relation was regarded as especially sacred, and not to be lightly dissolved; but, when dissolved, the dissolution was to be final. The right of divorce would appear to have belonged exclusively to the husband; and to make the act legal three steps were necessary: first, he must have a bill of divorcement drawn up; secondly, he must put it into his wife's hand; thirdly, he must send her away (Deut. xxiv. 1–4). A wife could contract no engagement, or even vow, independently of her husband, unless after divorce or his decease (Num. xxx. 6–15); and she had no power to separate herself from him. Marriage was forbidden among relatives (Lev. xviii.), as also with descendants of the seven nations that originally occupied the land of Canaan (Deut. vii. 1–6). It was a free act, and could not be consummated without the bride's consent. By a law known as the Levirite law, if a husband died without issue, his brother was required to take his widow to wife that he might raise up seed to him (Deut. xxv. 5–10).

3. *Master and slave.*—A servant was hired by his master, and received wages; a slave was the property of his master, who, however, was bound to treat him kindly, and must suffer penalty or loss if he treated him otherwise (Exod. xxi. 20, 26, 27). Of slaves there were two classes—(a) slaves that were Hebrew-born, and (b) slaves that were of alien blood. (a.) A Hebrew might

become a slave either by selling himself on account of poverty or debt, by being sold in punishment for theft, or, in the case of a girl, by being sold by her father. The Hebrew slave could claim his liberty at the end of six years (Exod. xxi. 2, 3), and his master, out of gratitude to the Lord for his own redemption, must not "send him away empty" (Deut. xv. 12-15). According to Lev. xxv., a Hebrew who sold himself on account of his poverty was treated as equal at least to a hired servant, and, if sold to a stranger sojourner, could be redeemed at any time by one of his brethren. If a Hebrew brought his wife with him into slavery, both were set free together; but if he married a wife in service and had children, they did not go free together with him, but he was permitted, by having his ear bored to the door-post, to bind himself to his master as a perpetual slave together with them (Exod. xxi. 4-6). (b.) Aliens might become slaves by purchase, by being taken captive in war, or as descendants of Canaanites; and these, with their offspring, were slaves for life (Num. xxxi. 26; Lev. xxv. 44-46) and heritable property, but always to be treated with consideration.

4. *The rich and the poor.*—The Jewish law is especially considerate of the poor, and makes especial provision for their relief. It requires every one who has the means to see to the supply of a neighbour's wants, by either lending him for return or giving him for nought (Deut. xv. 9-11). It evidently contemplates the unequal distribution of wealth in the state as a most serious evil, and the spirit of self-aggrandisement as absolutely ruinous to the common weal, as if it already forestalled the great principle of Christianity, which so unites man with man as to recognise in the poverty of one the poverty of all. The Hebrew prophets, accordingly, are never weary of urging on the nation regard for the poor and needy, and one of them goes so far as to identify justice to the indigent not only with the national welfare, but with the knowledge of God (Jer. xxii. 16). The privileges of the poor were the rights of gleaning in the fields, vineyards, and oliveyards after the ingathering, of reaping the produce of the Sabbatical year, of recovering their land on the year of Jubilee, of freedom from permanent bondage, of sharing in the tithes raised for the Levites, of being entertained at the feasts of Weeks and Tabernacles, of being paid their wages daily, and of protection against exorbitant usury, the curse of Oriental commerce.

5. *Debtor and creditor.*—Borrowing appears to have been permitted, and lending enjoined, only in circumstances of poverty induced by adversity; and the relation of debtor and creditor was one of simple borrowing and lending, the debtor fully intending to return the loan, and the creditor fully expecting it, there being no such thing contemplated as credit in the conduct of business. But in case the creditor should be too hard with the debtor, the latter, if unable to restore what he had borrowed, was released from his bond on the Sabbatical year, as the year of release proclaimed by the Lord (Deut. xv. 2 *seq.*). The lender was entitled only to the bare return of the loan, the relation between the parties being regarded as that of mutually helpful brethren.

6. *Strangers.*—The Jew was to give gratuitous entertainment to the stranger, and send him away with a blessing, remembering the time when he was a stranger in Egypt (Deut. x. 19), and he was bound also to see justice done to him (Deut. i. 16). By undergoing circumcision a stranger might become one of the chosen nation, and share in its privileges (Exod. xii. 48).

b. As regards Things: 1. *Property in land.*—The land belonged to the Lord, and was held by its holder direct from Him, for the benefit of the nation (Lev. xxv. 23). Every seventh, or Sabbatical, year, it was to be left idle, and the spontaneous crop upon it to be free to all (Lev. xxv. 3-7). Every fiftieth, or Jubilee, year, not only was the land to lie fallow, but all property in land was of right to return to its original owner (Lev. xxv. 10-17). If land was alienated through poverty, it could be redeemed at any time by its original owner or a kinsman, compensation being allowed to the present tenant for the loss of the crop of the years to run till the next Jubilee (Lev. xxv. 25-27). Land could be exchanged, might be given in dowry, and might be forfeited by disloyalty, but must in any case remain in the tribe. The purchase of land was originally before witnesses, afterwards by sealed bonds. A landmark could not be removed (Deut. xxvii. 17), and the crop must not be injured, although the wayfarer was free to pluck of the grapes or of the ears of corn, to relieve immediate necessity (Exod. xxii. 5, 6; Deut. xxiii. 24, 25).

2. *Inheritance.*—The sons were the sole heirs of the family property, both landed and personal, each receiving an equal share, except the eldest, whose portion was double, as on him devolved greater responsibilities than the rest (Deut. xxi. 17). Daughters receive no share, unless by will of the father, or unless there were no sons, but the inheritance reverted to their issue being males. Both sons and daughters failing, the estate went to the owner's brothers, failing whom, it went to the nearest kinsman, and was never alienated from the tribe (Num. xxxvii. 1-11).

3. *Debt.*—A debt was a loan; and, if it was not paid back, it was remitted on the seventh, or Sabbatical, year (Deut. xv. 1-11). It was a pure loan, and in return for the benefit no Israelite was permitted to take interest of another, because he was his brother (Exod. xxii. 25; Lev. xxv. 35-37), though he might do so of a stranger (Deut. xxiii. 20). A pledge could not be taken by force, it must be freely given, and it must not be a necessary of life (Deut. xxiv. 6, 10-13).

4. *Taxation.*—Prior to the monarchy, the only taxes imposed on the people were for the support of religion, and they were given and received as free-will offerings to the Lord in the form of small shares of some increment of wealth, viewed as from the Lord Himself. Once and again a poll-tax of a half-shekel (about 1s. 4d.) or so was levied for building or repairing the tabernacle or the temple, till it became at length a regular exaction. Under the monarchy the taxation was at first light, but under Solomon it became unbearably heavy; and it was the burdensomeness of this which led the tribes of the north to revolt from Solomon's successor, Rehoboam, who threatened he would make the burdens heavier still. These consisted of a tithe or tenth of the produce of the soil and of the flocks (1 Sam. viii. 15, 17), forced service in war (1 Sam. viii. 12; 1 Kings ix. 22) and on special occasions gifts to the king (1 Sam.

x. 27; xvi. 20). The burdens thus imposed affected the people both directly and indirectly, and they became absolutely crushing under foreign domination, and finally under the Roman rule, the community in this instance, as in so many others, being sacrificed to the exactions of those in power.

5. *Tithes*, i.e., tenths of all produce.—These were regarded as the Lord's, and must be offered to Him in the persons of His representatives the Levites, either in kind or by an equivalent, and one-fifth more, while the Levites were to give a tenth of these tithes to the high-priest (Lev. xxvii. 30-33; Num. xviii. 21-28). Besides tithes for the service of the Lord, there were also tithes exacted at certain times for the expense of religious festivals and for the poor (Deut. xiv. 22-29). Under this category may be included the first-fruits of the earth and the first-born of man and beast, which were regarded also as the Lord's, all of which last could be redeemed, the redemption-money of a man being five shekels, and of an unclean beast one shekel or a half (Num. xviii. 12-18).

6. *Labour and wages.*—Labour was devoted principally to the cultivation of the land, the tending and pasturing of flocks, and the practice of certain necessary crafts; and the wages of the hired labour of the poor were to be paid daily, at the peril of drawing down judgment from the Lord (Deut. xxiv. 15). Any one was free to occupy himself with any craft that pleased him; *i.e.*, there was no system of caste excepting in the service of the temple, which was confined to the tribe of Levi. All labour was regarded as honourable. But while special laws were laid down for justice in dealing, no encouragement was given to trade outside the land. The Mosaic Law contains no rules for the regulation of commerce.

II. THE CRIMINAL LAW bears partly on (a) Offences against God, and partly on (b) Offences against man. The punishments for these offences were either capital or secondary. The capital punishments were stoning to death; hanging, generally after death by other means; burning, also often after death by other means; strangling, and decapitation. To these may be added sawing asunder and precipitation, and later the Roman execution by crucifixion. The secondary punishments were retaliation (Exod. xxi. 24, 25), compensation (Exod. xxii.), stripes (Deut. xxv. 3), and scourging (Judg. viii. 16). The law of retaliation, or the *lex talionis*, as it was called, was a law which rendered any one who deliberately and maliciously injured another's person in certain respects liable to have similar injuries inflicted on himself.

a. *Offences against God.*—These were considered to be acts of treason, and were in the case of persons punishable with death by stoning, and in the case of places with utter destruction. (1.) *Idolatry.* This is literally worshipping something seen as representing the unseen, but it is essentially regarding or paying respect to anything as God which is not God, and idolatry in all its forms is represented as hateful to Jehovah and subversive of His worship. That worship is worship of God alone; it admits of no divided allegiance. (2.) *Practising divination.* This is forbidden in Deut. xviii. 9-22, and Lev. xix. 31, and condemned as an abomination to the Lord, who did not permit any attempt to hold intercourse with familiar spirits. (3.) *Blasphemy.* This offence is properly a felt and expressed contempt for God or any of His laws, and is regarded as not only hateful to God, but absolutely ruinous to the soul (Lev. xxiv. 14, 16, 23). (4.) *Sabbath profanation.* This was an offence against God, because the Sabbath was one of the tokens of God's covenant with Israel, and it was punished with death by stoning (Num. xv. 32-36).

b. *Offences against Man.*—These were :—(1.) *Disrespect to parents and sacred persons,* cursing in both cases being punishable with death (Exod. xxi. 17; 1 Kings xxi. 10-14). (2.) *Murder.* This offence was unpardonable, and punishable with death (Exod. xxi. 12-14). (3.) *Homicide.* This was slaying a man accidentally, and the slayer could only escape from being slain himself at the hands of the avenger of blood by making straight for a city of refuge, and remaining there till the death of the high-priest (Num. xxxv.). (4.) *Assault.* For personal injury by this means the penalty was according to the law of retaliation (Lev. xxiv. 19, 20). (5.) *Adultery.* The punishment for this offence was death (Deut. xxii. 22). (6.) *Seduction.* This offence could only be condoned by marriage, the granting of a dowry, and the forfeiture of the right of divorce. (7.) *Unnatural crimes.* For these the punishment was death or barrenness. (8.) *Theft.* The thief must make from twofold to fivefold restitution, and if he could not do so, he must be sold as a slave (Exod. xxii. 1-4).

III. THE CEREMONIAL LAW was twofold, according as it prescribed for (a) Acceptance with God, and (b) Holiness before God.

a. *Acceptance with God.*—This was by sacrifices and offerings, which were made regularly or occasionally, some in self-dedication, some propitiatory, and some eucharistic, and consisted of (1) burnt-offerings, (2) meal-offerings, (3) peace-offerings, and (4) sin- and trespass-offerings.

1. *The burnt-offering.*—This consisted of an offering to God by fire taken from the altar, where it burned continually, of a whole animal, and it symbolised the dedication of the entire life to God in an undying all-consuming zeal for His law. It was to be made daily on behalf of all the people (Exod. xxix. 38-42), to be double on the Sabbath (Num. xxviii. 9, 10), and to be a special feature of the great festivals (Num. xxviii. 11-xxix. 39).

2. *The meal-offering.*—This was "unbloody," consisting of pure flour, oil, and wine, seasoned with salt, and it was eucharistic, the flour in symbol that the support of life, the oil that its fulness, and the wine that its vigour are of the Lord. It was to be made at the morning and evening sacrifices (Exod. xxix. 40, 41), in the renewal of the shewbread every Sabbath (Lev. xxiv. 5-9), and specially on the Sabbath and at the great festivals (Num. xxviii. and xxix.).

3. *The peace-offering.*—This was "bloody," consisting of an animal from the herd or the flock, of which the flesh was to be eaten, the blood to be poured out, and the fat to be burned, in way of vow to observe the statute which required that the offerer should "eat neither fat nor blood" (Lev. iii.). It was to be in thank-offering, in vow or in freewill-offering (Lev. vii. 11-21).

4. *The sin- and trespass-offerings.*—These were propitiatory or expiatory, and consisted of the sacrifice of an animal, of which the blood was partly sprinkled before the vail of the sanctuary, partly put on the horns of the altar of incense, and the rest poured out at the foot of the altar of burnt-offering, and of which the flesh was either burnt without the camp or eaten by the priests in the holy place (Lev. iv.-vi.). They expressed confession of sin and a sense of its ill-desert—the sin-offering, it is thought, of sin in general or of offences which the person committing them has perpetrated unwittingly, and the trespass-offering of some particular offence of which the offender felt the guilt even before the community discerned it.

b. **Holiness before God.**—This expressed itself in special observances required of every Jew, as well as in the institution of the priesthood, and the consecration of certain places and certain days and seasons as holy to the Lord, already treated of. The people were required to confess themselves holy before God by (1) the dedication of their firstborn to God, (2) the observance of the distinction of clean and unclean in the matter of food, and (3) regard for the laws of purity and certain rites of purification.

1. *The dedication of the firstborn.*—The fruit of the womb and the fruit of the field were considered to belong to God, and the dedication of the first fruit of each to Him was an acknowledgment of His right of property in the whole. The dedication of this part was a virtual dedication of all.

2. *The distinction of clean and unclean.*—This distinction referred to food, and was one to be observed "between the beast that may be eaten and the beast that may not be eaten" (Lev. xi. 47); and it was enjoined to be observed because the people were to be holy unto the Lord; for He was holy, and had severed them from other people to be His (Lev. xx. 24-26). Certain things they must not eat because they were consecrated things, and certain others because they were abominable. Some of the animals that might be eaten are enumerated in Deut. xiv. 4-6; Lev. xi. 9; Deut. xiv. 11-20; Lev. xi. 21; and some of those that might not in Lev. xi. 12; Deut. xiv. Whosoever partook of, or even touched, these last was unclean, and, till purified, unfit to present himself before the Lord. Christ insisted on the indifference of this distinction, morally regarded, when He taught that it is not what enters the mouth, but what proceeds out of it, that defiles a man (Matt. xv. 17, 18).

3. *Moral and ceremonial purity.*—The laws that concern purity are laid down in Lev. xii.-xv., xviii., and xx., and are too numerous to be specified here; but they were all intended to enforce the necessity of personal holiness in approaching and appearing before God.

B. The Administration of the Laws.

Justice was administered by local judges, generally of the Levitical class, as presumably skilled in the law, and they exercised their office under the sanction of the supreme authority, to which there was liberty to appeal, and whose sentence was final. This supreme authority was claimed or asserted sometimes by the priesthood, sometimes by the princes of the congregation sometimes by the Sanhedrin, and even sometimes though illegally, by the king. The rule according to which judgment was in every case to be given must be found written in the law, which was ever regarded as the standard of all authority.

The judges referred to were termed "elders;" and their institution dates from the time of the sojourn of the children of Israel in the wilderness, when Moses, by suggestion of Jethro and at the command of the Lord, selected and set apart seventy of the chief men of the tribes to assist him in administering the affairs of the congregation. They were, when appealed to, to "judge righteously between every man and his brother," to have "no respect to persons," or any fear of man, only of God, and to bring any matter to Moses that was too "hard" for them (Deut. i. 16, 17). These judges had the power of inflicting corporal chastisement, exacting fines, and even passing sentence of death in capital offences, such severity being regarded as required of them at the hands of the holy God who dwelt in the midst of them. In primitive times the judges held sittings in an open place of the city daily, heard cases and decided disputes at the moment of their occurrence, and effect was given on the spot to their verdict. It was not till the days of David and Solomon that a national system of judicial administration was organised, and in the reign of the former the number of judges over the land amounted to six thousand, all of the tribe of Levi (1 Chron. xxiii. 4), and they were regarded as responsible to the king (1 Kings xxii. 27).

Among the Jews eventually there were three kinds of tribunals, each with its province clearly defined: (1) Petty Courts of three judges, with only civil jurisdiction, including cognisance of such crimes as involved a pecuniary penalty; (2) Provincial Sanhedrins of twenty-three judges, with jurisdiction as well in crimes of a more serious nature; and (3) the Great Sanhedrin (which see, p. 107), with supreme authority over the whole nation. In these courts the king had no authority; nor did he even appoint the judges, that being the privilege of the people. The Petty Courts were constituted to determine a particular case, and were then dissolved, two judges being appointed, one by each party, and these two naming a third. Townships consisting of a hundred and twenty families possessed a Provincial Sanhedrin, which was sometimes of temporary and sometimes of permanent institution.

As justice was administered according to the law, any well-educated Jew was eligible to be a judge, provided he were otherwise qualified. To be a member of a Sanhedrin he required to be a man of tried judgment and integrity, as well as knowledge and general ability. No man who did not earn his living by some useful industry or calling could be a judge—no caterer for mere pleasure, no gambler, no usurer; nor any man who was not humane as well as just in his dealings with other people, such as a slave-dealer; nor any one who had been guilty of seduction, nor one who had in any way an interest in the suit. A judge must, before all, be a modest man, and in good repute with his neighbours, as well as a general favourite in the community.

No conviction could be obtained without witnesses, and two was the legal number required. Evidence was not given on oath, but the penalty of false witness-bearing was severe, and on the witness it devolved to take the lead in executing sentence on the offender. An oath was sometimes resorted to where no witness or where only imperfect evidence could be had, and by means of it an accused person could clear himself of suspicion. Of oaths there were two kinds —one in which Jehovah was merely taken to witness, and one in which imprecation was also involved. The oath was administered by raising the hand, and also by putting the hand under the thigh of the person to whom a promise was made (Gen. xxiv. 2), or by dividing a victim and passing between or distributing the pieces (Gen. xv. 10, 17; Jer. xxxiv. 18). It was sometimes taken before the altar (1 Kings viii. 31). "Casting the lot" was also resorted to at times, but very rarely.

See books mentioned in chap. xxvi.; also E. W. Edersheim, *The Laws and Polity of the Jews.*

CHAPTER XXVIII.

JEWISH LEGALISM.

1. *Its Nature and Extent.*—Among the Jews everything was regulated by Law, and to observe this Law was the duty and distinction of every Israelite. He was trained from infancy to keep it, the possession of it was regarded as the most precious charge committed to him, and he would rather part with life itself than part with it.

2. *Its Motive.*—The motive to observe the Law was the belief that the weal or woe of the nation depended exactly on the degree of national conformity or nonconformity to its requirements, and the reward of keeping it and the penalty of breaking it were believed to be regulated according to strict principles of retributive justice. This principle, it was felt, was not, and could not be, carried out at once; but the realisation of it in a glorious future was confidently expected by believing Jews of the earlier period. In New Testament times this was looked for in the great judgment after the resurrection.

3. *Its Results.*—The result of this system was to externalise more and more the religious and moral life of the people, to the decay, and ultimate dissolution, of every religious and moral principle. The Law took cognisance mainly of the external action, and it justified or condemned according to mere external behaviour. The external character of the Law and the vexing exactions of its elaborate details were enormously aggravated by the traditional additions of the Pharisees in the nominal form of interpretation. No regard was had to the heart or the conscience, the seat and source of all moral and religious well-being; while the mind was distracted by attention to such a number of minute requirements as to swamp the thought of spiritual and higher interests. Thus there were no fewer than thirty-nine kinds of work that were prohibited to be done on the Sabbath, and each of these prohibitions was split up into a number of included ones, which had to be respected with equal scrupu-

losity. Reaping was forbidden, plucking the ears of corn was pronounced a species of reaping, and the act of doing so a sin. Making and tying a knot were forbidden, but other laws stated what kinds of such acts were, and what kinds were not, included in the prohibition. So with writing on the Sabbath, with baking and boiling, with kindling and extinguishing a fire, with the bearing of burdens, and such like. The same minuteness of legislation was necessary to determine what things were clean and what unclean. No fewer than twelve treatises of the Mishna, which constitutes the text of the Talmud, treat of matters pertaining to this subject alone. There were also minute directions concerning amulets, which derived their charm from Scripture passages attached, concerning prayers, also saying grace at meals, fasting, and such like; and the observance of these exhausted the powers of Hebrew devotion. Whoso was perfect in them, however, fulfilled all that was required of him, and was free from the discharge of every other obligation. The effect of all this was that "life was continual torment to the earnest man, who felt at every moment that he was in danger of transgressing the law; and where so much depended on the external form, he was often left in uncertainty whether he had really fulfilled its requirements. On the other hand, pride and conceit were almost inevitable for one who had attained mastership in the knowledge of the law. He could indeed say that he had done his duty, had neglected nothing, had fulfilled all righteousness. But none the less the supercilious and ostentatious spirit which this righteousness engendered was not the spirit which was acceptable to God, and it was condemned by the Founder of Christianity" (Luke xviii. 9-14; Matt. vi. 2, xxiii. 5).

See books mentioned in Chapter XXVI.

CHAPTER XXIX.

JEWISH MANNERS AND CUSTOMS.

REFERENCE is here made to the more peculiar of these manners and customs, and they are most conveniently arranged in alphabetical order.

Adoration.—This was either by a total, or by a partial and more formal, prostration of the body —in the latter case by falling on the knees, inclining the body forwards and touching the ground with the forehead; and this attitude was assumed not only as an act of worship, but as an expression of respect, and when often repeated it signified a profounder obeisance. In prayer it was customary to stand with the hands outspread to heaven.

Anointing.—Anointing the head or body with oil, usually olive-oil, was customary after a bath and preparatory to an entertainment, with a view to impart a healthy and bright appearance, so that it became a symbol of joy, as abstinence from it was a symbol of mourning. It was customary for a host to anoint the head of his guests, and it was by anointing that a person, as well as a thing, was consecrated from a secular to a sacred service. The process was symbolical of being endued with the Spirit.

Banquets.—These were mostly of a religious nature (see JEWISH FESTIVALS), but they were common also in connection with marriages, the weaning of the heir of a house, friendly partings, reunions, &c. They took place in the evening, the guests being dressed in gay clothing, and the entertainment conducted so as to conduce to cheerful sociality.

Bathing.—This, which was doubtless originally enjoined in a sanitary interest, was of frequent requirement for the removal of ceremonial impurity ; and ablution became the symbol of spiritual renewal, or rather the preparatory repentance or renunciation. The practice was eventually an accessory to luxurious living, and general indulgence in it a sign of effeminacy, and even national degeneracy or lapse into heathenism.

Beard.—The beard was cultivated both as a feature and as a badge of manhood, and to shave it, pluck the hairs of it, or neglect it was a token of sorrow or affliction. Great care was taken in dressing it, and it was the grossest of outrages to insult it.

Burial.—The Jews from the earliest times disposed of their dead by burial, and bodies so deposited were regarded as sacred, unless they were the remains of such as had been guilty of some profanation. Burial was generally by entombment, and where that was not possible, by interment. The burial places were outside the city walls, and the tombs were natural or artificial excavations in rock, with recesses or loculi in the walls, the access to which was closed by a large stone. The body, after death, was washed and anointed, swathed in fine linen with spices in the folds of it, and borne on a naked bier to the grave, followed by the mourners, who deposited it quietly in its resting-place without any formal burial-service. The burial of the dead was a sacred duty, and the denial of it held to be a sign of the Divine displeasure.

Circumcision.—The observance of this rite, though not peculiar to the Jews, was distinctive of the Jewish race among the tribes around them, specially those of Canaan, and it was a sign as well as a seal of inclusion among the chosen people. It was performed on every male child the eighth day after birth, and the penalty of its non-observance was death, or excision from the commonwealth of Israel and all its privileges. It was the custom to name the child on the occasion of its circumcision.

Crucifixion.—This form of punishment, which prevailed extensively among the civilised nations of antiquity, appears to have been introduced among the Jews by the Romans, by whom it was inflicted on slaves and the vilest criminals. Its execution was preceded by scourging, and by stripping the victim, who was required to carry the cross to the place of execution, which was always outside the city.

Dancing.—The dance among the Hebrews was symbolical of a joy not otherwise capable of the like emphatic expression, and was often accompanied with song and timbrel music. It was originally an outlet for religious enthusiasm,

but indulgence in it was regarded as less seemly in men than in women. Associated as it was with idolatrous rites, it fell in esteem as a vehicle for expressing religious emotions, and at length it was confined to occasions of ordinary festivity, though at such times it was looked on askance by the more rigid Jews as savouring of heathen laxity, and not consistent with strict morality.

Education.—Possibly, in Old Testament times, the Sons of the Prophets constituted educational colleges ; but we have no direct information on this point. Later, the synagogues were used as schools on the week days. The teaching was limited pretty much to instruction in the principles and precepts of the law and scripture knowledge generally. The teacher was always a married man, of the class of priest or scribe, and he was held in honour on account of his office (see THE SCRIBES, p. 92). At five a boy was to learn the law, beginning with extracts of the more important parts, the *Schema*, or Creed (Deut. ii. 4), the *Hallel*, or Festival Psalms (Psalms cxiv.-cxviii., cxxxvi.). At twelve he became responsible for obedience to the law. According to the *Pirhe Aboth* (v. 24) a boy was to enter on the study of the *Mishna* (or Commentary) at ten, and that of the *Gemara* (the more extended Commentary) at eighteen. It is presumed that it was customary to teach the better classes to read and write, and give them also some knowledge of accounts and such physical science as was available. What other learning a Jew might have he derived from other sources ; and every Jewish parent was bound to see that his son acquired skill in some useful craft, that he might thereby earn an honest living. The girls, besides a similar training in the law, were also trained to some useful industry, such as spinning, weaving, and needlework.

Hospitality.—The Jews, like the Semitic peoples generally, were famous for hospitality, and it was the duty of the head of the house to give food and shelter to any wearied wayfarer who might come under his roof (Lev. xix. 33, 34).

Kiss.—Kissing the lips was customary among relatives of both sexes as a token of affection (Gen. xxix. 11), while kissing the cheek was usual between individuals not so related of the same sex, and to some extent those of different sexes, in token of respect and formal salutation. In the Christian Church it was an expression of Christian brotherhood.

Lot.—Casting lots was often a species of divination, but among the Jews it was a form of appeal to God, and the result was regarded as His decision (Prov. xvi. 33). Recourse was had to it in the partition of lands or of spoil, in the detection of crime, and in appointments to certain offices.

Marriage.—Proposal of marriage was made by the relatives of the bridegroom to the parents of the bride ; and the proposal, if accepted, was followed by an espousal, in which the representatives of each were the contracting parties, the engagement being ratified by oaths and presents to the bride. By this proceeding the two became legally betrothed, and in the eyes of the law married people, and it only needed thereafter that the bridegroom should come some day with festive rejoicing and take his bride home to wife, though possibly after some formal ratification of the marriage oaths. For this ceremony he prepared with garlands and spices, and she by wearing a veil which covered her from head to foot, a peculiar girdle, and a chaplet on her forehead, beneath which her hair flowed freely. The ceremony itself was celebrated with pledging the wine-cup, and invocation of blessing, while the company walked round the married pair chanting hymns and showering rice on their heads. The home-going was in the evening, when the bridegroom, with his attendants and others playing on instruments or bearing torches, came to the house of the bride, who returned with him accompanied by her maidens, the procession being joined on the way by friends of the bridegroom with lamps burning. Festivities followed which lasted seven and sometimes fourteen days, and at which the guests were provided with wedding garments at the expense of their host.

Mourning.—The Jews gave expression to sorrow under any heavy affliction in various ways, such as by rending the seams of their garments, wearing sackcloth, casting ashes or dust on the person, dressing in sad-coloured clothing, laying aside of all ornaments, abstaining from food, beating the breast, plucking the hair of the head or the beard, even cutting the flesh, and, in general, with publicly expressed, but silent lamentations. The period of mourning was of varied duration, and extended to thirty, sometimes seventy, days. Hired professional female mourners, who made a great clamour with musical instruments, and loud, wild cries, were employed at funerals.

Obeisance.—This, on the part of an inferior to a superior, was by an inclination of the head and the body, with an extension of the hands, the palms being turned downwards; and the inclination was greater according to the depth of the feeling of respect, and according to the rank of the superior.

Salutations.—These were of two kinds, according as they were greetings on the occasion of meeting a friend or of writing him. In the former case it was the expression of a wish for his welfare, and was the same at parting as at meeting; and in the latter the writer placed his own name first, then that of the person addressed, with an expression wishing him joy. Sometimes a friend would salute another by placing his hand first on his forehead, then on his mouth, and then over his heart, to signify how entirely he was at his service.

Washing the Hands and Feet.—As the Jews ate out of a common dish without knives and forks, it was absolutely necessary that the hands should be perfectly clean; and the duty of washing them in pure water beforehand was regarded as matter of religious obligation, and regulated by strict ritual prescription. The washing of the feet was required from their wearing not shoes but sandals when walking, so tnat when a guest arrived at a house water

was provided for the purpose, the operation being performed by a menial of the household, and often, in token of great respect, by the host himself. On festive occasions the feet were anointed as well as washed.

See Van Lennep, *Bible Lands, &c.*, Vol. II.; Stapfer, *Palestine in the Time of Christ;* Thompson, *The Land and the Book;* Barrows, *The Manners and Customs of the Jews.*

CHAPTER XXX.

DRESS AND ORNAMENTS.

AMONG the Jews the dress of a man, on ordinary occasions, differed little from that of a woman, yet there were certain features by which the one was easily distinguishable from the other. Both wore an inner tight-fitting garment of cotton, linen, or wool, originally without sleeves, and reaching only to the knee, corresponding to our shirt, though translated "coat" in A. V., wearing which alone the person was reckoned naked; sometimes also a second "shirt" or "coat," an upper loose garment with ample sleeves, which extended to the feet; and an outer mantle, or shawl, of wool, conjectured to resemble a Scotch plaid in shape, which was variously used to wrap round the body, throw over the shoulders, or cover the head; only in the case of the women, the outer vesture appears to have been of ampler dimensions, and such as might veil at once both the head and the feet.

Anklets.—These are mentioned in Isa. iii. 18 as ornaments worn by women, and in ver. 20 as fastened by a chain, to force the wearer to walk with mincing steps. They were of the same material as the armlet (which see), those of the richer classes being often of solid gold, and those of the poorer of some baser metal, but in both cases worn to produce a tinkling effect.

Armlets.—These were worn by Jewish women, as elsewhere in the East by princes, and people of high degree. They were always of showy, if not rich, material; they often literally covered the arm, and were sometimes of great weight.

Bracelets.—These encompassed the wrists, were worn by men as well as women, were of the same material as the anklets and armlets, and were adopted from similar motives of pride.

Earrings.—These, which were generally of gold, with sometimes jewels attached, and circular, appear to have been worn both by men and women, and to have been originally adopted as amulets from superstitious motives. They were often of great weight.

Frontlets.—These, otherwise called "Phylacteries," were strips of vellum inscribed with certain texts of Scripture, enclosed in small cases made of layers of calf-skin, and attached to the forehead and the left arm, and also, in another form, to the doorposts of houses. The texts inscribed were Exod. xiii. 2-10, 11-16; Deut. vi. 4-9, 13-22. They were the workmanship of a privileged set of Scribes, who were required to be scrupulously careful in the execution of them, and bound to see that the letters were well and regularly written, and that there were no erasures or corrections. Originally subservient to acts of worship, they were eventually turned to superstitious account, and employed sometimes as charms, and sometimes for purposes of ostentation.

Girdle.—This was worn by both men and women, and was ordinarily of leather, though sometimes of embroidered linen and studded with jewels. It was fastened with a clasp or tied in a knot with the ends hanging down, and generally worn more loosely by women than men. Girdles were often of great value, and given as presents.

Head-dress.—The Hebrews originally wore no head-dress, employing for covering only a fold of the mantle ; and such a thing was first worn by way of ornament, or in symbol of dignity. It was of the nature of a turban, consisting of folds of linen wound round the head, of various devices and variously ornamented. In Palestine at the present day it is customary for girls to carry their dowries on their heads in the form of strings of coins hanging down on either side the face. Probably one of these coins is referred to in the parable of the lost piece of silver (Luke xv. 8-10).

Hem of Garment.—According to Num. xv. 38, 39, the hem of the garment was to be so wrought as to remind the wearer of his obligation to have regard to the law of the Lord ; but, in the hands of the Pharisees, it became more than a symbol, and was regarded as possessing something like a sacramental virtue. A special merit attached to regard for the fringes of the raiment. "Whoso takes care of these," says a Hebrew proverb, "deserves a good coat."

Horn.—The horn, worn attached to the head-dress, was a symbol of strength and honour, and was more or less expressive of sovereign authority. Silver horns are worn by married women among the Druses.

Nose-jewel.—This was a ring, generally of gold or silver, which passed through the right nostril, and was worn as an ornament by women. It was usually of 1½ inches diameter, and often of considerable weight. From it sometimes jewels were suspended.

Phylacteries.—See FRONTLETS, *supra.*

Sandals.—These were mere soles attached to the foot by thongs, which were often embroidered; they were worn among the Hebrews, instead of shoes, and they consisted of leather, felt, cloth, or wood, and sometimes, where possible, they were shod with iron. They were not worn within doors, only when going abroad, in which case the wearer often carried an extra pair. They were taken off at meals, on occasions of deep sorrow, and also on approaching a person or entering a place of peculiar sacredness, such as the Temple, in the case of the priests. To carry or unloose another's sandals, as being a menial's office, was a mark and confession of standing towards him in the humblest

relationship. To cast a sandal over anything was an expression of supreme contempt.

Veil.—The veil, as an article of female attire, was, as usual, of a light texture, and was worn partly for ornament and partly for concealment, as by a bride on the day of her marriage, and also by women of loose moral character. Hebrew women, maids as well as matrons, usually wore no veils.

See books mentioned in Chapter XXIX.

CHAPTER XXXI.

HOUSES, FOOD, AND MANNER OF LIVING.

THE **Houses** in Palestine were generally of one storey, except in towns, where they were often of three. They were all, or nearly all, flat-roofed, and without chimneys, for there were no fires in the apartments. When they were of three storeys, the principal apartment, called the upper room, was on the top floor, the bedrooms were on the second, while the ground-floor contained the ordinary sitting-rooms of the house. The front presented a dead wall, relieved only by a door and one or two latticed or projecting windows at the top. In the interior of a large dwelling there were generally two or more courts, into which the apartments opened, the innermost being, it would seem, reserved for the women and children, and accessible only to the master of the house and the female domestics. The upper apartments and the roof were reached by outside stairs, which arose from the court, and were generally concealed by foliage, or in some other way. An awning was sometimes spread over the courtyard. In the larger houses it was usual for a verandah to run round the courtyard, and if the house were of two or more storeys there would be a balcony covered with a second verandah. In the case of the paralytic who was let down through the "roof" to reach Christ, perhaps only the wooden roof of the verandah was torn up. The house-roof proper would be of beams, matted branches, and dried mud.

Diet.—The diet of the Hebrews, like that of the Orientals generally, was simple and light, and was mainly of vegetable quality, the staple article being bread. Except on festive occasions, flesh was seldom eaten, the chief animal products extensively used being milk, sour butter, and cheese. Besides its consumption in the form of bread, grain was eaten sometimes green and sometimes roasted ; and when baked into bread, it was usually accompanied with some seasoning, such as salt, or after being dipped into some sop, such as meat soup. Fruits, being abundant, were another means of subsistence, especially the fig and the grape, which were eaten both green and dried, and frequently, in the latter state, pressed into cakes. Apple, citron, date-palm, pomegranate, and sycamore trees were common, and the fruit of these too yielded a goodly supply of food. Of vegetables proper, the lentil and the bean, with other kinds of pulse, were largely in use for food, in addition to which cucumbers, leeks, and onions were held in general favour for the same purpose. Honey and oil were important articles of consumption, while among the condiments or spices there were, besides salt, which was the chief, cinnamon, mint, anise, mustard, and spice of certain nuts. Among the animals whose flesh was eaten were the ox, under three years of age, the calf, the lamb, the kid, fowl of various sorts, with their eggs, fish of certain kinds, and even locusts. The flesh of animals when cooked was usually eaten with bread or some other accompaniment, and never by itself.

Bath.—Bathing among the Jews was largely associated with ceremonial cleansing. Thus it was especially incumbent on the high-priest at his ordination (Lev. viii. 6), and on the Day of Atonement (xvi. 4, 24). In the time of Christ rigorous Jews took a bath after a visit to the market (Mark vii. 4). Even in early times baths were found in private houses (2 Sam. xi. 2). Pools, such as those of Siloam and Bethesda, seem to have been used as public baths. But the luxury and elaboration of bathing enjoyed among the Romans finds no counterpart in Jewish customs.

Bed.—By a bed in Scripture is generally to be understood a mattress, matting, or quilt, with a coverlet, for which last often an outer garment sufficed, the whole such as could be easily folded up and carried away. The bedstead was something slight and portable, and might be used as a litter, and even a bier.

Bread.—The better sort of bread was of wheat, and the more common of barley, or both mixed, to which the flour of beans, lentils, or millet was sometimes added, barley in this case being the chief ingredient. It was in the form of cakes, and a fresh supply was baked daily. The baking was done by the women of the household, and sometimes by professional bakers, the dough being kneaded in a trough and cooked on the hearth or in an oven.

Butter.—The butter of Scripture was merely curdled milk or cream, i.e., cheese unpressed and never, as with us, the product of the churn, the process of churning being entirely unknown to the Hebrews. This clotted cream appears to have been often allowed to ferment, a process which imparted to it a pleasant acid flavour.

Caves.—Owing to the prevailing character of the rock, which is chalky limestone, caves are numerous in the land of Palestine, and they were extensively resorted to as dwellings by the earlier inhabitants, as they still are occasionally by shepherds in the pastoral season. They were often used as burial-places and places of refuge, as well as haunts for robbers. The valley of Jehoshaphat is full of them, inhabited at this day by Arabs.

Ceilings.—These were met with only in the Temple, the palaces of the kings, or princely residences. They consisted of planks of cedar wood filling up the spaces between the beams or rafters. They were carved, ornamented with gold, and sometimes painted, specially with vermilion.

Chamber.—This term was applied specially to a royal sleeping apartment, and in ordinary houses of two storeys to the room on the uppermost floor, which was, as it were, the sanctuary of the dwelling, and had a window that looked out in the direction of the Temple.

Couch.—This was a framework for the bed (which see), used to recline on in the daytime, and it was often expensively decked and ornamented.

Drink.—Besides milk, already referred to, the Hebrews used beverages which consisted of barley and water, or fig-cake and water, recourse being had most frequently to the latter ingredient for refreshment. Unfermented wine seems to have been in common use as a beverage. By "strong drink" was meant the juice of any fruit, but specially the grape, that was of an intoxicating quality. Besides drink of this sort, the Jews used other beverages, such as a beer made of barley, and honey-wine. But the principal beverage was water.

Manna.—This was the miraculous food provided every day, except the Sabbath, for the children of Israel in the wilderness; and the word means "What is this?" that being the astonished exclamation of the Israelites when they saw it lying round the camp on the first morning (Exod. xvi. 14-36). It is described as lying on the ground in small grains like hoarfrost, as requiring to be gathered early every day, and as becoming offensive if kept till the morrow. It has been compared to truffles, small fungi that grow in the sand of the desert, and constitute the staple food of the Bedouin when travelling in the districts where they are found.

Meals.—The Jews would appear to have sat down to two chief meals a day—one of a light nature in the morning, about an hour before noon; and another, which was the principal meal, and of a more substantial nature, about sunset. Meals were originally and ordinarily eaten in a sitting posture, and it was only in later times that the practice, introduced from Syria and Babylon, began to prevail of reclining at them on couches. This was the custom in vogue in the days of Christ, the arrangement, called a *triclinium*, being a table in the centre, with couches generally for three men each, on three sides of it, the guests reclining with their bodies leaning forward and raised on the left elbow. The hands were washed and grace was said before and after eating; and the food, which was usually served in a common dish, though sometimes special portions were sent round, was eaten by dipping bread in it, or by using two pieces of it by way of forks. Meals of a sumptuous order were customary on the great festival days, and also in connection with birthdays, marriages, funerals, and all high occasions. At such times the guests were saluted with a kiss; sometimes they had their heads anointed with ointment and encircled with garlands, and occasionally their persons were decorated with a specially provided festive garment. The guests had their several places at the table allotted to them, and one of them was elected master of the ceremonies, and called the "governor of the feast" (John ii. 8).

Milk.—This, as all over the East, was among the Hebrews one of the chief articles of food, and was used both in its natural and in a curdled state (see BUTTER). The milk in most general use as well as esteem was that of the goat, although that of the cow, the sheep, and the camel was also employed for food.

Mirror.—Mirrors appear to have been chiefly used by the women, and were circular, highly polished plates of metal, with a handle attached, often ornamentally carved. The metal was a mixture of copper, tin, and lead, perhaps in the proportions, as found in the case of an Etruscan mirror, respectively of 8, 3, and 1.

Pillow.—Pillows, which appear to have consisted of a sheep or a goat's skin stuffed with cotton or wool, were used to support the head and shoulder when sleeping or reclining at meals. They were supported on a frame, and were placed under the armpit, so as to hold up the body.

Roof.—The roofs of the houses were usually flat, and protected by parapets of moderate height. They were reached by an outer staircase. In mild seasons they were used by the family both by day and night, and they served for an upper chamber in houses of only one storey high.

Soap.—Some vegetable alkali or some kind of potash seems to have been employed as soap. The word rendered "soap" in the English Bible, however, seems to stand for any substance with cleansing qualities.

Table.—See MEALS.

Tent.—The tent was the ordinary dwelling-house of the Hebrew till the time of his settlement in the land of Canaan, as was natural in his then nomadic life. At that time his occupation was that of shepherd, and his dwelling required to be such as could easily be removed from place to place. It would appear to have been a low, dark-coloured structure, nearly flat-roofed, consisting of skin or cloth of hair, which was raised by poles and tightened with cords. It contained at least two apartments, one for the men and another for the women.

Window.—This was a mere opening for air and light, to close which there was nothing better than a curtain or a frame of lattice work. Windows looked mainly to the rear of the dwelling, though projecting ones were sometimes met with in front, from which a side glance could be obtained along the lane or street.

Wine.—This was the produce of the fruit of the vine, and occasionally of the pomegranate and other fruits. Sometimes it was drunk in an unfermented, but more generally in a fermented, state, after the lees had been drained off. It is associated among the gifts of God with "corn and oil," and it appears along with them as one of the distinctive products or benefits of settled agricultural life. The introduction of the vine was connected with the establishment of a settled order of life. See books mentioned in Chapter XXIX.

CHAPTER XXXII.

ARMS, ARMOUR, AND ARMAMENTS.

Armour.—This included the coat of mail, or breastplate; the helmet; the large shield, or buckler; and the greaves for the legs. It was for defence, therefore, and not offence.

Armour-bearer.—He was an attendant on a warrior, who bore his heavy weapons for him, such as his shield and spear.

Army.—There was no regular army among the Jews till the erection of the kingdom, each tribe fighting under its own banner and leader, and often doing battle on its own behalf, as occasion summoned the clansmen to arms. Even under the kings it was some time before a standing army was organised, and then the formation of it was necessitated in consequence of the threatening attitude of the neighbouring nations, principally Syria on the north. Under David and Solomon, however, the military organisation was of some dimensions, and the force included horsemen and chariots, amounting even to thousands, the whole under officers holding different grades of rank (1 Kings ix. 22).

Artillery.—The term is applied to missile weapons of every kind, such as javelins and bows and arrows (1 Sam. xx. 40).

Band.—This was a Roman cohort, or the tenth part of a legion, and was understood to consist of 600 men; but it really consisted of 360 or so, divided into six centuries, each under a centurion. The Italian band (Acts x. 1) is supposed to have been composed of volunteers from Italy, and to have formed the procurator's body-guard. The Augustus band (Acts xxvii. 1) appears to have been formed of native troops, whose headquarters were Cæsarea.

Bows and Arrows.—The bows in use among the Jews were of great strength, and appear to have been bent with the aid of the foot. To wield them with effect required great skill as well as a powerful physique, and it was not given to every one to handle them with dexterity. They were used in hunting as well as war, and by the enemies as well as the armies of Israel. The bow-string was of natural fibrous cordage, and the arrow, which was carried in a quiver, was sometimes charged with matter on fire or with poison.

Coat of Mail.—This appears to have been a breastplate of scales of some sort for the protection of the body.

Greaves.—These were defences for the feet merely, like the upper part of a shoe, and not for the legs, and in some instances they were made of brass (1 Sam. xvii. 6).

Helmet.—This appears to have been of a round shape, and high.

Legion.—This was a body of Roman soldiers, nominally of 6000, sometimes only little more than 3000, men, and under the command of a tribune.

Quaternion.—This was a Roman guard of four soldiers, two of whom kept watch over a prisoner inside the cell and two at the door. It was relieved by another guard of four every three hours by day or night.

Shield.—Shields were of two kinds, one of larger and another of smaller dimensions. The larger covered the whole person, and the soldier who wielded it had some one to carry it for him when not engaged in fight. The smaller was a sort of buckler, and such as might be used in a hand-to-hand conflict with the sword.

Sling.—This was carried by shepherds, and employed by them to defend their flocks; and in the use of which certain Benjamites are said to have been very dexterous (Judg. xx. 16). The name was in the time of the monarchy applied to an engine of the nature of the catapult (2 Kings iii. 25 ; 2 Chron. xxvi. 15).

Spear.—There were three kinds of spears, of different dimensions. The largest mentioned in Scripture was that wielded by Goliath (1 Sam. xvii. 7) ; and the name given to it in the original is also applied to the spear of Saul (1 Sam. xxii. 6), which appears to have been both heavy and strong. The smaller spears were more of the nature of javelins, and some even akin to darts.

Sword.—This weapon is of early and frequent mention in Scripture, but little is known of the fashion of it or the mode of using it. It appears to have been shorter and lighter than the weapon of the same name with us, yet, when wielded by a powerful arm, to have been capable of inflicting fearful wounds with a single stroke. It had sometimes two edges, was provided with a sheath, and was suspended to the girdle. The buckling of it on was a declaration of war, and the whetting of it the sign of preparation for a bloody strife.

War Chariots.—These chariots were in common use among the enemies of Israel from the time when they were employed by Pharaoh against the Israelites as they fled out of Egypt, but they were not adopted by the people themselves till the days of David and Solomon. They constituted the heavy artillery of the army, and the chariots as well as the horses employed were imported chiefly from Egypt. They are often referred to in the prophets as symbolic of power (Ps. xx. 7; civ. 3; Jer. li. 21; Zech. vi. 1). They were semicircular, two-wheeled, and mounted from behind, where they were open. They carried two, sometimes three, persons, the driver to the left; and they were drawn by two or more horses, often of different colours.

CHAPTER XXXIII.

VESSELS, UTENSILS, AND IMPLEMENTS.

Baskets.—Baskets among the Jews, as with us, were usually of wickerwork, though sometimes also of network, and even ropework, and were of various forms, dimensions, and strength

of structure, according to the use they were put to. They were employed principally to contain bread, to carry it on the head or arm, or to store it up, and frequently also to hold and carry other articles of food, such as fruit. Pharaoh's baker dreamed he had three baskets on his head (Gen. xl. 16). These would be the flat, open baskets, often represented on Egyptian monuments. In the New Testament we meet with three kinds of baskets :—(1) The *kophinos*, a small hand basket, referred to in the feeding of the five thousand (Mark vi. 43); (2) the *spuris*, a large basket or hamper of twisted reeds, mentioned in the feeding of the four thousand (Mark viii. 8) ; (3) the *sargane*, a rope basket of large size, in one of which St. Paul was let down from the walls of Damascus (2 Cor. xi. 33).

Books. — These consisted of long stripes of parchment, written in pages usually on one side only and in two columns, with rollers attached to the extremities, the pages commencing from the right ; and they were read by unwinding the parchment from the left-hand roller and winding it on the right-hand one. This was called a roll (whence our " volume," from *volvo*, to roll), and each book of the Bible formed a separate one.

Bottles.—These were of prepared skin or of earthenware. The former were made, the larger ones of the skin of a goat, and smaller ones of the skin of a kid, by drawing the body of the animal out of it after the head and legs had been cut off, an opening being left where the head had been. These skins were prepared for use by being tanned, and were employed for holding wine and other liquors. When they ruptured, the rent was closed up usually either with a patch, or by gathering the sides up and tying them together. They were and are still used also as water-bags, and carried on the back. The earthenware or glass bottles are presumed to have been of Egyptian manufacture.

Candles.—The word "candle" is used inappropriately in the Bible for oil-lamps of earthenware, which burned with a wick that protruded from a small spout at the side, and which fitted on to, or were of a piece with, a lampstand, or "candlestick."

Carriage.—This word is used in Scripture in the sense of burden or baggage—that which is carried.

Cart.—This was an open or covered vehicle, usually with two wheels, drawn by oxen, not horses, and used for the conveyance of burdens and produce, as well sometimes as persons.

Knife.—Knives were used among the Jews chiefly for slaughtering animals, and also for other purposes, but rarely, if at all, at meals.

Lock and Key.—A lock was a hollow bolt with spikes that dropped into a groove and fastened the door, and the key was a beam with corresponding spikes to raise those of the bolt, so that it could be withdrawn. The key was often of some weight, and was the symbol of authority.

Mill.—This consisted of two circular stones of about two feet in diameter, the under one of which was the larger, had a slightly convex surface, and was fixed in the ground ; the upper was free, with a hole in the centre to admit the grain ; it had a corresponding concavity of surface, and it was worked by two upright handles near the edge, which were pushed to and fro usually by two women seated facing each other. The larger kind of mill was worked by an ass. It is the great stone of such a mill that Jesus names when He says : "And whosoever shall cause one of these little ones that believe on Me to stumble, it were better for him if a great millstone were hanged about his neck, and he were cast into the sea" (Mark ix. 42, R.V.).

Scrip.—This word stands for a leather bag, slung over the shoulders with a strap, and worn by peasants on a journey and shepherds when out on the hills, chiefly to carry their food.

Ship.—Ships, such as were used in the Mediterranean trade, were often of considerable tonnage, if we may judge from the one in which St. Paul was wrecked, that carried, besides cargo, 276 souls (Acts xxvii.). They were loosely built, so as to require girdings of ropes underneath to prevent the planks starting in rough weather, and they were steered by paddles, worked like oars from the ship's quarter. They had only one mast, square-rigged ; and the anchors—four in number in St. Paul's ship—were attached to the stern, and cast out at night against the danger of falling on breakers. The boats on the Sea of Galilee must have been a light craft, and at one time they were very numerous, though they are but few now.

Writing Materials.—Writing in Hebrew and Aramaic was from right to left. Originally it was on some durable material, such as stone or brass, and of the nature of engraving or carving done with a graver, lead being sometimes employed to fill up the cavities. For writing proper some kind of parchment was in common use, while the writing implement was a reed dipped in a black liquid of lamp-black dissolved in gall juice, which was held in an ink-horn, frequently suspended from the girdle. It is uncertain whether the Jews borrowed the use of papyrus-paper from the Egyptians to any extent. The Apostle John wrote on this paper (2 John 12). See books mentioned in Chapter XXIX.

CHAPTER XXXIV.

INSTRUMENTS OF MUSIC.

THE Instruments of Music in use among the Jews were of three kinds—Stringed Instruments, Wind Instruments, and Instruments of Percussion.

Bell.—Two Hebrew words are translated by the English word "bell" in the Authorised Version. One occurs in Zech. xiv. 20, and is akin to the Hebrew for a cymbal. It is translated in the LXX. by a word which means a bridle. In this case it appears to have been a cup of metal attached to a bridle, possibly to produce tink-ling effects. The other word, mentioned in Exod. xxviii. 33, &c., probably denotes what we understand by the word "bell." The bells used in the Tabernacle service were of gold.

Cithern.—The cithern was a sort of guitar of four or five chords, probably imported from Greece. It was played with the hand.

Cornet.—This was a loud-sounding trumpet, made of the horn of a ram or a chamois, and used in making proclamations or announcements of a formal kind.

Cymbals.—There were two species of cymbals, named respectively "loud" and "high-sounding," the former consisting of broad-rimmed shallow plates of metal, strapped singly or in pairs to each hand, and clashed together ; and the latter of conical vessels with a thin edge, one of which was brought sharply down on the other, so as to cause a shrill sound. They were used on solemn religious occasions only.

Dulcimer.—The dulcimer was a Babylonian instrument (Dan. iii. 5), and is considered by some to have been a stringed instrument played with hammers or little rods, and by others to have been a sort of bagpipe. This latter is the prevailing opinion.

Flute.—The flute is only mentioned in Dan. iii. 5, 7, 10, 15, and appears to have been a sort of Pan's pipes, or small organ.

Harp.—The harp was an instrument generally of ten strings, though sometimes it is said to have had as many as twenty-four, and even forty-seven strings. The shape of it is uncertain. Possibly it resembled our harp, but Jerome described it as like the Greek delta. It was played on either with the fingers or a plectrum. It was of early invention (Gen. iv. 21), and is the only stringed instrument mentioned in the Pentateuch.

Organ.—This instrument was originally formed of a collection of reeds like Pan's pipes, and similarly played, but was afterwards so improved in mechanism as well as enlarged as to justify its name "organ"—the pipes being inserted in some sort of wind-box, and the wind supplied by the mouth or bellows.

Pipe.—By this is meant sometimes a reed instrument with a mouthpiece, used on festive or solemn occasions, and sometimes a small flute. It was a domestic instrument known in private life.

Psaltery.—The psaltery was a large harp, and was so called from being one of the principal instruments used in the services of religious worship.

Ram's Horns.—See CORNET.

Sackbut.—The sackbut—only mentioned in Daniel—is a deep-toned wind-instrument with a slide, like a trombone ; but it is a mistranslation for a word that denotes a large, full-toned harp.

Shawm.—This is the name in the Prayer-Book

version of Psalm xcviii. 6 for the word translated "cornet" in the Authorised Version. (See CORNET.)

Tabret, Timbrel.—These two names are renderings of the same Hebrew word. The instrument referred to was a tambourine, and was used with cymbals as an accompaniment to dancing.

Trumpet.—There were three kinds of trumpets, two of them of horn, one crooked and one straight; and a third of silver, blown only by priests, and for purposes of solemn proclamation. Possibly some of these were the same as the cornets. (See CORNET.)

Viol.—This was a harp or psaltery of ten strings.
See Stainer, *Music of the Bible.*

CHAPTER XXXV.

ARTS AMONG THE JEWS.

Agriculture.—Though the Hebrews and their ancestors were originally a purely pastoral people, they changed their mode of life from the time of their settlement in the land of Canaan, and took with zest to the tillage of the soil; from that day the practice of agriculture became their chief occupation, while the land itself came to be regarded by them as the centre of their holiest affections. The soil of the country they now occupied was capable of producing fruits and grains in manifold variety, and its resources were at length enhanced by forming it into terraces and husbanding the water for its irrigation. Besides garden produce, the chief crops cultivated were wheat and barley, with pulse of various kinds, and the chief fruit-trees were the vine, the olive, and the fig. In preparing the grain for food the five chief processes were ploughing, sowing, reaping, threshing, and winnowing.

(*a.*) *Ploughing.*—The plough, a light instrument of wood with an iron tip, was used only on level land—the hoe being employed on steep and hilly parts—and generally it was drawn by only one yoke of oxen, while the ploughing itself was mere surface scratching. The operation was often repeated, and for the final time just before the season of rain.

(*b.*) *Sowing.*—This was usually after rain, and often without ploughing, the seed being thereafter either treated with a light harrowing or trampled under the hoofs of cattle.

(*c.*) *Reaping.*—Grain was reaped either with a sickle or by being pulled by the roots; and when the sickle was employed, sometimes only the ears were cut off, and sometimes the stalk with them. The corn was then gathered into sheaves or heaps till dry enough for harvesting.

(*d.*) *Threshing.*—The threshing-floor was a circular level spot of from 50 to 100 feet in diameter, and the process of threshing was usually by gathering the sheaves in the centre, and trampling out the grain with oxen, though sometimes an instrument like a flail was also employed, and later a sort of sleigh was dragged over the corn by oxen.

(*e.*) *Winnowing.*—This was done by tossing the grain with a broad shovel, called a fan, when a breeze was blowing, or by shaking it in a sieve, in order to separate the chaff from it.

Bread-baking.—This being a species of cooking, was originally and properly the business of the women of a household, although it was also, in the larger communities, carried on by men. A single baking for a family sufficed merely for a day, the bread being in the form of small thin cakes, and apt to become unpalatable after it was a day old. The bread was made by kneading the dough with the hands in a wooden trough, leaven being added afterwards, if required, and time allowed. When the process was complete, the dough was wrought, sometimes after being mixed with oil-seeds, &c., into round cakes, so small that three formed a meal, and these were then transferred to the oven and baked. The ovens were either jars that had been heated, or holes in the ground, presumably heated by being covered with fuel.

Brick-making.—The bricks which the Hebrews made in Egypt were probably of a Nile mud, such as required to be mixed with straw to give it the due coherence, and was, when moulded, dried in the sun. But even in Egypt, when the clay was of a quality to require no straw, it was baked in a kiln. Either way bricks were made by a number of men working together, each at a division of the work, and the whole operation was superintended by an overseer, called in the Egyptian brick-fields a "taskmaster." Assyrian bricks were sun-baked like the Egyptian. Babylonian bricks, however, were baked in kilns. The latter was the Jewish method of brick-making in Palestine (2 Sam. xii. 31).

Fishing.—Fish were caught by means of nets, or stakes, or hooks. The nets employed were the casting-net or the drag-net; the use of the latter, as being the larger, required the aid of a boat. The stakes were reeds stuck on the shore, and were rarely employed. The hook was the resource of the poor, and some kind of bait was used. The great fishing-field of Palestine was the Sea of Galilee, which abounded in fish.

Handicrafts.—These were such as working in metal, wood, and stone, spinning and weaving (see below, WEAVING), dyeing and tanning. The craftsmen connected with these arts were the makers of tools, goldsmiths, silversmiths, and coppersmiths; carpenters and masons; weavers, shoemakers, tailors, and tent-makers. Every Jew was required to teach his son some one or other of these crafts.

Medicine.—The Egyptians claimed to be the inventors of medicine. In the time of the Ptolemies dissection was practised at Alexandria. The treatment, however, was miserably ignorant, and the remedies employed were often disgusting concoctions from an absurd variety of natural objects. Medicine came very near to magic. Yet the references to physicians in the Gospels show that they were sought after and trusted (*e.g.*, Mark ii. 17; v. 26).

Mining.—That this art was known to the Hebrews we conclude from the use among them of metals not otherwise obtainable, and also from the graphic account given of the operations of the miner in the Book of Job. From Job xxviii. 1-11 we learn that the Jews were familiar with mining explorations, and with the devices to which the miner has recourse to coerce the depths of the earth into the surrender of its treasures. It has been said that this art among the Hebrews appears to have been limited to the quest after such metals as are obtainable in a pure state, and that there is no reason to believe that they knew the art of smelting such of them as are to be found only in the state of an ore. But we meet with repeated references to the refining of metals (e.g., Ps. xii. 6), and learn that the lead was burnt out of the ore (Jer. vi. 28-30).

Music.—The music of the Hebrews appears to have been for long of a very rude and simple kind, and to have been associated from the first with the dance on special occasions of rejoicing. Its origin is traced back to Jubal, who is called "the father of such as handle the harp and the organ" (Gen. iv. 21), and the sound of it was heard at every high and solemn moment throughout the history of the Jewish nation. It was especially cultivated in connection with the services of religion, and its development went parallel with the development of the Temple ritual. The use of it was generally a sign of joy, and the cessation a token of calamity and mourning. It was of a quality to soothe as well as to inspire; it had power to drive away the evil spirit from Saul (1 Sam. xvi. 19-23), and it aided the prophets as they prophesied and brought others into sympathy with the spirit that inspired them (1 Sam. x. 5-10).

See Chap. XXXIV., MUSICAL INSTRUMENTS.

Poetry.—See Chap. X., THE POETICAL BOOKS.

Pottery.—The potter's art must have been familiar to the Jews from the days of their sojourn in Egypt, as the wheel, which is the essential implement of the art in its developed form, was known to the Egyptians from the earliest antiquity. The clay, after being trodden into the due uniform softness, was placed on the wheel, where, as the latter revolved, it was shaped into a vessel by the hands of the potter, after which it was coated with some glazing substance and burnt in a furnace. The wheel was a small horizontal disc of wood, attached by a spindle to a larger wheel, which was worked either by the hand of an assistant or by the foot of the potter himself. But possibly some sort of rough clay-modelling by hand was practised, even before contact with Egypt, in making homely household vessels, as it is now practised by remote villagers in the East.

Weaving.—This is a very ancient art—probably practised by the Hebrews before the settlement in Goshen. In Egypt the art was carried to a comparatively high state of perfection, and there the Israelites would be able to acquire the skill which was manifested in the construction of the Tabernacle. The Egyptian loom was upright, but the modern Arab loom is horizontal. It is doubtful which way the Jewish loom was placed. The "beam" to which the warp was fixed is alluded to in Scripture (e.g., 1 Sam. xvii. 7); the shuttle which carried the woof and was thrown to and fro by the hand of the weaver (Job vii. 6); and also the pin on which the finished web was rolled (Judg. xvi. 14). Coarse fabrics, such as tent-cloth, sackcloth, and the "hairy garment" of the poor, were the most common products. Fine linen was more highly prized. Wool was woven for ordinary clothing, but any mixture of wool and flax was forbidden.

Writing.—The practice of writing among the Hebrews appears to date from the time of Moses. For books and important documents skins were used. In the New Testament we meet with the wooden tablet covered with wax (Luke i. 63), and also paper (2 John 12). Ink made of lamp-black dissolved in gall juice was in use both in Old Testament (Jer. xxxvi. 18) and in New Testament times (2 Cor. iii. 3; 2 John 12; 3 John 13). The writing was executed by a pointed style (Ps. xlv. 2; Jer. viii. 8); for rock engraving this was of iron (Job xix. 24), or even of a diamond (Jer. xvii. 1). Writing with ink was effected by means of a reed (3 John 13). The ink was carried in an "inkhorn" suspended at the girdle as is done in the East at the present day (Eze. ix. 2).

See books mentioned in Chapter XXIX.

CHAPTER XXXVI.

IDOLATRY AND DIVINATION.

A. IDOLATRY.

IDOLATRY is worship paid to that which is not God, or which only symbolises Him as though it were God. It is regarded throughout the Bible as directly counter to the worship of Jehovah, and fatal to the spiritual welfare of His people. Idols are usually designated in Scripture by names that imply similitude but unreality; or they are regarded as but objects of human device and workmanship, while epithets are applied to them expressive of their vanity, the grossness of their worship, and its evil consequences. The practice of idolatry was in direct violation of the constitution of the theocracy, and regarded as a breach of the covenant with Jehovah, comparable to nothing less than infidelity to a marriage vow. The inducements to indulge in it were too often the licentious observances which accompanied it; and it was long before the nation could tear itself away from such unholy indulgences and learn to content itself with the pure and simple worship of Jehovah alone.

Ashera. — The word Ashera, mistranslated "grove" in the A.V., does not stand for a place of worship, like the groves in which mysteries were sometimes celebrated, but for an object of worship, this word being used in two senses: *First*, as a proper name, it designates a particular goddess, mistakenly identified with Ashtoreth, who succeeded her as the consort of Baal. She was the goddess of fertility. *Second*, the word Ashera is used for the image, in the form of a trunk of a tree or a cone of stone, under the form of which the goddess was worshipped. The kings who cut down the "groves" of the A.V. —*i.e.*, the Asheras—did not fell forests; they hewed down idols.

Ashtoreth.—Ashtoreth (pl. Ashtaroth) was the principal goddess of the Canaanites, and the consort of Baal. She was at first typified under the form of a cow, with a star for emblem, earlier still as a conical stone in the image of a horn, the moon's or a cow's, or again as sitting on a lion, her head surrounded with a halo, in her right hand a thunderbolt, and in her left a sceptre. Originally Istar, the evening star, a Babylonian divinity, conceived of as at once both male and female, she came to be viewed at length as female only, and identified with the moon, representing the plastic power in nature, while Baal represented the creative.

Baal.—Baal (pl. Baalim), meaning Lord, Master, or Owner, was the native god of the land of Canaan, and was looked upon by the Canaanites as the giver of their corn and wine and oil, the god who presided over their labours as husbandmen and rendered the increase of their harvests. It was natural, when the Hebrews got possession of the land and entered into league with the Canaanites, that they should associate the worship of Baal, the god of the land, with that of Jehovah, the god of the nation; and this accordingly was the idolatry to which they were all along most prone. In a wider reference Baal was the god of the Phœnicians and Syrians, and also of the Babylonians, under the name of Bel, or Belus. In fact, the name is generic. Meaning "Lord," it did not necessarily stand for the same individual god among various nations. Nevertheless Baal was everywhere regarded as the god of the sun, in the light of the ruler and vivifier of nature, or as a sort of Asiatic Zeus. His crowning attribute appears to have been his strength. The Baal cult was conducted on the tops of hills, incense was frequently presented to him as well as sacrifices, and his priests danced round the altar and even cut themselves, while they made their offerings, in order the more to propitiate his favour (1 Kings xviii.). The name of *Baalism* has been given to the worship of Baal, which is definable as the worship of natural causes tending to the obscuration and denial of the worship of the Great First Cause, or prostration before the forces of nature apart from God and all thought of Him. (See ASHTORETH.)

Chemosh.—Chemosh was the national god of the Moabites, but we have no clue for determining what it was he symbolised or the character of the worship of him, except that this worship was idolatrous, and, as such, an abomination in the eyes of the servants of Jehovah (1 Kings xi. 7; 2 Kings xxiii. 13). On the famous "Moabite stone" Chemosh is praised for giving victory to his people, somewhat as Jehovah is honoured in Hebrew history for favouring the Jews.

Dagon.—Contrary to 1 Sam. v. 4, Dagon, the national god of the Philistines, has been represented under the form of a fish. It would appear that he had no such form. Originally one of the many divinities introduced into Canaan at an early period from Babylonia, he became a god of corn in the rich corn-growing plain of Philistia.

Diana.—Diana, or Artemis, was the twin-sister of Apollo, and a goddess of the Greeks, whose temple at Ephesus was one of the seven wonders of the world. As Apollo was represented as the typical image of the full bloom of manhood, so was Diana represented as the typical image of the full bloom of maidenhood, and both were worshipped as symbols of the strength and chastity of eternal youth. The sun was the emblem of the one and the moon was the emblem of the other, and they were each provided with bow and quiver to shoot down all who were not children of the light.

High Places.—These High Places, or Bamoth, were elevated spots, or hill-tops, on which altars were erected for worship, in the rude belief that, as they were nearer heaven, they were more favourable places for prayer and incense than the plains or valleys. Worship on such spots was almost universal among the Jews during and after the time of Solomon. In the time of Josiah the practice was finally put down, partly because it had degenerated into the worship of Baal, but also because the king was securing the centralising of worship at Jerusalem, as this was required to be in one spot by the book of Deuteronomy.

Moloch.—Moloch, or Milcom, the fire-god, was the chief god of the Ammonites, and his worship, which was common to all the nations of Canaan, was attended with cruelties which were especially revolting to the humane spirit of the Jewish religion. These were human sacrifices, ordeals by fire, mutilation, and even, it is said, the burning alive of little children, whose shrieks it was the custom to drown by the clash of cymbals.

Nehushtan.—This was believed to be the brazen serpent, made by Moses in the wilderness, which in after times became an object of superstitious reverence, and was even worshipped among the people of Israel. It was destroyed, along with other idolatrous relics, by King Hezekiah on his accession to the throne (2 Kings xviii. 4). Nehushtan signifies a piece of brass, and the name was given to it by Hezekiah to express his contempt for it as nothing more.

Queen of Heaven.—This deity, who is mentioned in Jer. vii. 18; xliv. 17, 18, 19, 25, is generally understood to be identical with the moon, viewed as an impersonation of the goddess Ashtoreth (which see).

Remphan.—Remphan is mentioned in Acts vii. 43 as the equivalent of Chiun in Amos v. 26. Possibly the Jews in Egypt had recognised the foreign Renpu worshipped in that country as identical with the object of worship mentioned by the Prophet. Chiun, however, seems to resemble the Egyptian goddess Ken. This Remphan, or Chiun, appears to have been a star-divinity, whose worship was of shepherd origin, and was practised by the Israelites in their wilderness wanderings, an image of whom they appear to have carried with them in some sort of shrine.

Rimmon.—This was worshipped as a Syrian god, and had a temple at Damascus called the house of Rimmon (2 Kings v. 18). He was identified with the Syrian sun-god, Hadad; but originally he was an Assyrian divinity.

Tammuz.—This god, who is mentioned only in Ezekiel, has been generally identified with the Greek Adonis, a youth of the most delicate beauty, who was fabled to have been mortally wounded by a boar, and thereafter immortalised by Venus, the memory of which event was celebrated annually with expressions first of mourning and then of joy all over the region of Asia Minor. Adonis appears to have been a symbol of the sun departing in winter and returning as youthful as ever in spring, and the worship of him a combined expression of the gloom connected with the presence of winter and the joy associated with the approach of summer.

B. DIVINATION.

Divination is a practice founded on the belief, mistakenly apprehended, however, that there is a certain sympathy between the world of nature and the world of spirit, and that certain signs discoverable by experience and observation in the one are significant and monitory of certain occurrences in the other. In practice the system was delusive, and gave rise to endless forms of imposture, which the too natural curiosity of man to pry into futurity only encouraged and intensified.

Amulets.—These were worn about the person under the belief that they possessed a virtue which would protect the wearer from the power of an enchantment, such, for instance, as might induce disease. These were of various sorts of forms, and their virtue was sometimes assumed to be native to them, as in certain stones, or animal substances (see the Book of Tobit), and sometimes to lie in some mystic or other symbol inscribed on them, as on the Phylacteries (which see).

Enchantments.—These were partly mere feats of legerdemain, and partly of the nature of spells, acting or presumed to act as a charm. The practice of having recourse to such was forbidden in Scripture (Lev. xix. 26), although it continued to exist among the Jews down to the times of the New Testament (Acts xiii. 6, 8; Gal. v. 20).

Magic.—Magic is the pretended art of summoning into play supernatural agencies or forces to produce miraculous effects or avert natural evils, and the practice of it is universal among all rude pagan nations. Indulgence in it was alien to the Jewish faith, yet the Jewish people had a native fondness for it, and we find them plying its arts in secret all through their history, from the time when Rachel stole away the Teraphim of her father (Gen. xxxi. 19) till the day when the imposture stood self-condemned in the presence of the power of the gospel (Acts xix. 13-20).

Teraphim.—These were small statues or images conceived as possessed of a certain magical virtue, which appear to have been occasionally consulted for purposes of divination. Regard for them in this light dates from patriarchal times, and a certain belief in them existed for long after among the children of Israel. Such were the images which Rachel abstracted from her father Laban, and it is clear that both he and she regarded them as treasures of no ordinary value (Gen. xxxi. 19, 30). They were worn as personal charms, or set up in houses as guardian deities.

See Robertson Smith, *Religion of the Semites*, and books on Old Testament Theology given in chapter xxvi.

CHAPTER XXXVII.

MALADIES AND DISEASES.

DISEASE among the Jews was traced partly to natural and partly to supernatural causes, and was viewed in both regards as the fruit or penalty of sin. The severer forms were sometimes held to be special divine inflictions, and evidences of a sinfulness of a deeper dye, especially such as were of sudden occurrence and of occult origin; and the power to heal such diseases was referred to as token of a power to forgive transgression. Disease was a ceremonial disqualification which unfitted even a consecrated person from officiating in any religious service. Many of the Jewish regulations in regard to cleanness had respect to disease springing from a natural root, and were required as much out of regard to the health of the community as purity in worship. In the former case the legislation referred to was intended to be preventive of skin diseases, and these were the most prevalent forms of disease among the Jewish people.

Blains.—This was a skin disease which showed itself in highly inflammatory ulcers. It is believed to have been the same as the black leprosy, and is elsewhere called the botch of Egypt (Deut. xxviii. 27), having been the sixth of the plagues which procured the deliverance of the children of Israel from the yoke of Pharaoh. It appears to have been a severe form of *elephantiasis*. The term is also applied to eruptions of a less violent and more harmless nature.

Blindness.—(1.) The inflammatory affection of the eye known as *ophthalmia* is very prevalent in the East, but especially in Syria and Egypt, and is due to various causes, such as the minute sharp particles of dust that fly about, the intense glare of light, the fall of the dew on the eyelids when asleep on the roofs, the remains of certain skin diseases, &c. Egyptian ophthalmia is highly contagious, and it has been known to spread rapidly as a fearful epidemic. Blindness, partial or total, as a consequence, prevails extensively, as well as weakness of the eyes. It is frequently regarded as a divine visitation, and the power to remove it is one of the attributes of the promised Messiah. (2.) *Cataract* is the most common cause of congenital blindness, and therefore this has been suggested as the disease referred to in John ix. (3.) Probably St. Paul (Acts ix. 8) and Elymas (Acts xiii. 11) were blinded by a sudden paralysis of the optic nerve.

Bloody Flux and Issue of Blood.—The former term is applied (Acts xxviii. 8) to a disease incident to males, and the latter to one incident to females, both being of the nature of hæmorrhage. Jehoram died of a chronic form of dysentery lasting for two years, and ending in the mortification and expulsion of parts of the intestines (2 Chron. xxi. 12-15).

Boils.—This term is applied to local eruptions, sometimes of the nature of a carbuncle, sometimes of an abscess, and in the original is suggestive of the accompaniment of great heat.

Botch.—This seems to be only a general name for boils and ulcers. (See BLAINS.)

Carbuncle.—See BOILS.

Consumption.—It is doubtful whether "consumption" among the Jews was that fell scourge of the English now called *phthisis*. The word seems to be used indefinitely for a wasting and emaciation of the system, having its seat in different parts of the body. Possibly pulmonary consumption was included under the name. Some form of consumption was often the result of severe internal abscesses. (See Deut. xxviii. 21, 22.)

Dysentery.—See BLOODY FLUX.

Emerods.—These are understood to have been what are called hæmorrhoids or bleeding piles, a disease very common in Syria at the present day.

Epilepsy.—This appears to have been not unfrequent in the times of Christ, and is referred to as a case of demoniac possession in Mark ix. 18.

Fever.—Fever of some kind is meant wherever in Scripture a burning affection is spoken of, as in Lev. xxvi. 16 and Deut. xxviii. 22, and it was the accompaniment of many diseases. In the former of the passages quoted ague is understood, in the latter possibly something like erysipelas. The swamps round about Lake Merom are as unwholesome as the Roman Campagna. In the hot, steaming valley of the Jordan and down by the Sea of Galilee—600 feet below the level of the Mediterranean Sea, and shut in on all sides by the mountains—the densely crowded population must have been peculiarly liable to malarious fever. It is not surprising, therefore, that we frequently meet with cases of fever in the gospel narratives of our Lord's Galilean ministry. It is interesting to note, moreover, that Jesus Christ planted the centre of His work of healing at Capernaum, the very heart of this unhealthy district.

Fiery Serpents.—Such a name might well be given to several species of snakes indigenous to the Arabian desert whose bite is followed by burning pain. But Küchenmeister has suggested that the terrible scourge of the Israelites described in Num. xxi. may not have been a snake at all, but a parasitic worm, known as *Filaria medinensis*, or Guinea worm, which—as Sir Risdon Bennett tells us in his "Diseases of the Bible"—was in ancient times reckoned among the serpents on account of its snake-like form. This has long been known as endemic on the borders of the Red Sea and in the Arabian desert. The horrible creature usually measures from one to three feet in length, but it has been found as long as six feet. It is about a tenth of an inch in breadth. It may be introduced into the system as a microscopic organism through drinking infected water, when it will develop and make its way to the surface of the body, producing frightful inflammation and pain as it tunnels outwards, till it emerges through the skin in a swollen place. Several of these disgusting parasites may be found in different parts of the body of one person.

Leprosy.—There is reason to believe that what is now known as leprosy is not the disease to which the name is given in the Bible. In the present day "leprosy" stands for the disease that is also called *elephantiasis*—the swelling, thickening, and diminished sensitiveness of the skin suggesting that of an elephant. This disease is of gradual approach and development. The face is the part most frequently affected. In severe cases the throat is involved and the voice becomes hoarse. Beginning in spots and blotches on the skin, the disease works its way into the flesh. Sometimes nodules like pears grow out on the skin. In another and more common form of the disease the body is slowly eaten away, till sometimes almost all traces of human features are lost, and finger-joints and then whole limbs decay away. It is a curious fact that this terrible malady is scarcely known to attack Jews. The leprosy of the Bible does not answer the description of *elephantiasis*. There we never read of the destruction of features and limbs. Yet the description of the disease in Lev. xiii., xiv., is minute and detailed. It is held by Sir Risdon Bennett and others that in the Bible the word "leprosy" stands for a variety of skin diseases. Even houses are said to be leprous when they are mildewed. Often the word is used for the "itch," sometimes perhaps for "ringworm," but most often for a disease called "psoriasis." This is a cutaneous disease, the essential characteristic of which is a rough scaly eruption on the skin. The scaly patches are sometimes of a pearly whiteness. The leper is then "white as snow." Evidently the question of the contagiousness of leprosy is affected by the fact that the name is given in a general sense. Some of the skin diseases are contagious—others not.

Lunacy and Demoniacal Possession.—The demoniacs of Scripture are persons described as possessed by demon or evil spirits, so that their will and reason are overborne, and they are plunged in a state of lunacy. This condition is sometimes associated with dumbness (Matt. ix. 32), blindness (Matt. xii. 22), and epilepsy (Mark ix. 17-27). It is generally associated with symptoms of mania (Matt. viii. 28; Mark v. 1-5), and the expression "to have a demon" is frequently taken as an equivalent of the expression "to be mad." Hence it has been suggested that what is called possession by a demon is simply insanity and a mere brain disease, accompanied sometimes by other bodily diseases. In favour of this view it has been urged that our Lord accommodated Himself to the prejudices of His hearers when He spoke as though He were expelling demons. It is known that mad people cannot be reasoned out of their delusions. A direct appeal along the line of the delusions would be the wisest and kindest way of saving the afflicted lunatics. Thus it has been said that Christ cured insane people who thought themselves possessed by demons by influencing their own minds through a command to the supposed demons to depart. On the other hand, it is to be remembered that the narrative says nothing of any such accommodation. It is plain, simple, and straightforward ; and it records the events referred to as if the possession were real, and not a subject of insane hallucination. We do not know the limits and powers of the inhabitants of the spiritual world, and there is nothing in experience to contradict the idea of actual demoniacal possession. We do not know whether insanity and disease even in the present day may not be in some way connected with Satanic influences.

Palsy.—This was of common occurrence, and different forms of the disease are referred to in Scripture. The case in which the centurion's servant was "grievously tormented" (Matt. viii. 6), and "sick and ready to die" (Luke vii. 2), was probably one of *progressive paralysis*, attended by muscular spasms, affecting the breathing, and rapidly tending towards a fatal termination. The man "sick of the palsy," who was "borne of four" (Matt. ix. 1–8), was probably suffering from severe general paralysis. Cases of blighted or "withered" limbs—such as that referred to in Matt. xii. 9–13 ; Mark iii. 1–5 ; Luke vi. 6–11—are often met with in the present day. One of the most common forms is known as *infantile paralysis*, and is caused by a disease in early life which arrests the development of a limb and leaves it shrunken and withered, but without other permanent bad results. Injury to the main nerve of a limb will arrest the nutrition and development of that limb, so that it becomes withered. Similar is the condition of *dropped hand*, known to painters and others as a result of lead-poisoning. Sir Risdon Bennett does not consider the case described in Luke xiii. 11–17, of "a woman which had a spirit of infirmity eighteen years, and was bowed together, and could in no wise lift up herself," to be one of paralysis strictly so called. He thinks her case "in all probability to have been such an one as is not unfrequently met with in the present day, even in the streets, in which there is a gradual wasting and relaxation of the muscles and ligaments of the back by which the trunk is held erect, so that the body falls forward, without there being any disease either of the brain or spinal cord, or any mental impairment."

Plague.—The words plague, pest, and pestilence are used indefinitely for various malignant epidemic diseases. But it is thought that the true plague—known as the *bubo-plague*—existed in early times, and may have been one of the scourges referred to in the Biblical narratives. Sir Risdon Bennett describes this as a "highly contagious malignant fever, attended by sudden and extreme prostration of all the powers, a leaden, sunken look of the eyes, erysipelatous inflammation of the skin, buboes, carbuncles,

and petechial patches, with diarrhœa." The "plague" referred to in 2 Chron. xxi. 14, 15, is plainly an epidemic of dysentery. With Jehoram the disease was chronic, and it ended fatally.

Scab and Scurvy.—These terms are applied to any skin disease milder perhaps than what would be called leprosy, and they were such as it would seem did not imply ceremonial uncleanness, though they disqualified a priest from the discharge of his official duties.

See Risdon Bennett, *Diseases of the Bible.*

CHAPTER XXXVIII.

NATURAL HISTORY OF THE BIBLE.

THE Natural History of the Bible will be considered under the three divisions of (A.) Animals, (B.) Plants, and (C.) Minerals, account being in the main given only of such as are of special interest. Their significance as symbols belongs more properly to the next chapter.

A. THE ANIMALS AND ANIMAL PRODUCTS OF THE BIBLE.

Adder.—In the Bible seven Hebrew words are used to denote the serpent tribe. The name adder represents in the A.V. four different serpents—the cobra (Ps. lviii. 4, 5—see ASP), the horned snake (Gen. xlix. 17), the viper (Ps. cxl. 3), and a snake in Prov. xxiii. 32, which is elsewhere called the "cockatrice," and may stand indefinitely for different species of vipers.

Ant.—This insect is celebrated for its wise instincts, its provident habits, and its industry. The belief, which was universal in ancient times, that it lays up store of food against winter, was only confirmed by observation a few years ago, although it had been known to lay by stores for lining its nest, and seen to carry in corn for this purpose.

Antelope.—See WILD BULL.

Ape.—This animal is only once mentioned in the Bible—in the account of the commodities imported by Solomon. It is not a native of Palestine, and was probably brought from India.

Asp.—Probably this is the Egyptian cobra, a poisonous snake which conceals itself in holes, from which it springs out violently when irritated ; it is a frequent subject for serpent-charming.

Ass.—From time immemorial the *domestic ass* has been in use as a beast of burden. In the East it is a powerful and nimble animal, and is cared for as much as the horse. It is frequently mentioned in Scripture as ridden, often richly harnessed, by persons of wealth and quality, so that Christ's riding one was a token of quiet dignity, not humiliation, as we are apt to fancy. The white varieties were highly prized. The *wild ass* is untamable, is remarkable for its shyness and fleetness, and wanders in droves about desolate and barren deserts.

Badger.—Possibly this term is applied in the A.V. to an animal of the seal tribe whose skin was used for the covering of the Tabernacle, and which abounds on the shores of the Red Sea; it is rendered "seal" in the R.V.

Basilisk.—In R.V. for the word rendered "cockatrice" in A.V. (Isa. xi. 8, &c.). It stands for a venomous snake, or perhaps, as Tristram suggests, a fabulous creature.

Bat.—Bats of various species are numerous in Palestine, especially in caves and about ruins. They were forbidden to be eaten, as being repulsive creatures. They were emblems of darkness and ignorance.

Bear.—The animal referred to under this name in the Bible is the well-known Syrian bear, once very abundant in Palestine, but since the country was denuded of forests it has been driven back to the Lebanon mountains, except during the snows of winter.

Bee.—Hive bees and wild bees abound in Palestine, but the allusions in Scripture are mostly to the latter, which were noted for the fury of their attacks on any who attempted to plunder them, and whom they assailed fiercely in swarms. They were especially abundant in the wilderness of Judæa, doubtless attracted by the marvellous profusion of wild flowers. "Honey from the rock" was obtained by rifling the nests of wild bees. The abundance of this honey is alluded to in the phrase, "a land flowing with milk and honey."

Beetle.—This word only occurs in Lev. xi. 21, 22; but though beetles abound in Palestine, in the Bible the name stands for some kind of locust.

Behemoth.—This animal is described in Job xl. 15-24, and is identified with the hippopotamus, of which and its habits the verses referred to give an exact description, although the Hebrew word simply means "beasts."

Bittern.—The bittern is a bird of the heron tribe, which haunts marshy desert places, and is extremely shy of the proximity of man. It lives on frogs, and utters a strange booming note, which is particularly weird when heard at night. Some regard the word "bittern" in the A.V., however, as a mistranslation, and would substitute "hedgehog" instead.

Boar, Wild.—This animal is noted in Ps. lxxx. 13 as lurking in the woods, and as destructive to the vineyards. It greatly infests the banks of rivers. The ravages wild boars work in the fields, often in a single night, are perfectly frightful.

Bull, Wild.—This name appears to have been given in Scripture to a large species of antelope, now known as the onyx (Deut. xiv. 5; Isa. li. 20).

Camel.—There is frequent mention of the camel in Scripture as a beast of burden and even draught, as well as for riding on, and as constituting no small item in the wealth of the early Hebrews. This was the one-humped camel. Its flesh was used as food in the East, but by the law of Moses was forbidden to be eaten, though its milk was not. A coarse cloth was woven of its hair, and John the Baptist is said to have been clothed with this. In the present day the Bedouins use the woven camel's hair for their cloaks and tent coverings.

Cankerworm.—This name was given to the larvæ, or caterpillar state, of the locust, and means literally the licker. These larvæ consume what has been left by the winged locust.

Cat.—This animal, though domesticated and even worshipped among the Egyptians, and employed by them in bird-catching, is not mentioned by the sacred writers, and is only once referred to in the Apocrypha (Baruch vi. 22).

Caterpillar.—See CANKERWORM.

Cattle.—The cattle of Palestine, i.e., the domesticated oxen, differ very little from our own. They were used for agricultural labour as well as sacrifice and food, a yoke comprising two, and the team being driven by a goad.

Chameleon.—This name, which occurs in Lev. xi. 30 in the A.V., is rendered "land crocodile" in the R.V., while the word "mole" of the A.V. in the same verse is rendered "chameleon." The word stands for some sort of land lizard.

Chamois.—This name is applied in the A.V. to the wild mountain sheep, which is grey like a goat, and considered a goat by the Arabs. It was familiar to the children of Israel in Egypt, and they might use its flesh for food (Deut. xiv. 5).

Cockatrice.—See BASILISK.

Coney.—This animal resembles the rabbit in external appearance and habits, but is nowise related to it, being neither ruminant nor rodent, but is known to naturalists as the *Hyrax Syriacus*, or rock-badger, an order by itself. It is a wary animal, lives in holes of the rocks, and is not formidable when attacked, being characterised in Prov. xxx. 26 as in company "a feeble folk."

Cormorant.—This is the name given in the A.V. to the pelican (which see), as well as for the bird known among us as the cormorant, a bird closely allied to the pelican.

Crane.—This is a large marsh bird of migratory habits, with a loud trumpet voice. It is four feet in height, and measures sometimes eight feet from wing to wing. Cranes migrate in troops, and darken the air like a cloud in their transit. But the word translated crane in the A.V. stands for the swift, and that translated swallow is the one designating the crane. This is corrected in the R.V.

Crocodile.—See LEVIATHAN.

Cuckoo.—By this name (Lev. ii. 16; Deut. xiv. 15) some think a species of sea-gull is meant. In the R.V. it is translated "sea-mew." But there are two species of cuckoo in Palestine.

Deer.—See HART.

Dog.—The dog was not held in the same honour among the Jews as with us, being employed merely to watch the house against robbers, to guard the flocks at night from wolves and jackals, and, as a scavenger, to clear the streets of carcasses and offal that might otherwise cause pestilence. Indeed, it was uniformly regarded with aversion and spoken of with contempt, being never made a companion of, and allowed to go masterless and prowl about like a wolf, doing so generally within some limited area, which it never crossed.

Dove.—The dove is mentioned more than fifty times in the Scriptures, and is the only bird enjoined in the Mosaic law to be offered in sacrifice. It is one of the earliest birds domesticated by man, and the only one which we have record of as domesticated among the Jews prior to the time of Solomon. The wild species as well as the tame were numerous in Palestine, and are frequently referred to in Scripture.

Dragon.—This name is applied in the A.V. sometimes to the jackal and sometimes to the Leviathan (which see). It is symbolically applied to Satan.

Dromedary.—A swift camel. (See CAMEL.)

Eagle.—The word so translated strictly designates not the eagle, but the Griffon or Great Vulture, as is evident from the "baldness," not characteristic of the eagle, ascribed to it in Micah i. 16. It is constantly referred to in Scripture as preying on the dead bodies of the slain, and it is distinguished for its strength, its swiftness, its power of flight, its keenness of vision, and length of vigorous life, as well as its care for its young ones.

Elephant.—The elephant is not mentioned in the Bible, although it was used in the Maccabæan war (1 Macc. vi. 30). But the Scripture writers are familiar with the nature of ivory, and make frequent mention of it in their writings, though the earliest allusion to it is as recent as the time of David (Ps. xlv. 8). The prevalence of the use of ivory was a sign of luxurious living. Solomon had a great throne of ivory (1 Kings x. 18.)

Falcon.—This bird is mentioned in Job xxviii. 7 (R.V.). The A.V. rendered the name "vulture" incorrectly. Possibly it stands for the kite.

Fallow-Deer.—This name is given to a species of antelope known as the *bubale* or wild cow of the Arabs. It has been described as between a calf and a stag in appearance. Its flesh was permitted to be eaten. In Deut. xiv. 5 the word "fallow deer" of the A.V. is rendered "roebuck" by the revisers.

Ferret.—See GECKO.

Fish.—No particular kind of fish is named in Scripture, though a distinction is made between the clean (those that have scales and fins) and the unclean (those that have not scales and fins, Lev. xi. 9–12). The Barbel and Bream are among the most common in the Jordan and the Sea of Galilee.

Flea.—This insect, though common in Palestine, is only twice referred to in the Bible (1 Sam. xxiv. 14; xxvi. 20.).

Fly.—Two Hebrew words are translated fly in the A.V.—one for the insect that constituted a plague in Egypt (Exod. viii.), possibly the mosquito; and the other in Eccles. x. 1, and Isa. vii. 18, perhaps in the latter case meaning the gadfly or some other blood-sucking fly.

Fox.—By this term the jackal is more frequently intended than the fox, though the latter also is sometimes referred to. The Hebrew word includes both animals. The fox is common in Syria, where there are two species, the Egyptian and the Syrian, the latter being a variety of the common fox of Europe.

Frog.—The frogs of the Bible are of a bright green colour and spotted, and they abound in the rivers and marshes of Egypt and Palestine, where their croaking at night is something deafening. They were regarded among the Jews as symbols of uncleanness.

Gazelle.—See ROEBUCK, by which name it is designated in the A.V.

Gecko.—This name appears in the R.V. (Lev. xi. 30) in place of the "ferret" of the A.V. It stands for a small reptile like a lizard, but with flatter pads on its toes.

Gier-Eagle.—This is the Egyptian vulture, and is of filthy habits, living not only on carrion, but on offal of all kinds, whereby it serves useful scavenger purposes, however.

Glede.—The bird to which this name is given in Deut. xiv. 13 is thought by Tristram to be the buzzard.

Gnat.—This insect is associated as a pest with the mosquito, and is referred to only once in Scripture as one of the smallest of insects (Matt. xxiii. 24).

Goat.—Goats constituted part of the wealth of the patriarchs; and they were frequently offered in sacrifice, as well as used for food. Living on tender twigs and the foliage of shrubs, by their browsing they were destructive to the growth of forests. Goats and sheep are often seen forming one flock, the latter on the level meadows, the former on the craggy heights above, but they never mingle or feed together. The milk of the goat is an important article of food, and the flesh of its young, the kid, very tender and excellent. Its skin is made into bottles for holding water or wine, and its hair woven into cloth, which is fine or coarse according to the variety of the animal. The Wild Goat has been identified with the Arabian Ibex, an animal closely akin to the Alpine Ibex.

Greyhound.—The revisers have retained this word in Prov. xxx. 31. But probably the original stands for the war-horse as suggested in the margin.

Grasshopper.—The name is given in the A.V. to what appears to have been a small species of locust of a brilliant colour, but somewhat difficult to identify.

Hare.—This animal was reckoned unclean, because, though presumed to chew the cud, it did not divide the hoof (Lev. xi. 6). It is not a ruminant, however, but a rodent, and as such seems to chew the cud when grinding its teeth and moving its jaw. There are two species found in Palestine, the Syrian resembling our own, and the Egyptian more like a rabbit.

Hart.—Deer were abundant in Palestine, and their flesh was esteemed a delicate food. They are mentioned in Scripture for their gentle, affectionate, and timid natures, their grace, sure-footedness, and swiftness.

Hawk.—The name is applied to the Kestrel tribe, and to all the smaller birds of prey.

Heron.—This was a marsh bird of several species, and was accounted unclean.

Hoopoe.—The "lapwing" of the A.V. is rendered "hoopoe" in the R.V. The latter bird visits Palestine in the summer.

Hornet.—The hornet is a large-sized wasp, of which four species occur in Palestine, and swarms of them often attack horses and cattle, goading them to madness and sometimes stinging them to death. They are regarded with terror.

Horse.—In Scripture the horse is associated with war. It was mounted by horsemen or yoked to chariots, the breed in use being peculiarly fitted for warlike purposes. War was its element, and a graphic account of it in this relation is given in the Book of Job (chap. xxxix. 19-25). Its hoof was hard, and unshod with iron. The Israelites were forbidden to multiply horses (Deut. xvii. 16), because horses were only used in war. The prohibition was equivalent to a command not to have a standing army. God was the safeguard of His people. It was only when the exigencies of war seemed to require it that the prohibition was disregarded.

Horse-leech.—This is a large kind of leech greedy of blood (see Prov. xxx. 15). It has been suggested that the original word stands for a "vampire," a blood-sucking ghoul.

Hyæna.—Probably this animal is referred to by Jeremiah (chap. xii. 9), as a "speckled bird," and by Isaiah (chap. xiii. 21), as a "doleful creature." It is very common in all parts of Palestine, having its favourite haunts in the woods, the deserts, and the tombs. It is a cowardly creature, and is abominated as unclean.

Jackal.—This animal is frequently referred to in Scripture, though the A.V. has "dragon" (Job xxx. 29; Isa. xxxiv. 13; Jer. x. 22, &c.) and "fox" (see Fox) where the jackal is meant. It abounds in Palestine, and is heard at night howling about the traveller's camp.

Kite.—The A.V. gives this name, in Deut. xiv. 13, to a bird which some take for the falcon. If that is correct, perhaps the word rendered "vulture" represents the kite.

Lapwing.—See Hoopoe.

Leopard.—The leopard was once common in Palestine, and it is frequently alluded to as a symbol of sly watchfulness and the fierce, sudden, swift attack of a foe. Its spotted skin is referred to in Jer. xiii. 23.

Leviathan.—This name occurs five times in Scripture, and, except in Ps. civ. 26, where some cetacean or whale-fish of the Mediterranean is meant, the Crocodile is undoubtedly to be understood. It is the monster reptile to the description of which chap. xli. of the Book of Job is devoted. The word "dragon" also is sometimes employed for the crocodile in reference to Egypt and the Nile, where it abounded.

Lice.—Some have said that the pests referred to in Exod. viii. 16, 17, were "gnats." But the description seems to point to their being "lice," as given in the A.V. In the margin of R.V. "sand-flies or fleas" is suggested.

Lion.—Several, as many as five, different names designate the lion in the original Hebrew, and it is mentioned 130 times in Scripture. Lions were at one time numerous in the forests of Palestine, but they have disappeared long since along with those forests. The short-maned variety appears to have been the more common; it was less formidable than the long-maned, and such as a stalwart shepherd might encounter single-handed. The lion is referred to in Scripture for its strength, its courage, its fierceness, its roar, and its vigilance in seeking for its prey.

Lizard.—Though only once mentioned in the A.V. of Scripture (Lev. xi. 30), the lizard is very common in Palestine; many varieties are found, some large, others exceedingly beautiful. The word translated "mole" in Lev. xi. 30 probably stands for a kind of lizard, as also does that translated "spider" in Prov. xxx. 28.

Locust.—The locust is referred to in the A.V. both as such and under the names of Beetle, Cankerworm, Caterpillar, Bald Locust, and Palmerworm; and a number of words, nine at least, are employed in the original to denote varieties of it, or some stage of its development. The habits of the insect, and the ravages it makes on vegetation, are well known, and often referred to in Scripture. It forms a palatable food, and is largely eaten by the natives.

Mole.—Any such animal as the mole is only once referred to in Scripture, in Isa. ii. 20, the animal mentioned in Lev. xi. 30 being a lizard. The name in the original points to any kind of burrowing animal. As no sort of mole is known in Palestine, and as the mole would not burrow among old ruins, perhaps a creature of the rat or weasel tribe is referred to. The word rendered "mole" in the A.V. is translated "chameleon" in the R.V. (which see).

Moth.—This insect is referred to in Scripture nearly always in connection with the destruction of clothing caused by its larvæ. Job (chap. iv. 19) refers to the fragility of its cocoon.

Mouse.—The mouse was unclean; and it was

employed as a scourge to chastise the Philistines for detaining the Ark of the Lord (1 Sam. v.). The original name means the "corn-eater," and denotes any small rodent, such as the dormouse, the rat, &c., of which there are twenty-three species in Palestine.

Mule.—There is no mention of this animal before the time of David, though there is frequently afterwards. It occurs as a royal animal, and was used by princes on state occasions, though it was also employed for carrying burdens. It was imported from abroad, from Egypt at first, as the Jews were forbidden to breed such animals (Lev. xix. 19). The mule is famous for its sure-footedness and its hardihood. The word "mule," in Esther viii. 10, 14, should be translated "dromedary," or "swift steed," and in Gen. xxxvi. 24 "hot-spring."

Night-hawk.—This word occurs as the name of one of the unclean birds in Lev. xi. 16 and Deut. xix. 15. Some have taken it for the Ostrich, others for the Egyptian Horned Owl. Tristram inclines to regard it as the Barn Owl, which is as common in Palestine as England.

Ospray.—This is also the name of one of the unclean birds, probably one of the smaller eagles (Lev. xi. 13).

Ossifrage.—This name, which means the "bone-breaker," is applied to the Bearded Vulture, the largest of the vulture tribe.

Ostrich.—The ostrich is referred to in Scripture oftener than appears in the A.V., it being mistaken sometimes for the "owl," as in Lev. xi. 16, and sometimes for the "peacock," as in Job xxxix. 13-18, where its habits are set forth.

Owl.—Various species of this bird are referred to in Scripture, and the references are numerous. The little owl is most frequently met with in Palestine (Ps. cii. 6).

Ox.—This name is given to all animals of the bovine race. (See CATTLE.)

Palmerworm.—See CATERPILLAR.

Partridge.—The partridge is twice mentioned in Scripture, in 1 Sam. xxvi. 20 and in Jer. xvii. 11, the reference in the one case being to hunting for the bird, and in the other to the disappointment it often experiences in hatching its eggs. It is still common in the wilderness.

Peacock.—This bird is not a native of Palestine, but of India or Ceylon, whence it was first imported among the precious and curious things introduced by Solomon.

Pelican.—This is a bird of the wilderness, that swallows great numbers of fish, disgorging them again to feed its young, which it does by pressing its bill on its breast; afterwards it will sit melancholy for hours with its bill so placed.

Pigeon.—See DOVE.

Porcupine.—This word probably stands for the Bittern. (See BITTERN.)

Pygarg.—This appears to be a large antelope. It is mentioned in Deut. xiv. 5, among the animals suitable for food.

Quail.—This bird is mentioned only as miraculously provided by way of food for the children of Israel in the wilderness. It is a small species of partridge of migratory habits, very abundant near the shores of the Mediterranean, and its flesh is delicate.

Raven.—This name is applied to all birds of the crow family, which were all unclean, as they fed principally on carrion. The provision that is made for the raven, and especially its young ones, is often referred to in illustration of the fatherly providence of God. Ravens are numerous in Palestine.

Roe, Roebuck.—By this name in the A.V. the Gazelle must be uniformly understood. It is celebrated in Scripture for its beauty, gracefulness, swiftness, and gentleness. It is abundant in Palestine, and is met with everywhere in herds, often of a hundred. It was reckoned a clean animal, and its flesh was used for food.

Satyr.—While this word may sometimes be used for a fabulous monster or a demon of the desert, it is thought by some also to stand for the "he-goat," and by others for the "baboon."

Scorpion.—This creature abounds in the wilderness of Sinai, and is found in Palestine also. It is dreaded for its venomous sting, which is most painful and sometimes deadly. It belongs to the spider tribe, and lurks in crevices and among ruins.

Serpent.—There are seven words in Hebrew for animals of the serpent class, and they are very loosely translated in the A.V. Sometimes the whole class is meant, and sometimes an individual species, such as the Adder, the Asp, the Cockatrice, and the Viper (which see). They are very numerous in Palestine. The serpent is especially distinguished and referred to for its subtilty.

Sheep.—The flesh, milk, and wool of the sheep have been of service to man from the earliest times, and flocks of sheep constituted the chief wealth of the patriarchs. It was preeminently the animal of sacrifice from Abel's time onwards, the lamb being especially selected as the type of innocence. The horn of the ram was converted sometimes into a trumpet, sometimes, and most commonly, into a flask to carry oil. The sheep is tended with great care, being watered daily and folded and watched over at night by the shepherds.

Snail.—The word so translated in Lev. xi. 30 probably stands for some sort of lizard, not for our snail.

Sparrow.—The Hebrew name for sparrow occurs upwards of forty times in the Old Testament, and is used for all varieties of small passerine birds.

Spider.—The spider is really referred to only twice in Scripture, and that in connection with its web (Job viii. 14 ; Isa. lix. 5), the word translated "spider" in Prov. xxx. 28 signifying the gecho, a kind of lizard.

Swallow.—Two Hebrew words are thus translated. One means "bird of freedom," and may stand for our swallow or for any other swiftly flying bird. The other stands for the crane, while that translated "crane" should be "swallow" or "swift."

Swan.—The name of the swan occurs in the A.V. in Lev. xi. 18 and Deut. xiv. 18, but the word is a mistranslation, and probably denotes the *Ibis*, a sacred bird of the Egyptians. In the R.V. it is rendered "horned owl."

Swine.—The swine were regarded with special aversion by the Jews, and classed by them among the most unclean of all prohibited animals, although about the time of Christ they appear to have been viewed with less abhorrence than formerly.

Tortoise.—This word occurs in the A.V. of Lev. xi. 29. The revisers have substituted "great lizard."

Turtle.—This is a division of the pigeon family, and consists of three species, of which the one known among us as the Turtle-dove is the most abundant in Palestine. It is migratory, and appears there in the second week of April, when it may be seen flying about in clouds.

Unicorn.—The animal so called was two-horned, and not one-horned, as this name implies. It was a strong wild animal of the ox tribe, with large horns, and of a fierce temper. It is known among naturalists as the Auroch, or the *Bos primogenius*. It is no longer to be found in Palestine.

Viper.—This name is often used to denote any poisonous snake, but as it occurs in Scripture it has been identified mostly with the Sand Viper, of small size, and common in Arabia and Syria as well as North Africa.

Vulture.—See EAGLE and FALCON.

Whale.—The word so rendered may mean any sea-monster, whether of the whale or shark tribe. Indeed, the word is also used for great terrestrial animals, crocodiles, and perhaps also great serpents. Whales, besides other cetacea, appear to have existed in the Mediterranean Sea at one time.

Wolf.—The wolf is the emblem of everything fierce and bloodthirsty, and is frequently referred to in Scripture in that light. It infests Palestine, and is to this day the dread of the shepherd.

Worm.—This word is used in the Bible for the larva of various kinds of insects, not for our common earth-worm. In Isa. li. 8 the larva of the clothes-moth is indicated. In Isa. lxvi. 24 it is the translation of a Hebrew word for the maggot that infests putrid dead bodies.

B. PLANTS AND THEIR PRODUCTS.

Algum or Almug Tree.—The wood of this tree, esteemed very precious, was imported from the East by Solomon, and has been identified by Max Müller with the Red Sandal-wood of India, which is heavy, fine-grained, and of a bright red colour.

Almond.—This is a small tree, is a native of Palestine, is allied to the peach and apricot, and gives forth its blossoms before its leaves, which it does early. The nut is well known ; it is originally covered with a pulp which withers in September. Aaron's rod was of this tree, and so were Jacob's "rods" (Gen. xxx. 37, R.V.).

Aloes.—This was the produce of some Judæan gum-tree, generally supposed to be the *Aquilaria agallochum*, a tree which reaches the height of 100 feet, and gives off a fragrant odour when beginning to decay. It is quite different from the aloes of medicine and the flowering aloes of modern gardens.

Anise.—This is mentioned only in Matt. xxiii. 23, and is an umbelliferous plant, not unlike fennel, known as Dill, much cultivated for its seeds, which are used both medicinally and for cooking.

Apple.—The apple of Scripture is generally believed to have been different from the fruit known as such among us, and is now identified by Dr. Tristram with the apricot, as that tree best answers to the descriptions in Scripture.

Ash.—The word "ash" mentioned in Isa. xliv. 14 must be a mistranslation, for the ash is not a native of Palestine, and the tree meant appears to be a species of pine. The R.V. has "fir."

Balm or Balsam.—Balm was a preparation from the gum or oil of a tree, of the genus *Balsamodendron*, that was possessed of medicinal virtues, especially in the cure of wounds. That of Gilead was most prized.

Barley.—This grain is more commonly met with in Palestine than any other. It is easily cultivated and early reaped, being gathered in generally three weeks before the commencement of the wheat harvest. It is largely used to feed horses and asses, as well as among the poor to bake into bread.

Bay.—The expression "bay tree" in Ps. xxxvii. (A.V.) is unwarranted, as the Hebrew means "native born ; " and the psalmist is only referring to any vigorous "green tree in its native soil " (R.V.).

Box.—In Isa. xli. 19 this tree is associated with the fir and the pine ; and "cypress" is suggested in the margin of the R.V. as an alternative. But in the R.V. of Ezek. xxvii. 6 the reference to inlaying suggests the hard box-wood known to us.

Bramble.—This term, together with Brier, Thorn, Thistle, &c., is applied indifferently in the A.V. to different thorny plants, to denote which there are as many as eighteen words in Hebrew, the combined heat and dryness of the climate of Palestine having a tendency to develop thorns even in plants where we would least expect them. Nevertheless in our Lord's time the word translated "bramble bush" (Luke vi. 44) was used for a Palestine variety of the common blackberry.

Brier.—See BRAMBLE.

Bulrush.—This name is given, probably, to the papyrus plant, which belongs to the sedge tribe, and at one time thickly covered the banks of the Nile, though it is now wholly extinct in lower Egypt. It is still found in Palestine.

Bush, The Burning.—Possibly this was a species of acacia now found at Sinai, resembling the Shittah tree.

Calamus.—This was an aromatic cane or reed imported from Arabia or India, the name being applied in Scripture to the aromatic substance extracted from it.

Camphire. — A mistranslation for Henna (which see).

Cane, Sweet.—See CALAMUS.

Caper.—See HYSSOP.

Cassia.—This was a pungent aromatic spice, derived, like cinnamon, from the bark of a tree, of the same family as the bay tree, presumed to be a native of India.

Cedar.—This name, though applied in Scripture to the Pine-tree family generally, and once to the juniper tree of Sinai (Lev. xiv. 4), is appropriated more especially to the cedar of Lebanon, which is the monarch of the forest, and serves as the symbol of majesty and vigorous expansive spiritual growth. The cedar is distinguished by its gnarled strength and its massive horizontally spreading branches. It grows rapidly and lives long.

Chestnut.—This word occurs twice in the A.V. (Gen. xxx. 37; Ezek. xxxi. 8), but is a mistranslation for the oriental Plane tree, which grows on the banks of rivers, such as the Jordan.

Cinnamon.—This is the well-known spicy bark of an Indian tree, stripped off and dried in the sun, used to compound ointments and as a perfume.

Cockle.—This is a weed of an offensive odour, as the Hebrew name suggests (Job xxxi. 40, R.V. marg., "noisome weeds").

Cucumber.—There are two species of cucumbers grown in Palestine. These vegetables form an important article of summer diet among the poor, who eat them with the rind on, and without any condiment.

Cummin.—This is a common umbelliferous plant, which is cultivated for the sake of its seeds, used as a spice and for medicine.

Dill.—See ANISE.

Ebony.—This is the heart-wood of a tree which grows in Southern India, and well known for its hardness, its dark colour, and its susceptibility of a fine polish.

Elm.—The name "elm" is applied in the A.V. to the Terebinth.

Fig Tree.—This tree, with its well-known fruit, is frequently mentioned in Scripture, and is native to the land of Palestine, where it yields an important article of daily food to the inhabitants. The destruction of the figs is ever regarded as one of the heaviest judgments that could overtake the people.

Fir Tree.—There are several species of fir trees found in Palestine, besides the cedar, the wood of which is used for building; but the Scotch fir and the larch are excepted from the number.

Fitches.—This is the translation in our version of two different words in the original, which denote, the one a ranunculus and the other a spelt, both cultivated for their seeds, which are used as those of the caraway. The R.V. substitutes the phrase "black cummin."

Flags.—These are river weeds of various kinds. (See BULRUSH.)

Flax.—This was early cultivated in Palestine and Egypt, and was the first material woven into cloth. The flax crop to be withholden was regarded in the light of a heavy judgment (Hos. ii. 9).

Frankincense. — This was the fragrant gum which exudes by slitting the bark of a tree native to Arabia, allied to the balsam tree and the terebinth; it yielded a rich perfume, and formed one of the ingredients of the holy incense.

Galbanum.—A gum resin of two umbelliferous plants, an ingredient in the incense.

Gall. — Two Hebrew words are translated "gall" in our Bible. One is used for the poison of serpents, and generally for what is bitter or poisonous; the other for the poppy.

Garlic.—A vegetable akin to the onion, which is much cultivated both in Egypt and in Syria.

Gopher Wood.—This is thought to have been the wood of the cypress tree.

Gourd.—The plant mentioned in Jonah iv. 5-10, the identification of which has given rise to much discussion. It is now generally believed to have been what is called the Bottle Gourd, or by botanists the *Cucurbita*, which has large leaves, is of rapid growth, and is used for shading arbours, as may still be seen in gardens about Sidon, though some have identified it with the castor-oil plant. The *Wild Gourd*, mentioned in 2 Kings iv. 39, is understood to be the colocynth, which sends out very long tendrils and bears a great quantity of

fruit. It is used as a medicine, and is bitter and drastic.

Grass.—The grasses of Palestine, of which there have been reckoned to be seventy different species, have been divided by Tristram into three groups: (1) a grass, met with on the downs of the south, which shoots up short and close after rain, and soon withers down; (2) a grass, met with on the coast, which grows tall and luxuriant in spring, and after the seed has ripened, sends up an after grass, affording food for cattle throughout the year; and (3) a grass, met with in the Jordan valley, which, forming seldom into turf, shoots up quickly and dies as quickly, leaving only scattered up and down the naked stems, now shaken of their seeds.

Hazel.—This name is given in the A.V. to the Almond tree.

Heath.—The "heath in the desert" (Jer. xvii. 6) is not our familiar heath, which is not found in the neighbourhood of Palestine. Probably the word stands for some bare, naked shrub, just able to exist in desert soil. Tristram takes it for a dwarf juniper.

Hemlock.—The Hebrew word "rosh," rendered "hemlock" in Hosea x. 4, and Amos vi. 12, refers to some bitter herb.

Henna.—A shrub found at Engedi, whose flowers, which grow in clusters, have a powerful fragrance. It yields a much-valued perfume; and from its leaves an astringent dye of a pasty consistence is obtained which imparts a rusty red colour, and when applied to hands or feet checks perspiration.

Husk.—This is the fruit or pod of the Carob tree, used as food for cattle, and only eaten by human beings when in the most abject poverty. It is sometimes called "St. John's bread."

Hyssop.—It has been difficult to identify this plant, but it is now presumed to have been the thorny Caper, a plant which grows out of the chinks of walls, as the hyssop was said to do (1 Kings iv. 33). It was used for sprinkling in ceremonies of purification.

Juniper.—The word thus translated stands not for a juniper, but for a broom with pink-white blossoms. This is a native of the desert, being the largest and most striking of the shrubs found there. It is manufactured into charcoal by the Arabs.

Leeks.—These were held in high favour among the Egyptians, and were much longed for by the children of Israel in the wilderness after the Exodus, in association with onions and garlic.

Lentils.—These were a species of vetch, of which there are several varieties. They sometimes form an ingredient in bread, and sometimes go to make up a pottage.

Lily.—This name appears to have been given to any brilliantly-coloured flower like a lily, such as a tulip, an anemone, or a ranunculus, and not to any lily proper. Tristram thinks the blood-red anemone best answers the description in Scripture.

Mandrake.—This is a native of Palestine as well as Mesopotamia, and belongs to the same family as the potato. It has scarcely any stem, bears a soft pulpy fruit like a plum, and grows from a root like the beet.

Melon.—Both the flesh and the water melon are largely cultivated in Palestine as well as in Egypt. The water melon, which sometimes weighs thirty pounds, serves for drink as well as food.

Millet.—There are several species of millet in Palestine. It is cultivated as a minor corn plant, and the seeds are eaten by the poorer classes both uncooked and baked into cakes. This must be distinguished from the black millet or *dhourra* of the Arabs.

Mint.—This familiar herb—of which three species are found in Palestine—was eaten by the Jews with meat, and was, according to some, the bitter herb taken with the paschal lamb.

Mulberry Tree.—The tree to which this name is given in the A.V. is believed to have been the Aspen Poplar.

Mustard Tree.—This is not properly a tree, but an herb, though it often grows in Palestine to a far greater height than with us. It has been found "as tall as a horse and his rider." There is therefore no reason to suppose that our Lord was referring to any other plant in Matt. xiii. 31.

Myrrh.—This is the gum of a tree still so called—a species of *Balsamodendron*—and was used in the holy ointment, as a perfume, for embalming, &c.

Myrtle.—This is the common tree so called, and is held in great favour in the East. It has dark glossy leaves and white flowers.

Nettle.—This plant is in some cases the common Stinging Nettle, but in others, as Job xxx. 7, Prov. xxiv. 31, and Zeph. ii. 9, the Prickly Acanthus.

Nuts.—Two kinds of nut trees are referred to in Scripture—the *Pistachia*, with oily, almond-like kernels, prized by the ancients as food and as medicine, in Gen. xliii. 11; and the familiar Walnut, in Cant. vi. 11.

Oak.—In the A.V. the Terebinth tree is sometimes, as in Gen. xxxv. 4, Judg. vi. 11, Ezek. vi. 13, mistaken for the oak, which it somewhat resembles in appearance. But in general the word "oak" stands for our oak tree. There are nine species of oak trees in Palestine, of which the prickly Evergreen Oak is the most abundant.

Oil Tree.—A tree of this name is three times referred to (in 1 Kings xi. 23; Neh. viii. 15; Isa. xli. 19). Though the original is wrongly rendered in the two former cases, in the third case it is identified with the Oleaster, a small, graceful shrub, common in Palestine, with hard, fine-grained wood, and yielding an inferior kind of oil.

Olive.—The prevalence of this tree is characteristic of Palestine, and its general cultivation the symbol of security and prosperity, of joy and plenteousness. It is an evergreen, the trunk gnarled, and the foliage dark green on the upper side of the leaves and grey beneath. It was cultivated for its wood, its fruit, and its oil.

Onion.—The onion was much cultivated in Egypt, where it formed an important article of food, and it was an object of desire to the Israelites in the wilderness, probably because of its cooling properties and its power to prevent thirst.

Palm Tree.—This tree was at one time abundant in Palestine, so much so that the land was known to the ancients as the land of palms. Its presence is noted in connection with more than one sacred spot in the history of the Jewish people, and Jericho is often characterised as "the city of palm trees." Its branches were used as the symbol of triumph.

Pine Tree.—This name occurs in Isa. xli. 19 and lx. 13, but the tree intended appears to be the Plane.

Pomegranate.—This is a fruit-bearing shrub of the myrtle family, seldom over eight or ten feet in height, the fruit being as large as an orange, and of a bright-red colour, and the compartments full of pink pips, whence its name, which means "grained apple." Its juice forms a cooling draught, and it is sometimes fermented into a wine, which is light.

Poplar.—This name occurs twice in the A.V. Perhaps the White Poplar, known in Europe as well as in Palestine, may be meant.

Pulse.—This term is used as descriptive of edible leguminous plants, such as beans and lentils (Dan. i. 12, 16; 2 Sam. xvii. 28).

Rose.—The rose referred to in the A.V. is not a true rose, and neither are the roses of Sharon or of Jericho there mentioned the same as those now so named. There are two words in the original so translated, and the one points to the Narcissus (Cant. ii. 1; Isa. xxxv. 1), while the other probably denotes the Oleander.

Rue.—This is a garden herb, referred to as tithed by the Pharisees (Luke xi. 42).

Rye.—This term is applied in the A.V. to spelt, a coarse wheat, rye not being a Syrian grain.

Saffron.—This plant is much esteemed for its perfume, and is of the crocus family.

Shittah Tree.—This is a species of Acacia, which abounds in the Arabian desert, and yields, besides gum arabic, a hard close-grained wood of an orange-brown colour called *shittim wood*—being the timber principally used in constructing the Tabernacle.

Spikenard.—This was a costly perfume obtained from a small, herbaceous plant, akin to our garden valerian, growing in India on the Himalayas.

Sweet Cane.—See CALAMUS.

Sycamine.—Among the Greeks this was the name of the Black Mulberry tree, which is now common in Palestine. But it does not appear that that tree was known there in Biblical times. In the Bible the word is used interchangeably with the word sycamore. In the LXX. sycamine is the universal rendering for the Hebrew word meaning "fig-tree," and therefore the presumption is that in Luke xvii. 6 it is equivalent to the sycamore of Luke xix. 4.

Sycamore or Sycomore.—This is a species of fig tree, and is not to be confounded with the plane tree so named by us. While the fruit is a fig, the leaf is like that of a mulberry, whence its name, which means a "fig-mulberry."

Tares.—This is a kind of rye-grass called bearded darnel, the seeds of which are poisonous. In its early stages the plant resembles wheat.

Teil or Terebinth Tree.—This, called also the Turpentine tree, is common in Palestine, and resembles the oak in appearance. It generally stands solitary. In many cases it is associated with some sacred memory, as in the case of the oak, or rather the terebinth of Mamre. This is said to have been the tree on which Judas hanged himself.

Thyme Wood.—Mentioned among the precious things of the Apocalyptic Babylon (Rev. xviii. 12); this is the wood of a cypress tree which grows on the Atlas Mountains.

Vine.—Palestine was renowned for its vines, which were both numerous and productive, and yielded excellent wines. They were grown on terraces along the hill-slopes, and sometimes trailed over the houses. At the present day vines sprawl over the ground without any support.

Wheat.—This was one of the special products of Palestine (Deut. viii. 8), and the reaping of it in May constituted one of the epochs of the Jewish year. The Heshbon wheat is a bearded kind, exceedingly prolific, bearing several ears on one stalk. Canon Tristram suggests that this is the "wheat of Minnith" exported from Palestine to Philistia, according to Ezek. xxvii. 17.

Willow.—There were several species of Willows in Palestine, the Weeping, called the Babylonian Willow, among the number, and they were all found growing by the watercourses.

Wormwood.—This was a bitter herb belonging to the great composite family that includes our daisies and dandelions, of which several species are met with in Palestine, and it is frequently referred to metaphorically in Scripture.

C. MINERALS—METALS AND PRECIOUS STONES.

Adamant.—The name was used for any stones of firm texture and extreme hardness, such as corundum, and the original is rendered " diamond " in Jer. xvii. 1.

Agate.—This precious stone is a semi-transparent variety of quartz, thought by some to be the same as the ruby. It was the second stone in the third row of the high-priest's breastplate.

Alabaster.—This word seems to have been used for a variety of gypsum, out of which vases, &c., were made in ancient times.

Amber.—This word occurs three times in Ezekiel as a name of a metallic alloy of uncertain composition, but of some bright-shining fiery colour. The original is translated "amber," as the equivalent to the words used in the LXX. and the Vulgate.

Amethyst.—This stone, a kind of quartz, is generally of a violet-blue colour. It formed the third in the third row of the high-priest's breastplate. The wearing of it was supposed by the Jews to induce pleasant dreams, and by the Greeks to be a charm against inebriation.

Antimony.—A mineral.

Beryl.—This precious stone was the first in the fourth row of the high-priest's breastplate, but it is of uncertain identification. It is presumed to be allied to the emerald, and to have been the same as *aqua marina*.

Bdellium.—Probably this word, which occurs in Gen. ii. 12 and Num. xi. 7, is used for some metal, and not for the gum that bears the name ; but it is impossible to identify the metal.

Brass.—The alloy known to us by this name was not known to the Jews. The word stands for copper or bronze. (See COPPER.)

Carbuncle.—This is a pellucid green stone, thought to be the same as the emerald.

Chalcedony.—This is a brilliant transparent green stone, our copper emerald, and is named after Chalcedon, the place where it was found.

Chrysolite.—This is a stone of a golden hue, streaked with green, and it is believed to have been a species of topaz. It is literally " gold-stone."

Chrysoprase.—This is a golden-spotted green stone. It is literally the "gold leek."

Copper.—This was partly found native in Palestine and partly imported from Cyprus, though it was familiar to the Jews principally in the form of bronze, the alloy of copper with tin.

Diamond.—This name was given to the third stone in the second row of the high-priest's breastplate. but it is variously understood to have been an onyx or a jasper.

Earth.—This word has three senses in Scripture, and denotes sometimes the soil or ground, sometimes the world or land, and sometimes dust.

Emerald.—This was the first stone in the second row of the high-priest's breastplate. The name, however, is used for several bright red stones.

Gold.—There are six names for gold in the original Scriptures. Though known from the earliest times, it does not appear to have been found in Palestine, but to have been imported from Arabia and the East.

Iron.—Though we are not told how the metal was procured, and though the name "iron" is often used in Scripture for anything strong or hard, there is no doubt that iron was known to the Jews, and that many of their implements were made of it.

Jacinth or Hyacinth.—This is a transparent stone of a dark-purple or blue colour.

Jasper.—This is a brilliant translucent stone, "clear as crystal" (Rev. xxi. 11), perhaps our diamond, and it was the twelfth stone in the high-priest's breastplate.

Lead.—This was known to and variously used by the Jews, being early found among the rocks of Sinai.

Ligure.—This was the first stone in the third row of the high-priest's breastplate, and was probably a jacinth.

Nitre.—This was not our saltpetre, but a native carbonate of soda. It is rendered "lye" in Jer. ii. 22 (R.V.).

Onyx.—This is an agate formed by alternate streaks of dark and white chalcedony.

Salt.—Salt is found in abundance on the southern shores of the Dead Sea, and it was extensively used by the Hebrews.

Sapphire.—This was the second stone in the second row of the high-priest's breastplate, and it has been identified with *lapis-lazuli*.

Sardius or Sardine.—This was a kind of agate, probably red in colour, and it occupied the first place in the first row of the high-priest's breast-plate.

Sardonyx.—This is a cornelian, with three-fold layers of spots or colours.

Silver.—This metal was abundant, but it was imported from Arabia and Spain.

Tin.—This was early known to the Jews, having been imported by the Phœnicians, and being generally used as an alloy.

Topaz.—This is a chrysolite of a greenish-yellow colour, obtained from an island in the Dead Sea.

Tristram, *The Natural History of the Bible;* Van Lennep, *Bible Lands, &c.,* Vol. I.; Groser, *Scripture Natural History.*

CHAPTER XXXIX.

GEOGRAPHY AND TOPOGRAPHY OF THE HOLY LAND.

THE Holy Land, or Palestine, is a small territory in the form of a truncated triangle, and about the size of Wales, being 140 miles in length from Dan in the north to Beersheba in the south, with a varying breadth from east to west of from 90 to 25 miles, the average being about 70 miles. It is situated at the south-east corner of the Mediterranean, is bounded on the west by that sea, on the north by the mountains of Lebanon, on the east by the heights of Moab, and the south by the Sinaitic desert. It lies obstructively athwart the great highway between the rival valleys of the Nile and the Euphrates. Palestine was properly bounded on the east by the Jordan, and, though lands were assigned to certain of the tribes of Israel on the opposite shore, these still continued to bear the names of their original occupants, and, reckoned from the south, were known as Moab, Ammon, Gilead, and Bashan.

1. PHYSICAL FEATURES.

Palestine is situated in a region of mountains which extend from Mount Taurus southward in two main branches or ranges—one range from Mount Lebanon along the west of the Jordan valley, which disappears in the desert to rise again in the heights of Sinai 250 miles south of Beersheba, and another range from Antilebanon, or Mount Hermon, along the east of the Jordan, forming the heights of Bashan, Gilead, and Moab, as far as Mount Hor in Edom, 250 miles from Dan. By these ranges the land is divided into four sections running lengthwise: (*a*) a level region forming the coast line, called the Maritime Plain ; (*b*) the hilly region forming the extension of Mount Lebanon, called the Mountains of Israel ; (*c*) the Jordan Valley ; and (*d*) the heights to the east of the Jordan forming the extension in table-land form of Mount Hermon, and called Eastern Palestine, to distinguish it from *a*, *b*, and *c*, which compose what has been called Western Palestine.

a. The Maritime Plain.—This plain is bounded on the north by the Leontes, a river which, issuing from between Lebanon and Antilebanon, falls into the Mediterranean 5 miles north of Tyre, and on the south by the desert beyond Gaza. It is intersected by Mount Carmel, where that hill juts out as a promontory seawards. The north section forms part of Phœnicia, and is very narrow ; the central section has an average width of 5 miles, and this includes the Bay of Acre, the only natural harbour of Palestine ; and the southern forms the Plain of Philistia, which extends in undulations 32 miles southward from Ekron to Gaza, with a breadth which varies from 9 to 16 miles.

b. The Mountains of Israel. — This region extends from Mount Hor in Lebanon to Beersheba, being interrupted to the south-east by the Bay of Acre by the Plain of Esdraelon (which see). It is throughout intersected by valleys, called Wadies, which slope on the one side into the Maritime Plain, and on the other

into the valley of the Jordan ; it is steeper, as well as more barren, on the east than the west ; and includes four most prominent points—Mount Gilboa, the hill of Samaria, Mounts Ebal and Gerizim, and the heights of Jerusalem and Bethlehem.

c. The Jordan Valley.—This is a gradually depressed extension southward of the plain between Lebanon and Antilebanon, down which flows the *Jordan*, a river that takes its rise in several streams at the roots of the Antilebanon, the most famous of which is near Cæsarea-Philippi, and loses itself in the waters of the Dead Sea, the surface of which is at a level 1290 feet below that of the Mediterranean, and the bottom as much as 1300 feet lower. The valley is of a width varying from an average of 2 or 3 to an average of 12 miles, becoming generally wider as it descends. It extended at one time as far as the Gulf of Akaba, carrying its waters along with it. This deep valley is characterised by some of the most remarkable geological phenomena in the world.

d. Eastern Palestine.—This region is a plateau spreading out eastward, and extending from Mount Hermon to Mount Hor in Edom. It included the densely-peopled lands of Bashan, Gilead, and Moab, which were, though allotted, never properly subject to Israel, but were always more or less independent.

2. CLIMATE AND ITS CONSEQUENCES.

The climate of Palestine is very varied, a circumstance due to the great diversity of level, which embraces a range of over 11,000 feet, extending, as it does, from the summit of Mount Hermon to the surface of the Dead Sea. The consequence of this is that among the plants and animals which it contains there are representatives of the flora and fauna of every other region of the globe from the Arctic circle to the tropics. The plants of northern Europe flourish on Lebanon, those of central Europe at the level of Jerusalem and Carmel, and those of the West Indies on the plain of Jericho near the Jordan ; while, as for the animals, some of them represent denizens of Alpine districts, and others the fauna of the plains of India and the rivers of Africa, thus supplying a natural symbolism that appeals more or less intelligibly to men of every nation.

3. MOUNTAINS.

Abarim.—A range of mountains in the land of Moab beyond the Dead Sea, steep in the west, and extending eastward into a plateau. It is seen as a great wall on the horizon to the east of Jerusalem, beyond the southern slope of Olivet (Num. xxvii. 12, xxxiii. 47, 48). It was round the north end of it that the children of Israel marched to the passage of the Jordan.

Antilebanon.—A range of mountains parallel to Lebanon on the east, which extends southward at a lower level through Gilead, Moab, and Edom as far as the eastern shores of the Red Sea.

Bamoth-baal (*i.e.*, Heights of Baal).—A mountain ridge south of Nebo in Moab, near which the children of Israel encamped, and the first of the heights which Balaam ascended at the instance of Balak to curse Israel (Num. xxii. 41).

Carmel.—The western extension of the range that, pursuing a north-westerly direction, bounds on the south the Plain of Esdraelon, and terminates in a rocky promontory 500 feet high, forming the southern boundary of the Day of Acre. Its highest point is 1742 feet above the sea, and the range about 15 miles long. It was distinguished for its vineyards and oliveyards, and it abounds to-day in the remains of winepresses, cisterns, and chambers for storing grain.

Ebal.—A mountain which rises to a height of 3077 feet above the sea on the north side of the narrow Vale of Shechem, and from the slopes of which the people responded to the curses which were pronounced by the Levites in the intervening valley (Josh. viii. 30–34). A level plateau constitutes the summit, and there are remains of cisterns and terraces on its sides.

Ephraim, Mount.—A mountainous district extending between Samaria and Bethel, a region of frequent resort for the disaffected in times of change and revolution.

Gerizim.—A mountain which rises to the height of 2848 feet above the sea on the south of the Vale of Shechem opposite Ebal (which see), and from the slopes of which the blessings were responded to by half the people. On this mountain the Samaritan temple was erected, ruins of which still remain. The Samaritan passover is still observed at this spot.

Gilboa.—A sickle-shaped range of hills, of which the highest point is 1400 feet, forming the south-eastern boundary of the Plain of Esdraelon.

Gilead.—A range of high land extending along the east of the Jordan, the summit of which, Jebel Osh'a, near Ramoth-Gilead, is 3597 feet above the sea, the general level being 2000 feet.

Hermon.—The three-peaked summit of Antilebanon, on the northern border of Palestine, which rises to a height of 9200 feet, and is covered with snow all the year round, except for about a fortnight towards the end of August. It is known by the name of *Shenir* and *Sirion*, or the "Breastplate," and *Sion*, or the "Elevated," which the word "Hermon" is also supposed to mean, and is famous for its dews, caused by the extremes of temperature. It is seen from all parts of Palestine, and the view from it is magnificent. Under the south-eastern peak, known as Baal-hermon, are the ruins of a temple once sacred to the worship of Baal.

Hermon, Little.—A range on the north-east border of Esdraelon, and south-west of the Sea of Galilee.

Hor.—A prominent peak, 4500 feet high, among the mountains to the extreme south in the direction of the "desert of Sinai," called *Jebel Harûn* (Aaron's Mount), has been identified by ancient tradition as the site of Aaron's burial.

Lebanon.—A range, extending north 100 miles, which rises to a height of 10,000 feet in the northern border of Palestine, and is divided into two by a valley which the Leontes and the Orontes water, the eastern being designated Antilebanon. It is celebrated in Scripture for its cool streams, its vines, and its cedars.

Moriah.—The site of the temple in Jerusalem (which see).

Nebo.—The flat summit of the ridge of Pisgah in Moab, which rises to a height of 2643 feet, and from which Moses is believed to have been permitted to behold the Land of Promise, and whence almost the whole of Palestine is visible.

Olivet.—A ridge to the east of Jerusalem with three summits, the loftiest of which is only 200 feet higher than the city, and 400 feet above the intervening valley of Kidron, while its height above the sea-level is 2600 feet. It is so called from the olive-trees with which it was at one time studded more thickly than now, and it is consecrated in the Christian memory as the scene of some of the most sacred events in the life of Christ.

Peor.—Peor, called also Baal-Peor, was the last of the three spots to which Balak conducted Balaam to curse Israel, and where Israel was tempted to sin against Jehovah. It was in the land of Moab, and commanded a full view of the land of Israel (Num. xxxiii. 28).

Pisgah.—A height east of the Jordan, in the south, from which Moses beheld the Land of Promise, and where he died (Deut. xxxiv. 1–5).

Salmon.—See ZALMON.

Tabor.—An all but isolated dome-shaped mountain on the north-eastern arm of the Plain of Esdraelon, some six or eight miles east of Nazareth, which rises to a height of 1850 feet, and is clothed with trees, the ruins of a fortress being on the top.

Zalmon.—This is commonly thought to be a mountain adjoining Gerizim, four or five miles south of Shechem, but possibly the name stands for some part of Ebal (which see).

Zion.—See JERUSALEM.

4. PLAINS AND VALLEYS.

Abel-shittim.—This word, meaning "acacia meadow," is a name for the Plains of Moab, at the south-eastern corner of the Plain of Jordan. Here the Israelites lay encamped when Balak summoned Balaam to curse them.

Achor.—"The valley" or pass of "trouble," which leads up from Ai to Jericho, and thence from Jericho to Jerusalem, where Achan was stoned (Josh. vii. 24–26). It was regarded as the key of the land (Hos. ii. 15).

Acre.—A rich plain along the sea-coast, forming the entrance to Esdraelon on the north-west.

Aijalon or Ajalon.—A broad fertile valley

stretching westward from Benjamin to Dan, and expanding into the Plain of Sharon.

Argob.—A wild, rugged, rocky region on the east of Bashan, over which Og was king, subsequently known as Trachonitis.

Baca.—The Valley of Rephaim (which see).

Beth-horon.—A pass leading into the valley of Ajalon from the north-west of Jerusalem, named after the town of Beth-horon.

Elah.—A fertile valley south-west of Jerusalem, in Dan, where David smote Goliath, and which was formerly famous for its terebinths, and is now famous for its acacias.

Esdraelon.—A flat and fertile plain in Galilee of great beauty and interest, called also the Valley of Jezreel, which, 9 miles broad at its centre, extends in a north-westerly direction from the Jordan at Bethshean towards the Bay of Acre, and is bounded on the north-east by Little Hermon, in the north-west by the Nazareth range, which rises from it precipitously, in the south-east by the mountains of Gilboa, and in the south-west by the range of Carmel. It is drained partly into the Jordan by the Jalud, and partly into the Mediterranean by the Kishon. It was the great battle-field of Palestine (Judg. iv., vi., vii.; 1 Sam. xxix. 1; 2 Kings xxiii. 29).

Eshcol.—A valley close to Hebron on the north, and from which the spies fetched the grapes to Kadesh-barnea as a sample of the fertility of the land. This is thought to be the same as the Valley of Mamre.

Gennesaret.—A small, flat, crescent-shaped plain, called also the "land of Gennesaret" (Matt. xiv. 34), on the north-west of the Sea of Galilee.

Golan.—A plain east of the Jordan and north of the Yarmuk, extending to the slopes of Hermon, known as the Jaulan.

Hinnom.—See JERUSALEM.

Jazar.—A valley 12 miles north-east of Heshbon descending to Abel-shittim.

Jehoshaphat, Valley of.—See JERUSALEM.

Jericho.—A deeply depressed plain, with a tropical climate, extending about 6 miles from the town of the same name as far east as the Jordan and as far south as the Dead Sea. It was at one time covered with palm-trees and famous for its balm, popularly called the "balm of Gilead."

Jeshimon.—The barren wilderness of Judah extending along the coast of the Dead Sea. It is sparsely inhabited by a people who speak a dialect of their own.

Jezreel.—See ESDRAELON.

Jordan.—A deep valley so called, of width from 2 to 12 miles, but which, generally speaking, widens as it descends, and is traversed by the Jordan river (which see). It is known among the Arabs as the "Ghor," or depression. The lower end, leading to the Gulf of Akabah, is known as the "Arabah."

Megiddo, Valley of.—A name for Esdraelon (which see).

Michmash.—A pass 4 miles south-east of Bethel.

Moreh.—A plain in Ephraim which joins the Plain of Shechem.

Rephaim.—A valley south of Jerusalem, by the road to Bethlehem.

Salt.—A valley on the south of the Dead Sea.

Sharon—A fertile section of the Maritime Plain between Carmel and Philistia.

Sorek.—A fair, open corn-valley, which was the scene of Samson's exploits, and through which flows a stream falling into the Mediterranean, 8 miles south of Joppa.

Tophet.—See JERUSALEM.

Zophim.—A field on the top of Pisgah.

5. RIVERS AND LAKES.

Arnon.—A river flowing in a deep narrow channel into the Dead Sea half way down its eastern shore, forming the southern boundary of Eastern Palestine, and dividing Ammon on the north from Moab on the south.

Belus.—A stream about 6 miles long, flowing into the north of the Bay of Acre.

Cherith.—A brook east of the Jordan, in the land of Manasseh, by the side of which Elijah took shelter.

Chinnereth.—Gennesaret. (See GALILEE, SEA OF.)

Dead Sea.—The name given to what is called in Scripture *the Salt Sea, the Sea of Arabah,* and *the East Sea,* and by the Latins *the Asphalt Lake.* It is formed by the waters of the Jordan, is 40 miles long, 10 miles broad, and in some parts 1300 feet deep, while its surface is 1290 feet below the level of the Mediterranean, so that its bed is about 2600 feet below this level, *i.e.,* as much as Jerusalem is above the Mediterranean. It contains more than one part in four of various salts. This extraordinary saltness of the Dead Sea is largely attributed to its having no outlet, the enormous evaporation produced by the intense heat keeping it at a normal level, while the rivers that feed it bring down salts in solution. But some of its ingredients seem to be due to hot springs in the sea bottom. Pitch or bitumen is found floating on its surface. It is enclosed east and west by steep mountains, which rise in some places to a height of 4000 feet above it.

Galilee, Sea of.—This, called also the Lake of Gennesaret, is an expansion of the Jordan, and is 12½ miles long by at the utmost 8 miles wide, its surface being 682 feet below the level of the Mediterranean. It is subject to sudden and violent storms. It is enclosed on all sides by steep mountains, except on the north-west, where the land is alluvial. Its shores were once in part clothed with corn-fields and trees, and well peopled; they are now barren and treeless, and almost without inhabitants except at Tiberias.

Huleh, Lake.—See MEROM.

Jabbok.—A brook which rises in the south-eastern part of Gilead, whence it bends away in a semicircle northward and westward, passing the base of Mount Gilead before it joins the Jordan fully half way down its course from the Sea of Galilee to the Dead Sea.

Jalud.—An affluent of the Jordan from the Plain of Esdraelon.

Jarmuk.—An affluent of the Jordan from Hauran, 4 miles below the Sea of Galilee.

Jordan.—The river Jordan was formerly said to rise at Cæsarea-Philippi, where a full swift stream suddenly bursts out of the cliffs at the foot of Hermon. But this is only one of three sources of the Jordan. Two other streams both come from more distant points. Five miles below Cæsarea-Philippi the first-mentioned stream is joined by the *Liddân*, a stream from Dan, and further down by the *Hashbâny*, a stream from the slopes of Hermon. Thus formed, its course for a time is within banks, after which it expands into lagoons that collect at length into a mass in Lake Merom or Huleh, 2 miles beyond which it plunges into a gorge, and rushes on for 9 miles as a torrent till its waters are collected again in the Sea of Galilee, to lose themselves finally in the Salt Sea, after winding along nearly 200 miles, though the distance is only 65 miles as the crow flies. At its rise it is 1080 feet, at Lake Huleh 7 feet above the sea-level, while at the Sea of Galilee 682 feet, and at the Dead Sea 1290 feet below that level.

Kishon.—A river which rises on the northern slope of Tabor and drains the west of the Plain of Esdraelon.

Leontes.—A river, called also the *Litany*, which, in first a south-westward, then a straight westward course, drains Cœle-Syria, and falls into the Mediterranean 5 miles north of Tyre, after a course of 55 miles.

Merom, Waters of.—A lake about 6 miles long by 4 miles broad, 11 miles north of the Sea of Galilee, derived from marshes formed by the waters of the Jordan in the early part of its course. It is also called Lake Huleh.

Orontes.—A river flowing north from between the Lebanons, and falling by way of Antioch into the Mediterranean after a course of nearly 100 miles.

6. ORIGINAL INHABITANTS.

Those known to primitive Scripture history were not the earliest inhabitants, but, like the Israelites after them, they had driven out and supplanted a prior aboriginal race, remnants of which were extant in the land as recently as the days of David (1 Sam. xxvii. 8-10). Gen. x. 15-18 and xv. 19-21 mention several nations who were in possession of the land when the Israelites invaded it. The chief of these were the *Canaanites*, who occupied the lowlands; the *Amorites* or "highlanders," a tall, fair, blue-eyed race, still extant in Palestine, who had their strongholds in the mountains, and held lordship over the fertile valleys adjoining (Judg. i. 35, 36); the *Perizzites*, who, like the Canaanites, dwelt in the plains, either along with them in some relation, or perhaps as a distinct people, though possibly their name only stands for "villagers" of no distinctive race; the *Hivites*, who are thought by some to have been cultivators of the soil, like the fellahîn of Egypt, and distinguished from the inhabitants of the towns; the *Jebusites*, who held the heights about Jerusalem; the *Girgasites*, who hovered somewhere on the northern outskirts of the country; the *Hittites*, a Mongolian race, who were entirely different in original position from the petty tribes with which they are associated in Jewish history, being scattered fragments of the once great Hittite Empire which had extended from Egypt through Syria and Asia Minor westwards and to the Euphrates in the East (see Hittites); the *Amalekites*, with the tribes of the Kenite and the Kennizzite, a nomad race, whose territory, with one exception (Judg. xii. 15), was chiefly on the southern borders of Palestine. These nations were all nature-worshippers, and Baal was their chief god.

7. POLITICAL DIVISIONS.

These varied from the days of the Patriarchs to the days of Christ.

a. In the days of the Patriarchs.—The Canaanite was still in the land, and Abraham, the first of the patriarchs, dwelt in it as a stranger, first at Shechem, then at Bethel or Luz, then at Mamre, near Hebron, the land at the first of these encampments being afterwards purchased by Jacob, who dug in it a well, known as his to this day. Abraham was living at Bethel when Lot left him, at Mamre when he witnessed the destruction of the cities of the plain, after which we find him located farther south in the neighbourhood of Gerar, on the borders of the Philistine country, till on the death of Sarah he finally appears as sojourning once more near Hebron. Isaac's connection with the land was limited pretty much to the spots last visited by his father, while Jacob takes a wider range and is found at Mizpeh, Mahanaim, and Succoth, as well as at spots associated with the sojourn of his grandfather.

b. As distributed among the Tribes after the Conquest.—To *Reuben* was assigned land between the Amorites and the Dead Sea; to *Gad*, land from the north of the territory of Reuben to the south of the Sea of Galilee; and to the *half-tribe of Manasseh*, land to the east and north-east of the latter sea. These territories are all on the east of the Jordan, and come up to the line of that river. To *Simeon* was assigned, apparently, the extreme south of Palestine west of the Dead Sea; to *Judah*, land to the west of the Dead Sea as far as the Mediterranean, inclusive of Philistia; to *Benjamin* and

Ephraim, the land north of Jerusalem to the neighbourhood of Shechem, from which two territories assigned to *Dan* stretched westward to the Mediterranean; to the *half-tribe of Manasseh,* and *Issachar,* land to the north of Ephraim and Dan nearly as far as the south-west of the Sea of Galilee; to *Zebulon,* land to the west of that sea; to *Naphtali* and *Asher,* lands to the north of Zebulon, those of the latter being on the coast of the Mediterranean.

c. In the days of the Kings.—In the time of David and Solomon the kingdom extended beyond the boundaries of Palestine proper, but on the death of the latter it split into two divisions, the northern being known as the kingdom of Israel and the southern as the kingdom of Judah, a separation which had appeared in the time of the Judges and during the usurpation of Ishbosheth while David was king of the south and reigning at Hebron, and which now continued down to the time of the Captivity. The northern, formed by the revolt of the ten tribes, was the larger, but the weaker; the southern, composed of the tribes of Judah and Benjamin, though smaller, was more compact.

d. In the days of Christ.—In the time of Christ, the Holy Land west of the Jordan was divided into *Galilee* in the north, *Samaria* in the centre, and *Judæa* in the south; to the east of the Jordan it was divided into *Gaulonitis* in the north. *Decapolis* in the centre, and *Perea* in the south. Galilee was divided into Upper and Lower Sections—the Upper to the north-west and the Lower to the west and south-west of the Sea of Galilee, while Judæa was divided into eleven districts.

8. Districts.

Abilene.—A tetrarchy on the eastern slope of Antilebanon, in a region fertilised by the Abana (Luke iii. 1).

Bashan.—A fertile region in Eastern Palestine of considerable extent, and at one time densely peopled, stretching from Hermon to the Jabbok, of which the eastern division was called *Argob,* or the "stony;" the southern *Hauran,* the northern *Geshur,* the north-western *Maachah,* and the south-western the *Land of Tob.* It was called *Batanæa* by the Romans.

Cœle-Syria (*i.e.,* the hollow of Syria).—A region 70 miles long by 7 miles broad, between Lebanon and Antilebanon, of the plain of which the valley of the Jordan before its depression was a continuation. The name was also used for an extensive tract of country east of the Jordan extending to Damascus and even to the borders of Egypt.

Decapolis.—A large district extending from the Sea of Galilee east and south, so called because embracing ten towns, including Damascus and Scythopolis, Pella, and Gadara. For the most part these were Greek cities, and Prof. Geo. A. Smith regards them as constituting an anti-Semitic league.

Galilee.—The northern division of Palestine, divided—as stated above—into Upper, which is highly mountainous, and Lower, which is at most only hilly. Its length averages 60 miles, and its breadth 30 miles.

Gaulonitis.—A district in the centre of Bashan east of the Sea of Galilee.

Geshur.—See BASHAN.

Gilead.—An elevated region, sometimes called Mount Gilead, and sometimes the Land of Gilead, of great beauty and fertility, which extends 25 miles southward from Bashan to beyond the Jabbok.

Hauran.—See BASHAN.

Ituræa.—A rich pastoral region in the north of Bashan, lying along the base of Hermon.

Judæa.—The southern division of Palestine, which extended from Samaria southward to the desert of Arabia, and from the country of the Philistines, or rather from the Mediterranean, eastward to the Dead Sea. It is very hilly, and is generally fertile, though barren to the east, a district known therefore as the *Wilderness of Judæa.*

Maachah.—See BASHAN.

Moab.—A region well adapted for pasturing flocks, extending along the eastern side of the Dead Sea, southward from Heshbon.

Negeb.—The south country about Beersheba (Gen. xiii. 3.; Num. xiii. 17).

Peræa.—A district extending from near the Sea of Galilee southwards to the Arnon.

Philistia.—A highly fertile undulating plain extending along the sea-coast from Joppa to the desert, being about 32 miles long and from 9 to 16 miles broad.

Samaria.—The central division of Palestine, the exact boundaries of which are uncertain. It included the land assigned to the tribe of Ephraim, and extended northward as far as Esdraelon.

Tob.—See BASHAN.

Trachonitis.—Argob. (See BASHAN.)

9. Towns and Historic Sites.

Abel-Meholah.—Elisha's birthplace, situated in the Jordan Valley, probably south of Beth-shean, nearly half way between the Sea of Galilee and the Dead Sea.

Abey.—At the north of the Plain of Esdraelon.

Accho, called afterwards **Ptolemais.** Situated at the foot of Mount Carmel, and inhabited by Phœnicians—the St. Jean d'Acre of the Crusaders.

Achshaph.—Probably the present village *El Yasîf,* north-east of Acre.

Adamah.—Five miles south-west of Tiberias.

Admah.—One of the five cities of the plain on the north of the Dead Sea.

Adullam.—In the Valley of Elah, 10 miles north-west of Hebron. It was a royal Canaanitish city, and David's hiding-place (1 Sam. xxii. 1).

Ænon.—In Samaria, to the north-east of Mount Ebal, and 7 miles north of Salem.

Ai.—A royal Canaanitish city 2 miles east of Bethel.

Amad.—Apparently *El 'Amûd*, north of Acre.

Anathoth.—Over the Mount of Olives, 3 miles north-east of Jerusalem. A Levitical city, the birthplace of Jeremiah.

Anem.—In the hills, west of the Plain of Esdraelon.

Antipatris.—A military town rebuilt by the Herods, upon the borders of Samaria, on the road between Jerusalem and Cæsarea, being 42 miles from the former and 26 miles from the latter.

Aphek.—A place 6 miles east of the Sea of Galilee.

Ar.—See RABBATH-MOAB.

Arimathæa.—See RAMAH.

Aroer.—(1.) A city of the Amorites, perhaps situated on the Arnon, on the edge of a deep ravine 15 miles from its mouth. (2.) Also a haunt of David, 12 miles south-east of Beersheba.

Ashdod.—One of the five Philistine cities on the red sandhills, 3 miles from the sea. It is also called Azotus.

Ashkelon.—A Philistine city on the sea-coast, 12 miles north of Gaza, famous for the worship of the Syrian Venus.

Ashtoreth-Karnaim.—A city of the Rephaim, and subsequently of Og, in Bashan, 4 miles east of Edrei, and 20 miles east of the Sea of Galilee.

Azotus.—See ASHDOD.

Baal Gad.—A town under Mount Hermon, supposed to be the same as Banias.

Baalath.—West of Beth-horon, and commanding the main road to Jerusalem.

Bahurim.—A village on the eastern slopes of Olivet, where Shimei came out to curse David. According to tradition the same as Alemeth of Benjamin, on the most northern of the roads from Jerusalem to the Jordan Valley.

Banias.—See CÆSAREA-PHILIPPI.

Beer-lahai-roi.—Hagar's well, identified by a doubtful tradition with a spot in the flat, chalky desert, 50 miles south of Beersheba.

Beeroth.—A Hivite town 2 miles from Bethel in the direction of Jerusalem.

Beersheba.—A town 27 miles south-west of

Hebron, the most southerly in Palestine, familiar in patriarchal story, lying in a pastoral district which abounded in wells.

Behen.—Eight miles east of Acre.

Bethabarah. — Major Conder identifies the Bethabara which some MSS. give as the place of our Lord's baptism (John i. 28) with 'Abara, just north of Bethshean ; but Prof. Geo. Adam Smith has pointed out that the name, meaning a "ford," was likely to be a common one for several places. Moreover, the best MSS. read "Bethany," which, Conder suggests, may be near Bashan. It is impossible to identify the place of the baptism with any certainty.

Bethany.—The town of Lazarus and his sisters, a little more than a mile east of Jerusalem, on the road to Jericho by the south of Olivet.

Bethaven.—A town on the borders of Benjamin and Ephraim, three-quarters of a mile east of Bethel—"The House of Naught," *i.e.*, "of idols," set over against "The House of God."

Bethel.—A town 20 miles south of Shechem and 10 miles north of Jerusalem, on the great watershed and highway that traverse the land, and famous in patriarchal history.

Beth-horon.—At the entrance of the valley of Ajalon, 10 miles north-west of Jerusalem.

Bethlehem.—The birthplace of Jesus Christ, standing 6 miles south of Jerusalem, on a narrow chalky ridge which runs eastward, and is protected by eastward deepening valleys of great fertility on the north and south.

Bethphage.—Thought by some to be a place on the Mount of Olives, near Bethany, on the road between Jericho and Jerusalem ; by others to be on the summit of the Mount of Olives ; and by others again to be the modern *Silwân*, at the junction of the valleys of Kidron and Hinnom.

Bethsaida.—A town on a little bay on the east of a ford of the Jordan, 2 miles up from the Sea of Galilee, known as Bethsaida-Julias, which the Tetrarch Philip rebuilt and named after the daughter of Augustus. A second Bethsaida was looked for on the north coast of the Sea of Galilee, further west, but it is now generally thought that there was only one town of that name.

Bethshean.—The chief city of Decapolis, on a mound commanding the eastern entrance to Esdraelon at the ford of Jordan.

Bethshemesh.—(1.) A Levitical city in the open corn valley of Sorek. (2.) Also the city of On or Heliopolis.

Bethshittah.—On the descent from the Plain of Esdraelon to the valley of the Jordan.

Bezek.—A place which has been discovered by the Palestine Exploration Society, in the very centre of Palestine, and on the eastern slope of Gilboa. It still bears its ancient name.

Bezer.—A city of refuge in Moab, 2 miles south of Dibon.

Bozrah.—(1.) A town in Edom, often referred to by the prophets. (2.) Also a town in Hauran.

Cæsarea.—A city on the sea-coast, 32 miles north of Joppa and 25 miles south of Carmel, founded by Herod the Great, and named after the Roman Emperor, where a temple was also erected to his honour. It became a most important garrison city.

Cæsarea-Philippi.—A town, called also Banias, at the foot of Mount Hermon, erected on the site of Baal-gad.

Cana.—Generally thought to be a place now called *Kefr Kenna,* a town 4 miles north of Nazareth; but a spring called *'Ain Kenna,* nearer Nazareth, is thought by some to mark the true site. The Crusaders fixed on *Kana,* further north. The question is still open.

Capernaum.—The centre of Christ's labours, a town on the north-west of the Sea of Galilee, not yet identified for certain. *Tel Hum,* at the north of the sea, with ruins of a fine marble synagogue, is the most popular site. But there is reason to think the city was on the plain of Gennesaret, therefore 2 or 3 miles further west and south, perhaps at *Khan Minyeh,* at the north-eastern extremity of the little plain.

Carmel.—A town 7 miles south of Hebron.

Chorazin.—A town north of *Tel Hum.* (See CAPERNAUM.)

Chozeba.—Possibly where the ruin *Kueizība* has been found, north-east of Hebron.

Cities of Refuge.—These were six: three east of the Jordan, viz., *Bezer, Golan,* and *Ramoth ;* and three on the west, viz., *Hebron, Kedesh,* and *Shechem.*

Dan.—A town, formerly Laish, at one of the sources of the Jordan, by the foot of Hermon.

Debir.—A Levitical city 12 miles south-west of Hebron—the Kirjath-sepher of the Hittites.

Dibon.—A town in Moab, 3 or 4 miles north of the Arnon, among the ruins of which the "Moabite stone" was found in 1868 by Dr. Klein. This stone, which is 4 feet high and 2 feet broad, and is now in the Louvre, describes a victory of Mesha, King of Moab, over the Israelites. It is in a shattered state ; but a squeeze of it taken at Damascus has been preserved.

Dio-Cæsarea.—A chief city of Galilee in Christ's time, 3 miles north of Nazareth.

Dor.—A town on the sea-shore, 12 miles south of Mount Carmel, at the north end of the Plain of Sharon.

Dothan.—A town 10 miles north of the city of Samaria.

Dumah.—(1.) A town 10 miles south-west of Hebron. (2.) The name also stands for a district of Mount Seir.

Ebenezer.—Placed by Christian hermits near Bethshemesh, but with no authority. The site is unknown.

Edrei.—The capital of Og, King of Bashan, on the south-western border of Argob—a subterranean city of caves, containing streets with shops and houses on each side, and a market-place.

Eglon.—A town captured by Joshua, 16 miles north-east of Gaza, and 2 or 3 miles east of Lachish.

Ekron.—A town of Philistia, on its northern border, 32 miles from Gaza, and 9 miles from the sea.

Elealeh.—A town in Moab, 4 miles north-east of Heshbon.

Emmaus.—(1.) A place about 2 miles south of Tiberias. (2.) For the village mentioned in Luke xxiv. a place 7½ miles north-west, and another 8 miles south-west, of Jerusalem have been suggested, both with uncertainty.

Endor.—A town in Issachar on the slopes of the Little Hermon range, 3 miles south from Tabor.

Engannim.—Seven miles south of Jezreel.

Engedi.—An oasis, a spot of rare beauty, once a place of palm-trees, called originally Hazazon-Tamar, on the west shore of the Dead Sea, 23 miles from its north end. It belonged at first to the Amorites.

Enrogel.—The same as Gihon—a spring flowing on the west side of the Kidron Valley, at the foot of the Ophel spur, now known as the Virgin's Fountain.

Ephratah.—See BETHLEHEM, of which this is another name.

Eshtaol.—One of Samson's resorts, in Dan, 1½ miles north-east of Zorah.

Gadara.—A town east of the Jordan, on the south bank of the Jarmuk.

Gamala.—On the Sea of Galilee, 10 miles north of Gadara.

Gath.—An inland city of Philistia, on the borders of Israel, probably near to Ekron.

Gaza.—A Philistine town, the gates of which Samson carried off by night, situated on a mound at the edge of the desert, 2 miles from the sea, a considerable place to this day.

Geba.—A frontier town of Judah and Israel.

Gebal.—A Phœnician city, also called Byblas, 40 miles north of Zidon, distinguished for its craftsmen and its worship of Adonis.

Gerar.—A place in a valley 10 or 12 miles south of Gaza, and 20 miles west of Beersheba.

Gethsemane.—Somewhere on the east side of the Kidron, at the foot of Olivet.

Gezer.—A town on the north border of Philistia, east of Joppa.

Gibbethon.—A town of Dan, thought to be 6 or 7 miles north-east of Lydda.

Gibeah.—(1.) A town north of Jerusalem and south of Geba. (2.) The name means a hill, and is applied to several places in elevated situations.

Gibeon.—A place on the northern slope of a hill 6 miles north of Jerusalem.

Gilgal.—(1.) The place where the Israelites held their camp after crossing the Jordan till they achieved the conquest of Canaan. It lay 3 miles east of Jericho. (2.) Also a place 5 miles south-west of Shiloh, with a school of the prophets. (3.) A place on the Plain of Sharon.

Golan.—A city of refuge east of the Jordan and north of the Jarmuk in the district of the same name.

Gomorrah.—In the north-west corner of the Dead Sea, where an echo of the name still lingers.

Hadadrimmon.—A place on the south edge of the Plain of Esdraelon, near Taanach.

Hamath.—A town, as well as a district, on the banks of the Orontes between Lebanon and Antilebanon—a Hittite centre.

Hazazon-Tamar.—See ENGEDI.

Hazor.—The city of Jabin, 4 miles west of the waters of Merom, and 4 miles south of Kedesh.

Hebron.—An ancient Hittite town and a city of refuge, originally called *Kirjath-arba—i.e.,* four cities—nearly 20 miles south of Jerusalem. It abounds still in vineyards and oliveyards, and its population at present is 10,000.

Helbon.—A place on Hermon.

Heshbon.—The royal city of the Amorites, 12 miles east of the north end of the Dead Sea. Its ruins are varied and considerable.

Hormah.—A Canaanitish town, south of the Dead Sea.

Ijon.—On the Hashbany, a branch of the Jordan, west of Banias.

Jabesh-Gilead.—In Gad, opposite Bethshean, about 6 miles south-east of Pella. Here the Benjamites got wives after the tribe had been nearly exterminated.

Jacob's Well.—A well, identified beyond doubt, 75 feet deep, and still sometimes containing water, situated at the point where the Vale of Shechem joins the Plain of Moreh, about 2 miles east of Nablûs. There is a vault over it now, and some remains of an ancient church.

Jahaz.—A Levitical city, north-east of Heshbon, probably where the Israelites overthrew Sihon, and got possession of all the land between the Arnon and the Jabbok.

Janoah.—In the hills, south-east of Tyre, possibly the modern *Yanûh.*

Jazer.—A place near Elealeh, 4 miles north-east of Heshbon.

Jebus.—The ancient Canaanite city which stood where Jerusalem was afterwards built.

Jericho.—A city situated on the south-western edge of the plain of Jordan, and the first taken by the Israelites after crossing the Jordan. Its site is 820 feet below the sea-level, and over 3000 below the level of Jerusalem. It is known as the "city of palm-trees."

Jerusalem.—Jerusalem, which originally belonged to the Jebusites, and was not in possession of the Israelites till the days of David, who conquered the place and made it the capital of his kingdom, was a strong city, being built on four hills, and surrounded by deep valleys, except on the north and north-west, where accordingly, as nowhere else, it was most open to hostile assault. The four hills are Mount Zion on the south-west, Acra on the north, Moriah on the east, with a south extension, named Ophel, and Bezetha on the north of Moriah, a valley called the Tyropœon Valley once separating the first of these, called also the Citadel of Zion, from the rest. The surrounding valleys are the Valley of Kidron or Jehoshaphat on the east, and the Valley of Hinnom or Gehenna on the south and south-west, Tophet terminating at its eastern extremity. On the east of the Kidron rises the Mount of Olives, to the south of which is the Hill of Offence, with the village of Siloam perched on its western slope, while to the south of Tophet rises the Hill of Evil Counsel, with the field of Aceldama on its north side. The mountains which are round the valleys are generally no higher than those on which the city stands, and only Mount Olivet looks down upon it, partly because it is higher and partly because the city slopes eastwards. The area which the city covered was at no time very great; probably it never exceeded 250 acres; it is at present less than 3 miles in circuit. It is not likely that the resident population ever amounted to more than 30,000. Jerusalem was and is still enclosed with walls, which were extended from time to time, the first surrounding only Mount Zion, a second including Mount Moriah and Acra, and a third of uncertain extent, sweeping round the north and north-west. Jerusalem has been besieged, overthrown, and rebuilt so many times that the present city stands on vast rubbish heaps, the ruins of ancient structures.

The deep Tyropœon Valley has been completely filled up.

Jeshimon.—"Solitude," the waterless desert which sinks down to the plateau of Engedi, overlooking the Dead Sea.

Jezreel.—A royal residence in the time of Ahab, situated on a kind of shelf on the western extremity of Gilboa, and commanding a view of the valley.

Jogbehah.—A town on the top of the hills of Gilead, north of Rabbath-Ammon.

Joppa.—The ancient port of Palestine, 35 miles from Jerusalem, now known as *Jaffa*. Here Hiram landed the cedars for the Temple, here Jonah took ship for Tarshish, thinking to escape from the presence of the Lord, and here was the residence of St. Peter when he was called to preach the gospel to the Gentile Cornelius.

Joseph's Tomb.—In the Vale of Shechem, a little to the north of Jacob's Well.

Kadesh.—On the Orontes, a stronghold of the Amorites and Hittites.

Kadesh-barnea.—On the northern edge of the Wilderness of Paran.

Kedesh.—(1.) One of the Cities of Refuge, 4 miles north-west of the Waters of Merom. (2.) A city of Issachar. (3.) A town in the extreme south of Judah.

Kerioth.—(1.) A place 4½ miles north of Arad. (2.) Also Ar of Moab.

Kirharesh (2 Kings iii. 25), **Kirhareseth** (Isa. xv. 17), **Kirheres** (Jer. xlviii. 31, 36).—A place 8 miles south of Ar in Moab.

Kirjath-Arba.—See HEBRON, of which this is another name.

Kirjath-Jearim.—Originally a Hivite town near Bethshemesh.

Lachish.—A primitive stronghold of the Amorites bordering on Philistia, the site of which is 15 miles east of Gaza. The ruins of it have been recently discovered by Mr. Petrie.

Laish.—The primitive name of Dan.

Libnah.—A priests' city near Lachish.

Luz.—An early name of Bethel.

Lydda.—A town 11 miles south-east of Joppa.

Machpelah, Cave of.—The burial-place of the Patriarchs, on the east of Hebron. It is surrounded by a wall 40 feet high, and the space enclosed is 197 feet long by 111 feet wide.

Madmenah.—A Benjamite village north of Jerusalem.

Madon.—A royal city of the northern Canaanites, near Hattin, west of the Sea of Galilee.

Magdala.—A little village on the west of the Sea of Galilee, north of Tiberias, the home of Mary Magdalene.

Mahanaim.—A place north of the Jabbok and near the Jordan.

Makkedah.—A cave south-west of Gezer.

Mamre, Plain or Oak of.—A secluded upland plain 2 miles north of Hebron.

Maon.—A place 8 miles south of Hebron.

Mareshah.—Micah's birthplace, on the eastern border of Philistia.

Medeba.—A city in the heart of Mishor, the great plain of Moab.

Megiddo.—Near Taanach, in the Plain of Esdraelon; the site has not been recovered.

Meroz.—A place 5 miles south of Bethshean.

Michmash.—In Benjamin, 4 miles south-east of Bethel.

Mizpeh.—A town in the land of Tob, *i.e.*, east of the Jordan, in the northern part of Gilead.

Nain.—A town nearly 8 miles south-east of Nazareth, on a hill at the end of the Little Hermon range, and looking westward over the Plain of Esdraelon. This town, where our Lord raised the widow's son, is within half-an-hour of Shunem, where Elisha effected a similar miracle.

Nazareth.—A highland town, perched like an eagle's nest in a secluded cleft in the range of hills on the north of the Plain of Esdraelon, being situated 1½ miles back from the front of the range and 140 feet beneath the summit. No highroad passed through this remote place in its mountain solitude. But from the top of the hill just above it a wide view would be seen —including a reach of the Mediterranean Sea, with the ships at anchor in the Bay of Acre, the Plain of Esdraelon, and the heights of Ephraim beyond, Tabor, and then the blue hills of Gilead across the deep Jordan Valley, with the snows of Hermon and Lebanon to the north.

Neapolis.—The Greek name of Shechem.

Nob.—A priest's village, north of Olivet, where the Tabernacle was when the Ark was at Kirjath-Jearim.

Ono.—In Sharon, 4 miles to the north of Lydda.

Ophel.—See JERUSALEM.

Ophni.—A place 3 miles north-west of Bethel.

Ophrah-Ephraim.—(1.) A place 4 miles north-ast of Bethel. (2.) Also another 6 miles south-west of Shechem.

Pella. — A town in Decapolis south-east of Bethshean, to which the disciples of Christ fled before the destruction of Jerusalem.

Peniel, or Penuel. — A place on the east of the Jordan and near the Jabbok, probably to the south of that stream.

Pirathon. — Possibly the modern *Fe'rôn*, a place west of Shechem.

Rabbath-Ammon. — The capital of the Ammonites, at the southern springs of the Jabbok.

Rabbath-Moab. — The ancient capital of Moab, south of the Arnon.

Ramah. — (1.) A town in Benjamin between Gibeon and Beeroth. (2.) Ramathaim-Zophim, Samuel's birthplace in "Mount Ephraim." Arimathea has been identified with this place. (3.) A town in Naphtali between Adamar and Hazor. (4.) A boundary town of Assher, apparently between Tyre and Sidon. (5.) Ramoth-Gilead (which see).

Ramoth-Gilead. — A strong place and city of refuge on a plain north of the Jabbok.

Ramoth-Lehi. — "The hill of the jaw." Somewhere on the borders of Philistia, but not discovered.

Rehoboth. — (1.) The place where Isaac stayed and dug a well, 15 miles south of Beersheba. (2.) "The city Rehoboth" is on the Euphrates above Babylon.

Riblah. — In Cœle-Syria, 35 miles beyond Baalbek.

Rimmon, The Rock. — East of Bethel some miles, the rock to which the 600 Benjamites fled for refuge after the slaughter of their tribe (Judg. xx. 47).

Salem. — Said by the Jews to be Jerusalem. But possibly it is the Salim where John was baptizing, or a place east of the Jordan. The title of Melchisedek, "King of Salem," may refer to no place, but may mean "King of Peace."

Salim. — A place a few miles east of Mount Ebal.

Samaria. — Capital of the district so called, built in a strong position on a conical hill by Omri, King of Israel (1 Kings xvi. 24), and the chief royal city of the northern kingdom.

Saphir. — Four or five miles north-east of Ascalon.

Sarepta. — A place 8 or 9 miles north of the mouth of the Leontes, associated with the life of Elijah.

Scythopolis. — Bethshean.

Shechem. — In the well-watered valley between Ebal and Gerizim, the chief city of refuge west of the Jordan, originally a Hivite town, and the place where Abraham built his first altar, and where Jehovah first appeared to him in the land of Canaan.

Shiloh. — In Ephraim, 12 miles south-west of Shechem, and 9½ miles north-west of Bethel, the first permanent site of the Tabernacle in Canaan, where lots were cast for division of the land, and the place of Samuel's upbringing.

Shunem. — Three and a half miles north of Jezreel; famous in the life of Elisha.

Sidon — An ancient Phœnician town 20 miles north of Tyre, and the original capital.

Siloam. — A village on the east side of the south end of the Kidron Valley, opposite to which in Jerusalem is the pool so called.

Sodom. — One of the cities of the plain, thought to have been in Abel-shittim, or the Plain of Moab.

Succoth. — On the east of the Jordan, about 1 mile north of the Jabbok.

Sychar. — On the south slope of Ebal, within a mile of Jacob's Well, now known as *'Askar*.

Taanach. — On the edge of the Plain of Esdraelon, 7 miles south-west of Jezreel.

Tadmor. — A city, called Palmyra by the Greeks, founded by Solomon in a remote eastern part of the Syrian desert to facilitate commerce with the East.

Tekoah. — A pastoral and market village 5 miles south of Bethlehem, Amos' birthplace.

Tiberias. — On the west of the Sea of Galilee, south of Magdala, named after the Emperor Tiberius by Herod Antipas, who founded it. Its original name was Rakkath. It is now an important Jewish centre.

Timnath. — A town in Dan, 4 miles south-west of Zorah, and on a lower level (Judg. xiv.).

Timnath-heres. — Joshua's portion, among the low chalk hills, 9 miles south-west of Shechem.

Tirzah. — Twelve miles north-east of Shechem, the capital of the northern kingdom before Samaria.

Tophet. — See JERUSALEM.

Tyre. — The chief of the cities of Phœnicia, celebrated for its wealth and commerce. It stood originally on two islands which were joined together by Hiram, and afterwards to the mainland by Alexander the Great.

Usdum. — Sodom.

Zarephath. — Sarepta.

Zeboim. — One of the cities of the plain, on the

west of the Jordan in the valley mentioned in 1 Sam. xiii. 18.

Zereda. — Probably the present *Surdeh*, in Mount Ephraim, west of Bethel.

Zidon. — Sidon.

Ziklag. — In the desert south of Beersheba.

Ziz. — Probably in the neighbourhood of En-gedi.

Zoar. — At the foot of the Moab mountains, by the northern end of the Dead Sea.

Zorah. — Samson's birthplace, in the Vale of Sorek, 13 miles west of Jerusalem.

See Conder, *Primer of Bible Geography*, a small useful handbook; also Geo. Ad. Smith, *The Historical Geography of the Holy Land;* Conder, *Tent Work in Palestine, and Heth and Moab;* Warren, *Underground Jerusalem;* Selah Merrill, *Galilee in the Time of Christ;* Stanley, *Sinai and Palestine;* Thomson, *The Land and the Book;* Porter, *Handbook for Syria and Palestine;* Hilprecht, *Exploration in Bible Lands.*

CHAPTER XL.

TOPOGRAPHY OF OTHER COUNTRIES AND PLACES CONNECTED WITH THE BIBLE.

Achaia. — Originally the name of a small state in the north of the Peloponnesus or the Morea, Achaia became under the Romans the name for the whole of Greece with the exception of Macedonia, and it is the designation of this region in the New Testament. The province, for such it then was under Rome, comes before us in connection with the ministry of St. Paul, and more especially four cities or towns contained in it. These are Athens, Corinth, Cenchrea, and Nicopolis. *Athens* was the most illustrious city not only of Greece but of the world, and among its citizens we meet with some of the most distinguished names that figure in the annals of human culture. Nevertheless it was not here but at Corinth that the gospel message was received with open welcome, though St. Paul himself sought to reason the *élite* of Athens into the faith of Christ (Acts xvii.). This was on the *Areopagus*, or *Mars' Hill*, which was one of the four hills within the compass of the city, a small, rocky elevation, overlooking the *market-place* to the south, where St. Paul had previously preached to the people of Christ and the resurrection. *Corinth* in the time of St. Paul was more a world-city than a Grecian; it was a busy trading centre between the east and west. The population therefore was of a very mixed character, and stood in various relations to the preaching of the cross. Though the Jewish section as a rule opposed it, others embraced it with eagerness, and became auxiliary to the spread of it far and wide. The city stood on an isthmus of the same name, between two seas, and had one port on the east and another on the west. *Cenchrea* was the eastern port of Corinth, and stood about 9 miles

from the city. It was the site of an apostolic church, of which Phœbe, mentioned in Rom. xvi. 1, was a member. *Nicopolis* is mentioned by St. Paul in Titus iii. 12 as a place where he proposed to winter, and possibly spent the last winter of his life. It was built by Augustus Cæsar in memory of the victory of Actium, on a low unhealthy spot by the borders of Macedonia.

Arabia. — This country, which extends away south-east of Palestine, chiefly concerns us as the home of a people of the same blood as the Hebrews, and eventually of kindred religion, and as containing within it on the north-west the *Wilderness of Sinai*. In this district dwelt the Midianites or Kenites and the Amalekites, the latter of whom were a source of much trouble to the children of Israel both before and after their settlement in Canaan, and among the former of whom Moses spent forty years of his life. The southern portion of it, 200 miles of utmost length and 150 miles of utmost breadth, known as the Sinaitic Peninsula, and abounding with grim, barren, rocky mountains and wastes, was the scene of the giving of the law and of much of the forty years' wandering after the Exodus. Here, as you go from the north-west southward, were the wilderness of *Etham*, the waters of *Marah*, the wells of *Elim*, the desert of *Sin*, the rock of *Rephidim*, and at length the heights of *Sinai*, under the shadow of which the Israelites encamped for a whole year. This mountain is difficult to identify, but the hill named "Jebel Mûsa," *i.e.*, the hill of Moses, which is the one to which tradition points, seems to be regarded with most favour as the real Sinai. At the foot of it on the north side is a plain where the congregation is believed to have assembled during the giving of the law. *Horeb* is by some identified with and by others distinguished from Sinai, while others again regard it as the name of the group to which the latter belonged. *Hazaroth* is north of the Sinai mountains, while the wilderness of *Shur* is north-west and that of *Paran* or the *Tih* north-east of the Sinaitic Peninsula.

Aramæa. — This name was given to the high land which extended to the north-east of Palestine from the mountains of Bashan as far as the Euphrates, or rather beyond it, so as to include Mesopotamia. It is nearly synonymous with Syria, and the epithets Aramaic and Syriac, as applied to the language especially, are interchangeable, except that the latter name is used for the later development of the language, especially in Christian literature.

Armenia. — A country forming a high table-land, the source of the Euphrates and Tigris, between the Caucasus mountains on the north and branches of Mount Taurus on the south, the Black Sea on the west, and the Caspian on the east. It is interesting to Bible students as the country in which the *Garden of Eden* is believed to have been situated, and as containing *Mount Ararat*, on which the ark rested, and which is 17,750 feet high.

Asia Minor. — Under the Romans this region was divided into a number of provinces, which were not always conterminous with the original racial and national divisions. In the New Testament the nomenclature follows this Roman arrangement.

a. THE PROVINCES : 1. *Cilicia.*—This province, level towards the sea, and mountainous on the north and the west, adjoined Syria, and its capital city was *Tarsus,* St. Paul's birthplace, on the banks of the Cydnus, a place of consequence under the Romans for its commerce and the cultivation of Greek learning.

2. *Cappadocia.*—This district lay to the north-east of Cilicia, beyond the sphere of St. Paul's labours. Pilgrims from it were present at Jerusalem on the day of Pentecost (Acts ii. 9), and St. Peter addresses his first epistle to Jews of the Dispersion scattered throughout the same region.

3. *Pamphylia.*—This province lay on the coast west of Cilicia, and contained the two cities first visited by Paul and Barnabas on their entrance into Asia Minor—*Perga,* on the river Cestius, where John Mark left them, a city celebrated for the worship of Artemis ; and *Attalia,* the chief seaport.

4. *Lycia* lay south of Caria, and its chief towns were *Myra,* near the sea (Acts xxvii. 5), and *Patara,* a seaport on the west (Acts xxi. 1).

5. *Galatia.*—This was a large province extending from Paphlagonia in the north to Pisidia in the south. It included several smaller divisions —(1.) Paphlagonia, not mentioned in Scripture. (2.) Galatia proper, inhabited by people of Gallic descent, the eastern outpost of some ancient immigration from Western Europe. (3.) Phrygian Galatia, including Iconium, Derbe, and Lystra. (4.) Taurus. (5.) Pisidia, which formed part of the great table-land of Asia Minor, and lay north of Pamphylia. It was approached by steep rugged passes infested by robbers, and its capital city was called *Antioch,* which in St. Paul's time was a Roman colony ; there, by his reception of the Gentiles, the apostle first provoked the violent hostility of the Jews. (6.) Isaurica. Prof. Ramsay has shown that when St. Paul refers to Galatia and the Galatians he means the large Roman province and its inhabitants, and not the people of Galatia proper. Thus it becomes most probable that the people addressed in the Epistle to the Galatians were the members of the churches he had founded in Antioch, Iconium, Lystra, and Derbe. Lycaonia (Acts xiv. 6) is an ethnological, not a topographical name.

6. *Asia.*—This province includes several divisions in the west of Asia Minor. (1.) Phrygia. This district formed somewhat vaguely the western section of the central region of Asia Minor, and was not a political division in the time of the Apostles, but only an ethnological one, *i.e.,* the region of a certain race. It contained the cities of *Colosse, Laodicea,* and *Hierapolis,* all three on the basin of the Meander, and near each other. (2.) Mysia, which lay west of Bithynia and Phrygia, and contained, besides its capital *Pergamos,* the small towns of *Assos* and *Adramythium,* as well as the world-famous district of *Troas. Pergamos* was at one time the seat of a powerful dynasty, and a centre of great wealth and luxury, and at length of pagan profligacy. (3.) Asia proper. This is part of what was also known as Lydia, and lay to the south of Mysia, and contained five of the seven churches addressed in the Revelation, namely, *Ephesus,*

Philadelphia, Sardis, Smyrna, and *Thyatira. Ephesus* was the chief city, not only of the district, but of the western region of Asia Minor ; it stood on the river Cayster, not far from the sea. It was famous for its wealth, its temple of Diana, or rather Artemis, and its connection with early Christianity ; it is now a ruin. *Sardis,* now also a ruin, was the ancient capital. *Smyrna* is on the coast, still a flourishing city and an important seaport. *Thyatira* lies north-east of Smyrna, and its inhabitants were famous for their skill in dyeing cloth. (4.) Caria lay to the south of Lydia, and formed the south-west corner of Asia Minor. The places in Caria mentioned in the New Testament were *Miletus,* an ancient and important town, which stood near the mouth of the Meander, 50 miles from Ephesus ; and *Cnidus,* a seaport on the point of the promontory of Triopium.

7. *Bithynia* lay west of Paphlagonia, and was the region which St. Paul was about to enter when he was summoned to preach the gospel in Europe. There appear to have been Christians here, probably of Jewish descent, when Peter wrote his first epistle. Nicæa and Chalcedon, where œcumenical councils were held, were in this district.

8. *Pontus.*—Pontus lay between Cappadocia and the Euxine, and is mentioned in the New Testament in connection with the former (which see).

b. THE ISLANDS.—The principal islands connected with Asia Minor were Cyprus, Crete, Clauda, Rhodes, Cos, Patmos, Samos, Chios, and Lesbos.

1. *Cyprus,* believed to be the same as *Chittim,* peopled originally by Phœnicians and at length by Greeks, is an island of the Mediterranean nearly as large as Palestine, situated to the south of Cilicia and the north-west of Syria. *Salamis* at the east and *Paphos* at the west end of the island, the former being the ancient capital and the latter the residence of the Roman governor, were visited by St. Paul and Barnabas in their first missionary tour (Acts xiii.).

2. *Crete* is a narrow island of hills and valleys 140 miles in length, which extends across the opening to the Archipelago, and it played an important part in the early history of Greece. St. Paul coasted along it on his voyage to Rome, touching at a roadstead in it called *Fair Havens.* It was the scene of Titus' labours.

3. *Clauda.*—A small island to the south of Crete, under the lee of which the ship in which St. Paul sailed to Rome found shelter from the gale which threatened to drive it on the African quicksands.

4. *Rhodes.*—An island 36 miles long, which was visited by St. Paul on his return to Syria from his third missionary tour, stood close to the south-western extremity of Asia Minor. It was famous in ancient and mediæval history.

5. *Cos* occupied the entrance to the Archipelago from the east, and St. Paul spent a night in it on his return from his third missionary tour after sailing from Miletus and before he reached Rhodes. It was celebrated for its wines, its light woven fabrics, and its medical school.

6. *Patmos,* the place of St. John's banishment and the scene of his visions, is a small, desolate, rocky island of the Ægean, some 15 miles in circumference west of Miletus.

7. *Samos* is an island of the Ægean, off the coast of Lydia, about 90 miles in circumference. It was the birthplace of Pythagoras, and St. Paul passed it on his voyage from Assos to Miletus.

8. *Chios* lay north of Samos, and is about the same size. St. Paul passed it on his last voyage from Troas to Jerusalem (Acts xx. 15).

9. *Lesbos* lay north of Chios, and its capital was *Mitylene*, at which St. Paul touched on his journey from Macedonia to Jerusalem (Acts xx. 14).

Assyria.—This country, said to have been named after Asshur, the son of Shem, originally lay wholly to the east of the Tigris and north of Babylonia, but gradually became extended so as to touch Armenia on the north, Mesopotamia, some think the Euphrates, on the west, the country about Bagdad on the south, and the Kurdistan mountains on the east. Its principal towns mentioned in the Bible were Nineveh, Rehoboth, Calah, and Resen. *Nineveh*, the capital, named after the Accadian god "Nin," stood from an obscure antiquity on the left bank of the Tigris till it was destroyed by the Medes and Babylonians (607 B.C.). It was "an exceeding great city," and was said to have been 60 miles in circumference, and surrounded by walls which were 100 feet high, the breadth of three chariots in width, and defended by 1500 towers, each 200 feet in height. Its ruins have of late years been discovered, and in part disinterred. The circuit of the ruined walls is found to be 7½ miles.

Babylonia.—This country, called also Chaldæa, though the latter name properly applies only to its southern portion, consists of a vast alluvial plain formed by the deposits of the Euphrates and the Tigris 400 miles along the rivers and 100 miles in width, and is bounded on the north by Mesopotamia, on the east by the Tigris, on the south by the Persian Gulf, and on the west by the Arabian Desert. The plains of *Shinar* and *Dura* formed parts of it, if they were not rather co-extensive with it—the same place under other names. *Ur of the Chaldees* has been identified as the *Uru* of the cuneiform inscriptions at Mugheir, situated west of the Euphrates, in Chaldæa proper, formerly near the Persian Gulf, now 150 miles from the sea. But Kittel argues against this identification, because he thinks Mugheir lies too far south. *Babylon*, the capital, though it existed before, being founded by Nimrod, first rose into prominence after the fall of Nineveh, and, when built and adorned by Nebuchadnezzar, it was one of the wonders of the world. It was in the form of a square, the sides of which were said to be 14 miles long, and the interior containing gardens parallel with the sides. It abounded in palaces and temples, and had hanging gardens arranged in terraces over each other. Here the Jews were captives for seventy years, till the city was taken by Cyrus and the seat of government transferred to Susa. Babylon is now in ruins, but among these have been found inscriptions confirmatory of the Scripture narratives and prophecies. The remains of the palace of Nebuchadnezzar have been exhumed, and seem to consist of pale yellow brick in fine cement. An inscription describing the conquest of Babylon by Cyrus in the time of Nabonidus was only published in 1882.

Chaldæa.—See BABYLONIA.

Cush.—See ETHIOPIA.

Dalmatia.—A Roman province on the east of the Adriatic, inhabited by tribes of a wild and roaming character, and visited by Titus.

Edom.—A region of considerable fertility and wealth, now desolate, peopled chiefly by the descendants of Esau. It lay south of Moab and Judæa, and was bounded by (and ultimately included) Arabia Felix on the east, and by the Red Sea on the west. Originally it was occupied by the Horites (cave-dwellers). It was ruled at various times by "dukes," and its tribes cherished a bitter hostility to the Jews. Here were *Mount Seir*, a rocky range, 20 miles broad, traversed by wadies once fertile and well-peopled, and running north to the east of the valley along which the Israelites marched; *Mount Hor*, a huge mountain of bare rock, full of chasms, on the top of which Aaron died and was buried; *Bozrah*, the ancient capital, southeast of the Dead Sea; *Elath*, a seaport at the head of the Gulf of Akabah; *Eziongeber*, an encampment of Israel, near Elah, where Solomon had a naval station; *Kadesh-Barnea*, a fertile oasis near a perennial spring not far from Mount Hor, whence the spies were sent, and the people driven back to wander forty years in the desert for their murmuring; *Petra*, or *Selah*, the now desolate rock-capital of Edom; *Teman*, now the village of Maan, in the south-east.

Egypt.—A country, called *Mizraim* in Scripture, consisting of the lower part of the Nile valley and its delta, and bounded on the north by the Mediterranean, on the east by Arabia and the Red Sea, on the south by Ethiopia, and on the west by Lybia. It is about 500 miles in length. It has been literally made by the soil which the river has deposited from time immemorial, and which extends only to a few miles east and west of its bed, till it expands into the broad delta in the north. In ancient times it was divided into Upper, Middle, and Lower Egypt. The following of its chief towns and regions are mentioned in Scripture:—*Alexandria*, in Lower Egypt, the Greek capital, founded by Alexander the Great, B.C. 332. It became an important seat of Greek learning and centre of influence in the development of later Judaism and early Christianity. *Goshen*, in a fertile district, along a branch of the Nile, in the eastern part of the delta of Lower Egypt. *Memphis*, called in the Hebrew Bible *Noph* (Isa. xix. 13) and *Moph* (Hos. ix. 6), the capital of the early kings of Lower Egypt, a few miles above Cairo, and in the neighbourhood of the Pyramids. *On*, called also *Heliopolis*, as well as *Aven* and *Bethshemish*—"house of the sun"—a city a few miles north-east of Cairo. *Pi-beseth*, or *Bubastis* (Ezek. xxx. 17), the city of the lion-headed goddess Bast, was near the modern Zagazig, 40 miles from Memphis. *Pithom* and *Rameses*, the treasure cities built by the Israelites in Lower Egypt. Quite recently Pithom was discovered by M. Naville, who has shown that it was the same place as Succoth, and was situated at *Tel-el-Maskhûtah*, where the first English victory was gained in 1882. Rameses has not been identified for certain; but it seems probable that the site of this city is close to *Tel-el-Kebir*. Thus the line of the Exodus is traced in the direction of Ismailia, up to which spot the Red Sea then reached. *Sin*, a military stronghold on the north-east of Lower Egypt. *Tahepanes*, a frontier city in the east part of Lower Egypt, now a desolate mound near *Kantarah*, on the Suez Canal; it was colonised by Jews after the capture of Jerusalem. *Thebes*, called *No-Amon*, the capital of Upper Egypt, fabled to have had a population of seven millions. *Zoan*, called *Tanis* by the Greeks, on the east branch of the Nile in Lower Egypt, the capital of the Hyksos and the later Pharaohs, the scene of the Divine judgments on behalf of Israel. The ruins still remain, half covered by sand, among the desolate marshes by Lake Menzaleh.

Elam.—See SUSIANA.

Ethiopia.—This region, called also Cush, lay to the south of Egypt, and it appears to have been nearly co-extensive with Nubia and Abyssinia. *Sheba*, which Josephus assigns to this region, appears to have been in Southern Arabia, along the opposite shore of the Red Sea. Possibly the name Ethiopia was given to the country of the south on both sides of the Red Sea—the east as well as the west.

Gog and Magog.—These names seem to denote respectively the Lydians and the land of Lydia as lying midway between Greece and the East.

Idumæa.—See EDOM, for which it is the Greek equivalent.

Illyricum.—A region on the east of the Adriatic.

Italy.—This country first comes into Scripture history mainly in connection with St. Paul's visit to Rome. The places mentioned in that relation were Rome itself, Appii Forum, the Three Taverns, Puteoli, and Rhegium. *Rome*, the city of the seven hills, seated on the Tiber, was the mistress of the world and the seat of world-empire in the days of Christ and at the founding of the Church. *Appii Forum* was on the Appian Way, some 43 miles south of Rome; here the apostle was met and escorted by the Roman Christians on his way to the city. *The Three Taverns* stood on the same road 10 miles nearer Rome. *Puteoli*, a landing-place for travellers to Rome, was upon the coast of the Bay of Naples. *Rhegium* was the first town St. Paul visited in Italy, and was situated on the Straits of Messina. *Melita*, where he was shipwrecked, is the island of Malta, to the south of Italy. *Sicily* is only referred to in Scripture as containing *Syracuse*, a city on its east coast, where St. Paul landed and remained three days on his way to Rome.

Kedar.—This name is applied to Arabia or a part of it.

Libya.—This region lay west of Egypt on the borders of the Mediterranean, but the name is sometimes given to the whole of Africa. Its most famous city, the chief of five, was *Cyrene*, where a number of Jews resided at the commencement of the Christian era; Simon, who was compelled to carry Christ's cross, belonged to this city.

Macedonia.—This region, where Christianity was first preached in Europe by St. Paul, was the northern division of Greece, and a Roman province in the days of Christ. The chief towns in it connected with the planting of the gospel were Philippi, Thessalonica, and Berea. *Philippi*, a Roman colony, and the seat of a prosperous Christian church, named after Philip of Macedon, was the chief city of the province, and stood on the borders of Thrace. *Thessalonica* was a busy seaport south of Philippi, and a centre of great importance in the founding of the Church. *Berea* is situated on the eastern slope of Mount Olympus.

Media.—This kingdom, which was of great antiquity, lay on the south-west of the Caspian Sea, on the east of the Zagros Mountains, and comprised part of the north and nearly all the north-west of modern Persia, into which it eventually merged. Its principal city was *Ecbatana*, presumed to be the same as *Achmetha* (Ezra vi. 2).

Meshech.—The territory of a Caucasian tribe on the shore of the Black Sea.

Mesopotamia.—This name, which means "between the rivers," is applied to a district lying to the south of Armenia, and bounded on the east by the Tigris and on the west and south-west by the Euphrates, and is called in Hebrew *Aram-naharaim*, or the Aram, *i.e.*, Syria, of the two rivers, a part of which is designated Padan-aram, or the Plain of Aram. It contains three or four places of note mentioned in the Bible—perhaps *Haran*, or *Charran*, some 20 miles south, where Abraham resided for a time after he left Ur, and where Nahor's family continued to dwell after his brother removed to Canaan; the river *Chebar*, a tributary of the Euphrates, where Ezekiel saw his vision (Ezek. i. 3, iii. 15, 23, x. 15, 22); and *Carchemish*, a strongly fortified city, at the confluence of the Chebar and the Euphrates, and in very early times a famous Hittite city.

Mizraim.—See EGYPT.

Ophir.—The application of this name, which is always associated with gold, is very uncertain, but it is most generally believed to have denoted a place towards India, probably east of the mouth of the Persian Gulf.

Persia.—Persia proper was a small territory which at length became the nucleus of a great empire, extending "from India even to Ethiopia," being bounded by Carmania on the east, Media on the north, Elam on the west, and the Persian Gulf on the south. It has been described as level and fertile in the centre, mountainous in the north, and sandy towards the shore.

Pethor.—The home of Balaam, on the Euphrates.

Philistia.—This district consisted of a plain which extended along the shore on the south-west of Palestine from Joppa to the desert, some 40 miles long by 15 miles broad. In Bible times it was, as it still is, of great fertility. Though originally allotted to the tribes of Dan, Judah, and Simeon, it was never possessed by them. The principal towns, described elsewhere (chap. xli.), were Ashdod, Askelon, Ekron, Gath, and Gaza, and in early times Gerar.

Phœnicia.—This celebrated region was limited to a narrow strip of territory on the north-west of Palestine between Lebanon and the sea. Its towns are elsewhere referred to (chap. xli.).

Phut.—A name for Lybia.

Seir, Mount.—See EDOM.

Susiana or Elam.—This region, the country of Chedor-laomer, lay to the south of Media and the east of the Tigris, and became subject first to Babylon and then to Persia. Its capital was *Shusan* or *Susa*, afterwards the capital of the Medes and Persians. It stood near the river Ulai, on the banks of which Daniel had divine revelations (Dan. viii. 2, 16).

Syria.—The name Syria, called Aram, or the Highlands, in Hebrew, is applied in Scripture to a region of vague extent stretching away from the north and south-east of Galilee included between the Mediterranean on the west and the Euphrates on the east, and of which *Damascus*

was the capital. Damascus, said to be the oldest city in the world, having existed 4000 years, is situated on the edge of a fertile plain watered by a river, called in Scripture Abana, and its tributary the Pharpar, which rises on the east side of Mount Hermon. It was the capital of the kings of Syria, and its neighbourhood was the scene of the conversion of St. Paul. Syria contained several states and cities, besides Damascus, referred to in Scripture ; such as *Aram-Maacha*, a small state at the foot of Mount Hermon, the chief town in which was *Abel Beth-Maachah ; Aram-Rehob*, a small state near the town of Dan ; *Arphad*, another associated with Hamath ; *Hamath* itself, between Lebanon and Antilebanon, of which *Riblah* was one of the towns, and *Baal-Gad* another ; *Tadmor*, or *Palmyra*, built by Solomon in the desert for commercial purposes ; *Antioch*, on the Orontes, 16 miles from the sea, where the disciples were first called Christians, and *Seleucia*, its seaport.

Tarshish.—(1.) This place, called Tartessus by the Greeks, was situated at the western limits of the Mediterranean, not far from Gibraltar. From an early date it was frequented by the merchants of the Phœnicians. (2.) 2 Chron. ix. 21 seems to point to another Tarshish in Yemen.

See Palmer, *The Desert of the Exodus ;* Palgrave, *Journey to Arabia ;* Ramsay, *Historical Geography of Asia Minor*, and *The Church in the Roman Empire ;* Geo. Smith, *Assyrian Discoveries ;* Layard, *Nineveh and Babylon ;* Ebers, *Egypt ;* Dawson, *Egypt and Syria.*

THE OLD TESTAMENT AND THE MONUMENTS.

MODERN discovery and research have thrown abundant and unexpected light upon the Old Testament, and have verified the historical accuracy of many parts of it. These confirmations of Scripture have been more especially furnished by the monuments of Babylonia, Assyria, and Egypt, which are contemporaneous with the events they record. It will be convenient to give some account of them under the several heads of (1) the Patriarchal Age, including the earlier chapters of Genesis, (2) the Exodus, (3) the Israelitish occupation of Palestine, and (4) the Exile.

1. **The Patriarchal Age.**—Among the cuneiform clay tablets or books of Babylonia and Assyria have been found accounts of the Creation, some of which are earlier than the time of Abraham. One of these accounts—which is, however, probably of a much later date, at all events in its present form—resembles in some respects the account of the Creation in the first chapter of Genesis. In the first tablet (or book) a description is given of the creation of the world out of the watery abyss of primeval chaos, in the fifth of the appointment of the heavenly bodies to rule the day and the night, and in the sixth of the creation of the animals. Between the first and the fifth is a long account of the war between Bel-Merodach, the Sun-god, and Tiamat (the Hebrew *tehôm* or "deep"), the dragon of darkness, who with her demoniac allies is finally overthrown. One half of her is made into the sky with the waters above the firmament, the other half into "the great deep," the origin of all springs and rivers.

No parallel to the Biblical account of Paradise has yet been found, but Eden is the Edin or "plain" of Babylonia, a name given to that country in the early cuneiform inscriptions, and Hiddekel (Gen. ii. 14) is Idikla, the primitive name of the Tigris. Inscriptions refer to the "sacred tree" which grew near Eridu, "the good city" (now Abu Shahrein), which once stood on the shore of the Persian Gulf in the south of Babylonia. The Biblical account of the Deluge presents a remarkable likeness to the Chaldæan account discovered by Mr. George Smith. This account was embodied in an epic poem which was composed before 2000 B.C., and its likeness to the Biblical narrative extends even to words and phrases. It states that all mankind were destroyed by the flood on account of their sins, with the exception of the few who, with certain animals, found refuge in the ship of Xisuthros, the Chaldæan Noah; that the flood raged for seven days; that three birds, a dove, a swallow, and a raven, were sent out to see if the earth were dry, the raven alone not returning to the ship; and that when Xisuthros had

landed on the top of Mount Nizir to the northeast of Assyria and had offered sacrifice, a rainbow was "lifted up" over it in token of its acceptance.

Much light has been cast by the monuments on the tenth chapter of Genesis. Gomer is the Gimirrâ of the Assyrians, the Cimmerians of Greek history; the names of Casluhim and Caphtorim have been found in an Egyptian text at Kom Ombo; and Heth or the Hittites have proved to be an important people with Mongoloid features, and a peculiar art and system of writing, who descended from the mountains of the Taurus, overrunning Syria and establishing themselves in Kadesh on the Orontes, "in the land of the Amorites." Here they contended on equal terms with the Egyptian kings of the nineteenth dynasty. Their power declined before the time of David, and the capture of Carchemish by the Assyrians in 717 B.C. completed their overthrow.

The ruins of Ur, where Abraham was born, have been discovered at Mugheir in Babylonia, on the western side of the Euphrates. It was famous for its temple of the Moon-god, like Haran, where another temple of the Moon-god was built by the Babylonians. The campaign of Chedor-laomer (Gen. xiv.) has been fully vindicated by the inscriptions. Long before the days of Abraham the Babylonian kings, Sargon of Accad and his son, had conquered Palestine, and even marched to Sinai, and *cir.* 2200 B.C. a Babylonian king still claimed rule in "the land of the Amorites." The cuneiform tablets found at Tel-el-Amarna in Upper Egypt show that the Babylonian language and script were known throughout Western Asia, and prove how long and great must have been the influence of Babylonia in Canaan. In the age of Abraham Babylonia was divided into more than one state under the suzerainty of Elam, and one of these states, Larsa, was ruled by Eri-aku, the Arioch of Genesis, who calls himself the son of Kudur-Mabug, "the father of the Amorite-land." Mabug was the name of an Elamite deity like Lagamar, whose name enters into that of Chedor-laomer (Kudur-Lagamar). Mr. Pinches has lately found the names of Kudur-Lagamar, "the King of Elam," and Tudkhula or Tid'al in connection with Eri-Aku.

2. **The Exodus.**—The site of Pithom (Pa-Tum) has been excavated by Mr. Naville, who has also identified the land of Goshen (Kosem in Egyptian) between Zagazig and Tel-el-Kebîr. As the inscriptions found at Pithom show that Pithom was built by Ramses II. of the nineteenth Egyptian dynasty (1348-1281 B.C.), Ramses II., whose mummy is now in the Museum at Cairo, must have been the Pharaoh of the Oppression.

The cuneiform tablets of Tel-el-Amarna, which consist mainly of letters and despatches to the Pharaoh from the kings of Babylonia, Assyria, and Mesopotamia, and the Egyptian governors of Palestine, indicate that "the new king" of Exod. i. 8 was the founder of the nineteenth dynasty. They further prove that the Mosaic age was one of high literary activity throughout the ancient East. The Pharaoh of the Exodus would have been either Meneptah or Seti II., the successors of Ramses II. It may be noted that Pharaoh is a title, in Egyptian Per-âa, signifying "the great house" or "palace." The Israelitish conquest of Canaan must have been effected after the beginning of the reign of Ramses III. of the twentieth dynasty, since that monarch overran the south of Palestine. Egypt had just been attacked by northern tribes, in whose train had come the king of Aram-Naharaim, called Mitanni by its inhabitants. This throws light on Judges iii. 8. In an inscription of Meneptah, discovered by Professor Petrie in 1896, mention is made of "the Israelites."

3. **The Settlement in Palestine.**—Shishak (1 Kings xiv. 25) was the founder of the twenty-second Egyptian dynasty, and the names of the places he captured in Judah (and also in the south of Israel) are engraved on the wall of the temple of Karnak (Thebes) in Upper Egypt. His great-grandson, Osorkon II., who states that he had been victorious in Syria, is probably the Zerah of 2 Chron. xiv. 9. The famous "Moabite Stone" of King Mesha, son of Chemosh-melech, discovered on the site of Dibon in 1868, brings us to the reign of Ahab (2 Kings iii. 4). It is one of the oldest examples of alphabetic writing, the letters resembling those used at the time by the Israelites. It shows that the Moabite language was very closely allied to Hebrew. In it Mesha describes the victories he had gained over Israel, and ascribes them to his god Chemosh. Quite as interesting as the Moabite Stone is the early Jewish inscription, probably of the time of Hezekiah, which was found in 1880 in the subterranean tunnel that conveys the water of the Virgin's Spring—the only natural spring in or about Jerusalem—to the Pool of Siloam. The inscription states that the tunnel of 1708 feet in length was begun simultaneously at the two ends of the cliff, and that the workmen met within a few feet of one another in the middle.

With the reign of Ahab, Assyria began to intervene in the affairs of Palestine, and the monuments enable us to correct the chronology of the later kings of Judah and Israel, so long the despair of historians. In 853 B.C. Shalmaneser II. of Assyria defeated at Karkar a league formed by Hamath, Arvad, Ammon, and other states, under the leadership of Hadad-ezer of Damascus (the Ben-hadad of the Old Testament), to which "Ahab of Israel" contributed 2000 chariots and 10,000 men. In 840 B.C. Hazael, the successor of Hadad-ezer, was again defeated and driven into Damascus, and Jehu (Yahua) of Samaria, like the Phœnician cities, sent tribute to the Assyrian king. Some forty years later another Assyrian king captured Damascus, making its king, Marih, tributary. He also claims the conquest of Samaria and Palastu or Philistia. In 745 B.C. the older Assyrian dynasty came to an end, and the throne was seized by

Pulu (Pul), who was proclaimed king on the 13th of Iyyar (April) under the name of Tiglath-pileser III. He at once set about establishing an Assyrian empire over the whole of Western Asia. A highly-trained and disciplined standing army was formed, and a bureaucracy established, centralised in the person of the monarch, who appointed the numerous civil and military officers. Conquered provinces and cities were placed under Assyrian governors, and their principal inhabitants transported to another part of the empire. In 738 B.C. Hamath, which had been assisted by Azariah of Judah, was annexed, and the princes of the west, including Rezon of Damascus and Menahem of Samaria, offered homage (2 Kings xv. 19). Four years latter Ahaz (termed Jehoahaz in the inscriptions) called in the aid of Tiglath-pileser against Rezon (Rezin in the Old Testament) and Pekah. In 732 B.C. Damascus was taken and made an Assyrian city and Rezon was slain (2 Kings xvi. 9). Hosea had already been appointed king of Samaria in place of Pekah. In December 727 B.C. Tiglath-pileser died, and the crown was usurped by Ululâ, who took the name of Shalmaneser IV. (2 Kings xvii. 3). While besieging Samaria he died, December 722 B.C., and another usurper, Sargon, became king. Sargon took Samaria along with fifty chariots, carried the upper and military classes, 27,280 persons in all, into captivity, and placed the city under an Assyrian prefect. Sargon was an able general, and reduced the whole of Western Asia to subjection. Babylonia had been conquered by Tiglath-pileser III. in 727 B.C., but on the death of Shalmaneser it had recovered its independence under Merodach-baladan, the chief of the Kaldâ or Chaldæans, who lived in the marshes at the mouth of the Euphrates. In 711 B.C. Merodach-baladan formed a league against the common foe with Judah, Edom, Moab, and Egypt (Isa. xxxix.); Ashdod, where an usurper Yavan, "the Greek," was reigning, being the centre of disaffection in the West. Ashdod, however, was captured by the Tartan (Ass. Turtannu) or "commander-in-chief" (Isa. xx. 1), and in 709 Merodach-baladan was driven out of Babylonia.

Sargon was murdered by a soldier in 705 B.C., and succeeded by his son Sennacherib on the 12th of Ab or July. Merodach-baladan ventured again into Babylonia, but was soon forced to return to the marshes, and in 701 B.C. Sennacherib invaded Palestine, where Hezekiah had revolted, in reliance on the help of Egypt. Phœnicia, Ammon, Moab and Edom submitted to the invader. A new king was set over Ashkelon, and Hezekiah was compelled to restore to Ekron its prince, whom he had imprisoned in Jerusalem. Tirhakah, the Ethiopian king of Egypt, was defeated at Eltekeh, and Hezekiah vainly tried to appease Sennacherib by rich and numerous gifts. The Assyrians, however, devastated Judah, destroyed its cities, including Lachish, the capture of which is represented on a monument now in the British Museum, and carried into captivity 200,150 persons. Jerusalem was next besieged, but the Assyrian army perished before it, and Sennacherib was compelled to retreat homeward (2 Kings xix. 35, 36). The following year saw him in Babylonia, where he drove Merodach-baladan out of the marshes, and forced him to fly to the opposite coast of the Persian Gulf. Sennacherib returned no more to the West, and on the 20th of Tebet, or December 681 B.C., he was murdered by two of his sons. The Assyrian army was at the time carrying on war against Ararat or Armenia, under the command of another son, Esar-haddon, and for forty-two days the conspirators had possession of Nineveh. Then they fled to Erimenas, king of Ararat (2 King xix. 37), and a decisive battle was fought on the 12th of Iyyar (April) near Malatiyeh, which resulted in the victory of Esar-haddon. He was proclaimed king, and on the 8th of Sivan (May) was crowned at Nineveh.

Esar-haddon restored Babylon, which had been rased to the ground by his father (in 689 B.C.), and conquered Egypt. Manasseh of Judah appears as one of his tributaries. He died on the 10th of Marchesvan (October) 668 B.C., while on the way to Egypt, and was succeeded by his son Assur-bani-pal, who is possibly the Asnapper of Ezra iv. 10. His destruction of "No of Amon," that is Thebes in Upper Egypt, is alluded to in Nah. iii. 8. He also conquered Elam, the last civilised power which resisted Assyria. In 606 B.C., however, Nineveh and the Assyrian empire fell together, and the Babylonian empire of Nebuchadrezzar rose upon its ruins. The buildings of Nebuchadrezzar at Babylon made it the wonder of the world. In 568 B.C. he attacked Egypt (Jer. xliii. 10-13), "Phut of the Ionians" being mentioned in connection with the campaign.

The last king of the Babylonian empire was Nabonidos, the son of Nebo-balasu-ikbi (556-538 B.C.). The inscriptions of this king and of his conqueror Cyrus have given us a detailed account of the fall of the Babylonian empire.

Cyrus, though of Persian descent, was king of Anzan in Elam, which had been conquered by his great-grandfather, and he did not become king of Persia till 548 B.C., the year after his conquest of Ecbatana in Media (cf. Isa. xxi. 2). In 538 B.C. he entered Babylonia, where the population in the south had revolted, Nabonidos having made himself unpopular by endeavouring to abolish the local cults and centralise Babylonian religion in Babylon. The Babylonian army was defeated at Opis in the northern part of the country, and a few days later (on the 14th of Tammuz or June) Sippara surrendered. Gobryas, the governor of Kurdistan, was then sent against Babylon, which opened its gates on the 16th of Tammuz "without fighting," and Nabonidos, who had concealed himself, was taken prisoner. On the 3rd of Marchesvan (October) Cyrus arrived at Babylon and proclaimed a general amnesty, which was communicated by Gobryas to "all the province of Babylon," of which he had been made governor. Soon afterwards the wife of Nabonidos died, and Cambyses, the son of Cyrus, conducted the funeral. Cyrus had already been crowned "King of Babylon," and along with his son offered sacrifices to ten times the usual amount to the Babylonian gods Bel-Merodach and Nebo. He also issued an edict allowing the foreign exiles in Babylonia to return to their homes, together with the statues of their deities. Belshazzar, the son of Nabonidos, is named in the inscriptions, and he was probably "the king's son" who commanded the Babylonian army at Sippara. He is last mentioned as having paid the tithe due from his sister to the temple of the Sun-god at Sippara on the 5th of Ab (July) 538 B.C.

THE

SACRED BOOKS OF NON-CHRISTIAN RELIGIONS.

ALL the religions of civilised nations are represented by sacred books, most of which are regarded by their adherents as more or less inspired and of corresponding divine authority. In some cases these books are preserved in a definite canon ; in others they shade off by imperceptible degrees into later and less authoritative works, the universal tendency being to give the highest rank to what are regarded as the oldest writings. The science of comparative religion has taught us to classify the several cults of the world according to the ethnical affinities of the people among whom they had their origin and development. With the exception of the three great missionary faiths, Christianity, Mohammedanism, and Buddhism, all the religions of the world admit of a geographical and national definition ; and in every case the most scientific as well as the simplest method of procedure will be to arrange the sacred books of the world according to the racial divisions of the peoples they severally represent.

1. **Egyptian.**—The one supremely sacred book of ancient Egypt is that known among Egyptologists as *The Book of the Dead*, the original title of which is *Per-em-hru, i.e.*, "Coming forth by day." The oldest version of this work was discovered by M. Maspero during his explorations of the pyramids of Sakkara in 1880–84, in the form of inscriptions on the tombs of Unas of the fifth dynasty, and Pepi I., Pepi II., Teta, and Mer-en-ra of the sixth dynasty. These inscriptions cannot be later than 3500 B.C., and therefore it is clear the work itself must be still more ancient, for time must be allowed for the collection of its contents and the attainment of its position of authority. Although it would appear from later inscriptions that the pyramid texts continued in use as recently as A.D. 200, a fresh collection of texts was made about 1700 B.C., on the establishment of the eighteenth dynasty and the rising of the Theban hierarchy of the temple of Amen at Thebes. In the year 1888 the trustees of the British Museum were fortunate enough to secure a magnificent papyrus roll of this text, some seventy-eight feet long, carefully written and richly illustrated. Dr. Budge has published a translation of this valuable manuscript. About 600 B.C., when the capital was transferred to Sais in Lower Egypt, a still later edition of the Book of the Dead was drawn up by the priests of the temple of Neith, and it was from the Turin papyrus of this version, which was regarded as the standard text until recent discoveries brought the much more ancient text to light, that Birch's translation was made (1867). We are now in a much better position for understanding the original character of this wonderful book.

The work consists of a series of separate religious compositions ; and the successive editions that have now come to light make it evident that it is a gradual accretion, additions having been made from time to time. Primarily it is a ritual for the dead, that is to say, it is supposed to be composed for the use of the dead. This is how it came to be found inscribed on the interior walls of tombs, or in papyrus form buried with mummies in their sarcophagi. Its object is to guide the dead to the attainment of immortality. To this end it is based on the myth of Osiris. The life and death and subsequent revival of Osiris are patterns of the experience men must pass through if they would follow the god on to his immortality. The aim of the dead man therefore must be to assimilate his experience to that of his great prototype. Various prayers and charms are supplied to enable him thus to identify himself with Osiris.

2. **Chinese.** — *a. Confucianism.* — The books now recognised as of highest authority in China are the 5 *King* and the 4 *Shoo.* "King" means the adjustment of the threads of a web, and is used to represent that which is regulative, *i.e.*, canonical ; "Shoo" simply means writing, *i.e.*, scripture, or books, *i.e.*, Bible. The authorship or compilation of the 5 King is popularly ascribed to Confucius, who was born in the year 551 B.C. ; but Dr. Legge has shown that with respect to most of this literature Confucius is "transmitter, not creator." The 5 King consist of the following books :—(1) *Yih*, "The Book of Changes," a work to the study of which Confucius is said to have devoted fifty years, adding appendices of his own. The date of its origin must be earlier than 1143 B.C. It contains sixty-four short essays enigmatically and symbolically expressed, for the most part on moral, social, and political themes. A curious feature of this work is its system of lineal figures, each of these figures being representative of some idea which is discussed in the elucidation of the meaning of the lines. (2) *Shoo*, "The Book of History," which professes to give a historical record of the period from 2357 B.C. to 627 B.C. (3) *She*, "The Book of Poetry," a collection of various odes, some of them but indifferent, but others pronounced to be very graceful. (4) *Leki*, "The Record of Rites," dealing with rules of propriety and ceremonial usages. (5) *Chan Tsew*, "Spring and Autumn," a chronicle of events from 721 B.C.

to 480 B.C. which is held to be rightly ascribed to Confucius.

The 4 Shoo are the books of the four philosophers. (1) *Lun-Yu,* called by Dr. Legge "Confucian Analects," is chiefly occupied with the sayings of Confucius. (2) *Ta-Hëo,* or "Great Learning," is now generally attributed to Tsan Sin, a disciple of Confucius. (3) *Chung-Yung,* or "The Doctrine of the Mean," is ascribed to Kung Keih, a grandson of Confucius. (4) The works of Mencius coming later were slow in attaining a classical position, but they are now authoritative representatives of Confucianism. The whole of this literature is to be considered as moral rather than as religious. It is true we meet with the name of God in it as a relic of earlier ideas, but the worship which it sometimes encourages is ancestor worship. The moral tone of the teaching of Confucius is pure and lofty. Dr. Legge has not found a single impure expression in all the ancient literature of China, a fact in remarkable contrast with the character of the recent literature of the Celestial Empire, or indeed that of any other modern people.

b. Taouism.—Lao-tse, the founder of Taouism, was a contemporary of Confucius, a few years senior, and the young philosopher is said to have resorted to him for advice. While Confucianism may be described as the rationalistic Aristotelianism of China, Taouism may be called the Chinese Neo-Platonism. Lao-tse aimed at rendering man immortal by means of the contemplation of God and the repression of the bodily passions. His system degenerated into alchemy, divination, and the invocation of spirits. (1) The chief book of the sect is *Tao-tih-king,* or the "Book of Reason and Virtue," ascribed to the founder. Other books are (2) the *Kan-ying-peen,* or "Book of Rewards and Punishments," and (3) *Yin-chin-wan,* or "Book of Secret Blessings."

The third religion of China—Buddhism—is a foreign importation, and Chinese Buddhist writings are of late origin and secondary value.

3. **Aryan.**—*a. Hindu.*—All the Aryan religions —Indian, Persian, and European—like the languages in which they are embedded, have elements in common, and give evidence of a common origin. Among these, that represented by the ancient Sanskrit literature comes nearest to the primitive type, and here we have the most elementary form of those religious ideas which appear later in the myths and practices of the various Aryan races. The most ancient and sacred Sanskrit writings are described as Vedas, from a root that means knowledge; they are supposed to contain unwritten knowledge, the breath of Brahman, the self-existent one. They fall into three divisions—*Mantra,* hymns of prayer and praise; *Brahmana,* sacrificial precepts in the form of commentaries on the Vedic hymns; and *Aranyakas,* or "Forest Books," i.e., books which should be studied in the solitude of the forest, among which are the *Upanishads,* the philosophical writings of the early Hindus.

(1) The word *Mantra* signifies literally "the instrument for conveying thought;" but it is used to signify inspired speech or writing. The Mantras consist of four collections of hymns and chants called *Samhitas:*—The *Rig-veda,* or Veda of praise; the *Sama-veda,* or Veda of

chants and tunes; the *Yajur-veda,* or Veda of prayers; and the *Atharva-veda,* the Veda of the Atharvans. Of these four Vedas the three first are called the *trayi-vidya,* i.e., the three-fold science; the fourth, the *Atharva-veda,* is a later collection that came to be assigned to a fourth class of Brahmans, to whom at first no particular text-book was given. This deals in hymns and spells that reveal the dread of malevolent powers. Very different is the tone of the earlier Vedas, which are cheerful and sunny, and devoted to a free and joyous nature-worship. The most ancient and venerable collection is that of the Rig-veda, consisting of 1028 hymns, the greater part of which was put together about 1000 B.C., having come down from still more ancient times. Here we meet with the primitive gods of Aryan mythology—Indra, the rain-giving expanse (Jupiter Pluvius); Agni, fire (Latin, Ignis); Surya, the sun (Greek, Ἥλιος), which together constitute the Vedic chief triad. Secondary deities are Ushas, the goddess of dawn; Prithivi, the broad one, i.e., the earth; Varuna, heaven (Οὐρανός), the stern guardian of ordinances, &c. The other Mantras repeat many of the hymns contained in the Rig-veda. Thus the Yajur-veda borrows a number of these hymns, consisting as it does simply of hymns and texts arranged for sacrificial use. The Sama-veda also borrows from the primary collection of the Rig-veda, but it arranges its materials to suit the ceremonies of the cult of Soma, an intoxicating juice—the Indian Bacchus worship.

(2) The *Bramanas* are commentaries on the Samhitas regarded especially from a sacrificial point of view. Those on the two first collections of Samhitas are purely professional text-books for the use of the priests.

(3) The *Upanishads* have their roots in the Rig-veda, and are of various ages, the earliest dating from before B.C. 600. In these ancient writings of Hindu philosophy, while the forms of the Aryan mythology are respected, the universe is resolved into a system of idealistic pantheism. Thus the first Upanishad begins, "Let a man meditate on the syllable OM. For the Udgitra (a portion of the Sama-veda) is sung, beginning with OM. The essence of all things is the earth, the essence of the earth is water, the essence of water plants, the essence of plants man, the essence of man speech, the essence of speech the Rig-veda," &c.

Later writings, which do not claim to be inspired, are the *Grihya-sutras,* collections of aphoristic rules relating to domestic life; the *Dharma-sastras,* or law books, and chief among the latter the "Laws of Manu." These books were originally manuals written by the teachers of the Vedic schools for the guidance of their pupils; subsequently they were raised by the Brahmans to the rank of sacred law books. Manu is regarded as the progenitor of the human race, by nature as belonging both to gods and men, and he is treated as the founder of the social and moral order.

The Vedas represent the classic religion of India, and the study of them—written as they are in Sanskrit, a dead language—is necessarily confined to scholars. In the present day the popular worship is divided among the followers of Siva and the much larger number of devotees of Vishnu; Krishna, the human incarnation of

Vishnu, affording a centre of peculiar attraction. Consequently the later Hindu writings, those in which legends of Krishna are narrated, have come to assume the position of the chief religious books of India. The principal of these works is the *Maha-bharata*, an immense epic poem containing stores of Hindu traditions, legendary history, philosophy, ethics, &c. The most popular portion of this poem is the *Bhagavat-Gita*—"the lay of the adorable one." Another epic is the *Rama-ayana*, which recounts the heroic achievements of Rama, the seventh incarnation of Vishnu. The earliest version of both of these poems has been fixed at about 500 B.C. In this literature is developed the Hindu doctrine of *Trimurti*, the threefold manifestation of God—as Brahma, the creator; Vishnu, the preserver; and Siva, the destroyer and renovator.

Subsequent to these works are the *Puranas*, which are devoted to the exaltation of different divinities, and the *Tantras*, composed to give prominence to the female counterpart of Siva.

b. Buddhist. — Buddhism, the most widely-spread religion in the world, numbering some 500,000,000 adherents, springs from the life and teaching of the Hindu reformer Gautama, the son of the "king of Sakya," a tribe the headquarters of which was situated some 100 miles north-east of Benares. The date of Gautama's death is fixed by Max Müller at 477 B.C., instead of the year 543 B.C., as was previously supposed. The Buddhist writings fall into two classes—the books of southern Buddhism, and the books of northern Buddhism.

(1) *Southern Buddhism.*—The chief authoritative scriptures of Buddhism are the Pali scriptures from Ceylon. These consist of the *Pitakas*, or "collections," which are the canonical books of the southern Buddhists and Commentaries on them. The canon is said to have been determined about B.C. 250 at the council of Pataliputra on the Ganges. Buddhist tradition assigns it to a much earlier date, soon after the death of Buddha, but on no valid grounds. Gautama left no writings; but there is every reason to believe that the Pali scriptures contain a true version of his teachings. The following are the four great doctrines of Buddhism, probably as formulated by the founder:—(a) That misery always accompanies existence. (b) That all modes of existence result from passion or desire. (c) That there is no escape from existence except by the destruction of passion and desire. (d) That this end may be reached by following the fourfold way. The "Paths" of this way are marked by four stages—awakening, to see the evil of existence; the suppression of impure desires and revengeful feelings; the suppression of all other evil desires in the following consecutive order—ignorance, doubt, heresy, unkindness, vexation; finally nirvana. There is much difference of opinion as to the meaning of this word nirvana. By some it is taken as equivalent to extinction of being, by others as pointing to a state of perfect peace and restfulness. There can be no doubt that to the Buddhist, since all existence is an evil, the supreme end to be aimed at is a total cessation of being. But Mr. Rhys Davids has brought forward a number of passages from the Buddhist scriptures which seem to make it perfectly apparent that the restfulness which follows the suppression of all desire and passion is called nirvana. While, however, this is an end to be aimed at, it is not the supreme and final end. The pure Buddhist believes neither in God nor in spirit. Therefore death is the end of the individual existence. But the Hindu doctrine of the transmigration of souls, grafted on to man's natural instinct of immortality, is too strong for him. He cannot but believe in a future life. Here comes in the doctrine of karma. Although there is no soul to survive death, the effects of a man's life remain, and the total sum of these effects, the grand resultant of all his actions, desires, and passions, is called karma. This karma calls another life into existence, the new life being shaped by the old life as its direct fruit and therefore representing and perpetuating its character. But when nirvana is reached, the karma, which has been gradually attenuated by the suppression of desire, entirely vanishes, so that at death there is nothing to produce another life, and the sum of existence is diminished, the supreme end of existence is aimed at. Melancholy and even appalling as this view of life and its issues may appear to us, it indicates a great advance on Hinduism. While Gautama swept away the whole collection of ancient gods and their myths, he taught that salvation was not to be attained either by sacrifice or by asceticism. The evil was too internal for these outward remedies. People were to learn to master their own passions and practise kindness one to another. But there was no confession of man's weakness, and no saviour. The gospel of Buddhism only shows man how he is to save himself. Later Buddhism developed its own ritual, and converted Buddha into a god.

(2) *Northern Buddhism.*—This is the religion of an enormous number of people in China and Thibet, but its sacred literature is less known than the Pali scriptures, and of later date. The *Lalita Vistara*, partly in prose and partly in verse, is the standard Sanskrit account of the legendary life of the Buddha among the northern Buddhists. According to M. Foucaux, who translated it from Thibetan into French, this version was made by the sixth century A.D. The age of the original Sanskrit is uncertain. The "Book of the Great Renunciation," which gives the account of Gautama's abandonment of his princely home in pursuit of the higher life, has passed from the Sanskrit into Chinese. Most of the Chinese Buddhist works are of late date, and only represent the degeneration of the Buddhism.

c. Zoroastrian.—It has been commonly assumed that Zoroaster was a religious reformer who instigated a revolt against the idolatry prevalent among the people of north-west India, where the faith which bears his name originated; but it is now clear that, although some religious hero may have existed to give a historical starting-point to the traditions of the supposed founder, Zoroastrianism represents not a revolt from, but rather a gradual development of, the ancient Aryan faith. It spread westwards, and soon after the time of Cyrus became the religion of Persia. The Mohammedan conquests were followed by the conversion of the greater part of the population of Persia to the Muslim faith, and in the present day the Zoroastrian religion is only maintained by the small body of people known as Parsees, most of whom reside in India, whither their fathers had fled from Mohammedan persecutions. The *Zend-Avesta* is the Zoroastrian scriptures. It is a liturgical collection, and, as Mr. Darmesteter, its translator, remarks, "It bears more likeness to a prayer-book than to the Bible." As we have it in the present day it is a collection of fragments. It is divided into two parts. The first part, the Avesta proper, contains the Vendidad, a compilation of religious laws and mythical tales; the Visperad, a collection of litanies; and the Yasna, which is also composed in part of litanies, with the addition of five hymns, called Gathas, written in an older dialect than the general language of the Avesta. The second part, known as the *Khorda-Avesta*, or "Little Avesta," consists of short prayers for the faithful, to be recited at certain moments of the day, month, or year, and in presence of the different elements. While the more primitive parts of the Zend-Avesta come down from times before the rise of the Persian empire, the work was added to from time to time, and the whole completed some time before the fourth century A.D. In the development of Zoroastrianism from the original Aryan faith one god emerges into solitary existence on the side of good, while evil, which was acknowledged in the older faith, is greatly magnified, so that the result is a dualism, with a conflict between Ormazd, the good god, and Ahriman, the prince of evil. The object of religion is to obtain purity. Death is the great impurity, and all contact with death defiles. Where death is strongest the defiling influence is also most potent. Thus a body just dead, or even a dying person while still alive, gives out more defilement than a decaying corpse. Contact with death brings one under the influence of Ahriman. The earth is sacred, therefore it must not be defiled by burial. Fire is still more sacred as a gift from heaven; still less then must fire be defiled by cremation. On these principles the Parsee mode of disposing of the dead is determined, when the corpse is lifted above the earth and left on the "tower of silence," which, by a symbolical action, is supposed to be separated from the earth. Formally regarded, this system is very artificial and external. But, on the one hand, its rules for preventing defilement to a large extent agree with the laws of health; and, on the other hand, to an awakened conscience the external defilement of death and the need of continual purifications could not but suggest the moral death of sin, and the call for a deeper purification. Among the ceremonial remedies for defilement prescribed by the Zend-Avesta we meet with the purely spiritual atonement of repentance which includes the avowal of guilt. Some sins, however, are inexpiable, to be punished with death in this world and with torments in the next.

d. Greek.—The mythology of the Greek, Latin, and Teutonic races has been shown to be of one family with the more primitive myths contained in the Sanskrit writings of the Indian Vedas. Its manifestation in European literature came to have the weight of scriptural authority attached to it. Homer was held to be inspired, and the Iliad became the Bible of the Greeks, so that at Alexandria grammarians discussed the theological meanings of phrases from the great epic, and interpreted them so as to suit the exigencies of contemporary philosophy, and rhetoricians preached from them as from authoritative texts, thereby, as Dr. Hatch showed, preceding the Christian custom of textual preaching, and so starting the like process among the Christian fathers who were trained in their schools.

4. *Semitic.*—The brick libraries of the Babylonians, with the account of the Creation, the Flood, and other statements concerning the antiquity of the race and the relation of mankind to the gods, may be said to contain the elements of a Babylonian book of Genesis; but we are not yet in a position to point to anything like a canon of Chaldee scriptures. The Old Testament is the Bible of the Jews, and the Samaritan version of the Pentateuch the Bible, and practically the fetich, of the dwindling relic of the ancient sect that is still to be found at Nablus. But it is when we turn to Mohammedanism that we light on the one book apart from the works included in the Christian canon that has been accepted by a Semitic people as inspired scripture.

The Koran.—Unlike the sacred books of other religions the Mohammedan scriptures are later than the appearance of Christianity, and bear indications of Christian influences. Mohammed was born about A.D. 571, and he died in the year 632. Since at his death no collection of the Koran had been made, and only scattered fragments were in the hands of certain of his followers, the text had to be collected and arranged, and Omar employed Zaid ibn Thabit, a native of Medina, who had acted as amanuensis to Mohammed, to perform this all-important task. Thus the Koran was got together from "palm leaves, skins, blade bones, and the hearts of men." The chapters, or *surahs*, as they are called in the Arabic—a word that means primarily the courses of bricks in a wall—were arranged in no order, but simply according to their length. When they are arranged chronologically they fall into two main divisions—first, those put forth by the prophet at Mecca, and, second, those composed at Medina after the flight. There is a marked distinction between these two classes of surahs. The earlier chapters are charged with all the moral earnestness and high enthusiasm of an inspired soul, and they indicate the prophet's sincere and glowing conviction of his mission; but in the later chapters he appears more as the military commander.

In all probability Mohammed could neither read nor write, and the Jewish and Christian elements in the Koran are all traditional and legendary. In the grand, simple, early Meccan surahs the prophet's sole purpose is to bring men to a belief in the one God. Thus the fundamental article of the Mohammedan creed is set forth in the famous brief surah on "Unity," "Say, 'He is God, one God, the eternal. He begets not and is not begotten; nor is there like unto him, one.'" Subsequently Mohammed developed the idea of the mercifulness of God. The absolute supremacy of God runs through all the teachings of the prophet in the Koran. The will of Allah must be done; this great thought fell in with the common tendency of the Oriental to fatalism; and theoretically the Mohammedan is a fatalist, though not to the exclusion of human responsibility, besides belief in God. According to the Koran, angels exist as sexless beings created of fire, who neither eat, nor drink, nor propagate their species. The chief archangels are Gibra'il (Gabriel), "the faithful spirit," called also "the holy spirit;" Mika'il (Michael), the guardian angel of the Jews; Israfil, the archangel who will sound the last trumpet at the resurrection; and Azra'il, the angel of death. Every human being has two angels appointed, one on his right hand and the other on his left, to record all his actions. There are also lower existences created out of fire, called *ginn*, both good and evil. God has sent five chief prophets—Adam, the chosen of God; Noah, the prophet of God; Abraham, the friend of God; Jesus, the Spirit of God; and Mohammed, the friend of God. Each prophet prepares for his successor—thus, Jesus prepares for Mohammed. But Mohammed himself is "the seal of the prophets," and he is reported to have said, "There is no prophet after me." The practical duties of *Islam* (a word that means "submission") are—(1) The profession of faith, which is expressed in the creed,

"There is no god but God, and Mohammed is the Apostle of God;" (2) prayer; (3) fasting; (4) almsgiving; (5) pilgrimage. Mohammed confirmed the degradation of woman and the institution of slavery. He did not himself bring about these conditions of society which are among the most unhappy features of Islam to-day; he found them already existing, and he took steps to ameliorate them, enjoining a more just treatment both of women and of slaves than was prevalent among the Arabs of his day. Faithful women are to be admitted to Paradise. In these matters, as Prof. Palmer remarks, "the real fault lies in the unelastic nature of the religion." Mohammed would allow of no change; the Koran was the revealed will of God for all time. Hence what was advanced and enlightened in his day is retrograde and mischievous now, and herein is one marked distinction between the teaching of Mohammed and that of our Lord Jesus Christ, which can never be superseded because it is without flaw, perfect, and always in advance of human achievement.

AN ITINERARY

OF THE CHILDREN OF ISRAEL FROM EGYPT TO CANAAN.

TIME.	STATIONS.	MODERN OR OTHER NAME.	REFERENCES.
Y. M. D. 1. 1. 15.	1. RAMESES	prob. Tel El Kebir	Ge. 47. 11. Ex. 1. 11.-12. 37. Nu. 33. 3, 5.
	2. SUCCOTH	Pithom, prob. Tel el Maskhûtah	Ex. 12. 37.-13. 20. Nu. 33. 5, 6.
	3. ETHAM	in Wady Tumeilat	Ex. 13. 20. Nu. 33. 6, 7.
	4. PI-HAHIROTH	near Ismailieh	Ex. 14. 2 9. Nu. 33. 7, 8.
	5. MARAH	prob. Ain Howarah, or Wady Amârah	Ex. 15. 23. Nu. 33. 8, 9.
	6. ELIM	Wady Gharandel, or Wady Useit	Ex. 15. 27.-16. 1. Nu. 33. 9, 10.
	7. BY THE RED SEA	Mouth of Wady Feiran	Nu. 33. 10.
1. 2. 15.	8. IN THE WILDERNESS OF SIN	El Markha	Ex. 16. 1.-17. 1. Nu. 33. 11, 12.
	9. DOPHKAH	in Wady Feiran	Nu. 33. 12, 13.
	10. ALUSH	" "	Nu. 33. 13, 14.
	11. REPHIDIM		Ex. 17. 1, 8.-19. 2. Nu. 33. 14, 15.
1. 3. 15.	12. MOUNT SINAI	in Sufsafeh Mountains, perhaps Jebel Mûsa	Ex. 16. 1.-19. 1, 2, 11, 18, 20, 23.-24. 16.-31. 18.-34. 2, 4, 29, 32. Le. 7. 38.-25. 1.-26. 46.-27. 34. Nu. 1. 1, 19.-3. 1, 4, 14.-9. 1, 5.-10. 12.-26. 64.-28. 6.-33. 15, 16. De. 33. 2. Jud. 5. 5. Ne. 9. 13. Ps. 68. 8, 17. Ac. 7. 30, 38. Ga. 4. 24, 25.
	13. TABERAH	site unknown	Nu. 11. 3. De. 9. 22.
	14. KIBROTH-HATTAAVAH	" "	Nu. 11. 34, 35.-33. 16, 17. De. 9. 22.
	15. HAZEROTH	Ain Hudhera	Nu. 11. 35.-12. 16.-33. 17, 18. De. 1. 1.
2. 2. 20.	16. WILDERNESS OF PARAN	desert of El-Tih	Ge. 21. 21. Nu. 10. 12.-12. 16.-13. 3, 26.-De. 1. 1.-33. 2. 1 Sam. 25. 1. 1 Ki. 11. 18. Hab. 3. 3.
2. 5.	17. KADESH-BARNEA	Ain Kadeis	Nu. 13. 26.-20. 1, 14, 22.-27. 14.-32. 8.-33. 36, 37.-34. 4. De. 1. 2, 19, 46.-2. 14.-9. 23.-32. 51. Jos. 10. 41.-14. 6, 7.-15. 3. Ju. 11. 16. 17. Ps. 29. 8. Eze. 47. 19.-48. 28.
	18. RIMMON PAREZ	prob. in the region of El-Tih	Nu. 33. 19.
	19. LIBNAH	prob. El-Beyâneh	Nu. 33. 20.
	20. RISSAH	Rasa	Nu. 33. 21.
	21. KEHELATHAH	site not known	Nu. 33. 22.
	22. MOUNT SHAPHER	prob. Jebel-esh-Shureif or Jebel Sherâfeh	Nu. 33. 23.
	23. HARADAH	prob. 'Aradeh	Nu. 33. 24.
	24. MAKHELOTH	not known	Nu. 33. 25.
	25. TAHATH	prob. Elt 'hi	Nu. 33. 26.
	26. TARAH	not known	Nu. 33. 27.
	27. MITHCAH	"	Nu. 33. 28.
	28. HASHMONAH	prob. Heshmon (Josh. 15. 27), Ain Hasb	Nu. 33. 29.
	29. MOSEROTH	west of Arabah, beneath El-Mahrah	Nu. 33. 30.
	30. BENE-JAAKAN	prob. near wells of Mayein	Nu. 33. 31.
	31. HOR-HAGIDGAD	not known	Nu. 33. 32.
	32. JOTBATHAH	prob. Wady Tabah	Nu. 33. 33, 34. De. 10. 7.
	33. EBRONAH	on shore of Elanitic Gulf	Nu. 33. 34.
	34. EZION-GEBER	Wady Ghadyân	Nu. 33. 35, 36. De. 2. 8. 1 Ki. 9. 26.-22. 48.-2 Ch. 8. 17.-20. 36.
40. 1.	35. KADESH	Ain Kadeis	Nu. 33. 36.
	36. MOUNT HOR	Jebel Neby Haroun	Nu. 20. 22, 23, 25, 27.-21. 4.-33. 37, 38, 39, 41. De. 32. 50.
	37. ZALMONAH	prob. Alem Maan	Nu. 33. 41.
	38. PUNON	prob. Anezeh	Nu. 33. 42.
	39. OBOTH	prob. El-Alsa	Nu. 21. 10, 11.-33. 43, 44.
	40. IJE-ABARIM, OR IIM	in desert east of Moab	Nu. 21. 11.-33. 44, 45.
	41. DIBON, OR DIBON-GAD	Dhiban	Nu. 21. 30.-32. 3, 34.-33. 45, 46. Jos. 13. 9. 17. Is. 15. 2. Je. 48. 18, 22.
	42. ALMON-DIBLATHAIM	site unknown	Nu. 33. 46. Eze. 6. 14.
	43. NEBO	near Pisgah, mountains of Moab	Nu. 32. 3, 38.-33. 47. De. 32. 49.-34. 1. 1 Ch. 5. 8. Ezr. 2. 29.-10. 43. Ne. 7. 33. Is. 15. 2. Je. 48. 1, 22.
41. 1. 10.	44. IN THE PLAINS OF MOAB, NEAR JORDAN	part of El-Ghor, or the Valley of the Jordan	Nu. 22. 1.-33. 48.

CHRONOLOGY OF THE BIBLE.

1. The Old Testament.—From time to time various attempts have been made to settle the chronology of the Bible on a sound and consistent basis. The most famous of these is contained in Archbishop Usher's *Annales Veteris et Novi Testamenti*, published in 1650–54. Owing to its being adopted by printers of the Bible, and set at the head of their pages, Usher's chronology acquired a factitious authority, and came to be treated popularly almost as an integral part of the sacred text. And yet, reliable as it is in many parts, it could never be regarded as unassailable. Early in the nineteenth century Dr. Hales brought out an elaborate work in four volumes entitled *A New Analysis of Chronology*, in which he made considerable departures from Usher's tables. Since his time criticism and discovery have combined to throw a flood of light on the whole problem, with the result that, while some of the older dates have received marvellous confirmations, others are proved to be plainly wrong, and some, again, left open to considerable debate. Under these circumstances it does not seem just to head every page of the Bible with a date. To continue to do so would be to imply a fixity of chronology throughout which no serious student of the subject can now pretend to have established. In many cases where we are fairly certain of the period it is impossible to fix on the exact year; in many cases, while a high degree of probability attaches to a certain date, strict accuracy forbids us to set it down without qualification in a way that implies absolute certainty. It is better to be sure of the knowledge we really possess than to lay claim to a large territory of debatable ground. On the other hand, it is a great satisfaction to find that recent research has brought to light facts that help to settle some of the most important dates by means of evidence that was not within the reach of the older students of Scripture chronology.

The difficulties that beset the subject manifest themselves immediately we begin to inquire concerning the materials out of which Usher and Hales constructed their systems. These are chiefly taken from the Bible itself; but it is not always easy to interpret the Biblical references to periods of time. The three texts—*i.e.,* the Hebrew, the Samaritan Pentateuch, and the Greek of the Septuagint—differ among themselves. Thus for the age of Adam at the birth of his first-born the Hebrew and Samaritan texts give 130 years, the LXX. 230; for the age of Lamech at the birth of his first-born the Hebrew has 182 years, the Samaritan 53, and the LXX. 188. It may be observed that Josephus keeps most close to the LXX., which also is usually followed by the writers of the New Testament; while our Bibles represent the Hebrew text of the Old Testament. Then it is especially in the transmission of numbers that errors of transcription would have crept in, since some Hebrew letters that represent different figures are remarkably alike in form, so that copyists might easily have mistaken one for another. Add to these considerations critical questions concerning the authorship, re-editing, and later recensions of some of the Old Testament books, and it will be seen that there must be difficulties especially with the earlier dates. Geology has its say concerning the earliest of all. Nobody can suppose that the world was created just in the year 4004 B.C., which is Usher's date for that event.

While criticism has thus busied itself in unsettling a wrongly constructed chronology, the interpretation of ancient monuments has helped to determine some of the most interesting dates. These monuments are practically contemporary writings. They are not subject to the errors of the copyist, such as are sure to appear in the case of documents that have been transmitted to us by means of a number of hands, till the oldest MSS. now available may be, as in the case of books of the Old Testament, some two thousand years later than the original. The Egyptian hieroglyphics and the Assyrian cuneiform writings in stone or brick are original autographs or contemporary copies. We do not get much help from Egypt for the settling of chronology. Two points, however, may here be noted—the reign of the Hyksos, or shepherd kings, at the time of the Hebrew migration thither; and the identification of Ramses II. with the Pharaoh of the Oppression, illustrated by M. Naville's discovery of the treasure city of Pithom. The Exodus would appear to have taken place in the reign of his son Meneptah, and about 1320 B.C. Very much more is to be learnt from the Assyrian monuments. A cuneiform list of Babylonian kings goes back to the time of Abraham. Prof. Schrader has identified Arioch, king of Ellassar, with *Iri-Aku* in this list and, less certainly, other names in Gen. xiv., and fixes the date of these kings at about 2010 B.C. Prof. Sayce fixes on the year about 2000 B.C. This, then, would seem to be the time of Abraham. Here is our starting-point; attempts to settle earlier dates in the chronology of Genesis must be very precarious. Coming down to a later period, we have a most important aid in the Assyrian "Eponym lists." These were found in inscriptions brought to England by Layard and others, and were first interpreted by Sir Henry Rawlinson. George Smith, the Assyriologist, translated and published them. They consist of a canon of chronology, giving the name of a king or high official for every year from 900 B.C. to 666 B.C.. Some of these names are met with in the history of Israel, and in one copy of the list there is a parallel series of events, some of which can be identified with events mentioned in the sacred history. Thus the eponym year (i.e., second complete year of reign) of Shalmaneser, who made war with Ahab, is found to be 858 B.C. ; the year of Tiglath-Pileser's accession, 745 B.C. ; that of Sargon, the conqueror of Samaria, 722 B.C.; that of Sennacherib, 705 B.C. Schrader has identified the following dates of Israelite history from references in the Assyrian inscriptions :—

Ahab—854 B.C., Battle of Karkar.
Jehu—842 B.C., Payment of tribute.
Azariah (Uzziah)—742-740 B.C.
Menahem—738 B.C., Payment of tribute.
Pekah—734 B.C., Defeat by Tiglath-Pileser.
Hoshea—728 B.C., Last year of tribute ; 722 B.C., Fall of Samaria.
Hezekiah—Sennacherib's campaign.
Manasseh—681-673 B.C., 668 B.C., about 647 B.C., Revolt of Sammughes.

One of the notes of contemporary events is invaluable in settling the dates of the whole period. At the ninth year of King Asur-dan-ils (the eponym year Purilsagali) it is stated, "In the month Silvan the sun suffered an eclipse." Now it has been ascertained by means of astronomical calculations that the sun eclipsed on June 15th, 763 B.C., and that no other eclipse took place near this time. Thus we get a definite date from which to calculate all the other eponym years.

Now when we compare the dates ascertained by reference to the eponym canon with those deduced from the Hebrew text we find that, although they do not tally in all cases, on the whole they confirm the general outline of chronology derived from the Bible. Neither Usher's nor Hales' chronologies can be retained without considerable alteration, and yet, when we look over the whole period, we find that the relative positions of most of the names and events hold their old proportions.

We have less assistance for settling the dates of the intermediate period. In the first place, there are discrepancies with regard to the duration of the residence of the Hebrews in Egypt. The Hebrew text gives it as 430 years (Ex. xii. 40). But in the LXX. this period is made to include the previous sojourn of the patriarchs in Canaan. This reckoning was followed by the Samaritan version, Josephus, the Targum, and apparently St. Paul, when he wrote of the law coming 430 years after the covenant with Abraham (Gal. iii. 17). If, however, the dates given above for Abraham and the Exodus are correct, we must retain the Hebrew reckoning of 430 years in Egypt.

According to 1 Kings vi. 1, Solomon's temple was begun in the 480th year after the Exodus. The total period of the successive oppressions and deliverances given in the book of Judges amounts to 410 years. If we add to this,'at one end, the 40 years in the wilderness and the time of Joshua, and at the other end, 40 years each for Saul and David, and also the time of Samuel, which may be variously reckoned, we have to exceed the time given in 1 Kings. It is possible that some of the judges were contemporary in

different parts of the country. Inasmuch as the number of years given for the reigns of the three first kings—Saul, David, and Solomon—is just 40, a favourite number among the Jews, typical of completeness, it would seem to be most safe not to take this too absolutely, and to admit the possibility that it may be given as a round number to represent a full, long reign. If so, the dates of these kings can only be set down with a more or less approximate attempt at accuracy. Here we have no contemporary records to assist us. But from this point onwards it becomes possible to determine the chronology with tolerable assurance of correctness.

In his work, *The Assyrian Canon*, George Smith drew out a list of the kings of Judah and Israel that differed very little from the chronology of Usher ; but Schrader has shown the necessity of making more serious alterations, as the dates cited above, when compared with Usher's dates, will indicate. Kamphausen contributed an important monograph on the subject, pointing in the same direction. In a valuable note appended to his translation of Schrader's work on the cuneiform inscriptions, Principal Whitehouse has shown good reason for amending Kamphausen's series of dates at one or two places.

In the tables of patriarchs and judges Usher's and Hales' dates are given, not as though either of them can be held to be reliable for the early periods, but because these lists represent the relative order of the names as they appear in the Bible. That is to say, with these earlier names the chronology must be read as literary rather than as historical. In the case of the kings we have arrived at a more definite chronology, and here the older lists are given, not at all as suggested alternatives for possible adoption, but in order that the reader may see at a glance what changes have been made. The new list represents the chronology as corrected by the monuments. This list itself is for the most part Kamphausen's ; the alternative dates in brackets are those of Whitehouse's emendations. One or two additional dates have been inserted on the basis of Schrader's facts and arguments and other evidences.

2. **The New Testament.**—The chronology of the New Testament can be fixed at several points by reference to contemporary events in Roman and Jewish history, with the occasional further aid of astronomical data. The following are the more important guiding facts.

a. The Life of Christ.—The now prevalent manner of reckoning dates from the supposed time of the birth of our Lord was introduced by the Roman abbot Dionysius Exiguus in the sixth century, on an evident miscalculation probably derived from the understanding that the fifteenth year of Tiberius (Luke iii. 1, 23) was calculated from the commencement of that emperor's sole rule, although there is reason to believe that the reference is to the time when Tiberius was associated with Augustus in the imperial government. The date of the birth of Christ must be earlier than the commencement of the Christian era, because Herod's death occurred earlier. According to the gospel narrative Jesus was born in the days of Herod (Matt. ii. 1 ; compare Luke i. 5, 26), but, according to Josephus, Herod died just before the

Passover, A.U. 750 (*i.e.*, 4 B.C.). Josephus adds, "And that night there was an eclipse of the moon" (*Antiq.*, xvii. 6. 4); now it has been calculated astronomically that the moon was eclipsed on March 13, 4 B.C. Thus the date of Josephus has received a singular confirmation. Jesus, therefore, must have been born in the year 4 B.C., if not earlier. Then, turning to St. Luke's date, "the fifteenth year of Tiberius," we find that Tiberius commenced to reign conjointly with Augustus A.D. 11; St. Luke's date, therefore, will be A.D. 26. If Jesus were just thirty years of age at this time, we should have B.C. 4 as the date of His birth, in agreement with what we learn elsewhere. St. Luke's date referred to the commencement of John's ministry. That of Jesus began a little later, probably A.D. 27, when he would still be "about" thirty years of age if born in 4 B.C. It is not easy to determine the duration of our Lord's ministry. According to the synoptics it might have lasted no more than one year. But St. John's notes of time are much more full than those of the other evangelists, and he mentions three Passovers (John ii. 13; vi. 4; xi.

55), and perhaps four. The question of a fourth Passover turns on a reference to a feast in John v. 1, which some take to be a Passover, and others a different festival, such as the Dedication, or, more probably, the Purim. If there were three Passovers the ministry of our Lord would extend to over two years; if four, to over three years. The general opinion is that it lasted over three years and so included four Passovers. It is quite possible that it was even longer, for we have no express statements as to its length.

b. The Apostolic Age.—The date of the great Christian Pentecost is determined by that of the death and resurrection of Jesus Christ, and is thus fixed at May A.D. 30. We learn from Josephus that Herod Agrippa died in A.D. 44. This fixes the date of the martyrdom of James, which preceded it (Acts xii. 2, 20-23). The chronology of St. Paul's life is chiefly determined by reference to the succession of Festus to Felix, which took place in A.D. 60 or 61, probably 60. For the determination of this important date see Conybeare and Howson, *Life and Epistles of St. Paul*, vol. ii. Appendix ii.

CHRONOLOGICAL TABLE

OF THE

PATRIARCHS AND THE JUDGES,

ACCORDING TO USHER AND HALES.

THE PATRIARCHS.

THE JUDGES.

THE PATRIARCHS.	USHER.	HALES.
	B.C.	B.C.
Adam	4004	5411
Seth	3874	5181
Enos	3769	4976
Cainan	3679	4786
Mahalaleel	3609	4616
Jared	3544	4451
Enoch	3382	4289
Methusalah	3317	4124
Lamech	3130	3937
Noah	2948	3755
Shem	2446	3155[?]
(*Flood*)	2348	3155
Arphaxad	2346	3153
Salah	2311	3018
Eber	2281	2880
Peleg	2247	2954
(*Tower of Babel*)	..	..
Reu	2217	2624
Serug	2185	2492
Nahor	2155	2362
Terah	2131	2289
Abram	1996	2153
Isaac	1896	2053
Jacob	1836	1993

THE JUDGES OF ISRAEL.	USHER.	HALES.
	B.C.	B.C.
Moses (born)	1571	1728
Exodus	1491	1648
Joshua	1451	1618
Under king of Mesopotamia 8 years.		
Othniel	1405	1564
Ehud	1325	1506
Oppressed by Moab 18 years.		
Shamgar	1325	1506
Under Jabin, king of Canaan, 20 years.		
Deborah, the Prophetess	1285	1604
Delivered to Midian 7 years.		
Gideon	1245	1359
Abimelech	1236	1319
Tola	1233	1316
Jair	1210	1293
Oppressed by Philistines and Ammonites 18 years.		
Jephthah	1188	1253
Ibzan	1182	1247
Elon	1175	1240
Abdon	1165	1230
Delivered to Philistines 40 years.		
Eli, the High Priest	1156	1182
Samson	1137	1202
Samuel, the Prophet	1116	1122

N.B.—Probably some of these Judges were contemporary.

A COMPARATIVE CHRONOLOGICAL TABLE
OF THE KINGS AND PROPHETS OF JUDAH AND ISRAEL

The Kings of Israel before the Revolt of the Ten Tribes.

		USHER.	HALES.	KAMPHAUSEN.
SAUL	REIGNED 40 YEARS	B.C. 1095	B.C. 1110	B.C. 1037
DAVID	— 40 —	,, 1055	,, 1070	,, 1018
SOLOMON	— 40 —	,, 1015	,, 1030	,, 978
TEMPLE BEGUN		,, 1012	,, 10:7	,, 975
TEMPLE FINISHED		,, 1005	,, 1020	,, 968

	JUDAH.				ISRAEL.				
Prophets.	Kings.	Usher.	Hales.	Kamphausen, White-house, Etc.	Usher.	Hales.	Kamphausen, White-house, Etc.	Kings.	Prophets.
		B.C.	B.C.	B.C.	B.C.	B.C.	B.C.		
Shemaiah...	Rehoboam	975	990	**938**	975	990	**938**	Jeroboam	Man of God from Judah.
	Abijah, or Abijam.	958	973	921					Ahijah.
Oded	Asa...............	955	970	918					
Azariah					954	968	916	Nadab...........	
Hanani......					953	966	914	Baasha	
					930	943	891 [900]	Elah	
					929	942	890 [900]	Zimri	
					929	942	890 [900]	Omri	
					918	931	878 [875]	Ahab...........	Elijah.
Jehu, son of Hananī	Jehoshaphat	914	929	877					Micaiah.
					898	909	856 [853]	Ahaziah..........	Elisha.
Jahaziel.....					896	907	854 [852]	Joram, or Jehoram	
Eliezer	Jehoram, or Joram	892	904	852				854	*Battle of Karkar* ..
	Ahaziah, or Azariah	885	896	843					
	Athaliah..........	884	895	842	884	895	842	Jehu	
	Jehoash, or Joash.	878	889	837					
Zechariah, son of Je-hoiada..					856	867	815	Jehoahaz	Jonah (?).
					841	850	798	Joash, or Jehoash.	
	Amaziah..........	839	849	797	825	834	782	Jeroboam II.	
	Interregnum, 11 years, according to Hales........		820						
							763	*Eclipse of Sun (Amos viii. 9)....*	Hosea.
Zechariah (who had un-derstanding in the visions of God, 2 Ch. xxvi. 5).	Uzziah, or Azariah	810	809	777	784	793		{ *Interregnum, 22 years, according to Hales........*	Amos.
					773	771	741	Zachariah	
					772	771	741	Shallum	
					772	770	741	Menahem	
					761	760	738	Pekahiah..........	
					759	758	736	Pekah	
	Jotham, regent....			750				*Anarchy..........*	
Isaiah	Jotham, king......	758	757	736					
Micah	Ahaz..............	742	741	735	739	738	730	} Hoshea..........	Oded.
					730	728	[734]		
Nahum	Hezekiah	726	725 {	714 [726]	} 721	719	722	The Kingdom of Is-rael overthrown by the Assyrians	
Joel (?)......	Manasseh	698	696	685 [697]				*Shalmaneser, king of Assyria, came up against Samaria in the sixth year of the reign of Hoshea, and after a siege of three years, took the city, carried Israel away into Assyria (722 B.C.), and having re-moved them to the cities of Halah and Habor, by the river Gozan, and into the cities of the Medes, he placed Assyrians in the cities of Samaria in their room.*	
	Amon.............	643	641	641					
Jeremiah....	Josiah	641	639	639					
Habakkuk ..	Jehoahaz	610		608					
Zephaniah..	Jehoiakim	610	608	608					
Ezekiel......	Jehoiachin, or Je-coniah.......	599		597					
Daniel									
Obadiah	Zedekiah	599	597	597					
	Jerusalem destroyed and Judah car-ried captive	588	586	586					
	GOVERNORS OF JERUSALEM AFTER THE CAPTIVITY.							*Persian Kings.*	
Haggai......	Zerubbabel	536		536				536 First year of Cyrus.	
	Dedication of Temple			515				529 Cambyses. 521 Darius Hystaspes. 486 Xerxes I. 478 Esther queen.	
Zechariah...	Ezra	457		458				465 Artaxerxes Longimanus.	
Malachi....	Nehemiah	445		444				424 Darius Nothus.	

Contemporary with Rehoboam was Sesonchis of the 22nd Dynasty in Egypt; with Jehoshaphat, Mesha, king of Moab, and Ethbaal, king of Tyre; with Athaliah, Dido, who founded Carthage. During Uzziah's long reign the First Olympiad (776 B.C.) takes its rise; and Rome was founded (753) in the reign or regency of Jotham.

CHRONOLOGICAL TABLE

OF NEW TESTAMENT HISTORY.

NEW TESTAMENT HISTORY.	CONTEMPORARY EVENTS.
B.C.	**B.C.**
4 Birth of Jesus Christ.	Augustus, Emperor of Rome. 27
	Death of Herod. 4
	A.D.
A.D.	Cyrenius (Quirinius), Governor of Syria 6
8 First visit to the Temple.	(second time).
	Revolt of Judas of Galilee.
	Tiberius, colleague of Augustus. 12
	Death of Augustus. 14
	Caiaphas, High Priest. 25
	Pontius Pilate, Procurator. 26
27 Baptism of Jesus Christ.	
30 Crucifixion and resurrection of Jesus Christ.	
Descent of the Holy Spirit at Pentecost.	
35 Martyrdom of St. Stephen.	
Conversion of St. Paul (?).	
	Caligula, Emperor. 37
	Herod Agrippa I., King of Judæa and Samaria.
38 St. Paul's first visit to Jerusalem.	
	Claudius, Emperor. 41
44 Martyrdom of the Apostle James.	Death of Herod Agrippa I. 44
St. Paul's second visit to Jerusalem.	
The Epistle of St. James (?).	
45 St. Paul's first missionary journey:—	
Antioch to Cyprus, Pisidia, Derbe, Lystra, &c., and back.	
50 Jerusalem council. St. Paul's third visit.	
51 St. Paul's second missionary journey:—	Conquest of Britain. Caractacus a prisoner. 51
Antioch to Cilicia, Lycaonia, Galatia, Troas, Philippi, Thessalonica, Beræa, Athens, Corinth.	
52 St. Paul at Corinth, remaining 1½ years.	Claudius banishes Jews from Rome. 52
53 *1 and 2 Thessalonians.*	Antonius Felix, Procurator. 53
54 St. Paul's fourth visit to Jerusalem. Short stay at Corinth. Third missionary journey commenced.	Nero, Emperor. 54
St. Paul at Ephesus two years.	
	Revolt of Sicarii (Acts xxi. 38). 55
57 *1 Corinthians* (from Ephesus); *2 Corinthians* (from Macedonia).	
58 *Galatians* and *Romans* (from Corinth).	
St. Paul's fifth visit to Jerusalem. Imprisonment at Cæsarea, lasting two years.	
60 St. Paul before Festus, and sent to Rome. Two years a prisoner there in hired house.	Porcius Festus, Procurator. 60
	War with Boadicea in Britain. 61
62 Epistles to *Philippians, Ephesians, Colossians,* and *Philemon* (from Rome).	Josephus at Rome. 62
63 St. Paul released (?).	
64 St. Paul visits Crete and Macedonia.	Fire of Rome. 64
1 Timothy and *Titus.*	Nero's persecution.
66 *2 Timothy* (from Rome).	Beginning of war between the Jews and Rome. 66
Martyrdom of St. Paul and St. Peter (?).	
About this time the *Synoptic Gospels* written, also perhaps *Jude* and *1 and 2 Peter.*	
	Vespasian, General, in Palestine. 67
68 St. John's *Apocalypse.*	Galba, Emperor. 68
Epistle to *Hebrews* (?).	Otho, Vitellius, and Vespasian, Emperors. 69
	Destruction of Jerusalem. 70
	Titus, Emperor. 79
	Destruction of Pompeii and Herculaneum. 79
	Domitian, Emperor. 91
	Domitian's persecution. 95
96 St. John's *Epistles and Gospel* (?).	Nerva, Emperor. 96
98 Death of St. John (?).	Trajan, Emperor. 98

THE GREAT

PROPHECIES AND ALLUSIONS TO CHRIST
IN THE OLD TESTAMENT,

**WHICH ARE EXPRESSLY CITED, EITHER AS PREDICTIONS FULFILLED IN HIM, OR APPLIED TO
HIM IN THE NEW TESTAMENT.**

FROM HALES' ANALYSIS OF SACRED CHRONOLOGY

FIRST SERIES:

DESCRIBING CHRIST IN HIS HUMAN NATURE, AS THE PROMISED SEED OF THE WOMAN, IN THE GRAND CHARTER OF
OUR REDEMPTION (GEN. iii. 15); AND HIS PEDIGREE, SUFFERINGS, AND GLORY IN HIS SUCCESSIVE
MANIFESTATIONS OF HIMSELF UNTIL THE END OF THE WORLD.

I. THE SEED OF THE WOMAN.—Ge. 3.
15. Gal. 4. 4. 1 Tim. 2. 15. Rev. 12. 5.

II. BORN OF A VIRGIN.—Ps. 22. 10;
69. 8; 86. 16; 116. 16. Isa. 7. 14; 49. 1.
Je. 31. 22. Mi. 5. 3. Mat. 1. 23. Lu.
1. 26-35.

III. OF THE FAMILY OF SHEM.—Ge.
9. 26.

IV. OF THE RACE OF THE HEBREWS.—
2 Cor. 11. 22. Phi. 3. 5.

V. OF THE SEED OF ABRAHAM.—Ge.
12. 3; 18. 18; 22. 18. Mat. 1. 1.
Jno. 8. 56. Ac. 3. 25.

VI. OF THE LINE OF ISAAC.—Ge. 17.
19; 21. 12; 26. 4. Ro. 9. 7. Gal.
4. 23-28. He. 11. 18.

VII. OF JACOB OR ISRAEL.—Ge. 28.
4-14. Ex. 4. 22. Nu. 24. 7-17. Ps.
135. 4, &c. Is. 41. 8; 49. 6. Je. 14. 8.
Lu. 1. 68; 2. 30. Ac. 28. 20.

VIII. OF THE TRIBE OF JUDAH.—Ge.
49. 10. 1 Ch. 5. 2. Mi. 5. 2. Mat.
2. 6. He. 7. 14. Re 5. 5

IX. OF THE HOUSE OF DAVID.—2 Sa.
7. 12-15. 1 Ch. 17. 11-14. 2 Ch. 6.
42. Ps. 89. 4-36; 132. 10-17. Isa.
9. 7; 11. 1; 55. 3, 4. Je. 23. 5, 6.
Am. 9. 11. Mat. 1. 1. Lu. 1. 69;
2. 4. Jno. 7. 42. Ac. 2. 30; 13. 23.
Ro. 1. 3. 2 Ti. 2. 8. Re. 22. 16.

X. BORN AT BETHLEHEM, THE CITY
OF DAVID.—Mi. 5. 2. Mat. 2. 6.
Lu. 2. 4. Jno. 7. 42.

XI.—ADORED BY THE MAGI.—Ps. 72.
10-15.

XII. HIS PASSION OR SUFFERINGS.—
Ge. 3. 15. Ps. 22. 1-18; 31. 13;
89. 38-45. Is. 53. 1-12. Da. 9. 26.
Zec. 13. 6, 7. Mat. 26. 31. Lu. 24.
26. Jno. 1. 29. Ac. 8. 32-35; 26. 23.

XIII. HIS BETRAYAL. — Ps. 41 9.
Zech. 11. 12.

XIV. DESERTION.—Zech. 13. 7.

XV. HIS DEATH ON THE CROSS.—Nu.
21. 9. Ps. 22. 16; 31. 22. Isa. 53.
8, 9. Da. 9. 26. Mat. 20. 19; 26. 2.
Jno. 3. 14; 8. 28; 12. 32, 33. 1 Co.
15. 3. Col. 2. 15. Phi. 2. 8.

XVI. HIS ENTOMBMENT AND EMBALM-
MENT.—Isa. 53. 9. Mat. 26. 12. Mar.
14. 8. Jno. 12. 7; 19. 40. 1 Cor. 15. 4.

XVII. HIS RESURRECTION ON THE
THIRD DAY. Ps. 16. 10; 17. 15;
49. 15; 73. 24. Mat. 12. 40; 16. 4;
27. 63. Jno. 1. 17; 2. 19. Ac. 2.
27-31; 13. 35. 1 Co. 15. 4.

XVIII. HIS ASCENSION INTO HEAVEN.
—Ps. 16. 11; 24. 7; 47. 5; 68. 18;
110. 1; 118. 19. Jno. 20. 17. Ac. 1.
11; 2. 33. Eph. 4. 8-10. He. 1. 3;
2. 9. Rev. 12. 5.

XIX. HIS SECOND APPEARANCE AT
THE REGENERATION. — Is. 40. 10;
62. 11. Je. 23. 5, 6. Da. 7. 13, 14.
Ho. 3. 5. Mi. 5. 3. Hag. 2. 7.
Mat. 24. 3-30; 26. 64. Jno. 5. 25.
He. 9. 28. Rev. 20. 4; 22. 20.

XX. HIS LAST APPEARANCE AT THE
END OF THE WORLD.—Job 19. 25-29.
Ps. 50. 1-6. Ec. 12. 14. Da. 12. 2, 3.
Mat. 25. 31-46. Jno. 5. 28-30. Ac.
17. 31 ; 24. 25. Re. 20. 11-15.

SECOND SERIES:

DESCRIBING HIS CHARACTER AND OFFICES, HUMAN AND DIVINE.

I. THE SON OF GOD.—Ps. 2. 7; 72. 1.
Pr. 30. 4. Da. 3. 25. Mat. 3. 17;
17. 5. Mar. 1. 1. Lu. 1. 35. Jno.
1. 34-50; 3. 16-18; 20. 31. Ro. 1. 4.
He. 1. 1-5. 1 Jno. 4. 14. Rev. 1. 5, 6.

II. THE SON OF MAN.—Ps. 8. 4, 5.
Da. 7. 13. Mat. 16. 13; 26. 64. Jno.
1. 51; 3. 13; 5. 27. He. 2. 7. Re.
1. 13; 14. 14.

III. THE HOLY ONE, OR SAINT.—
Deut. 33. 8. Ps. 16. 10; 89. 19.
Is. 10. 17; 29. 23; 49. 7. Ho. 11. 9.
Hab. 1. 12; 3. 3. Mar. 1. 24. Lu.
1. 35; 4. 34. 1 Jno. 2. 20.

IV. THE SAINT OF SAINTS.—Dan. 9. 24.

V. THE JUST ONE, OR RIGHTEOUS.—
Ps. 34. 19, 21. Is. 41. 2. Je. 23. 5.
Zec. 9. 9. Mat. 27. 19-24. Lu. 1. 17;
23. 47. Ac. 3. 14; 7. 52; 22. 14.
Ja. 5. 6. 1 Jno. 2. 1, 29.

VI.—THE WISDOM OF GOD.—Pr. 8.
22-30. Mat. 11. 19. Lu. 11. 49. 1 Co.
1. 24.

VII. THE ORACLE (OR WORD) OF THE
LORD OR OF GOD.—Ge. 15. 1-4. 1 Sa.

3. 1-21. 2 Sa. 7. 4. 1 Ki. 17. 8-24.
Ps. 33. 6. Is. 40. 8. Je. 25. 3. Mi.
4. 2. Lu. 1. 2. Jno. 1. 1-14; 3. 34.
He. 4. 12; 11. 3. 1 Pe. 1. 23. 2 Pe.
3. 5. Re. 19. 13.

VIII. THE REDEEMER OR SAVIOUR.—
Ge. 48. 16. Job 19. 25-27. Ps. 19. 14.
Is. 41. 14; 44. 6; 47. 4; 59. 20; 62.
11; 63. 1. Je. 50. 34. Mat. 1. 21.
Lu. 2. 11. Jno. 1. 29; 4. 42. Ac.
5. 31. Ro. 11. 26. Re. 5. 9.

IX. THE LAMB OF GOD.—Is. 53. 7.
Jno. 1. 29. Ac. 8. 32-35. 1 Pe. 1. 19.
Re. 5. 6; 13. 8; 15. 3; 21. 22; 22. 1.

X. THE MEDIATOR, INTERCESSOR, OR
ADVOCATE.—Job 33. 23. Is. 53. 12;
59. 16. Lu. 23. 34. 1 Ti. 2. 5. He.
9. 15. 1 Jno. 2. 1. Re. 5. 9.

XI. SHILOH, THE APOSTLE.—Ge. 49. 10.
Ex. 4. 13. Mat. 15. 24. Lu. 4. 18.
Jno. 17. 3; 20. 21. He. 3. 1.

XII.—THE HIGH PRIEST.—Ps. 110. 4.
Is. 59. 16. He. 3. 1; 4. 14; 5. 10;
9. 11.

XIII. THE PROPHET LIKE MOSES.—
Deut. 18. 15-19. Lu. 24. 19. Ma.

6. 15. Jno. 1. 17-21; 6. 14. Ac. 3.
22, 23.

XIV. THE LEADER, OR CHIEF CAP-
TAIN.—Jos. 5. 14. 1 Ch. 5. 2. Is.
55. 4. Da. 9. 25. Mi. 5. 2. Mat.
2. 6. He. 2. 10.

XV. THE MESSIAH, CHRIST, KING OF
ISRAEL.—1 Sa. 2. 10. 2 Sa. 7. 12.
1 Ch. 17. 11. Ps. 2. 2; 45. 1, 6;
72. 1; 89. 38. Is. 61. 1. Da. 9. 26.
Mat. 2. 2-4; 16. 16. Lu. 23. 2. Jno.
1. 41-49; 6. 69. Ac. 4. 26, 27; 10. 38.

XVI. THE GOD OF ISRAEL.—Ex. 24.
10, 11. Jos. 7. 19. Ju. 11. 23. 1 Sa.
5. 11. 1 Ch. 17. 24. Ps. 41. 13. Is.
45. 3. Eze. 8. 4. Mat. 15. 32. Jno.
20. 28.

XVII. THE LORD OF HOSTS, OR THE
LORD.—2 Sa. 7. 26. 1 Ch. 17. 24.
Ps. 24. 10. Is. 6. 1-5. Mal. 1. 14.
Ro. 12. 19. Phi. 2. 9-11.

XVIII. KING OF KINGS AND LORD OF
LORDS.—Ps. 89. 27; 110. 1. Da. 7.
13, 14. Mat. 28. 18. Jno. 3. 35;
13. 3. 1 Co. 15. 25. Ep. 1. 20-22.
Col. 3. 1. Re. 19. 16.

THE

HARMONY OF THE FOUR EVANGELISTS,

CHRONOLOGICALLY ARRANGED.

(For Index to the Parables, see page 39.)

PART I.	MATTHEW.	MARK.	LUKE.	JOHN.
The Evangelical History before Jesus's Public Ministry; containing the space of Thirty Years and Six Months.				
SECT.				
1. The Word	——	——	——	1. 4.
2. Luke's Preface	——	——	1. 1—4.	
3. John's Preface	——	——		1. 1—18.
4. Annunciation of the birth of John the Baptist	——	——	1. 5—23.	——
5. The conception of Elisabeth	——	——	1. 24, 25.	——
6. The salutation of Mary	——	——	1. 26—38.	——
7. Mary visits Elisabeth	——	——	1. 39—56.	——
8. John the Baptist is born	——	——	1. 57—79.	——
9. An angel appears to Joseph	1. 18—25.	——	——	——
10. The birth of Jesus	1. 25.	——	2. 1—7.	——
11. The genealogies of Jesus	1. 1—17.	——	3. 23—38.	——
12. An angel appears to the shepherds, who visit Jesus	——	——	2. 8—20.	——
13. The circumcision of Jesus	1. 25.	——	2. 21.	——
14. The presentation of Jesus in the temple	——	——	2. 22—38.	——
15. The Magi. Jesus's flight into Egypt. Herod's cruelty. Jesus's return	2. 1—23.	——	2. 39.	——
16. Jesus as a child	——	——	2. 40.	——
17. Jesus goes to the Passover when he is twelve years of age	——	——	2. 40—52.	——
18. Jesus as a youth	——	——	2. 51.	——
19. Of John the Baptist, and his ministry	3. 1—12.	1. 1—8.	{ 1. 80. / 3. 1—18. }	1. 15—28.
PART II.				
The Transactions of about Six Months, from Jesus's Baptism until the beginning of the ensuing Passover.				
20. The baptism of Jesus	3. 13—17.	1. 9—11.	3. 21, 22.	1. 32—34.
21. The temptation of Jesus	4. 1—11.	1. 12, 13.	4. 1—13.	
22. The testimony of John the Baptist to Jesus, and its effects	——	——	——	1. 19—51.
23. The marriage feast at Cana in Galilee	——	——	——	2. 1—11.
PART III.				
The Transactions of Twelve Months, from the beginning of the First Passover.				
24. Jesus visits Capernaum	——	——	——	2. 12.
25. Jesus goes to Jerusalem at the Passover, and casts the traders out of the temple	——	——	——	2. 13—25.
26. Jesus's discourse with Nicodemus	——	——	——	3. 1—21.
27. Jesus tarries and baptizes in Judea. John the Baptist asserts the superior dignity of Jesus	——	——	——	3 22—36.
28. Passing through Samaria, he meets the woman of Sychar	——	——	——	4. 1—42.
29. Baptist's imprisonment	4. 12; 14. 3.	1. 14; 6. 17.	3. 19, 20.	3. 24.
30. Jesus retires into Galilee after the Baptist's imprisonment	4. 12. / 14. 3—5.	1. 14, 15. / 6. 17—20.	4. 14, 15. / 4. 43—45.	——
31. In Galilee Jesus exercises his public ministry. In Cana he heals the son of King Herod's officer, who lay sick at Capernaum	4. 12.	1. 14, 15.	4. 14.	4. 43—54.
32. Jesus goes to Nazareth, where he preserves his life by miracle; and then fixes his dwelling at Capernaum	4. 13—16.	——	4. 15—31.	——
33. The call of Simon and Andrew, and likewise of James and John; with the miracle which preceded it	4. 18—22.	1. 16—20.	5. 1—11.	——
34. Jesus in the synagogue at Capernaum heals a demoniac	——	1. 21—28.	4. 31—37.	——
35. Peter's wife's mother and many others are healed. Jesus, attended by some of his disciples, teaches and works miracles throughout Galilee	8. 14—17. / 4. 23—25.	} 1. 29—39.	4. 38—44.	——
36. Jesus heals a leper	8. 2—4.	1. 40—45.	5. 12—16.	——
37. Jesus stills the storm	8. 18—27.	4. 35—41.	8. 22—25.	——
38. The demoniacs in Gadara	8. 28—34.	5. 1—20.	8. 26—39.	——
39. Jairus' daughter and a woman healed	9. 18—26.	5. 21—43.	8. 40—56.	——

SECT.	MATTHEW.	MARK.	LUKE.	JOHN.
40. The blind men and demoniac	9. 27—34.	——	——	——
41. Jesus heals a paralytic	9. 2—8.	2. 1—12.	5. 17—26.	——
42. Matthew the publican	9. 9—13.	2. 13, 17.	5. 27—32.	——
43. The disciples not fasting	9. 14—17.	2. 18—22.	5. 33—39.	——

PART IV.

The Transactions of Twelve Months, from the beginning of the Second Passover.

	MATTHEW.	MARK.	LUKE.	JOHN.
44. The healing of an infirm man at Bethesda in Jerusalem	——	——		5. 1—47.
45. Jesus vindicates his disciples for plucking ears of corn on the sabbath	12. 1—8.	2. 23—28.	6. 1—5.	——
46. Jesus heals a man with a withered hand on the sabbath, withdraws himself from the Pharisees, and heals many	12. 9—21.	3. 1—12.	6. 6—11.	——
47. Jesus retires to a mountain, calls his disciples to him, chooses twelve, is followed by a great multitude, heals many	10. 2—4.	3. 13—19.	6. 12—19.	——
48. The sermon on the mount	5. 1—48. 6. 1—34. 7. 1—29.	——	6. 20—49.	——
49. The servant of the centurion is healed	8. 5—13.	——	7. 1—10.	——
50. The widow's son is raised from the dead at Nain	——	——	7. 11—17.	——
51. Jesus's answer to the disciples sent by John the Baptist	11. 2—19.	——	7. 18—35.	——
52. Jesus's reflections in consequence of his appeal to his mighty works	11. 20—30.	——	——	——
53. A woman, who had been a sinner, is publicly re-assured of forgiveness by Jesus, while sitting at meat with a Pharisee	——	——	7. 36—50.	——
54. During Jesus's second circuit through Galilee he heals a demoniac; and the Scribes and Pharisees blaspheme the Holy Spirit	9. 35. 12. 22—37.	6. 6. 3. 20—30.	8. 1—3. 11. 14—23.	——
55. Parables. The reason why Jesus used them. An explanation of one	13. 1—53.	4. 1—34.	8. 4—18. 13. 6—10. 13. 18—22.	——
56. The Scribes and the Pharisees are reproved for seeking a sign	12. 38—45.	——	11. 16. 11. 29—36. 11. 24—26.	——
57. Who are truly blessed	——	——	11. 27—28.	——
58. Jesus regards his true disciples as his nearest relations	12. 46—50.	3. 31—35.	8. 19—21.	——
59. Jesus, sitting at meat with a Pharisee, denounces woes against the Pharisees, Scribes, and teachers of the law	——	——	11. 37—54.	——
60. Jesus instructs his disciples and the multitude.	——	——	12. 1—59.	——
61. The calamities of certain Galileans, a warning to the Jews	——	——	13. 1—9.	——
62. Jesus revisits Nazareth, and is again rejected there	13. 54—58.	6. 1—6.	——	——
63. The occasion of sending the apostles to preach and work miracles	9. 36—38.	——	——	——
64. The twelve are instructed and sent forth	10. 1, 5—42. 11. 1.	6. 7—11.	9. 1—5.	——
65. Jesus continues his tour through Galilee				——
66. The twelve preach repentance, and work miracles, everywhere		6. 12, 13.	9. 6.	——
67. The death of John the Baptist	14. 6—12.	6. 21—29.		——
68. Herod hears of Jesus's fame, and desires to see him	14. 1, 2.	6. 14—16.	9. 7—9.	——
69. The twelve return		6. 30, 31.	9. 10.	——
70. Five thousand are fed on five loaves and two fishes	14. 13—21.	6. 32—44.	9. 10—17.	6. 1—14.
71. Jesus walks on the sea. Miracles at Gennesaret	14. 22—36.	6. 45—56.		6. 15—21.
72. Jesus's discourse with the multitude in Capernaum; in the synagogue of that city; and with his disciples. Peter's confession	——	——	——	6. 22—71. 7. 1.

PART V.

The Transactions of Twelve Months, from the beginning of the Third Passover.

	MATTHEW.	MARK.	LUKE.	JOHN.
73. Jesus's discourse with the Pharisees and Scribes, with the multitude, and with his disciples, about eating with unwashed hands	15. 1—20.	7. 1—23.	——	——
74. Jesus heals the daughter of a Syro-phenician woman	15. 21—28.	7. 24—30.	——	——
75. Jesus restores a person to hearing and speech	15. 29—31.	7. 31—37.	——	——
76. Jesus feeds more than four thousand with seven loaves and a few small fishes	15. 32—39.	8. 1—10.	——	——
77. The Pharisees and Sadducees again ask a sign. *See Section 56*	16. 1—4.	8. 11, 12.	——	——
78. The disciples are cautioned against the leaven of the Pharisees, of the Sadducees, and of Herod	16. 4—12.	8. 13—21.	——	——
79. Jesus restores a blind man to sight near Bethsaida	——	8. 22—26.	——	——
80. Peter repeats his confession that Jesus was the Christ. *See Section 72*	16. 13—20.	8. 27—30.	9. 18—21.	——
81. Jesus plainly foretells his sufferings and resurrection, rebukes Peter, exhorts all to self-denial	16. 21—28.	8. 31—38. 9. 1.	9. 22—27.	——

SECT.	MATTHEW.	MARK.	LUKE.	JOHN.
82. Jesus's transfiguration: his discourse with the three disciples as they were descending from the mountain	17. 1—13.	9. 2—13.	9. 28—36.	——
83. Jesus casts out a dumb and deaf spirit	17. 14—21.	9. 14—29.	9. 37—43.	——
84. Jesus again foretells his sufferings and resurrection	17. 22, 23.	9. 30—32.	9. 43—45.	——
85. Jesus works a miracle to pay the tribute money	17. 24—27.	——	——	——
86. The disciples contend who should be the greatest. Jesus's conduct and discourse on that occasion	18. 1—35.	9. 33—50.	9. 46—50.	——
87. Fire from heaven	——	——	9. 52—56.	——
88. Answers to disciples	8. 19—22.	——	9. 57—62.	——
89. Seventy disciples are instructed and sent out	——	——	10. 1—16.	——
90. Jesus goes to Jerusalem at the feast of tabernacles. His conduct and discourses during the feast	——	——	——	7. 2—53
91. A woman taken in adultery is brought before Jesus	——	——	——	8. 2—11.
92. Jesus discourses with the Scribes and Pharisees, with those who believed in him, and, v. 33, with the unbelieving Jews	——	——	——	8. 12—59.
93. Jesus restores to sight one blind from his birth	——	——	——	9. 1—41.
94. The good shepherd	——	——	——	10. 1—21.
95. The seventy return	——	——	10. 17—24.	——
96. A teacher of the law is instructed how to attain to eternal life	——	——	10. 25—37.	——
97. Jesus is received into Martha's house	——	——	10. 38—42.	——
98. The disciples are again taught how to pray	6. 9—13.	——	11. 1—13.	——
99. Jesus restores a woman who had been bowed down for eighteen years	——	——	13. 10—21.	——
100. Jesus replies to the question, Are there few that be saved?	——	——	13. 22—35.	——
101. The transactions when our Lord ate bread with a chief Pharisee on the sabbath	——	——	14. 1—24.	——
102. Jesus states to the multitude the difficulties attending a profession of his religion	——	——	14. 25—35.	——
103. Jesus defends himself against the Pharisees and Scribes for instructing publicans and sinners	——	——	15. 1—32.	——
104. Jesus instructs his disciples by the parable of the unjust steward. The Pharisees are reproved	——	——	16. 1—31.	——
105. Jesus further instructs his disciples	——	——	17. 1—10.	——
106. The Samaritans will not receive Jesus. James and John reproved for their zeal against them	——	} 9. 51—56.	} 17. 11.	——
107. Jesus cleanses ten lepers	——	——	17. 12—19.	——
108. The Pharisees ask when the kingdom of God should come. Our Lord's answer	——	——	17. 20—37.	——
109. Jesus speaks a parable to his disciples, and another to certain who trusted in themselves that they were righteous	——	——	18. 1—14.	——
110. Jesus enters Judea. The Pharisees question him about divorces	19. 1—12.	10. 1—12.	——	——
111. Jesus lays his hands on young children, and blesses them	19. 13—15.	10. 13—16.	18. 15—17.	——
112. Jesus's discourse in consequence of being asked by a rich man how he should attain eternal life	19. 16—30.	10. 17—31.	18. 18—30.	——
113. Labourers in the vineyard	20. 1—16.	——	——	——
114. Jesus, as he is going up to Jerusalem, foretells his sufferings to the twelve apart. See Sections 81 & 84	20. 17—19.	10. 31—34.	18. 31—34.	——
115. The ambitious request of James and John	20. 20—28.	10. 35—45.	——	——
116. Jesus restores sight to two blind men near Jericho	20. 29—34.	10. 46—52.	18. 35—43.	——
117. Jesus keeps the feast of dedication at Jerusalem	——	——	——	10. 22—39.
118. Jesus goes again to Bethabara (John i. 28) after the feast of dedication; and remains there till a fit occasion calls him into Judea	——	——	——	10. 40—42.
119. Jesus raises Lazarus from the dead. The consequences of this miracle	——	——	——	11. 1—54.
120. Meeting of the Sanhedrim	——	——	——	11. 45—53.
121. Christ in Ephraim	——	——	——	11. 54—57.
122. Jesus visits Zaccheus, a chief of the publicans	——	——	19. 1—28.	——
123. Jesus arrives at Bethany six days before the Passover	——	——	——	12. 1, 9—11.
124. Jesus proceeds to Jerusalem, amidst the acclamations of the disciples and of the multitude. The transactions there	21. 1—11. 14—17.	11. 1—10.	19. 29—44.	12. 12—50.
125. The barren fig-tree. The temple cleansed	21. 18, 19. 12, 13.	11. 12—19.	19. 45—48.	——
126. The disciples observe that the fig-tree was withered away	21. 20—22.	11. 20—26.	——	——
127. Jesus's discourse with the Priests, Scribes, and Elders in the temple	21. 23—46. 22. 1—14.	11. 27—33. 12. 1—12.	} 20. 1—19.	——
128. The Pharisees and Herodians, the Sadducees, and one of the Pharisees who was a Scribe, question Jesus. Jesus questions the Pharisees	22. 15—46.	12. 12—37.	20. 20—44.	——
129. Jesus, in the hearing of his disciples and of the multitude, reproves the Scribes and Pharisees to their face with a divine eloquence	23. 1—39.	12. 38—40.	20. 45—47.	——
130. Jesus prefers the widow's offering to the gifts of the rich	——	12. 41—44.	21. 1—4.	——

SECT.	MATTHEW.	MARK.	LUKE.	JOHN.
131. Jesus foretells the destruction of the temple as he takes his final leave of it: and, on the Mount of Olives, teaches four of his apostles what were the signs of his coming to destroy the Jews, and to close the Mosaic dispensation	24. 1—51. 25. 1—30.	13. 1—37.	21. 5—36.	——
132. Jesus describes the proceedings at the last day. How Jesus hitherto employed himself during the week	25. 31—48.	——	21. 37, 38.	——
133. The transactions on the fourth day of the week in which Jesus was crucified	26. 1—16.	14. 1—11.	22. 1—6.	12. 2—8.

PART VI.

The Transactions of Three Days, from the Day on which the Fourth Passover was killed, to the end of the day before the Resurrection.

SECT.	MATTHEW.	MARK.	LUKE.	JOHN.
134. Jesus prepares to keep the passover . . .	26. 17—19.	14. 12—16.	22. 7—13.	——
135. Jesus sits down with the twelve. There is an ambitious contention among the twelve . . .	26. 20.	14. 17.	22. 14, 24—30. 22. 15—18.	——
136. Jesus washes the feet of his disciples . . .	——	——	——	13. 1—20.
137. Jesus foretells that Judas would betray him. The conduct of the disciples, and of Judas . .	26. 21—25.	14. 18—21.	22. 21—23.	13. 21—35.
138. Jesus foretells to the apostles the fall of Peter, and their common danger	26. 31—35.	14. 27—31.	22. 31—38.	13. 36—38.
139. Jesus breaks and distributes the bread to his disciples	26. 26.	14. 22.	22. 19.	1 Cor. 11. 23, 24.
140. Jesus comforts his disciples	——	——	——	Jn.14.1—31.
141. Jesus presents the cup to his disciples . . .	26. 27—29.	14. 23—25.	22. 20.	1 Cor. 11. 25.
142. Jesus resumes his discourse to his disciples . .	——	——	——	Jn.15.1—27. 16. 1—33.
143. Jesus's prayer	——	——	——	17. 1—26.
144. Jesus's agony in Gethsemane	26. 30, 36, 46.	14. 26, 32—42.	22. 39—46.	18. 1.
145. Jesus is betrayed	26. 47—56.	14. 43—52.	22. 47—53.	18. 2—12.
146. Jesus is brought before Annas and Caiaphas. Peter denies him thrice	26. 57, 58. 26. 69, 75.	14. 53, 54. 14. 66—72.	22. 54—62.	18. 13—18. 18. 24—27.
147. Jesus stands before Caiaphas, and then before the whole Jewish Council. He confesses himself to be the Christ, and is pronounced guilty of death	26. 57, 59—68.	14. 53, 55—65.	22. 66—71. 22. 63—65.	18. 19—23, 28.
148. Jesus is taken before Pilate	27. 1, 2, 11—14.	15. 1—5.	23. 1—5.	18. 28—38.
149. Pilate sends Jesus to Herod	——	——	23. 6—12.	——
150. Herod sends Jesus again to Pilate. Pilate seeks to release him	27. 15—23.	15. 6—14.	23. 13—23.	18. 39, 40.
151. Pilate, having scourged Jesus, and having repeated his attempts to release him, delivers him to the clamours of the Jews. The soldiers insult him, and lead him away to crucify him	27. 26—31.	15. 15—20.	23. 23—25.	19. 1—16.
152. Judas repents, and destroys himself	27. 3—10.	——	Acts 1. 18,19. L. 23. 26—33.	——
153. Jesus is led away to be crucified . . .	27. 32—34.	15. 21—23.		19. 17.
154. What happened while Jesus was on the cross, till he expired	27. 35—50.	15. 24—37.	23. 33—46.	19. 18—30.
155. What happened at Jesus's death. Who were present during the crucifixion. The remaining transactions of the day	27. 51—61.	15. 38—47.	23. 45, 47—56.	19. 31—42.
156. The transactions on the day after the crucifixion	27. 62—66.	——	——	

PART VII.

Transactions of 40 days, from the day of the Resurrection to the Ascension.

SECT.	MATTHEW.	MARK.	LUKE.	JOHN.
157. The transactions on the day of the resurrection, before the first visit of the women to the sepulchre	28. 2—4. 27, 52, 53.	16. 1.		——
158. The first visit of the women to the sepulchre . .	28. 1, 5—8.	16. 2—8.	24. 1—11. 24. 12.	20. 1, 2.
159. Peter and John visit the sepulchre . . .	——	——		20. 3—10.
160. Jesus appears first to Mary Magdalene . . .	——	16. 9—11.	——	20. 11—18.
161. Jesus's second appearance	28. 9, 10.	——		——
162. The conduct of the Roman soldiers and Jewish rulers	28. 11—15.	——		——
163. Jesus, having been seen of Peter, appears to the two who went to Emmaus	——	16. 12, 13.	24. 13—36.	1 Cor.15,part of ver. 5.
164. Jesus appears to the Apostles in the absence of Thomas	——	16. 14—18.	24. 36—49.	20. 19—23.
165. Jesus appears to the Apostles, Thomas being present	——	——	——	20. 24—29.
166. The Apostles go into Galilee. Jesus appears at the Sea of Tiberias	28. 16.	——		21. 1—24.
167. Jesus's appearance on a mountain in Galilee .	28. 16—20.	——	——	——
168. Other appearances of Jesus	1 Cor. 15. 6,7.	——	——	——
169. Jesus's ascension	——	16. 19, 20.	24. 50—53.	Acts 1. 3—8. Acts 1. 9—12.
170. John's conclusion	——	——	——	Jn. 20. 30,31. Jn. 21. 25.

PARABLES.

1. OLD TESTAMENT.

The trees choosing a king	Judg. ix. 7–15.	The potter's vessel	Jer. xix. 1–13.
The ewe lamb	2 Sam. xii. 1–4.	The two baskets of figs	Jer. xxiv. 1–4.
The widow's two sons	2 Sam. xiv. 6–11.	The great eagles and the vine	Ezek. xvii. 1–10.
The escaped captive	1 Kings xx. 35–40.	The lion's whelps	Ezek. xix. 1–9.
Micaiah's vision	1 Kings xxii. 19–23.	The two sisters	Ezek. xxiii. 1–4.
The thistle and the cedar	2 Kings xiv. 9.	The boiling pot	Ezek. xxiv. 3–5.
The unfruitful vineyard	Isa. v. 1–7.	The cedar in Lebanon	Ezek. xxxi. 1–9.
The ploughman	Isa. xxviii. 28, 29.	The valley of dry bones	Ezek. xxxvii. 1–10.
The linen girdle	Jer. xiii. 1–8.	The plumbline	Amos vii. 7–9.
The potter	Jer. xviii. 1–4.	The basket of summer fruit	Amos viii. 1, 2.

2. NEW TESTAMENT.

(See Harmony of the Four Evangelists, page 166.)

	SECT.		SECT.
Why Jesus spoke in parables	55	The choosing the highest seat	101
The house on the rock and the house on the sand	48	The great supper	101
The two debtors	53	The proposal for building a tower	102
The relapsing demoniac	56	The king going to war	102
The rich man's ground	60	The salt having lost its savour	102
The returning from a wedding	60	The lost sheep	103
The barren fig-tree	55	The lost piece of silver	103
The sower	55	The prodigal son	103
The tares	55	The unjust steward	104
The casting seed into the ground	55	The rich man and Lazarus	104
The mustard seed	55	The master and servant	105
The leaven	55	The importunate widow	109
The hidden treasure	55	The Pharisee and publican	109
The pearl	55	The labourers in the vineyard	113
The net cast into the sea	55	The ten pounds	122
The good householder	55	The two sons	127
The new cloth and old garment	55	The cruel husbandmen	127
The new wine and old bottles	43	The wedding garment	127
The rich fool	60	The fig-tree putting forth leaves	131
The plant not planted by God	73	The thief	131
The strayed sheep	86	The man taking a far journey	131
The king and his debtors	86	The faithful and evil servant	131
The shepherd and sheep	94	The ten virgins	131
The good Samaritan	96	The talents	131
The importunate friend	98	The sheep and the goats	132

MIRACLES.

1. OLD TESTAMENT.

(a.) Under Moses.

Aaron's rod becoming a serpent	Ex. vii. 10–12.
The ten plagues :—	
1. Water made blood	Ex. vii. 20–25.
2. Frogs	,, viii. 5–14.
3. Lice	,, viii. 16–18.
4. Flies	,, viii. 20–24.
5. Murrain	,, ix. 3–6.
6. Boils and blains	,, ix. 8–11.
7. Thunder and hail	,, ix. 22–26.
8. Locusts	,, x. 12–19.
9. Darkness	,, x. 21–23.
10. Death of the firstborn	,, xii. 29, 30.
The Red Sea divided	,, xiv. 21–31.
The waters of Marah sweetened	,, xv. 23–25.
The manna	,, xvi. 14–35.
Water from the rock at Rephidim	,, xvii. 5–7.
Death of Nadab and Abihu	Lev. x. 1, 2.
Fire consuming the people at Taberah	} Num. xi. 1–3.

Death of Korah, Dathan, and Abiram	} Num. xvi. 31–35.
Aaron's rod budding	,, xvii. 6–8.
Water from the rock at Meribah	,, xx. 7–11.
The brazen serpent	,, xxi. 8, 9.

(b.) Under Joshua.

The Jordan stopped	Josh. iii. 14–17.
The fall of Jericho	,, vi. 6–20.
Sun and moon stayed	,, x. 12–14.

(But probably this was in some way an apparent rather than an actual miracle among the heavenly bodies.)

(c.) Under the Judges.

The strength of Samson	Judg. xiv.–xvi.
The water in a hollow place	,, xv. 19.
Dagon's falls and the emerods	1 Sam. v. 1–12.
Men of Bethshemeth smitten	,, vi. 19.

MIRACLES.

(d.) UNDER THE KINGS.

Death of Uzzah	2 Sam. vi. 7.	
Jeroboam's hand withered and altar destroyed	}1 Kin. xiii. 4–6.	
By Elijah :—		
The widow's cruse supplied	,, xvii. 14–16.	
The widow's son raised from the dead	} ,, xvii. 17–24.	
The sacrifice at Carmel consumed	} ,, xviii. 30–38.	
Ahaziah's troops consumed by fire	}2 Kin. i. 10–12.	
The dividing of Jordan	,, ii. 7, 8.	
Elijah translated to heaven	,, ii. 11.	
By Elisha :—		
The dividing of Jordan	,, ii. 14.	
The waters of Jericho sweetened	,, ii. 21, 22.	
Mocking children (Heb. young men) destroyed by bears	} ,, ii. 24.	
Water supplied to Jehoshaphat and the allied army	} ,, iii. 16–20.	
The widow's oil increased	,, iv. 2–7.	

The Shunammite's son raised from the dead	}2 Kin. iv. 32–37.	
Deadly pottage corrected	,, iv. 38–41.	
100 men fed with 20 loaves	,, iv. 42–44.	
Naaman's leprosy cured and transferred to Gehazi	} ,, v. 10–27.	
The axe-head floated	,, vi. 5–7.	
The Syrian army smitten and cured	} ,, vi. 18–20.	
Resurrection of a dead man on Elisha's bones	} ,, xiii. 21.	
Sennacherib's army destroyed	,, xix. 35.	
Return of the shadow on the sundial of Ahaz	} ,, xx. 9–11.	
Uzziah smitten with leprosy	2 Chr. xxvi. 16–21.	
Jonah's deliverance	Jonah ii. 1–10.	

(e.) DURING THE CAPTIVITY.

Shadrach, Meshach, and Abednego uninjured in the furnace	}Dan. iii. 19–27.	
Daniel uninjured in the lions' den	,, vi. 16–23.	

2. NEW TESTAMENT.

(a.) BY JESUS CHRIST. (*Arranged in chronological order. These are only the miracles of which detailed accounts are given. There are allusions in the Gospels to a great many more miracles.*)

(SEE HARMONY OF THE FOUR EVANGELISTS, PAGE 166.)

	SECT.
Water turned into wine	23
Nobleman's son healed	31
Draught of fishes (first)	33
Cure of demoniac in synagogue	34
Healing of Peter's wife's mother and others	35
Cleansing a leper	36
Stilling a storm	37
The legion of demons cast out	38
The woman with the issue of blood healed	39
The daughter of Jairus raised to life	39
Two blind men receiving sight	40
A dumb demoniac cured	40
A paralytic healed	41
The impotent man at Bethesda healed	44
The man with a withered hand cured	46
The centurion's servant healed	49
The widow's son at Nain raised to life	50
The blind and dumb demoniac cured	54
Feeding the 5000	70

	SECT.
Jesus walking on the sea	71
The daughter of the Syrophœnician woman healed	74
A deaf and dumb man cured	75
Feeding the 4000	76
A blind man at Bethsaida gradually restored	79
The curing of a demoniac child	83
The stater found in the fish's mouth	85
The man born blind receiving sight	93
An infirm woman restored	99
A man with the dropsy cured	101
Ten lepers cleansed	107
Blind Bartimæus receiving sight	116
The resurrection of Lazarus	119
The barren fig-tree cursed	126
The ear of Malthus restored	145
Draught of fishes (second)	166

The resurrection of Jesus Christ and His subsequent appearances, Sects. 157 to 169.

(b.) RECORDED IN THE ACTS OF THE APOSTLES.

The gift of the Holy Spirit at Pentecost	}Acts ii. 1–4.	
The cripple at the Beautiful gate cured	} ,, iii. 1–10.	
The death of Ananias and Sapphira	,, v. 1–11.	
Various miracles	,, v. 12.	
The Apostles delivered from prison	,, v. 21–23.	
St. Stephen's miracles	,, vi. 8.	
St. Philip's miracles	,, viii. 13.	
Conversion of St. Paul	,, ix. 1–9.	
St. Paul's sight restored by means of Ananias	} ,, ix. 17–19.	
St. Peter cures Æneas of palsy	,, ix. 32–35.	
St. Peter raises Dorcas to life	,, ix. 36–43.	

St. Peter is delivered from prison	Acts xii. 5–11.	
The blinding of Elymas the sorcerer	,, xiii. 11.	
Various miracles by Paul and Barnabas at Iconium	} ,, xiv. 3.	
St. Paul heals a cripple at Lystra	,, xiv. 8–10.	
St. Paul cures the maid with a spirit of divination at Philippi	} ,, xvi. 16–18.	
Paul and Silas set free by an earthquake	} ,, xvi. 26.	
Many miracles by St. Paul at Ephesus	} ,, xix. 11, 12.	
St. Paul unhurt by a viper's bite	,, xxviii. 3–6.	
St. Paul cures the father of Publius and others	} ,, xxviii. 7–10.	

I

PASSAGES

IN THE OLD TESTAMENT QUOTED OR ALLUDED TO IN THE NEW TESTAMENT.

This list contains not only the direct or indirect citations, but also the allusions which are particularly worthy of attention; and the passages are given in the order of the books of the New Testament.

The mere allusions are marked *a*.

MATTHEW.

Chap.	1. 23. . .	Isa.	7.	14.
,,	2. 6. .	Mic.	5.	2.
,,	2. 15. . .	Hos.	11.	1.
,,	2. 18. .	Jer.	31.	15.
,,	3. 3. . .	Isa.	40.	3.
,,	4. 4. .	Deut.	8.	3.
,,	4. 6. . .	Psa.	91.	11, 12.
,,	4. 7. .	Deut.	6.	16.
,,	4 10. .	Deut.	6.	13.
,,	4. 10. .	Deut.	10.	20.
,,	4. 15, 16.	Isa.	9.	1, 2.
,,	5. 5. .	ᵃPsa.	37.	11.
,,	5. 21. . .	ᵃEx.	20.	13.
,,	5. 21. .	Deut.	5.	17.
,,	5. 27. . .	ᵃEx.	20.	14.
,,	5. 27. .	Deut.	5.	18.
,,	5. 31. . .	ᵃDeut.	24.	1.
,,	5. 33. .	ᵃEx.	20.	7.
,,	5. 33. . .	ᵃLev	19.	12.
,,	5. 38. .	ᵃEx.	21.	24.
,,	5. 38. . .	ᵃLev.	24.	20.
,,	5. 38. .	Deut.	19.	21.
,,	5. 43. . .	ᵃLev.	19.	18.
,,	7. 23. .	Psa.	6.	8.
,,	8. 4. . .	ᵃLev.	14.	2.
,,	8. 17. .	Isa.	53.	4.
,,	9. 13. . .	Hos.	6.	6.
,,	10. 35, 36.	ᵃMic.	7.	6.
,,	11. 5. . .	ᵃIsa.	35.	5.
,,	11. 5. .	ᵃIsa.	29.	18.
,,	11. 10. . .	Mal.	3.	1.
,,	11. 14. .	ᵃMal.	4.	5.
,,	12. 3. . .	ᵃ1 Sam.21.		6.
,,	12. 5. . .	ᵃNum.	28.	9, 1.
,,	12. 7. . .	Hos.	6.	6.
,,	12. 18. .	Isa.	42.	1.
,,	12. 40. . .	ᵃJon.	1.	17, &c.
,,	12. 42. .	ᵃ1 Ki.	10.	1.
,,	13. 14. .	Isa.	6.	9, 10.
,,	13. 35. .	Psa.	78.	2.
,,	15. 4. . .	Ex.	20.	12.
,,	15. 4. .	Deut.	5.	16.
,,	15. 4. . .	Ex.	21.	17.
,,	15. 4. .	ᵃLev.	20.	9.
,,	15. 4. . . ᵃProv.		20.	20.
,,	15. 8, 9.	Isa.	29.	13.
,,	17. 2. . .	Ex.	34.	29.
,,	17. 11. .	Mal.	3.	1.
,,	17. 11. .	ᵃMal.	4.	5.
,,	18. 16. .	ᵃDeut.	19.	15.
,,	19. 4. . .	ᵃGen.	1.	27.
,,	19. 5. .	Gen.	2.	24.
,,	19. 7. . .	Deut.	24.	1.
,,	19. 18. .	Ex.	20.	12, &c.
,,	19. 19. . .	Lev.	19.	18.
,,	21. 5. .	Zec.	9.	9.
,,	21. 9. . .	Psa.	118.	26.
,,	21. 13. .	Isa.	56.	7.
,,	21. 13. .	Jer.	7.	11.
,,	21. 16. .	Psa.	8.	2.
,,	21. 33. . .	Isa.	5.	1.
,,	21. 42. .	Psa.	118.	22, 23.
,,	21. 44. . .	ᵃIsa.	8.	14.
,,	21. 44. .	ᵃZec.	12.	3.
,,	21. 44. . .	ᵃDan.	2.	34, 35, 44.
,,	22. 24. .	Deut.	25.	5.

MATTHEW.

Chap.	22. 32. . .	Ex.	3.	6.
,,	22. 37. .	Deut.	6.	5.
,,	22. 39. . .	Lev.	19.	18.
,,	22. 44. .	Psa.	110.	1.
,,	23. 35. . .	ᵃGen.	4.	8.
,,	23. 35. . .	ᵃ2 Chr.	24.	21, 22.
,,	23. 38. . .	ᵃPsa.	69.	25.
,,	23. 38. .	ᵃJer.	12.	7.
,,	23. 38. .	ᵃJer.	22.	5.
,,	23. 39. .	ᵃPsa.	118.	26.
,,	24. 15. . .	ᵃDan.	9.	27.
,,	24. 15. . .	ᵃDan.	8.	13.
,,	24. 15. . .	ᵃDan.	11.	31.
,,	24. 15. . .	ᵃDan.	12.	11.
,,	24. 29. . .	ᵃIsa.	13.	9, 10.
,,	24. 29. .	ᵃJoel	3.	15.
,,	24. 29. . .	ᵃEze.	32.	7.
,,	24. 37. .	ᵃGen.	7.	4.
,,	25. 41. . .	Psa.	6.	8.
,,	26. 31. .	Zec.	13.	7.
,,	26. 64. . .	Dan.	7.	13.
,,	26. 67. .	ᵃIsa.	50.	6.
,,	27. 9, 10.	Zec.	11.	13.
,,	27. 35. .	Psa.	22.	18.
,,	27. 43. . .	ᵃPsa.	22.	8.
,,	27. 46. .	Psa.	22.	1.

MARK.

Chap.	1. 2, 3.	Mal.	3.	1.
,,	1. 2, 3.	Isa.	40.	3.
,,	1. 44. .	ᵃLev.	14.	2.
,,	2. 25, 26.	ᵃ1 Sa.	21.	6.
,,	4. 12. .	Isa.	6.	9.
,,	7. 6, 7.	Isa.	29.	13.
,,	7. 10. .	Ex.	20.	12.
,,	7. 10. . .	Deut.	5.	16.
,,	7. 10. .	Ex.	21.	17.
,,	7. 10. . .	Pro.	20.	20.
,,	9. 11. .	ᵃMal.	4	5.
,,	9. 44. . .	ᵃIsa.	66.	24.
,,	10. 4. .	ᵃDeut.	24.	1.
,,	10. 6. .	Gen.	1.	27.
,,	10. 7. .	Gen.	2.	24.
,,	10. 19. .	Ex.	20.	12, &c.
,,	11. 17. .	Isa.	56.	7.
,,	11. 17. .	Jer.	7.	11.
,,	12. 1. .	ᵃIsa.	5.	1.
,,	12. 10, 11.	Psa.	118.	22, 23.
,,	12. 19. .	Deut.	25.	5.
,,	12. 26. . .	Ex.	3.	6.
,,	12. 29, 30.	Deut.	6.	4, 5.
,,	12. 31. .	Lev.	19.	18.
,,	12. 36. .	Psa.	110.	1.
,,	13. 14. . .	ᵃDan.	9.	27.
,,	13. 14. .	ᵃDan.	8.	13.
,,	13. 14. . .	ᵃDan.	11.	31.
,,	13. 14. . .	ᵃDan.	12.	11.
,,	13. 24. . .	ᵃIsa.	13.	9, 10.
,,	13. 24. .	ᵃJoel	3.	15.
,,	14. 27. . .	Zec.	13.	7.
,,	14. 62. .	Dan.	7.	13.
,,	15. 28. .	Isa.	53.	12.
,,	15. 34. .	Psa.	22.	1.

LUKE.

Chap.	1. 9, 10.	ᵃLev.	16.	17.
,,	1. 17. .	Mal.	4.	5, 6.

LUKE.

Chap.	1. 33. . .	ᵃMic.	4.	7.
,,	1. 55. .	ᵃGen.	22.	18.
,,	1. 73. . .	ᵘGen.	22.	16.
,,	2. 21, 22.	ᵃLev.	12.	3, 4.
,,	2. 23. . .	Ex.	13.	2.
,,	2. 24. .	Lev.	12.	8.
,,	2. 34. . .	ᵃIsa.	8.	14, 15.
,,	3. 4, 5, 6.	Isa.	40.	3, 4, 5.
,,	4. 4. .	Deut.	8.	3.
,,	4. 8. .	Deut.	6.	13.
,,	4. 8. .	Deut.	10.	20.
,,	4. 10, 11.	Psa.	91.	11, 12.
,,	4. 12. .	Deut.	6.	16.
,,	4. 18, 19.	Isa.	61.	1, 2.
,,	4. 25, 26.	ᵃ1 Ki.	17.	1, 9.
,,	4. 25, 26.	ᵃ1 Ki.	18.	1, 2.
,,	4. 27. . .	ᵃ2 Ki.	5.	14.
,,	5. 14. .	Lev.	14.	2.
,,	6. 3, 4.	ᵃ1 Sa.	21.	6.
,,	6. 24. .	ᵃAmos	6.	1.
,,	7. 27. . .	Mal.	3.	1.
,,	8. 10. .	Isa.	6.	9.
,,	10. 4. . .	ᵃ2 Ki.	4.	29.
,,	10. 27. .	Deut.	6.	5.
,,	10. 27. . .	Lev.	19.	18.
,,	10. 28. . .	ᵃLev.	18.	5.
,,	11. 30. . .	ᵃJon.	1.	17.
,,	11. 31. .	ᵃ1 Ki.	10.	1.
,,	11. 51. . .	ᵃGen.	4.	8.
,,	11. 51. .	ᵃ2 Chr.	24.	21, 22.
,,	13. 27. .	Psa.	6.	8.
,,	13. 35. .	ᵃPsa.	118.	26.
,,	13. 35. . .	ᵃJer.	12.	7.
,,	13. 35. .	ᵃJer.	22.	5.
,,	14. 8. . .	ᵃProv.	25.	6.
,,	14. 26. .	ᵃMic.	7.	6.
,,	17. 3. . .	ᵃLev.	19.	17.
,,	17. 27. .	ᵃGen.	7.	7.
,,	17. 29. . .	ᵃGen.	19.	24.
,,	17. 32. .	ᵃGen.	19.	26.
,,	18. 20. .	Ex.	20.	12.
,,	18. 20. .	Deut.	5.	17, 18, &c.
,,	19. 46. .	Isa.	56.	7.
,,	19. 46. .	Jer.	7.	11.
,,	20. 9. . .	ᵃIsa.	5.	1.
,,	20. 17. .	Psa.	118.	22, 23.
,,	20. 18. .	ᵃIsa.	8.	14.
,,	20. 18. .	ᵃZec.	12.	3.
,,	20. 18. .	ᵃDan.	2.	44.
,,	20. 28. .	Deut.	25.	5.
,,	20. 37. . .	ᵃEx.	3.	6.
,,	20. 42, 43.	Psa.	110.	1.
,,	22 37. . .	Isa.	53.	12.
,,	23. 29. .	ᵃIsa.	54.	1.
,,	23. 30. . .	ᵃHos.	10.	8.
,,	23. 46. .	Psa.	31.	5.

JOHN.

Chap.	1. 23. . .	Isa.	40.	3.
,,	1. 51. .	ᵃGen.	28.	12.
,,	2. 17. . .	Psa.	69.	9.
,,	3. 14. .	ᵃNum.	21.	8, 9.
,,	3. 36. . .	Hab.	2.	4.
,,	4. 20. .	Deut.	12.	5.
,,	4. 37. . .	ᵃMic.	6.	15.
,,	5. 10. .	Jer.	17.	21, 27.

JOHN.

Chap.	5. 38.	. .	Deut.	4. 12.
„	6. 31.	.	Psa.	78. 24.
„	6. 45.	. .	Isa.	54. 13.
„	6. 49.	.	a Ex.	16. 15.
„	7. 22.	.	a Lev.	12. 3.
„	7. 38.	.	a Isa.	55. 1.
„	7. 38.	. .	a Isa.	58. 11.
„	7. 38.	. .	a Isa.	44. 3.
„	7. 38.	. .	a Zec.	13. 1.
„	7. 38.	. .	a Zec.	14. 8.
„	7. 42.	. .	a Psa.	89. 4.
„	7. 42.	. .	a Psa.	132. 11.
„	7. 42.	. .	a Mic.	5. 2.
„	8. 5.	.	a Lev.	20. 10.
„	8. 5.	.	a Deut.	22. 21.
„	8. 17.	.	Deut.	19. 15.
„	9. 31.	. .	a Prov.	28. 9.
„	10. 35.	.	Psa.	82. 6.
„	12. 13.	. .	a Psa.	118. 26.
„	12. 14, 15.		Zec.	9. 9.
„	12. 34.	. .	2 Sam.	7. 13.
„	12. 34.	.	a Psa.	89. 30, 37.
„	12. 34.	. .	a Psa.	110. 4.
„	12. 38.	.	Isa.	53. 1.
„	12. 40.	. .	Isa.	6. 9.
„	13. 18.	.	Psa.	41. 9.
„	15. 25.	. .	Psa.	109. 3.
„	15. 25.	.	Psa.	35. 19.
„	17. 12.	.	a Psa.	41. 10.
„	17. 12.	.	a Psa.	109. 8, 17.
„	19. 24.	. .	Psa.	22. 18.
„	19. 28.	.	a Psa.	69. 21.
„	19. 36.	. .	Ex.	12. 46.
„	19. 36.	.	a Num.	9. 12.
„	19. 37.	.	Zec.	12. 10.
„	20. 17.	.	a Psa.	22. 22.

ACTS.

Chap.	1. 20.	. .	Psa.	69. 2.
„	1. 20.	.	Psa.	109. 8.
„	2. 17.	. .	Isa.	44. 3.
„	2. 17.	.	Joel	2. 28.
„	2. 25.	.	Psa.	16. 8.
„	2. 30.	.	a 2 Sam.	7. 12.
„	2. 30.	. .	a Psa.	89. 4.
„	2. 31.	.	Psa.	16. 10.
„	2. 34.	. .	Psa.	110. 1.
„	3. 22, 23.		Deut.	18. 15, 19.
„	3. 25.	. .	Gen.	22. 18.
„	3. 25.	.	a Gen.	12. 3.
„	4. 11.	. .	Psa.	118. 22, 23.
„	4. 11.	.	a Isa.	28. 16.
„	4. 25, 26.		Psa.	2. 1, 2.
„	7. 3.	.	Gen.	12. 1.
„	7. 6, 7.		Gen.	15. 13, 14.
„	7. 8.	.	a Gen.	17. 10.
„	7. 9.	. .	a Gen.	37. 28.
„	7. 9.	.	a Gen.	39. 1.
„	7. 17.	. .	a Ex.	1. 7.
„	7. 20.	.	a Ex.	2. 2.
„	7. 24.	. .	a Ex.	2. 11.
„	7. 26.	. .	Ex.	2. 13, 14.
„	7. 30.	. .	a Ex.	3. 2.
„	7. 32.	.	Ex.	3. 6.
„	7. 33, 34.		Ex.	3. 5,7,8, 10.
„	7. 35.	.	Ex.	2. 14.
„	7. 37.	. .	Deut.	18. 15.
„	7. 38.	.	a Ex.	19. 3.
„	7. 40.	. .	Ex.	32. 1.
„	7. 42, 43.		Amos	5. 25, 26.
„	7. 44.	. .	a Ex.	25. 40.
„	7. 45.	.	a Josh.	3. 14.
„	7. 46.	. .	a 2 Sa.	7. 2.
„	7. 46.	. .	a Psa.	132. 5.
„	7. 49, 50.		Isa.	66. 1, 2.
„	8. 32, 33.		Isa.	53. 7, 8.
„	10. 34.	. .	a Deut.	10. 17.
„	10. 34.	.	a Job	34. 19.
„	13. 17.	. .	a Isa.	1. 2.
„	13. 17.	. .	a Ex.	13. 14, 16.
„	13. 18.	. .	a Deut.	1. 31.
„	13. 22.	. .	1 Sa.	13. 14.
„	13. 22.	. .	Psa.	89. 20.
„	13. 33.	. .	Psa.	2. 7.
„	13. 34.	. .	Isa.	55. 3.
„	13. 35.	. .	Psa.	16. 10.
„	13. 36.	. .	a 1 Ki.	2. 10.
„	13. 41.	. .	Hab.	1. 5.
„	13. 47.	. .	Isa.	49. 6.
„	13. 47.	. .	a Isa.	11. 10.
„	15. 16, 17.		Amos	9. 11, 12.
„	17. 31.	. .	a Psa.	9. 9.
„	17. 31.	. .	a Psa.	96. 13.
„	17. 31.	. .	a Psa.	98. 8.
„	23. 5.	.	Ex.	22. 28.
„	28. 26, 27.		Isa.	6. 9, 10.

ROMANS.

Chap.	1. 17.	. .	Hab.	2. 4.
„	1. 22.	.	a Jer.	10. 14.
„	1. 23.	. .	Psa.	106. 20.
„	2. 6.	. .	Psa.	62. 12.
„	2. 6.	. .	a Prov.	24. 12.
„	2. 11.	. .	a Deut.	10. 17.
„	2. 11.	. .	2 Chr.	19. 7.
„	2. 11.	.	a Job	34. 19.
„	2. 24.	. .	Isa.	52. 5.
„	2. 24.	.	Eze.	36. 20.
„	3. 4.	. .	Psa.	116. 11.
„	3. 4.	.	Psa.	51. 4.
„	3. 10, 11, 12.		Psa.	14. 1, &c.
„	3. 13.	. .	Psa.	5. 9.
„	3. 13.	. .	Psa.	140. 3.
„	3. 14.	.	Psa.	10. 7.
„	3. 15.	.	Prov.	1. 16.
„	3. 15, &c.		Isa.	59. 7.
„	3. 18.	.	Psa.	36. 1.
„	4. 3.	.	Gen.	15. 6.
„	4. 7, 8.		Psa.	32. 1, 2.
„	4. 11.	.	Gen.	17. 10.
„	4. 17.	. .	Gen.	17. 5.
„	4. 18.	. .	Gen.	15. 5.
„	7. 7.	. .	Ex.	20. 17.
„	7. 7.	. .	Deut.	5. 21.
„	8. 36.	. .	Psa.	44. 22.
„	9. 7.	. .	Gen.	21. 12.
„	9. 9.	. .	Gen.	18. 10.
„	9. 12.	. .	Gen.	25. 23.
„	9. 13.	. .	Mal.	1. 2, 3.
„	9. 15.	. .	Ex.	33. 19.
„	9. 17.	. .	Ex.	9. 16.
„	9. 20.	.	a Isa.	45. 9.
„	9. 21.	. .	a Jer.	18. 6.
„	9. 25.	.	Hos.	2. 23.
„	9. 26.	. .	Hos.	1. 10.
„	9. 27, 28.		Isa.	10. 22, 23.
„	9. 29.	. .	Isa.	1. 9.
„	9. 33.	. .	Isa.	8. 14.
„	9. 33.	. .	Isa.	28. 16.
„	10. 5.	. .	Lev.	18. 5.
„	10. 5.	. .	Eze.	20. 11.
„	10. 6.	. .	a Deut.	30. 12.
„	10. 8.	. .	Deut.	30. 14.
„	10. 11.	. .	Isa.	28. 16.
„	10. 13.	. .	Joel	2. 32.
„	10. 15.	. .	Isa.	52. 7.
„	10. 15.	. .	Nah.	1. 15.
„	10. 16.	. .	Isa.	53. 1.
„	10. 18.	. .	Psa.	19. 4.
„	10. 19.	.	Deut.	32. 21.
„	10. 20, 21.		Isa.	65. 1, 2.
„	11. 1.	.	a Psa.	94. 14.
„	11. 3.	. .	1 Ki.	19. 14.
„	11. 4.	. .	1 Ki.	19. 18.
„	11. 8.	. .	Isa.	29. 10.
„	11. 8.	. .	a Isa.	6. 9.
„	11. 9, 10.		Psa.	69. 22, 23.
„	11. 26, 27.		Isa.	59. 20, 21.
„	11. 34.	. .	Isa.	40. 13.
„	11. 35.	.	a Job	41. 11.
„	12. 9.	. .	a Amos	5. 15.
„	12. 16.	.	Prov.	3. 7.
„	12. 16.	. .	a Isa.	5. 21.
„	12. 19.	.	Deut.	32. 35.
„	12. 20.	.	Prov.	25. 21, 22.
„	13. 9.	.	Ex.	20. 13, 17.
„	13. 9.	. .	Deut.	5. 17, 20.
„	13. 9.	. .	Lev.	19. 18.
„	14. 11.	. .	Isa.	45. 23.
„	15. 3.	. .	Psa.	69. 9.
„	15. 9.	. .	Psa.	18. 49.
„	15. 10.	. .	Deut.	32. 43.
„	15. 11.	. .	Psa.	117. 1.
„	15. 12.	. .	Isa.	11. 10.
„	15. 21.	. .	Isa.	52. 15.

1 CORINTH.

Chap.	1. 19.	. .	Isa.	29. 14.
„	1. 20.	. .	a Isa.	44. 25.
„	1. 20.	. .	a Isa.	33. 18.
„	1. 31.	.	Jer.	9. 24.
„	2. 9.	. .	Isa.	64. 4.
„	2. 16.	. .	Isa.	40. 13.
„	3. 8.	. .	a Psa.	62. 12.
„	3. 19.	. .	Job	5. 13.
„	3. 20.	. .	Psa.	94. 11.
„	5. 13.	. .	a Deut.	17. 9.
„	5. 13.	. .	a Deut.	19. 19.
„	5. 13.	. .	a Deut.	24. 7.
„	6. 16.	. .	Gen.	2. 24.
„	9. 9.	. .	Deut.	25. 4.
„	10. 1.	. .	a Ex.	13. 21.
„	10. 1.	. .	a Ex.	14. 22.
„	10. 1.	. .	a Num.	9. 18.
„	10. 3.	. .	a Ex.	16. 15.
„	10. 4.	. .	a Ex.	17. 6.
„	10. 6.	. .	a Num.	11. 4.
„	10. 4.	. .	a Num.	20. 11.
„	10. 5.	. .	a Num.	26. 64, 65.
„	10. 7.	. .	Ex.	32. 6.
„	10. 8, 10.		a Num.	25. 1, 9.
„	10. 8, 10.		a Num.	21. 4.
„	10. 8, 10.		a Num.	14. 2, 36.
„	10. 8, 10.		a Psa.	106. 14, 19.
„	10. 20.	.	Deut.	32. 17.
„	10. 20.	.	Psa.	107. 37.
„	10. 26, 28.		Psa.	24. 1.
„	10. 26, 28.		Deut.	10. 14.
„	14. 21.	.	Isa.	28. 11, 12.
„	14. 34.	. .	a Gen.	3. 16.
„	15. 3.	.	a Isa.	53. 8, 9.
„	15. 3.	. .	a Psa.	22.
„	15. 3.	. .	a Psa.	40.
„	15. 4.	. .	a Psa.	16. 10.
„	15. 25.	. .	Psa.	110. 1.
„	15. 27.	. .	Psa.	8. 6.
„	15. 32.	. .	Isa.	22. 13.
„	15. 45.	. .	Gen.	2. 7.
„	15. 54.	. .	Isa.	25. 8.
„	15. 55.	. .	Hos.	13. 14.

2 CORINTH.

Chap.	3. 13.	. .	a Ex.	34. 33.
„	4. 13.	. .	Psa.	116. 10.
„	5. 17.	. .	Isa.	43. 18, 19.
„	6. 2.	. .	Isa.	49. 8.
„	6. 16.	. .	Lev.	26. 11, 12.
„	6. 17, 18.		Isa.	52. 11, 12.
„	6. 17, 18.		Jer.	31. 1, 9.
„	6. 17, 18.		2 Sa.	7. 14.
„	8. 15.	. .	Ex.	16. 18.
„	9. 7.	.	a Prov.	11. 25.
„	9. 9.	. .	Psa.	112. 9.
„	9. 10.	.	Isa.	55. 10.
„	10. 17.	.	Jer.	9. 24.
„	13. 1.	.	Deut.	19. 15.

GALATIANS.

Chap.	2. 6.	. .	Deut.	10. 17.
„	2. 16.	.	a Psa	143. 2.
„	3. 6.	. .	a Gen.	15. 6.
„	3. 8.	. .	Gen.	12. 3.
„	3. 8.	. .	a Gen.	22. 18.
„	3. 10.	.	Deut.	27. 26.

GALATIANS.

Chap.	3. 11.	. .	Hab.	2. 4.
,,	3. 12.	. .	Lev.	18. 5.
,,	3. 13.	. .	Deut.	21. 23.
,,	3. 16.	. .	Gen.	22. 18.
,,	3. 17.	. .	*a* Ex.	12. 40.
,,	4. 22.	. .	*a* Gen.	21. 2, 9.
,,	4. 22.	. .	*a* Gen.	16. 15.
,,	4. 27.	. .	Isa.	54. 1.
,,	4. 30.	. .	Gen.	21. 10.
,,	5. 14.	. .	Lev.	19. 18.

EPHESIANS.

Chap.	2. 17.	. .	*a* Isa.	57. 19.
,,	4. 8.	. .	Psa.	68. 18.
,,	4. 25.	. .	Zec.	8. 16.
,,	4. 26.	. .	Psa.	4. 4.
,,	5. 31.	. .	Gen.	2. 24.
,,	6. 2, 3.	.	Ex.	20. 12.
,,	6. 2, 3.	.	Deut.	5. 16.
,,	6. 9.	. .	*a* Deut.	10. 17.
,,	6. 9.	. .	*a* Job	34. 19.
,,	6. 17.	.	*a* Isa.	59. 17.

PHILIPP.

Chap.	2. 10.	. .	*a* Isa.	45. 23.
,,	4. 5.	. .	*a* Psa.	119 & 141.
,,	4. 5.	. .	*a* Psa.	145. 18.

COLOSS.

Chap.	2. 11.	.	*a* Deut.	10. 16.
,,	3. 25.	. .	*a* Deut.	10. 17.
,,	3. 25.	. .	*a* Job	34. 19.

1 THESS.

Chap.	5. 8.	.	*a* Isa.	59. 17.
,,	5. 15.	. .	*a* Prov.	17. 13.

2 THESS.

Chap.	2. 4.	. .	*a* Dan.	11. 36.
,,	2. 8.	.	*a* Isa.	11. 4.
,,	2. 8.	. .	Hos.	6. 5.

1 TIMOTHY.

Chap.	2. 13.	. .	*a* Gen.	1 and 2.
,,	2. 14.	. .	*a* Gen.	3. 6.
,,	5. 18.	. .	Deut.	25. 4.
,,	6. 7.	.	*a* Job	1. 21.
,,	6. 7.	. .	*a* Ecc.	5. 14.
,,	6. 7.	. .	*a* Psa.	49. 17.

2 TIMOTHY.

Chap.	2. 19.	. .	*a* Num.	16. 5.
,,	3. 8.	. .	*a* Ex.	7. 11, 22.

HEBREWS.

Chap.	1. 5.	. .	Psa.	2. 7.
,,	1. 5.	. .	2 Sa.	7. 14.
,,	1. 6.	. .	Psa.	97. 7.
,,	1. 7.	. .	Psa.	104. 4.
,,	1. 8, 9.	.	Psa.	45. 6, 7.
,,	1. 10. 11, 12.		Psa.	102. 25, 26, 27.
,,	1. 13.	. .	Psa.	110. 1.
,,	2. 6.	. .	Psa.	8. 4.
,,	2. 12.	. .	Psa.	22. 22.
,,	2. 13.	. .	Isa.	8. 18.
,,	2. 13.	. .	Psa.	18. 2.
,,	2. 13.	. .	2 Sa.	22. 2.
,,	3. 2.	. .	*a* Num.	12. 7.
,,	3. 7-11.	.	Psa.	95. 7-11.
,,	3. 15-19.	.	Psa.	95. 7-11.
,,		. .	*a* Num.	14. 29, &c.
,,	4. 3.	. .	Psa.	95. 11.
,,	4. 4.	. .	Gen.	2. 3.
,,	4. 7.	. .	Psa.	95. 7, 8.
,,	5. 4.	. .	*a* 1 Ch.	23. 13.
,,	5. 4.	. .	2 Ch.	26. 18.
,,	5. 5.	. .	Psa.	2. 7.
,,	5. 6.	. .	Psa.	110. 4.
,,	6. 13, 14.		Gen.	22. 16, 17.
,,	7. 1.	. .	*a* Gen.	14. 18.
,,	7. 17, 21.		Psa.	110. 4.

HEBREWS.

Chap.	8. 5.	. .	Ex.	25. 40.
,,	8. 8, 9, 10, 11, 12.		Jer.	31. 31, 32, 33, 34.
,,	9. 2.	.	*a* Ex.	25.
,,	9. 2.	.	*a* Ex.	40. 4.
,,	9. 13.	.	*a* Lev.	16. 14.
,,	9. 13.	. .	Num.	19. 17.
,,	9. 20.	. .	Ex.	24. 8.
,,	10. 5, 6.		Psa.	40. 6.
,,	10. 12, 13.		*a* Psa.	110. 1.
,,	10. 16, 17.		Jer.	31. 33, 34.
,,	10. 27.	.	*a* Isa.	64. 1, 2.
,,	10. 28.	. .	*a* Deut.	17. 6.
,,	10. 30.	.	Deut.	32. 35, 36.
,,	10. 37, 38.		Hab.	2. 3, 4.
,,	11. 3.	.	*a* Gen.	1. 1.
,,	11. 4.	.	*a* Gen.	4. 4.
,,	11. 5.	.	*a* Gen.	5. 24.
,,	11. 7.	.	*a* Gen.	6. 8, 14.
,,	11. 8.	.	*a* Gen.	12. 1, 4.
,,	11. 13.	. .	Gen.	23. 4.
,,	11. 13.	.	*a* Gen.	47. 9.
,,	11. 13.	.	*a* Psa.	39. 12.
,,	11. 17.	.	*a* Gen.	22. 9.
,,	11. 18.	.	*a* Gen.	21. 12.
,,	11. 20.	.	*a* Gen.	27. 27, 28.
,,	11. 21.	.	Gen.	47. 31.
,,	11. 21.	.	Gen.	48. 16.
,,	11. 22.	.	*a* Gen.	50. 25.
,,	11. 23.	.	*a* Ex.	2. 2.
,,	11. 28.	.	*a* Ex.	12. 11, 18.
,,	11. 29.	.	*a* Ex.	14. 22.
,,	11. 30.	.	*a* Jos.	6. 20.
,,	11. 31.	.	*a* Jos.	2. 1.
,,	11. 31.	.	*a* Jos.	6. 17, 23.
,,	11. 32.	.	*a* Jud.	6. 4, 11, 15.
,,	11. 32.	.	*a?* 1 Sa.	7.
,,	11. 32.	.	*a?* 2 Sa.	2.
,,	11. 33.	.	*a?* 2 Sa.	8.
,,	11. 33.	.	*a?* Jud.	14.
,,	11. 33.	.	*a?* Dan.	6.
,,	11. 34.	.	*a?* Dan.	3.
,,	11. 35.	.	*a?* 2 Ki.	4. 20.
,,	12. 5, 6.		Prov.	3. 11, 12.
,,	12. 9.	. .	*a?* Num.	27. 16.
,,	12. 12, 13.		*a* Isa.	35. 3.
,,	12. 12, 13.		*a* Prov.	4. 26.
,,	12. 15.	. .	*a* Deut.	29. 18.
,,	12. 16.	.	*a* Gen.	25. 33.
,,	12. 18.	.	*a* Ex.	19. 16.
,,	12. 20.	.	Ex.	19. 12, 13.
,,	12. 21.	.	Deut.	9. 19.
,,	12. 26.	.	Hag.	2. 6.
,,	12. 29.	.	Deut.	4. 24.
,,	13. 5.	.	Deut.	31. 8.
,,	13. 5.	.	Josh.	1. 5.
,,	13. 6.	.	Psa.	118. 6.
,,	13. 11.	.	*a* Lev.	4. 12, 21.
,,	13. 11.	. .	*a* Lev.	16. 27.
,,	13. 11.	. .	*a* Num.	19. 3.
,,	13. 14.	. .	*a* Mic.	2. 10.

JAMES.

Chap.	1. 10.	. .	*a* Isa.	40. 6.
,,	1. 12.	. .	Job	5. 17.
,,	1. 19.	.	*a* Prov.	17. 27.
,,	2. 1.	.	*a* Lev.	19. 15.
,,	2. 1.	.	*a* Prov.	24. 23.
,,	2. 8.	.	Lev.	19. 18.
,,	2. 11.	. .	Ex.	20. 13, 14, 15.
,,	2. 21.	. .	*a* Gen.	22. 9.
,,	2. 23.	. .	Gen.	15. 6.
,,	2. 25.	.	*a* Josh.	2. 1.
,,	2. 25.	. .	*a* Josh.	6. 17, 23.
,,	4. 6.	. .	Prov.	3. 34.
,,	5. 3.	.	*a?* Prov.16.	27.
,,	5. 11.	. .	*a* Job	1. 21, 22.
,,	5. 11.	. .	*a* Job	42. 1-17.
,,	5. 17, 18.		*a* 1 Ki.	17. 1.
,,	5. 17, 18.		*a* 1 Ki.	18. 41.

1 PETER.

Chap.	1. 16.	. .	Lev.	11. 44.
,,	1. 24, 25.		Isa.	40. 6.
,,	2. 3.	. .	*a?* Psa.	34. 8.
,,	2. 4.	.	*a* Psa.	118. 22.
,,	2. 6.	. .	Isa.	28. 16.
,,	2. 7.	.	Psa.	118. 22, 23.
,,	2. 9.	.	Ex.	19. 6.
,,	2. 10.	.	*a* Hos.	2. 23.
,,	2. 17.	.	*a* Prov.	24. 21.
,,	2. 22.	.	Isa.	53. 9.
,,	2. 24.	. .	Isa.	53. 5.
,,	3. 6.	.	*a* Gen.	18. 12.
,,	3. 10, 11, 12.		Psa.	34. 13, &c.
,,	3. 14, 15.		? Isa.	8. 12, 13.
,,	3. 20.	.	*a* Gen.	6. 3, 12.
,,	4. 8.	. .	Prov.	10. 12.
,,	4. 18.	.	*a* Prov.	11. 31.
,,	5. 5.	.	*a* Prov.	3. 34.
,,	5. 7.	.	*a* Psa.	55. 22.

2 PETER.

Chap.	2. 5.	. .	*a* Gen.	7. 23.
,,	2. 5.	.	*a* Gen.	8.
,,	2. 6.	.	*a* Gen.	19.
,,	2. 15, 16.		*a* Num.	22.
,,	2. 22.	. .	Prov.	26. 11.
,,	3. 4.	.	*a* Eze.	12. 22.
,,	3. 5, 6.		*a* Gen.	1. 1, 2, 6.
,,	3. 5, 6.		*a* Gen.	7. 21.
,,	3. 8.	.	*a* Psa.	90. 4.
,,	3. 10.	.	*a?* Psa.102.	26, 27.
,,	3. 13.	.	*a* Isa.	65. 17.
,,	3. 13.	.	*a* Isa.	66. 22.

1 JOHN.

Chap.	1. 8.	.	*a* Prov.	20. 9.
,,	3. 5.	.	*a* Isa.	53. 4.
,,	3. 12.	.	*a* Gen.	4. 8.
,,	3. 12.	.	*a?* Num.22.	
,,	3. 12.	.	*a* Num.	16. 1, 31.

REVELAT.

Chap.	1. 4.	.	*a* Ex.	3. 14.
,,	1. 6.	.	*a?* Ex.	19. 6.
,,	1. 7.	. .	*a?* Dan.	7. 13.
,,	1. 7.	.	*a?* Isa.	40. 5.
,,	1. 7.	.	*a?* Zec.	12. 10-14.
,,	1. 8.	.	*a* Isa.	41. 4.
,,	1. 8.	.	*a?* Isa.	44. 6.
,,	1. 12.	.	*a?* Zec.	4. 2.
,,	1. 14, 15.		*a?* Dan.	7. 9.
,,	1. 14, 15.		*a?* Dan.	10. 5, 6.
,,	1. 14, 15.		*a?* Eze.	1. 27.
,,	1. 14, 15.		*a?* Eze.	8. 2.
,,	1. 14, 15.		*a?* Eze.	43. 2.
,,	1. 16.	.	*a?* Isa.	49. 2.
,,	1. 17.	.	*a?* Dan.	8. 17.
,,	1. 17.	.	*a?* Dan.	10. 8, &c.
,,	1. 17.	.	*a?* Isa.	44. 6.
,,	2. 1.	.	*a?* Deut.23.	14.
,,	2. 7.	.	*a?* Gen.	2. 9.
,,	2. 14.	.	*a?* Num.25.	1.
,,	2. 14.	.	*a?* Num.31.16.	
,,	2. 20.	.	*a?* 1 Ki.	16. 31.
,,	2. 20.	.	*a?* 1 Ki.	21. 23.
,,	2. 20.	.	*a?* 2 Ki.	9. 33.
,,	2. 23.	.	*a?* Jer.	17. 10.
,,	2. 27.	.	*a?* Psa.	2. 9.
,,	3. 7.	.	*a?* Isa.	22. 22.
,,	3. 7.	.	*a?* Job	12. 14.
,,	3. 9.	.	*a?* Isa.	60. 14.
,,	3. 17.	.	*a?* Hos.	12. 8.
,,	3. 19.	.	*a?* Prov.	3. 11, 12.
,,	3. 21.	.	*a?* Psa.110.	1.
,,	4. 2, 3.		*a?* Eze.	1. 26, 28.
,,	4. 5.	.	*a?* Ex.	19. 16.
,,	4. 5.	.	*a?* Eze.	1. 13.
,,	4. 5.	.	*a?* Isa.	6.
,,	4. 5.	.	*a?* Zec.	4. 2.
,,	4. 6.	.	*a?* Eze.	1. 22.
,,	4. 6.	.	*a?* Ex.	24. 10.

REVELAT.

Chap.		Ref.
4. 6.	a? Eze.	1. 5.
4. 6.	a? Eze.	10. 12.
4. 7.	a? Eze.	1. 10.
4. 8.	a? Isa.	6. 2.
5. 1.	a? Eze.	2. 9.
5. 6.	a? Isa.	53. 7.
5. 6.	a? Zec.	4. 10.
5. 6.	a? 2 Ch.	16. 9.
5. 8.	a? Psa.	141. 2.
5. 10.	a? Ex.	19. 6.
5. 11.	a? Dan.	7. 10.
6. 8.	a? Eze.	14. 21.
6. 12, 13.	a? Isa.	24. 18, 23.
6. 12, 13.	a? Isa.	13. 13.
6. 12, 13.	a? Hag.	2. 6.
6. 12, 13.	a? Joel	2. 31.
6. 12, 13.	a Isa.	34. 4.
6. 14.	a Psa.	102. 26.
6. 14.	a Isa.	34. 4.
6. 15, 16.	a? Isa.	2. 9, &c.
6. 15, 16.	a? Isa.	2. 19, &c.
6. 15, 16.	a Hos.	10. 8.
6. 15, 16.	a Isa.	13. 13.
6. 15, 16.	a Psa.	110. 5.
6. 15, 16.	a Joel	2. 11.
7. 2, &c.	a? Eze.	9. 2, &c.
7. 16.	Isa.	49. 10.
7. 17.	Isa.	25. 8.
8. 3.	a Lev.	16. 12, &c.
8. 3.	a? Ex.	30. 8.
8. 3.	a Psa.	141. 2.
8. 5.	a? Eze.	10. 2.
8. 7.	a Joel	2. 30.
8. 7.	a Ex.	9. 23.
8. 8.	a? Ex.	7. 20.
8. 11.	a Jer.	9. 15.
8. 12.	a? Eze.	32. 7.
9. 4.	a Eze.	9. 6.
9. 6.	a Jer.	8. 3.
9. 7, 8, 9.	a Joel	2. 4.
9. 7, 8, 9.	a Joel	1. 6.
9. 7, 8, 9.	a Joel	2. 5.
9. 20.	a Psa.	115. 4.
9. 20.	a Psa.	135. 15.
10. 2.	a Eze.	2. 9.
10. 3.	a Jer.	25. 30.
10. 4.	a Dan.	8. 26.
10. 5.	a Dan.	12. 7.
10. 8, &c.	a Eze.	2. 8.
10. 11.	a? Jer.	1. 9, 10.
11. 1.	a? Eze.	40. 3, 5.
11. 1.	a? Eze.	41. 13.
11. 1.	a? Eze.	40. 47.
11. 2.	a? Dan.	7. 25.
11. 4.	a Zec.	4. 3, 11.
11. 5.	a? 2 Ki.	1. 9-12.
11. 6.	a 1 Ki.	17. 1.
11. 6.	a Ex.	7. 20.
11. 7.	a Dan.	7. 21.
11. 10.	a Esth	9. 22.
11. 15.	a? Dan.	2. 44.
11. 15.	a Dan.	7. 14.
11. 18.	a Psa.	2. 1-5.
11. 18.	a Psa.	46. 6.
11. 18.	a? Dan.	7. 10, 22.
11. 18.	a Psa.	115. 13.
11. 18.	a? Dan.	11. 44.
12. 1, 2.	a? Mic.	4. 9, 10.
12. 1, 2.	a? Isa.	66. 7.

REVELAT.

Chap.		Ref.
12. 3.	a Dan.	7. 7.
12. 4.	a? Dan.	8. 10.
12. 5.	a Isa.	66. 7.
12. 5.	a? Psa.	2. 10.
12. 6.	a? Dan.	7. 25.
12. 7.	a? Dan.	10. 13, 21.
12. 7.	a? Dan.	12. 1.
12. 14.	a? Dan.	7. 25.
12. 14.	a? Dan.	12. 7.
13. 1.	a? Dan.	7. 3, 7.
13. 2.	a Dan.	7. 5, 6.
13. 5, 6.	a Dan.	7. 8.
13. 5, 6.	a Dan.	7. 25.
13. 7.	a? Dan.	8. 10, 24.
13. 7.	a Dan.	5. 19.
13. 7.	a Dan.	2. 37.
13. 10.	a Isa.	14. 2.
13. 10.	a Gen.	9. 6.
13. 14.	a? Dan.	3.
14. 1.	a Psa.	2. 6.
14. 1.	a Isa.	59. 20.
14. 5.	a Psa.	32. 2.
14. 8.	a Isa.	21. 9.
14. 8.	a Jer.	51. 8.
14. 8.	a? Dan.	4. 31.
14. 10.	a? Psa.	75. 8.
14. 10.	a Isa.	51. 22.
14. 10.	a Jer.	25. 15.
14. 11.	a Isa.	34. 10.
14. 14.	a? Dan.	7. 13.
14. 14.	a Isa.	19. 1.
14. 15.	a? Joel	3. 13.
14. 19, 20.	a Joel	3. 13.
14. 19, 20.	a Isa.	63. 3.
14. 19, 20.	a Lam.	1. 15.
15. 3.	a Ex.	15. 11.
15. 4.	a Jer.	10. 7.
15. 4.	Psa.	86. 9.
15. 7.	a Eze.	10. 7.
15. 8.	a Eze.	10. 4.
15. 8.	a Isa.	6. 4.
15. 8.	a 1 Ki.	8. 11.
16. 2.	a? Ex.	9. 10.
16. 3, &c.	a? Ex.	7. 19, 20.
16. 6.	a? Ex.	7. 21.
16. 6.	a? Eze.	16. 38.
16. 10.	a? Ex.	10. 22.
16. 12.	a? Isa.	11. 15, 16.
16. 12.	a? Jer.	50. 38.
16. 14, 16.	a? Zep.	3. 8.
16. 14, 16.	a? Joel	3. 2.
16. 14, 16.	a? Zec.	14. 2.
16. 21.	a? Ex.	9. 24, 34.
17. 1.	a Jer.	51. 13.
17. 2.	a Jer.	51. 7.
17. 3.	a? Dan.	7. 7, 8.
17. 4.	a? Jer.	51. 7.
17. 8.	a? Dan.	7. 11.
17. 12.	a Dan.	7. 20, 24.
17. 14.	a Dan.	8. 25.
17. 15.	a Isa.	8. 7.
17. 15.	a Jer.	47. 2.
18. 2.	Isa.	21. 9.
18. 2.	a Jer.	51. 8.
18. 2.	a Isa.	13. 21.
18. 3.	Jer.	51. 7.
18. 3.	a Nah.	3. 4.
18. 4.	a Isa.	52. 11.
18. 4.	a Jer.	50. 8.

REVELAT.

Chap.		Ref.
18. 4.	a Jer.	51. 6, 9, 45.
18. 6.	a Jer.	50. 15, 29.
18. 6.	a Psa.	137. 8.
18. 7, 8.	a Isa.	47. 7, &c.
18. 7, 8.	a Jer.	50. 31.
18. 11.	a Eze.	27. 27.
18. 11.	a Isa.	23.
18. 18.	a Isa.	34. 10.
18. 20.	a Isa.	44. 23.
18. 20.	a Jer.	51. 48.
18. 21.	a? Jer.	51. 63, 64.
18. 22.	a Isa.	24. 8.
18. 22.	a Jer.	7. 34.
18. 22.	a Jer.	25. 10.
18. 23.	a Isa.	23. 8.
18. 24.	a Jer.	51. 49.
19. 2.	a Deut.	32. 4, 41.
19. 3.	a Isa.	34. 10.
19. 5.	a Psa.	135. 1, 20.
19. 5.	a Psa.	115. 13.
19. 8.	a Psa.	45. 14.
19. 8.	a Isa.	61. 10.
19. 11.	a? Psa.	72. 2, &c.
19. 12.	a Dan.	10. 6.
19. 13.	a Isa.	63. 1.
19. 15.	a Psa.	2. 9.
19. 15.	a Lam.	1. 15.
19. 15.	a Isa.	63. 3.
19. 17, 18.	a? Isa.	34. 6.
19. 17, 18.	a Eze.	39. 17-20.
19. 19.	a Psa.	2. 2.
19. 20.	a? Isa.	30. 33.
19. 20.	a? Dan.	1. 7-11.
20. 4.	a? Dan.	9. 22, 27.
21. 1.	a Isa.	65. 17.
21. 2.	a? Eze.	40 & 48.
21. 3.	a Eze.	37. 27.
21. 4.	a Isa.	25. 8.
21. 4.	a Isa.	65. 19.
21. 5.	a Isa.	43. 19.
21. 6.	a Isa.	51. 1.
21. 10.	a Eze.	40. 2.
21. 12.	a Eze.	48. 31.
21. 15.	a Zec.	2. 1.
21. 15.	a Eze.	40. 3.
21. 19.	a Isa.	54. 11, 12.
21. 23.	a Isa.	60. 19.
21. 23.	a? Eze.	48. 35.
21. 24, 25.	a Isa.	60. 3, 11, 20.
21. 27.	a? Isa.	52. 1.
21. 27.	a Eze.	44. 9.
22. 1, 2.	a Zec.	14. 8.
22. 1, 2.	a Eze.	47. 1, 7, 12.
22. 3.	a? Zec.	14. 11.
22. 5.	a Isa.	24. 23.
22. 5.	a Isa.	60. 19.
22. 5.	a Eze.	48. 35.
22. 10.	a? Dan.	8. 26.
22. 10.	a? Dan.	12. 4.
22. 12.	a Isa.	40. 10.
22. 13.	a Isa.	41. 4.
22. 13.	a Isa.	44. 6.
22. 16.	a Isa.	11. 1, 10.
22. 17.	a Isa.	55. 1.
22. 18.	a Deut.	4. 2.
22. 18.	a Deut.	12. 32.

THE NAMES, TITLES, AND CHARACTERS

OF THE

SON OF GOD JESUS CHRIST OUR LORD,

IN THEIR VARIETY, AS FOUND IN THE SCRIPTURES.

"THEY ARE THEY WHICH TESTIFY OF ME."

The Headings are designed to direct the mind to various Aspects of the Person, and Glories of the Lord. Examine each text with the context, in Proof that the Son of God is the Speaker, or the One spoken of.

I.—AND SIMON PETER ANSWERED AND SAID, THOU ART THE CHRIST, THE SON OF THE LIVING GOD.—Mat. 16. 16.

The Son	1 Jno. 4. 14.
The Son of God	Jno. 1. 34.
The Son of the living God	Mat. 16. 16.
His only begotten Son	Jno. 3. 16.
The only begotten Son of God . . .	Jno. 3. 18.
The Son of the Father	2 Jno. 3.
The only begotten of the Father .	Jno. 1. 14.
The only begotten Son, which is in the bosom of the Father	Jno. 1. 18.
The first born of every creature .	Col. 1. 15.
His own Son	Ro. 8. 32.
A Son given	Is. 9. 6.
One Son (His well-beloved) . . .	Mar. 12. 6.
My Son	Ps. 2. 7.
His dear Son (or the Son of His love) .	Col. 1. 13.
The Son of the Highest	Lu. 1. 32.
The Son of the Blessed	Mar. 14. 61.

Secret, Ju. 13. 18.—Wonderful, Is. 9. 6.

TESTIMONY BORNE TO THE SON BY THE FATHER, BY JESUS HIMSELF, BY THE SPIRIT, BY ANGELS, SAINTS, MEN, AND DEVILS.

My Beloved Son, Mat. 17. 5 .	God the Father.
I am the Son of God, Jno. 10. 36 .	Jesus Himself.
The Son of God, Mar. 1. 1	The Spirit in the word.
The Son of God, Lu. 1. 35 ; 2. 11 .	Gabriel.
This is the Son of God, Jno. 1. 34	John Baptist.
The Christ the Son of God, Jno. 20. 31 .	John, Apostle.
He is the Son of God, Ac. 9. 20 .	Paul, Apostle.
Thou art the Son of God, Mat. 14. 33	Disciples.
Rabbi, thou art the Son of God, Jno. 1. 49	Nathanael.
The Christ the Son of God, Jno. 11. 27 .	Martha.
Jesus Christ is the Son of God, Ac. 8. 37	Eunuch.
Truly this was the Son of God, Mar. 15. 39	Centurion.
Thou art the Son of God, Mar. 3. 11	Unclean Spirits.
Thou Son of the Most High God, Mar. 5. 7	The Legion.

II.—UNTO THE SON HE SAITH, THY THRONE, O GOD, IS FOR EVER AND EVER.—He. 1. 8.

God . . Jno. 1. 1; Mat. 1. 23;	Is. 40. 3.
Thy throne, O God, is for ever and ever	He. 1. 8.
The Mighty God	Is. 9. 6.
The Everlasting God	Is. 40. 28.
The True God	1 Jno. 5. 20.
My Lord and my God . . .	Jno. 20. 28.
God my Saviour	Lu. 1. 47.
Over all, God blessed for ever, Amen .	Ro. 9. 5.
The God of the whole earth . .	Is. 54. 5.
God manifest in the flesh . .	1 Ti. 3. 16.
Our God and Saviour (*marg.*) .	2 Pe. 1. 1.
The Great God, and our Saviour Jesus Christ	Tit. 2. 13.
Emmanuel, God with us . .	Mat. 1. 23.

The God of Abraham . } Ex. 3. 2, 6	As to the Angel of the Lord who spake as the God of Abraham being the Son of God, comp. Ju. xiii. 18, 22 (*mar.*), with Is. ix. 6; also Da. iii. 25, 28.
The God of Isaac	
The God of Jacob	

The Highest, Lu. 1. 76.

III.—VERILY, VERILY, I SAY UNTO YOU, BEFORE ABRAHAM WAS, I AM.—Jno. 8. 58.

HOLY, HOLY, HOLY IS JEHOVAH OF HOSTS.— Is. 6. 3.

Jehovah	Is. 40. 3.
The Lord Jehovah	Is. 40. 10.
Jehovah my God	Zec. 14. 5.
Jehovah of Hosts . . . Is. 6. 3 ;	Jno. 12. 41.
Jehovah God of Hosts . Ho. 12. 4, 5 ;	Ge. 32. 24.
The King Jehovah of hosts . .	Is. 6. 5.
The Strong and Mighty Jehovah .	Ps. 24. 8.
Jehovah, mighty in battle . .	Ps. 24. 8.
The Man, Jehovah's Fellow . .	Zec. 13. 7.
Jehovah-tsidkenu . . .	Je. 23. 6.
(the Lord our righteousness)	
The Lord . . . Ro. 10. 13 ;	Joel 2. 32.
The Lord of Glory	1 Cor. 2. 8.
The Same . . . . He. 1. 12 ;	Ps. 102. 27.
I am . . . . Ex. 3. 14 ;	Jno. 8. 24.
I am (before Abraham was) . .	Jno. 8. 58.
I am (whom they sought to kill) . .	Jno. 18. 5, 6.
I am (the Son of Man lifted up) .	Jno. 8. 28.
I am (the Resurrection and the Life) .	Jno. 11. 25.

IV.—HE IS BEFORE ALL THINGS, AND BY HIM ALL THINGS CONSIST.—Col. 1. 17.

The Almighty, which is, and which was, and which is to come . . .	Re. 1. 8.
The Creator of all things . .	Col. 1. 16.
The Upholder of all things . .	He. 1. 3.
The Everlasting Father . . .	Is. 9. 6.
(or Father of Eternity)	
The Beginning	Col. 1. 18.
The Beginning and the Ending .	Re. 1. 8.
The Alpha and the Omega . .	Re. 1. 8.
The First and the Last . . .	Re. 1. 17.
The Life	1 Jno. 1. 2.
Eternal Life	1 Jno. 5. 20.
That Eternal Life which was with the Father	1 Jno. 1. 2.
He that liveth	Re. 1. 18.

V.—NO MAN HATH SEEN GOD AT ANY TIME, HE HATH DECLARED HIM.—Jno. 1. 18.

The Word	Jno. 1. 1.
The Word was with God . .	Jno. 1. 1.
The Word was God . . .	Jno. 1. 1.
The Word of God	Re. 19. 13.
The Word of Life	1 Jno. 1. 1.
The Word was made flesh . .	Jno. 1. 14.
The Image of God	2 Cor. 4. 4.
The Image of the Invisible God .	Col. 1. 15.
The Express Image of his Person .	He. 1. 3.
The Brightness of his Glory . .	He. 1. 3.
Wisdom	Pr. 8. 12, 22.
The Wisdom of God . . .	1 Cor. 1. 24.
The Power of God	1 Cor. 1. 24.
My Messenger	Is. 42. 19.
The Messenger of the Covenant .	Mal. 3. 1.
The Angel of Jehovah . . .	Ge. 22. 15.
The Angel of God . Ge. 31. 11, 13 ;	Ex. 14. 19.
The Angel of his presence . .	Is. 63. 9.

NAMES AND TITLES OF THE SON OF GOD.

VI.—Thou hast made Him a little lower than the Angels.—He. 2. 7.

The Man	Jno. 19. 5.
The Man Christ Jesus	1 Ti. 2. 5.
A Man approved of God . . .	Ac. 2. 22.
The Second Man, the Lord from Heaven	1 Co. 15. 47.
The Son of Man	Mar. 10. 33.
The Son of Abraham . . .	Mat. 1. 1.
The Son of David	Mat. 1. 1.
The Son of Mary	Mar. 6. 3.
The Son of Joseph (reputed) . .	Jno. 1. 45.
The Seed of the Woman . . .	Ge. 3. 15.
The Seed of Abraham . . .	Ga. 3. 16, 19.
Of the Seed of David . . .	Ro. 1. 3.

VII.—Lo, I come to do Thy will, O God.—He. 10.

The Babe	Lu. 2. 12.
The Child	Is. 7. 16.
The Young Child	Mat. 2. 20.
A Child Born	Is. 9. 6.
The Child Jesus	Lu. 2. 43.
Her First Born Son . . .	Lu. 2. 7.
The Sent of the Father . . .	Jno. 10. 36.
The Apostle	He. 3. 1.
A Prophet	Ac. 3. 22, 23.
A Great Prophet . . .	Lu. 7. 16.
The Prophet of Nazareth . . .	Mat. 21. 11.
A Prophet, mighty in deed and word .	Lu. 24. 19.
A Servant	Phi. 2. 7.
The Servant of the Father . .	Mat. 12. 18.
My Servant, O Israel	Is. 49. 3.
My Servant, the Branch . .	Zec. 3. 8.
My Righteous Servant . . .	Is. 53. 11.
A Servant of Rulers . . .	Is. 49. 7.
A Nazarene	Mat. 2. 23.
The Carpenter	Mar. 6. 3.
The Carpenter's Son (reputed) . .	Mat. 13. 55.

He humbled Himself . . . unto death.

A Stranger and an Alien . . .	Ps. 69. 8.
A Man of Sorrows	Is. 53. 3.
A Worm, and no Man . . .	Ps. 22. 6.
Accursed of God	De. 21. 23.
or the Curse of God (*marg.*)	

VIII.—God hath given Him a Name which is above every name.—Phi. 2. 9, 10.

Jesus	Mat. 1. 21.
Jesus Himself	Lu. 24. 15.
I, Jesus	Re. 22. 16.
A Saviour, Jesus	Ac. 13. 23.
The Saviour of the World . .	1 Jno. 4. 14.
A Saviour, which is Christ the Lord	Lu. 2. 11.
Jesus Christ	Re. 1. 5.
The Lord Jesus Christ . . .	Col. 1. 2.
Our Lord Jesus Christ, Himself .	2 Thes. 2. 16.
Jesus the Christ	Mat. 16. 20.
Jesus Christ, our Lord . . .	Ro. 5. 21.
Jesus Christ, the Righteous .	1 Jno. 2. 1.
Jesus Christ, the same yesterday, to-day, and for ever . . .	He. 13. 8.
Jesus of Nazareth	Ac. 22. 8.
Jesus Christ of Nazareth . .	Ac. 4. 10.
Lord Jesus	Ac. 7. 59.
Christ Jesus	1 Ti. 1. 15.
Christ	Mat. 23. 8.
Messiah, which is called Christ .	Jno. 4. 25.
Anointed . . .	Ps. 2. 2 ; Ac. 4. 26.
Christ, the Lord	Lu. 2. 11.
The Lord Christ	Col. 3. 24.
The Christ of God . . .	Lu. 9. 20.
The Lord's Christ . . .	Lu. 2. 26.
The Christ, the Son of the Blessed .	Mar. 14. 61.
The Christ, the Saviour of the World .	Jno. 4. 42.

IX.—Worthy is the Lamb that was slain to receive Power, Riches, Wisdom, Strength, Honour, Glory, and Blessing.—Re. 5. 12.

The Lamb of God	Jno. 1. 29.
A Lamb without blemish, and without spot	1 Pe. 1. 19.
The Lamb that was Slain . . .	Re. 5. 12.
A Lamb as it had been Slain . .	Re. 5. 6.
The Lamb in the midst of the Throne	Re. 7. 17.
The Bridegroom . . .	Mat. 9. 15 ; Re. 21. 9.
The Lamb (the Temple of the City) .	Re. 21. 22.
The Lamb (the Light of the City) .	Re. 21. 23.
The Lamb (the overcomer) . . .	Re. 17. 14.

X.—I will set up One Shepherd over them, and He shall feed them.—Eze. 34. 23.

One Shepherd	Jno. 10. 16.
Jehovah's Shepherd	Zec. 13. 7.
The Shepherd of the Sheep . .	He. 13. 20.
The Way	Jno. 14. 6.
The Door of the Sheep . . .	Jno. 10. 7.
The Shepherd of Israel . . .	Eze. 34. 23.
The Shepherd and Bishop of Souls .	1 Pe. 2. 25.
The Good Shepherd . . .	Jno. 10. 11.
(that laid down His life)	
The Great Shepherd	He. 13. 20.
(that was brought again from the dead)	
The Chief Shepherd . . .	1 Pe. 5. 4.
(that shall again appear)	

XI.—The Tree of Life, in the midst of the Paradise of God.—Re. 2. 7.

The Root of Jesse	Is. 11. 10.
The Root of David	Re. 5. 5.
The Root and Offspring of David .	Re. 22. 16.
A Rod out of the stem of Jesse .	Is. 11. 1
A Branch out of his roots . .	Is. 11. 1.
The Branch	Zec. 6. 12.
The Branch of the Lord . .	Is. 4. 2.
The Branch of Righteousness . .	Je. 33. 15.
A Righteous Branch . . .	Je. 23. 5.
The Branch strong for Thyself .	Ps. 80. 15.
The Vine	Jno. 15. 5.
The True Vine	Jno. 15. 1.
The Tree of Life	Re. 2. 7.
The Corn of Wheat . . .	Jno. 12. 24.
The Bread of God . . .	Jno. 6. 33.
The True Bread from Heaven .	Jno. 6. 32.
The Bread which came down from Heaven	Jno. 6. 41.
The Bread which cometh down from Heaven	Jno. 6. 50.
The Bread of Life . . .	Jno. 6. 35.
The Living Bread	Jno. 6. 51.
The Hidden Manna	Re. 2. 17.
A Plant of Renown . . .	Eze. 34. 29.
The Rose of Sharon . . .	Ca. 2. 1.
The Lily of the Valleys . . .	Ca. 2. 1.
A Bundle of Myrrh	Ca. 1. 13.
A Cluster of Camphire . . .	Ca. 1. 14.

XII.—I am the Light of the world : he that followeth Me shall have the Light of Life.—Jno. 8. 12.

The Light	Jno. 12. 35.
The True Light	Jno. 1. 9.
A Great Light	Is. 9. 2.
A Light come into the World . .	Jno. 12. 46.
The Light of the World . .	Jno. 8. 12.
The Light of Men . . .	Jno. 1. 4.
A Light to lighten the Gentiles .	Lu. 2. 32.
A Light of the Gentiles . . .	Is. 42. 6.
A Star	Nu. 24. 17.
The Morning Star	Re. 2. 28.
The Bright and Morning Star . .	Re. 22. 16.
The Day Star	2 Pe. 1. 19
The Day-spring from on High . .	Lu. 1. 78.
The Sun of Righteousness . . .	Mal. 4. 2.

XIII.—THE NAME OF THE LORD IS A STRONG TOWER.— Pr. 18. 10.

The Strength of the Children of Israel	Joel 3. 12-16.
A Strength to the Poor .	Is. 25. 4.
A Strength to the Needy in distress	Is. 25. 4.
A Refuge from the Storm . .	Is. 25. 4.
A Covert from the Tempest . .	Is. 32. 2.
The Hope of His People . .	Joel 3. 12-16.
or Place of Repair (marg.)	
or Harbour of His People (marg.)	
A Horn of Salvation . . .	Lu. 1. 69.

XIV.—THEY DRANK OF THAT SPIRITUAL ROCK THAT FOLLOWED THEM, AND THAT ROCK WAS CHRIST.— 1. Cor. 10. 4.

The Rock	Mat. 16. 18.
My Strong Rock . . .	Ps. 31. 2.
The Rock of Ages (marg.) . .	Is. 26. 4.
The Rock that is higher than I .	Ps. 61. 2.
My Rock and my Fortress . .	Ps. 31. 3.
The Rock of my Strength . .	Ps. 62. 7.
The Rock of my Refuge . .	Ps. 94. 22.
A Rock of Habitation (marg.) .	Ps. 71. 3.
The Rock of my Heart (marg.) .	Ps. 73. 26.
The Rock of my Salvation .	2 Sa. 22. 47.
My Rock and my Redeemer (marg.) .	Ps. 19. 14.
That Spiritual Rock . . .	1 Co. 10. 4.
The Rock that followed them .	1 Co. 10. 4.
A Shadow from the Heat . .	Is. 25. 4.

XV.—OTHER FOUNDATION CAN NO MAN LAY THAN THAT IS LAID, WHICH IS JESUS CHRIST.—1 Cor. 3. 11.

The Builder . . .	He. 3. 3; Mat. 16. 18.
The Foundation	1 Co. 3. 11.
A Sure Foundation . .	Is. 28. 16.
A Stone	Is. 28. 16.
A Living Stone	1 Pe. 2. 6.
A Tried Stone	Is. 28. 16.
A Chief Corner-stone . . .	1 Pe. 2. 6.
An Elect Stone	1 Pe. 2. 6.
A Precious Stone . . .	1 Pe. 2. 6.
The Head Stone of the Corner .	Ps. 118. 22.
A Stone cut out without hands .	Da. 2. 34, 45.
But unto them which are disobedient	
A Stone of Stumbling . . .	1 Pe. 2. 8.
A Rock of Offence . . .	1 Pe. 2. 8.

XVI.—IN HIS TEMPLE EVERY WHIT OF IT UTTERETH HIS GLORY (marg.)—Ps. 29. 9.

The Temple	Re. 21. 22.
A Sanctuary	Is. 8. 14.
The Minister of the Sanctuary and of the True Tabernacle . . .	He. 8. 2.
Minister of the Circumcision . .	Ro. 15. 8.
The Veil (His flesh) . . .	He. 10. 20.
The Altar	He. 13. 10.
The Offerer	He. 7. 27.
The Offering	Ep. 5. 2.
The Sacrifice	Ep. 5. 2.
A Ransom (His life) . . .	Mar. 10. 45.
The Lamb	Re. 7. 9.
The Lamb Slain	Re. 13. 8.
Within the Veil	
The Forerunner (for us entered, even Jesus)	He. 6. 20
The Mercy-seat (or Propitiation) .	Ro. 3. 25.
The Priest	He. 5. 6.
The High Priest	He. 3. 1.
The Great High Priest . . .	He. 4. 14.
The Mediator	1 Ti. 2. 5.
The Daysman	Job 9. 33.
The Interpreter	Job 33. 23.
The Intercessor	He. 7. 25.
The Advocate	1 Jno. 2. 1.
The Surety	He. 7. 22.

XVII.—A GIFT IS AS A PRECIOUS STONE IN THE EYES OF HIM THAT HATH IT; WHITHERSOEVER IT TURNETH, IT PROSPERETH.—Pr. 17. 8.

The Gift of God . . .	Jno. 3. 16; Jno. 4. 10.
His Unspeakable Gift . . .	2 Co. 9. 15.
My Beloved, in whom my soul is well pleased	Mat. 12. 18.
Mine Elect, in whom my soul delighteth .	Is. 42. 1.
Thy Holy Child Jesus . . .	Ac. 4. 27.
The Chosen of God	Lu. 23. 35.
The Salvation of God . . .	Lu. 2. 30.
The Salvation of the daughter of Zion .	Is. 62. 11.
The Redeemer	Is. 59. 20.
The Shiloh (Peace Maker) . . .	Ge. 49. 10.
The Consolation of Israel . .	Lu. 2. 25.
The Blessed	Ps. 72. 17.
The Most Blessed for ever . .	Ps. 21. 6.

XVIII.—WHO WAS FAITHFUL TO HIM THAT APPOINTED HIM.—He. 3. 2.

The Truth	Jno. 14. 6.
The Faithful and True . .	Re. 19. 11.
A Covenant of the People . . .	Is. 42. 6.
The Testator or Covenantor . .	He. 9. 16, 17.
The Faithful Witness . . .	Re. 1. 5.
The Faithful and True Witness .	Re. 3. 14.
A Witness to the People . .	Is. 55. 4.
The Amen	Re. 3. 14.

XIX.—HE THAT IS HOLY, HE THAT IS TRUE.—Re. 3. 7.

The Just	1 Pe. 3. 18.
The Just One	Ac. 7. 52.
Thine Holy One	Ac. 2. 27.
The Holy One, and the Just . .	Ac. 3. 14.
The Holy One of Israel . .	Is. 49. 7.
The Holy One of God . .	Mar. 1. 24.
Holy, Holy, Holy . . .	Is. 6. 3; Jno. 12. 41.

XX.—THAT IN ALL THINGS HE MIGHT HAVE THE PRE-EMINENCE.—Col. 1. 8.

The Beginning of the Creation of God	Re. 3. 14.
My First Born	Ps. 89. 27.
The First Born from the dead . .	Col. 1. 18.
The First Begotten of the dead .	Re. 1. 5.
The First Born among many Brethren	Ro. 8. 29.
The First Fruits of them that slept .	1 Co. 15. 20.
The Last Adam	1 Co. 15. 45.
The Resurrection	Jno. 11. 25.
A Quickening Spirit . . .	1 Co. 15. 45.
The Head (even Christ) . . .	Ep. 4. 15.
The Head of the Body the Church .	Col. 1. 18.
The Head over all things to the Church	Ep. 1. 22.
The Head of every Man . . .	1 Co. 11. 3.
The Head of all Principality and Power	Col. 2. 10.

XXI.—GIRD THY SWORD UPON THY THIGH, O MOST MIGHTY, WITH THY GLORY AND THY MAJESTY.— Ps. 45. 3.

The Captain of the Host of the Lord	Jos. 5. 14.
The Captain of Salvation . .	He. 2. 10.
The Author and Finisher of Faith .	He. 12. 2.
A Leader	Is. 55. 4.
A Commander	Is. 55. 4.
A Ruler	Mi. 5. 2.
A Governor	Mat. 2. 6.
The Deliverer	Ro. 11. 26.
The Lion of the Tribe of Judah .	Re. 5. 5.
An Ensign of the People . .	Is. 11. 10.
The Chiefest among 10,000 (in an army) .	Ca. 5. 10.
or Standard Bearer (marg.)	
A Polished Shaft	Is. 49. 2.
The Shield	Ps. 84. 9.

XXII.—ALL POWER IS GIVEN UNTO ME IN HEAVEN AND IN EARTH.—Mat. 28. 18.

The Lord	1 Co. 12. 3.
One Lord	Ep. 4. 5.
God hath made that same Jesus both Lord and Christ	Ac. 2. 36.
Lord of Lords	Re. 17. 14.
King of Kings	Re. 17. 14.
Lord both of the dead and living	Ro. 14. 9.
Lord of the Sabbath	Lu. 6. 5.
Lord of Peace	2 Thes. 3. 16.
Lord of all	Ac. 10. 36.
Lord over all	Ro. 10. 12.

XXIII.—HIM HATH GOD EXALTED TO BE A PRINCE AND A SAVIOUR.—Ac. 5. 31.

The Messiah the Prince	Da. 9. 25.
The Prince of Life	Ac. 3. 15.
A Prince and a Saviour	Ac. 5. 31.
The Prince of Peace	Is. 9. 6.
The Prince of Princes	Da. 8. 25.
The Prince of the Kings of the earth	Re. 1. 5.
A Prince (among Israel)	Eze. 34. 24.
The Glory of thy people Israel	Lu. 2. 32.
He that filleth all in all	Ep. 1. 23.

XXIV.—HE SHALL REIGN FOR EVER AND EVER.—Re. 11. 15.

The Judge	Ac. 17. 31.
The Righteous Judge	2 Ti. 4. 8.
The King	Zec. 14. 16.
King of Kings	Re. 19. 16.
Lord of Lords	Re. 19. 16.
A Sceptre (out of Israel)	Nu. 24. 17.
The King's Son	Ps. 72. 1.
David their King	Jer. 30. 9.
The King of Israel	Jno. 1. 49.
King of the daughter of Zion	Jno. 12. 15.
The King of the Jews (born)	Mat. 2. 2; Mar. 15. 2.
The King of the Jews (crucified)	Jno. 19. 19.
The King of Saints	Re. 15. 3.
or King of Nations	
King over all the Earth	Zec. 14. 9.
The King of Righteousness	He. 7. 2.
The King of Peace	He. 7. 2.
The King of Glory	Ps. 24. 10.
The King in his beauty	Is. 33. 17.
He sitteth King for ever	Ps. 29. 10.
Crowned with a Crown of Thorns	Jno. 19. 2.
Crowned with Glory and Honour	He. 2. 9.
Crowned with a Crown of pure Gold	Ps. 21. 3.
Crowned with many Crowns	Re. 19. 12.

ALLUSIONS, CHARACTERISTICS, AND EPITHETS.

As a Refiner's Fire	Mal. 3. 2.
As Fuller's Soap	Mal. 3. 2.
As the Light of the Morning when the sun riseth, even a morning without clouds	2 Sa. 23. 4.
As the Tender Grass by clear shining after rain	2 Sa. 23. 4.
As a Tender Plant (to God)	Is. 53. 2.
As a Root out of a dry ground (to man)	Is. 53. 2.
As Rain upon the mown grass	Ps. 72. 6.
As Showers that water the earth	Ps. 72. 6.
As Rivers of Water in a dry place	Is. 32. 2.
As the Shadow of a great Rock in a weary land	Is. 32. 2.
As an Hiding Place from the wind	Is. 32. 2.
As Ointment poured forth	Ca. 1. 3.
Fairer than the Children of Men	Ps. 45. 2.

A glorious high Throne from the beginning is the place of our sanctuary	Je. 17. 12.
For a Glorious Throne to his father's house	Is. 22. 23.
A Crown of Glory	Is. 28. 5.
A Diadem of Beauty	Is. 28. 5.
A Stone of Grace (marg.)	Pr. 17. 8.
A Nail fastened in a sure place	Is. 22. 23, 24.
A Brother born for adversity	Pr. 17. 17.
A Friend that sticketh closer than a brother	Pr. 18. 24.
A Friend that loveth at all times	Pr. 17. 17.
His Countenance is as the sun	Re. 1. 16.
His Countenance is as Lebanon	Ca. 5. 15.
Yea, He is altogether lovely	Ca. 5. 16.
This is my Beloved, and this is my Friend	Ca. 5. 16.

CONSIDER HIM

He was Obedient		Phi. 2. 8.
,, ,,	Meek, Lowly	Mat. 11. 29.
,, ,,	Guileless	1 Pe. 2. 22.
,, ,,	Tempted	He. 4. 15.
,, ,,	Oppressed	Is. 53. 7.
,, ,,	Despised	Is. 53. 3.
,, ,,	Rejected	Is. 53. 3.
,, ,,	Betrayed	Mat. 27. 3.
,, ,,	Condemned	Mar. 14. 64.
,, ,,	Reviled	1 Pe. 2. 23.
,, ,,	Scourged	Jno. 19. 1.
,, ,,	Mocked	Mat. 27. 29.
,, ,,	Wounded	Is. 53. 5.
,, ,,	Bruised	Is. 53. 5.
,, ,,	Stricken	Is. 53. 4.
,, ,,	Smitten	Is. 53. 4.
,, ,,	Crucified	Mat. 27. 35.
,, ,,	Forsaken	Ps. 22. 1.
He is Merciful		He. 2. 17.
,, ,,	Faithful	He. 2. 17.
,, ,,	Holy, Harmless	He. 7. 26.
,, ,,	Undefiled	He. 7. 26.
,, ,,	Separate	He. 7. 26.
,, ,,	Perfect	He. 5. 9.
,, ,,	Glorious	Is. 49. 5.
,, ,,	Mighty	Is. 63. 1.
,, ,,	Justified	1 Ti. 3. 16.
,, ,,	Exalted	Ac. 2. 33.
,, ,,	Risen	Lu. 24. 6.
,, ,,	Glorified	Ac. 3. 13.

For unto us a Child is born, unto us a SON is given, and the government shall be upon HIS shoulder; and His name shall be called Wonderful, Counsellor, The Mighty God, The Everlasting Father, The Prince of Peace. —Is. 9. 6.

Then He said unto them, O fools, and slow of heart to believe ALL that the Prophets have spoken !

And beginning at Moses, and ALL the Prophets, He expounded unto them in ALL the Scriptures the things concerning HIMSELF. —Lu. 24. 25, 27.

That all should Honour the SON, even as they Honour the Father. He that Honoureth not the SON, Honoureth not the Father which hath sent Him.— Jno. 5. 23.

THE LORD IS MY PORTION.

My Maker, Husband		Is. 54. 5.
,,	Well Beloved	Ca. 1. 13.
,,	Saviour	2 Pe. 3. 18.
,,	Hope	1 Ti. 1. 1.
,,	Brother	Mar. 3. 35.
,,	Portion	Je. 10. 16.
,,	Helper	He. 13. 6.
,,	Physician	Je. 8. 22.
,,	Healer	Lu. 9. 11.
,,	Refiner	Mal. 3. 3.
,,	Purifier	Mal. 3. 3.
,,	Lord, Master	Jno. 13. 13.
,,	Servant	Lu. 12. 37.
,,	Example	Jno. 13. 15.
,,	Teacher	Jno. 3. 2.
,,	Shepherd	Ps. 23. 1.
,,	Keeper	Jno. 17. 12.
,,	Feeder	Eze. 34. 23.
,,	Leader	Is. 40. 11.
,,	Restorer	Ps. 23. 3.
,,	Resting Place	Je. 50. 6.
,,	Meat (His flesh)	Jno. 6. 55.
,,	Drink (His Blood)	Jno. 6. 55.
,,	Passover	1 Co. 5. 7.
,,	Peace	Ep. 2. 14.
,,	Wisdom	1 Co. 1. 30.
,,	Righteousness	1 Co. 1. 30.
,,	Sanctification	1 Co. 1. 30.
,,	Redemption	1 Co. 1. 30.
,,	All and in All	Col. 3. 11.

I. THE names of the smaller *Measures of length* among the Hebrews have been borrowed from some of the members of the human body, as *digit, handbreadth,* or *palm, span, foot, cubit.* The following are the measures of length mentioned in Scripture :—

1. The *digit,* or *fingerbreadth,* אצבע, *etzbá,* is said to contain the breadth of six barleycorns, where thickest, and equal to rather more than three-fourths of an inch.

2. The *handbreadth,* or *palm,* טפח, *tophach,* is the width of a man's four fingers laid flat, *i.e.,* four digits, or rather more than 3½ inches.

3. The *span,* זרת, *zereth,* is the measure from the thumb to the little finger expanded, equal to three palms, or about 11 inches.

4. The *cubit,* אמה, *ammah,* is the measure of a man's arm, from the elbow to the extremity of the middle finger. The ancient Hebrew cubit was about 1 foot 5½ inches. In Roman times a longer cubit was in use, measuring 1 foot 9 inches.

5. The *fathom,* ὀργυιά, is the distance between the hands stretched out, including the breast, equal to 5 or 6 feet.

6. The *reed,* קנה, *kaneh,* was six cubits and a hand-breadth, or about 10 feet 10 inches.

7. The *stadium,* στάδιον, contained 600 Greek feet, or 625 Roman feet, or 125 Roman paces, *i.e.,* 606 English feet, nearly equal to a furlong, or the eighth part of an English mile.

8. A *mile,* μίλιον, so called from *mille,* a thousand, contained among the Romans 1000 paces, or 8 stadia, rather less than an English mile.

II. *Of Measures of capacity,* some of which were for liquids, and some for things dry, the following are mentioned in Scripture :—

1. The *log,* לג, the smallest measure for liquids, was one-fourth of a cab, and one-seventy-second of an ephah, about three-fourths of a pint.

2. The *cab,* קב, κάβος, was one-sixth of a seah, and contained 24 eggs, or 3½ pints English.

3. The *omer,* עמר, was a measure for things dry (Ex. xvi. 36), containing one-tenth of an ephah, about 5 pints English.

4. The *hin,* הין, was a measure of liquids (Ex. xxix. 40), equal to about one gallon and a half English.

5. The *seah,* סאה, or σάτον, was a measure of things dry, containing one-third of an ephah, and equal to about two gallons and a half English.

6. The *ephah,* איפה, was a measure of dry things containing three sata, or seahs, equal to about seven gallons and a half English.

7. The *bath,* בת, or βάτος (Lu. xvi. 6), was a measure of liquids, of the same capacity as the ephah, "the tenth part of an homer" (Eze. xlv. 14).

8. The *lethech,* לתך, was a measure of dry things, and contained fifteen seahs, as EPIPHANIUS states, equal to sixteen pecks English.

9. The *homer,* or *chomer,* חמר, a measure of dry things, contained ten ephahs (Eze. xlv. 11), equal to thirty-two pecks English.

10. The *cor,* כר, or κόρος, was a measure both for liquids and solids, of the same capacity as the homer (Eze. xlv. 14; Lu. xvi. 7).

BESIDES these measures, peculiar to the Hebrews, there are three others mentioned in the New Testament, belonging to other nations.

1. The *sextarius,* or ξέστης, rendered a *pot* (Mar. vii. 4), was a Roman measure of liquids, equal to about a pint English.

2. The *chœnix,* χοῖνιξ, rendered a *measure* (Re. vi. 6), was a Grecian measure of capacity equal to two sextarii, about a quart, corn-measure.

3. The *metretes,* μετρητής, rendered *firkin* (Jno. ii. 6), contained seventy-two sextarii, *i.e.,* about nine English gallons.

III. As the Hebrew *Coins* were originally *Weights,* and as it is by their respective weight that their value is ascertained, it will be necessary to treat of both at once.

1. The *gerah,* גרה, rendered a *piece of money,* was one-twentieth of a shekel (Ex. xxx. 13), weighing nearly 11 grains, in value about 1¼d.

2. The *beka,* בקע, was a half-shekel (Ge. xxiv. 22; Ex. xxxviii. 26), weighing about 4 dwt. 13½ grains, in value rather more than 1s. 1½d.

3. The *shekel,* שקל, according to which all the other weights and coins are computed, has been variously estimated at from 218 grains and four-sevenths to 273 grains and three-fifths ; and consequently in value from 2s. 3d. to 3s., according to the old reckoning of the value of silver. But the depreciation of silver throws out all calculations dependent on comparison with a gold coinage, and its fluctuations prevent us from fixing the value of a silver monetary system.

4. The *maneh,* מנה, or *mina,* in gold was equal in weight to 100 shekels (1 Ki. x. 17), or about 3 lb. 9 oz. 1 dwt. 3 grains ; and consequently, reckoning gold at £4 an ounce, was in value rather more than £180. But, in silver, it weighed only 60 shekels (Eze. xlv. 12), or 2 lb. 6 oz. ; and as a coin it was only equal to 50 shekels, or about £5, 14s.

5. The *talent,* ככר, *kikkar,* weighed 3000 shekels, or 114 lb. 15 dwt. A talent of silver, according to the old value of the metal relative to gold, equalled about £400. A talent of gold was worth £6000.

BESIDES these coins, proper to the Hebrew nation, the following Greek and Roman coins are mentioned in the New Testament :—

1. The *mite,* or *λεπτόν,* called by the later Jews פרוטה, *peruta,* the eighth, *i.e.,* of an assarium, was equal to half a quadrans (Mar. xii. 42), or about three-eighths of a farthing.

2. The *farthing,* κοδράντης, or *quadrans,* so called from *quatuor,* four, was a Roman brass coin, in value about three-fourths of a farthing.

3. The *assarium,* ἀσσάριον, or *as,* rendered a *farthing* (Mat. x. 29), and called by the Rabbins איסר, *isor,* who say that it contained eight mites, was equal to the tenth part of a denarius, about three farthings and one-tenth of our money.

4. The *penny,* or *denarius,* δηνάριον, so called because in ancient times it consisted *denis assibus,* of ten asses, was a Roman silver coin, equal to about 8½d. of our money. Considering the impossibility of establishing a silver value, it may be more helpful to reckon by the market worth of the denarius. According to Matt. xx. 9, this was equal to a labourer's day wages.

5. The *drachma,* δραχμή, of Attica, was equal in value to the Roman denarius (Lu. xv. 8).

6. The *didrachma,* δίδραχμον, or *double drachm,* rendered by our translators *tribute money* (Matt. xvii. 24), was consequently equal to 1s. 5d.

7. The *stater,* στατήρ, a Grecian coin, was, as appears from Matt. xvii. 27, equal in value to two *didrachmas,* or four Attic drachms,

TABLES

OF

MEASURES, WEIGHTS, AND COINS.

1. SHORTER MEASURES OF LENGTH.

	Eng. feet.	inch.
Digit	0	0¾
Palm	0	3½
Span	0	11
Ancient cubit	1	5½
Roman cubit	1	9
Fathom, varied, about	6	0

2. LONGER MEASURE.

	Eng. yds.
Stadium, or Furlong	202
Mile (Roman)	1614

Day's journey, about	30 miles
Sabbath day's journey	2000 paces
or 6 furlongs, about	1212 yards

3. JEWISH MONEY.

	£	s.	d.
Gerah	0	0	1¼
Bekah	0	1	1½
Shekel, or 2 Bekahs	0	2	3
Maneh, or mina Hebraica	5	14	0
Silver talent	400	0	0
Gold talent	6000	0	0
A solidus aureus, or sextula	0	12	0½
Imperial aureus	1	1	0
Pound, or mina	4	0	0

4. JEWISH WEIGHTS.

	Troy weight.			
	lbs.	oz.	dwt.	gr.
Gerah	0	0	0	12
Beka	0	0	4	13½
Shekel	0	0	10	0
Maneh	2	6	0	0
Talent	125	0	0	0

5. GREEK AND ROMAN MONEY.

	£	s.	d.	far.
Mite (λεπτόν), about	0	0	0	0⅜
Farthing (κοδράντης), about	0	0	0	0¾
As (ἀσσάριον), or farthing	0	0	0	3¹⁄₁₀
Penny, denarius (δηνάριον), or drachma	0	0	8	2
Didrachma	0	1	5	0
Stater	0	2	10	0
Attic mina	3	4	7	0
Attic talent	193	15	0	0

The Italian mina, or Roman libra or pound, was ninety-six denarii, equal to about £3, 8s.

Seventy-two libras made a Roman talent, equal to about £240.

Note.—In the preceding Tables, silver is valued at 5s. and gold at £4 per oz. The depreciation of silver makes the silver values only relative. It is impossible to fix them absolutely. See note on talent on page 180.

6. JEWISH LIQUID MEASURES.

	gall.	pints.
Caph	0	0½
Log	0	0¾
Cab	0	3½
Hin	1	4
Seah	2	4
Bath, or ephah	7	4
Corus, chomer, or homer	75	0

7. JEWISH DRY MEASURES.

	English Corn Measure.		
	pecks.	gall.	pints.
Gachal	0	0	0½
Cab	0	0	2
Omer, or gomer	0	0	5
Seah	1	0	1
Ephah	3	0	3
Letech	16	0	0
Corus, chomer, or homer	32	0	0

8. GREEK AND ROMAN MEASURES.

Sextarius	0	1
Metretes (Firkin)	9	0
Chœnix (measure)	0	2

JEWISH CALENDAR.

The CIVIL year, from which the Jews "computed their jubilees, dated all contracts, and noted the birth of children and the reigns of kings."

The ECCLESIASTICAL or SACRED year, from which the festivals were computed. This mode of reckoning is the one generally adopted by the sacred writers.

The following table shows the correspondence of both the Civil and Sacred calendars with our own :—

Name.	No. of Days.	Month of Sacred Year.	Month of Civil Year.	Corresponding with
Nisan or Abib	30	1st	7th	March—April.
Jyar or Zif	29	2nd	8th	April—May.
Sivan or Sisan	30	3rd	9th	May—June.
Thammuz	29	4th	10th	June—July.
Ab	30	5th	11th	July—August.
Elul	29	6th	12th	August—September.
Tizri	30	7th	1st	September—October.
Hesvan or Bul	29	8th	2nd	October—November.
Chisleu	30	9th	3rd	November—December.
Thebeth	29	10th	4th	December—January.
Shebat	30	11th	5th	January—February.
Adar	29	12th	6th	February—March.

Ve-Adar, or Second Adar, every third year.

The Hebrew months being *lunar* ones of twenty-nine and thirty days each, their year was eleven days shorter than ours, and therefore the several divisions of each could not precisely coincide. This deficiency of eleven days was compensated for by adding a *thirteenth* month every *three* years. The supplementary month they called *Ve-Adar*.

Their day was twofold : the *natural*, consisting of from ten to fourteen hours, which commenced at sunrise, and the *civil*, beginning at sunset and ending at sunset, which ran through the twenty-four hours ; and the night was divided into four watches in the time of our Lord, and also into hours The first began at sunset ; the second at nine o'clock ; the third at midnight ; the fourth at three in the morning, and continued until sunrise.

Their natural day was divided into four equal parts. The first watch began at sunrise, and corresponded to our six A.M. at the equinoxes, and continued until nine o'clock ; the second began at nine, and continued till noon ; the third began at noon, and ended at three in the afternoon (which is sometimes termed the ninth hour) ; the fourth began at three, and continued till sunset.

Six seasons appear to have been recognised. They are enumerated in Gen. viii. 22. They may be compared with our months, as follows :— ·

1. SEED-TIME, middle of October to middle of December.
2. WINTER,   middle of December to middle of February.
3. COLD,   middle of February to middle of April.
4. HARVEST,   middle of April to middle of June.
5. SUMMER,   middle of June to middle of August.
6. HEAT,   middle of August to middle of October.

In the beginning of our year, therefore, we find ourselves advanced about a fortnight into the Jewish season of winter.—*Bible Months*, by W. H. GROSER, B.Sc., published by the Sunday School Union.

FAMILY OF THE HERODS.

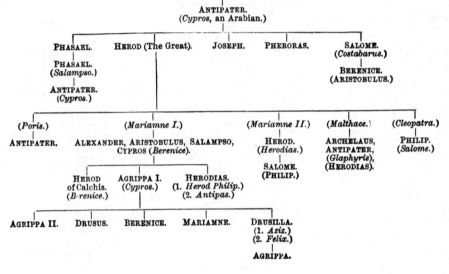

ANTIPATER (Governor of Idumæa).

ANTIPATER.
(*Cypros*, an Arabian.)

PHASAEL.   HEROD (The Great).   JOSEPH.   PHERORAS.   SALOME.
                                                              (*Costabarus.*)

PHASAEL.   BERENICE.
(*Salampso.*)   (ARISTOBULUS.)

ANTIPATER.
(*Cypros.*)

(*Poris.*)   (*Mariamne I.*)   (*Mariamne II.*)   (*Malthace.*)   (*Cleopatra.*)

ANTIPATER.   ALEXANDER, ARISTOBULUS, SALAMPSO,   HEROD.   ARCHELAUS,   PHILIP.
              CYPROS (*Berenice*).   (*Herodias.*)   ANTIPATER,   (*Salome.*)
                                                                     (*Glaphyris*),
                                                     SALOME.   (HERODIAS).
                                                     (PHILIP.)

          HEROD   AGRIPPA I.   HERODIAS.
          of Calchis. (*Cypros.*)   (1. *Herod Philip.*)
          (*B·renice.*)   (2. *Antipas.*)

AGRIPPA II.   DRUSUS.   BERENICE.   MARIAMNE.   DRUSILLA.
                                                    (1. *Aziz.*)
                                                    (2. *Felix.*)

                                                    AGRIPPA.

INDEX OF PROPER NAMES,

WITH THEIR ACCENTUATION AND MEANINGS.

PRONUNCIATION.

Original (probably)—*a* as *ah ; e* as *ay ; i* as *e ; o* as *oh ; u* as *oo ; c* as *k ; ch* as German *ch ; g* hard **;**
iah as *yah ; j* as *y.*

Anglicised (in usage)—*a* as in "tale"; *e* as in "eel"; *i* as in "it"; *ī* as in "kite"; *o* as in "toll"; *u* as
in "rule"; *c* as in "cake"; *ch* as in "chord"; *g* as in "gun"; *iah* in one
syllable like "yah"; *j* as in "jar."

HAR'-SHA, magician.
HA'-RUM, high.
HA'-RUZ, active.
HA'-SAD-I'-AH, loved by Jehovah.
HA'-SHEM, fat.
HASH'-UB, thoughtful.
HASH'-UM, rich.
HA-TI'-PHA, seized.
HAU'-RAN, cave land.
HA-VIL'-AH, region of sand, or village.
HA'-VOTH-JA'-IR, villages of Jair.
HA'-ZA-EL, seen by God.
HA'-ZAR, town.
HAZE-E'-ROTH, villages.
HA'-ZIEL, seen of God.
HA'-ZOR, inclosure, castle.
HE'-BER, companionship, fellowship.
HE'-BREW, immigrant, from the other side.
HEB'-RON, confederacy.
HEL'-BON, fruitful.
HE'-LI, same as ELI.
HE'-MAN, reliable, faithful.
HEN, favour.
HEPH'-ZI-BAH, my delight in her.
HER'-MAS, the god Mercury.
HER-MOG'-E-NES, born of Hermes or Mercury.
HER'-MON, high mountain peak.
HER'-OD, heroic.
HE-RO'-DI-ANS, adherents of Herod.
HE-RO'-DI-AS, feminine of Herod.
HESH'-MON, riches.
HETH, Assyrian, Hatti.
HEZ-E-KI'-AH, might of Jehovah.
HEZ'-RON, inclosure.
HID'-DE-KEL, circling.
HI'-EL, God lives.
HI-ER-AP'-O-LIS, sacred city.
HIL-KI'-AH, Jehovah my portion.
HIN'-NOM, gracious or rich.
HI'-RAM, noble.
HIT'-TITES, descendants of Heth.
HI'-VITES, villagers.
HO'-BAB, beloved, befriended.
HO'-BAH, hidden.
BO'-DESH, new moon.
HO-DI'-AH, Jehovah his praise.
HOG'-LAH, partridge.
HOPH'-NI, fighter, pugilist.
HOR, mountain.
HO'-REB, parched waste place.
HO'-RI, cave-dweller.
HOR'-MAH, doomed or devastated place.
HOR-O-NA'-IM, two caverns.
HO-SAN'-NA, save, we pray.
HO-SE'-A, help, deliverance, salvation.
HO-SHAI'-AH, freed by Jehovah.
HO-SHE'-A, same as HOSEA.
HO'-THAM, signet.
HUL'-DAH, weasel.
HUM'-TAH, fortress.
HU'-PHAM, dweller by shore.
HUR, pit.
HUSH'-A-Î, quick, agile.
HY-MEN-Æ'-US, belonging to Hymen.

IB'-HAR, He (God) chooses.
IB-NEI'-AH, Jehovah builds.
ICH'-A-BOD, no glory, inglorious.
I-CON'-I-UM, a town of Asia Minor.
ID'-DO, loving.
I-DU-MÆ'-A, same as EDOM.
I'-GAL, he will redeem.
IG-DAL-I'-AH, the Lord is great, or whom He makes great.
I'-IM, ruins.
I'-JE-A-BAR'-IM, ruin-heaps of Abarim.
I'-JON, a ruin.
IL'-A-Î, most high.
IL-LYR'-I-CUM, a district on the Adriatic.
IM'-LAH, filler, fulfiller.
IM-MAN'-UEL, God with us.
I'-RAD, wild ass.
I'-SAAC, laughter.
I-SAI'-AH, Jehovah is salvation.
IS-CAR'-I-OT, man of Kerioth.
ISH-BO'-SHETH, man of shame.
ISH'-HOD, man of glory.
ISH'-MA, high, husband.
ISH'-MA-EL, whom God hears.

ISH'-MA-EL-ITES, descendants of Ishmael.
ISH-MAI'-AH, the man Jehovah hears.
ISH'-MER-A-Î, the man Jehovah keeps.
IS'-RA-EL, soldier of God.
IS'-RA-EL-ITES, descendants of Israel.
ITH'-A-MAR, land of palms.
ITH'-I-EL, God with me.
ITH'-NAN, strong.
IT-U-RÆ'-A, land of Jetur.
I'-VAH, destruction, overthrow.

JA-A-LAM, hidden.
JA-A-ZA-NI'-AH, whom God always hears.
JAB'-BOK, pouring out, stream.
JA'-BESH, dry, arid.
JA'-BESH-GIL'-E-AD, Jabesh of Gilead.
JA'-BEZ, causing pain.
JA'-BIN, considered by God.
JAB'-NE-EL, built by God.
JA'-CHAN, troubled.
JA'-CHIN, firm, strong.
JA'-COB, supplanter.
JA'-DA, wise.
JAD'-DUA, skilled.
JA'-DON, a judge.
JA'-EL, wild she-goat, chamois.
JA'-HAZ, trampled down with the feet.
JAH'-DAI, directed by Jehovah.
JAH'-DI-EL, made glad by God.
JAH'-DO, union.
JAH'-LE-EL, hope in God.
JAH'-ZE-EL, God allots.
JA'-IR, enlightened of God.
JA-I'-RUS, same as JAIR.
JA'-KEH, (?) pious.
JA'-LON, passing the night.
JAM'-BRES, corruption of Mambres.
JAMES, same as JACOB.
JA'-MIN, right hand.
JAM'-LECH, he makes to reign.
JAM'-NES, an Egyptian magician.
JA'-PHETH, fair one, spreading widely.
JA'-REB, adversary, contentious.
JA'-SON, healer, same as JESUS or JOSHUA.
JA'-VAN, Ionian.
JEB'-U-SITES, descendants of Jebus.
JEC-O-NI'-AH, established by God.
JED'-ID-I'-AH, beloved of God.
JED-U'-THUN, praised, praising.
JE-GAR'-SA-HA-DU'-THAH, heap of testimony, witness-heap.
JE-HI'-AH, Jehovah liveth.
JE-HI'-EL, God liveth.
JE-HO'-A-HAZ, held fast by Jehovah.
JE-HO'-ASH, supported by Jehovah.
JE-HOI'-A-CHIN, appointed of Jehovah.
JE-HOI'-A-DA, known of Jehovah.
JE-HOI'-A-KIM, set up by Jehovah.
JE-HO'-IA-RIB, Jehovah will contend.
JE-HON'-A-DAB, Jehovah is a liberal giver.
JE-HO'RAM, exalted by Jehovah.
JE-HOSH'-A-PHAT, Jehovah, or whom He judges.
JE-HOSH'-E-BA, Jehovah's oath.
JE-HOSH'-UA, help of Jehovah.
JE-HO'-VAH, destructive.
JE-HO'-VAH-JI'-REH, Jehovah will provide.
JE-HO'-VAH-NIS'-SI, Jehovah my banner.
JE-HO'-VAH-SHAL'-OM, Jehovah is peace.
JE-HO'-VAH-SHAM'-MAH, Jehovah ir there.
JE-HO'-VAH-TSID-KE'-NU, Jehovah our righteousness.
JE-HO'-ZA-BAD, Jehovah gives.
JE-HO'-ZA-DAK, Jehovah is just.
JE'-HU, Jehovah is He.
JE-HU'-DI, a jew.
JE-MI'-MA, a dove.
JEPH'-THAH, Jehovah is opener.
JE-PHUN'-NEH, prepared.
JER'-E-MAI, dwelling on high.
JER-E-MI'-AH, exalted, or appointed by God.
JE-RE'-MOTH, high places.
JER'-I-CHO, place of fragrance.
JER-O-BO'-AM, whose people are many.
JE-RUB-BA'-AL, fighter with Baal.
JE-RU'-SA-LEM, city of the god of peace.
JESH-A'-NAH, old.
JESH-AR-EL'-AH, well-pleasing to God.
JE'-SHER, uprightness.

JE-SHIM'-ON, the waste, desert.
JESH'-U-A, Jehovah the salvation.
JESH-U'-RUN, the upright one, the beloved.
JES'-SE, wealth.
JE'-SUS, Saviour.
JETH'-LAH, lofty.
JETH'-RO, pre-eminent.
JE'-TUR, enclosure.
JE'-UZ, counsellor.
JEW'-RY, Judea.
JEWS, inhabitants of Judea.
JEZ'-E-BEL, unmarried.
JEZ'-RE-EL, God scatters or plants.
JO'-AB, Jehovah is father.
JO-AN'-NA, gift of Jehovah.
JO'-ASH, bestowed or supported by Jehovah.
JOB, the much afflicted.
JOCH'-E-BED, whose glory is Jehovah.
JO'-ED, God his witness.
JO'-EL, Jehovah is God, or mighty.
JO-HA'-NAN, Jehovah's gift.
JOHN, God's gift, or grace.
JOK'-TAN, small.
JON'-A-DAB, Jehovah is a liberal giver.
JO'-NA, Greek for Johanan.
JO'-NAH, a dove.
JO'-NAS, same as JONA.
JON'-A-THAN, Jehovah's gift.
JOP'-PA, beauty.
JO'-RAM, exalted of Jehovah.
JOR'-DAN, descending, flowing down.
JOS'-E-DECH, to whom Jehovah is just.
JO'-SEPH, he shall add.
JO'-SES, helped of Jehovah.
JOSH'-U-A, Jehovah the Saviour.
JO-SI'-AH, God is healer, or healed by Jehovah.
JO'-THAM, Jehovah is upright.
JOZ'-A-CHAR, remembered of Jehovah.
JU'-BAL, player on the lyre.
JU'-DAH, praised.
JU'-DAS, same as JUDAH.
JUDE, same as JUDAH.
JU-DE'-A, land of Judah.
JU'-DITH, Jewess.
JU'-LI-A, feminine of Julius.
JU'-PI-TER, father of day.
JUS'-TUS, just.
JUT'-TAH, extended.

KA'-DESH, sanctuary.
KA'-DESH-BAR'-NE-A.
KAD'-MON-ITES, easterns, orientals.
KA'-NAH, place of reeds.
KAR-NA'-IM, of the two horns.
KE'-DAR, black skin, black-skinned.
KE-DE'-MOTH, eastern parts.
KE'-DESH, sanctuary.
KE-I'-LAH, fortress, castle.
KE'-NAZ, hunting.
KEN'-E-ZITE, a descendant of Kenaz.
KE'-NITES, descendants of Kain.
KER'-I-OTH, cities.
KE-TU'-RAH, incense.
KE-ZI'-A, cassia.
KE'-ZIZ, cut off.
KIB'-ROTH-HAT-TA'-A-VAH, graves of lust.
KIB-ZA'-IM, two heaps.
KID'-RON, the turbid (brook).
KIR, a wall, a walled place, citadel.
KIR-HE'-RES, fortress of brick.
KIR-JATH-A'-IM, double city.
KIR-JATH-AR'-BA, stronghold.
KIR-JATH-BA'-AL, city of Baal.
KIR'-JATH-HU'-ZOTH, city of streets.
KIR'-JATH-JE'-A-RIM, city of forests.
KIR-JATH-SAN'-NAH, city of instruction.
KIR-JATH-SEPH'-ER, city of the brook.
KISH, a bow.
KI'-SHON, winding, twisting.
KITH'-LISH, fortified.
KIT'-RON, burning.
KO'-A, prince.
KO'-HATH, assembly.
KO'-RAH, bald.
KO'-RE, partridge.
KOZ, thorn.

LA'-BAN, white, beautiful.
LA'-CHISH, invincible, impregnable.

O'-PHIR, plenty.
OPH'-RAH, fawn.
OR'-EB, raven.
OR'-EN, pine.
O'-RI-ON, the giant.
OR'-NAN, (?) joyful.
OTH'-NI, Jehovah is my strength.
OTH'-NI-EL, lion of God.
O'-ZEM, strength.
OZ'-NI, hearing.

PA'-A-RAI, possibly a mistake for Naarai.
PA'-DAN, plain ploughed by oxen.
PA'-DAN-A'-RAM, the plain of Aram.
PAL-ES-TI'-NA, land of immigration, or stranger.
PAL'-LU, distinguished.
PAM-PHYL'-I-A, a region of Asia Minor.
PA'-PHOS, a town in Cyprus.
PAR'-A-DISE, a park.
PA'-RAN, cavernous.
PAR'-ME-NAS, abiding, steadfast.
PAR'-SHAN-DA'-THA, (?) given to Persia.
PAR'-THI-ANS, men from Parthia.
PAR-VA'-IM, eastern regions.
PASH'-UR, extension, expansion.
PAT'-A-RA, a city of Lycia.
PATH'-ROS, southern land.
PAT'-MOS, an island in the Ægean.
PAUL, little.
PE-DA'-I-AH, redeemed of Jehovah.
PE-DAH'-EL, God redeemed.
PE'-KAH, with open eyes.
PE-KA-HI'-AH, Jehovah has opened the eyes.
PEL-A-TI'-AH, deliverance from God.
PE'-LEG, division.
PE'-LET, liberation.
PEL'-ETH-ITES, runners.
PE-NI'-EL, face of God.
PE-NIN'-NAH, coral.
PEN'-TE-COST, fiftieth.
PE-NU'-EL, same as PENIEL.
PE'-OR, a hole.
PE-RA'-ZIM, breaches.
PE'-REZ, breach.
PE'-REZ-UZ'-ZAH, breach of Uzzah.
PER'-GA, a city of Pamphylia.
PER'-GA-MOS, a city of Mysia.
PER'-IZ-ZITES, villagers.
PE'-TER, a rock.
PE-THAH-I'-AH, whom Jehovah looses.
PE-UL'-TA-Ī, Jehovah's deed.
PHAL'-TI, Jehovah's deliverance.
PHAL'-TI-EL, God's deliverance.
PHAN'-U-EL, same as PENIEL.
PHA'-RAOH, great house.
PHA'-RAOH-NE'-CHO, Pharaoh the lame.
PHA'-RI-SEES, separatists.
PHAR'-PAR, mobility, nimbleness.
PHE'-BE, shining, the moon.
PHE-NI'-CE, palm-tree.
PHE-NIC'-IA, same as PHENICE.
PHI'-CHOL, (?) attentive.
PHIL-A-DEL'-PHI-A, brotherly love.
PHI-LE'-MON, affectionate.
PHI-LE'-TUS, beloved.
PHIL'-IP. lover of horses.
PHIL-IP'-PI, town founded by Philip of Macedon.
PHIL-IS'-TI-A, same as PALESTINA.
PHIL'-IS-TINES, inhabitants of Philistia.
PHIL-OL'-O-GUS, lover of learning.
PHIN'-E-HAS, brazen or serpent's mouth.
PHLEG'-ON, burning with zeal.
PHRYG'-I-A, country in Asia Minor.
PHY-GEL'-LUS, litt e, fugitive.
PI-BE'-SETH, city of Bast.
PI-HA-HI'-ROTH, place of reeds or rushes.
PI'-LATE, armed with a dart.
PI'-LE-HA, (?) ploughman.
PIL'-TA-Ī, whom Jehovah delivers.
PI'-NON, darkness.
PIS'-GAH, a height, a peak.
PI-SID'-I-A, district in Asia Minor.
PI'-SON, outpouring, water-court.
PI'-THOM, house of Tum, or the setting sun.
PLEI'-A-DES, stars of the sailors.
PON'-TI-US, belonging to the sea.
PON'-TUS, the sea.
PO-RA'-THA, given by fate.

POT'-I-PHAR, gift of the sun-god.
POT-I-PHE'-RAH, same as POTIPHAR.
PRIS-CIL'-LA. dear, ancient.
PROCH'-O-RUS, choir-leader.
PTOL-E-MA'-IS, city of Ptolemy.
PUB'-LI-US, common.
PU'-AH, splendour.
PU'-DENS, modest.
PUL, strong, powerful.
PUR, a lot.
PU'-RIM, lots.
PU-TE'-O-LI, wells, a town of Italy.

QUAR'-TUS, fourth.

RA'-A-MAH, the quivering mane.
RA-AM'-SES, son of the sun.
RAB'-BAH, chief.
RAB'-BI, master.
RAB-BO'-NI, my master.
RAB'-MAG, chief of the Magi.
RAB'-SAR-IS, chief of the heads.
RAB'-SHA-KEH, chief of the princes.
RA'-CHEL, an ewe.
RAG'-U-EL, friendship with or friend of God.
RA'-HAB, roomy, violent, turbulence.
RA'-KEM, variegated.
RAK'-KATH, shore.
RAM, high.
RA'-MAH, high place.
RA'-MATH-A'-IM, double high place.
RA'-MATH-LE'-HI, height of Lehi.
RAM'-E-SES, same as RAAMSES.
RAM-I'-AH, Jehovah is high.
RA'-MOTH-GIL'-E-AD, heights of Gilead.
RA'-PHU, heated.
RE'-BA, a fourth.
RE-BEC'-CA, noose, fettering cord.
RE'-CHAB, the horseman.
RE'-CHAB-ITES, descendants of Rechab.
REL-EL-AI'-AH, trembling for Jehovah.
RE'-GEM-ME'-LECH, the king's friend.
RE'-HOB, broad place.
RE-HO-BO'-AM, enlarger of the people.
RE-HO'-BOTH, wide spaces, suburbs.
RE'-HUM, compassionate.
RE'-I, friendly.
REI-AI'-A, Jehovah has seen.
REM-A-LI'-AH, adorned of God.
REM'-PHAN (uncertain).
RE-PHA'-IM, giants.
REPH'-I-DIM, rests, stays.
RE'-SAN, head of the spring.
REU'-BEN, lo ! a son, or Jehovah has seen.
REU'-EL, friend of God.
REZ'-IN, firm, strong.
RE'-ZON, lean.
RHE'-GI-UM, a breaking.
RHO'-DA, a rose.
RIB'-A-Ī, contentious.
RIM'-MON, pomegranate, the air-god.
RIM'-MON-PA'-REZ, pomegranate of the breach.
RIN'-NAH, a shout.
RIS'-SAH, a river.
RIZ'-PAH, a hot coal.
ROME, city of Romulus.
RU'-FUS, red.
RU-HA'-MAH, compassionate.
RU'-MAH, height.
RUTH, friend, friendship.

SAB-A'-OTH, hosts.
SA-BE'-ANS, people of Seba, or Saba, or Sheba.
SA'-CAR, hire.
SAD'-DU-CEES, disciples of Zadok.
SAL'-A-MIS, a city of Cyprus.
SA'-LEM, peace.
SAL'-LA-Ī, exaltation.
SAL'-MA, a garment.
SAL'-MON, shady, or casting a shade.
SAL-MO'-NE, a promontory of Crete.
SA-LO'-ME, peaceable, perfect.
SA-MA'-RI-A, a ward, a guard.
SA-MAR'-I-TANS, people of Samaria.
SAM'-LAH, a garment.
SAM-O-THRA'-CIA, an island in the Ægean.
SAM'-SON, of or like the sun.
SAM'-U-EL, name of God, heard of God.

SAN-BAL'-LAT, the moon-god has given life.
SAN'-HE-DRIN, the Council.
SAN-SAN'-NAH, palm branch.
SAP-PHI'-RA, beautiful.
SA'-RAH, queen.
SA'-RA-Ī, queen in Canaanitish.
SA-REP'-TA, same as ZAREPHATH.
SA'-RID, a survivor.
SA'-TAN, adversary.
SAUL, asked for.
SCE'-VA, left-handed.
SCYTH'-I-AN, a man of Scythia.
SE-BA, Saba in Arabia.
SE'-BAT, (?) red.
SE-CUN'-DUS. second.
SE'-GUB, exalted.
SE'-IR, rugged, shaggy.
SE'-LAH, a musical direction.
SE'-LA-HAM-MAH'-LE-KOTH, rock of escapes.
SEN-NACH'-E-RIB, the moon increases brethren.
SEPH-AR-VA'-IM, the two Sipparas.
SER'-A-PHIM, burning ones.
SE'-RED, fear.
SER'-GI-US, a Roman proconsul.
SE'-RUG, a shout.
SETH, substitute.
SE'-THIN, hidden.
SHAD'-DA-Ī, almighty.
SHAD'-RACH (uncertain).
SHA'-GE, wanderer.
SHAL'-LUM, recompense.
SHAL-MA-NE'-ZER, show in favour.
SHAL'-MA-Ī, (?) peaceful.
SHA'-MA, obedient.
SHAM'-MAH, desolation.
SHAM-MU'-AH, renowned.
SHA'-PHAM, bald.
SHA'-PHAN, jumper, a rock-badger.
SHA'-PHAT, a judge.
SHA-RE'-ZER, defend the king.
SHA'-RON, a plain.
SHA'-VEH, same as SHARON.
SHE'-AL, prayer.
SHE-AR-JA'-SHUB, the remnant shall return.
SHE'-BA, an oath, Saba in Arabia.
SHEB'-NA, tenderness, or tender age.
SHE'-BU-EL, God's captive.
SHE-CHAN-I'-AH, Jehovah dwells.
SHE'-CHEM, shoulder, ridge.
SHE-DE-UR, hurling fire.
SHE-HAR-I'-AH, Jehovah seeks.
SHE'-LAH, request.
SHE-LEM-I'-AH, when Jehovah repays.
SHE'-LEPH, drawing out.
SHE'-LESH, a triad.
SHE-LO'-MI, peaceful.
SHEM, name.
SHE'-MA, fame.
SHEM-AI'-AH, heard of Jehovah.
SHE-MI'-NITH, eighth.
SHE-MI'-RA-MOTH, highest name.
SHEN, tooth.
SHEPH-A-TI'-AH, defended by Jehovah.
SHE'-PHI, baldness.
SHESH-BAZ'-ZAR (uncertain).
SHE'-THAR-BOZ'-NA-Ī, star of brightness.
SHE'-VA, variety.
SHIB'-BO-LETH, a flood, or ear of corn.
SHIG-GAI'-ON, wandering.
SHIG-I'-O-NOTH, same as SHIGGAION.
SHI'-HON, ruin.
SHI-LO'-AH, tunnel, conduit.
SHI'-LOH, rest.
SHIM'-E-A, renown, famous.
SHIM'-E-I, renown.
SHIM'-EON, hearkening.
SHIM'-RATH, watchfulness.
SHIM'-RI, watchful.
SHI'-NAR, lion-land.
SHIPH'-RAH, beauty.
SHIPH'-TAN, judicial.
SHI'-SHA, brightness.
SHIT'-TIM, acacias.
SHO'-A, opulent.
SHO-SHAN'-NIM, lilies.
SHU'-LAM-ITE, peaceful.
SHU'-NAM-ITE, a native of Shunem.

OBSOLETE AND AMBIGUOUS WORDS.

ABHORRING, an object of abhorrence. Isa. lxvi. 24.

ABIDE, to wait for. Acts xx. 23.

ABJECT, an outcast, a worthless person. Ps. xxxv. 15.

ABUSE, to ill use. 1 Cor. vii. 31.

ACCEPT, to receive with favour. Gen. xxxii. 20.

ACCEPTABLE, agreeable, well-pleasing. Deut. xxxiii. 24.

ACCOMPLISH, to make complete. Luke ii. 21.

ACCURSE, to curse. Gal. i. 8.

ACQUAINT, to make oneself acquainted with. Job xxii. 21.

ADAMANT, literally *invincible*, a hard stone, diamond. Ezek. iii. 9.

ADDICT, to devote oneself. 1 Cor. xvi. 15.

ADJURE, to bind by oath. Matt. xxvi. 63.

ADMIRATION, astonishment. Rev. xvii. 6.

ADO, doing, stir, tumult. Mark v. 39.

ADVANTAGE, to benefit. Luke ix. 25.

ADVENTURE, to happen. Acts xix. 31.

ADVENTURES, AT ALL, at random. Lev. xxvi. 21m.

ADVERSARY, an opponent in a lawsuit. Matt. v. 25.

ADVERTISE, to inform. Num. xxiv. 14.

ADVICE, to take advice, consult. Judg. xix. 30.

ADVISE, to consider, reflect. 1 Chron. xxi. 12.

ADVISEMENT, consideration, deliberation. 1 Chron. xii. 19.

AFFECT, to aim at, strive at, after. Gal. iv. 17.

AFFECTION, passion. Col. iii. 5.

AFFECTIONED, affected, disposed. Rom. xii. 10.

AFORE, beforehand. Rom. ix. 23.

AFORETIME, of old. Neh. xiii 5.

AFTER, according to. Ps. xxviii. 4.

AGONE, ago. 1 Sam xxx. 13.

ALBEIT, although it be. Ezek. xiii. 7.

ALL, sometimes used as *any* or *every*. Heb. vii. 7.

ALL TO BRAKE, broke all to pieces. Judg. ix. 53.

ALLEGE, to adduce proof. Acts xvii. 3.

ALMSDEED, an act of charity. Acts ix. 36.

ALONG, at full length. Judg. vii. 13.

ALWAY, always. Phil. iv. 4.

AMAZEMENT, confusion, as well as wonder. 1 Pet. iii. 6.

AMBASSAGE, an embassy. Luke xiv. 32.

AMBUSHMENT, an ambuscade. 2 Chron. xiii. 13.

AMERCE, to fine. Deut. xxii. 19.

AMIABLE, lovely. Ps. lxxxiv. 1.

ANCIENT, an elder. Isa. iii. 14.

ANCRE, variant spelling of anchor. Acts xvii. 29.

AND, used as *if*. Gen. xliv. 30.

ANGER, to make angry. Ps. cvi. 32.

ANGLE, a fishing-rod with line and hook. Isa. xix. 8.

ANON, at once. Matt. xiii. 20.

ANY WHILE, for any length of time. Mark xv. 44.

ANYTHING, in any way. Num. xvii. 13.

APACE, swiftly. Ps. lxviii. 12.

APPARELLED, clothed. 2 Sam. xiii. 18.

APPARENTLY, manifestly. Num. xii. 6.

APPLE OF THE EYE, the eye-ball. Ps. xvii. 8.

APPOINT, expressly name. Gen. xxx. 28.

APPOINTED, equipped. Judg. xviii. 11.

APPREHEND, to take hold of. Phil. iii. 12.

APPROVE, to prove. Acts ii. 22.

ARK, a chest. Exod. ii. 3.

ARMHOLE, the arm-pit. Jer. xxxviii. 12.

ARRAY, dress. 1 Tim. ii. 9.

ARROGANCY, arrogance. 1 Sam. ii. 3.

ARTIFICER, a skilled workman. Gen. iv. 22.

ARTILLERY, missile weapons, bow and arrows. 1 Sam. xx. 40.

AS. for *as if*. Acts x. 11.

ASK AT, to inquire of. Dan. ii. 10.

ASSAY, to attempt, try. Deut iv. 34.

ASSWAGE, lessen, subside. Gen viii. 1.

ASTONIED, astonished. Job xvii. 8.

ASTROLOGIAN, astrologer. Dan. ii. 27.

ATTENDANCE, attention. 1 Tim. iv. 13.

ATTENT, attentive. 2 Chron. vi. 40.

ATTIRE, a woman's head-dress. Prov. vii. 10.

ATTIRE, to put on a head-dress. Lev. xvi. 4.

AUDIENCE, hearing. Gen. xxiii. 13.

AUL, the old spelling of awl. Exod. xxi. 6.

AVENGEMENT, revenge. 2 Sam. xxii. 48m.

AVOID, to make empty. 1 Sam. xviii. 11.

AVOUCH, to acknowledge, avow. Deut. xxvi. 17.

AWAIT, ambush. Acts ix. 24.

BAKEMEATS, the work of a baker. Gen. xl. 17.

BAKEN, baked. Lev. ii. 4.

BANQUET, to drink. Esther vii. 1.

BARBARIAN, not a Greek. 1 Cor. xiv. 11.

BARBAROUS PEOPLE, foreigners. Acts xxviii. 2

BASE, low, humble, not necessarily evil. 1 Cor. i. 28.

BATTLE, a body of troops. 1 Chron. xix. 9.

BEAST, living creature. Rev. iv. 6.

BECAUSE, in order that. Matt. xx. 31.

BEEVES, plural of beef, oxen. Lev. xxii. 19.

BEHALF, ON THIS, on this account. 1 Pet. iv. 16.

BESOM, a broom. Isa. xiv. 23.

BESTEAD, situated. Isa. viii. 21.

BETHINK, to call to mind. 1 Kings viii. 47.

BETIMES, in good time. Gen. xxvi. 31.

BEWRAY, accuse, discover. Matt. xxvi. 73.

BID, to invite. Matt. xxii. 9.

BLAIN, a boil or blister. Exod. ix. 9.

BLASPHEMER, a slanderer.

BLAZE, to spread far and wide. Mark i. 45.

BOLLED, swollen, podded for seed. Exod. ix. 31.

BONNET, a head-dress whether of a man or of a woman. Exod. xxviii. 40.

BOOK, any formal writing. Job xxxi. 35.

BOOTIES, plunder. Hab ii. 7.

BOSS, a knob. Job xv. 26.

BOTCH, a boil. Deut. xxviii. 35.

BOWELS, compassion. Phil. i. 8.

BOWMAN, an archer. Jer. iv. 29.

BRASS, copper. Deut. viii. 9.

BRAY, to knead. Prov. xxvii 22.

BREACH, a creak. Judg. v. 17.

BRIGANDINE, a kind of scale armour. Jer. xlvi. 4.

BROIDED, braided. 1 Tim. ii. 9.

BRUIT, noise, rumour. Jer. x. 22.

BUFFET, to beat. 2 Cor. xii. 7.

BUNCH, a hump. Isa. xxx. 6.

BY, against, with reference to. 1 Cor. iv. 4.

BY AND BY, immediately. Matt. xiii. 21.

BY THAT, by the time that. Exod. xxii. 26.

BYWORD, a proverb. Job xvii. 6.

CABINS, vaults or cellars. Jer. xxxvii. 16.

CANDLESTICK, a lamp-stand. Matt. v. 15.

CANKER, a cancer. 2 Tim. ii. 17.

CANKERED, rusted. Jas. v. 3.

CAREFUL, full of care, anxious. Dan. iii. 16.

CARELESS, free from care. Ezek. xxx. 9.

CARR

CARRIAGE, baggage, something to be carried. Acts xxi. 15.

CAST, to consider, plan. Luke i. 29.

CAST ABOUT, to go round, turn Jer. xli. 14.

CAUL, a small cap. Isa. iii. 18.

CAUSEWAY, a paved road. 1 Chron xxvi. 16.

CHAFED, heated, angry. 2 Sam. xvii. 8.

CHALLENGE, to claim. Exod. xxii. 9.

CHAMBERING, wanton living. Rom. xiii. 13.

CHAMPAIGN, CHAMPION, a plain. Deut. xi. 30.

CHANEL-BONE, collar-bone. Job xxxi. 22m.

CHAPITER, the capital of a column. Exod. xxxvi. 38.

CHAPMAN, a merchant. 2 Chron. ix. 14.

CHARGER, a dish. Matt. xiv. 8.

CHARGES, TO BE AT, to pay the cost. Acts xxi. 24.

CHARITY, love. 1 Cor. xiii.

CHECK, reproof, rebuke. Job xx. 3.

CHEEK TEETH, the molar teeth. Joel i 6.

CHEER, the countenance, aspect. Matt. ix. 2.

CHIDE, to scold, quarrel, contend noisily. Exod. xvii. 2.

CHODE. past tense of chide. Gen. xxxi. 36.

CHOLER, anger. Dan. viii. 7.

CHURL, a countryman. Isa. xxxii. 5.

CIELED, panelled, wainscotted. 2 Chron iii. 5.

CIELING, wainscotting. 1 Kings vi. 15.

CLEAN, entirely. Josh. iii. 17.

CLEAR, innocent. Gen. xxiv. 8.

CLEAR, to acquit. Exod. xxxiv. 7.

CLEAVE, to adhere. Gen. ii. 24.

CLIFT, cleft. Exod. xxxiii. 22.

CLOUTED, patched. Josh. ix. 5.

CLOUTS, patches. Jer. xxxviii. 11.

COASTS, border country. Matt. viii. 34.

COAT, a woman's gown. Cant. v. 3.

COCKATRICE, a corruption of crocodile, but standing for a serpent. Isa. xi. 8.

COLLOPS, lumps of meat. Job xv. 27.

COLOUR, pretext. Acts xxvii 30.

COME A , come near. Dan. vi. 24.

COME BY, to get possession of. Acts xxvii. 16.

COMFORT, to strengthen. Judg. xix. 5.

COMMEND. to commit to one's charge. Acts xiv. 23.

COMMUNE WITH, converse with. Luke vi. 11.

COMMUNICATE, to share, to impart. Gal. ii. 2.

COMMUNICATION, conversation. Luke xxiv. 17.

COMPACT, firmly fitted. Ps. cxxii. 3.

COMPASS, n., circumference. Exod. xxvii. 5.

COMPASS, v., to go all round. Matt. xxiii. 15.

COMPASS, TO FETCH A, to make a circuit. Acts xxviii. 13.

COMPOUND, compounded. Exod. xxx. 25.

COMPREHEND, to include. Isa. xl. 12.

CONCEIT, conception, imagination. Prov. xviii. 11.

DECE

CONCISION, cutting, mangling. Phil. iii. 2.

CONCUPISCENCE, evil desire, lust. Rom. vii. 8.

CONFECTION, a compound of spices and drugs. Exod. xxx. 35.

CONFECTIONARY, a confectioner. 1 Sam. viii. 13.

CONFUSION, used in the strong sense of destruction. Isa. xxiv. 10.

CONSCIENCE, consciousness. 1 Cor. viii. 7.

CONSIST, to stand firm, subsist. Col. i. 17.

CONTAIN, to be continent. 1 Cor. vii. 9.

CONTEST, to call to witness. Exod. xix. 21m.

CONVENIENT, fitting, suitable, becoming. Acts xxiv. 25 ; Rom. i. 28.

CONVENT. to convene. Jer. xlix. 19m.

CONVERSATION, (1) behaviour, Gal. i. 13 ; (2) disposition, Heb. xiii. 5; (3) citizenship, Phil. iii, 20.

CONVERT to turn round. Isa. vi. 10.

CONVINCE, to convict. John viii. 46.

CONVOCATION, assembly. Exod. xii. 16.

CORN, a grain. John xii. 24.

COTES, huts, sheds. 2 Chron. xxxii. 28.

COUCH, to lie. Deut. xxxiii. 13.

COUNT, an account, a reckoning. Exod. xii. 4.

COUNTERVAIL, counterbalance. Esther vii. 4.

COUSIN, a kinsman, or kinswoman. Luke i. 36.

COVERT, a hiding-place, shelter. 1 Sam. xxv. 20.

COVET, to desire. 1 Cor. xii. 31.

CRACKNELS, crisp cakes. 1 Kings xiv 3.

CRAFT, handicraft, trade. Acts xviii. 3.

CRAVE, to ask for. Mark xv. 43.

CRAW, the crop of a bird. Zeph. iii. 1m.

CREATURE, a created thing. Rom. i. 25.

CRIB, a manger for cattle. Isa. i. 3.

CRISPING PINS, curling irons. Isa. iii. 22.

CRUSE, a small vessel for liquids. 1 Kings xiv, 3.

CUMBERED, too much occupied, troubled. Luke x. 40.

CUMBRANCE, encumbrance. Deut. i. 12.

CUNNING, knowledge, skill. 1 Kings vii. 14.

CUSTOM, tribute, tax. Ezra iv. 13.

DAM, the mother bird. Deut. xxii. 6.

DAMN, to judge, condemn. 2 Thess. ii. 12.

DAMNABLE, destructive. 2 Pet. ii. 1.

DAMNATION, condemnation. Rom. iii. 8.

DANGER, IN, liable to. Matt. v. 22.

DAYSMAN, an arbitrator. or umpire. Job ix. 33.

DAYSPRING, dawn, daybreak. Luke i. 78.

DAY-STAR, the morning star. 2 Pet. i. 19.

DEAL, a part. portion. Exod. xxix. 40.

DEBATE, strife, contention. Isa. lviii. 4.

DECEASE, to die. Matt. xxii. 25.

ESCH

DECENTLY, in a becoming manner. 1 Cor. xiv. 40.

DECK, to cover, adorn. Prov. vii. 16.

DECLARE, to make clear, explain. Matt. xiii. 36.

DECLINE, to turn aside. Exod. xxiii. 2.

DEFENCED, fortified. Isa. xxv. 2.

DEGREE, rank, station. 1 Tim. iii. 13.

DEMAND, to ask. 2 Sam. xi. 7.

DENOUNCE, to announce. Deut. xxx. 18.

DEPUTY, the proconsul. Acts xiii. 7.

DESCRIBE, to trace, mark out. Josh. xviii. 4.

DESCRY, to observe, reconnoitre. Judg. i. 23.

DESIRE, to regret. 2 Chron. xxi. 20.

DESPITE, contempt. Heb. x. 29.

DESPITEFULLY, spitefully, maliciously. Matt. v. 44.

DETERMINATE, determined upon. Acts ii. 23.

DIET, a daily allowance. Jer. lii. 34.

DISALLOW, disapprove. Num. xxx. 5.

DISANNUL, to annul entirely. Gal. iii. 17.

DISCIPLINE, instruction. Job xxxvi. 10.

DISCOMFIT, to defeat, rout. Exod. xvii. 13.

DISCOVER, to uncover, lay bare. Ps. xxix. 9.

DISHONESTY, disgrace, shame. 2 Cor. iv. 2.

DISPENSATION, stewardship, administration. 1 Cor. ix. 17.

DISPOSITION, appointment, arrangement. Acts vii. 53.

DISSOLVE, to solve. Dan. v. 16.

DO TO WIT, to make known. 2 Cor. viii. 1.

DOCTOR, a teacher. Luke ii. 46.

DOCTRINE, teaching. Mark iv. 2.

DOTE, to be mad or foolish. Jer. l. 36.

DRAG, a drag-net. Hab. i. 15.

DRAUGHT, DRAUGHT-HOUSE, a privy. Matt. xv. 17.

DREDGE, a mixture of oats and barley. Job xix. 6m.

DRESS, to trim. Gen. ii. 15.

DUKE, a leader, chieftain. Gen. xxxvi 15.

DURE, to endure, last. Matt. xiii. 21.

EAR, to plough. Deut. xxi. 4.

EARING, ploughing. Gen. xlv. 6.

EARNEST, a pledge. 2 Cor. i. 22.

EDIFY, to build up. Acts ix. 31.

EFFECT, purport, meaning. Ezek. xii. 23.

ELEMENTS, rudiments. Gal. iv. 9.

EMERODS, hæmorrhoids, the disease of piles. 1 Sam. v. 6.

EMINENT, lofty. Ezek. xvi. 24.

ENDAMAGE, to injure, damage. Ezra iv. 13.

ENDUE, to endow. Gen. xxx. 20.

ENLARGE, to set at liberty. 2 Sam. xii. 37.

ENSAMPLE, example. 1 Cor. x. 11.

ENSIGN, a standard or flag. Isa. v. 26.

ENSUE, follow and overtake. 1 Pet. iii. 11.

ENTREAT, to treat, deal with. Gen. xii. 16.

EQUAL. just. right. Ps. xvii. 2.

ESCHEW, shun, avoid. Job i. 1.

ESTA

ESTATE, a state, condition. Gen. xliii. 7.

EVILFAVOUREDNESS, ugliness, deformity. Deut. xvii. 1.

EXCHANGER, a money-changer, banker. Matt. xxv. 27.

EXERCISED, made familiar. 2 Pet. ii. 14.

EXORCIST, one who casts out evil spirits by adjuration. Acts xix. 13.

EXPECT, to await. Heb. x. 13.

EXPRESS, modelled, exact. Heb. i. 3.

FAIN, glad, gladly. Luke xv. 16.

FALL, to happen. Ruth iii. 18.

FAME, report, tidings. Gen. xliv. 16.

FASHION, to make, shape. Gen. vi. 15.

FAT, a vessel, vat. Joel ii. 24.

FAT, to fatten. Luke xv. 23.

FAVOUR, face, or appearance. Ps. xlv. 12.

FEAR, cause or object of fear. Gen. xxxi. 42.

FEARFUL, timorous, faint-hearted. Matt. viii. 26.

FEARFULNESS, fear. Ps. lv. 5.

FETCH ABOUT, to bring about, contrive. 2 Sam. xiv. 20.

FINE, refine. Job xxviii. 1.

FIRSTLING, the first offspring. Gen. iv. 4.

FITCHES, vetches. Isa. xxviii. 25, 27.

FLOURISH, to blossom. Eccles. xii. 5.

FOLDEN, folded. Nah. i. 10.

FOOTMEN, foot-soldiers, infantry. Num. xi. 21.

FOR ALL, although, notwithstanding. John xxi. 11.

FORBEAR, to be indulgent to, or patient with. Col. iii. 13.

FORESHIP, the bow of the ship. Acts xxvii. 30.

FORNACE, the old form of furnace. Deut. iv. 20.

FORTH OF, out of, or from. Gen. viii. 16.

FOWL, a bird generally. Gen. i. 20.

FRANKLY, freely Luke vii. 42.

FRAY, the root of the verb affray. Deut. xxviii. 26.

FRET, to corrode. Lev. xiii. 55.

FROWARD, cross, perverse. Deut. xxxii. 20.

FURNITURE, equipment, accoutrements. Gen. xxxi. 34.

GAD, to rove about without any good purpose. Jer. ii. 36.

GAINSAY, to contradict. Luke xxi. 15.

GARNER, granary. Matt. iii. 12.

GENDER to beget, engender. Job xxxviii. 29.

GENERATION, offspring, progeny. Matt. iii. 7.

GLISTERING, glistening. Luke ix. 29.

GOODLY, fair, handsome. Gen. xxxix. 6.

GOODMAN, the master of the house. Matt. xx. 11.

GOVERNOR, the man at the helm. Jas. iii. 4.

GRACE, favour. Ruth ii. 2.

GRAFF, graft. Rom. xi. 17.

GRIEVE, to inflict bodily pain. Gen. xlix. 23.

GRUDGE, to grumble, murmur. Ps. lix. 15.

LODG

HABERGEON, a little coat of mail covering the head and shoulders. Exod. xxviii. 32.

HALE, to pull with force. Luke xii. 58.

HALT, lame, crippled. Matt. xviii. 8.

HALT, to limp. Gen. xxxii. 31.

HARNESS, accoutrements in general. 1 Kings xx. 11.

HARNESSED, armed. Exod. xiii. 18.

HASTE. to hasten. Gen. xviii. 7.

HELVE, the handle. Deut. xix. 5.

HOISE, to hoist. Acts xxvii. 40.

HOLPEN, helped. Ps. lxxxiii. 8.

HONEST, honourable, comely. Rom. xii. 17.

HONESTY, becoming deportment. 1 Tim. ii. 2.

HOSEN, the old plural of hose. Dan. iii. 21.

HOUGH, to cut the hamstrings. Josh. xi. 6.

HUNGERBITTEN, famished. Job xviii. 12.

HUSBANDMAN, a farmer. Gen. ix. 20.

HUSBANDRY, tillage. 1 Cor. iii. 9.

ILL-FAVOURED, bad-looking. Gen. xli. 3.

IMPLEAD, to indict, accuse. Acts xix. 38.

INHABITER, an inhabitant. Rev. viii. 13.

INSTANT, urgent. Luke xxiii. 23.

INSTANTLY, urgently. Luke vii. 4.

JANGLING, prating, babbling, idle talking. 1 Tim. i. 6.

JEOPARDY, danger, risk. Luke viii. 23.

JEWEL, an ornament. Exod. iii. 22.

KERCHIEF, a covering for the head. Ezek. xiii. 18.

KINDREDS, families. Ps. xxii. 27.

KINE, the plural of cow. Gen. xxxii. 15.

KNIT, firmly fastened. Judg. xx. 11.

KNOP, a bud. Ex. xxv. 31.

LACE, a band. Exod. xxviii. 28.

LARGE, wide, spacious. Judg. xviii. 10.

LATCHET, a lace, thong. Mark i. 7.

LAVER, any vessel for washing. Exod. xxxviii. 8.

LEASING, a lie, falsehood. Ps. iv. 2.

LEES, sediment, dregs. Isa. xxv. 6.

LESSER, smaller. Gen. i. 16.

LET, to hinder. 2 Thess. ii. 7.

LET BE, to cease. Matt. xxvii. 49.

LEWD, ignorant, unlearned. Acts xvii. 5.

LIEN, past participle of the verb to lie. Gen. xxvi. 10.

LIGHT, to come down. Ruth ii. 3.

LIGHTEN, to illuminate. 2 Sam. xxii. 29.

LIKE, to please. Deut. xxiii. 16.

LIKE, to prefer. 1 Chron. xxviii. 4.

LIKEN, to compare. Matt. vii. 26.

LIKING, condition, plight. Job xxxix. 4.

LIST, to will, please, like. Matt. xvii. 12.

LIVELY, living. 1 Pet. i. 3.

LODGE, to pass the night. Gen. xxiv. 23.

OCCU

LODGE, a hut. Isa. i. 8.

LOFT, an upper room. Acts xx. 9.

LOOK, to expect. Isa. v. 2.

LOVER, an intimate friend. Ps. xxxviii. 11.

LUCRE, gain. 1 Tim. iii. 3.

LUST, to desire strongly. Jas. iv. 2.

LUST, strong desire, pleasure. 1 John ii. 16, 17.

LUSTY, stout, vigorous. Judg. iii. 29.

MAGNIFICAL, magnificent. 1 Chron. xxii. 5.

MAGNIFY, to make great. Josh. iii. 7.

MAKE, to feign, pretend. Josh. viii. 15.

MAKE, to do. Judg. xviii. 3.

MAKEBATE, a causer of strife. 2 Tim. iii. 3m.

MAN OF WAR, a warrior, soldier. Exod. xv. 3.

MANICLES, manacles. Jer. xl. 1m.

MANSIONS, dwelling-places, resting-places. John xiv. 2.

MARISH, a marsh. Ezek. xlvii. 11.

MASTERY, superiority. Exod. xxxii. 18.

MATTER, fuel. Jas. iii. 5.

MAUL, a mallet. Prov. xxv. 18.

MAW, the stomach. Deut. xviii. 3.

ME THINKETH, it seems to me. 2 Sam. xviii. 27.

MEAN, common, lowly. Prov. xxii. 29.

MEAT, food. Gen. i. 29, 30.

MEET, proper. Heb. vi. 7.

MEMORIAL, memory. Ps. ix. 6.

MERCHANTMAN, merchant. Matt. xiii. 45.

MERRY, joyful. Jas. v. 13.

MESS, a dish of meat (derived from O. Fr. mes). Gen. xliii. 34.

METE, to measure. Exod. xvi. 18.

METEYARD, a measuring rod. Lev. xix. 35.

MILCH, milk-giving. Gen. xxxii. 15.

MINCING, tripping. Isa. iii. 16.

MIND, will, consent. Philem. 14.

MIND, to care for. Phil. iii. 19.

MIND, to intend, purpose. Acts xx. 13.

MINDED, determined. Matt. i. 19.

MINISH, to diminish. Exod. v. 19.

MINISTER, to supply, furnish. 2 Cor. ix. 10.

MORROW, morning. Josh. v. 11.

MORTIFY. put to death. Rom. viii. 13.

MOTE, a small particle. Matt. vii. 3.

MOTIONS, emotions, impulses. Rom. vii. 5.

MUNITION, means of defence. Isa. xxix. 7.

NAUGHT, worthless, bad. 2 Kings ii. 19.

NAUGHTINESS, wickedness. 1 Sam. xvii. 28.

NAUGHTY, bad, wicked. Prov. vi. 12.

NEPHEW, a grandson. Judg. xii. 14.

NETHER, lower. Exod. xix. 17.

NOISOME, hurtful, noxious. Ps. xci. 3.

OBEISANCE, obedience. Gen. xxxvii. 7.

OBSERVATION, observance. Neh. xiii. 14m.

OBSERVE, to treat with respect. Mark vi. 20.

OCCUPIER, a trader. Ezek. xxvii. 27.

OCCUPY, to trade. Luke xix. 13.

OCCU

OCCURRENT EVIL, evil chance. 1 Kings v. 4.

OUCHES, the sockets in which precious stones are set, also the jewels themselves. Exod. xxviii. 13.

OUTMOST, utmost. Deut. xxx. 4.

OUTWENT, outstripped. Mark vi. 33.

OVERLIVE, to outlive. Josh. xxiv. 31.

PAINFUL, full of pain. Ps. lxxiii. 16.

PALSY, paralysis. Matt. iv. 24.

PAP, the nipple of the breast. Luke xi. 27.

PAPER REED, the papyrus plant. Isa. xix. 7.

PARCEL, piece, portion. Josh. xxiv. 32.

PARTAKER, an accomplice. Ps. l. 18.

PASSENGER, passer by, wayfarer. Prov. ix. 15.

PASSIONS, feelings, dispositions. Jas. v. 17.

PASTOR, a shepherd. Jer. xxiii. 1.

PATE, the crown of the head. Ps. vii. 16.

PEACE, TO HOLD ONE'S, to be silent. Exod. xiv. 14.

PECULIAR, one's own. Exod. xix. 5.

PERADVENTURE, perhaps. Gen. xxxi. 31.

PERSECUTE, to pursue. Ps. vii. 1.

PERSUADE, to use persuasion, but not necessarily to prevail. Acts xix. 8.

PILL, to peel. Gen. xxx. 37.

PILLED, bald. Lev. xiii. 40m.

PITIFUL, full of pity. Lam. iv. 10.

PLAINNESS, sincerity, frankness. 2 Cor. iii. 12.

PLAT, a plot or small portion of ground. 2 Kings ix. 26.

PLATTER, a dish. Matt. xxiii. 25.

POINT OUT, to assign. Num. xxxiv. 7.

POLL, to cut the hair of the head. 2 Sam. xiv. 26.

PORT, a gate. Neh. ii. 13.

PORTER, a gate-keeper. John x. 3.

POSSESS, to seize, take possession of. Acts xvi. 16.

POST, runner. 2 Chron. xxx. 6.

POTTAGE, broth, soup. Gen. xxv. 29.

POWER, a force, used of an army. 2 Chron. xxxii. 9.

PRACTISE, to plot. Ps. xxxvii. 12m.

PREFER, to advance, to put before. John i. 15.

PRESENTLY, instantly. 1 Sam. ii. 16.

PRESS, a crowd. Mark ii. 4.

PRESSFAT, the vat of an olive or wine-press. Hag. ii. 16.

PREVENT, to go before. 1 Thess. iv. 15.

PROFESS, to declare openly. Matt. vii. 23.

PROFIT, to benefit. Mark viii. 36.

PROLONG, to defer, postpone. Ezek. xii. 25.

PROPER, one's own. 1 Cor. vii. 7.

PROVE, to test, try. Exod. xvi. 4.

PUBLICAN, from Lat. *publicanus*, one who farmed the public taxes. Matt. v. 46.

PURCHASE, to win, acquire. 1 Tim. iii. 13.

PURTENANCE, the intestines of an animal. Exod. xii. 9.

PUT TO THE WORSE, to worst, defeat. 2 Kings xiv. 12.

SHIP

QUICK, living, alive. Ps. lv. 15.

QUICKEN, to make alive. Eph. ii. 1.

QUIT, to discharge a duty, and so to free oneself from the obligation of it. 1 Cor. xvi. 13.

QUIT, set free, acquitted. Exod. xxi. 19.

RAGGED, rugged. Isa. ii. 21.

RANGES, chimney racks. Lev. xi. 35.

RASE, to level with the ground, from Fr. *raser*. Ps. cxxxvii. 7.

RAVENING, plunder. Luke xi. 39.

RAVIN, to prey with rapacity. Gen. xlix. 27.

RAY, array. 1 Sam. xvii. 20m.

READY, swift, quick. Ps. xlv. 1.

READY, near, at the point. Luke vii. 2.

REASON, to converse. Acts xxiv. 25.

REBATEMENT, literally a diminution. 1 King iv. 6m.

RECEIPT, a place for receiving. Matt. ix. 9.

RECORD, witness. Phil. i. 8.

REFRAIN, to bridle, restrain. Prov. x. 19.

REINS, kidneys. Ps. vii. 9.

RELIGIOUS, professing religion in the outward form. Jas. i. 26.

RENT, the old form of "rend." Jer. iv. 30.

REPLENISH, to fill, not *to fill again*. Gen. i. 28.

REPORT, fame, reputation. Acts vi. 3.

REPROOF, reply. Ps. xxxviii. 14.

REPROVE, refute, disprove. Job vi. 25.

REQUIRE, to ask, without demanding as a right. 2 Sam. xii. 20.

REREWARD, the rear-guard of an army. 1 Sam. xxix. 2.

RESEMBLE, to liken, compare. Luke xiii. 18.

REVIVE, to come to life again. Rom. xiv. 9.

RINGSTRAKED, marked with rings. Gen. xxx. 35.

RIOT, dissolute, or luxurious living. Titus i. 6.

RIOTOUS, luxurious, dissolute. Luke xv. 13.

ROAD, a riding, especially a plundering excursion, a raid. 1 Sam. xxvii. 10.

SAVE, SAVING, except. Neh. iv. 23.

SAVOUR, taste, flavour. Matt. v. 13.

SCALL, an eruption of the skin. Lev. xiii. 30–37.

SCRABBLE, to scrawl. 1 Sam. xxi. 13.

SCRIP, a small bag. Matt. x. 10.

SEAR, to dry up, scorch. 1 Tim. iv. 2.

SECURE, careless, void of care. Job xi. 18.

SECURELY, carelessly. Prov. iii. 29.

SEEK, to resort to. Deut. xii. 5.

SEETHE, to boil. Exod. xvi. 23.

SENT, the old and more correct spelling of "scent." Job xiv. 9.

SHAKED, shook. Ps. cix. 25.

SHAMBLES, a butcher's stall. 1 Cor. x. 25.

SHAMEFACEDNESS, bashfulness, modesty. 1 Tim. ii. 9.

SHERD, shred, fragment. Isa. xxx. 14.

SHIPMASTER, the captain of a ship. Jonah i. 6.

SHIPMEN, sailors. Acts xxvii. 27.

TIRE

SHOELATCHET, the lace or thong of a shoe. Gen. xiv. 23.

SILLY, literally simple, harmless, guileless. Hos. vii. 11.

SILVERLING, a piece of silver. Isa. vii. 23.

SINCERE, pure, unadulterated. 1 Pet. ii. 2.

SIT AT MEAT, sit down to table. Matt. ix. 10.

SITH, since. Ezek. xxxv. 6.

SLANG, the past tense of "sling." 1 Sam. xvii. 49.

SLEEP, ON, asleep. Acts xiii. 36.

SLEIGHT, artifice. Eph. iv. 14.

SLICE, a frying-pan. Lev. ii. 5m.

SOD, SODDEN, the preterite and past participle of seethe. Gen. xxv. 29; Exod. xii. 9.

SOOTHSAYER, literally a "truth-sayer," hence a foreteller, a diviner. Isa. ii. 6.

SOOTHSAYING, divination. Acts xvi. 16.

SPEED, fortune. Gen. xxiv. 12.

SPRING, the dawn. 1 Sam. ix. 26.

SPRING, young shoots. Ezek. xvii. 9.

STABLISH, establish. 2 Sam. vii. 13.

STONY, rocky. Matt. xiii. 5.

STOUTNESS, stubbornness. Isa. ix. 9.

STRAIN AT, a misprint for "strain out." Matt. xxiii. 24.

STRAIT, a narrow place. Job xxxvi. 16.

STRAIT, narrow. Matt. vii. 13.

STRAKE, the past tense of "strike." Acts xxvii. 17.

STRIPE, a stroke, blow. Exod. xxi. 25.

STUFF, baggage of an army or traveller. 1 Sam. x. 22.

SUNDER, IN, asunder. Ps. xlvi. 9.

SWADDLE, to swathe, bandage. Lam. ii. 22.

SWADDLING-BAND, a bandage used for infants. Job xxxviii. 9.

SWADDLING-CLOTHES, the bandages used in swaddling infants. Luke ii. 7.

TABER, to beat as a taber or tabret. Nah. ii. 7.

TABERNACLE, a tent. Matt. xvii. 4.

TABLE, a writing tablet. Luke i. 63.

TABLET, an ornament on a necklace. Exod. xxxv. 22.

TACHE, a fastening or catch. Exod. xxvi. 6.

TARGET, a shield. 1 Sam. xvii. 6.

TARRY, to stay, wait for. Gen. xix. 2.

TAVERNS, shops. Acts xxviii. 15.

TELL, to count. Gen. xv. 5.

TEMPERANCE, self-restraint. Acts xxiv. 25.

TEMPT, to try, put to the test. Gen. xxii. 1.

TEMPTATION, trial. Deut. iv. 34.

TENDER EYED, weak-eyed. Gen. xxix. 17.

THOUGHT, anxiety, hence "to take thought" is "to be anxious." Matt. vi. 25.

THROUGH-AIRED, airy. Jer. xxii. 14m.

THROUGHLY, thoroughly. Matt. iii. 12.

TILLER, a cultivator. Gen. iv. 2.

TIRE, a head-dress. Isa. iii. 18.

TIRE

TIRE, to attire, adorn with a tire. 2 Kings ix. 30.

TITTLE, apparently a diminutive of tit, small. Matt. v. 18.

TORMENTOR, a torturer, executioner. Matt. xviii. 34.

TRAFFICKERS, merchants. Isa. xxiii. 8.

TRANSLATE, to remove, transfer. Heb. xi. 5.

TRANSLATION, removal. Heb. xi. 5.

TRAVAIL, labour, toil. Isa. liii. 11.

TRAVAIL, to be in labour. Gen. xxxv. 16.

TRAVEL. *See* TRAVAIL. Lam. iii. 5.

TREATISE, narrative. Acts i. 1.

TROW, to think, believe. Luke xvii. 9.

TRUMP, trumpet. 1 Cor. xv. 52.

TURN AGAIN, to return. Ruth i. 11.

TURTLE, a turtle-dove. Cant. ii. 12.

TUTOR, a guardian. Gal. iv. 2.

TWAIN, two. 1 Sam. xviii. 21.

UNCTION, literally "anointing." 1 John ii. 20.

UNDERSETTERS, props, supports. 1 Kings vii. 30.

UNDERTAKE, to be surety. Isa. xxxviii. 14.

UNJUST, dishonest. Luke xvi. 8.

UNWASHEN, unwashed. Matt. xv. 20.

UNWITTINGLY, without knowing. Lev. xxii. 14.

USE, to practise. Lev. xix. 26.

USURY, formerly denoted "interest." Matt. xxv. 27.

UTMOST, outermost. Num. xxii. 36.

UTTER, to give out, disclose. Lev. v. 1.

UTTER, outer. Ezek. x. 5.

VAGABOND, a wanderer. Gen. iv. 12.

VAIN, empty, worthless. Exod. v. 9.

VAUNT, to boast. 1 Cor. xiii. 4.

VENIME, venom. Deut. xxxii. 33.

VENISON, flesh of beasts taken in hunting, game. Gen. xxv. 28.

VENTURE, AT A, at random. 1 Kings xxii. 34.

VERY, true. John vii. 26.

WHILE

VESTURE, dress, clothing. Ps. xxii. 18.

VEX, to torment, harass. Matt. xv. 22.

VEXATION, torment, trouble. Deut. xxviii. 20.

VILE, cheap, worthless. Jer. xxix. 17

VIRTUE, might, power. Mark v. 30.

VOCATION, calling. Eph. iv. 1.

VOID, empty. Gen. i. 2.

VOLUME, a roll. Heb. x. 7.

WAG, to move. Matt. xxvii. 39.

WAIT, ambush, watch. Jer. ix. 8.

WAIT UPON, to watch, attend. Ps. cxxiii. 2.

WAKE, to watch. 1 Thess. v. 10.

WALLOW THYSELF, roll thyself. Jer. vi. 26.

WARD, guard, prison. Gen. xl. 3.

WARE, merchandise. Neh. x. 31.

WARE, aware, literally "wary, cautious." Acts xiv. 6.

WASHPOT, a vessel for washing in. Ps. lx. 8.

WASTER, a spendthrift. Prov. xviii. 9.

WATCHING, (1) waking, awake, Luke xii. 37; (2) wakefulness, sleeplessness, 2 Cor. vi. 5.

WAX, to grow. Exod. xxii. 24.

WAXEN, grown. Gen. xix. 13.

WAY, (1) road, Gen. xvi. 7; (2) a course of life, Acts xix. 9.

WAYFARING, travelling. Isa. xxxiii. 8.

WAYMARK, a guide-post. Jer. xxxi. 21.

WAYS, "any ways," equivalent to "any wise." Lev. xx. 4.

WEALTH, weal, or well-being generally. 2 Chron. i. 12.

WEALTHY, prosperous. Jer. xlix. 31.

WEDLOCK, TO BREAK, to commit adultery. Ezek. xvi. 38.

WELL FAVOURED, good-looking. Gen. xxix. 17.

WELLSPRING, a spring, or fountain. Prov. xvi. 22.

WENCH. a girl, applied generally to one of low birth. 2 Sam. xvii. 17.

WHEN AS, when. Matt. i. 18.

WHILE AS, while. Heb. ix. 8.

YOKE

WHILES, while. Matt. v. 25.

WHISPERER, a secret informer, talebearer. Rom. i. 29.

WHIT (A.S. *wiht*), a thing. John vii. 23.

WHOLE, hale, healthy. Matt. ix. 12.

WHOLESOME, healthy, healing. 1 Tim. vi. 3.

WIMPLE, a covering for the neck. Isa. iii. 22.

WINEBIBBER, a drunkard. Matt. xi. 19.

WINEFAT, the vessel into which the liquor flows from a wine-press. Mark xii. 1.

WINK, to connive. Acts xvii. 30.

WISE, manner, way. Matt. 1. 18.

WIST, knew. Mark ix. 6.

WIT, to know. 2 Cor. viii. 1.

WITCH, used of a man. Deut. xviii. 10.

WITH, a twisted branch of a tree. Judg. xvi. 7.

WITHAL, likewise. 1 Kings xix. 1.

WITNESS, evidence. Mark xiv. 55.

WITTINGLY, knowingly. Gen. xlviii. 14.

WITTY, skilful, ingenious. Prov. viii. 12.

WONT, accustomed. Mark x. 1.

WORSHIP, reverence, honour. Luke xiv. 10.

WORTHY, deserving, whether of good or ill. Rom. i. 32.

WOT, WOTTETH, the present tense of wit. Gen. xxi. 26.

WOULD NONE OF, refused. Prov. i. 25.

WREATHEN, twisted. Exod. xxviii. 14.

WREST, to twist, pervert. Ps. lvi. 5.

WROTH, wrathful, angry. Gen. iv. 5.

YEARN, to stir with emotion. Gen. xliii. 30.

YESTERNIGHT, corresponding to "yesterday." Gen. xix. 34.

YOKEFELLOW, comrade. Phil. iv. 3.

See WRIGHT, *The Bible Word Book*— a work to which the compiler of this list is largely indebted.

ALPHABETICAL INDEX OF THE HOLY SCRIPTURES:

COMPRISING THE NAMES, CHARACTERS, AND SUBJECTS, BOTH OF

THE OLD AND NEW TESTAMENTS.

AHAZ

Ki. 16; 2 Ch. 28; encouraged by Isaiah, Is. 7.

AHAZIAH, *king of Judah; his history*, 2 Ki. 8.24-29; 9.16-28; 2 Ch. 22.

AHAZIAH, *king of Israel; his history*, 1 Ki. 22.40,49,51-53; 2 Ki. 1.

AHIJAH, *a prophet; his prophecies*, 1 Ki. 11.29-36; 14.5-16.

AHIKAM, *father of Gedaliah, son of Shaphan (the scribe)*, 2 Ki. 22.12-20; 25.22; Je. 26.24.

AHIMAAZ, *high priest; his history*, 2 Sa. 15.27; 17.17-22; 18.19-30.

AHIMELECH, *high priest, great-grandson of Eli; his history*, 1 Sa. 21.1-9; 22.9-21.

AHIMELECH, *grandson of the former*, mentioned 2 Sa. 8.17; 1 Ch. 18.16; 24.3,6,31.

AHITHOPHEL, *David's counsellor; account of*, 2 Sa. 15.12,31,34; 16.15-23; 17.1-23; Ps. 41.9; 55.12; 109.

AHITUB, *high-priest, grandson of Eli;* 1 Sa. 14.3; 22.11,20.

AI, *a city of Canaan*, mentioned Josh. 7.1-5; 8.1-29.

ALEXANDER, one of that name mentioned in Mar. 15.21; Ac. 4.6; 19. 33; 1 Ti. 1.20; 2 Ti. 4.14.

ALEXANDER *the Great, his victories foretold*, Da. 8.5,21; 10.20; 11.3,4.

ALEXANDRIA, *a city in Egypt, founded by Alexander*, mentioned Ac. 6.9; 18.24; 27.6.

ALLEGORY, the history of Hagar and Sarah said to be, Ga. 4.22-31.

ALMOND TREE, hoary locks compared to, Ec. 12.5.

ALMS-GIVING recommended, De. 15.7; Lu. 3.11; 11.41; Ep. 4.28; 1 Ti. 6.18; He. 13.16; 1 Jno. 3.17; will be rewarded, Ps. 41.1; 112.9; Pr. 14.21; 19.17; 22.9; 28.27; Mat. 25.32-40; Lu. 6.38; 14.13,14; 1 Ti. 6.18,19; He. 6.10; the neglect of it will be punished, Job 20.19,20; Pr. 21.13; Eze. 18.12,13; Mat. 25.41-46; to be given chiefly to the saints, Ro. 12.13; 2 Co. 9.1; Ga. 6.10; not to the idle, 2 Th. 3. 10; according to men's ability, Mar. 12.43; Ac. 11.29; 1 Co. 16.2; 2 Co. 8.12; 1 Pe. 4.11; cheerfully and speedily, Pr. 3.27; Ro. 12.8; 2 Co. 8.11; 9.7; not from ostentation, Pr. 20.6; Mat. 6. 1; directions for, Deut. 15.7,8; Lu. 3.11; 11.41; 1 Co. 16.2; 2 Co. 9.7; Eph. 4.28; 1 Tim. 6.17,18; Heb. 13. 16; 1 Jno. 3.17; Gal. 6.10.

ALPHA and OMEGA, Rev. 1.8,11; 21.6; 22.13. See *Christ.*

ALPHEUS *(supposed to be Cleophas), the father of James and Jude*, Mat. 10.3; Lu. 6.15; 24.18; Jno. 19.25; Ac. 1.13.

ALPHEUS, *father of Matthew*, Mar. 2.14.

ALTAR *of burnt-offering*, Ex. 27; 38.1.

ALTAR *of incense*, Ex. 30.1; 37.25.

ALTAR *of brass*, in the temple of Solomon, 2 Ch. 4.1.

ALTAR *built by the Reubenites*, Josh. 22.10.

ALTAR, Christ compared to an, He. 13.10.

ALTARS, how to be made, Ex. 20.24; Deut. 27.5; erected for the worship of the true God, Ge. 8.20; 12.7,8; 13.4,18; 22.9; 26.25; 33.20; 35.1-7; Ex. 17.15; Ezr. 3.1-6.

AMALEK, Ge. 36.12; Ex. 17.8,13; 17.16; Deut. 25.17; Jud. 7.12; 1 Sam. 14.47; 15.*&*; 27.9; 30.17; 2 Sam. 1.10-15.

ANGE

AMASA, *Absalom's general*, mentioned 2 Sa. 17.25; 20.4-13.

AMAZIAH, *king of Judah; his history*, 2 Ki. 12.21; 13.12; 14.1-20; 2 Ch. 25.1.

AMAZIAH, *a priest of Bethel*, Am. 7. 10-17.

AMBASSADOR, *earthly*, 2 Ch. 32.31; *heavenly*, 2 Co. 5.20.

AMBER, Eze. 1.4,27; 8.2.

AMBITION, instances of, Mat. 18.1-4; 20.20,21; 23.8; Lu. 22.24; punishment, Pr. 17.19; Isa. 14.12.

AMEN, used as a petition or confirmation, Nu. 5.22; De. 27.15-26; 1 Ki. 1.36; 1 Ch. 16.36; Ne. 5.13; 8.6; Is. 65.16; Mat. 6.13; 1 Co. 14. 16; Re. 22.20.

AMETHYST. See *Jewels.*

AMMONITES, *descendants of Ammon*, Ge. 19.38; mentioned De. 2.19; 23. 3; Ju. 10.7; 11.32; 1 Sa. 11.11; 2 Sa. 10; 12.26; 2 Ch. 26.8; 27.5; Je. 25.21; 49.1-6; Eze. 21.28; 25.1-10; Am. 1.13; Zep. 2.8.

AMNON, *a son of David; his history*, 2 Sa. 3.2; 13.1-33; 1 Ch. 3.1.

AMON, *king of Judah; his history*, 2 Ki. 21; 19.23; 2 Ch. 33.20-25.

AMORITES, *one of the families of Canaan*, mentioned Ge. 15.16; 48. 22; De.20.17; Jo. 3.10; 10.5; 24.8-12,18; Ju. 1.34-36; 6.10; 11.19-23; 1 Sa. 7.14; 2 Sa. 21.2; Eze. 16.3,45.

AMOS, *father of Isaiah*, Is. 1.1.

AMOS, *the prophet*, Amos 1., etc.

AMRAM, *the father of Aaron, Moses, and Miriam*, Ex. 6.20; 1 Ch. 6.3.

ANAKIM, *a race of giants*, Nu. 13.33; De. 9.2; Josh. 11.21.

ANANIAS and SAPPHIRA, their sin and punishment, Ac. 5.1-11.

ANANIAS, *high priest*, mentioned Ac. 23.2-5; 24.1.

ANANIAS, *a disciple of Jesus*, mentioned Ac. 9.10-18; 22.12.

ANATHEMA, 1 Co. 16.22.

ANATHOTH, *a city of the priests*, 1 Ki. 2.26; 1 Ch. 6.60; Je. 11.21-23.

ANCHOR, mentioned Ac. 27.29,30; spiritual, He. 6.19.

ANCIENT of days, Da. 7.26.

ANDREW, *one of the twelve apostles, his call*, Mat. 4.18; Jno. 1.40-44; mentioned Mar. 13.3; Jno. 6.8; 12. 22.

ANGELS, said to be wise, good, and immortal, 2 Sa. 14.17,20; Ps. 103. 20; Mat. 25.31; Lu. 20.36; elect, 1 Ti. 5.21; are appointed as guardians of men, Ps. 34.7; 91.11; Ec. 5.6; He. 1.14; spirits of men called so, Mat. 18.10; Ac. 12.15; ignorant of the day of judgment, Mat. 24. 36; desire to know what the apostles knew, 1 Pe. 1.12; are in great numbers, De. 33.2; Ps. 68.17; Da. 7.10; Mat. 26.53; Lu. 2.13; He. 12.22; Jude 14; Re. 5.11; are in the immediate presence of God, Lu. 1.19; are of different ranks, Da. 10. 13; Jude 9; are subject to Christ, Heb. 1.6; 1 Pe. 3.22; not to be worshipped, Col. 2.18; Re. 19.10; 22.9; they worship God, Ne. 9.6; Ps. 148. 2; *messengers of God*, sent to Sodom, Ge. 19.1-22; to David, 2 Sa. 24.16, 17; to Elijah, 1 Ki. 19.5-7; smite the Assyrians, 2 Ki. 19.35; to Zacharias, Lu. 1.19; to Mary, Lu. 1.26; deliver Peter, from prison, Ac. 12.7-10; smite Herod, Ac. 12.23; appear to the shepherds, Lu. 2.9-14; attend Christ on earth, Mat. 4.11; Mar. 1. 13; Lu. 22.43; roll the stone from

APOS

his sepulchre, Mat. 28.2; at his ascension, Ac. 1.10; to accompany Jesus at his second coming, Mat. 25.31; sometimes the LORD appeared as one; to Abraham, Ge. 18. 17-33; 22.15; to Jacob, 31.11; 32. 24-30; 48.16; to Moses, Ex. 3.2, etc.; to Joshua, Jo. 5.13-15; to the Israelites, Ju. 2.1-5; to Gideon, Ju. 6.11-23; to Manoah, Ju. 13.3-21; some that sinned, 2 Pe. 2.4; Jude 6; their ministry. Heb. 1.14; Gen. 19.1-15; Dan. 9.21,22; 10.18,19; Lu. 2.10; 15.10; Matt. 4.11; Lu. 22.43; Matt. 28.2; 13.41; 1 Thess. 4.16; their number, Rev. 5.11; Heb. 12. 22.

ANGER, general advice to repress it, Ps. 37.8; Pr. 16.32; 17.14; 19.11; Ep. 4.26,31; Col. 3.8; Ja. 1.19; exposes a man, and makes him incapable of friendship, Pr. 22.24; 25.8,28; a mark of folly or madness, Job 5.2; Pr. 12.16; 14.29; 27.3; 29.20; may bring a man to destruction, Pr. 19.19; Mat. 5.22; one of the works of the flesh, Ga. 3.20; comes from pride, Pr. 13.10; 21.24; its effects on others, Pr. 15.1,18; 26.21; 29.22; 30.33; may be innocent, Ep. 4.26; how pacified, Pr. 21.14; 25.15; Ec. 10.4; Mat. 5.25; Ro. 12.19-21; examples of it, Ge. 4.5-8; 39.19,20; 49.6; Nu. 20.10,11; 22.27; 1 Sa. 18.11; 20.30,33; Ps. 106.33; Jonah 4.1; Lu. 4.28; of reasonable anger, Ge. 6.6,7; 30.1,2; 31.36; Ex. 4.14; Le. 10.16; Nu. 16.15; 31.14; Ps. 7.11; Mar. 3.5.

ANNA, her character and prophecy, Lu. 2.36,38.

ANNAS, *high priest*, Lu. 3.2; Jno. 18.13,24; Ac. 4.6.

ANOINTED, the, 1 Sam. 2.35; 24.10; 26.9; 1 Ch. 16.22; Ps. 132.10; Isa. 61.1; Lu. 4.18; Ac. 4.27; 10.38; Christ was anointed by several women, as a proof of their love and reverence, Mat. 26.6,7; Lu. 7.37-47; Jno. 12.3.

ANOINTING, *a Jewish ceremony*, Le. 16.32; 1 Sa. 16.12; 1 Ki. 19.16; typical, Ex. 28.41; 29.7; 40.15; 40.9-11; 30.31,32; spiritual, Heb. 1.8,9; 2 Co. 1.21,22; 1 Jno. 2.20,27.

ANTI-CHRIST, his coming foretold, 2 Th. 2.3-9; 1 Ti. 4.1; said to come, 1 Jno. 2.18.

ANTIOCH, *a city of Syria;* Ac. 13.1; Gal. 2.11; the term *Christian* first used there, Ac. 11.26.

ANTIPAS, *a Christian martyr*, Re. 2.13.

ANXIETY, about worldly things, forbidden, Mat. 6.25-34; 13.22; Lu. 12.22-31; Jno. 6.27; 1 Co. 7.32; Ph. 4.6; 1 Ti. 6.8; 1 Pe. 5.7.

APOLLOS, *an eloquent preacher; account of*, Ac. 18.24-28; 19.1; 1 Co. 1.12; 3.4-6.

APOLLYON, Rev. 9.11. See *Devil.*

APOSTACY, Ge. 6.1-6; Mat. 13.20,21; 1 Co. 5; 2 Pe. 2.17-22; 1 Jno. 2.19; of angels, Jude 6; of man, Gen. 3.6; of Israel, Ex. 32.7,8; Is. 1.4-6; of disciples, Jno. 6.66; of the latter days, 1 Tim. 4.1-3.

APOSTLES, their appointment and powers, Mat. 10; Mar. 3.13-19; 16. 15; Lu. 6.13-16; sent out, Mar. 6.7-13; Lu. 9.1-6; their power of binding and loosing, Mat. 16.19; 18.18; Jno. 20.23; 1 Co. 5.3-5; 2 Th. 3.6,14; to do greater works than even Jesus had done, Jno.

APPI

14.12; their words were the words of God, Mat. 10.20,40; 2 Co. 5.20; 1 Th. 2.13; witnesses of Christ's resurrection, Lu. 24.50,51; Ac. 1. 22; 1 Co. 15.4-9; their sufferings, Mat. 10.16; Lu. 21.16; Jno. 15.20; 1 Co. 4.9; Paul one, Ac. 9.1-20; 13.2; 22.1-20; 23.11; 26.13-20; Ro. 1.1; 11.13; 1 Co. 15.8-10; 2 Co. 12.1-12; Ga. 1.1,11-24; 2.7; Ep. 1.1; 3.2-8; Col. 1.1; 1 Ti. 1.1; 2 Ti. 1.1; Tit. 1.1; false ones complained of, 2 Co. 11.13.

APPII FORUM, Ac. 28.15.

APPLE of the eye, De. 32.10; Ps. 17.8; Pr. 7.2; Zech. 2.8.

AQUILA, mentioned Ac. 18.2,18; Rom. 16.3; 1 Cor. 16.19.

ARABIA, *a country of Asia,* mentioned *historically,* 1 Ki. 10.1-15; 2 Ch. 9.1-14; Ps. 72.10,15; Gal. 1.17; *prophetically,* Is. 21.13; Je. 25.24.

ARABIANS, mentioned *historically,* 2 Ch. 17.11; 26.7; Je. 3.2; Ac. 2.11; *prophetically,* Is. 13.20.

ARARAT, *a mountain in Armenia* upon which the ark rested, Ge. 8.4.

ARAUNAH, *or* ORNAN, *a Jebusite,* his transaction with David, 2 Sa. 24.16-25; 1 Ch. 21.15-18.

ARCHELAUS, *a king under Cæsar,* Mat. 2.22.

ARCTURUS, *a star,* mentioned Job 9.9; 38.32.

AREOPAGUS, *Mars' hill,* Paul's presence there, and speech, Ac. 17.19-34.

ARISTARCHUS, *an early convert,* and prisoner with Paul, Ac. 19.29; 20.4; 27.2; Col. 4.10; Phil. 24.

ARK of Noah described, Ge. 6.14-16; 1 Pet. 3.20; of the covenant, its history, Ex. 25.10-21; 37.1-9; Jos. 3.15-17; 4.11; 6.11; 1 Sa. 4.5,11; 5; 6; 7.1,2; 2 Sa. 6; 15.24; 1 Ki. 8.3; 1 Ch. 13.15,16; 2 Ch. 5; in heaven, Rev. 11.19.

ARMAGEDDON, battle of, Re. 16.16.

ARMOUR, Goliath's, 1 Sa. 17.5; Saul's refused by David, 1 Sa. 17. 38,39; the Christian's, Rom. 13.12; 2 Cor. 6.7; 10.4; Ep. 6.13, etc.

ARTAXERXES, *or* SMERDIS, *an usurper of the Persian throne,* mentioned Ezr. 4.

ARTAXERXES, *Longimanus.* See *Ahasuerus.*

ASA, *king of Judah,* his history, 1 Ki. 15.8-24; 2 Ch. 14; 15; 16.

ASAHEL, *Joab's brother,* 2 Sa. 2.18-32; 3.27,30; 23.24; 1 Ch. 2.16; 11.26.

ASAPH, *a devout Levite, author of many Psalms,* 1 Ch. 6.39; 16.7; 25; 26.1; 2 Ch. 5.12; 29.30; 35.15; Ne. 12.46.

ASAPH, *keeper of the forest* of the king of Persia, Ne. 2.8.

ASCENSION, the, Mar. 16.19; Lu. 24.51; Acts 1.9-11; typified, Lev. 14.4-7; 16.15; foretold, Ps. 68.18; Jno. 6.62; 7.33; 14.28; 16.5; 20. 17; necessary, Jno. 16.7; its object, Ro. 8.34; Heb. 9.24; Jno. 14.2; its result, Acts 2.32,33; Eph. 2.4-7.

ASHDOD, *a city of the Philistines,* mentioned Jos. 15.47; 1 Sa. 5; 2 Ch. 26.6; Ne. 13.23,24; Is. 20.1; prophecies of, Je. 25.20; Am. 1.8; 3.9; Zep. 2.4; Zec. 9.6.

ASHER, *one of the twelve sons of Jacob,* his birth, Ge. 30.13; his blessing, 49.20; his inheritance, Jos. 19.24; his descendants, Num. 1.40; 26.44; 1 Ch. 7.30; Anna, Lu. 2.36.

BAAL

ASHES, Gen. 18.27; Job 30.19; 2 Sa. 13.19; Est. 4.1; Job. 2.8; 42.6; Jon. 3.6; Mat. 11.21.

ASHTAROTH, Ju. 2.13; 1 Sa. 12.10.

ASKELON, *a city of the Philistines,* Ju. 1.18; 14.19; 1 Sa. 6.17; Je. 25. 20; Zeph. 2.4.

ASP, *a poisonous serpent,* De. 32.33; Job 20.14,16; Is. 11.8; Ro. 3.13. See *Serpent.*

ASS of Balaam, speaks, Nu. 22.28-30; 2 Pet. 2.16; wild, described, Job 39.5-8; Hos. 8.9; Christ riding on one, Zech. 9.9; Mat. 21.1,11; Jno. 12.14,15.

ASSEMBLIES of Christians enjoined, He. 10.25; delighted in, Ps. 27.4; 42.1; 122.1, etc.; a blessing follows, Ps. 118.26; 134.1, etc.; 135.3; Mal. 3.16,17; Mat. 18.20; instances of, Lu. 24.33-36; Jno. 20.19-29; Ac. 1.13,14; 2.1-42; 4.23-31; 5.20,21,25, 42; 10.33-48; 12.5; 13.2,14-48; 16.13; 17.2; 20.7-11,17-36; 28.23-31.

ASSISTANCE, divine, necessary in all our undertakings, Jno. 15.5; 1 Co. 15.10; 2 Co. 3.5; Ph. 2.13; 1 Ti. 1.12; promised upon proper application, Ps. 37.4,5; Is. 58.9; Je. 29.12,13; Mat. 7.11; 21.22; Lu. 11.5-13; 18.1-14; Jno. 15.7; Ja. 1.5; 1 Jno. 3.22; 5.14,15; instances and acknowledgments of such, Ge. 24; 1 Sa. 1; 2 Ki. 19; 20; 2 Ch. 33.13; Job 42.10; Ps. 3.4; 118.5; 120.1. See *Reason* and *Understanding.*

ASSURANCE, of Sonship, Heb. 3.14; Ro. 8.16; 1 Jno. 3.2; of eternal life, 1 Jno. 3.14; Jno. 10.28,29; of abiding union with Christ, Jno. 17.24; Rom. 8.38,39.

ASSYRIA, 2 Ki. 15.29; 17; 19.35; Is. 37.36; prophecies of, Is. 8; 10. 5; 14.24-27; 30.31; 31.8; Mic. 5.6; Zep. 2.13; its departed glory described, Eze. 31.3.

ASTROLOGERS, Is. 47.13; La. 1.20; 2.27; 4.7; 5.7.

ATHALIA, *wife of Jehoram, king of Judah,* her history, 2 Ki. 8.26; 11.1, etc.; 2 Ch. 22; 23.

ATHEISTS, Ps. 14.1; 53.1.

ATHENS, *a city in Greece;* Paul preaches there, Ac. 17.15-34; 1 Th. 3.1.

ATONEMENT, Ex. 30.16; *annual day of,* Le. 16; 23.26-32; sacrifices on it, Nu. 29. 7-11; CHRIST an atonement for the sins of the world, Is. 53; Dan. 9.24; Mat. 20.28; Ro. 3.25; 5.6-19; 2 Co. 5.21; Ga. 1.4; 3.13; Tit. 2.14; He. 9.28; 1 Pe. 1. 19; 2.24; 3.18; 1 Jno. 2.2; 4.10; Rev. 1.5; 13.8; of God, Zac. 13.7-9; Isa. 53.10; Jno. 3.16; through love, 1 Jno. 4.10; Ro. 5.8; 8.32; 2 Co. 5. 18,19; how accomplished, Lev. 17. 11; Heb. 9.22; Eph. 1.6,7; Col. 1. 14; 1 Jno. 1.7; Rev. 7.14; 12.11; its result, Heb. 2.9; Isa. 53.5,6; 1 Pet. 2.24; Jno. 1.29; Rom. 5.10,11; 3.24,25; Gal. 1.3,4; Rom. 5.9; Heb. 10.14; 1 Th. 1.10; Heb. 9.28.

AUGUSTUS CÆSAR, Lu. 2.1.

AZARIAH, *or* UZZIAH, *king of Judah;* his history, 2 Ki. 14.21,22; 15.1-7; 1 Ch. 3.12; 2 Ch. 26.1,23; Ze. 14.5.

AZARIAH, *the son of Oded,* prophesies in the time of Asa, 2 Ch. 15.1-7.

BAAL, destruction of his altar and priests, Ju. 6.25-35; 1 Ki. 18.20-40; 2 Ki. 10.18-29; 11.18; 23.4,5; an

BAR-J

idol worshipped under the form of a bull, instances of, Nu. 22.41; Ju. 2.13; 1 Ki. 16.31,32; 2 Ki. 17.16; 21.3.

BAAL-PEOR, Nu. 25.3; De. 4.3; Ps. 106.28; Ho. 9.10.

BAASHA, *king of Israel,* his history, 1 Ki. 15.16-34; 16.1-14.

BABEL, the building of it, and the confusion of tongues there, Ge. 11.

BABYLON, *the capital of Chaldea,* mentioned 2 Ki. 17.30; 20.12-18; 2 Ch. 32.31; its destruction foretold, Is. 13; 14.4; 21.2-9; 47,48; Je. 25. 12-14; 50; 51, etc.

BABYLON, mystical, Re. 14.8; 16; 19; 17; 18.

BACA, Ps. 84.6.

BACKBITING, Ps. 15.3; Pr. 25.23; 2 Cor. 12.20.

BACKSLIDE, *to decline in religion,* Pr. 14.14; Je. 2.19; 3.12-14; Ho. 14.4; Lu. 9.62; Jno. 5.14; He. 10.38.

BADGER, its skin used as a covering to the tabernacle, Ex. 25.5; 26.14; 35.7; Nu. 4.10,11.

BAG, Hag. 1.6; Lu. 12.33; Jno. 12.6; 13.29.

BAKER, Ge. 40.1; 41.10; Jer. 37.21.

BALAAM, his history, Nu. 22.1, etc.; 23.1, etc.; 24.1, etc.; 31.8; Jos. 13. 22; 24.9; his sin mentioned, De. 23.4; Jude 11; Re. 2.14.

BALANCES, Lev. 19.35; Pr. 11.1; 16.11; Ho. 12.7.

BALD, 2 Ki. 2.23.

BALM, *a precious gum,* Ge. 37.25; Eze. 27.17. See *Figures.*

BANDS, Ps. 2.3; 73.4; Ho. 11.4; Zech. 11.7.

BANNER, Ps. 20.5; 60.4; Cant. 2.4.

BAPTISM, of John, Mat. 3.1-12; Mar. 1.1-8; Lu. 3.3-21; Jno. 1.19, 25-31; 3.23; Jesus questions the Pharisees concerning it, Mat. 21.25-27; Mar. 11.29-32; Lu. 20.4-7; to be administered to all Christian converts, Mat. 28.19; Mar. 16.16; instances of, Ac. 2.41; 8.12-38; 9. 17,18; 10.44-48; 16.13-15,29-34; 18. 4-8; 19.3,4; 1 Co. 1.13-17; 16.15; Christ submitted to it as our example, Mat. 3.13.17; Mar. 1.9-11; Lu. 3.21,22; Jno. 1.32,33; He compared His sufferings to it, Lu. 12. 50; an emblem of the death and resurrection of Christ, Ro. 6.3-5; Col. 2.12; compared to the saving of Noah by water, 1 Pe. 3.21; of water by John, Mat. 3.11-15; Mar. 1.4; Mat. 3.5,6; Mar. 1.8,9; Lu. 3. 12; 7.29; Mat. 3.7; Lu. 7.30; of fire, Mar. 10.38,39; Lu. 12.49-51; Mat. 3.11; of the Holy Ghost, Mat. 3.11-16; Ac. 1.5; 2.1-4; 8.14-17; 10.36-38,44; 18.24,25; 19.1-6; in the name of the Lord Jesus, Acts 2.38; 41; 8.12-17,36-38; 9.17,18; 22.16; 10.44-48; in the name of the Trinity, Mat. 28.18,19; its symbolical character, 1 Co. 10.2; 12.13; 15.29; Gal. 3.27; Eph. 4.3-5; Rom. 6.3,4; Col. 2-13.

BARABBAS, *a robber and murderer,* the account of him, Mat. 27.16-21; Mar. 15.6-11; Lu. 23.18-25; Jno. 18.40.

BARAK, *a Jewish deliverer,* the account of him, Ju. 4.6, etc.; his and Deborah's song, 5.1, etc.; Heb. 11.32.

BARBARIANS, Ac. 28; Rom. 1.14; 1 Cor. 14.11.

BAR-JESUS. See *Elymas.*

I4

BOTT

BOTTLES made of leather, mentioned Jos. 9.4; of wine, 1 Sa. 25.18; Ho. 7.5; old and new, Job 32.19; Mat. 9.17.

BOTTOMLESS pit, Re. 9.1; 11.7; 17.8; Satan bound, Re. 20.1,2.

BOW in the cloud, Ge. 9.13.

BOW, weapon, Ge. 48.22; 49.24; Ps. 44.6; Rev. 6.2.

BOWELS of mercies, Ge. 43.30; Ps. 25.6; Is. 63.15; Ph. 2.1; Col. 3.12.

BOZRAH, or Bezer, mentioned in history, Ge. 36.33; De. 4.43; Jos. 20.8; in prophecy, Is. 34.6; 63.1; Je. 48.24; 49.13,22; Am. 1.12; Mi. 2.12.

BRASS. See Figures.

BREAD, food, Ge. 47.12; Ex. 23.25; De. 8.3; Mat. 4.4; manna so called, Ex. 16; CHRIST calls Himself so, Jno. 6.31-58; also He is so in the Lord's Supper, Lu. 22.19; 24.30; Ac. 2.42,46; 20.7,11; 1 Co. 10.16; 11.23,24; unleavened, Ge. 19.3; 1 Co. 5.8; believers are so, 1 Co. 10. 17. See Shew-bread, and Types.

BREAST-PLATE of the high-priest, Ex. 28.15-30; 39.8-21; of righteousness, Ep. 6.14; of faith and love, 1 Th. 5.8.

BREATH of life from God, Ge. 2.7; Job 12.10; 33.4; Ps. 104.29; Ac. 17.25.

BRETHREN, to forgive each other, Mat. 5.22,23,24; 18.21,22; Gal. 6.1; 2 Th. 3.13-15; to confess their faults, and pray for each other, Ja. 5.16; to love each other, Ro. 12.10; 1 Th. 4; He. 13.1. See Brother and Brothers.

BRIBERY censured, Ex. 23.8; De. 16.19; Job 15.34; Pr. 17.23; 29.4; Ec. 7.7; Is. 5.23; Ez. 13.19; Am. 2.6; examples of it, Ju. 16.5; 1 Sa. 8.3; 1 Ki. 15.9; Mat. 26.14,15; 28. 12; Ac. 8.18; 24.26.

BRICKS, mentioned Ge. 11.3; Ex. 1.14; 5; forbidden for an altar, Is. 65.3.

BRIDEGROOM, heavenly, Mat. 9.15; 25.1; Jno. 3.29.

BRIMSTONE and fire, employed to execute God's wrath, Gen. 19.24; De. 29.23; Luke 17.29; predicted as a future punishment, Ps. 11.6; Is. 30.33; 34.9; Eze. 38.22; Re. 9. 17,18; 14.10; 19.20; 20.10; 21.8.

BROTHER, Levitical law concerning, De. 25.5; Mat. 22.24; anger with, Mat. 5.22. See Brethren.

BROTHERS, examples of enmity between them, Gen. 4.8; 27.37; Ju. 9.1-5; 2 Sa. 13.28; 2 Ch. 21.4; Lu. 12.13.

BUCKLER, or target. See Shield.

BURDEN, Ps. 55.22; Is. 58.6; 2 Cor. 5.4; Ps. 38.4; of Christ, Mat. 11. 30; used of prophecy, 2 Ki. 9.25; Is. 13.1; 15.1; 17.1; 19.1; 23.1; Ne. 1.1.

BUNDLE of life, 1 Sam. 25.29.

BURIAL, the want of it a calamity, De. 28.26; Ps. 79.2; Ec. 6.3; Is. 14.19; Je. 7.33; 16.4,6; 25.33; 34. 20; of Sarah, Ge. 23.19; of Abraham, 25.9; of Isaac, Ge. 35.29; of Jacob, Ge. 50.7-14; of Joseph, Ge. 50.26.

BURNING BUSH, Ex. 3.2; Mar. 12. 26; Lu. 20.37; Ac. 7.35.

BURNT-OFFERINGS. See Offerings.

BUSINESS, injunctions for the right discharge of it, Pr. 19.15; Ro. 12. 11; Ep. 4.28; 1 Th. 4.11; 2 Th. 3. 10,12.

CARE

BUSY-BODIES censured, Pr. 20.3; 26.17; 1 Th. 4.11; 2 Th. 3.11; 1 Ti. 5.13; 1 Pe. 4.15. See Tale-bearing; Whisperings.

CÆSAR, a name used by the Roman Emperors; four mentioned in Scripture, Augustus, Lu. 2.1; Tiberius, Lu. 3.4; Claudius, Ac. 11.28; Nero, Ph. 4.22; 2 Ti. 4.16,17.

CÆSAREA, a city on the shores of the Mediterranean, named so in honour of Cæsar, mentioned Ac. 8.40; 9.30; 10; 11.11; 12.19; 18.22; 21.16; 23. 23; 25.

CÆSAREA PHILIPPI, a place near the springs of Jordan, built by Philip the tetrarch, mentioned Mat. 16.13; Mar. 8.27.

CAIAPHAS, high-priest of the Jews, account of, Mat. 26.27; Mar. 14.53; Lu. 22.54; Jno. 11.49,50; 18.13,14.

CAIN, the first born son of Adam, his history, Ge. 4; 1 Jno. 3.12; Jude 11.

CAINAN, son of Enos, Ge. 5.9-14; Lu. 3.37.

CALAMITIES. See Afflictions.

CALEB, one of the twelve spies, his history, Nu. 13.1; 14.1-10; 26.65; 32.12; De. 1.36; Jos. 41.6, etc.; 15.13-19; Ju. 1.12-15.

CALF, golden, made by Aaron, Ex. 32; Ac. 7.41; of Samaria, Ho. 8.5, 6; two by Jeroboam, 1 Ki. 12.28-33.

CALLING, whereunto, 1 Co. 1.9; Ro. 8.30; 1 Th. 4.7; Gal. 5.13; 1 Co. 7.15; Col. 3.15; 2 Pe. 1.3; 2 Th. 2.14; 1 Pe. 5.10; God unchangeable, Ro. 11.29.

CALVARY, Lu. 23.33.

CANA, Jesus' first miracle there, Jno. 2; 4.46.

CANAAN, the son of Ham, cursed, Gen. 9.25.

CANAAN, the land of, promised to Abraham, Ge. 12.7; 13.14; its boundary, Ex. 23.31; Nu. 34.1-12; Jos. 1.3,4; conquered by Joshua, Jos. 11.16; its kings enumerated, Jos. 12.9; the names of those who were to divide it, Nu. 34.16, etc.; how to be divided, Nu. 26.52, etc.; divided by lot, Jos. 14.1; its borders not conquered, Jos. 13.1; the reason given, Ju. 2.3.

CANAANITES, idolatrous, to be extirpated, Ex. 23.31; 34.11; Nu. 33. 52; De. 20.16,17; not wholly conquered by Joshua, Jos. 16.10; 17. 12; Ju. 1.27, etc.; 2.20-23; 3.1, etc.

CANDLE, Job 18.6; 21.17; Ps. 18. 28; Pr. 20.27; Mat. 5.15.

CANDLESTICK, in the tabernacle, Ex. 25.31-37; 37.17-23; Le. 24.4; Zech. 4.2; Rev. 1.12.

CAMEL, an eastern beast of burden, Ge. 12.16; 1 Sa. 27.9; 30.17; 2 Ki. 8.9; 1 Ch. 5.21; 12.40; Es. 8.10; Job 1.3; John's dress made of their hair, Mat. 3.4.

CAPERNAUM, a city on the sea of Galilee, Mat. 4.13,17; 8.5; 11.23; 17.24; Jno. 4.46; 6.17.

CAPPADOCIA, a province of Asia, mentioned Ac. 2.9; 1 Pe. 1.1.

CAPTIVITY of Israel, foretold, Le. 26.23; De. 28.36; Am. 3; 4; 7.11-17; accomplished, 2 Ki. 17.3-18; of Judah, Is. 39.6; Je. 13.19; 20.4; 25.11; accomplished 2 Ki. 25; 2 Ch. 36; alluded to, Ps. 137; return from, Ezra 1; Ne. 2; Ps. 126.

CARBUNCLE. See Jewels.

CARE, worldly, Mat. 6.25; Lu. 8.14;

CHED

Ph. 4.6; Martha's, Lu. 10.41; exhortation, Ps. 37.5; 55.22; Pr. 16.3; 1 Pet. 5.7; Ph. 4.6.

CARPENTER, Zech. 1.20.

CARMEL. See Mountains.

CARMEL, a district in the tribe of Judah, Jos. 15.55; 1 Sa. 15.12; Is. 37.24.

CARNAL, applied to the state of the mind, Jno. 3.6; Ro. 8.5-7; 1 Co. 3. 1-4; Col. 2.18.

CASSIA, used in making the sacred perfume, Ex. 30.24; Ps. 45.8.

CASTOR and Pollux, one of the twelve signs of the Zodiac, a ship's figure head, Ac. 28.11.

CATTLE, Sabbath-day laws concerning them, Mat. 12.11; Lu. 13.15; 14.5.

CAVES, places of safety, Ge. 19.30; Jo. 10.16; 1 Sa. 13.6; He. 11.38.

CEDAR, a tree, 2 Sa. 7.2; 1 Ki. 4.33; Ps. 80.10; 92.12; the temple of Solomon built with it, 1 Ki. 6.15; supplied by Hiram, 1 Ki. 5.6.

CEDRON. See Kedron.

CELIBACY, advised in particular cases, Mat. 19.12; 1 Co. 7.

CENCHREA, a town, mentioned Ac. 18.18; Ro. 16.1.

CENSERS, brazen vessels for incense, Le. 10.1; 16.12; golden, 1 Ki. 7.50; 2 Ch. 4.22; He. 9.4; Rev. 8.3-5.

CENTURION, a Roman officer, several honourably mentioned, Mat. 8.5-13; Lu. 7.2-10; Mat. 27.54; Lu. 23.47; Ac. 27.43.

CEPHAS, Jno. 1.42; 1 Cor. 1.12; 3. 22; 9.5; Gal. 2.9.

CHAIN of gold, used as an honour, Ge. 41.42; Dan. 5.29; on camels, Ju. 8.26.

CHALCEDONY. See Jewels.

CHALDEANS, Job 1.17; 2 Ki. 24.2; an eastern nation, appointed to punish the Israelites, Hab. 1.6; to be punished, Hab. 2.5, etc.

CHANCE, excluded by Divine Providence, Ps. 91.3, etc.; Pr. 16.33; Mat. 6.26; 10.29,30; Lu. 12.6,7.

CHARGE of God to Adam, Ge. 2.16; to Moses and Aaron, Ex. 6.13; of Moses to Joshua, De. 31.7,8; of God to Joshua, Jos. 1.2-9; of Joshua to the people, Jos. 23; of David to Solomon, 1 Ki. 2.1-9; 1 Ch. 22.6-19; of Jehoshaphat to the judges, 2 Ch. 19.6,9; of Jesus to the apostles, Mat. 10; to the seventy, Lu. 10.1-12; to Peter, Jno. 21.15-19; to the apostles before his ascension, Mat. 28.18-20; Mar. 16.15,16; of Paul to the elders of Ephesus, Ac. 20.17-35; to Timothy, 1 Tim. 5.21.

CHARIOT of fire, 2 Ki. 2.11.

CHARIOTS of war, Ex. 14.7; Ps. 20. 7; 68.17.

CHARITY and benevolence recommended, Ex. 23.4; Le. 19.18; De. 15.7; 22.1; Job 31.16, etc.; Pr. 19. 17; 24.17; 25.21; Ec. 11.2; Mat. 7.12; 22.39; Ja. 2.8; an example, Lu. 10.25-37; characterised, 1 Co. 8.1; 13.1-8; 13.13; exhortation, 1 Pet. 4.8; 1 Tim. 1.5; Col. 3.14; 1 Co. 16.14. See Affection and Love.

CHASTISEMENT. See Afflictions.

CHASTITY recommended, Col. 3.5; 1 Th. 4.3; 1 Ti. 5.2; Tit. 2.5; an example of in Joseph, Ge. 39.7; in Job, 31.1-11.

CHEAT. See Robbery.

CHEBAR, a river in Chaldea, mentioned Eze. 1.1; 3.15; 10.15,20.

CHEDORLAOMER, King of Elam, mentioned Ge. 14.10-17.

CHEE

CHEERFULNESS described, Pr. 12. 25; 15.13,15; 17.22.

CHERUBIM, Ge. 3.24; where to be placed, Ex. 25.18-20; for the temple, 1 Ki. 6.23; 2 Ch. 3.10-13; Ps. 80.1; Eze. 41.18. See *Visions*.

CHILDLESSNESS, a curse, Le. 20. 20; Je. 22.30.

CHILDREN to be instructed, Ge. 18.19; De. 4.9; 6.7; 11.19; Ps. 78. 5; Ep. 6.4; a blessing, Ps. 127.3-5; 128.3; if good, Pr. 10.1; 15.20; 23.24; 27.11; 29.3; but if bad a curse, Pr. 17.21; 19.13; 28.7; 29.15; *their duty*, to regard the directions of their parents, Le. 19.3; Pr. 1.8; 6.21; 13.1; 15.5; 23.22; Ep. 6.1; Col. 3.20; Christ's example, Lu. 2. 51; not to grieve, nor rob, nor despise their parents, Pr. 19.26; 28. 24; a curse rests on the disobedient, De. 27.16; complaint, Eze. 22.7; to honour and maintain them, Ex. 20.12; De. 5.16; Ep. 6.2,3; the smiting of their parents punishable with death, Ex. 21.15; Le. 20.9; De. 21.18, etc.; converts to Christianity called so by the apostles, Ga. 4.19; 1 Jno. 2.1; Christ calls his disciples, Jno. 13.33; to suffer for the sins of their parents, Ex. 20.5; De. 5.9; this reversed, De. 24.16; Eze. 18.1, etc.; of God, by nature, Eph. 2.3; by faith, Gal. 3.26; 1 Jno. 5.1; Jno. 1.12; their true sonship, Gal. 4.4-7; 1 Jno. 3.1,2; Ro. 8.14,16; of the devil, Mat. 23.15; Jno. 8.44; 1 Jno. 3.10; Jno. 6.70; Ac. 13.10. See *Training*.

CHITTIM, Is. 23.1-12; Dan. 11.30.

CHLOE, *a Corinthian convert*, 1 Cor. 1.11.

CHRIST, His names, titles, and characters. See *the Names, Titles, and Characters of the Son of God.*

CHRIST above Moses, He. 3.5,6; and all the Levitical priests, He. 7.21; 8.1, etc.; co-eternal with the FATHER, Jno. 1.1; 17.5; Col. 1.17; He. 13.8; co-equal with the FATHER, Zec. 13.7; Mat. 16.15; 17.10; 28. 18; Ph. 2.6; Col. 1.16: 2.9; of one substance with the FATHER, Jno. 10.30,38; 12.45; 14.9; 17.11,22; the FATHER spoken of as greater, Jno. 14.28; superior to all created beings, Ro. 9.5; 14.9,11; Ph. 2.9,10; Col. 2.10,15; 1 Pet. 3.22.

CHRIST one with his disciples, Jno. 17.21; He. 2.11, etc.

CHRIST, perfect man, Mat. 4.2; 8. 24; 23.38; Jno. 1.14; 4.6; 11.35; 12.27; 19.28; Ph. 2.7; He. 2.14; without sin, Lu. 1.35; though tempted as other men, 2 Co. 5.21; He. 4.15; 7.26; 1 Pet. 2.22; 1 Jno. 3.5; learned obedience by suffering, He. 5.8.

CHRIST, perfect God, this appears, 1. *By His being expressly so called*, Is. 9.6; Mat. 1.23; Jno. 1.1; Ro. 9.5; Col. 2.9; 1 Tim. 3.16; He. 3.4; 1 Jno. 3.16; 2. *By His forgiving sins*, Mat. 9.2; Lu. 5.20; 7.48; 3. *By His miracles*, Jno. 3.2; 5.36; 10.25,38; 14.10; 4. *By His knowing men's thoughts*, Mat. 9.4; 12.25; Mar. 2.8; Lu. 5.22; 6.8; 9.47; 11. 17; Jno. 2.24; 6.61; 21.17; 5. *By His raising Himself from the dead*, Jno. 2.19; 10.17; 6. *By His promising and sending the Holy Ghost*, Jno. 14.26; 15.26; Ac. 2.4; 7. *By creation, omnipotence, and omniscience, etc.*,

CHRY

being ascribed to Him, Jno. 1.3; Ph. 3.21; Col. 1.16; He. 1.2.

CHRIST the Messiah spoken of by the prophets, Lu. 24.27; Jno. 1.45; 4.25; 5.39,46; 11.27; Ac. 28.23.

CHRIST came down from heaven, Jno. 3.13,31; 6.38,50; 16.28; for our sakes, Mat. 18.11; Lu. 19.10; Jno. 3.17; 10.10; 12.47; incarnate of the Virgin Mary, Mat. 1.18; Lu. 1.35; died for our sins, Is. 53.8; Da. 9.26; Mat. 20.28; Ro. 4.25; 5.6; 1 Co. 15.3; Ga. 1.4; Ep. 5.2; He. 9.28.

CHRIST abolished death, 2 Ti. 1.10; rose again the third day, Lu. 24.1, 46; Ac. 2.24; 3.15; 4.10; 5.30; 10.40; 17.31; Ro. 10.9; 1 Co. 6.14; 15.3,4; 1 Th. 1.10; He. 13.20; 1 Pe. 3.18; ascended up to heaven, Mar. 16.19; Lu. 24.51; Ac. 1.2,9; Ep. 4. 8; 1 Ti. 3.16; intercedes there for His people, Ro. 8.34; He. 7.25; 1 Jno. 2.1; Re. 8.3,4; and prepares mansions for them, Jno. 14.2; sitteth on the right hand of God, Mat. 16.19; Ac. 7.56; Ep. 1.20; Col. 3.1; He. 1.3; 8.1; 10.12; 12.2; 1 Pe. 3.22.

CHRIST, all power given to Him, Mat. 28.18; Ep. 1.20,21; will come again to judge the world, Ac. 1.11; 1 Th. 4.16; 2 Ti. 4.1; will reject the workers of iniquity, Mat. 7.21; His mediatorial reign will have an end, 1 Co. 15.2; but His kingdom shall endure for ever, Ps. 10.16; 45.6; 89.19-37; 145.13; Is. 9.7; Da. 4.3,34; 6.26; 7.14; Re. 11.15.

CHRIST expected by the Jews at the time of His coming, Mar. 15.43; Lu. 2.25,38; 3.15; Jno. 1.25,45; 4.25; 10.24; 11.27.

CHRIST the pattern that we ought to follow, Mat. 11.29; Jno. 13.15; Ph. 2.5; 1 Pe. 1.15; 2.21; 1 Jno. 2.6.

CHRIST the object of the believer's *faith*, Jno. 6.69; 14.1; Ac. 16.31; *hope*, 1 Cor. 15.12-22; Ep. 2.12; Col. 1.5,23,27; 1 Th. 1.3; 5.8; 1 Ti. 1.1; Tit. 2.13; He. 6.18-20; 7.19; 1 Pe. 1.3,21; 1 Jno. 3.3; *love*, Jno. 21.15-17; 1 Co. 16.22; Ep. 6.24; 1 Pe. 1.8.

CHRIST, promises connected with belief in Him, Jno. 3.15,16,36; 6. 40-47; 20.29,31; curses connected with unbelief, Jno. 3.18,36; 1 Jno. 5.10-12.

CHRIST came to fulfil the law, Mat. 5.17.

CHRIST was trusted in by Abraham and the Patriarchs, Jno. 8.56; He. 11.

CHRIST represented as seated on a white horse, Re. 19.11; His message to the seven churches, Re. 1; 2; 3.

CHRIST not to be denied, Mat. 10.33; Mar. 8.38; Lu. 9.26; 12.9; Ro. 1.16; 1 Jno. 2.23; but confessed, Mat. 10. 32; 19.28,29; Lu. 12.8. See *Confession*.

CHRIST preached at Rome of contention, Ph. 1.16. See *Jesus*.

CHRISTS, false, Mat. 7.15; 24.4,5, 11,24; Ac. 20.29; 2 Th. 2.8; 1 Ti. 4.1; Rev. 13.

CHRISTIANS, Ac. 11.26; the salt of the earth, Mat. 5.13; the light of the world, Mat. 5.14-16; their privileges, Ro. 8.14, etc.; He. 12.22-24; 1 Pe. 2.5, etc.; 1 Jno. 3.1,2; one with Christ and the Father, Jno. 17.11,21; all one body, 1 Co. 10.17; 12.13; Ep. 4.15,16; the temple of God, 1 Co. 3.16. See *Union*.

CHRYSOLITE. See *Jewels*.

201

COMM

CHRYSOPRASUS. See *Jewels*.

CHURCH, *holy catholic*, how to be understood, Jno. 10.16; Ro. 12.5; 1 Co. 10.17; 12.13-31; Ga. 3.28; He. 11.40; 12.23; sometimes means the whole congregation of faithful people, Mat. 16.18; Ac. 2.47; 14.27; Ep. 3.10,21; Col. 1.24; called the whole family, Ep. 3.15; sometimes a national, local, or private congregation, Mat. 18.17; Ac. 14.27; 18. 22; Ro. 16.5; 1 Co. 14.23; 3 Jno. 9; sometimes the place of worship, 1 Co. 11.18; 14.19,34.

CHURCH, reverence to be observed in it, Lev. 26.2; Ps. 93.5; Ec. 5.1; Je. 7.30; Eze. 5.11; 1 Co. 11.1, etc.; 14; instances of profanation condemned, 2 Ki. 21.4; 2 Ch. 33.7; Mat. 21.12; Jno. 2.13-16.

CILICIA, *a country in Asia Minor*, birth-place of Paul, mentioned Ac. 6.9; 15.23,41; 21.39; 22.3; 27.5; Ga. 1.21.

CIRCUMCISION instituted, Ge. 17. 10-14,23,24,25; instances, 34.24; Ex. 4.25; 12.48; Jos. 5.2-5; in what it really consists, Ro. 2.25-29; 3.30; 4.9-12; 1 Co. 7.19; Ga. 5.6; 6.15; Ph. 3.3; Col. 2.11; 3.11; abolishment of it, Ac. 15.1, etc.; Ga. 5.2; the spiritual meaning, De. 10.16; 30.6; Ro. 2.25-29; Ph. 3.3; Col. 2. 11; seal of Abraham's faith, Ro. 4. 10-13.

CIRCUMSPECTION recommended, Ro. 12.17; 2 Co. 8.21; Ep. 5.15; Ph. 4.8; 1 Th. 4.12; 1 Pe. 2.12; 3.16. See *Watchfulness*.

CITIES of Refuge. See *Refuge*.

CIVILITY recommended, Ro. 12.10; 13.7; 1 Pe. 2.17.

CLAUDIA, *a Roman convert*, 2 Ti. 4. 21.

CLAUDIUS. See *Cæsar*.

CLAUDIUS LYSIAS, *the Roman tribune*, mentioned Ac. 21.31,33; 22. 24; 23.10,26.

CLEMENT, *a Christian preacher*, Ph. 4.3.

CLEOPAS, *a disciple of Jesus*, Lu. 24. 18; Jno. 19.25.

CLOUD, pillar of, conducted the Israelites, Ex. 13.21; 14.19; Nu. 9.15; Ne. 9.19; Ps. 78.14; 1 Cor. 10.1; employed as a figure, Ps. 36.5; 57. 10; 68.34; 97.2; 104.3.

COLLECTION for poor believers, Ac. 11.29; Ro. 15.26-28; 1 Co. 16.1; 2 Co. 8.1-4; 9.1, etc.

COLLEGE, *a school*, 2 Ki. 22.14; 2 Ch. 34.22.

COLOSSE, *an ancient city in Phrygia*, mentioned Col. 1; 2; 3; 4.

COMFORTER, Jno. 14.26; 15.26; 16.7.

COMMANDMENTS, *the ten*, delivered by God, Ex. 20; 31.18; De. 5.6; were written on stone, Ex. 31.18; broken, Ex. 32.19; renewed, Ex. 34.1-4; De. 10.1-5; not abrogated by Christ, Mat. 5.17; 19.17; 22.35-40; Mar. 10.17-19; Lu. 10.25-28; 18.8-20.

COMMUNION. See *Lord's Supper*. Mal. 3.16; Ac. 2.42; 20.7; 1 Co. 1. 9; 10.16; 2 Co. 13.14; Ph. 1.4,5; 2.1; 3.10; 1 Jno. 1.3,6,7; with the Father, 1 Jno. 1.3,7; Jno. 14.28; with the Son, 1 Co. 1.9; 1 Jno. 1.3; Phil. 3.10; Rev. 3.20; with the Spirit, 2 Co. 13.14; 1 Co. 12.13; Phil. 2.1,2; necessary to a godly walk, Amos 3.3; warnings, 2 Co. 6. 14; 1 Jno. 1.6; Heb. 13.14. See *Fellowship*.

EKRON, *a city of Philistia*, mentioned Ju. 1.18; 1 Sa. 5.10; 6.17; 7.14; Am. 1.8; Zep. 2.4; Zec. 9.5,7.

ELAH, *king of Israel*, his history, 1 Ki. 16.8-10.

ELAH, *father of Hoshea*, 2 Ki. 15.30; 17.1; 18.1,9.

ELAM, *Shem's eldest son*, Ge. 10.22; 14. 1; Je. 49.34; to be restored, Je. 49. 39.

ELAMITES, mentioned Ezra 4.9; Ac. 2.9.

ELDAD, endued with a spirit of prophecy, Nu. 11.26,27.

ELDERS, seventy, appointed by Moses, Ex. 24.1; Nu. 11.16; a name given to magistrates, Ge. 50.7; 1 Sa. 16.4; 2 Ki. 6.32; Ez. 8.1; a title assumed by the apostles, 1 Pe. 5.1; 2 Jno. 1; 3 Jno. 1; given to the governors of Christian churches, their qualifications and duty, Ac. 11.30; 14.23; 15.4,6; 16.4; 20.17; 1 Ti. 5.1,19; Tit. 1.5; Ja. 5.14; 1 Pe. 5.1; the twenty-four, Rev. 4.4; 7. 11; 14.3.

ELEAZAR, *the third son of Aaron*, his history, Ex. 6.23,25; 28.29; Le. 10. 16; Nu. 3.2,4,32; 4.16; 16.39; 20. 26-28; 26.60,63; 27.22; 31.12,54; 34. 17; Jos. 17.4; 24.33; 1 Ch. 6.3,4; 24.1-6.

ELEAZAR, *son of Abinadab*, 1 Sa. 7.1.

ELEAZAR, *one of David's mighty men*, 2 Sa. 23.9; 1 Ch. 11.12; and others of the same name, 1 Ch. 23.21,22; 24.28; Ezra 88.33.

ELECT, referring to CHRIST, Is. 42.1; Mat. 12.18; 1 Pe. 2.6; angels, 1 Tim. 5.21; to the Israelites, Is. 65.9,22; to saints, Mat. 24.22; Ro. 8.33; Col. 3.12; Tit. 1.1.

ELECTION an act of love, Deut. 7.6-8; irrespective of any merit in the objects of it, Ro. 9.11,12,16; to salvation or eternal life, Ac. 13.48; 1 Th. 5.9; eternal, Ep. 1.4; 3.11; 2 Th. 2.13; sovereign, Ro. 8.28; Ep. 1.11; 2 Ti. 1.9; personal, Mat. 20. 23; 25.34; 2 Ti. 2.19; of individuals, Jos. 24.2,3; Neh. 9.7; Acts 7.2,3,5; Mal. 1.2,3; Ro. 9.11,13; 1 Sa. 16.12; Ps. 89.34-36; Lu. 5.27,28; Mat. 4. 18-22; Gal. 1.15,16; of Israel, Deut. 7.6-8; Isa. 45.4; Ro. 11.5-7,23,25,32, 33; Ps. 33.12.

ELECT lady, 2 Jno.

ELHANAN, *one of David's mighty men*, mentioned 2 Sa. 21.19; 23.24; 1 Ch. 11.26; 20.5.

ELI, *high priest and judge of Israel*, his history, 1 Sa. 1.12-17,25-28; 2. 11-36; 3; 4.1-18.

ELI, Eli, Mat. 27.46; Mar. 15.34.

ELIAKIM, *son of Hilkiah*, 2 Ki. 18.18-37; 19.2; Is. 22.20,25; 36; 37.

ELIAKIM, *Josiah's son*, 2 Ki. 23.34-37; 2 Ch. 36.4-8.

ELIAS, Mat. 16.14; 17.3-12; 27.47, 49; Mar. 15.35,36.

ELIASHIB, Ne. 3.1; 13.4.

ELIEZER, *Abram's servant*, Ge. 15.2; 24.

ELIEZER, *son of Moses*, Ex. 14.4; 1 Ch. 23.15,17.

ELIEZER, *a prophet*, 2 Ch. 20.37.

ELIHU, *one of Job's friends*, his speeches, Job, chapters 32 to 37.

ELIJAH, *a prophet of Israel*, his history, 1 Ki. 17; 18; 19; 21.17-29; 2 Ki. 1; 2.1-14; 9.36; 10.10,17; 2 Ch. 21.12-15; Lu. 4.25,26.

ELIJAH, prophetically promised, **Mal.** 4.5; fulfilled, Mat. 11.14; 16. **14**; 17.3-12; Mar. 6.15; 9.4-13; Lu.

1.17; 9.8,19,28-36; Jno. 1.20,25; Paul's allusion to him, Ro. 11.1-5; James's, Ja. 5.17,18.

ELIMELECH, *Naomi's husband*, Ru. 1.1-3.

ELIPHAZ, *one of Job's three friends*, his speeches, Job 2.11-13; 4; 5; 15; 22; 32.1; 42.7,8.

ELIZABETH, *the mother of John the Baptist*, her history, Lu. 1.5-25,40-58.

ELISHA, *a prophet of Israel*, his history, 1 Ki. 19.15-21; 2 Ki. 2; 3.11-27; 4; 5; 6; 7; 8; 9.1; 13.14-21; Lu. 4.27.

ELKANAH, *the father of Samuel*, his history, 1 Sa. 1.

ELNATHAN, *grandfather to king Jehoiachin*, his history, 2 Kings 24.8; Je. 26.22; 36.25; others of the name returned from captivity, Ezra 8.16.

ELON, *a judge of Israel*, his history, Ju. 12.11,12.

ELYMAS, or Bar-jesus, *a sorcerer*, Ac. 13.6-11.

EMBALMING of bodies, Ge. 50.2,3, 26; 2 Ch. 16.14; Jno. 19.39,40.

EMERALD, *a precious stone*, Ex. 28. 18; 39.11; Ez. 27.16; 28.13; Re. 4. 3; 21.19.

EMERODS, *a disease*, mentioned De. 28.27; 1 Sa. 6.5-12; 6.

EMMANUEL. See *Immanuel*.

EMMAUS, *a town of Judea*, mentioned Lu. 24.13.

EMIMS, *giants*, mentioned Ge. 14.5; Deut. 2.10.

ENCHANTMENTS, *magical charms*, forbidden, Le. 19.26; De. 18.9-12; Is. 47.9; the effect of the gospel on this sin, Ac. 19.18-20.

ENDOR, *the witch of*, 1 Sa. 28.7-25.

ENEAS, mentioned Ac. 9.33,34.

ENEMIES, laws concerning the treatment of them, Ex. 23.4; Pr. 24.17; 25.21; Mat. 5.44; Lu. 6.27,36; Ro. 12.14-21; *example*, Job 31.29-31; David, 1 Sa. 24; 26; Ps. 35.4-15.

ENGEDI, *a city near the Dead sea*, mentioned Jos. 15.62; 1 Sa. 23.29; 24.1; 2 Ch. 20.2; Ca. 1.14; Ez. 47. 10.

ENMITY spoken of, Ge. 3.15; Ro. 8. 7; Ja. 4.4.

ENOCH, *an antediluvian saint*, his life, Ge. 5.18-24; Lu. 3.37; He. 11. 5; Jude 14.

ENOCH, *a son of Cain*, Ge. 4.17,18.

ENON, *the place where John baptized*, Jno. 3.23.

ENOS, *the son of Seth*, Ge. 4.26; 5.6-11.

ENVY condemned, Job 5.2; Ps. 37.1; Pr. 3.31; 14.30; 23.17; 24.19; 27.4; Ro. 13.13; 1 Co. 3.3; Ga. 5.21; Ja. 3.14; 5.9; 1 Pe. 2.1; *examples*, Ge. 4.5-13; 26.14; 30.1; 37.4,11; Nu. 16; 1 Sa. 18.8,9; Es. 5.13.

EPAPHRAS, *a helper of the apostles*, Col. 1.7; 4.12.

EPAPHRODITUS, *a Christian brother*, mentioned by Paul, Ph. 2.25-30; 4. 18.

EPHAH, *son of Midian*, Ge. 25.4; *a place*, Is. 60.6; *a measure*, Ex. 16. 36; Le. 19.36. See *Vision*.

EPHESUS, *a city of Asia Minor*, mentioned Ac. 18.19; 19; 20.16-38; 1 Co. 15.32; 16.8,9; 1 Ti. 1.3; 2 Ti. 1.18; 4.12.

EPHPHATHA, Mar. 7.34.

EPHRAIM, *Joseph's second son*, his history, Ge. 41.52; 48; that of his

descendants, Nu. 1.10,32,33; 2.18; 7.48-53; 13.8; 26.35; Ju. 17; 18; 19; 1 Ch. 7.20-28; 9.3; 2 Ch. 15.9; 25.10; their possessions, Jos. 16; 17.14-18; 20.7; 21.5,20,21; Ju. 1.29; 2.9; 7.24,25; 8.1-3; 12; 1 Sa. 1.1; 2 Ki. 5.22; 1 Ch. 6.66,67; 2 Ch. 13. 19; 17.2; Jno. 11.54; the name used for Israel generally, Ps. 78.9, etc.; Je. 7.15; prophecies concerning them, Is. 7; 9.9-21; 11.13; 28. 1-3; Je. 4.15; 31; 50.19; Eze. 37.15-28; 48.5,6; Ho. 5; 6; 7; 8; 9; 10; 11; 12; 13; 14; Ob. 19; Zech. 9. 10-17; 10.7-12.

EPHRATAH, Ge. 35.16; Ps. 132.6; Mi. 5.2.

EPHRON, *the Hittite*, mentioned Ge. 23.10; 25.9; 49.30; 50.13.

EPICUREANS, *a sect of philosophers*, mentioned Ac. 17.18.

EQUITY, *the great rule*, Le. 19.18; Mat. 7.12; 22.39; Ro. 13.8; Ja. 2.8.

ERASTUS, *a Christian convert*, Ac. 19.22; Ro. 16.23; 2 Ti. 4.20.

ESAR-HADDON, *king of Assyria*, 2 Ki. 19.37; Ezra 4.2; Is. 37.38.

ESAU, *Isaac's eldest son*, his history, Ge. 25.21-34; 26.34,35; 27; 28.6-9; 32; 33.1-16; 35.29; his possession, De. 2.1-8; Jos. 24.4; Ro. 9. 10-13; He. 12.16,17; his wives and descendants, Ge. 36; 1 Ch. 1.35-54; prophecies concerning them, Je. 49.7-22; Ob. 1, etc.; Mal. 1.2-4; He. 11. 20. See *Edom*.

ESHCOL, *the place whence the spies obtained the bunch of grapes*, mentioned Nu. 13.23-27.

ESTHER, *a captive Jewess, made queen of Persia*, her history. The book of Esther.

ETHAN, *a wise man*, mentioned 1 Ki. 4.31.

ETHIOPIA, mentioned 2 Ki. 19.9; Es. 1.1; Job 28.19; Ac. 8.26-40; prophesied against, Is. 18.1-7; 20; 45.14; Ez. 30; 38.5; Zep. 3.10.

EUNICE, *Timothy's mother*, mentioned Ac. 16.1; 2 Ti. 1.5.

EUNUCH, *the Ethiopian*, Ac. 8.27.

EUNUCHS, laws and promises connected with them, De. 23.1; Is. 56. 4,5; our Lord's remark on them, Mat. 19.12. See *Philip*.

EUPHRATES, *a river in the garden of Eden*, Ge. 2.14; 15.18; mentioned afterwards, De. 11.24; Jos. 1.4; 2 Sam. 8.3; prophetically, Je. 13.1-8; Re. 9.14; 16.12.

EUROCLYDON, Ac. 27.14.

EUTYCHUS, mentioned Ac. 20.7-12.

EVANGELISTS, *preachers of the gospel*, their duty, Ep. 4.11,12; 2 Ti. 4.5; Philip so called, Ac. 21.8. See *Philip*.

EVE, *the first woman*, her history, Ge. 1.26-31; 2.18-25; 3; 4.1,2,25; 5.2; mentioned by Paul, 2 Co. 11.3; 1 Ti. 2.13,14.

EVIL, *as iniquity*, 1 Ki. 16.25; Ec. 9. 3; *as calamity*, Job 2.10; Is. 45.7; Am. 3.6; *as malignity*, Pr. 24.19,20; Mat. 5.39; Ro. 12.21; *as sin and suffering*, Mat. 6.13.

EVIL-MERODACH, *Nebuchadnezzar's son*, mentioned 2 Ki. 25.27-30; Je. 52.31.

EXACTION censured, De. 15.2; Ne. 5.1-13; 10.31; Pr. 28.8; Ez. 22.12; 45.9; Lu. 3.13; 1 Cor. 5.10.

EXAMINATION of self, Ps. 4.4; 77. 6; 119.59; La. 3.40; Hag. 1.5,7; Mat. 7.3; Lu. 15.17,18; 1 Co. 11.28; 2 Co. 13.5; Ga. 6.4; 1 Jno 3.20,21.

FIGU

spots, for our innate depravity, Je. 13.23; *linen* (clean and white), the righteousness of the saints, Re. 19. 8,14; *lions*, for the Israelites, Ez. 19.1-9; *Lucifer* (literally the morning star), for a proud tyrant, Is. 14. 12; *locusts*, for desolating judgments, Joel 1.4; 2.25; *marrow*, for the secret thoughts, He. 4.12; for gospel blessings, Ps. 63.5; Is. 25.6; *medicine*, for counsel, Is. 1.6; Je. 30.13; 46.11; *naked*, for spiritual destitution, Re. 3.17,18; *night*, for adversity, Is. 21.11,12; ignorance, Ro. 13.12; death, Jno. 9.4; *oven*, for the day of wrath, Mal. 4.1; *owl*, for desolation, Job 30.29; Ps. 102.6; Is. 13.21; Mi. 1.8; *partridge*, for insignificance, 1 Sa. 26.20; *pearl*, for Christian experience, Mat. 7.6; for CHRIST, Mat. 13.45,46; *pelican*, for solitude, Ps. 102.6; *pilgrimage*, for human life, Ge. 47.9; Ex. 6.4; Ps. 119.54; *pilgrims*, for Christians, He. 11.13; 1 Pe. 2.11; *potsherds*, for worthless men, Is. 45.9; *princess*, for Jerusalem, La. 1.1; *prison*, for affliction, Ps. 142.7; Is. 42.7; *queen*, for the church of Christ, Ps. 45.9; for the anti-christian church, Re. 18; for the moon, Je. 44.17,25; *rags*, for our righteousness, Is. 64.6; *Rachel*, for the women of Israel, Je. 31.15; *razor*, for deceit, Ps. 52.2; *reed*, for anything fragile, 2 Ki. 18.21; Is. 36. 6; 42.3; Mat. 11.7; *rock*, for the natural heart, Je. 23.29; Lu. 8.6; for the state of nature, Is. 51.1; for JEHOVAH-JESUS, De. 32; 1 Sa. 2.2; 2 Sa. 22.2,3,32,47; 23.3; Ps. 28.1; 31.2,3; 42.9; 61.2; 62.2,7; 78.35; 89.26; 94.22; 95.1; Is. 17.10; 26.4; 32.2; Mat. 7.24,25; 16.18; Ro. 9.33; 1 Co. 10.4; 1 Pe. 2.8; *scarlet*, for aggravated sins, Is. 1.18; Re. 17.4; *scorpion*, for malice, Ez. 2.6; *shadow*, for our natural life, Job 14.2; 17.7; *shipwreck*, for false profession, 1 Ti. 1.19,20; *shuttle*, for natural life, Job 7.6; *sow and reap*, for cause and effect, Job 4.8; Pr. 11.18; 22.8; Hos. 10.12,13; Ga. 6.7,8; *stiffnecked*, for self-willed, Ex. 32.9; De. 10.16; Ac. 7.51; *stone*, for CHRIST, Is. 28.16; Da. 2.34; Ep. 2.20; 1 Pe. 2.4,6-8; for believers, Ep. 2.21,22; 1 Pe. 2.5; *stubble*, for the wicked, Job 21.17,18; Ps. 83.13; Is. 47.14; Mal. 4.1; *sword*, for the word of God, Ep. 6.17; He. 4.12; *thirst*, for desire, Ps. 42.1,2; 63.1; Is. 55.1; Mat. 5.6; Jno. 7.37; *vail*, for darkness of mind, 2 Co. 3.14-16; *vapour*, for life, Ja. 4.14; *vine*, for Israel, Ez. 15.1-6; *virgin*, for Israel, 2 Ki. 19.21; Is. 37.22; Je. 14.17; 18.13; 31.4,21; *water*, for trouble, Ps. 69.1; for a multitude, Is. 8.7; for the gospel, Is. 55.1; for the SPIRIT, Is. 12.3; 35.6,7; 44.3; Jno. 4.10; 7.37, 38; *waves*, for afflictions, Ps. 42.7; 88.7; *white raiment*, for victory, Re. 3.4; 4.4; 7.9-13; 15.6; 19.8,14; *white stone*, of acquittal, Re. 2.17; *wind*, for destruction, Je. 49.36; 51. 1; Da. 7.2; for the SPIRIT, Jno. 3. 8; *wine*, for GOD's anger, Ps. 75.8; Is. 51.17; 63.6; Je. 25.15; *winepress*, for judgment, Is. 63.1-6; La. 1.15; Re. 14.19,20; 19.15; *wings*, for protection, Ps. 17.8; 36.7; 57.1; 61.4; 63.7; for the wind, Ps. 18.10; 104.3; *wolves*, for rapacious deceivers, Ez. 22.27; Zep. 3.3; Mat. 7.15; 10.16; Lu. 10.3; Ac. 20.29.

FORG

FIGURES, prophetical, *Aholah and Aholibah*, Ez. 23; *Bands*, Zec. 11.7; *beasts*, various, Da. 7.8; Re. 4.6-9; 11.7; 13; 15.2; 16.13; 17; 19.19, 20; 20.10; *Beauty*, Zec. 11.7; *cedar*, 2 Ki. 14.9; Ez. 17; Am. 2.9; *Mahershalal-hash-baz*, Is. 8.1-8; *pot*, Je. 1.13; Ez. 24.3-11; *roll* (flying), Zec. 5.1.

FIRE, pillar of, Ex. 13.21; God as fire, Ex. 3.2; 13.21; De. 4.12; Is. 6.4; Mal. 3.2; Rev. 1.14; God's word, Je. 23.29; God, a consuming, Heb. 12.29.

FIRE *from heaven*, employed for destruction, Ge. 19.24; Ex. 9.23,24; Le. 10.2; Nu. 11.1-3; 16.35-37; 2 Ki. 1.9-15; as a proof of the Divine acceptance of the sacrifice, Le. 9.24; Ju. 6.21; 13.19,20; 1 Ki. 18.38; 2 Ch. 7.1.

FIRMAMENT, *the visible heaven*, Ge. 1.17,20; Ps. 19.1; Ez. 1.22; Da. 12.3.

FIRST-BORN, laws relating to, Ex. 13.2,12-15; 22.29; 34.19,20; De. 15. 19; 21.15-21. See *Birthright*.

FIRST-FRUITS, the law relating to them, Ex. 22.29; 23.16,19; 34.26; Nu. 28.26; De. 26.

FIR-TREE, Is. 41.19; 55.13; 60.13; Ho. 14.8.

FISHERMEN, most of the apostles were, Mat. 4.18; Mar. 1.16; Lu. 5. 1-11; Jno. 21.7.

FISHES created, Ge. 1.20; one swallows Jonah, Jon. 1.17; miraculous draughts, Lu. 5.6; Jno. 21.6; one caught to pay tribute, Mat. 17.27.

FLATTERY, detestable, Job 17.5; 32. 21,22; Ps. 12.3; Pr. 24.24; 26.28; 28.23; 29.5; Is. 5.20; 1 Th. 2.5.

FLEECE, Gideon's, Ju. 6.37.

FLESH, after the flood, to be eaten, Ge. 9.3; signifying human nature, Jno. 1.14; 1 Ti. 3.16; 1 Pe. 3.18; our corrupt nature, Ro. 7.5; 8.9,12; 13.14; Ga. 5.19; 1 Pe. 2.11; 2 Pe. 2.10.

FLIES. See *Plagues*.

FLINT, water brought miraculously from, Nu. 20.11; De. 8.15; Ps. 114. 8; 1 Cor. 10.4; used figuratively, Is. 50.7; Ez. 3.9.

FLOOD. See *Deluge*.

FOLLY, *evil*, Ps. 5.5; Pr. 1.7,22; 3. 35; 10.18; 13.19; 14.8; 19.1; 26.11; 28.26; Je. 4.22; 5.4; Mar. 7.22; Tit. 3.3. See *Fool*.

FOOD for man, Ge. 1.29. See *Flesh*.

FOOL, *a silly person*, 1 Sa. 26.21; Ps. 92.6; 107.17; Pr. 10.8,23; 12.15,16, 23; 13.16,20; 14.9,16; 17.7,28; 18.2; 19.1; 29.11; Ec. 2.16; 5.3; 10.2,3-5,14; Mat. 23.17; 25.2.

FOOLISHNESS, the gospel accounted so by the world, 1 Co. 1.18-23; 2.14; the wisdom of the world accounted so by God, 1 Co. 3.19.

FOOTSTOOL, Solomon's, 2 Ch. 9.18, 19; the earth called GOD's footstool, Is. 66.1; Mat. 5.35; Ac. 7.49; the temple also, 1 Ch. 28.2; Ps. 99.5; 132.7; La. 2.1; and his enemies, Ps. 110.1; Mat. 22.44; Mar. 12.36; Lu. 20.43; Ac. 2.35; He. 1.13; 10.13.

FORBEARANCE recommended, Mat. 18.33; 1 Cor. 13.4,7; Ep. 4.2; Col. 3.13; 1 Th. 5.14; manifested by GOD to man, Ps. 50.21; Ec. 8.11; Mat. 18.27; Ro. 2.4; 2 Pe. 3.9,15.

FOREKNOWLEDGE. See GOD.

FORERUNNER. See CHRIST.

FORGETFULNESS *of God and his*

FUTU

laws, dangerous, De. 4.9; 6.12; 8. 11; 2 Ki. 17.38; Ps. 44.17,20; Pr. 3.1; He. 13.16; Ja. 1.25; *of favours*, censured, Ec. 9.15; example, Ge. 40.23.

FORGIVENESS *of sins* promised by God on repentance, Ex. 34.6,7; 2 Ch. 7.14; Ps. 32.1; 103.3; 130.4; Pr. 28.13; Is. 1.18; 55.7; Je. 31.34; Da. 9.9,24; Mar. 1.4; Lu. 1.77; 3. 3; 24.47; Ac. 2.38; 5.31; 8.22; 10. 43; 13.38; Ro. 3.25; Col. 1.14; He. 8.12; Ja. 5.15; 1 Jno. 2.12; how obtained, 1 Jno. 1.9; Is. 43.25; Ps. 25.11; Heb. 9.22; 2 Co. 5.18,19,21; Is. 53.4,5; 1 Pet. 2.24; Heb. 9.26-28; Ro. 4.6-8; Ac. 5.30,31; 10.43; already bestowed, Ep. 1.7; Col. 1. 14; 2.13; 1 Jno. 2.12; Heb. 10.1,2; to be sought with the whole heart, De. 4.29; 1 Ch. 28.9; Ps. 119.2; Je. 29.13; 1 Th. 5.17; *of injuries*, recommended, Pr. 19.11; enjoined, Mat. 5.23; 6.14,15; 18.21; Mar. 11. 25; Lu. 6.36; 17.4; Ep. 4.32; Col. 3.13; Ja. 2.13.

FORNICATION forbidden to the Israelites, Le. 19.29; De. 23.17; laws and cautions *in general*, Pr. 6. 25; 7; 22.14; 23.27; 31.3; Ec. 7.26; Ho. 4.11; Mat. 15.19; Mar. 7.21; Ac. 15.20; Ro. 1.29; 1 Co. 5.9; 6.9, 18; 2 Co. 12.21; Ga. 5.19; Ep. 5.3; 1 Th. 4.3; 1 Ti. 1.10; He. 12.16; Re. 2.14,20; laws *in particular*, Ex. 22.16; Le. 19.20; De. 22.28; 23.18; motives to avoid it, Pr. 2.16-20; 5. 3-13; 6.24-35; 7; 9.18; 29.3; 1 Co. 6.18; Ep. 5.5; Col. 3.5; He. 13.4; Jude 7; Re. 21.8; 22.15; examples, of Judah, Ge. 38.15-26; of Zimri and Cozbi, Nu. 25.1-15; of Samson, Ju. 16.1-3; spiritual, Ez. 16.29; Ho. 1. 2,3; Rev. 14.8; 17.2; 18.3; 19.2.

FOUNDATION. See *Christ*.

FOUNTAIN. See *Christ*.

FOX, *a wild animal*, mentioned historically, Ju. 15.4,5; La. 5.18; comparatively, Mat. 8.20; figuratively, Lu. 13.32.

FRANKINCENSE, a *sweet-scented gum*, used in the incense, Ex. 30.34; Le. 2.1; Mat. 2.11.

FRAUD. See *Deceit*.

FREEDOM, *true*, Jno. 8.36; Ro. 6. 16-18; *false*, 2 Pe. 2.19.

FREE woman, Ga. 4.25.

FRIENDS, the value of them, Pr. 17. 17; 18.24; 27.9,17; how separated, Pr. 17.9; danger from unfaithful ones, Ps. 55.12; Pr. 19.5; examples, of Jael, Ju. 4.18-22; of Delilah, 16. 4-21; of Joab, 2 Sa. 3.27; 20.9,10; of Judas, Mat. 26.47-50.

FRINGES *on garments*, laws concerning them, Nu. 15.37-39; De. 22.12; Mat. 23.5.

FROGS. See *Plagues*. See *Visions*.

FRONTLETS, Ex. 13.6; De. 6.8.

FRUGALITY recommended, Pr. 18. 9; Jno. 6.12.

FRUITS, used figuratively for proofs, Mat. 3.8; 7.16; 2 Co. 9.10; Ga. 5. 22,23; Ph. 1.11; Ja. 3.17.

FURLONG, *the eighth part of a mile*, Lu. 24.13; Jno. 6.19; 11.18.

FURNACE, *natural*. See *Figures*; *figurative*, De. 4.20; Ez. 22.17-22; Mat. 13.42.

FUTURE state mentioned, or alluded to, in the Old Testament, 2 Sa. 12. 23; Job 19.25; 21.30; Ps. 9.17; 16. 11; 17.15; Pr. 14.32; Ec. 3.17; 11. 9; Da. 12.13. See *Heaven*.

FUTURE state, no marriages in it,

GAAL

Lu. 20.34; our bodies changed for it, 1 Co. 15.42,51, etc.; the happiness of it, Re. 7.15; 21.4.

GAAL, spoken of, Ju. 9.

GABRIEL, *an archangel*, appears to Daniel, Da. 8.16-27; 9.21-27; to Zacharias, Lu. 1.19; to the Virgin Mary, Lu. 1.26.

GAD, *one of the sons of Jacob*, his history, Ge. 30.11; 35.26; 46.16; 49.19; his descendants, Nu. 1.24,25; their inheritance, Nu. 32; 34.14; Jos. 13.24-28; 1 Ch. 5.11; their duty, De. 27.13; Jos. 4.12,13; 22.9; their blessing, De. 33.20,21.

GAD, *David's seer*, mentioned 2 Sa. 24.11-19; 1 Ch. 21.9-18; 29.29; 2 Ch. 29.25.

GADARENES, Mat. 8.28; Mar. 5.1; Lu. 8.26.

GALILÆANS, Lu. 13.1; Ac. 1.11; 2.7.

GALLIO, *the Roman deputy of Achaia*, mentioned Ac. 18.12-17.

GAMALIEL, *a doctor of the law*, mentioned Ac. 5.34-40; 22.3.

GAMES, public, 1 Cor. 9.24; Phil. 3. 12; 1 Ti. 6.12; 2 Ti. 5.2; 4.7; Heb. 12.1.

GARDEN, Ge. 2.8; Jno. 18.1.

GATES of heaven, Ge. 28.7; Ps. 24.17; of death and hell, Ps. 9.13; Mat. 16. 8; of the grave, Is. 38.10; strait, Mat. 7.13,14.

GATH, *a city of the Philistines*, mentioned 1 Sa. 5.8,9; 27.4; 1 Ki. 2.39, 40; 2 Ki. 12.17; 1 Ch. 18.1; 2 Ch. 26.6.

GAZA, *a city of the Philistines*, mentioned Ju. 16; Ac. 8.26; prophesied against, Je. 47; Am. 1.6-8; Zep. 2. 4; Zech. 9.5.

GEDALIAH, *governor of Judah*, 2 Ki. 25.22-25; Je. 40; 41; 43.6.

GEDOR, mentioned 1 Ch. 4.39-43.

GEHAZI, *Elisha's servant*, his history, 2 Ki. 4; 5.20-27; 8.4,5.

GENEALOGIES of Adam, Ge. 5; of Noah, Ge. 10; of Shem, Ge. 11.10; of Terah, Ge. 11.27; of Abraham, Ge. 25; of Jacob, Ge. 29.31; of Esau, Ge. 36; of Israel and Judah, their origin, 1 Ch. 1; 2; 3; 4; 5; 6; 7; 8; 9; of David, Ruth 4.7-22; of JESUS *nominally*, Mat. 1.1-18; *actually* (Joseph's name being according to Jewish custom substituted for Mary's), Lu. 3.23, etc.

GENEROSITY recommended, De. 15. 7-11; Pr. 11.24-26; 18.16; 21.26; 1 Co. 16.3; 17; 2 Co. 9; instances of, 2 Ch. 28.15; Je. 40.13-16.

GENNESARETH, *a lake in the land of Canaan*, Lu. 5.1; called by Moses, *Chinnereth*, Nu. 34.11; in the New Test. *the sea of Galilee*, Mat. 4.18; 15.29; Mar. 1.16; *the sea of Tiberias*, Jno. 6.1,23; incidents which occurred there, Mat. 8.23-26; Mar. 4.1,35-41; Lu. 5.1-11; 8.22-26; Jno. 21.1-14.

GENTILES, their heathen state, Ro. 1.21; 2.14,15; 1 Co. 12.2; Ep. 2.1, 11,12; 4.17-19; intimations of their admission to the blessings of the gospel, Is. 42.1-12; 49.6,22; 60.2,3; 65.1; Je. 16.19; Hos. 2.23; Joel 2. 32; Mi. 4.1; Zep. 3.9; Mal. 1.11; Mat. 8.11; Lu. 2.32; 3.6; 24.47; Jno. 10.16; Ac. 10.15; their admission, Ac. 8.37; 10; 11; Ro. 11; their recognition, Ac. 15; Ep. 2.

GENTLENESS recommended, 2 Ti. 2.24; Tit. 3.2; CHRIST an example,

GOD

2 Co. 10.1; the apostles, 1 Th. 2.7. See *Meekness*, also HOLY SPIRIT.

GERAR, *a city of the Philistines*, mentioned Ge. 20.1; 26.6.

GERIZIM. See *Mountains*.

GERSHON or GERSHOM, *one of the sons of Levi*, Ge. 46.11; Nu. 3.17, etc.

GERSHON, *son of Moses*, Ex. 2.22.

GETHSEMANE, *the garden of Mount Olivet* to which our Lord resorted, Mat. 26.36; Mar. 14.32; Lu. 22.39; Jno. 18.1.

GIANTS, before the flood, Ge. 6.4; subsequently in the land of Canaan, Nu. 13.33; De. 2.10; 3.11; 1 Sa. 17; 2 Sa. 21.16-22; 1 Ch. 20.4-8.

GIBEAH, *a city in the tribe of Benjamin*, mentioned Ju. 19; 20; 1 Sa. 10.26; 14.2; 15.34; 2 Sa. 21.6.

GIBEON, *a city of Canaan, the inhabitants of which artfully deceived* Joshua, Jo. 9; 10; 2 Sa. 2.13; 20.8; 1 Ki. 3.5; 1 Ch. 21.29; used as a comparison, Is. 28.21.

GIDEON, *one of the judges or deliverers of Israel*, his history, Ju. 6.11; 40; 7; 8; He. 11.32.

GIFT of God, Jno. 4.10; 2 Cor. 9.15; Ac. 2.38.

GIFTS or contributions, Ex. 35.21-29; Nu. 7; Mar. 12.41-44; Lu. 21.1-4; Ac. 2.45; 4.34-37; 10.4; 11.29,30; Ro. 15.25-33; 1 Co. 16.1-3; 2 Co. 9; Ga. 2.10; Ph. 4.9-18.

GIFTS, *spiritual*, Ps. 29.11; 68.18-35; Ro. 12.6; Ja. 1.5,17; 4.6; rules concerning the exercise of them, 1 Co. 12; inferior to love, 1 Co. 13; and to preaching, 1 Co. 14.

GILBOA. See *Mountains*.

GILEAD, *prophetically or figuratively* mentioned, Ps. 60.7; 108.8; Ca. 4.1; 6.5; Je. 8.22; 46.11; 50.19; Ob. 19; Mi. 7.14; Zec. 10.10; *naturally*. See *Mountains*.

GILEAD, *Jephthah's father*, Ju. 11.1,2.

GILEAD, *Manasseh's grandson*, Nu. 26.29,30.

GILGAL, *a place near Jordan*, mentioned Jos. 4.19-24; 9.6; Ju. 2.1; 1 Sa. 7.16; 10.8; 11.14,15; 13; 15. 33; in prophecy, Ho. 4.15; Am. 4. 4; 5.5.

GIRDLE, Ex. 28.4; Jer. 13.1.

GIRGASHITES, *a tribe of the Canaanites*, Ge. 10.15,16; 15.21; Jos. 24.11.

GLASS, 1 Co. 13.12; 2 Co. 3.18; sea of, Rev. 4.6; 15.2.

GLEANINGS *at the harvest and vintage*, Le. 19.9,10; 23.22; De. 24.20, 21; Ruth 2.15.

GLORY of GOD, the peculiar display of it, called the *Shekinah*, Ex. 3.2-5; 13.21,22; 19; 24.16,17; 40.34-38; Le. 9.23,24; 16.2; Nu. 14.14; 2 Ch. 7.1-3.

GLORY of GOD manifest in his works of nature, Ps. 8; 19.1; 139.14; 145. 1; Ro. 1.20; and in those of grace, 2 Co. 3.18; 4.6.

GLORIFY GOD, our duty to, 1 Co. 6.20; 10.31.

GLUTTONY, censured, De. 21.20; Pr. 23.1,20; 25.16; 1 Pe. 4.3.

GNASHING of teeth, *rage*, Ps. 35.16; Ac. 7.54; *anguish*, Ps. 112.10; Mat. 8.12; 13.42,50; 22.13.

GOATS, wild, described, Job 39.1; 4. See *Figures*.

GOD, HIS NATURE is Trinity in Unity, Ge. 1.26; Ex. 3.14; 20.2,3; De. 4. 35,39; 5.6,7; 6.4; 32.39; Ps. 86.10; Is. 37.16; 43.10-14; 44.6; 45.5; Mat. 3.16,17; 28.19; Mar. 1.10,11; Lu. 3.

GOD

22; 24.49; Jno. 14; 15; 16; 17.3; Ac. 1.4-8; 2.36-38; 1 Co. 8.4-6; 2 Co. 13.14; Ga. 3.20; Ep. 2.18; 4.6; 1 Ti. 2.3; He. 9.14; 1 Jno. 5.7; Jude 20.21; a Spirit, Jno. 4.24; invisible, Ex. 33.20; Jno. 1.18; 5.37; Ro. 1. 20; Col. 1.15; 1 Ti. 1.17; 6.16; He. 11.27; 1 Jno. 4.12; living and true, Je. 10.10; Da. 4.34; 6.26; Ac. 14.15; 1 Th. 1.9; He. 9.14; 10.31; eternal, De. 33.27; Ps. 9.7; 90.24; 93.2; 102.12,24,27; 104.31; 135.13; 145. 13; Is. 40.28; 57.15; 63.16; Je. 10. 10; La. 5.19; Da. 4.3; Ro. 1.20; 2 Co. 4.18; 1 Ti. 1.17; 6.16; Re. 4.9; first and last, Is. 41.4; 44.6; 48.12; Re. 1.8; 22.13; unsearchable, Job 5.9; 11.7; Ps. 145.3; Ec. 8.17; Ro. 11.33; Ep. 3.8; unchangeable, Nu. 23.19; 1 Sa. 15.29; Mal. 3.6; He. 1. 12; Ja. 1.17; blessed or happy, Ps. 119.12; Ro. 1.25; 1 Ti. 1.11; 6.15; love, 1 Jno. 4.8,16; light, Jno. 1.4-9; 1 Jno. 1.5-7; life, Jno. 1.4; 5.26; 11.25; Col. 3.4; 1 Jno. 1.2; HIS PREROGATIVES: God and Lord alone, 2 Ki. 19.15; Ne. 9.6; Ps. 86.10; Is. 37.16,20; none else, or beside Him, De. 4.35; 2 Sa. 7.22; 22.32; 2 Ki. 5. 15; Is. 44. 6,8; 45.5,6,14,18,21,22; 46.9; Ho. 13.4; none with Him, De. 32.39; none like Him, Ex. 8.10; 9.14; 15.11; De. 33.26; 2 Sa. 7.22; 1 Ch. 17.20; Ps. 35.10; 86.8; 89.6; Is. 40.18; 46.5-9; Je. 10.6,7; sole object of worship, Ex. 20.3-5; De. 4.39; Lu. 4.8; the only Lawgiver, Ex. 19; 20; De. 4.14; Is. 33.22; Ja. 4.12; the universal Governor, De. 8. 18; 1 Ch. 29.12; 2 Ch. 1.12; Job 1. 21; 9.12; Ps. 75.7; 103.19; 135.6; Da. 4.17,35; brings good out of evil, Ge. 45.8; 50.20; Job 5.12; Ps. 33.10; 76.10; Je. 16.9,33; 19.21; Ph. 1.12; the Creator and Upholder of all things, Ge. 1; Ne. 9.6; Job 26.7; Ps. 33.6; 89.11; 148.5,6; Pr. 3.19,20; Is. 45.18; Je. 38.16; Zec. 12.1; Ac. 17.28; Col. 1.16,17; Re. 4.11; is to be feared, Ps. 33.8; 76.7; to be loved, Mat. 22.37-40; to be obeyed, Ac. 5.29; his superiority to idols, Is. 40.12-31; 41.21-24; 44.6-20; 45.20-25; 46.5-10; Je. 10.6-15; HIS ATTRIBUTES: immutability, Ex. 3.14,15; Mal. 3.6; Ro. 1.23; He. 13. 8; Ja. 1.17; omnipotence, Ge. 17.1; 18.14; Ex. 15.7; Job 9.4-12; 23.13; 37.23; 42.2; Ps. 62.11; 68.35; 135. 6; 145.12; Is. 14.24; 26.4; 40.29; Je. 32.17; Da. 3.17,20; 4.35; Mat. 9. 6; Lu. 1.37; Ro. 1.20; 2 Co. 12.9; omniscience, 1 Sa. 2.3; Job 26.6; 28.24; 34.21; Ps. 33.13,14; 44.21; 94.9; 139.1-16; Pr. 15.11; Je. 32.19; Mat. 6.18; 9.4; 10.29; 12.25; Mar. 5.30; 12.15; Jno. 2.24; 6.61; 16.19; Ac. 15.18; He. 4.12,13; 1 Jno. 3.20; omnipresence, 1 Ki. 8.27; 2 Ch. 6. 18; Ps. 139.7-11; Pr. 15.3; Je. 23. 24; Ep. 1.23; foreknowledge, Ge. 8. 22; 1 Ki. 22.28; Jno. 6.64; 13,1,3, 11; 18.4; 19.28; Ro. 8.29; 2 Ti. 1. 9; 1 Pe. 1.2,20; truth and faithfulness, Jos. 21.43-45; Is. 65.16; 2 Co. 1.18-20; He. 10.23; 11.11; 2 Pe. 3. 9,13; Re. 15.3; justice, Ge. 18.25; De. 24.16; 32.4; Job 34.7-19; 35.14; Ez. 18; Ac. 17.31; Re. 15.3; 19.1 2; holiness, Ex. 3.5; 19; Le. 19.2; Jos. 5.15; 1 Sa. 2.2; 6.20; 2 Sa. 6.6,7; Is. 6; Jno. 17.11; Re. 4.8; 15.4; goodness and mercy, Ge. 20.6; 34. 6; Ps. 57.10; 86.5; 100.5; 103.8; 119.64; 145.9; Is. 30.18; Joel 2.13;

GODL

Mat. 19.17; 2 Co. 1.3; 1 Jno. 1.9; wisdom, Job 9.4; 36.5; Ps. 92.5; 104.24; 147.4,5; Is. 28.29; Ro. 16. 27; 1 Co. 3.19,20; 1 Ti. 1.17; perfect, De. 32.4; Mat. 5.48; the marks of His sons, Ro. 8.14,15; Ga. 4.6; 1 Jno. 5.4,5,18; description of His throne in a vision, Is. 6.1-3; Re. 4.

GODLINESS, *delight in God*, Ge. 39. 9; Ps. 4.3; 48.14; 73.24,25; La. 3. 24; 1 Ti. 4.8; 6.6; 2 Pe. 2.9; 3.11.

GODS, *great men*, so called, Ex. 22. 28; Ps. 82.1; 138.1; Jno. 10.34,35; 1 Co. 8.5: and GODDESSES, *heathen ones*, mentioned Nu. 2.58; Ju. 2.13; 8.33; 16.23; 1 Sa. 5; 1 Ki. 11.5,7, 33; 2 Ki. 1.2,3; 5.18; 17.29-31; 19. 37; Is. 46.1; Ez. 8.14; Da. 3; Am. 5.26; Ac. 7.43; 14.12; 19.24.

GOG *and* MAGOG, mentioned Ez. 38. 39; Re. 20.8.

GOLD, employed as a comparison, Ps. 19.10; as a simile, Job 23.10; 1 Pe. 1.7; Re. 21.18,21.

GOLGOTHA. See *Mountains*.

GOLIATH, *a giant of Gath*, mentioned 1 Sa. 17; 21.9; 22.10; 2 Sa. 21.15-22; 1 Ch. 20.4-8.

GOMORRAH. See *Sodom*.

GOSHEN, *a province in Egypt*, mentioned Ge. 45.10; 46.34; 47.4,6,27; Ex. 8.22; 9.26; *a place in Canaan*, mentioned Jos. 10.41; 11.16; 15.51.

GOSPEL, the GLAD TIDINGS OF SALVATION, Mat. 4.23; 24.14; Lu. 2.10; Mar. 16.15,16; Ac. 13.26; Rom. 1. 16; 10.3,6,9,10; 11.6; 1 Co. 1.18; 2 Co. 5.18,19; Ep. 3.2; 1 Pe. 1.25; preached to Abraham, Ga. 3.8; to the poor, Mat. 11.5. See *Cruden's Concordance*, under the words *Salvation, Save, Saved, Saviour*, etc. *Believe, Believed*, etc. *Faith, Justification, Justify*, etc. *Blood, Blood of Christ, His Blood*, etc. *Remission, Atonement, Sin*, etc. *Death, Life*, etc. etc.

GOURD, *a plant of rapid growth*, mentioned Jon. 4.6-10; wild, mentioned 2 Ki. 4.39.

GRACE, its source, Jno. 1.14,16,17; Ro. 1.7; 16.20,24; 1 Co. 1.3; 2 Co. 13.4; Gal. 1.3; 2 Ti. 1.9; 1 Pe. 5.10; Re. 22.21; its character, free and undeserved, Ac. 20.24; 2 Co. 8.9; Ep. 2.5; 1 Ti. 1.14; 2 Ti. 1.9; justifying, Ro. 3.24; 11.6; 1 Co. 15.10; Ep. 2. 8; Tit. 3.7; purifying, Tit. 2.11; He. 12.28; strengthening, 2 Co. 12.9; 2 Ti. 2.1; He. 4.16; 13.9; its use, Ro. 5.17; 15.15; Ep. 3.8; 2 Co. 4. 15; 6.1; Tit. 2.11; who are partakers of it, Ep. 6.24; Ja. 4.6; 1 Pe. 5.5; as a principle in the believer, Ro. 12.3,6; 15.15; 2 Co. 8.6,7; Gal. 2.9; Col. 3.16; 4.6; in the sense of kindness or gifts from one to another, 1 Co. 16.3; 2 Co. 8.19; its manifestation in Jesus on earth, Lu. 2.40; 4.22; the characteristic of future blessing, 1 Pe. 1.13.

GRAFF or graft, believers so called, Ro. 11.17-25; the word of God so called, Ja. 1.21.

GRATITUDE recommended, 2 Sa. 9; 2 Ki. 4.13. See *Praise*.

GRAPES, laws respecting them, Le. 25.5,11; Nu. 6.3; De. 23.24; 24.21; the bunch from Eshcol, Nu. 13.20-24; used as emblems, Ge. 49.11; Is. 5.1-12; 17.6; 24.13; Ez. 18.2; Ho. 9.10; Re. 14.18.

GRASS, man as, Ps. 37.2; 90.5; 103. 15; Is. 40.6; Ja. 1.10; 1 Pe. 1.24.

HAND

GRASSHOPPER, Ec. 12.5; Is. 40.22; Am. 7.1.

GRAVE, triumph over it, Job 19.25-27; Ps. 30.3; 49.15; Is. 38.18; Ho. 13.14; 1 Co. 15.55.

GRAVITY enjoined, 1 Ti. 3.4,8,11; Tit. 2.2,7.

GRECIANS, apply to Jesus, Jno. 12. 20-22; many of them converted, Ac. 11.19-21; 17.4.

GREECE or *Grecia*, mentioned *prophetically*, Da. 8.21-25; 10.20; 11.2; Zec. 9.13; *historically*, Ac. 20.2.

GRIEF for the loss of friends, Ge. 23. 2; 50.1; 2 Sa. 1.11,12; 3.31; Jno. 11.35; Ph. 2.27; should not be immoderate, 2 Sa. 12.20; 1 Co. 7.30; 1 Th. 4.13.

GROVES, Ge. 21.33; De. 16.21; Ju. 6.25; 1 Ki. 15.13; 2 Ki. 17.16; 21.3.

GRUDGING. See *Hospitality*.

GUIDE, GOD will be one to His people, Ps. 25.9; 32.8; Is. 40.11; 42.16; 48.17; 49.10; 57.18; 58.11; by his word, Ps. 119.105; 2 Ti. 3.16; by his providence, Ps. 37.23; Pr. 16.9; by his HOLY SPIRIT, Ez. 36. 27; Jno. 16.13.

GUILE, injunctions concerning, Ps. 32.2; 34.13; Jno. 1.47; 1 Pe. 2.1; 3.10. See *Deceit*.

HABAKKUK, only mentioned in his prophecy.

HABITS, not easily changed, Pr. 22. 6; Je. 13.23.

HADAD, *the Edomite*, mentioned 1 Ki. 11.14.

HAGAR, *Abraham's bond-woman and wife*, her history, Ge. 16; 21.9-21; her descendants, 1 Ch. 5.10,20; Ps. 83.6; the history of Sarah and Hagar an allegory, Ga. 4.22-31.

HAGGAI, Ezra 5; 6.14. See his prophecy.

HAIL, employed to execute the wrath of God, Ex. 9.23; Jos. 10.11; predictions, Is. 28.2,17; 30.30; Ez. 13. 13; Re. 8.7; 11.19; 16.21.

HALLELUJAH, *praise the Lord*, Ps. 106; 111; 113; 146; 148; 149; 150; Re. 19.1-4,6.

HALLOWED, *made holy*, Ex. 20.11; 28.38; Le. 22.32; Mat. 6.9.

HAM, his history, Ge. 9.22-27; his descendants, 10.16; 1 Ch. 1.8-16.

HAMAN, *a Persian noble*, his history, Es. 3; 4; 5; 6; 7; 8.1-7.

HAMATH, Nu. 34.8; Jos. 13.5; 2 Ki. 18.34.

HAMOR, his history, Ge. 34; Ac. 7. 16.

HANANI, *the prophet*, 2 Ch. 16.17.

HANANI, *a returned captive*, Ezra 10. 20; Ne. 1.2; 7.2; 12.36.

HANANIAH, *the false prophet*, mentioned Je. 28.

HANANIAH. See *Shadrach*.

HANANIAH, *son of Zerubbabel*, 1 Ch. 3.19.

HAND of God, 2 Ch. 30.12; Ne. 2.18; De. 2.15; Job 2.10; 1 Pe. 5.6.

HANDS, imposition of, in blessing, Ge. 48.14; Mat. 19.13,15; in dedicating sacrifices, Ex. 29.10; Le. 1.4; in ordaining to offices, Nu. 8.10; 27. 18; De. 34.9; Ac. 6.6; 1 Ti. 4.14; 5.22; 2 Ti. 1.6; in miraculous cures, Mar. 6.5; 16.18; Lu. 13.13; Ac. 9. 17; 28.8; at the impartation of the HOLY SPIRIT, Ac. 8.17; 19.6; lifted up in prayer, Ex. 17.11,12; Ps. 28.2; 63.4; 88.9; 134.2; 141.2; 143.6; washed publicly, De. 21.6,7; Mat. 27.24.

HEAR

HANGING, an infamous death, Ge. 40.22; Nu. 25.4; De. 21.22,23; Jos. 10.26; 2 Sa. 21.8,9; Es. 7.10; 9.14; crucifixion so called, Ga. 3.13.

HANNAH, *the wife of Elkanah*, her history, 1 Sa. 1; 2.1-21.

HAPPINESS, wherein it consists, Ps. 1; 32.1; 40.4; 106.3; 112.1; 119.1; 128.1; Pr. 3.13; 29.18; Is. 56.2; Mat. 5.3-11; Lu. 6.20-22; 11. 28; 12.43; Jno. 13.17; Ro. 4.7; 14. 22; Ja. 1.12; Re. 14.13.

HARAN, *son of Terah*, Ge. 11.26-32.

HARAN, *son of Caleb*, 1 Ch. 2.46.

HARAN, *son of Shimei*, 1 Ch. 23.9.

HARAN, *a place so called between Ur and Canaan*, Ge. 11.31,32; 12.1-4; 27.43; 28.10; 29.4; 2 Ki. 19.12.

HARDENED heart, Ex. 7.13; 8.15; De. 15.17; 1 Sa. 6.6; He. 3.8; Pr. 38.14; Jno. 12.40.

HARLOT, Je. 3.3; Mat. 21.31,32; 1 Co. 6.15; figurative, Is. 1.21; Je. 2. 20; Ez. 16.23; Ho. 2; Re. 17.18.

HARMLESS, Mat. 10.16; Ho. 7.26; Ph. 2.15.

HARP, *a musical instrument*, Ge. 4. 21; used by David, 1 Sa. 10.5; 1 Ch. 25.3; Ps. 33.2; 43.4; 57; Re. 14.2.

HART or *Deer, a quadruped*, De. 12. 15; 14.5; 1 Ki. 4.23; Ps. 42.1; Is. 35.6.

HARVEST, promise, Ge. 8.22; feast, Ex. 23.16; 34.21; Is. 9.3; 16.9; of the world, Je. 8.20; Mat. 13.30; Re. 14.15.

HATRED in the heart condemned, Le. 19.17; Pr. 10.12,18; 26.24 ˙ 1 Jno. 2.9; 3.15.

HAUGHTINESS. See *Pride*.

HAVEN, *a sea-port*, Ge. 49.13; Ps. 107.30; Ac. 27.8,12.

HAWK described, Job 39.26.

HAZAEL, *captain and afterwards king of Syria*, his history, 1 Ki. 19. 15-17; 2 Ki. 8.7-15,28,29; 9.14,15; 10.32,33; 12.17,18; 13.22-25.

HAZOR, *a city of Canaan*, its history, Jos. 11.10,11; 15.21-23; Ju. 4.2; 1 Ki. 9.15; 2 Ki. 15.29; Je. 49.28-33.

HEAD, CHRIST is, of His body, the church, Ep. 5.23; of all things, Ep. 1.22; Col. 2.10. See *Union*. See *Body*.

HEALTH, the value of it, and how preserved, Pr. 3.7,8; Ac. 27,34; 1 Ti. 5.23.

HEARING, to be with profit, De. 4. 9,10; Mat. 7.24; Ro. 2.13; He. 2.1; 12.25; Ja. 1.22.

HEART, in its natural state, is utterly depraved, Ge. 6.5; 8.21; Ps. 51.5; 58.3; Pr. 6.18; 22.15; Ec. 8. 11; 9.3; Is. 53.6; Mat. 15.19; Ro. 3.10-18; at enmity with God, showing itself in pride and rebellion, Ex. 5.2; De. 5.29; Job 21.14,15; Ps. 10. 4; 73.6,11; 101.5; Pr. 11.20; 21.4; Is. 9.9,10; Je. 5.23; 49.16; Ez. 14. 4; Ho. 13.16; Ob. 3; Ro. 1.28; 3. 18; 8.7; 9.20; 1 Co. 2.14; insensible to its own state, De. 29.4; Ps. 119. 70; Ez. 11.19; Mat. 13.15; the prerogative of GOD to search it, 1 Sa. 1. 13; 16.7; 1 Ch. 29.17; Ps. 44.21; Pr. 16.1,9; Je. 11.20; 17.10; He. 4. 12; and to change it, see HOLY SPIRIT; the effects of this change, it sorrows for sin, Ps. 34.18; 51.17; Is. 57.15; 61.1; 66.2; it abhors evil, and loves GOD's law, Job 42.6; Ps. 1.2; 40.8; 119.97,113,163; Is. 6. 5; Ro. 7.21-23; it bows to Divine authority, Ps. 119.11,32,105,111,112; 131.1,2; Je. 15.16; Ep. 6.6; it

211

ISRA

numbered in the wilderness, Nu. 1. 2-46; again in the plains of Moab, Nu. 26; enter into a covenant with God, Ex. 19.20; De. 29.10; called a peculiar people, De. 26.18; their privileges, De. 4.33-38; 7.6; 1 Ch. 17.21,22; Ro. 9.4,5; the order of their encampment, Nu. 2; of their marches, Nu. 10.14-28; all their stations in the wilderness, Nu. 33; murmur at Taberah, Nu. 11.1-3; on the death of Korah, Nu. 16.41; at the return of the spies, Nu. 14.1; punished for it, Nu.14.26-45; all the murmurers perished in the wilderness, Nu. 26.64; defeat the Canaanites at Hormah, Nu. 21.1-3; join in the worship of Baal-peor, Nu. 25.1-5; their various rebellions enumerated, De. 9; Ju. 2; 3.7; repent when oppressed by their enemies, Ju. 10.10; their ingratitude to the family of Gideon, Ju. 8.35; their war with the tribe of Benjamin, Ju. 19.29,30; 20; 21; defeated by the Philistines, and the ark taken, 1 Sa. 4; desire a king, 1 Sa. 8.5; their request granted, see *Saul, David, and Solomon.* The kingdom was divided under Rehoboam, who governed Judah and Benjamin, the ten tribes being given to Jeroboam. *See their histories;* the line of Israel until carried captive into Assyria, was, Jeroboam, Nadab, Baasha, Elah, Zimri, Omri, Ahab, Ahaziah, Joram, Jehu, Jehoahaz, Joash, Jeroboam II., Zachariah, Shallum, Menahem, Pekahiah, Pekah, Hoshea; line of Judah until carried captive into Babylon, was, Rehoboam, Abijam, Asa, Jehoshaphat, Joram, Ahaziah, Athaliah, Joash, Amaziah, Uzziah, Jotham, Ahaz, Hezekiah, Manasseh, Amon, Josiah, Jehoahaz, Jehoiakim, Jehoiachin, Zedekiah; *see the Chronological Table;* carried captive to Babylon, 2 Ki. 25.11; 2 Ch. 36.20; Je. 39.5; return from their captivity, Ez. 1; the number that returned, Ez. 2; Ne. 7; their history recapitulated, Ps. 78; 105; 106; 107; their rebellions enumerated and lamented, Ezra 9.5-15; Ne. 9.7-38; Eze. 20.5; their degeneracy complained of, Is. 1; 43.22; Am. 2.9-16; Mi. 3; 6; 7; Zep. 3; Zec. 7.5; Mal. 1; 2; 3; and their rejection and dispersion foretold, Le. 26.28-39; De. 4.27,28; 28.15-68; Ho. 9.17; their sufferings for their sins, Is. 1. 7; 3.1; 5.24; 7.17-25; 9.8-21; 10; 17.4,9; 22; 24; 25; 28.17; 29; 30; 32.9; 42.24,25; 50.1; 51.17; 57.17; 59.2; 63.10; 64.5; 65.2-16; Je. 13. 22; 14.17; 15; 16.10; 17.1; 18.11; Eze. 6; 7; 8.18; 9; 12.18-20; 14; 16; 21; 22; 23; Ho. 2.1-13; 3.4; 4; 13; Am. 2; 4; 6; 8; 9.1-8; Mi. 1; 2.1; Zep. 1; the restoration of Israel foretold, De. 30.1-9; Is. 1.26; 4.2-6; 11.11; 14.1-3; 18; 27.9,12; 29.18; 30.18; 32.15; 44.22; 49.9-26; 51.11; 54.6-17; 60; 65.9; 66.8; Je. 12.15; 16.14,15; 23.8; 30; 31; 32. 36,44; 33.14,20,21; 46.27,28; 50.4; Eze. 6.8; 11.16,19; 12.22; 16.60; 20.33; 28.24; 29.21; 36.26; Da. 12. 1; Ho. 3.5; Am. 9.14,15; Zep. 3.13; Zec. 8; 12.10; 13; represented by the revival of dead bones, Ez. 37; by the olive tree, Ro. 11; their prosperity in the last times, Is. 2; 9.1-7; 12; 25.6; 26; 28.5,16; 35; 40.1,11; 41; 51.22; 52.12; 62.4;

JEBU

65.17; Ez. 17.22; Ho. 1.7,10; 2.14; 13.9,14; Joel 2.21,28; 3; Am. 9.11; Ob. 17; Mi. 2.12; 4; Zep. 3.14-20; Zec. 2; 8.2; 13.9; 14; the nations that have oppressed them will suffer for it, Is. 17.12; 33.1; 34; 49.25; 54.3; 60.16; 61.5; 63.1-6; 66.20-24; Je. 46.28; Joel 3.2-8; Mi. 5.8; 7.16, 17; Zep. 3.8; Hag. 2.22; Zec. 10.5-12; 12.4,9; 14.12; in Israel will all nations be blessed, Is. 42.1; 49.6; 56.3-8; 60.3; 62.2; 65.1; 66.19; they will no more be two kingdoms, but one, Ez. 37.22; their history a warning to Christians, 1 Co. 10.6. See *Jews.*

ISSACHAR, *one of the sons of Jacob,* Ge. 30.18; 35.23; his blessing, Ge. 49.14,15; his descendants, 1 Ch. 7. 1; their appointment, De. 27.12; their inheritance, Jos. 19.16-23.

ITUREA, *a province in Syria,* mentioned Lu. 3.1.

IVORY, its former abundance, 1 Ki. 10.18; 22.39; 2 Ch. 9.21; Am. 3.15; 6.4.

JABBOK, Ge. 32.22.

JABESH-GILEAD, mentioned Ju. 21; 1 Sa. 11; 31.11-13; 2 Sa. 2.4,5; 21.12-14.

JABEZ, mentioned 1 Ch. 4.9,10.

JABIN, *king of Hazor,* mentioned Jos. 11.1-5; Ju. 4.

JACHIN, *a pillar of the temple,* 1 Ki. 7.21; 2 Ch. 3.17.

JACOB, *Isaac's youngest son,* his history, Ge. 25.24-34; 27; 28; 29; 30; 31; 32; 33; 34; 35; 37; 42; 43; 44; 45; 46; 47; 48; 49; 50.

JACOB'S well, Jno. 4.5.

JAEL, mentioned Ju. 4.18-24.

JAILER of Philippi, his conversion, Ac. 16.22-36.

JAIR, *a judge of Israel,* his history, Ju. 10.3-5.

JAIRUS, *the father of the young girl restored to life by our Lord,* Mat. 9. 18; Mar. 5.22-43; Lu. 8.41-56.

JAMES I., apostle, son of Zebedee, and brother of John, Mat. 4.21; 10. 2; 17.1; Mar. 1.19,29; 3.17; 5.37; 9. 2; 10.35,41; 13.3; 14.33; Lu. 5.10; 6.14; 8.51; 9.28,54; Ac. 1.13; 12.2.

JAMES II., apostle, son of Alpheus, brother or cousin to Jesus, Mat. 10. 3; 13.55; 27.56; Mar. 3.18; 6.3; 15. 40; 16.1; Lu. 6.15,16; Ac. 1.13; 12. 17; 15.13; 21.18; 1 Co. 15.7; Gal. 1.19; 2.9,12; Ja. 1.1; Jude 1.

JANNES and JAMBRES, mentioned 2 Ti. 3.8.

JAPHETH, *son of Noah,* his descendants, Ge. 10.1-5; 1 Ch. 1.5.

JARED, *one of the antediluvian patriarchs,* Ge. 5.15-20; Lu. 3.37.

JASHOBEAM, *one of David's mighty men,* 1 Ch. 11.11,16,17.

JASHER, book of, Jos. 10.13; 2 Sa. 1.18.

JASON, mentioned Ac. 17.5-9; Ro. 16.21.

JAVAN, mentioned Ge. 10.2; his territory or descendants, Is. 66.19; Ez. 27.13,19.

JAVELIN, *an ancient weapon,* Nu. 25. 7; 1 Sa. 18.10,11.

JAW-BONE of an ass, Ju. 15.15,19.

JEALOUS God, Ex. 20.5; Ps. 78.58; 1 Co. 10.22.

JEALOUSY, the law concerning it, Nu. 5.11.

JEBUSITES, mentioned Ge. 15.21; Nu. 13.29; Jos. 15.63; Ju. 1.21; 19. 11; 2 Sa. 5.6-9.

JESU

JEDUTHUN, *one of the four masters of the temple music,* 1 Ch. 16.38,41,42. See also Ps. 39; 62, etc.

JEHOAHAZ (Shallum), *king of Judah,* his history, 2 Ki. 23.31-34; 2 Ch. 36. 1-4; prophecy concerning him, Je. 22.9-12.

JEHOAHAZ, *king of Israel,* his history, 2 Ki. 10.35; 13.1-9.

JEHOIACHIN (Coniah or Jeconiah), *king of Judah,* his history, 2 Ki. 24. 6-16; 25.27-30; 2 Ch. 36.8-10; Je. 52.31-34; prophecy concerning him, Je. 22.24-30.

JEHOIADA, *the high priest,* his history, 2 Ki. 11.4-21; 12.1-16; 2 Ch. 22.11,12; 23; 24.1-22.

JEHOIAKIM, *king of Judah,* 2 Ki. 23.34-37; 24.1-6; 2 Ch. 36.4-8; Da. 1.2; prophecy concerning him, Je. 22.18,19.

JEHORAM or Joram, *king of Judah,* his history, 1 Ki. 22.50; 2 Ki. 8.16-29; 2 Ch. 21.

JEHORAM, *king of Israel,* succeeds Ahaziah, 2 Ki. 1.17; 3; 5.5-8; 6.24-33; 7; 8.1-6; 9.15-24.

JEHOSHAPHAT, *king of Judah,* his history, 1 Ki. 15.24; 22.1-50; 2 Ch. 17; 18; 19; 20; 21.1.

JEHOVAH or JAH, *the most solemn name given to* GOD, *signifying "the self-existent,"* Ex. 6.3; Ps. 83.18; Is. 12.2; 26.4; distinguished in the English Bible by capital letters. See CHRIST and HOLY GHOST. This name given to altars and remarkable places, signifying the "Lord will provide," Ge. 22.14; "the Lord my banner," Ex. 17.15; "the Lord send peace," Ju. 6.24; "the Lord is there," Ez. 48.35; "the Lord our righteousness," Je. 23.6.

JEHU, *king of Israel,* his history, 2 Ki. 9.10.

JEHU, the prophet, mentioned 2 Ch. 19.2; 20.34.

JEPHTHAH, *a judge of Israel,* his history, Ju. 11; 12.1-7; mentioned He. 11.32.

JEREMIAH, *the prophet,* his history, 2 Ch. 35.25; see his prophecy particularly. See also the Lamentations.

JERICHO, account of, Jos. 2.1; 3.16; 6; 24.11; 1 Ki. 16.34; 2 Ki. 25.5; Lu. 10.30; He. 11.30.

JEROBOAM, *first king of the ten tribes,* his history, 1 Ki. 11.26-40; 12; 13; 14.1-20; 15.34.

JEROBOAM II., *king of Israel,* his history, 2 Ki. 13.13; 14.16,23-29.

JERUSALEM, its history as a city, Ju. 1.8,21; 2 Sa. 5.6-10; 2 Ki. 25.4-7; 2 Ch. 36.17-21; Je. 39.1-14; 52.4-23; Ne. 3; 4; 5; 6; 11; 12.27-43; threatenings and expostulations, Je. 1.15; 2; 3; 4; 5; 6; 7; 8; 9; 10; 11; Ez. 21; 22; see Lamentations; figurative representations, Is. 3.26; Ez. 4; 5; 16; prophecy of its re-erection, Je. 31.38-40; its future name and signification, Ez. 48.30-35; Ga. 4.26; Re. 21.

JESHUA, *one who returned from the captivity,* Ezra 2.2; 3.2.

JESHURUN, *a name given to Israel,* De. 32.15; 33.5,26; Is. 44.2.

JESSE, *David's father,* mentioned Ru. 4.22; 1 Sa. 16; his descendants, 1 Ch. 2.13.

JESUS CHRIST, his divinity, Co. 2. 9; 1 Tim. 3.16; Jno. 1; 1.14,18; Co. 1.15-19; 1 Co. 15.47; Heb. 1.2,3; 1 Co. 2.8; Jno. 1.3; 10.30-36; 14.8,9; 10,13,14; Phil. 2.6,10,11; Isa. 45.21-

214

LOAV

LOAVES, multiplied, Mat. 14.17 ; 15. 32 ; Mar. 6.13 ; Lu. 9.12 ; Jno. 6.5.

LOCUSTS, Ex. 10.4 ; Pr. 30.27 ; Na. 3.7 ; Re. 9.7 ; used for food, Mat. 3.4. See *Plague.*

LOIS, *Timothy's grandmother,* 2 Ti. 1.5.

LOQUACITY reproved, Pr. 10.8,19 ; 12.16 ; 29.11 ; Ec. 5.3 ; 10.14.

LORD, *when printed in capital letters in our Bibles, is the translation of the word* JEHOVAH, *and is equally applied to* F·THER, SON, *and* HOLY SPIRIT, compare Ge. 2.4-8 ; Is. 6.1 with Jno. 12.41 ; also Je. 31.31-34 with He. 10.15-17.

LORD, *when in our translation printed in small characters, signifies either a king,* Ge. 40.1 ; 2 Sa. 19.19,20 ; *a prince or noble,* Ga. 42.10-30 ; *a prophet,* 1 Ki. 18.7 ; 2 Ki. 2.19 ; *a husband,* Ge. 18.12.

LORD'S DAY. See *Sabbath.*

LORD'S SUPPER, called communion, cup of the Lord, Lord's table, 1 Co. 10.16,21 ; the feast, 1 Co. 5.8 ; breaking of bread, Ac. 2.42 ; 20.7 ; instituted, Mat. 26.26 ; Mar. 14.22 ; Lu. 22.19 ; observed frequently, probably weekly, by the first disciples, Ac. 2.42,46 ; 20.7,11 ; rules concerning the observance of it, 1 Co. 5.7,8 ; 11.17-29.

LOT, *nephew of Abraham,* his history, Ge. 11.27,31 ; 12.5 ; 13.1-12 ; 14 ; 18.16-33 ; 19 ; 2 Pe. 2.6-8.

LOTS, the ancient manner of settlement, approved by God, Le. 16.8 ; Nu. 26.55,56 ; Jos. 7 ; 1 Sa. 10.20-24 ; 14.40-44 ; Pr. 16.33 ; Ac. 1.26 ; in this way the Roman soldiers divided the garments of our Lord, Mat. 27. 35 ; prophesied of, Ps. 22.18.

LOVE of God to His people, its nature, Is. 54.10 ; Je. 31.3 ; Ho. 14. 4 ; Zep. 3.17 ; Jno. 3.16 ; 17.23 ; Ro. 5.8 ; 8.39 ; 2 Co. 13.14 ; Ep. 1.2-6 ; 2. 4-6 ; 2 Th. 2.16 ; 1 Jno. 3.1,2 ; 3.16 ; 4.16 ; of CHRIST, Jno. 13.1 ; 15.12, 13 ; Ro. 8.35 ; 2 Co. 5.14 ; Ep. 3.19 ; 5.2,25 ; of the SPIRIT, Ro. 15.30 ; 2 Co. 13.11.

LOVE to God required, De. 6.5 ; 10. 12 ; rendered by his children, Ph. 1.9 ; 1 Jno. 2.5 ; 4.19 ; how shown, Job 23.3-6 ; Ps. 19.7-10 ; 27.4 ; 42.1, 2 ; 51.3,4 ; 63.1-8 ; 84 ; 116.1 ; Is. 26.8,9 ; 1 Jno. 4.20,21 ; 5.1-3 ; 2 Jno. 6 ; to CHRIST, its nature, Mat. 10. 37-42 ; Jno. 14.15,21,23 ; 21.15-17 ; 1 Pe. 1.7,8 ; to his word, Ps. 119. 97,119,127,159,167.

LOVE, brotherly, enjoined, Jno. 13. 34 ; 15.12,17 ; Ro. 12.9,10 ; 13.8 ; 1 Co. 13 ; Ga. 5.6,13 ; 6.2 ; Col. 3.14 ; 1 Th. 3.12 ; 4.9 ; Ep. 5.2 ; Ph. 2.1 ; 1 Ti. 1.5 ; He. 13.1 ; 1 Pe. 1.22 ; 3.8 ; 4.8 ; 1 Jno. 2.9 ; 3.10,23 ; 4.7,11,20, 21 ; 2 Jno. 5 ; its genuineness shown, Le. 19.17 ; Ps. 119.63 ; Mat. 18.15-17 ; 25.40 ; Ac. 2.42-47 ; 4.32 ; Ro. 12 ; 1 Co. 12.26,27 ; 2 Co. 2.4,10 ; 8 ; !; 12.14-19 ; 13.11,12 ; Ga. 4.15 ; 6. [-10 ; Ep. 1.15,16 ; 6.18,19 ; Ph. 1.3-5; Col. 1.3,4 ; 1 Th. 1.2,3 ; 5.11-15 ; Phile. 8.9 ; He. 10.24,25 ; 13.1-3 ; 1 Jno. 3.17,18 ; 2 Jno. 1.2 ; 3 Jno. 1-8. See *Affection* and *Charity.*

LOVE of our country commendable, Ne. 2.3 ; Ps. 25.22 ; 51.18 ; 122.6-9 ; 126 ; 137.5 ; Ro. 10.1.

LOVE of the world forbidden, Mat. 6. 24 ; 13.22 ; 19.22 ; 1 Ti. 6.9 ; 2 Ti. 4. 10 ; Ja. 1.27 ; 4.4 ; 1 Jno. 2.15.

LOWLINESS. See *Humility.*

MAN

LUCIUS *of Cyrene,* mentioned Ac. 13. 1 ; Ro. 16.21.

LUCRE, *worldly riches,* the love of, forbidden, 1 Sa. 8.3 ; Mat. 6.24 ; Lu. 16.1-13 ; 1 Ti. 3.3 ; Tit. 1.7,11 ; 1 Pe. 5.2 ; 1 Jno. 2.15.

LUKE, *the evangelist,* his history is much mingled with the apostle Paul's, as he evidently accompanied him in many of his travels, Ac. 16. 12 ; 20.1 ; 27.1 ; 28.13-16 ; was at Rome with him, 2 Ti. 4.11 ; Phile. 24 ; called the beloved physician, Col. 4.14 ; he wrote the gospel which bears his name, and the Acts.

LUKEWARMNESS censured, 1 Ki. 18.20-46 ; Mat. 8.21 ; Lu. 9.57-62 ; Ac. 26.29 ; Re. 3.15.

LUSTS of the flesh, to be crucified, Mat. 5.29 ; 15.19 ; Ro. 8.13 ; 1 Co. 9.27 ; Ga. 5.16,19-21 ; Col. 3.5 ; 1 Th. 4.5 ; 1 Pe. 2.11.

LUZ, *the ancient name for Bethel, and also of another city built to commemorate it,* Ge. 28.19 ; Ju. 1.22-26.

LYCAONIA, mentioned Ac. 14.6-20.

LYCIA, mentioned Ac. 27.5.

LYDDA, an early Christian church formed there, Ac 9.32-38.

LYDIA, a convert, her history, Ac. 16.13-15,40.

LYING, forbidden, Le. 19.11 ; Pr. 24. 28 ; Ep. 4.25 ; Col. 3.9 ; hateful to God, Pr. 6.16,17,19 ; 12.22 ; threatened with punishment, Ps. 5.6 ; 52. 1-7 ; Pr. 12.19 ; 19.5,9 ; Re. 21.8,27 ; abominable in the sight of men, Ps. 101.7 ; 119.163 ; 120.2 ; Pr. 13.5 ; 19.22 ; characteristic of a fool and wicked man, Ps. 58.3 ; Pr. 10.18 ; 14.5,25 ; Is. 30.9 ; comes from the devil, Jno. 8.44 ; Ac. 5.3 ; examples of, Ge. 4.9 ; 18.15 ; 27.18,19 ; 1 Ki. 13.18 ; 2 Ki. 5.25 ; Ac. 5.1-11. See *Deceit.*

LYSIAS, *a Roman governor,* mentioned Ac. 21.31-40 ; 22.26-30 ; 23. 15-30.

LYSTRA, Paul and Barnabas taken for gods there, Ac. 14.6-23.

MACEDONIA, Paul called to, Ac. 16. 9 ; Paul in, Ac. 17.

MACHPELAH, Ge. 23 ; 25.9 ; 49.30.

MAGI, or wise men, Mat. 2.1-12.

MAGICIANS of Egypt, Ge. 41.8 ; Ex. 7.11,22 ; 8.7,18 ; of Babylon, Da. 2. 1-13 ; 5.7,11.

MAGISTRATES, Jewish commands respecting them, Ex. 22.28 ; De. 17. 8-12 ; Ac. 23.5 ; to be obeyed by Christians, Ro. 13.1-7 ; Tit. 3.1 ; 1 Pe. 2.13-17.

MAHANAIM, Ge. 32 ; 2 Sa. 2.8 ; 17. 24.

MAHER-SHALAL-HASH-BAZ, Is. 8.1.

MALCHUS, Mat. 26.51 ; Jno. 18.10.

MALICE forbidden, Pr. 17.5 ; 24.17 ; 1 Co. 5.6 ; 14.20 ; Ep. 4.31 ; Col. 3. 8 ; Tit. 3.3 ; 1 Pe. 2.1,16 ; examples of, Ge. 4.8 ; 27.41 ; 31 ; 34.25 ; 37.5, 18 ; 1 Sa. 19.10 ; 2 Sa. 3.27 ; Es. 3. 6-15 ; Mar. 6.17 ; 11.18.

MALEFACTORS, Jewish law concerning, De. 21.22,23 ; the two, Lu. 23.32.

MAMMON, Mat. 6.24 ; Lu. 16.9. See *Lucre.*

MAMRE, *Abraham's residence in Canaan,* mentioned Ge. 13.18 ; 14. 13,24 ; 18.1 ; 23.17-19 ; 35.27. See *Hebron.*

MAN, his primeval dignity, Ge. 1.26, 27 ; 2.7 ; Ps. 8.5 ; Ec. 7.29 ; his fall,

MARY

Ge. 3.17 ; 6.5 ; 8.21 ; Ps. 14.3 ; Je. 17.9 ; universal corruption **of** his nature, Job 14.4 ; Ps. 51.5 ; Jno. 3. 6 ; Ro. 3.23 ; 7.18 ; Ga. 5.17 ; Ep. 2. 1-3 ; his mortality, Job 7.10 ; 14 ; Ps. 62.9 ; 78.39 ; 103.14 ; 144.4 ; 146. 3 ; Ec. 12.7 ; Ro. 5.12 ; 1 Co. 15.22 ; 1 Pe. 1.24 ; the great business of his life, Ec. 12.13 ; Am. 4.12 ; Mar. 8.36 ; Lu. 10.27 ; 2 Pe. 1.10 ; his dignity restored by CHRIST, 1 Co. 15.49 ; Ep. 5.25,27 ; Ph. 3.21 ; Col. 3.4,10 ; He. 2.10 ; 2 Pe. 1.4 ; 1 Jno. 3.2.

MANASSEH, *Joseph's eldest son,* his history, Ge. 41.51 ; 48 ; that of his descendants, Nu. 1.10 ; 7.54-59 ; 26. 29-34 ; 1 Ki. 15.19,20 ; 1 Ch. 5.23-26 ; 7.14-17 ; 2 Ch. 30.1-11 ; 31.1 ; his inheritance, Jos. 13.29-31 ; 17 ; mentioned in prophecy, Eze. 48.4,5.

MANASSEH, *king of Judah,* his history, 2 Ki. 21 ; 2 Ch. 33.

MANDRAKES, Ge. 30.14 ; Cant. 7.13.

MANGER, Lu. 2.7.

MANNA given and described, Ex. 16 ; Nu. 11.7-9 ; Ps. 78.23-25. See *Types.*

MANOAH, *Samson's father.* See *Samson.*

MAN-SLAUGHTER, laws respecting it, Ge. 4.4-15 ; 9.6 ; Nu. 35.22-34 ; De. 19.4-6 ; Jos. 20.1-6.

MAN-STEALING, laws against it, Ex. 21.16 ; De. 24.7.

MARAH, *place of halting for the Israelites,* mentioned Ex. 15.23-26.

MARANATHA. See *Anathema.*

MARBLE, mentioned in the building of the temple, 1 Ch. 29.2 ; and in the Persian monarch's habitation, Es. 1.6.

MARK. See *John.*

MARRIAGE, its institution, Ge. 2. 21-24 ; its nature, Mat. 19.4-9 ; 1 Co. 6.16 ; 7.10,11 ; Ep. 5.31 ; unlawful ones, Le. 18 ; with strangers forbidden to the Israelites, Ge. 34.14, 15 ; De. 7.3,4 ; Jos. 23.12,13 ; Ez. 10 ; Ne. 13.23-31 ; lawful for all Christians, 1 Co. 7.38 ; 1 Ti. 5.14 ; He. 13.4 ; St. Paul's advice on the subject, 1 Co. 7 ; when prudent, 1 Ti. 5.14 ; the happiness of a suitable one, Pr. 12.4 ; 18.22 ; 19.14 ; 31.10-31 ; the misery of an unsuitable one, Pr. 12.4 ; 19.13 ; 21.9,19 ; 25.24 ; 27. 15 ; the ancient mode of celebrating it, Ge. 29.22 ; seen by our LORD'S parables, Mat. 22.1-12 ; 25.1-10 ; our LORD sanctioned it by His presence, Jno. 2.1-10 ; none in heaven, Mat. 22.30 ; Mar. 12.25 ; Lu. 20.35. See *Types.*

MARTHA, *the sister of Lazarus,* her history, Lu. 10.38-42 ; Jno. 11.1-44 ; 12.2.

MARTYRDOM, the commands of CHRIST concerning it, Mat. 10.28, 37 ; 16.24-27 ; Mar. 8.34-38 ; Lu. 14. 26 ; will be amply rewarded, Mat. 5.10 ; Ro. 8.17 ; 2 Ti. 1.12 ; 2.12 ; 1 Pe. 4.13 ; Re. 2.10 ; 6.11 ; 7.14-17 ; instances of, Ac. 7.54-60 ; 12.2. See He. 11.26-40. See *Sufferings.*

MARY, *the mother of Jesus,* her pedigree, Lu. 3.23-38 (Joseph, her husband's name, being, according to Jewish custom, substituted for hers) ; her history, Mat. 1.18-25 ; 2. 11-23 ; 12.46-50 ; 27.56 ; 28.1 ; Mar. 3.31-35 ; 15.40,47 ; 16.1 ; Lu. 1.26-56 ; 2 ; 8.19-21 ; 24.1-10 ; Jno. 2.1-12 ; 19.25-27 ; Ac. 1.14.

MARY MAGDALENE, Mat. 27.56,61 ;

PAVI

Ga. 1.11-24; 2.1-16; 1 Ti. 1.12,13; 2 Ti. 4.10-18; his character, 1 Co. 9. 15-23; 2 Co. 1.24; 4; 6.3-10; 7.2; 11; 12.14; Col. 1.23,24; *his writings —the Epistles to the Romans, the Corinthians,* etc.

PAVILION, naturally, *a tent,* 1 Ki. 20.12,16; Je. 43.10; GOD describes himself as such to his people, Ps. 27.5; 31.20; the darkness is such to him, 2 Sa. 22.12; Ps. 18.11.

PEACE, to be cultivated, Ps. 34.14; 133.1; Pr. 3.30; 15.17; 17.1,14; 20. 3; 25.8; Zec. 8.19; Mat. 5.9; Mar. 9.50; Ro. 12.8; 14.19; 2 Co. 13.11; 1 Th. 5.13; 2 Ti. 2.22; He. 12.14; 1 Pe. 3.11; by what means, Pr. 15.1; 25.9,15; Col. 3.13; 1 Th. 4.11; the gift of JESUS to his people, Jno. 14. 27; Ph. 4.7; Ja. 3.17,18.

PEACE-OFFERINGS. See *Offerings.*

PEARL. See *Figures.*

PEACOCK, mentioned 2 Ch. 9.21; Job 39.13.

PEKAH, *king of Israel,* his history, 2 Ki. 15.25-31; prophesied against, Is. 7.1-9.

PEKAHIAH, *king of Israel,* his history, 2 Ki. 15.22-26.

PELATIAH, *the prophet,* mentioned Eze. 11.13.

PELEG, mentioned Ge. 10.25.

PELICAN, De. 14.17; Ps. 102.6.

PENS, *instruments so called, whether used for writing or engraving,* Ju. 5. 14; Job 19.24; Ps. 45.1; Je. 17.1; 3 Jno. 13.

PENTECOST, or *the feast of weeks,* how to be observed, Le. 23.9-21; De. 16.9; the descent of the SPIRIT upon it, Ac. 2.

PENUEL, *the place of Jacob's wrestling,* Ge. 32.22-32; Ju. 8.8-17; 1 Ki. 12. 25.

PENNY, *a Roman coin, value about sevenpence three-farthings,* mentioned Mat. 20.1-16; Mar. 6.37; 12.15-17; Re. 6.6.

PEOPLE of God, their duty to God's ministers, De. 12.19; 14.27; 18.6-8; Mat. 10.14; Lu. 10.16; 1 Co. 4.1; 9.14; Ga. 6.6; 1 Th. 5.12,13; 1 Ti. 5.17; He. 13.7,17.

PEOR. See *Mountains.*

PERDITION, the future lot of the impenitent, Jno. 17.12; Ph. 1.28; 2 Th. 2.3; 1 Ti. 6.9; He. 10.39; 2 Pe. 3.7; Re. 17.8,11.

PERFECT, GOD is absolutely, De. 32. 4; 2 Sa. 22.31; Mat. 5.48; so his law, Ps. 19.7; man cannot be, in this life, Job 9.20; 15.14; Pr. 20.9; Ro. 3.10; 1 Jno. 1.8; is to be aimed at, De. 18.13; 1 Ki. 8.61; Mat. 5.48; Lu. 6.36; 2 Co. 13.9,11; Ep. 5.1-8; Col. 4.12; 1 Th. 3.10; He. 13.20,21; 1 Pe. 5.10; believers are so by virtue of their union to Christ, Col. 2.10; and will manifestly be so in the consummation of all things, Ro. 8; Ep. 4.13; Col. 1.28; He. 12.23; the Saviour's prayer to his Father for this, Jno. 17.

PERGA, mentioned Ac. 13.14; 14.25.

PERGAMOS, the message of CHRIST to the church there, Re. 2.12-17.

PERIZZITES, *a tribe of ancient Canaanites,* Ge. 13.7; 15.20; Ju. 1. 4; 2 Ch. 8.7.

PERJURY forbidden, Ex. 20.16; Le. 6.3; 19.12; De. 5.20; Eze. 17.16-20; Zec. 5.4; 8.17; 1 Ti. 1.10; an instance, 2 Ch. 36.13.

PERSECUTION, 2 Ti. 3.12; Jno. 16. 33; Ph. 1.29; the cause, Jno. 15.18-

PHIL

21; Gal. 4.28,29; 5.11; how to behave under it, Mat. 5.44; 10.22; Ro. 12.14; 1 Co. 4.12; 2 Co. 12.10; 1 Pe. 4.19; the blessing connected with it, Mat. 5.10; 16.25; Mar. 8. 35; Lu. 9.24; 1 Pe. 4.14; Ja. 1.2; Re. 6.9; 7.13.

PERSEVERANCE in duty enjoined, Mat. 24.13; Lu. 9.62; Ac. 13.43; 1 Co. 15.58; 16.13; Col. 1.23; 2 Th. 3. 13; 1 Ti. 6.14; He. 3.6,14; 10.23,38; 2 Pe. 3.17; Re. 2.10,25; of the saints insured, Job 17.9; Ps. 94.14; 125.1, 2; Pr. 4.18; Is. 54.4-10; Je. 31.3; 32.38-40; Jno. 3.5,6,14,15; 5.24; 10. 27,28; 17.1-12; Ac. 20.28; Ro. 8.29-39; Ep. 1; 3.10-12; Ph. 1.6; 2 Th. 2.13,14; Tit. 2.14; 3.5; He. 13.5.

PERSIA, *an ancient kingdom of Asia,* historically mentioned, 2 Ch. 36. 20; Es. 1.3,14,18; Eze. 27.10; 38.5; prophetically, Da. 8.20; 10.13,20; 11.2.

PERSIANS, mentioned in prophecy, Is. 21.2; Da. 5.28.

PERSONS of men not regarded by God, De. 10.17; 2 Ch. 19.7; Job 34. 19; Ac. 10.34; Ro. 2.11; Ga. 2.6; Ep. 6.9; Col. 3.25; 1 Pe. 1.17. See *Partiality.*

PESTILENCE, threatened on the Israelites for disobedience, Le. 26. 25; Nu. 14.12; De. 28.21; Mat. 24. 7; instances, Nu. 14.37; 16.46-50; 25.9; 2 Sa. 24.

PETER, *the chief apostle to the Jews,* his history, Mat. 4.18-20; 10.2; 14. 22-33; 16.13-23; 17; 26.31-75; Mar. 3.16; 16.7; Lu. 5.1-11; 6.14; 22.54-62; Jno. 1.40-44; 13.6-10; 18.10-27; 20.1-10; 21; Ac. 1.10-26; 3; 4; 5; 8.14-25; 9.32-43; 10; 11.1-18; 12.1-19; Ga. 2.7-21; his writings, the two epistles which bear his name.

PHARAOH, *king of Egypt,* mentioned Ge. 12.15-20.

PHARAOH, *king of Egypt,* mentioned Ge. 40; 41; 45.16-20; 47.

PHARAOH, *king of Egypt,* mentioned Ex. 1.8-22; 2.5-10,23.

PHARAOH, *king of Egypt,* mentioned Ex. 3; 4.21-23; 5; 7; 8; 9; 10; 11; 12.29-32; 14.

PHARAOH, *king of Egypt,* mentioned 1 Ki. 3.1; 7.8; 9.16,17; 11.15-22; 2 Ch. 8.11.

PHARAOH, *king of Egypt,* mentioned 2 Ki. 18.20-24.

PHARAOH NECHOH, mentioned historically, 2 Ki. 23.29-35; prophetically, Je. 46.

PHARAOH HOPHRA, mentioned in prophecy, Je. 44.30; Eze. 29; 30.20-31; 32.

PHARAOH'S daughter, Ex. 2.5-10; Ac. 7.21.

PHARISEES, severely censured, Mat. 5.20; 16.6,12; 23; Mar. 8.15; Lu. 11.37-44; 12.1; 16.14,15; 18.9-14.

PHEBE, mentioned Ro. 16.1,2.

PHENICIA, *a province of Syria,* mentioned Ac. 11.19; 15.3; 21.2.

PHENICE, mentioned Ac. 11.19.

PHICHOL, *of Gerar,* mentioned Ge. 21.22.

PHILADELPHIA, Christ's message to the church there, Re. 3.7-13.

PHILEMON, *a friend of the apostle Paul's.* See *the epistle to him.*

PHILIP, *the apostle,* his history, Mat. 10.3; Mar. 3.18; Lu. 6.14; Jno. 1. 43-46; 6.5-7; 12.21,22; 14.8,9; Ac. 1.13; 8.

PHILIP, *the deacon or evangelist,* mentioned Ac. 6 ᶠ; 21.8.

PLEI

PHILIP, *Herod's brother,* **mentioned** Mat. 14.3; Mar. 6.17; Lu. 3.1,19.

PHILIPPI, mentioned Ac. 16.12-40.

PHILISTIA, *the land of the Philistines,* mentioned Ge. 21.34; Ex. 13.17; Jos. 13.2; 2 Ki. 8.2; Ps. 60.8; 87.4; 108.9.

PHILISTINES, their history, Ge. 26. 14-22; Ju. 3.31; 14; 15; 16; 1 Sa. 4; 5; 6; 7; 13.11-23; 14; 17; 18. 20-27; 19.8; 24.1; 27; 28.15; 29; 31; 2 Sa. 5.17-25; 23.9-12; 2 Ch. 21. 16; 26.6,7; 28.18; Is. 2.6; prophecies against, Is. 11.14; Je. 25. 20; 47; Eze. 25.15-17; Am. 1.6-8; Ob. 19; Zep. 2.5-7; Zec. 9.5,6.

PHILOSOPHY, heathen, the folly of it, 1 Co. 1.19,20; 2.6; Col. 2.8.

PHINEHAS, *the son of Eleazar,* his history, Ex. 6.25; Nu. 25.7-13; 31. 6; Jos. 22.11-34; 24.33; 1 Ch. 6.4; 9.2; Ps. 106.30.

PHINEHAS, *the son of Eli,* his history, 1 Sa. 1.3; 2.22-34; 4.11-22; 14.3.

PHRYGIA, *a country of Asia Minor,* mentioned Ac. 16.6; 18.23.

PHYGELLUS, and *Hermogenes,* mentioned 2 Ti. 1.15.

PHYLACTERIES, *strips of parchment with passages from the law written on,* worn by the Jews, through falsely interpreting Ex. 13.9,16; Nu. 15.38, 39; Mat. 23.5.

PHYSICIAN, Mat. 9.12; Lu. 4.23; 5. 31.

PIGEONS, used in Jewish offerings, Le. 1.14-17; 5.7-10; 12.8; Mat. 21. 12; Lu. 2.24.

PI-HAHIROTH, *on the Red Sea,* Ex. 14.2.

PILATE, *the Roman governor in Judea when* CHRIST *was condemned,* Mat. 27.11-24; Mar. 15.1-15; Lu. 23.1-25; Jno. 18.28-40.

PILGRIMAGE and *Pilgrim.* See *Figures.*

PILLARS, remarkable ones, Ge. 28. 18; 35.20; Jos. 24.26; 2 Sa. 18.18; two in the temple of Solomon, 1 Ki. 7.15-21; 2 Ch. 3.17.

PISGAH. See *Mountains.*

PISIDIA, *a province in Asia Minor,* mentioned Ac. 13.14; 14.24.

PISON, *a river,* Gen. 2.11,12.

PIT, as used for prisoners, Ge. 37.22-24; Is. 24.22; 51.14; Je. 38.6-13; Zec. 9.11; meaning the grave or hades, Job 17.16; 33.18; Ps. 28.1; 30.3,9; 55.23; 88.4-6; 143.7; Is. 14. 15; 38.17,18; Eze. 26.20; 32.23; a tank for water, Ex. 21.33,34; Le. 11.36; 2 Ki. 18.31; Is. 30.14; Je. 14.3; a hiding-place from an enemy, 1 Sa. 13.6; 2 Sa. 17.9; Je. 41.7-9. See *Caves.*

PITCH, used in building the ark, Ge. 6.14; also that of Moses, Ex. 2.3.

PITCHER, Ge. 24.15; Ju. 7; Mar. 14.13; Lu. 22.10.

PITY required of us, Job 6.14; Ps. 41.1,2; Pr. 28.8-10. See *Mercy.*

PLAGUE, inflicted as a punishment, Ge. 12.17; Nu. 14.37; 16.46-50; 25. 9; 2 Sa. 24.15,16.

PLAGUES of Egypt, Ex. 7; 8; 9; 10; 11; 12.29,60.

PLANT, Ps. 128.3; 144.12; Is. 5.7; 53.2; Je. 2.21.

PLEASURE, its vanity, Ec. 2.1; lovers of it warned, Lu. 8.14; 16. 19-31; Ph. 3.19; 2 Ti. 3.4; He. 11. 25; 1 Pe. 4.3; 2 Pe. 2.13.

PLEDGES, laws concerning them, De. 24.10-13.

PLEIADES, Job 9.9; 38.31.

PLEN

PLENTY, to be thankful for it, De. 16.10; Ps. 103.1-5.

PLOWING, Levitical law concerning, De. 22.10.

PLOWSHARES, Is. 2.4; Joel 3.10; Mi. 4.3.

PLUMMET, 2 Ki. 21.13; Is. 28.17; Amos 7.8; Zec. 4.10.

POISON of serpents, De. 32.24,33; Job 20.16; Ps. 58.4; Ro. 3.13; Ja. 3.8.

POLLUTE, ceremonially, Ex. 20.25; 2 Ki. 23.16; morally, Eze. 20.13,31; 23.30; 36.18.

POLYGAMY, laws against, Ge. 2.24; Mat. 19.4-6; Mar. 10.6-8; Ro. 7.3; 1 Co. 7.2.

POLYTHEISM forbidden and censured, Ex. 20.2-6; Is. 43.10; 44.8; Ho. 13.4.

POMEGRANATES, the fruit, mentioned Nu. 13.23; De. 8.8; the representation on the high priest's dress, Ex. 28.33,34; 39.24-26; on the pillars of the temple, 1 Ki. 7.18-20; 2 Ki. 25.17; 2 Ch. 3.16.

POOL *of Bethesda*, account of, Jno. 5.1-7.

POOLS, mentioned Ex. 7.19; 2 Sa. 2. 13; 4.12; Ne. 3.15; Is. 35.7; Jno. 9.7.

POOR, frequently good men are so by the appointment of God, 1 Sa. 2. 7; Ps. 75.7; promises for them, Job 5.15,16; 36.15; Ps. 9.18; 68. 10; 69.33; 72.2; 102.17; 109.31; 113.7; 140.12; Is. 14.30; Ja. 2.5; duty of the rich to relieve them, Le. 25.35; De. 15.7; Ps. 41.1; 112. 9; Pr. 3.9,10,27; 11.24,25; 14.21,31; 17.5; 19.17; 21.13; 22.9; 28.27; Is. 58.6-10; Mat. 25.34-46; Mar. 10. 21; 1 Ti. 6.17-19; their advantages, Ps. 37.16; Ec. 5.12; on a level with the rich, Pr. 22.2; Mat. 11.5; Lu. 7.22; Ja. 1.9,10; 2.5; their condition sometimes preferable, Pr. 15.16; 16. 8; 19.1; 28.6; Mat. 19.23; Lu. 6.20; the inconvenience of poverty, Pr. 14.20; 18.23; 19.4,7; 30.9; Ec. 9. 15; often occurs through vice and idleness, Pr. 6.6-15; 10.4; 13.4; 19. 15; 20.13; 23.21; 28.19.

POTIPHAR, Ge. 39.

POTTAGE, remarkable circumstances connected with it, Ge. 25.29-34; 2 Ki. 4.38-41.

POTTER. See *Types.*

POWER, of man vain when opposed to God, Job 1; 12.17; 34.24; Ps. 33. 16; 44.6; Lu. 1.51.

POWER of God, a motive to obedience, Ps. 76.7; Is. 26.4; Mat. 10.28; 1 Pe. 5.6.

PRAISE of God, exhortation to it, Ps. 22.23; 67.3; 69.34; 119.164; Is. 38.19; Ac. 2.47; motives to it, Ps. 9.1; 26.7; 28.7; 57.9,10; 63.3; 75.1; 89.1; 103.1-5; 104.24; 106.1; 111.1,2; 139.14; 150.1,2; Is. 12.2,4, 5; 44.23; Lu. 1.64; 2.10-38; Ro. 6. 17; 1 Co. 15.57; 2 Co. 2.14; 8.16; 9.15; Ep. 1; Ph. 1.3; Col. 1.3,4; 1 Th. 2.13; 3.9; 2 Th. 1.3; 1 Pe. 1. 3,4; Re. 1.5,6; 5.12,13; 7.9,10; 15; and way of doing it, Ps. 13.6; 18. 49; 21.13; 30.4; 33.3; 34.1; 35.28; 47.7; 104.33; 138.1; 145.2; 147.1; Is. 42.10; 48.20; 49.13; Mat. 26.30; Ac. 16.25; 1 Co. 14.15; Ep. 5.19; Col. 3.16; He. 13.13; Ja. 5.13.

PRAISE of men, no proper principle of action, Mat. 6.1; Ga. 5.26; Ph. 2.3.

PRAYER, the obligation and use of

PRED

it, 2 Ch. 7.14; Ps. 105.4; Is. 63.15, etc.; Mat. 5.44; 6.6; 7.7; Lu. 18. 1; Ph. 4.6; Col. 4.2; 1 Ti. 2.1; 1 Pe. 1.17; proper to precede great undertakings, 2 Ki. 4.33-35; Ac. 1. 24; preparation for it, Ps. 66.18; 145.18; Pr. 15.8,29; 28.9; Is. 1.15; 29.13,14; 59.2; Mar. 7.6; 11.25; Jno. 9.31; 1 Ti. 2.8; Ja. 1.6; 4.3; should be offered in faith, Mat. 21. 22; Mar. 11.24; He. 11.6; with fervour, Ps. 59.17; Lu. 11.8; 18.1; Ro. 12.12; Ep. 6.18; frequency, Ps. 55.17; 86.3; Lu. 2.37; 21.36; 1 Th. 3.10; 5.17; 1 Ti. 5.5; 2 Ti. 1.3; 1 Pe 4.7; without ostentation, Lu. 18. 1-14; without vain repetitions, Ec. 5.2; Mat. 6.7; for all men, 1 Ti. 2.1; in the name of CHRIST, Jno. 14.13; 15.16; 16.23; Ep. 5.20; He. 13.15; 1 Pe. 2.5; with dependence on the HOLY SPIRIT, Ro. 8.15,26; for wisdom, Ja. 1.5; Pr. 3.5,6; for deliverance, Job 27.8-10; Ps. 34.15; 50.15; He. 4.16; for guidance, Ps. 37.5; Pr. 16.3; the Spirit's help, Lu. 11.13; Ro. 8.26; Ep. 2.18; 6. 18; Jude 20,21; instances of different kinds—mental, Ex. 14.15; 1 Sa. 1.13; private, Da. 6.10; Mat. 14.23; Ac. 9.11; 10.9; family, Jos. 24.15; social, 1 Ki. 8.22-54; Ezra 9.5-15; Ne. 9; Ps. 5; Hab. 3; Lu. 1.10; Ac. 1.14; 2.42; 12.12; 16.13,16; 21.5; CHRIST our example, Mat. 14.23; 26.36-44; Mar. 6.46; 14.32-38; Lu. 6.12; 22. 41-45; 23.34; Jno. 11.41-43; 17; promises of an answer to it, Ps. 34. 15,17; 145.18; Is. 30.19; Je. 29.12; Mat. 7.7; Jno. 15.7; Ja. 1.5; 5.15; 1 Pe. 3.12; 1 Jno. 3.22; 5.14; examples of it, Ge. 24.12-60; 32.9-28; Ex. 32.11,31-34; Nu. 14.13-20; Ju. 6.17-24,36-40; 13.8-20; 16.28-30; 1 Sa. 1.10-28; 2 Sa. 7.18-29; 1 Ch. 29. 10-19; 2 Ki. 19.15-20; 20.2-7; 2 Ch. 33.11-13; 14.11-15; 20.6-18; Es. 4. 16,17; 5.1-3; Da. 9; Am. 7.2,5; Jon. 2; Lu. 13.13; Ac. 10.1-8.

PRAYER, for others. See *Intercession.*

PRAYER, forms of it, Nu. 6.22-27; 10.35,36; De. 21.8; 26; Mat. 6.9-13; Lu. 11.2-4.

PREACHING the gospel, called prophesying, 1 Co. 14.1; teaching, Mat. 28.19; a Divine appointment, Mat. 28.19; Mar. 16.15; Lu. 9.60; 24.46,47; Ac. 10.42; 1 Co. 1.17-29; 2 Co. 5.20; rules for, 1 Co. 14; instances of the manner and subjects of the apostles' preaching, Ac. 4.2; 5.42; 8; 9.20,27; 10.36-48; 11.19,20; 13.5,38-52; 14.15,25; 15.35,36; 17.3, 13,18; 19.13; 20.7,25; 28.31; Ro. 10.8; 16.25; 1 Co. 1.17-31; 2.2; 4; 9.16,18,27; 15.11-14; 2 Co. 4.5; 10. 14; 11.4; Ga. 1.8,16,23; 2.2; 5.11; Ep 2.17; 3.8; Ph. 1.15-18; Col. 1. 23,24; 1 Ti. 3.16; 2 Ti. 4.2,17; Tit. 1.3; He. 4.2,6; 1 Pe. 3.19; instances of usefulness, Ac. 2.41; 4.4; 8.35-40; 10.34-38; 16.14,15,31-34; 1 Co. 3.6,7; the power, Ac. 4.13; 1 Co. 1. 18; 2 Co. 3.5,6; the manner, 1 Co. 1.17; 2.4; 2 Ti. 4.1,2; the reward, 1 Co. 9.14,18.

PRECEPTS of virtue, Book of Proverbs.

PREDESTINATION, *the fore-appointment of events by* GOD, Ge. 3.15; 12. 3; 49.10; Is. 46.9; Mat 16.18; Lu. 18.31-33; Jno. 7.30; 8.20; 13.21; Ac. 16.7; Ro. 9.9; Ep. 4.1,11; such as—the establishment of Israel in Canaan, Ge. 12.7; 13.15; Ex. 7.4;

PRIN

Ps. 105.6-45; the choice of particular persons to advance his glory, and to effect his purposes, Pharaoh, Ex. 7.3,4; 9.16; the Canaanites, Jos. 11. 20; their own sins the cause of being thus used, Ge. 15.16; Da. 5. 20; Ro. 9.14-22; He. 3.13; 1 Pe. 2. 8; Jude 4; Cyrus, Is. 44.28; Jeremiah, Je. 1.5; Paul, Ac. 9.15; Ga. 1.15; also, of some persons to eternal life and glory, Lu. 10.20; 12.32; Ac. 2.47; 13.48; Ro. 8.28; 9; Ep. 1.4; 1 Th. 5.9; 2 Ti. 1.9; also by producing good from men's evil intentions, Ge. 50.20; Job 5.12; Ps. 33.10; 127.1; Pr. 19.21; and, disposing of the good things of this world according to his will and pleasure, De. 8.18; 1 Ch. 29.12; 2 Ch. 1.11,12; Job 1.21; 9.12; Ps. 75. 7; Da. 4.17. See *Election.*

PREJUDICE, effects of it, 1 Sa. 10. 27; Mat. 13.55; Lu. 19.14; Jno. 1. 46; 7.48,52; 9.16; Ac. 2.13; 17.18; 21.28; 22.22.

PRESBYTERY, 1 Ti. 4.14.

PRESENCE, divine, 1 Ch. 16.27; Ps. 16.11; 68.8; Is. 64.1; Hab. 3; Heb. 9.2; Re. 5.8,11.

PRESENTS, mentioned Ge. 20.14; 24.22,53; 32.13; 43.11; 45.22; 1 Sa. 16.20; 17.18; 18.4; 1 Ki. 10.10; 2 Ki. 5.5; Mat. 2.11.

PRESERVATION, daily, from God, Ps. 3.5; 4.8; 121.8; La. 3.22; Mat. 6.11; Ac. 17.28.

PRESUMPTION, reproved, Nu. 15. 30; De. 17.12; Pr. 27.1; Lu. 12.18-21; Ja. 4.13; prayer against it, Ps. 19.13.

PREVARICATION, an instance of, Ge. 12.11-20; 20. See *Lying.*

PRICE, Mat. 26.15; of wisdom, Job 28.13; pearl of great, Mat. 13.46.

PRIDE condemned, Ps. 101.5; 138.6; Pr. 3.7; 6.16-19; 8.13; 16.18; 21.4; 26.12; 29.23; Is. 5.21; Je. 9.23; 45. 5; Lu. 1.51; 18.9; Ro. 12.16; 1 Co. 4.7; 8.2; 2 Co. 10.18; Ga. 6.3; Ph. 2.3; Ja. 4.6; motives to guard against it, Ps. 12.3; 18.27; Pr. 13. 10; 15.25; 16.5,18; 17.19; 28.25; Is. 14.13-17; the marks of it, Mat. 23.5; Lu. 11.43; Jno. 7.18; Nu. 16; Es. 3; Da. 4.30; Ac. 8.9,10; 12.21-23.

PRIESTS, to be the family of Aaron, Ex. 28.1; laws concerning them, Ex. 19.22; Le. 6.8-23; 7.28-38; 8; 9; 21; 22.1-25; Nu. 3.1-4; 18; their genealogies, 1 Ch. 6.50-60; 9. 10-13; divided into orders by David, 1 Ch. 24.1-19; which of them returned from the captivity, Ne. 12; prophecies of their return, Ez. 44. 15-31; their departure from God exposed, Hos. 5.1; 6.9; Mal. 2.

PRIESTS, HIGH, first Aaron, afterwards the eldest son of the eldest branch of his family, his dress, Ex. 28; 39; his peculiar office, Le. 16; general laws, see *Priests.* Usually the judge of Israel, 1 Sa. 7.15-17; 8. 1-6; concerned in the condemnation of JESUS, Mat. 26.3-5,57-66; Lu. 22. 54-71; Jno. 18.10-28; a type of JESUS CHRIST, who is *the Great High-Priest*, Ps. 110.4; Ro. 8.34; He. 4.14; 5.4.5; 6.20; 7; 8; 9; 10. 1-22; 1 Jno. 2.1; the sacrifice *Himself*, Is. 53.5-10; Mat. 20.28; Jno. 10.11; Ep. 5.2; Tit. 2.14; He. 9.11 28.

PRINCE of Peace. See *Christ.*

PRINCE of this world. See *Devil.*

PRIN

PRINCIPALITY, *the chief or first*, Ep. 1.21; 3.10; 6.12; Col. 2.15.

PRISCILLA, Ac. 18; Ro. 16.3; 1 Cor. 16.

PRISONERS, our duty towards them, Mat. 25.36; He. 13.3.

PROFESSION of belief, 1 Ti. 6.12; He. 3.1; 4.14; 10.23.

PROFITABLE, what really is so, 1 Ti. 4.8; 2 Ti. 3.16.

PROMISES of GOD to be depended upon, Nu. 23.19; De. 7.9; Ps. 89.3, 34; 105.8; Is. 41.10; 42.16; Je. 32. 40; La. 3.31,32; Lu. 1.45; 2 Co. 1. 20; He. 13.5; Ja. 1.17; particular ones, to Noah, Ge. 8.21; 9.9-17; to Abraham, 12.7; 13.14-17; 15. 1-6; 17.1-22; 18.10-14; 22.15-18; to Hagar, 16.10; 21.17,18; to Isaac, 26.2-4; to Jacob, 28.13-15; 31.3; 32.12; 35.11-13; 46.3,4; to David, 2 Sa. 7.12-17; to Solomon, 2 Ch. 1. 7-12; 7.12; to mankind, and to his people (see *Covenant*); to the stranger, the fatherless, and the widow, De. 10.18; Ps. 10.14,18; 68. 5; 146.9; Pr. 15.25; 23.10,11; Je. 49.11; Ho. 14.3; the poor, Ps. 9.8; 12.5; 69.33; 72.12,13; 102.17; 107. 41; 109.31; 113.7; of temporal blessings, Ex. 23.25; Le. 26.6; Ps. 34.9,10; 37.3,23; 91.1-4; 102.28; 112.2; 121.3; 128.2; Pr. 3.6,33; 14. 11,26; Is. 32.18; 33.16; Mat. 6.25-32; Ph. 4.19; of spiritual blessings in this life, of pardon and reconciliation, Ex. 34.7; 65.3; 103.3,13; 130. 4,8; Is. 1.18; 27.5; 43.25; 44.22; 45.25; 46.13; 53.11; Je. 31.34; 33. 8; Ez. 33.16; 36.25; Mi. 7.18,19; Ro. 5.9,10; Ep. 2.13-17; Col. 1.21-23; adoption, Is. 63.16; Ro. 9.26; 2 Co. 6.18; of strength and succour, Ps. 37.39; 94.22; Is. 40.29-31; 41. 10; 49.14-16; 54.9,10; Ho. 13.9,10; Ro. 16.20; 1 Co. 10.13; 2 Co. 12.9; of his love and care, Ps. 42.8; 103. 13,17; Is. 30.18; 43.4; 63.9; Je. 31. 3; Ho. 14.4; Zep. 3.7; Zec. 2.8; 1 Pe. 5.7; of answers to prayer (see *Prayer*); of increase in holiness and wisdom, Ps. 1.3; 92.12-15; Is. 2.3; 29.18,24; Je. 31.12; Ho. 14.5,6; Mal. 4.2; Jno. 15.2,5; Ja. 1.5; of support in death, Ps. 23.4; 37.37; 73.26; Pr. 14.32; Is. 25.8; Ho. 13. 14; Ro. 8.38,39; 1 Co. 15.55-57; of the Holy Spirit in all His offices (see HOLY SPIRIT); after death the immediate happiness of the soul, Lu. 16.25; 23.43; 2 Co. 5.8; Ph. 1. 21,23; He. 12.23; Re. 14.13; the resurrection of the body to eternal blessedness, Job 19.26,27; Ps. 33. 19; Is. 26.19; Da. 12.2,3; Mat. 13. 43; 25.34,46; Lu. 20.35,36; Jno. 5. 28,29; 6.39,40,54; 10.28,29; 11.25; 14.2,3; Ro. 2.6,7; 8.11,17-23,38,39; 1 Co. 1.7,8; 15.12-57; 2 Co. 4.17,18; 5.1,4; Ph. 3.20,21; Col. 3.3,4; 1 Th. 4.15,17; 5.23,24; 2 Pe. 1.10,11; 1 Jno. 3.2; Re. 2.10; 7.15-17; 21. 22,23; including both, Ps. 84.11; Ro. 8.30; Ep. 1.3-14; 2 Pe. 1.3,4.

PROMOTION, whence it springs, Ps. 75.6,7; instances of, Ge. 39; 41; Ex. 2; 3; 2 Ki. 9; Ps. 78.70,71.

PROPHECIES relating to CHRIST: general ones, declaring the coming of a Messiah, Ge. 3.15; De. 18.5; Ps. 89.20; Is. 2.2; 9.6; 28.16; 32. 1; 35.4; 42.6; 49.1; 55.4; Eze. 34. 24; Da. 2.44,45; Mi. 4.1; Zec. 3.8; his excellency and dignity, and the design of his mission, Ge. 12.3; 49.

PROP

10; Nu. 24.19; De. 18.18; Is. 59. 20; Je. 33.15,16; his divinity, Ps. 2.11,12; 45.7; 72.7,8; 110.1; Is. 9. 6; 25.9; 40.10; Je. 23.6; Mi. 5.2; Mal. 3.1; the nation, tribe, and family he was to descend from, Ge. 12.1-3; 18.18; 21.12; 22.18; 26.4; 28.14; 49.8; Ps. 18.50; 89.3,4,29,36; 132.11; Is. 11.1; Je. 23.5; 33.15; the time when he was to appear, Ge. 49.10; Nu. 24.17; Da. 9.24; Hag. 2.7; Mal. 3.1; the place of his birth, Nu. 24.17,19; Mi. 5.2; that a messenger should go before him, Is. 40.3; Mal. 3.1; 4.5; that he was to be born of a virgin, Ge. 3.15; Is. 7. 14; Je. 31.22; that he was to be worshipped by the wise men, Ps. 72.10,15; Is. 60.3,6; that there should be a massacre at Bethlehem, Je. 31.15; that he should be carried into Egypt, Ho. 11.1; that he was to be distinguished by peculiar grace and wisdom, and by the descent of the Holy Spirit upon him, Is. 11.2; 42.1; 61.1; that he should be a prophet, De. 18.15; that he should preach the word of the Lord, Is. 2.3; 61.1,2; Mic. 4.2; that he should work miracles, Is. 35.5,6; that he should cast the buyers and sellers out of the temple, Ps. 69.9; that he should be a priest and offer sacrifice, Ps. 110.4; that he should be hated and persecuted, Ps. 22.6; 35.7,12; 109.2; Is. 49.7; 53.3; that the Jews and Gentiles should conspire to destroy him, Ps. 2; 22.12; that he should ride triumphantly into Jerusalem, Ps. 8.2; Zec. 9.9; that he should be sold for thirty pieces of silver, Zec. 11.12; that he should be betrayed by one of his own familiar friends, Ps. 41.9; 55. 12; that his disciples should forsake him, Zec. 13.7; that he should be accused of false witnesses, Ps. 27.12; 35.11; 109.2; that he should not plead upon his trial, Ps. 38.13; Is. 53.7; that he should be insulted, buffeted, and spit upon, Ps. 35.15, 21; that he should be scourged, Is. 50.6; that he should be crucified, Ps. 22.14,17; that he should thirst and that they should offer him gall and vinegar to drink, Ps. 22.15; 69.21; that they should part his garments, and cast lots upon his vesture, Ps. 22.18; that he should be mocked by his enemies, Ps. 22. 16; 109.25; that his side should be pierced, Zec. 12.10; also his hands and his feet, Ps. 22.16; Zec. 13.6; that he should be patient under his sufferings, Is. 53.7; that he should pray for his enemies, Ps. 109.4; that a bone of him should not be broken, Ps. 34.20; that he should die with malefactors, Is. 53.9,12; that he should be cut off in the midst of his days, Ps. 89.45; 102. 24; that there should be an earthquake at his death, Zec. 14.4; and a remarkable darkness, Am. 5.20; 8.9; Zec. 14.6; that he should be buried with the rich, Is. 53.9; that he should rise again from the dead, Ps. 16.10; 30.3; 41.10; Ho. 6.2; that he should ascend into heaven, and sit on the right hand of God, Ps. 16.11; 24.7; 68.18; 110.1; 118. 19; that his betrayer should die suddenly and miserably, Ps. 55.15, 23; 109.17; that the potter's field should be bought with the pur-

PUBL

chase money, Zec. 11.13. Compare *Christ.*

PROPHECIES accomplished: compare Ge. 15.13 with Ex. 2.24,25; 6. 1-8; 12.40,41; Ge. 18.10 with 21.1; 37.5-11 with 42.6; Jos. 6.26 with 1 Ki. 16.34; 1 Sa. 2.34 with 4.11; 1 Sa. 28.19 with 31.2-6; 1 Ki. 13.2 with 2 Ki. 23; 1 Ki. 13.22 with 23. 30; 1 Ki. 14.10-14 with 15.29; 16.3 with 11,12; 17.1 with 18.41-44; 20. 22 with 26; 1 Ki. 21.19 with 22.38; 21.21,22 with 2 Ki. 10.11; 1 Ki. 21. 23 with 2 Ki. 9.34-37; 3.17 with 20; 7.1 with 18; 7.2 with 19.20; 10.30 with 15.12; 13.14-19 with 25; 19.7 with 36,37; 20.17 with 24.13; 25. 13-17.

PROPHECIES spoken by Christ, Mat. 12.40; 17.22; 20.18; 24.2,11; 26.21, 32,34; Mar. 9.31; 10.32,39; 13.14-37; 16.17; Lu. 9.22; 13.33; 18.31-33; 19.43; 21.6; 22.21,31; Jno. 2. 19; 6.70; 11.23; 12.23; 13.18,38; 14.16,26; 15.26; 16.2,32; 21.18; Ac. 1.5,8.

PROPHECY, 2 Pe. 1.19-21; Rev. 19. 10; Amos 3.7; De. 29.29; Ge. 18.17; Jno. 15.14,15; 1 Pe. 1.10,11.

PROPHECY, a sure word, 2 Pe. 1.19-21.

PROPHETS, their duty, 1 Sa. 12.23; Is. 58.1; 62.6; Je. 1.8,17; 23.28; Eze. 2.6; 3.9,11,17; threatenings concerning, Je. 23.33-35; 25.4; 26. 5; Am. 8.11; promises concerning, Is. 30.20; Je. 3.15; false ones spoken of, De. 13.1-3; 18.20; 1 Ki. 13.18; 22.22-24; Is. 56.10; Je. 6.13; 14.13-17; 23.1,9; Eze. 22.25; 34.2; Mi. 3.11; Mal. 1.6,7; judgments denounced against them, De. 13.5; Je. 14.15; 23.31,32; 25.34,35; 28. 15,16; 29.31,32; Eze. 13.3; 14.9; foretold to arise in the Christian church, Mat. 7.15; 24.11,24; Ac. 20.29; 1 Ti. 4.1; 2 Pe. 2.1.

PROPHETS, the name given to Christian teachers, 1 Co. 14.

PROPHETESSES spoken of, Ex. 15. 20; Ju. 4.4; 2 Ki. 22.14; Ne. 6.14; Lu. 2.36; Ac. 21.9.

PROPITIATION. See *Christ.*

PROSELYTE, a convert to Judaism, Ac. 2.10; 6.5; 13.43.

PROSPERITY, no evidence of the favour of God, Job 12.6; 20.5; 21. 7-18; Ps. 17.10; 37.1; 73.3,13,18; 92.7; Ec. 8.14; 9.2; Je. 12.1; Hab. 1.16; Mal. 3.14; Mat. 5.45; Lu. 13. 1-3; 16.19-31; Jno. 9.2; Ac. 28.4; Ja. 5.1-5; is a dangerous state, De. 6.10-12; Pr. 1.32; 30.8; Lu. 6.24; 12.16-21; Ja. 5.1; of nations, causes thereof, Le. 26.3; De. 7.12; 28.1; Ju. 2.20.

PROVERBS, their use, Pr. 1.1, etc.

PROVIDENCE OF GOD asserted, Ex. 21.13; Job 1.12; 2.6; 5.6; 23.14; Ps. 65.9; 75.6; 105.14; 113.7; 127. 1; 147.6; Pr. 16.9,25; 19.21; 20.24; 21.30; Je. 10.23; Mat. 6.26; 10.29-31.

PRUDENCE recommended, Pr. 12. 16,23; 13.16; 14.8; 15.5; 19.11; 22. 3; 27.11,12; Mat. 10.16; Ja. 3.13.

PSALTERY, 2 Sa. 6.5; 2 Ch. 9.11; Da. 3.5.

PTOLEMAIS, *a sea-port of Canaan*, mentioned Ac. 21.7.

PUBLIC worship, rules concerning, 1 Co. 11; 14.40.

PUBLICAN, Mat. 18.17; Lu. 18.10.

PUBLICANS, Mat. 5.46; Lu. 5.27; 7.29; 15.1.

ALPHABETICAL INDEX OF THE HOLY SCRIPTURES.

SEAL

SEALING, the antiquity and use of it, Ge. 38.18; Ex. 28.11; 1 Ki. 21.8; Ne. 9.38; Es. 3.12; Je. 32.10; Da. 6.17; Mat. 27.66.

SEALS, Ge. 38.18; Job 38.14; Ca. 8. 6; seven, Re. 5.1.

SEARCHER of hearts, 1 Ch. 28.9; Ps. 7.9; Je. 17.10.

SECOND coming of Christ, Ac. 1.11.

SECOND death, Re. 20.14.

SECRET things, De. 29.29; Job 15. 8; actions will be revealed, and come to judgment, Job 31.4; 34.21, 22; Ps. 139.12; Pr. 5.21; Ec. 12.14; Je. 32.19; Mat. 10.26; Lu. 8.17; 12.2; Ro. 2.16; 1 Co. 4.5; He. 4.13.

SECRETS not to be revealed, Pr. 17. 9; 25.9; Mi. 7.5. See *Delilah*.

SEED of the woman, Ge. 3.15; Re. 12.

SEER, 1 Sa. 9.9; 2 Sa. 24.11.

SEIR, Mount. See *Mountains*.

SELF-DENIAL, a Christian duty, Mat. 5.29,30; 16.24; 18.8,9; Mar. 8.34; Lu. 9.23; 1 Co. 8.13; 9.17-27; 10.23; 2 Co. 10.5; Ga. 5.24; Tit. 2. 12; Christ our great example, Mat. 4.8; 8.20; Jno. 13.12-17; 2 Co. 8.9; Ph. 2.5-7.

SELF-RENUNCIATION, Is. 64.6; Mat. 6.10; 16.25; 26.39; Mar. 8.35; Lu. 9.24; 1 Co. 3.18-20; 2 Co. 12. 10; Ph. 3.7-9.

SELLING, frauds forbidden, Le. 19. 13,36; 25.14; Pr. 11.1; 16.11; 20. 10,23.

SENNACHERIB, king of Assyria, account of, 2 Ki. 18.13-37; 19; Is. 36; 37.

SENSUALITY censured, Am. 6.1-4; Lu. 16.19-31; Ja. 5.1-5.

SEPULCHRES, spoken of, Ge. 23.6; Ju. 8.32; 1 Sa. 10.2; 2 Sa. 2.32; 4. 12; 17.23; 21.14; 1 Ki. 13.31; 2 Ki. 9.28; 13.21; 21.26; 23.16,17,30; Ne. 2.3,5; Is. 22.16; Mat. 23.27,29; 27. 60; Lu. 11.47; Ac. 2.29; 7.16; whited, Mat. 23.27. See *Grave*.

SERAPHIM. See *Vision*.

SERGIUS PAULUS, the governor of Cyprus, a Christian convert, Ac. 13. 7-12.

SERPENT. See *Devil*.

SERPENTS, sent as a punishment, Nu. 21.4-9. See *Types*.

SERUG, Abraham's great-grandfather, Ge. 11.22,23.

SERVANTS, Jewish laws concerning them, Ex. 21.1-11,20-27; De. 23.15; 24.14,15; general commands concerning them, Pr. 18.9; Ep. 6.5-8; Col. 3.22-25; 1 Ti. 6.1,2; Tit. 2.9, 10; 1 Pe. 2.18-25.

SETH, son of Adam, Ge. 4.25; 5.2-8.

SEVEN, a sacred number among the Jews, Ge. 2.2; Ex. 20.8-11; Le. 25; Ps. 12.6; 119.164; Pr. 24.16; Is. 4.1.

SEVENTY elders appointed to relieve Moses, Ex. 24.1; Nu. 11.16-29.

SEVENTY disciples sent out by Jesus, Lu. 10.1-20.

SEVENTY weeks, Daniel's prophecy of, Da. 9.24-27.

SHADOW. See *Figures*.

SHADRACH, Meshach, and Abednego, Da. 1.3-20; 2.49; 3.8-30.

SHALLUM, king of Israel, his history, 2 Ki. 15.10-15; Je. 22.11.

SHALMANESER, king of Assyria, account of, 2 Ki. 17; 18.9-12.

SHAME, just cause of it, Ge. 3.7-10; 2 Sa. 10.4,5; Ezra 9.6; Ps. 25.3; Pr. 13.5; Is. 1.29; 42.17; Je. 2.26; 3.25; Lu. 13.17; 16.3; Jno. 3.20; unreasonable, 2 Ki. 2.17; Mat. 10.33;

SIGN

Mar. 8.38; Lu. 9.26; Ro. 1.16; 2 Ti. 1.8.

SHAMGAR, one of the deliverers of Israel, Ju. 3.31.

SHAMMAH, one of David's worthies, 2 Sa. 23.11-17.

SHAPHAN. See *Scribes*.

SHARON, more than one place so called in Canaan, 1 Ch. 5.16; 27.29; Ca. 2.1.

SHAVING, a rite of purification, Le. 14.8; Nu. 6.9; Ac. 18.18; 21.24; a token of humiliation, Job 1.20; 2 Sa. 10.4.

SHEAVES, De. 24.19; Ps. 126.6; Mi. 4.12; Mat. 13.30.

SHEBA. See *Queens*.

SHEBNA. See *Scribes*.

SHECHEM, his history, Ge. 34; a city, mentioned Jos. 24.

SHEEP, 2 Sa. 24.17; Ps. 74.1; 79.13; 100.3; Ez. 36.38; Mat. 15.24; 25. 32; Jno. 10.2; 1 Pe. 2.25; the chosen animal for sacrifice, see *Sacrifice* and *Offerings*.

SHEM, son of Noah, his history, Ge. 11.10; his descendants, 10.21-32; 11.10-32; 1 Ch. 1.17. See *Noah*.

SHEMAIAH, the prophet, spoken of, 2 Ch. 12.5-7.

SHEPHERDS, prophets so called, Eze. 34; Zec. 11.3. See CHRIST.

SHESHBAZZAR, supposed to be Zerubbabel. See *Zerubbabel*.

SHEW-BREAD, ordered, Le. 24.5-9; 1 Sa. 21.6; Mar. 2.26; Lu. 6.4; He. 9.2.

SHIBBOLETH, Ju. 12.6.

SHIELD, a piece of defensive armour, anciently in use, 1 Sa. 17.6,7; 1 Ki. 10.16,17; 14.27,28; 1 Ch. 5.18; 12. 34; 2 Ch. 14.8; God is to His people, Ge. 15.1; De. 33.29; Ps. 33.20; 84. 11; faith is to Christian, Ep. 6.16.

SHILOH, Ge. 49.10; Jos. 18.1,51; Je. 7.12.

SHIMEI, account of, 2 Sa. 16.5-12; 19.18-23; 1 Ki. 2.36-46.

SHIPS, Noah's ark the first, Ge. 6.14-16; 7; 8; early in use, Ge. 49.13; Ju. 5.17; 1 Ki. 9.26-28; 22.48,49; 2 Ch. 20.36.

SHISHAK, king of Egypt, spoken of, 1 Ki. 14.25,26.

SHITTIM wood. See *Temple*.

SHOE, taken off, Ex. 3.5; De. 25.9. See *Redemption of Land*.

SHOUTING, Jos. 6.5; 1 Sa. 4.5; 2 Sa. 6.15; Ps. 47.1.

SHUNEM, a city of Issachar, Jos. 19. 17,18; mentioned in history, 1 Sa. 28.4; 2 Ki. 4. See *Abishag*.

SHUSHAN, the ancient capital of Persia, Ne. 1.1; Es. 2.8; 3.15; 8.15; Da. 8.2.

SICK, to be visited, 2 Ki. 8.29; Job 2.11; Mat. 25.36; Ja. 5.4.

SICKLE, natural, mentioned De. 16. 9; 23.25; spiritual, Joel 3.13; Re. 14.14-17; 18.19.

SICKNESS, why permitted, De. 28. 22; Job 5.17; Ps. 94.12; how to behave under it, 2 Ki. 20; Ja. 5.14. See *Afflictions*.

SIDON, historically spoken of, Ge. 10.15,19; Mar. 3.8; 7.31; Lu. 4.26; Ac. 12.20; 27.3; its destruction foretold, Eze. 28.20-22.

SIGNS, requested or given, Ge. 9.13; 15.8; 24.14,15; Ex. 3.12; 4.8,9,17; 28; Jos. 2.12-18; Ju. 6.36-40; 1 Sa. 10.2; 14.8-12; 1 Ki. 13.3; 2 Ki. 20. 8-11; Is. 7.14; Mat. 12.38-40; 16.1-4; Mar. 8.11; Lu. 11.16; Jno. 2.18, 19; 6.30.

SMYR

SIHON, king of the Amorites, conquered, Nu. 21.21-31; De. 2.26-37; Ps. 105.11; 136.19.

SILAS, or Silvanus, a fellow-preacher with Paul, his history, Ac. 15.22-41; 16.20-40; 17.1-15; 2 Co. 1.19; 1 Th. 1.1; 2 Th. 1.1; 1 Pe. 5.12.

SILENCE, sometimes proper, Ps. 39; Pr. 11.12; 17.28; 26.4; 1 Ti. 2.11; Ja. 1.19; in heaven, Re. 8.1.

SILOAM. See *Bethesda*.

SILVER, Ex. 26.19; Nu. 7.13; as money, Ge. 23.15; 44.2.

SIMEON, one of the twelve patriarchs, his history, Ge. 29.33; 34; 35.23; 42.24; 43.23; 46.10; his blessing, Ge. 49.5-7; his descendants, Ex. 6. 15; Nu. 1.22,23; 26.12-14; 1 Ch. 4. 24-27; 12.25; their inheritance, Jos. 13.1-9.

SIMEON, a good old man who was waiting for the Saviour, Lu. 2.25-35.

SIMILITUDE. See *Figures*.

SIMON, the brother of Jesus, Mat. 13.55; Mar. 6.3.

SIMON, the Canaanite, called Zelotes, an apostle, Mat. 10.4; Mar. 3.18; Lu. 6.15.

SIMON, surnamed Peter. See *Peter*.

SIMON, the Pharisee, Lu. 7.36-50.

SIMON, the leper, Mat. 26.7; Mar. 14.3.

SIMON, the father of Judas Iscariot, Jno. 6.71; 12.4.

SIMON, the Cyrenian, Mat. 27.32; Mar. 15.21; Lu. 23.26.

SIMON, the tanner, Ac. 9.43; 10.6,17 32.

SIMON, Magus, Ac. 8.9-24.

SIMPLICITY, signifying meekness, Ps. 19.7; 116.6; ignorance, Pr. 1.22; 7.7; 9.4; Ro. 16.18; folly, Pr. 1.32.

SIN, lawlessness, Jno. 15.22; Ro. 3.20; 4.15; 1 Co. 15.56; Ja. 1.15; 1 Jno. 3.4; 5.17; incident to all men, 1 Ki. 8.46; Job 15.14; 25.4; Ps. 130.3; Pr. 20.9; 24.16; Ec. 7.20; Ja. 3.2; 1 Jno. 1.8; comes from the heart, Mat. 15.19; Ja. 1.14; presumptuous, the danger of it, Nu. 15.30; Ps. 19. 13; Lu. 12.47; Ro. 1.32; He. 10.26; against the HOLY SPIRIT, unpardonable, Ex. 23.21; Mat. 12.31,32; Mar. 3.28,29; Lu. 12.10; He. 10.29; 1 Jno. 5.16; national, Is. 1.24; 30.1; Je. 5.9; 6.27; Mat. 23.35; 27.25.

SINAI. See *Mountains*.

SINCERITY required, Jos. 24.14; 1 Sa. 12.24; 16.7; 1 Ch. 28.9; 29.17; Ps. 32.2; 73.1; Mat. 5.8; Ro. 12.9; Ph. 1.10; Col. 3.22.

SINGING in Divine worship, 1 Ch. 6. 32; 13.8; Ne. 12.28; Mat. 26.30; Ac. 16.25; recommended, Ps. 95.1; 96.1; 98; 100; 1 Co. 14.15; Ep. 5. 19; Col. 3.16; Ja. 5.13.

SISERA, account of, Ju. 4; 5.

SLANDER, censured, Ex. 23.1; De. 22.19; Ps. 15.3; 50.19,20; 64.3,4; 101.5; Pr. 10.18; Ro. 1.29.30; 2 Co. 12.20; Tit. 3.2; Ja. 4.11; how to be borne, Mat. 5.11; 1 Co. 4.12, 13.

SLAVE. See *Servants*.

SLEEP, not to be indulged in too much, Pr. 6.4,9; 20.13; 23.21; 34. 33; 1 Th. 5.6.

SLING, an ancient weapon, Ju. 20.16; 1 Sa. 17.40-49; 2 Ki. 3.25; 2 Ch. 26.14.

SLOW to speak, Ja. 1.19.

SLUGGARD, described, Pr. 6.6-11; 10.26; 13.4; 20.4; 26.16.

SMYRNA, Christ's message to the church there, Re. 2.8-11.

225

SO

SO, *king of Egypt*, spoken of, 2 Ki. 17.4.

SOBRIETY of mind and body recommended, 1 Th. 5.8; Tit. 2.2,4,6; 1 Pe. 1.13; 4 7; 5.8.

SODOM, destroyed, Ge. 19; the vileness of the inhabitants continued, 1 Ki. 14.24; 22.46; their sin denounced, La. 18.22; 20.13; De. 23. 17; Ro. 1.27; 1 Co. 6.9; 1 Ti. 1.10.

SOLDIERS, their duty, Lu. 3.14.

SOLITUDE, often desirable, Mat. 6.6; 14.23; Mar. 1.35; Lu. 5.16; 9.28.

SOLOMON, *king of all Israel*, his history, 2 Sa. 5.14; 12.24; 1 Ki. 1; 2; 3; 4; 5; 6; 7.1,51; 8; 9; 10; 11; 1 Ch. 22; 28; 29; 2 Ch. 1; 2; 3; 4; 5; 6; 7; 8; 9; his writings, the Books of Proverbs, Ecclesiastes, and Canticles.

SON. See *Children*.

SONS of GOD. See *Adoption*.

SONSHIP, Jno. 1.12,13; Ro. 8.14-17; **Gal.** 4.4-7; Heb. 2.11; 1 Jno. 3.1,2; **Ep.** 1.4,5; 1 Jno. 3.9,10.

SONGS, in time of rejoicing, Ge. 31. 27; Ex. 26.13; instances, Ex. 15.1-21; Nu. 21.17,18; De. 32.1-45; Ju. 5; 1 Sa. 2.1-10; 2 Sa. 22; Lu. 1.46-55,68-80; 2.13,29; Re. 5.9,19.

SORCERY, Is. 47.9; Ac. 8.9; Re. 21.8.

SORROW, just causes of it, 2 Sa. 12. 13; 1 Ki. 21.27; Ps. 119.136,158; **Mat.** 26.75; Ph. 2.27; good effects of it, Ps. 34.18; 51.17; 126.6; Ec. 7.3; Is. 57.15; Mat. 5.4; 2 Co. 7. 10; Ja. 4.10; bad effects of it, Pr. 12.25; 15.13,15; 17.22.

SOSTHENES, *an early convert*, Ac. 18.17; 1 Co. 1.1.

SOUL, Ge. 2.7; signifying person, Ge. 12.5,13; De. 13.6; Ps. 40.14; 94.17, 21; Pr. 11.25; 27.7; Ro. 2.9; 13.1; for the affections or feelings, Ge. 34. 8; 1 Sa. 18.1; Job 3.20; Pr. 13.19; the vital principle, Job 12.10; Ps. 107.5; Ec. 12.7; La. 1.11; Mat. 10. 28; 1 Th. 5.23; He. 4.12; 10.39; exists in a separate state, Ec. 3.21; Mat. 22.32; Lu. 16.22; 23.43; Ph. 1.23; worth of the, Mat. 16.26.

SOUR grapes, Je. 31.29; Ez. 18.2.

SOUTH, king of, Da. 11; queen, Mat. 12.42.

SOW and REAP. See *Figures*.

SPAIN, spoken of, Ro. 15.24,28.

SPEAR, *an ancient weapon*, Jos. 8.18; 1 Sa. 17.7; 26.7; 2 Ch. 11.12; Jno. 19.34.

SPEECH, rules for the proper government of it, Pr. 4.24; 10.10,19; 15.4; 17.20; 18.6,7,13,21; Ec. 10.12,13; **Mat.** 5.22; 12.36; Ep. 4.29; 5.4; **Col.** 3.6; 4.6; 1 Th. 5.11; Tit. 3.2; **Ja.** 1.26; 3.2; 1 Pe. 3.10; the benefit of it when seasonable, Pr. 12.25; 15.23; 16.24; 25.11,15.

SPICES, used in the tabernacle worship, Ex. 30.34-38; in perfuming the person, Ex. 2.12; Ps. 45.8; Pr. 7.17; in burying the dead, 2 Ch. 16. 14; Mar. 16.1; Lu. 23.56; Jno. 19. 40.

SPIES sent to view the land of Canaan, their account, Nu. 13; 14; De. 1.22-46; Jos. 2.

SPIKENARD, *a perfume*, Ca. 1.12; 4. 14; Mar. 14.3-9; Jno. 12.3-7.

SPIRIT of GOD. See HOLY SPIRIT.

SPIRIT of Christ, Ro. 8.9; of antichrist, 1 Jno. 4.3; of truth, Jno. 14.17; 15.26; of bondage, Ro. 8.15.

SPIRITS, signifying pretenders, to be tried, Mat. 7.15; 1 Jno. 4.1; Re. 2. 2; in prison, 1 Pe. 3.19.

SWIN

SPIRITUAL body, 1 Co. 15.44; Ph. 3.21; 1 Jno. 3.2.

SPIRITUAL gifts. See HOLY SPIRIT.

SPRINKLING of blood, Ex. 12.22; He. 11.28; of the blood of Christ, He. 10.22; 12.24; 1 Pe. 1.2.

STABILITY recommended, Ps. 17.3-5; Pr. 24.21; Mar. 13.13; 1 Co. 15. 58; Ep. 4.14; 1 Th. 5.21; He. 10. 23; 13.9; Ja. 1.6.

STAR in the east, Mat. 2.2; morning, Re. 22.16.

STEALING, forbidden, Ex. 20.15; Le. 19.11; Ps. 50.18; Zec. 5.4; Mat. 15.19; 1 Co. 6.10; Ep. 4.28; 1 Pe. 4.15.

STEPHEN, *the deacon*, his history, Ac. 6; 7.

STEWARD, in earthly things, Ge. 15. 2; 24; 43; 44; Lu. 8.3; in spiritual, 1 Co. 4.1,2; Tit. 1.7; 1 Pe. 4.10.

STOCKS, Job 13.27; 33.11; Pr. 7.22; Je. 20.2; Ac. 16.24.

STOICS, Ac. 17.18.

STONE, corner, Ps. 118.22; Mat. 21. 42; 1 Pe. 2.6.

STONES, precious. See *Jewels*.

STONING, *a capital punishment* among the Jews, Le. 20.2,27; 24.14, 16,23; Nu. 15.32-36; De. 13.1-11; 22.21,24; Jos. 7.25; 1 Ki. 21.13; Ac. 7.58; 14.19.

STRENGTH and stature. See *Giants*.

STRIFE. See *Quarrels*.

STRIPES, De. 25.3; 2 Co. 11.24.

STUDY, Ec. 12.12.

STUMBLING-BLOCK, Is. 8.14; Ro. 9.32; 1 Co. 1.23; 8.9; 1 Pe. 2.8.

SUBMISSION to the will of GOD. See *Resignation*.

SUCCOTH, *a city of Canaan*, Ge. 33. 17; Jos. 13.27; Ju. 8.5-16; 1 Ki. 7. 46; Ps. 60.6.

SUCCOTH, *in Egypt*, Ex. 12.37; 12. 30.

SUFFERINGS, how to be borne, exemplified by the Apostles, Ac. 5. 40; 9.16; 13.50,51; 14.19,20; 16.23-25; 20.24; 21.13; 1 Co. 4.12; 2 Co. 1.4; 4.8-18; 6.4,5; 11.23-33; Ph. 1. 29,30; 1 Ti. 4.10; 1 Pe. 2.19; 3.14; 4.12-19; Re. 12.11.

SUFFERINGS of CHRIST, Is. 53; Mat. 2.13-15; 8.20; 11.19; 26.56,67; 27.27-35,46; Mar. 14.34-36,65; 15. 19-24; Lu. 22.41-44; 23.33; Jno. 12. 27; 18.22,23; 19.1-18; 1 Pe. 2.21-24.

SUN, Ge. 1.14; not to be worshipped, De. 4.19; 17.3; Job 31.26,27; Eze. 8.16,18; miraculous events connected with it, Jos. 10.12,13; 2 Ki. 20.9-11; Lu. 23.44,45; Ac. 26.13,14; of righteousness, Mal. 4.2.

SUPERSTITION, censured, Ec. 11.4; Je. 10.2; Jon. 2.8; Gal. 4.10.

SUPPER, natural, spoken of, Mar. 6. 21; Lu. 14.12; Jno. 12.2; spiritual or symbolical, Re. 19.9,17. See *Parables*. See *Lord's Supper*.

SUPPLICATION. See *Prayer* and *Intercession*.

SURETYSHIP, the danger of it, Pr. 6.1-5; 11.15; 17.18; 20.16; 27.13.

SUSANNA, honourably mentioned, Lu. 8.3.

SWALLOW, Ps. 84.3; Pr. 26.2; Is. 38. 14; Je. 8.7.

SWEARING, forbidden, Mat. 5.34-37; Ja. 5.12.

SWINE, forbidden to the Jews for food, De. 14.8; Is. 65.3,4; their destruction, Mat. 8.30-32; Mar. 5. 11-13; Lu. 8.32,33; typical, Mat. 7. 6; 2 Pe. 2.22.

TEMP

SWORD of the Lord, Ge. 3.24; Ju. 7. 18; Ps. 45.3; Is. 66.16; Je. 12.12; Ez. 21.4; Zeph. 2.12.

SYCAMORE, or Sycamine tree, bearing *a kind of fig*, mentioned 1 Ki. 10.27; 1 Ch. 27.28; Ps. 78.47; Lu. 19.4.

SYMPATHY, recommended, Ec. 7.2, 4; Ro. 12.15; 1 Co. 12.26; Ga. 6.2; He. 13.3; 1 Pe. 3.8; CHRIST our example, Mat. 25.40; He. 4.15.

SYNAGOGUES, *places of worship among the Jews*, mentioned Ps. 74.8; Mat. 4.23; 6.2,5; 10.17; 12.9; 13. 54; 23.1-7; Lu. 4.16; Jno. 6.59; Ac. 13.5; 18.4.

SYRACUSE, *in Sicily*, mentioned Ac. 28.12.

SYRIA, historically mentioned, 2 Sa. 8; 2 Ki. 5; 6; 7; 8; 13; 16; Is. 7; Ez. 27.16-18; Mat. 4.24; Lu. 2.2; Ac. 15.23,41; 18.18; 21.3; Ga. 1. 21; prophetically, Am. 1.5.

SYRO-PHŒNICIAN woman, account of, Mar. 7.25-33.

TABERAH, the Israelites sojourn there, Nu. 11.1-3; Ps. 78.21.

TABERNACLE ordered to be built, and described, Ex. 25; 26; 27; 36; 37; 38; preparations for it, Ex. 35; set up, Ex. 40.

TABERNACLES, feast of. See *Festivals*.

TABITHA. See *Dorcas*.

TABLES of stone. See *Commandments*.

TABOR. See *Mountains*.

TABRET, Ge. 31.27; 1 Sa. 18.6.

TADMOR, *now Palmyra*, its history, 1 Ki. 9.17,18; 2 Ch. 8.4.

TALE-BEARING, censured, Le. 19. 16; Pr. 11.13; 17.9; 18.8; 20.19; 26.20,22; 1 Ti. 5.13; 1 Pe. 4.15. See *Busy-bodies*.

TAMAR, *daughter-in-law of Judah*, Ge. 38.

TAMAR, *the daughter of David*, 2 Sa. 13.

TAPESTRY, spoken of, Pr. 7.16; 31. 22.

TARES. See *Parable*.

TARGET. See *Shield*.

TARSHISH, or Tarsus, *chief city of Cilicia*, mentioned in history, Jno. 1.3; 4.2; Ac. 9.11; 11.25; 21.39; 22.3.

TARSHISH, *son of Javan*, Ge. 10.4; 1 Ch. 1.7.

TATNAI, account of, Ezra 5; 6.

TEACHERS, false, their character described, and Christians warned against them, Ro. 16.17; 2 Co. 11. 13; Ga. 1. 7-9; Ph. 3.2; Col. 2.8, 18; 1 Ti. 1.7; 4.2; 6.3; 2 Ti. 3.2-5, 13; Heb. 13.9; 2 Pe. 2.

TEACHING of the HOLY SPIRIT, described, Job 40.4,5; Ps. 119.18-20; Is. 6.5; 2 Co. 3.18; Ja. 1 22-25.

TEARS. See *Afflictions*.

TEKOA, widow of, 2 Sa. 14.

TEMAN, *grandson of Esau*, Ge. 36.11, 15,16; 1 Ch. 1.53; inheritance, Je. 49.20; Ez. 25.13; Am. 1.12.

TEMPERANCE, recommended, Pr. 23.1-3; Ga. 5.23; Ep. 5.18; Tit. 1. 8; 2.2; 2 Pe. 1.6.

TEMPLE, the materials prepared by David, 1 Ch. 28.29; built by Solomon, 1 Ki. 6; 7; the dedication of it, 8; repaired by Joash, 2 Ki. 12; by Hezekiah, 2 Ch. 29; by Josiah, 2 Ch. 34; burned by the Chaldeans, 2 Ki. 25.9; 2 Ch. 36.19; a new one built after the captivity, Ezra 3; 5;

INTRODUCTION

GREEK OF THE NEW TESTAMENT.

A. THE GREEK CHARACTERS.

1. The **Alphabet** consists of twenty-four letters, seven being vowels and seventeen consonants.

A α (Alpha)	= a	N ν (Nu) = n
B β (Beta)	= b	Ξ ξ (Xi) = x
Γ γ (Gamma)	= g	O o (Omikron) = ŏ
Δ δ (Delta)	= d	Π π (Pi) = p
E ε (Epsilon)	= ĕ	P ρ (Rho) = r
Z ζ (Zeta)	= z	Σ σς (Sigma) = s
H η (Eta)	= ē	T τ (Tau) = t
Θ θ (Theta)	= th	Y υ (Upsilon) = u
I ι (Iota)	= i	Φ φ (Phi) = ph
K κ (Kappa)	= k	X χ (Chi) = ch
Λ λ (Lambda)	= l	Ψ ψ (Psi) = ps
M μ (Mu)	= m	Ω ω (Omega) = ō

2. **Sounds of Vowels and Diphthongs.** — The prevailing vowel sounds in Greek are *a, e, o,* and the language abounds in diphthongs. α = *a* in *bat, bar;* ε = *e* in *the, then;* η = *ey* in *they;* ι = *i* and *ee;* o = *o* in *not;* υ = *u* in French; ω = *ow* in *own;* αι = *aye;* αυ = *ow* in *how;* ει = *ei* in *height;* ευ = *ew* in *few;* οι = *oi* in *foil;* ου = *oo* in *foot;* υι = *we* in *we.*

Note. — Of consonants, γ is hard, as in *get,* and = *ng* before κ, γ, χ or ξ; ζ = *ds;* χ = *ch* in German.

3. **Quantity of Vowels.** — ε and o are short, η and ω long; α, ι, υ vary.

Note. — When η or ω forms a diphthong with ι, the ι is subscribed: thus, ῃ, ῳ.

4. **Contractions of Vowels.** — These take place in connection with terminal changes in nouns, adjectives, and verbs. (*a.*) α before α, ε or η contracts into α; before o, ω, into ω. (*b.*) ε before α contracts into α or η; before ε, into ει; before o, into ου; before a long vowel or diphthong is absorbed. (*c.*) o before α and a long vowel contracts into ω; before ε and o, into ου; before a diphthong is absorbed.

5. **Consonants and their Combinations.** — The Consonants are divided into Mutes, Liquids, and Sibilants. (*a.*) The Mutes are the Labials π, β, φ; the Gutturals κ, γ, χ; the Dentals τ, δ, θ, in the order severally of *smooth, middle* and *aspirate.* (*b.*) The Liquids are λ, μ, ν, ρ. (*c.*) The Sibilants are σ, ζ, ξ, ψ.

Note. — π, β, φ with ς become ψ; κ, γ, χ with ς become ξ; and τ, δ, θ (and ντ) with ς become σ; to which components, therefore, ψ, ξ, and σ can be resolved back. Before μ, π, β, φ become μ; κ, γ, χ become γ, and τ, δ, θ become σ; ν becomes μ before π, β, φ; γ before κ, γ, χ, and is assimilated before liquids. π becomes φ and κ becomes χ before a rough breathing. Two successive syllables cannot begin with an aspirate. If two mutes combine, the latter is always a dental. When two mutes come together, smooth combines with smooth, middle with middle, and aspirate with aspirate.

6. **Breathings.** — There are two, a soft (᾿), not sounded, and a rough (῾) = *h*. Every initial vowel and diphthong has one or other; υ always the rough, as also ρ: thus, ὕλη, ῥόδον. Double ρ has both: thus, Πύρρος.

7. **Accents.** — There are three, the acute (´), the grave (`), and the circumflex (῀). This last frequently indicates contraction.

8. **Punctuation.** — The punctuation marks are comma (,), semicolon (·), period (.), interrogation (;).

Note. — A diaeresis (¨) indicates the separation of two vowels; an apostrophe (᾿) the elision of one.

B. THE PARTS OF SPEECH AND THEIR INFLEXIONS.

Inflexion. — The Article, the Noun, the Adjective, and the Pronoun inflect, *i.e.,* undergo changes in the final syllable, to express number, gender, and case. Verbs also inflect to express person, number, tense, mood, and voice; inflexion in the former being called *Declension,* and in the latter *Conjugation.* Thus a noun is said to be declined, and a verb conjugated. The extent to which the verb suffers inflexion contributes greatly to the expressiveness of the language.

Genders and Numbers. — The same as in English, only there is in Classic Greek, though not in the New Testament, a dual number to express two or a pair.

Note. — In the inflexions given below the dual is therefore omitted.

Cases. — These are developed by inflexion, where we use prepositions, and are five in number. Nominative (*N.*), the case of the subject; Genitive (*G.*), expressed by *of* or *from;* Dative (*D.*), expressed by *to* or *for;* Accusative (*A.*) = Objective; Vocative (*V.*) = Nominative of address, usually the same as the Nominative.

I. The Article. — 1. *The Definite* = the, is thus declined :—

	Mas.	Fem.	Neut.		Mas.	Fem.	Neut.
Sing. N.	ὁ,	ἡ,	τό.	*Pl. N.*	οἱ,	αἱ,	τά.
G.	τοῦ,	τῆς,	τοῦ.	*G.*	τῶν,	τῶν,	τῶν.
D.	τῷ,	τῇ,	τῷ.	*D.*	τοῖς,	ταῖς,	τοῖς.
A.	τόν,	τήν,	τό.	*A.*	τούς,	τάς,	τά.

2. *The Indefinite,* τις, *any* = *a,* is thus declined :—

	M. & F.	Neut.		M. & F.	Neut.
Sing. N.	τις,	τι.	*Pl. N.*	τινες,	τινα.
G.	τινος,	τινος.	*G.*	τινων,	τινων.
D.	τινι,	τινι.	*D.*	τισι,	τισι.
A.	τινα,	τι.	*A.*	τινα,	τινα.

Note. — These are types of the declension of all nouns, adjectives, and pronouns. As in them, the dat. sing. ends always in ι, the gen. pl. in ων; and the acc. neut. is like the nom. neut., which in the plur. always ends in α.

II. Nouns. — Nouns are declined in three different ways, called respectively 1st, 2nd, and 3rd Declensions, the type of the first being the fem. of ὁ; of the second, the mas. and neut. of ὁ; and of the third, τις. The 1st and 2nd inflect by altering, and the 3rd by adding to, the final syllable.

1. *The First Declension.* — Nouns in this declension end in η or α (fem.), ης or ας (mas.), and decline thus :—

Those in η, N. τιμή, *honour*; G. τιμῆς; D. τιμῇ, &c., like ἡ exactly.

Those in a, after a consonant, δόξ-α, *glory*, -ης, -ῃ, -αν, &c.; after a vowel and ρ, σκι-ά, *a shadow*, -ᾶς, -ᾷ, -αν, &c.

Those in ης and ας follow the same rules, only they have οὗ in G. and α in V.; as, N. μαθητ-ής, *a disciple*; G. -οῦ; D. -ῇ, &c.

2. *The Second Declension.*—Nouns in this declension end in ος (mas. or fem.) and ον (neut.), and decline thus:—

Those in ος: N. λόγος, *a word*; G. λόγου; D. λόγῳ, &c., like ὁ.

Those in ον: N. δῶρον, *a gift*; G. δώρου; D. δώρῳ, &c., like τό.

Note 1.—ο and ε preceding ος or ον contract by rules A. 4.

Note 2.—A few nouns in this declension end in ως and ων, and substitute ω for ο throughout.

3. *The Third Declension.*—Nouns in this declension have various terminations, and are of all genders. The norm of their declension is given in τις, viz., G. sing. ος, D. ι, A. a or ν, N. plur. ες, G. ων, D. σι, A. ας or α. The stem, or part of the word to which the case-endings are appended, is obtained from the gen. by dropping the ος; and the nom. is formed from it (a) by adding ς if it end in a mute: thus, G. λαίλαπ-ος, λαιλαπ, N. λαίλαψ, *a storm*; G. παιδ-ός, παιδ, N. παῖς, *a boy*; G. γίγαντ-ος, γιγαντ, N. γίγᾱς, *a giant*; (b) by lengthening the vowel before ν or ρ: thus, G. ποιμέν-ος, ποιμεν, N. ποιμήν, *a shepherd*; G. ῥήτορ-ος, ῥητορ, N. ῥήτωρ, *an orator*; (c) by dropping τ as well as ος: thus, G. σῶμ-ατ-ος, σωματ, N. σῶμα, *a body*, because the language admits of no final consonant except either ν, ρ, or ς.

Contractions are frequent in the inflected parts. (a) Nouns with nom. in ης, ος, ω, and ως contract in all the cases except N. and V. sing. (b) Those in ις, ι, υς, υ, besides having generally ε for ι or υ in all the oblique cases, contract in D. sing. and N. and A. pl. (c) Those in ευς contract similarly. (d) Those in N. ας, G. ατος, drop the τ and contract.

Note.—" Oblique " is applied to all cases except the nom., which is not properly a case.

III. Adjectives.—1. *Adjectives in the positive* decline like nouns, and, like the art., they have each three genders. They are of three classes— (1) those which decline like the article; (2) those with the mas. and neut. after the 3rd declension, and the fem. after the 1st; (3) those all after the 2nd declension or after the 3rd.

First Class.—To this belong such as σοφ-ός, -ή, -όν, *wise*, and ἅγι-ος, -α, -ον, *holy*. To it also may be referred N. μέγ-ης, ἀλή, -α, G. μεγάλου, -άλης, -άλου, *great*; and N. πολ-ύς, -λή, -ν, G. πολλ-οῦ, -ῆς, -οῦ, *much*.

Second Class.—To this belong such as N. εὐθ-ύς, -εῖα, -ύ, G. εὐθ-έος, -είας, -έος, *straight*; N. μέλ-ας, -αινα, -αν, G. μέλ-ανος, -αίνη, -ανος, *black*; N. ἑκ-ών, -οῦσα, -όν, G. ἑκ-όντος, -ούσης, -όντος, *willing*; N. π-ᾶς, -ᾶσα, -ᾶν, G. π-αντός, -άσης, -αντός, *all*.

Third Class.—To this belong such as N. αἰώνι-ος, -ος, -ον, G. αἰώνι-ου, -ου, -ου, *eternal*; N. ἀληθ-ής, -ής, -ές, G. ἀληθ-οῦς, -οῦς, -οῦς (contracted from εος), *true*; N. μείζ-ων, -ων, -ον, G. μείζ-ονος, -ονος, -ονος, *greater*, and all comparatives in ων.

2. *Comparison of Adjectives.*—Adjectives of the first class are compared by dropping ς and adding τερ-ος, -α, -ον, for the comparative, and τατ-ος, -η, -ον, for the superlative: thus, μικρός, *little*, μικρο, μικρό-τερος, -τατος. The ο becomes ω if the previous syllable is short: thus, σοφός, *wise*, σοφω, σοφώ-τερος, -τατος. Those of the second class generally add τερος and τατος to the neut., sometimes εστερος and εστατος.

Adjectives such as ἡδύς, *sweet*, take ιων, ιστος.

To this class belong ταχ-ύς, *swift*, which has θάσσων, τάχιστος; καλός, *beautiful*, καλλίων, κάλλιστος; and μέγας, *great*, μείζων, μέγιστος.

Certain are irregular, as ἀγαθός, *good*, βελτίων, βέλτιστος, also κρείσσων, κράτιστος; κακός, *bad*, κακίων, κάκιστος, also χείρων, χείριστος; μικρός, *little*, ἐλάσσων, ἐλάχιστος; and πόλυς, *much*, πλείων, πλεῖστος.

3. *Numerals.*—These consist of (a) cardinals, of which from one to three are declined, and from 200 onward; and (b) ordinals, all of which are declined like adjectives of the first class.

(a) The elementary cardinal numbers are—

1 εἷς, μία, ἕν.	9 ἐννέα.
2 δύο.	10 δέκα.
3 τρεῖς, τρία.	20 εἴκοσι.
4 τέσσαρες (ττ).	30 τριάκοντα.
5 πέντε.	100 ἑκατόν.
6 ἕξ.	200 διακόσιοι
7 ἑπτά.	1,000 χίλιοι.
8 ὀκτώ.	10,000 μύριοι.

εἷς is of the 1st and 3rd declension. N. εἷς, μία, ἕν; G. ἑνός, μιᾶς, ἑνός, &c.

Note.—οὐδ-είς (-εμία, -έν) and μηδ-είς (-εμία, -έν), *none*, are declined like εἷς.

(b) The elementary ordinal numbers are—

πρῶτος, first.	ἕκτος, sixth.
δεύτερος, second.	ἕβδομος, seventh.
τρίτος, third.	ὄγδοος, eighth.
τέταρτος, fourth.	ἔννατος, ninth.
πέμπτος, fifth.	δέκατος, tenth.

IV. Pronouns.—There are eight classes of pronouns.

1. *Personal.*—1st Sing. N. ἐγώ, *I*; G. ἐμοῦ, μοῦ; D. ἐμοί, μοί; A. ἐμέ, με. Pl. N. ἡμεῖς; G. ἡμῶν; D. ἡμῖν; A. ἡμᾶς.

2nd Sing. N. σύ, *thou*; G. σοῦ; D. σοί; A. σέ. Pl. N. ὑμεῖς, &c., as ἡμεῖς.

3rd Sing. N. αὐτός, αὐτή, αὐτό, *he, she, it*, declined like the article.

Note.—αὐτός attached to a noun = *himself, herself*, &c.; with the art. prefixed = *the same*.

2. *Reflexive.*—Reflexive pronouns can occur only in the oblique cases, and are formed in the first person of ἐμ-, in the second of σε-, in the third of ἑ-, with the oblique cases of αὐτος affixed: thus, G. ἐμαυτ-οῦ, -ῆς, -οῦ; σεαυτ-οῦ, -ῆς, -οῦ; ἑαυτοῦ (or αὑτοῦ), -ῆς, -οῦ, &c.

The plural is formed of the oblique cases plural of the personals, αὐτὸς being joined therewith in agreement.

3. *Possessive.*—ἐμὸς, *my*; σὸς, *thy*; ἡμέτερος, *our*; ὑμέτερος, *your*; declined like adjectives of the first class.

Note.—For the possessive of the 3rd pers. the gen. of the 3rd personal or the 3rd reflexive is used.

4. *Demonstrative.*—(a.) N. ὅδε, ἥδε, τόδε, *this* (here); being the Art. with δε undeclinable.

(b.) N. οὗτος, αὕτη, τοῦτο, *this* (near); G. τούτου, ταύτης, τούτου, &c.; Pl. N. οὗτοι, αὗται, ταῦτα; G. τούτων, τούτων, τούτων, &c.

(c.) ἐκεῖν-ος, -η, -ο, *that*, declined like the Art.

Note.—τοιοῦτος, *such*; οἷος, *as* = its relative; τοσοῦτος, *so great*; ὅσος, *as* = its relative; τοσοῦτοι, *so many*; ὅσοι, *as* = its relative; τηλικοῦτος, *so great in size*; are compounds of οὗτος.

5. *Relative.*—ὅς, ἥ, ὅ, *who* or *which*, is declined like the Art., the stem being ὁ, whereas that of the Art. is το, and the rough breathing (ʹ) taking the place of τ throughout (see *Note* above).

6. *Interrogative.*—τίς, τίς, τί, *who?* or *what?* (see The Article).

ποῖος, *of what kind?* πόσος, *how much?* πόσοι, *how many?* πηλίκος, *how great?*

7. *Indefinite.*—τις, τις, τι (unaccented), *any* (see The Article).

ὅστις, *whoever, whatever,* is a compound of ὅς and τις, which are declined conjointly. *G.* sometimes ὅτου. Other compounds of τις are οὔτις and μήτις, *no one.*

ὁ δεῖνα, *such a one,* occurs in Matt. xxvi. 18.

8. *Distributive.*—ἀλλ-ος, -η, -ο, *another;* ἕτερ-ος, -α, -ον, *other;* and ἕκαστ-ος, -η, -ον, *each;* all declined like the art. or adj. of first class. ἀλλήλων, *of each other,* is used only in G. D. and A. pl.

V. The Verb.—1. *Voices.*—Verbs have three Voices—Active, Middle, and Passive. The Active and the Middle may be either transitive or intransitive, although the Middle is properly the form which the verb assumes when the action affects the agent; thus Act. φαίνω, *I show;* Mid. φαίνομαι, *I show myself,* i.e., *I appear.*

2. *Moods.*—There are five Moods: the Indicative, which asserts simply; the Subjunctive (or Conjunctive), which asserts conditionally; the Optative, which expresses a wish; the Imperative, which commands; the Infinitive, which names the action, and = to a verbal noun. Besides these there are Participles attached to all the tenses, = verbal adjectives.

3. *Tenses.*—There are six Tenses: three Principal—Present, Future, and Perfect; and three Historical — Imperfect, Aorist, and Pluperfect. There are two forms of the Perfect, as also of the Aorist, a First and a Second.

4. *Conjugations* or *Modes of Inflexion.*—There are two: the First in ω, the Second in μι.

5. *Augment.*—This is either ἐ prefixed to the past ind. of a verb when it begins with a consonant, called the Syllabic augment, as τύπτω, imperf. ind. ἔτυπτον; or it is a lengthening of its initial vowel, called the Temporal, as ἄγω, imperf. ind. ἦγον.

Note.—The augment in compound verbs is prefixed to the roots, as προσ-βάλλω, προσ-έβαλλον, and sometimes the vowel of the prefix is either dropped before it or contracted with it. If the root begins with ρ the ρ is doubled, thus, ῥίπτω, ἔῤῥιπτον.

6. *Reduplication.*—This occurs in the perfect tenses, through all the moods, and consists in prefixing the initial consonant with ε: thus, τύπτω, perf. τετύφα.

Note.—If the verb begins with a vowel, the vowel is merely lengthened; and if the initial consonant is an aspirate it is changed into its smooth. Verbs beginning with σ do not reduplicate.

7. *Personal Endings.*—These are modified forms of fragments of personal pronouns.

As the Article served and was given as model of the declension of nouns, so εἰμί, *to be,* is here given as model of the conjugation of verbs.[1]

PRES. IND., *I am*

Singular.			*Plural.*		
1st Pers.	2d Pers.	3d Pers.	1st Pers.	2d Pers.	3d Pers.
εἰμί,	εἶ,	ἐστί.	ἐσμέν,	ἐστέ,	εἰσί(ν).

PRES. SUB., *I may be.*

| ὦ, | ἦς, | ἦ | ὦμεν, | ἦτε, | ὦσι(ν). |

PRES. OPT., *I might be.*

| εἴ-ην, | -ης, | -η. | -ημεν, | -ητε, | -ησαν. |

IMP., *Be thou.*

| —— | ἴσθι, | ἔστω. | —— | ἔστε, | ἔστωσαν. |

PRES. INF., εἶναι, *to be.*

PRES. PART., ὤν, οὖσα, ὄν, *being.*

IMPERF. IND., *I was.*

| ἦν, | ἦσθα, | ἦν. | ἦμεν, | ἦτε, | ἦσαν. |

---

1 See the "Practical Guide to the Greek Testament," pp. 17-24. Bagster, London.

FUT. IND., *I shall be.*

| ἔσ-ομαι, | -η, | -ται. | -όμεθα, | -εσθε, | -ονται. |

FUT. INF., ἔσεσθαι, *to be about to be.*

FUT. PART., ἐσόμενος, *about to be.*

A. FIRST CONJUGATION—ACTIVE VOICE—τύπτω, *I strike.*

PRES. IND., *I strike.*

Singular.			*Plural.*		
1st Pers.	2d Pers.	3d Pers.	1st Pers.	2d Pers.	3d Pers.
τυπτ-ω,	-εις,	-ει.	-ομεν,	-ετε,	-ουσι(ν).

PRES. SUBJ., *I may strike.*

| τύπτ-ω, | -ης, | -η. | -ωμεν, | -ητε, | -ωσι(ν) |

PRES. OPT., *I might strike.*

| τύπτ-οιμι, | -οις, | -οι. | -οιμεν, | -οιτε, | -οιεν. |

PRES. IMP., *Strike thou.*

| —— | τύπτ-ε, | -ετω. | —— | -ετε, | -ετωσαν. |

PRES. INF., τύπτ-ειν, *to strike.*

PRES. PART., τύπτ-ων, -ουσα, -ον, *striking.*

Note.—The Subjunctive merely lengthens the vowel of the Indicative. The Optative shows a preference for diphthongs.

IMPERF. IND., *I was striking.*

| ἔτυπτ-ον, | -ες, | -ε. | -ομεν, | -ετε, | -ον. |

FUT. IND., τύψω, *I shall strike.*

The moods of this tense inflect like PRES.

Note.—The Fut. has no Subjunctive.

1st AORIST IND., *I struck.*

| ἔτυψ-α, | -ας, | -ε. | -αμεν, | -ατε, | -αν. |

1st AOR. SUBJ., *I may strike.*

| τύψ-ω, | -ης, | -η. | -ωμεν, | -ητε, | -ωσι(ν). |

1st AOR. OPT., *I might strike.*

| τύψ-αιμι, | -αις, | -αι. | -αιμεν, | -αιτε, | -αιεν. |

1st AOR. IMP., *Strike thou.*

| —— | τύψ-ον, | -ατω. | —— | -ατε, | -ατωσαν. |

INF., τύψαι, *to strike.*

PART., τύψ-ας, -ασα, -αν, *having struck.*

2nd AORIST IND., *I struck.*

ἔτυπον, like Imperf. Ind. Other moods inflect like Pres., dropping augment.

1st PERF. IND., *I have struck.*

| τέτυφα, | -ας, | -ε. | -αμεν, | -ατε, | -ασι(ν). |

INF., τετυφέναι, *to have struck.*

PART., τετυφ-ώς, -υῖα, -ος. *G.,* -ότος, -υίας, -ότος, *having struck.*

Note.—Subj. and Opt. like Pres. They preserve the reduplication.

1st PLUPERF. IND., *I had struck.*

| ἐτετύφ-ειν, | -εις, | -ει. | -ειμεν, | -ειτε, | -εισαν. |

2d PERF. IND., *I have struck.*

τέτυπα, inflects as 1st Perf.

2d PLUPERF. IND., *I had struck.*

ἐτετύπειν inflects as 1st Pluperf.

Note.—The participles in ων decline like ἕκων and in ας like πᾶς (which see).

MIDDLE VOICE.

PRES. IND., *I strike myself.*

| τύπτ-ομαι, | -η, | -εται. | -όμεθα, | -εσθε, | -ονται. |

PRES. SUBJ., *I may strike myself.*

| τύπτ-ωμαι, | -η, | -ηται. | -ώμεθα, | ησθε, | -ωνται. |

PRES. OPT., *I might strike myself.*
τυπτ-οίμην, -οιο, -οιτο. | -οίμεθα, -οισθε, -οιντο.

PRES. IMP., *strike thyself.*
— ου, εσθω. | — εσθε, εσθωσαν.

PRES. INF., τύπτεσθαι, *to strike one's self.*

PRES. PART., τυπτόμενος, *striking one's self.*

IMPERF. IND., *I was striking myself.*
ἐτυπτ-όμην, -ου, -ετο. | -όμεθα, -εσθε, -οντο.

FUT. IND., *I shall strike myself.*
τύψομαι, &c., inflects like Pres. Ind.
Note.—The Fut. has no Subjunctive or Imperative.

1st AORIST IND., *I struck myself.*
ἐτυψ-άμην, -ω, -ατο. | -άμεθα, -ασθε, -αντο.

1st AOR. SUBJ., *I may strike myself.*
τύψ-ωμαι, -ῃ, -ηται. | -ώμεθα, -ησθε, -ωνται.

1st AOR. OPT., *I might strike myself.*
τυψ-αίμην, -αιο, -αιτο. | -αίμεθα, -αισθε, -αιντο.

1st AOR. IMP., *Strike thyself.*
— τύψ-αι, -άσθω. | — -ασθε, -άσθωσαν.

INF., τύψασθαι, *to strike one's self.*

PART., τυψάμενος, *having struck one's self.*

2d AORIST IND., *I struck myself.*
ἐτυπόμην, inflects like Imperf. Other moods like Pres., dropping the augment.
Note—All the participles of the Middle decline like adj. of the first class in ος.

PASSIVE VOICE.

The Pres., *I am struck,* &c., inflects in all the moods like Pres. Middle.

IMPER., *I was struck,* inflects like Imperf. Middle.

1st FUT. IND., *I shall be struck.*
τυφθήσ-ομαι, inflects like Pres. Mid.

2d FUT IND., *I shall be struck.*
τυπήσ-ομαι, inflects like Pres. Mid.

1st AORIST IND., *I was struck.*

Singular.			*Plural.*		
1st Pers.	2d Pers.	3d Pers.	1st Pers.	2d Pers.	3d Pers.
ἐτύφθ-ην,	-ης,	-η.	-ημεν,	-ητε,	-ησαν.

1st AOR. SUBJ., *I may be struck.*
τυφθ-ῶ, -ῇς, -ῇ. | -ῶμεν, -ῆτε, -ῶσι(ν).

1st AOR. OPT., *I might be struck.*
τυφθ-είην, -είης, -είη. | -είημεν, -είητε, -είησαν.

1st AOR. IMP., *Be thou struck.*
— τύφθ-ητι, -ητω. | — -ητε, -ήτωσαν.

INF., τυφθῆναι, *to be struck.*

PART., τυφθ-είς, -εῖσα, -εν. G., -εντος, &c. *having been struck.*

2d AORIST IND., *I was struck.*
ἐτύπην, inflects throughout like 1st Aor.

PERF. IND., *I have been struck.*
τέτυ-μμαι, -ψαι, -πται. | -μμεθα, -φθε, -μμένοι εἰσί(ν)

PERF. SUBJ., *I may have been struck,* the Subj. of εἰμί with the part. τετυμμένος.

PERF. OPT., *I might have been struck,* the Opt. of εἰμί with the part. τετυμμένος.

IMP., *Be thou struck.*
— τέτυ-ψο, -φθω. | — -φθε, -φθωσαν

INF., τετύφθαι, *to have been struck.*

PART., τετυμμένος, *having been struck.*

PLUPF. IND., *I had been struck.*
ἐτετύ-μμην, -ψο, -πτο, -μμεθα, -φθε, -μμένοι ησαν.

2. *Classes of Verbs in* ω.—There are five classes of these, according as the final letter, after dropping ω, is a labial, as πέμπω, *I send ;* a guttural, as λέγω, *I say;* a dental, as πείθω, *I persuade ;* a liquid, as βάλλω, *I throw;* or a vowel, as λύω, *I loose;* and they are designated correspondingly, as Labial, Guttural, Dental, Liquid, and Pure verbs, the Pure being those whose final letter is a vowel.

3. *Formation of the Tenses.*—The *Imperfect* is formed by changing ω of act. into ον, ομαι of mid. and pass. into ομην, and prefixing the augment (which see).

The *Future Act.* is formed (*a*) by adding σω to the root in labials, as πέμπω, πέμψω ; in gutturals, as λέγω, λέξω ; and in dentals, as πειθω, πεισω ; (*b*) by shortening the penult in liquids, as βαλλω, βαλῶ ; (*c*) by lengthening the vowel before σω in pure verbs, as ποιεω, ποιήσω.

Note.—Liquids in the fut. inflect thus : -ῶ, εῖς, εῖ, οῦμεν, εῖτε, οῦσι.

The *Fut. Mid.* changes ω of fut. act. into ομαι; of liquids ῶ into οῦμαι.

The *First Aorist Act.* changes ω of the fut. into α and prefixes the augment : thus πέμψω ἔπεμψα. Liquids lengthen the shortened penult of the fut., as ῐ into ῑ, ε into ει, or α into η.

Note.—Verbs in ππ have a simpler stem in π, β, or φ ; in σσ one in γ ; in ζ one in γ or δ ; in εν one in ν ; in ει one in ι, and in general a long syllable has a simpler short.

The *First Aorist Mid.* adds μην to the active.

The *Second Aorist* is formed from the primitive root of the verb by adding ον, and prefixing the augment.

The *First Perfect Active* may be formed by adding κα to dental, liquid, and pure verbs ; ά to labials and gutturals, and prefixing the reduplication (which see).

Note.—Liquids in νω drop ν, or change it into γ, and some change ε and ει into α.

The *First Pluperfect* is formed from the perf. by prefixing the augment, and changing α into ειν.

The *Second Perfect* affixes α to the stem, and reduplicates, the form of the stem being generally strengthened.

The *First Aorist Passive* is formed by adding θην to the root, and prefixing the augment.

The *Second Aorist Passive* by changing ον of the 1st aor. act. into ην.

The *First Future Pass.* by changing θην of 1st aor. into θήσομαι, and dropping the augment.

The *Second Future Pass.* by changing ην of 2d aor. into ησομαι, and dropping the augment.

The *Perfect Pass.*—Its personal endings are: sing., μαι, σαι, ται; pl., μεθα, θε, μενοι ειςί.

Before μ, π β φ become μ; before σ, ψ; before τ, π.

Before μ, κ γ χ become γ; before σ, ξ; before τ,· κ.

Before μ, τ δ θ become σ, before σ are dropped, before τ become σ.

The *Pluperfect Passive* changes μαι of perf. pass. into μην and prefixes the augment. It inflects μην, σο, το, &c.

Contracted Verbs.—Verbs in αω, εω, and οω contract all through the pres. and imperf. tenses, according to the rules given for contractions of vowels in A 4.

B. SECOND CONJUGATION—ACTIVE VOICE.

Verbs of this conjugation have, at most, only three tenses — a present, an imperfect, and a second aorist. They are formed from simpler stems in α, ε, ο, or υ. Thus ἵστημι, *to cause to stand*, from στα by lengthening α into η before μι = I, and reduplicating with ι; similarly, τίθημι, *to place*, from θε; δίδωμι, *to give*, from δο; and δείκνυμι, *to show*, from δεικνυ, only this last does not reduplicate.

The verbs ἵστημι, τίθημι, and δίδωμι are conjugated as follows :—

PRES. IND.

	Singular.			Plural.	
1st Pers.	2d Pers.	3d Pers.	1st Pers.	2d Pers.	3d Pers.
ἵστ-ημι,	-ης,	-ησι(ν).	-αμεν,	-ᾶτε,	-ᾶσι(ν).
τίθ-ημι,	-ης,	-ησι(ν).	-εμεν,	-ετε,	-εᾶσι(ν).
δίδ-ωμι,	-ως,	-ωσι(ν).	-ομεν,	-οτε,	-οᾶσι(ν).

PRES. SUBJ.

Same as in 1st Conj., only δίδ-ωμι has ω throughout.

PRES. OPT.

ἱστ-αίην,	-αίης,	-αίη.	-αῖμεν,	-αῖτε,	-αῖεν.
τιθ-είην,	-είης,	-είη.	-εῖμεν,	-εῖτε,	-εῖεν.
διδ-οίην,	-οίης,	-οίη.	-οῖμεν,	-οῖτε,	-οῖεν.

PRES. IMP.

ἵστ-η, -ατω, &c. τίθ-ει, -ετω, &c. δίδ-ου, -οτω, &c.

PRES. INF.

ἱστάναι. τέθεναι. δίδοναι.

PRES. PART.

ἱστ-άς, -ασα, -αν. τιθ-είς, εῖσα, έν. διδ-ούς, -οῦσα, -ον.

IMP. IND.

ἵστ-ην,	-ης,	-η.	-αμεν,	-ατε,	-ασαν.
ἐτίθ-ην,	-ης,	-η.	εμεν,	-ετε,	-εσαν.
ἐδίδων,	-ως,	-ω.	-ομεν,	-οτε,	-οσαν.

2d AORIST IND.

ἔστ-ην,	-ης,	-η.	-ημεν,	-ητε,	-ησαν.
Pl.,	ἔθ-εμεν,	-ετε,	-εσαν.	ἐδ-ομεν,	-οτε, -οσαν.

2d AOR. SUBJ.

στῶ, θῶ, δῶ, as in Pres. Subj.

2d AOR. OPT.

σταίην, θείην, δοίην, as in Pres. Opt.

2d AOR. IMP.

στη-θί, -τω. θ-ές, -έτω. δ-ός, -ότω.

2d AOR. INF.

στῆναι. θεῖναι. δοῦναι.

2d AOR. PART.

στάς. θείς. δούς. As in Pres. Part.

MIDDLE AND PASSIVE.

PRES. IND.

	Singular.			Plural.	
	ἵστα-,	τίθε-,	διδο-,	with—	
1st Pers.	2d Pers.	3d Pers.	1st Pers.	2d Pers.	3d Pers.
μαι,	σαι,	ται.	μεθα,	σθε,	νται.

PRES. SUBJ.

ἱστ-, τιθ-, with ῶμαι, ῇ, ῆται, &c. διδῶμαι, -ω, -ῶται, &c.

PRES. OPT.

ἱσταί-, τιθεί-, διδοί-, with μην, ο, το, -μεθα, σθε, ντο.

PRES. IMP.

ἵστα-, τίθε-, δίδο-, with σο, σθω, σθε, σθωσαν.

PRES. INF.

ἵστασθαι. τίθεσθαι. δίδοσθαι.

PRES. PART.

ἱστάμενος, τιθέμενος, διδόμενος.

IMPERF. IND.

	ἱστα-,	ἐτιθέ-,	ἐδιδό-,	with—	
μην,	σο,	το.	μεθα,	σθε,	ντο.

2d AORIST IND.

	ἐθέ-,	ἐδό,	with—		
μην,	ου,	το.	μεθα,	σθε,	ντο.

2d AOR. SUBJ.

θῶμαι, θῇ, &c. δῶμαι, δῷ, &c.

2d AOR. OPT.

θεί-, δοί-, with μην, ο, το, &c.

2d AOR. IMP.

θοῦ, θέσθω. δοῦ, δόσθω.

2d AOR. INF.

θέσθαι. δόσθαι.

2d AOR. PART.

θέμενος. δόμενος.

Note.—The remaining tenses of these verbs, and of others of the same conjugation, are formed and inflected like those of the first. Thus of ἵστημι (from στα) the fut. act. is στήσω; 1st aor. act., ἔστησα; perf. act., ἔστηκα; of τίθημι (from θε), fut. act., θήσω; 1st aor. act., ἔθηκα, perf. act., τέθεικα; of δίδωμι (from δο), fut. act., δώσω; 1st aor. act., ἔδωκα; perf. act., δέδωκα.

φημί, *to say* (from φα), is like ἵστημι, substituting φ for ιστ; thus, 3d sing. pres., φησί; 3d pl., φασί; 3d sing. imperf., ἔφη.

δύναμαι, *to be able* (from δυνα), is like the mid. of ἵστημι; also ἐπίσταμαι, *to know*.

εἰμί, *to be* (already given); εἶμι, *to go*; and ἵημι, *to send*, are of this conjugation.

εἶμι, *to go* (stem ι), pres. sing., εἶμι, εἶ, εἶσι; pl., ἴμεν, ἴτε, ἴασι; imp., ᾖειν, like a plup. act.; imp. sing., ἴθι, ἴτω; pl., ἴτε, ἴτωσαν; subj., ἴω, like sub. of εἰμί; opt., ἰοίμι-, οις, &c.; inf., ἰέναι; part., ἰών, ἰοῦσα, ἰόν.

ἵημι, *to send* (stem ἑ), conjugates like τίθημι; substituting, in the pres. and imperf., ἱ for τιθ, and ' for θ in 2d aor. Its fut. is ἥσω; 1st aor., ἧκα; perf., εἷκα; perf. pass., εἷμαι. This verb occurs frequently compounded with ἀπό, as ἀφίημι, *to let go*.

Verbal Adjectives.—These are adjectives derived from verbs, and are formed by adding τός or τέος to the stem; those in τός implying possibility, and those in τέος obligation or necessity. Thus from αἴρεω, *to take*, we have αἱρετός, *that may be taken*, and αἱρετέος, *that should* or *must be taken*.

VI. Adverbs.—Adverbs are formed from nouns, adjectives, pronouns, verbs, and prepositions. Those from nouns are sometimes nouns in acc., as σήμερον, *to-day*; sometimes nouns in dat., as πεζῇ, *a-foot*; or in one word with a preposition, as παραχρῆμα, *immediately*. Those from adjectives end in ως, as ἀληθῶς, *truly*; ὄντως, *really*; or they take the form of the sing. or pl. neut., as πρῶτον, *firstly*; ἴσα, *equally*. Some from prepositions end in ω, as ἄνω, *upwards*; εἴσω, *within*. Certain end in ιστί, as Ἑλληνιστί, *in Greek*. Those from pronouns are formed from some case of the relative ὅς, prefixing π to interrogatives, and τ to demonstratives, as ποῖ, *whither*; τοῖ, *thither*; οὗ, *where*. Terminals, θι or σι, answer the question *where?* δε or σε, *whither?* and θεν, *whence?* thus οὐράνοθι, *in heaven*; οὐρανόνδε, *to heaven*; οὐρανόθεν, *from heaven*. Terminal -κις means *times*, as ἑπτάκις, *seven times*. The negative adv. οὐ, *not*, becomes οὐκ before a vowel, and οὐχ before an aspirate.

To these may be added certain particles used as prefixes; as ἀ, *intensive*; in ἀτενίζω, *to gaze intently*; ἀ or ἀν, *privative* = *un* in English; δυς = *un* in English, and ἡμι = *half*.

Comparison of Adverbs.—The comparative of an adv. is the neut. sing. of the comparative, and its superlative the neut. plur. of the superlative of the adjective from which it comes; as posit., σοφῶς, *wisely*; comp., σοφώτερον; super., σοφώτατα.

VII. Prepositions.—Prepositions are more common in New Testament than in classic Greek; and they all require the object to be in a particular case. They all primarily denote local relation, that, *viz.* of rest in a place, motion to it, or motion from it, to the first of which the dative answers, to the second the accusative, and to the third the genitive.

A. Prepositions that govern the Gen. only, are:—

ἀντί: 1. lit. *over against*; 2. *instead of*; 3. *for*; 4. *corresponding to.*
ἀπό: 1. lit. *away from*; 2. *from*, 3. *after*; 4. *by.*
ἐκ or ἐξ: 1. lit. *out of*; 2. *after* or *since*; 3. *from.*
πρό: 1. lit. *in front of*; 2. *before* (in place and time).
Note.—ἀπό is from the exterior, ἐκ the interior.

B. Those that govern the Dat. only, are :—

ἐν: 1. lit. *within*; 2. *in*; 3. *amongst*; 4. *by*; 5. *on.*
σύν: 1. lit. *together with*; 2. *in company with*; 3. *by help of.*

C. Those that govern Acc. only, are:—

εἰς: 1. lit. *into*; 2. *to* or *unto*; 3. *as far as*; 4. *amongst.*
ἀνά: 1. lit. *up through*; 2. *up*; 3. *during.*

D. Those that govern Gen. and Acc. are :—

διά: lit. *through*; with Gen. 1. *through*; 2. *by means of*; with Acc. *on account of.*
κατά: lit. *down through*; with Gen. 1. *down from*; 2. *against*; with Acc. 1. *down*; 2. *through*; 3. *as far as*; 4. *as regards*; 5. *according to.*
μετά: lit. *among*; with Gen. *amongst* or *with*; with Acc. *after.*
ὑπέρ: lit. *above*, with Gen. 1. *over*; 2. *beyond*; 3. *for*; with Acc. *beyond.*

E. Those that govern three cases are :—

ἀμφί: lit. *on both sides*, does not occur in N.T.
ἐπί: lit. *upon*, with Gen. 1. *on*; 2. *towards*; 3. *over*; 4. *before*; 5. *in the time of*; with Dat. 1. *upon*; 2. *on the ground of*; 3. *in addition to*; 4. *dependent on*; with Acc. 1. *upon*; 2. *to*; 3. *as respects*; 4. *against.*
παρά: lit. *beside*; with Gen. *from*; with Dat. 1. *beside*; 2. *with*; with Acc. 1. *beside*; 2. *contrary to*; 3. *beyond*; 4. *because of.*
περί: lit. *all round*; with Gen. 1. *about*; 2. *concerning*; with Dat. *round*; with Acc. 1. *around*; 2. *about*; 3. *as regards.*
πρός: lit. *close towards*; with Gen. 1. *towards*; 2. *touching*; with Dat. *close by*; with Acc. 1. *towards*; 2. *to* or *unto*; 3. *with*; 4. *concerning.*
ὑπό: lit. *below*; with Gen. 1. *from under*; 2. *by*; with Dat. *close under*; with Acc. 1. *under*; 2. *close upon.*

VIII. Conjunctions.—Of these there are several classes.

1. Conjunctive, as καί, *and, also, even*; καί, or τε, . . . καί, *both . . . and.*
2. Disjunctive, as ἤ . . . ἤ, *either . . . or*; εἴτε, . . . εἴτε, *whether . . . or.*
3. Adversative, as ἀλλά, δέ, *but*; μέν . . . δέ, *indeed . . . but*; οὔτε . . . οὔτε; μήτε . . . μήτε, *neither . . . nor*; οὐ . . . οὐδέ . . . οὐδέ, *not . . . nor even . . . nor yet.*
4. Comparative, as ὡς, *as*; κάθως, ὥσπερ, *just as.*
5. Temporal, ὡς, ὅτε, ἐπειδή, *when.*
6. Conditional, as εἰ, ἐάν (εἰ ἄν), *if.*
7. Causal, as ὅτι, διότι, *because*; γάρ, *for*; ἐπεί, *since.*

8 Inferential, as οὖν, *therefore*; ἄρα, *then*; διό, *wherefore.*
9 Final, as ἵνα, *in order that*; ὡς, ὅπως, *so that*; μή, *that not.*
10. Emphatic, as γε, *at least*; δή, *indeed.*
Note.—The particle ἄν may be always understood as referring to a supposed case.

C. SYNTAX.

The Subject.—The subject of a finite verb, *i.e.*, a verb in the ind., the subj., or the opt. mood, is always in the nominative; but the subject of an infinitive is always in the accusative. With impersonal verbs it may be in the acc. or dat., as δεῖ με, *it behoves me = I must.*
Note.—1. When there are two nominatives in a sentence with a substantive verb, such as *be, become, &c.*, the one with the article is the subject. 2. The subject, unless emphatic, is usually unexpressed when it is a pronoun, when the predicate suggests it, or when the context does.
The *Predicate.*—1. The predicate agrees in number and person, as well as otherwise where possible, with the subject. Exceptions — 1. A neuter plural generally takes a verb in the singular. 2. A collective noun often takes a verb in the plural (Luke xix. 37). 3. An adjective used as predicate is often neuter when the subject is masculine or feminine, some neuter noun being understood (see Matt. vi. 34; 2 Cor. ii. 6).
Two or more singular subjects take a verb in the plural, or in the singular, in agreement with one and understood to the rest. If the subjects are of different persons, the verb is plural, but in agreement with the first person rather than the second, and the second rather than the third, or it agrees with one and is understood to the rest. If it is of different genders, the predicate agrees with the mas. rather than fem., and with fem. rather than neut.
Note.—When the verb "to be" forms part of the predicate it is often omitted, particularly in general propositions and proverbial sayings, and in connection with verbals in τέος and other expressions of necessity and duty.

The Article.—The article plays an important part in Greek. It is never omitted where it is absolutely necessary, and never employed where it is quite superfluous. It was originally a demonstrative pronoun, as may be seen in Acts xvii. 28, and as it continued to be in the phrase ὁ μὲν . . . ὁ δέ, *this . . . that*; and it agrees, like an adjective, with some noun expressed or understood. Its uses are: (*a.*) to particularise, as ὁ φίλος, *the friend*; ἡ κρίσις, *the judgment*; (*b.*) to generalise, as οἱ ἄνθρωποι, *men universally*; ὁ ἐργάτης, *the labourer generally*; (*c.*) to point out the subject, as Θεὸς ἦν ὁ λόγος, *the Word was God*; (*d.*) in connection with the proper name of a person well known or already mentioned, particularly in the oblique cases, as τοῦ Ἰησοῦ, *the Jesus* just mentioned; (*e.*) to represent a possessive pronoun, τὰ τέκνα, *his, her, &c., children.* It is construed—(*a.*) with adjectives, as οἱ πραεῖς, *the meek* (people); τὸ δικαίον, *the just* (thing); (*b.*) with participles, as ὁ σπείρων, *the* (man) *sowing = he who sows*; τὸ ῥηθέν, *the* (thing) *spoken = that which is spoken*; (*c.*) with infinitives, τὸ σπείρειν, *sowing*; τοῦ σπείρειν, *of sowing, &c.*; (*d*) with a dependent Gen., as οἱ τοῦ Χριστοῦ, *the* (disciples) *of Christ*; τὰ τοῦ πνεύματος, *the* (things) *of the Spirit*; (*e*) with a prepositional phrase, as ὁ ἐν τοῖς οὐρανοῖς, *the* (one, *i.e.* he who is) *in the heavens*; οἱ περὶ Παῦλον, *the* (men) *round Paul, i.e.* Paul and his companions; (*f.*) with an adverb, as οἱ νῦν, *the* (men) *now*; τὰ ἄνω, *the* (things) *above*; (*g.*) with demon. and poss. pronouns, as οὖτος ὁ ἄνθρωπος, *this man*; ὁ ἐμὸς πατήρ, *my father.* The article is

omitted when accompanied with a definite expression.

Note 1. — When used with Θεός, the article points out the God of revelation or grace ; when used with Χριστός and Ἰησοῦς, the reference is to these names as appellatives, equal the one to the Messiah and the other to the Saviour ; when used with πνεῦμα ἅγιον, the Holy Spirit is meant ; when used absolutely with νόμος, the law of Moses is meant.

The Noun. Number, Gender, and Case.—1. *Number* —The sing. is often used for the pl. with the art collectively, as ὁ Ἰουδαῖος, Rom. iii. 1; and distributively, as in τὸ σῶμα, 1 Cor. vi. 19. The pl. is often used for the sing , as in Matt. ii. 20, and in the names of places, as well as of virtues and vices, Mark vii. 22 ; 2 Pet. iii. 11.

2. *Gender.*—The neut. is sometimes applied to persons, 2 Thess. ii. 6.

3. *Case.*—Case, as already said, is terminal inflexion to express such relations as we employ prepositions to indicate. To define the relation more exactly a preposition is also frequently employed, and more so in the New Testament than in classic Greek, for the reason that, as the writers of the New Testament were Hebrews, and not Greeks, the prepositional force of the Greek inflexion was less familiar to them. The nom. and acc., as expressing essential relations, are the principal cases ; the Gen. and Dat., as expressing subordinate ones, are secondary.

Nominative.—This is the case of the subject, and also of the predicate after a substantive verb. It is sometimes used absolutely, this is, without being grammatically connected with any other word in the sentence, to call attention to the subject spoken of, Acts vii. 40 ; Rev. ii. 26. This has been called the *suspended Nominative.* It is used for voc. in Matt. xi. 26 ; Luke viii. 54.

Genitive —This case for the most part expresses such relations as we denote by the prepositions *of* and *from*, such ideas, viz., as possession, separation, and derivation, and indicates that to which a thing may be referred as proceeding from it, belonging to it, or otherwise intimately connected with it. It is often represented by the possessive in English. It expresses frequently an objective relation, as φόβος Ἰουδαίων, *fear of the Jews;* ἀγάπη τοῦ Θεοῦ, *love to God.* It is governed by partitive words and comparatives, as πολλοί τῶν Φαρισαίων, *many of the Pharisees;* μείζων τοῦ κυρίου αὐτοῦ, *greater than his master.* It follows all verbs of the senses except sight, as well verbs expressive of desiring, caring for, and ruling, and verbs and adjectives of plenty and want. Time when and place where are expressed by the Gen., and also the price of a thing. A noun or pronoun and a participle are put in the Gen. called the Gen. Absolute, when, while expressing some circumstance of time or manner, neither is grammatically connected with any other word in the sentence ; as, τοῦ Ἰησοῦ γεννηθέντος, *Jesus being born* (see Matt. ii. 1). This case is represented by the ablative in Latin and the nominative in English.

Dative.—This is the case in which a noun is put when it denotes the object in relation to whom or which something is done, whether for advantage or disadvantage. It is used after verbs of benefiting and hurting, pleasing and serving, believing and following, as well as adjectives denoting equality, similarity, suitability, and the like. It frequently expresses the cause, manner, means, or instrument of an action, as well as the time when and the place where a thing happens. The Dat., with such verbs as "be" and "become," denotes the possessor, as ἀργύριον οὐκ ἔστι μοι, *money is not to me = I have no money.*

Accusative.—The Accusative is the case in which a noun is placed when it is the immediate object of an action expressed by a transitive verb. Verbs of asking, teaching, concealing and depriving take an acc. both of person and thing. Intransitive verbs take an acc. of kindred meaning, as it were adverbially, thus, ἐχάρησαν χαρὰν μεγάλην, *they rejoiced with great joy.* The acc. is used to limit the application of an attribute, as καλὸς τὸ σῶμα, *beautiful in body;* also as the subject of an infinitive, as ἐν τῷ καθεύδειν τοὺς ἀνθρώπους, *while men slept.* The acc. also expresses duration of time and distance.

The *Adjective.* — Adjectives, including participles, agree with their substantives in gender, number, and case, though an author, having regard to the sense more than the form of the words, sometimes makes the adj. plural when the substantive is sing., and mas. when it is neut. The substantive is often understood, generally when the application is obvious, occasionally also when it may not be so, as in ἡ οἰκουμένη, translated "world," where supply γῆ, *land* (Rom. x. 18). When an adj. applies to two or more substantives, it is often given in agreement with one, and understood to the rest. As an adverb is sometimes used for an adj., so an adj. in agreement with the subject is sometimes used where we use an adv., as ἑκών, for "willingly." Other parts of speech perform the function of the adj., such as a noun in the genitive, a preposition with a noun, a noun in apposition, and an appellative.

Degrees of comparison.—An adj. in the comparative either governs the genitive or is followed by ἤ, *than*, in which latter case the noun following is put in the same case as the subject of comparison. Sometimes the second member of the comparison is omitted, as in Acts xviii. 26 ; John xix. 11. The superlative also governs the genitive, and is sometimes used for the comparative, as in John i. 15, 30. As in Hebrew, the superlative is expressed by ἐν, *among*, after an adj., as "blessed among women" in Luke i. 42, and by a noun or adj., followed by its genitive plural, as in "holy of holies," Heb. ix. 3.

Pronouns.—1. The *personal* as subject is seldom expressed, except when it is emphatic. To express possession, the gen. of the personal pron. is generally employed, and not the possessive pron., as πάτερ ἡμῶν, *our Father,* lit. *Father of us.* 2. The *possessive pronoun* is seldom expressed, except for emphasis, and it has often an objective meaning, as φιλία ἡ ἐμή, *friendship towards me.* The article, as noticed, is often used for the poss. pron. 3. *Adjective pronoun.*—This, though in the oblique cases it stands for the third personal, αὐτὸς properly is, and it is always emphatic, being translatable by *self, selves,* whether added to substantives or pers. pronouns. 4. *Reflexive pronouns.*—These are used in reference to the principal subject, and are sometimes employed in place of reciprocal ones. The reflexive of the third pers. is often used instead of the others. 5. *The Relative Pronoun.*—The relative agrees with its antecedent in gender, number, and person, but its case is determined by the part it plays in its own clause. It is sometimes attracted into the case of its antecedent, as in Acts i. 1, and sometimes into the gender of its own predicate, as in Gal. iii. 16. Sometimes the antecedent is omitted, as in Mat. x. 27, and sometimes it occurs in the rel. clause, as in Rom. vi. 17. 6. *The Indefinite Pronoun.*—τις is often equal to the indefinite article *a,* and, when it is so, it stands second, as ἀνήρ τις, *a certain man.*

The Verb—The Voices.—1. The *active voice* is sometimes transitive and sometimes intransitive in meaning, that is, it sometime~ expresses an action which passes over to an object and sometimes one which is confined to the agent. Many verbs of motion which are properly transitive are used intransitively ; a reflexive pronoun signifying "self" being understood, as is the case with βάλλω, *to throw*, when it means *to rush*. 2. The *middle voice* expresses an action done to, done for, or done at the instance of, the subject, and so is ascribed to it. 3. In the *passive voice* the object of the active—the indirect, if a person, as well as the direct—is made the subject, and the agent is under government of ὑπό, *by*, with the gen., and at times of παρά and πρός.

The Tenses.—1. The *Present* states (*a.*) what is, or is going on, or just now ; (*b.*) what is habitually or universally true (Matt. vii. 18), and (*c.*) in lively narrative what is past as if it were present (Matt. iii. 13), as also (*d.*) in certain cases what is about to be (John xx. 17). 2. The *Imperfect* states what was going on at a certain past time or was customary. It is properly the descriptive tense, and represents an action in its continuance and progress. It also indicates what one was proceeding to do. 3. The *Future* expresses futurity indefinitely, as well as what is required or enjoined to be. Conjoined with οὐ μή it expresses a strong negation. 4. The *Aorist* is a strictly past or preterite tense. It is sometimes equal to the perfect with "have," and to the pluperfect with "had," and sometimes emphasizes the completion of the act (John xiii. 31). 5. The *Perfect* properly denotes what is just completed, also what still is, if the effect remains.

The Moods.—1. The *Indicative* asserts a thing positively and as a matter of fact, as ἔλεγε, *he said* ; ἦλθεν, *he came*. It is also used interrogatively in the same reference. 2. The *Subjunctive* or *Conjunctive* asserts a thing conditionally or as dependent on something else, and it chiefly occurs in dependent propositions, as λέγω, ἵν᾽ εἰδῇς, *I speak, that you may know*. It is also used in exhorting, as ἴωμεν, *let us go* ; in deliberative questions, as τί ποιῶμεν, *what shall we do?* and in prohibitions (Matt. vi. 2). The subjunctive properly expresses the condition of something else ; thus ἐὰν θέλῃς, δύνασαι, *if t..u wilt, thou canst* (Matt. viii. 2). 3. The *Opt..ive* is in the New Testament confined pretty mu.h to the expression of a wish, as μὴ γένοιτο, *may it not be*. In classic Greek it is employed as a conjunctive dependent on past tenses, the subjunctive being so employed as dependent on principal tenses. *Note.*—According to Winer, "The indicative denotes the *actual*, the conjunctive and optative that which is merely *possible* ; the conjunctive being used for the possible as dependent on circumstances, and the optative for the possible as conceived by the mind." 4. The *Imperative* commands or entreats, and sometimes permits ; the *aor. imp.* requiring a thing of immediate obligation or to be done at once ; the *pres. imp.* requiring a thing of lasting obligation, or to be done always or regularly. *Note.*—The presents and aorists of the subjunctive and the infinitive are similarly distinguished. 5. The *Infinitive* properly expresses the notion of the verb absolutely, that is, without limitation to any subject, and is often equal to a verbal noun. It possesses the governing power of the verb, and when used as a noun is conjoined with the neut. of the Art. It may be used as subject or object, and is frequently dependent on another verb. When it takes a subject, that subject is in the accusative, unless it is the same as that of the governing verb, in which case it is in the nominative ; and when used as a noun the article suffers inflexion. With the Genitive of the Article

it expresses purpose, as τοῦ ἀπολέσαι, *in order to kill*. It is sometimes redundant, as in τὸ νῦν εἶναι, *the now being*=for the present. 6. The *Participle*, extensively used in Greek, partakes of the nature of the verb and the adjective ; of the verb **as** undergoing modification to express voice and tense, as well as in possessing its governmental power ; of the adjective as in concord with a substantive. Conjoined with the article it is equal to a noun or a relative clause, as ὁ σπείρων, *the sower* ; ὁ τεχθείς, *he that is born* (Matt. ii. 2) ; to which it is sometimes equivalent without the article. When a participle applies to the object of a verb it agrees with it, as οἶδα ἄνθρωπον θνητὸν ὄντα, *I know that man is mortal* ; but when the object is the same person as the subject, it agrees with the subject, as οἶδα θνητὸς ὤν, *I know that I am mortal*.

The Moods in Subordinate Clauses.—1. *Objective Clause.*—When a clause is the objective to a verb of thinking, knowing, seeing, believing, declaring, &c., its verb is in the indicative with ὅτι, *that*, in the infinitive with accusative, or in the form of a participle with accusative, unless indeed the subject of the inf. or the part. is the same as that of the governing verb (see 5 and 6 in preceding sections).

Note.—ὅτι is sometimes used to introduce a quotation, being then equal to inverted commas with us.

2. *Clauses of Time.*—These are expressed by such conjunctions as ὅτε, ἐπεί, *when* ; ἕως, *until*, with the verb in the indicative, when an actual occurrence is meant, and in the subjunctive with ἄν, when a contingent is ; as ἐπειδάν, *whenever*. πρίν, *before*, is used with the inf. as well as wit ι the ind. and subj.

3. *Clauses of Purpose.*—Purpose is expressed by such particles as ἵνα, *to the end that* ; ὅπως, *so that* ; ἵνα μή, *that not*, &c., with the verb in the subjunctive mood. ὥστε = *with a view to*, takes the inf. = *so that*, it takes the ind. or the inf. Purpose is often expressed by the simple infinitive, as well as by the inf. with the gen. of the article.

4. *Clauses of Condition and Consequence.*—The condition, or protasis as it is called, takes εἰ, *if*, with the ind. or opt. or ἐάν = εἰ ἄν with the subj.; and the consequence, or apodosis as it is called, takes the ind. with or without ἄν. (*a.*) εἰ with the ind. in the protasis assumes the hypothesis as a fact and is followed by the ind. (Matt. iv. 3) or the imper. (John vii. 4) in the apodosis. (*b.*) εἰ with the opt. assumes something that may possibly take place (1 Pet. iii. 14 ; 1 Cor. xiv. 10), or chance to be (Acts xxiv. 19). (*c.*) ἐάν with the subj. supposes a thing, from which the ind. in the apodosis states something else will certainly follow (Matt. xvii. 20). (*d.*) εἰ with the ind., having ind. and ἄν in principal clause, asserts that if a certain thing had been, another would have been, which yet is not (Luke vii. 39 ; John v. 46).

5. *Relative Clauses.*—The relative takes the ind. when the reference is to a definite object, and the subj., usually with ἄν, when the reference is to an indefinite.

6. *Interrogative Clauses.*—These are introduced (*a.*) by interrogative words such as τίς, *who?* or (*b.*) by interrogative particles, such as ἤ. An interrogative word with the ind. asks as a fact ; with the subj. it asks with uncertainty. ἤ, simply asks; οὐ and οὐκοῦν, expect "yes" for answer ; ἆρα-μή and μῶν, expect "no."

7. *Negative Clauses.*—οὐ (οὐκ, οὐχ) goes with the ind. and denies a fact, positively and absolutely ; it stands in all independent propositions ; μή goes with the subj. opt. and the imp. and negatives a supposition, or what is mere matter of thought.

It denies conditionally, and is used after all particles denoting condition, supposition, or intention, in questions implying doubt or fear, in prohibitions, exhortations, and wishes, with the infinitive and the art. This distinction applies to the compounds of οὐ and μή. μή after verbs of fearing = *that*, μὴ οὐ = *that not*. οὐ μή, is used in emphatic prohibitions = *by no means*.

In prosecuting the study of the Greek New Testament, to the grammar of which the above is an introduction, the student is referred to the "Greek Student's Manual," published by the Messrs. Bagster. It contains the whole Greek text, together with the English version, in parallel columns, an excellent Greek-English Lexicon, and a Practical Guide to the Grammar of the Greek Testament. In the study a comparison of the original with the version in use is strongly recommended.

INTRODUCTION
TO THE
HEBREW OF THE OLD TESTAMENT.

A. THE HEBREW CHARACTERS.

HEBREW, like all the other languages of the Semitic stock, is written from right to left, and all the letters of the alphabet are Consonants, to which, some centuries after the language ceased to be spoken, an ingenious set of Vowel Marks of a phonetic order was added, called Points, to ensure correct reading (see chap. iii., 1. The Hebrew).

The Letters.—The letters of the alphabet are twenty-two in number, and the following table gives the forms, names, and powers of them.

Forms.	Names.	Power.
א	A'-leph	a slight breath
ב or בּ	Beth	bh, b [sound
ג or גּ	Gi'-mel	gh, g, as in *give*
ד or דּ	Dá-leth	dh, d
ה	He	h
ו	Vav, Waw	v, or more gener-
ז	Zá-yin	z [ally w
ח	Kheth	ch, as in the Ger.
ט	Teth	ṭ [*ch*
י	Yodh	y
כ or כּ final ך or ךּ } Kaph	kh, k
ל	Lá-medh	l
מ fin. ם	Mem	m
נ fin. ן	Nun	n
ס	Sá-mech	ş
ע	A'-yin	a throat sound
פ or פּ fin. ף	Pe	ph, p
צ fin. ץ	Tsá-dë	ts
ק	Koph	k
ר	Resh	r
שׁ	Shin	sh
שׂ	Sin	s
ת or תּ	Taw, Tau	th, t

In naming these letters, as also the vowels following, sound *a* as *ah*, *e* as *ay*, *i* as *ee*, and *u* as *oo*. When ב, ג, ד, כ, פ, ת take a dot in the middle of them, they drop the aspirate, and sound *b*, *g* (hard), *d*, *k*, *p*, and *t* respectively.

Note 1.—א, ה, ח, ע are called gutturals, but they are more properly breathings. To the last of these the Spanish Jews give the sound of *ng*, which is recommended to those who find gutturals troublesome.

Note 2.—א, ה, ו, and ' are called *vowel-letters*, as having been originally used to represent vowels, and they still frequently serve as vowels in combination with the points (which see). Of these א represented the sound *a*, ו *o* and *u*, ' *e* and *i*, and ה *a*, *e*, and *o* final, but not *i* and *u*. When a "vowel-letter" combines, as in long chirek and shurek, with a point, it is said to quiesce, and such letters are called *quiescent*. These *quiescents* are consonants at the beginning of a syllable, but silent at the end of a syllable after a full vowel.

The Points.—Of these there are ten—five representing a long or open sound, and five generally a short or shut. They are appended to the letters which they *follow* in pronunciation, and are all, when simple, except the mark for *o* (which stands over the left shoulder of the letter it accompanies), written below the letters, as it were outside the words.

The five representing long sounds are—

Forms.	Names.	Power.	Example.
ֵ	Kamets	a in *farm*	בָּ, *bah*.
ֵ	Tserë	a in *fame*	בָּ, *bay*.
ִ	{ Long Chirek	i in ma- chíne }	בִּ, *bee*.
ֹ and ֹ	Cholem	o in *bone*	בוֹ or בֹ, *bow*
ֹ	Shurek	u in *true*	בוּ, *boo*.

The five representing short (or common) are—

	Pathach	a in *bad*	בַּד, *bad*.
ֶ	Sĕghol	e in *pen*	בֶּד, *bed*.
ִ	{ Short Chirek }	i in *pin*	בִּד, *bid*.
ָ	{ Kamets Chatuph }	o in *hot*	בָּד, *bod*.
ֻ	Kibcuts	u in *put*	בֻּד, *bud*.

Note 1. ֵ and ֻ are sometimes long like ֵ. and ' respectively.

Note 2. ֵ at the end of a word before a guttural, and which disappears under inflexion, is called *furtive pathach*, as in רוּחַ, pronounced *rú-ach*.

Besides these ten vowel marks, there are other four of a less distinct quality. These consist of—

ְ Shĕvá (Simple), ĕ, as in *believe*.

And three Compound Shevas called Chatephs—

ֲ Chateph-Pathach, ă, as in *a*bound.

ֱ Chateph-Seghol, ĕ, as in b*e*neath.

ֳ Chateph-Kamets, ŏ, as in c*o*llection.

Simple Sheva accompanies all consonants, except final ones, that have no vowel of their own; it is added, however, to final Kaph, thus, ךְ, and, when two consonants end a word, to each of them. Compound Shevas are mostly used under the gutturals.

Note 1.—שְׁ = *so* when it has no vowel under it, as אֲנָ, *só-ne;* שְׁ = *sho* when the preceding letter has no vowel, thus מֹשֶׁה, *mó-she.* שְׁ = *sho* when there is no vowel under it, and שְׁ = *os* when no vowel precedes it.

Note 2.—וֹ = *ov* when a vowel follows, as לוֹךְ, *lo-ve;* and = *vo* when a vowel precedes. עָוֹן = *a-von.*

Note 3.—וֹ = *vv* when there is a vowel before it and a vowel after it, as הַוָּה, *Hav-vah,* the dot in the centre being a Daghesh forte (which see).

Note 4.—ֹ = *o, i.e.,* Kamets-Chatuph, when it is unaccented and sheva follows, Daghesh forte, or Chateph-Kamets, also when it enters into a final syllable, or when another *o* follows, though there is no accent.

Note 5.—When Sheva stands under a consonant it merely divides the syllables, and, being silent, is called *quiescent sheva.* It is only when it stands under the first letter of a syllable that it is sounded, and then it is called *audible sheva.*

Note 6.—After a short vowel Sheva belongs to the preceding syllable, and is quiescent; after a long vowel, it belongs to the following, and is audible. The compound shevas always belong to the following syllable.

Accents.—These are marks, distinct from the points, written above or below Hebrew words, serving partly as accents, partly as signs of logical relation, and partly as musical notes. In connection with these, it is enough here to mention the *Metheg* (ֽ) and the *Makkeph* (־). Metheg is used to give a certain distinction or emphasis to a syllable, and accompanies all vowels followed by a compound sheva; and Makkeph connects two words into one, while it throws the accent on the latter, as כָּל־יוֹם, kol-yŏm, *every day.*

Note.—Hebrew is a strongly accented language, and the accent generally falls on the last syllable, though also on the penult, of the word. Its position determines to a great extent those vowel changes which are so characteristic of the inflexions of Hebrew nouns and verbs.

Daghesh.—This is a point in the body of a letter, and serves a twofold purpose : 1. *D. lene* occurs in the aspirated letters, to make them hard, which they become in the beginning of a sentence, in the beginning of a word, after another ending in a consonant, and in the middle of a word after quiescent sheva. These letters dispense with the Daghesh only when preceded by a vowel sound. 2. *D. forte* indicates the doubling of a letter, and it is distinguished from the *D. lene* in being both preceded and followed by a vowel.

Note.—When a Daghesh occurs in ה—thus, הּ—it is called a *Mappik,* and indicates that the guttural retains its power as a consonant, otherwise it is not sounded.

The Gutturals.—These, together with ר, cannot be doubled, but they tend to lengthen the preceding vowel. They take an *a* sound before them in preference to any other vowel, and a compound sheva in preference to a simple. In a final syllable they prefer a pathach.

Syllables.—1. Every syllable must begin with a consonant, unless it happen to be ו. If it begins with two, the first takes sheva.

2. Every syllable must terminate either in a long vowel, in a short followed by a consonant, or in a short followed by metheg or an accent. A final syllable may, and alone can, end in two consonants.

3. A long vowel without an accent cannot take the following consonant in the same syllable, nor even with an accent if the consonant is needed to commence the following syllable.

4. Neither simple sheva nor a compound sheva constitutes the vowel of a syllable.

5. Sheva is never vocal unless it begin a word or follow an open syllable.

6. When ע, ח, ה, stand at the end of a word with pathach under it, pathach is sounded before them (see The Points, *Note* 2).

Note.—An open syllable, which is one that ends with a vowel, is long, unless sometimes when it has the accent. A close or shut, which is one that ends with a consonant, is short, unless sometimes when it has the accent.

B. THE PARTS OF SPEECH AND THEIR INFLEXIONS.

I. The Article.—There is only one article in Hebrew, the definite, הַ = *the,* which, however, never appears in this form. It is an inseparable particle prefixed to words, the ה being assimilated into the following consonant, which is accordingly doubled, as הַשֶּׁשׁ, *the sun,* for הַלְשֶׁשׁ. When the consonant following is a guttural the pathach of the article is changed into kamets, unless the guttural be ה or ח, in which case the pathach remains, as הָאָב, *the father;* הַחֹרֶשׁ, *the month.* The reason of this rule is that a guttural does not admit of a daghesh forte.

II. The Pronouns.—Of these there are four classes : Personal, Demonstrative, Relative, and Interrogative.

Personal.—Of these only the nominative is represented by a separate word, the genitive and other cases being represented by fragmentary forms of them, named *pronominal suffixes*, appended to nouns, verbs, and particles undeclined ; those after nouns representing possessive pronouns, those after verbs representing the object direct or indirect, and those after particles the gen. or acc. case. The nominative forms are as follows :—

Singular.		Plural.	
1st pers. אֲנִי, אָנֹכִי, *I.*		נַחְנוּ, אֲנַחְנוּ, *we.*	
2d pers. mas. אַתָּה, *thou.*		אַתֶּם, *ye.*	
——— fem. אַתְּ, *thou.*		אַתֵּן, אַתֶּן, *ye.*	
3d pers. mas. הוּא, *he.*		הֵם, הֵמָּה, *they.*	
——— fem. הִיא, *she.*		הֵן, הֵנָּה, *they.*	

Demonstrative.—These are :—

Sing. mas. זֶה, fem. וֹאת, *this;* plur. com. אֵל, אֵלֶּה, *these.*

,, ,, הוּא, fem. הִיא, *that;* plur. mas. הֵמָּה הֵם; fem. הֵן, הֵנָּה, *those.*

,, ,, הַלָּזֶה; fem. הַלָּזוּ, *yonder.*

Relative.—The only relative pron. is אֲשֶׁר, *who, which, what.* It is unaffected by gender or number, and is sometimes abbreviated into שֶׁ- or שֶׁ-. Gender and number, as well as person, is often indicated by a pronoun affixed to a member of the sentence, as אֲשֶׁר רֹאשׁוֹ, *who his head,* for *whose head.*

Interrogative. — There are two interrogatives מִי, *who?* for persons, and מָה, מַה-, *what?* for things. These are also used indefinitely for *whoever* and *whatever* respectively.

III. Nouns.

Nouns are divided into primitives and derivatives, and inflect, that is, undergo terminal changes, to express gender and number. There are but two genders—mas. and fem. ; and three numbers—sing., dual, and plur. The same may be said of the adjective.

Gender.—The fem. appends דָה-, also ת-, or in gutturals הֿ- to the mas., but if the mas. end in a vowel ת only is added. So that nouns so ending are fem., as also names not so ending of females, towns, countries, and members of the body generally; but names, howsoever ending, of males and occupations of males, of nations, rivers, and mountains, are masculine. Not a few words are of both genders, such as אֶרֶץ, *the earth.*

Number.—1. *Mas. Nouns.*—Mas. nouns add יִם- to the sing. to form the plur., but if the sing. end in ה- only ם is usually added. Nouns ending in הֶ- drop ה- before adding יִם-. 2. *Fem. Nouns.* —Fem. nouns add וֹת for the same purpose, or substitute וֹת for ה- or ת- of the sing. Those in ית- form the plur. in יוֹת -, as sing. עִבְרִית, pl. עִבְרִיּוֹת. 3. To form the dual the termination יִם- is added to both genders, but the feminine ה- changes into ת-.

Note.—Only nouns and certain numerals have a dual in Hebrew.

The Construct State.—In Greek and Latin when one noun is dependent on another it is the dependent word that is modified, but in Hebrew it is the governing. Thus in the expression "head of the king," the Greek and the Latin require the word "king" to be modified, whereas the Hebrew modifies the word "head," to indicate the relation implied in our word "of." A Hebrew word in this case is said to be in the Construct State, and the dependent word, if another in turn does not depend on it, in the Absolute State. The noun in the construct state is a shortened form of the absolute ; thus דָּבָר, *a word,* but a word of a king is דְּבַר מֶלֶךְ. Plurals and Duals masculine form their construct state by changing their respective terminations יִם- and יִם- into יֵ-; feminines by changing ה-ָ and ת-ַ into ת-ַ, and verbals like רֹאֶה, *a seer,* by changing ה-ֶ into הֵה-. Nouns in יֵ-, like חַי, *life,* take יֵ-.

Note.—The shortening of the vowels in the construct state is due to the advance of the tone.

Noun Prefixes.—These supply the place of inflexion met with in other languages, and are four in number, viz. : בְּ, *in, with, by;* לְ, *to, for, towards;* כְּ, *as, like;* מִי, *from, out of.* בְּ, לְ, כְּ regularly take sheva, but they take chirek when another sheva immediately follows, because two shevas cannot follow each other at the beginning of a word. If a compound sheva follows, they take the short vowel of the compound, followed by Metheg. Before an accented syllable the בְּ becomes בָּ. מִי is from מִן, the נ being assimilated into the following letter, or else the בְּ changed into מֵ- before a guttural.

Pronominal Suffixes.—These, as said, are fragments, representing the genitive, of the personal pronouns affixed to nouns to indicate possession, by the annexation of which the noun undergoes certain vowel changes. These suffixes are as follows :—

Of a Noun sing.	Of a Noun. pl.
1st PERS. SING. COMMON.	
ִ-	ַי-, *my.*
2d PERS. SING. MAS.	
ךָ, in pause, ךָ-	יךָ-ֶ, *thy.*
2d PERS. SING. FEM.	
ךְ, דֵך-	יִךְ-ַ, *thy.*
3d PERS. SING. MAS.	
וֹ, הוּ-, הוּ; וֹ-;	יהוּ-ֶ, יו-ָ, יו-ָ, *his.*
3d PERS. SING. FEM.	
הָ; ה-ָ; הָ-;	יהָ-ֶ, *her.*
1st PERS. PL. COM.	
נוּ; נוּ-ֵ;	ינוּ-ֵ, *our.*
2d PERS. PL. MAS.	
כֶם	יכֶם-ֵ, *your.*

2d PERS. PL. FEM.

כֶן   יׁכֶן ־ָ, *your.*

3d PERS. PL. MAS.

הָם ; ־ָם מוֹ־ ־ֵּ־   יהָם ־ָ, ־ֵימ, *their.*

3d PERS. PL. FEM.

הֶן, הֵן, | ־ָ   יהֶן ־ָ, *their.*

These suffixes are appended in the case of סוּס, *a horse*, thus :—

SING. OF THE NOUN.

סוּסִי, *my horse;* mas. סוּסְךָ, *thy horse;* fem. סוּסֵךְ, *thy horse;* mas. סוּסוֹ, *his horse;* fem. סוּסָה, *her horse;* com. סוּסֵנוּ, *our horse;* mas. סוּסְכֶם, *your horse;* fem. סוּסְכֶן, *your horse;* mas. סוּסָם, *their horse*; fem. סוּסָן, *their horse.*

PLUR. OF THE NOUN.

סוּסַי, *my horses;* mas. סוּסֶיךָ, *thy horses;* fem. סוּסַיִךְ, *thy horses;* mas. סוּסָיו, *his horses;* fem. סוּסֶיהָ, *her horses;* com. סוּסֵינוּ, *our horses;* mas. סוּסֵיכֶם, *your horses;* fem. סוּסֵיכֶן, *your horses;* mas. סוּסֵיהֶם, *their horses;* fem. סוּסֵיהֶן, *their horses.*

Declension. — This is the name given to the changes which nouns undergo on receiving the plural termination, on passing into the construct state, or on the annexation of a pron. suffix; on the principle, which pervades the language, that every addition to a word, by throwing the tone forward, tends to shorten the preceding changeable vowel or vowels. The general rule being that if the tone advances one syllable one of the vowels is shortened, and if it advances two syllables both are. According to these changes, due to inflexion, nouns have been grouped under no fewer than *nine* declensions, the first comprising all those, such as סוּס, in which the vowel is unchangeable.

IV. Adjectives.—There are comparatively few adjectives in Hebrew, the deficiency being supplied by substantives (see under SYNTAX, The Noun, 1.).

Numerals.—These are of two classes, Cardinal and Ordinal.

1. *The Cardinals.*—The cardinal אֶחָד, *one,* is an adjective and is construed in agreement with its noun ; the others are properly nouns, each with a fem. as well as a mas. form, and sometimes in the construct state before, sometimes in apposition with, the word which they quantify. The tens are the plurals of the digits, but twenty is the plural of ten, and for a hundred there is a distinct word. The following are the cardinals up to ten in the absolute mas. : שְׁנַיִם, *two;* שְׁלֹשָׁה, *three;* אַרְבָּעָה, *four;* חֲמִשָּׁה, *five;* שִׁשָּׁה, *six;* שִׁבְעָה, *seven;* שְׁמֹנָה, *eight;* תִּשְׁעָה, *nine;* עֲשָׂרָה, *ten.*

2. *The Ordinals.*—These, except רִאשׁוֹן, *the first,*

are generally formed by appending ־ִי to the Cardinals.

The Verb.—The Verb is the most important part of speech in the language, and it yields the majority of its root-words. Its root consists of three letters, and is generally found in the 3d sing. mas. of the Preterite, from which, together with the Infinitive, all the other parts are derived. These derivations are effected by changes chiefly in the vowels and by the addition of supplementary particles. Such inflexional changes give rise to what are usually called Conjugations, of which there are seven, the first being named Kal, i.e. *light,* because it presents the verb in its simplest form, unburdened with formative additions as the others are, and the rest deriving their names from the modification of פָּעַל, *to do,* which was formerly used by way of example. The seven conjugations of the verb קָטַל are :—

1. Kal	קָטַל,	*to kill.*
2. Niphal	נִקְטַל,	*to be killed.*
3. Piël	קִטֵּל,	*to kill many.*
4. Pual	קֻטַּל,	Pass. of Piël.
5. Hiphil	הִקְטִיל,	*to cause to kill.*
6. Hophal	הָקְטַל,	Pass. of Hiphil.
7. Hithpaël	הִתְקַטֵּל,	*to kill one's self.*

It will thus be seen that the so-called Conjugations are more properly Voices, three Active, a Simple (1), an Intensive (3), a Causative (5), with their respective Passives (2, 4, 6) and a Reflexive (7), which (2) also properly is.

Moods. — Verbs in Hebrew have only three moods, an Indicative, an Imperative, and an Infinitive, together with a Participle, the Subjunctive being generally expressed by the Imperfect.

Tenses.—There are properly no Tenses, the so-called Preterite expressing a finished action = the Perfect, and the so-called Future an unfinished = the Imperfect, neither having reference to time. These so-called tenses are frequently changed into one another by prefixing the letter *vav,* hence called *Vav Conversive.* This vav was conceived of as changing a past into a future, and *vice versa,* but it is now considered as changing a perfect into an imperfect, and *vice versa,* and is hence called *Vav Consecutive.* The vav so used is a particle ordinarily with simple copulative power = *and,* but in this case it has a certain sequential force = *and so.*

Inflexion.—The verb suffers inflexion to express person, and this is done by adding pronominal suffixes to the stem. Thus in the Preterite, or Perfect rather, the 3d sing. mas. takes no suffix, but the 3d fem. takes ־ָה (*she*), the 2d mas. תָּ, and 2d fem. תְּ (*thou*), and the 1st תִּי (*I*), the 3d plur. וּ (*they*), 2d mas. תֶּם, and 2d fem. תֶּן (*you*), 1st נוּ (*we*). The Future, or Imperfect rather, prefixes

‎־ּ in 3d sing. and plur. mas., ‎ָה in 3d sing. and plur. fem., and 2d mas. and fem. of both numbers, ‎אָ in 1st sing. and ‎נ‍ in 1st plur., while 2d sing. fem. adds ‎־ִי, the 3d and 2d plur. mas. adds ‎ו, and 3d and 2d plur. fem. adds ‎ּהָ.

Kal.—All this will be best understood by the conjugation of ‎קָטַל in Kal.

Pret.	Sing.	Plur.
3d mas.	‎קָטַל, *he killed.*	‎קָטְלוּ, *they killed.*
3d fem.	‎קָטְלָה, *she killed.*	
2d mas.	‎קָטַלְתָּ, *thou killedst.*	‎קְטַלְתֶּם, *ye killed.*
2d fem.	‎קָטַלְתְּ, *thou killedst.*	‎קְטַלְתֶּן, *ye killed.*
1st com.	‎קָטַלְתִּי, *I killed.*	‎קָטַלְנוּ, *we killed.*

Inf. absol., ‎קָטוֹל, *to kill :* Inf. constr., ‎קְטֹל, *to kill.*

Imp. mas. ‎קְטֹל, *kill thou.*   Mas. ‎קִטְלוּ, *kill ye.*
Imp. fem. ‎קִטְלִי, *kill thou.*   Fem. ‎קְטֹלְנָה, *kill ye.*

Fut.	Sing.	Plur.
3 m.	‎יִקְטֹל, *he will kill.*	‎יִקְטְלוּ, *they will kill.*
3 f.	‎תִּקְטֹל, *she will kill.*	‎תִּקְטֹלְנָה, *they will kill.*
2 m.	‎תִּקְטֹל, *thou wilt kill.*	‎תִּקְטְלוּ, *ye will kill.*
2 f.	‎תִּקְטְלִי, *thou wilt kill.*	‎תִּקְטֹלְנָה, *ye will kill.*
1 m.	‎אֶקְטֹל, *I will kill.*	‎נִקְטֹל, *we will kill.*

Part. act., ‎קֹטֵל, *killing :* Part. pass., ‎קָטוּל, *being killed.*

Note 1.—From this it will be seen that the vowels of the two tenses are different, and that, as in nouns, they undergo modifications due to throwing forward the tone.

Note 2.—The prefixes, equally with the suffixes, are fragments of personal pronouns.

Note 3.—The 3d preterite of Kal has sometimes a Tsere and sometimes a Cholem in the second syllable as well as a pathach, as ‎כָּבֵד, *he was heavy,* ‎יָכֹל, *he was able.*

Note 4.—The infinitive, as seen in the example, has two forms, an absolute, which admits neither prefix nor suffix, and a construct, which admits both.

Note 5.—The imperative holds of the inf. and is formed similarly to the future.

Note 6.—It will be seen there are two participles in Kal, an active called Poël, and a passive called Patül, both after the original example in ‎קָטַל, and both generally forming their plurals and feminines like nouns.

Niphal.—The characteristic syllable of this conjugation is ‎הִנ. This appears in the infinitive construct, the future, and the imperative, but is abbreviated in the preterite and participle into ‎נ. It represents generally the passive of Kal and inflects like it, but its proper meaning is reflexive like the middle voice in Greek.

Piel.—The characteristic of this conjugation is seen in the doubling, by means of Daghesh forte,

of the middle radical or stem letter. It is properly the intensive of Kal and denotes generally the frequent or continuous repetition of the act. It has sometimes reference to many objects and is sometimes causative, as is seen in ‎לִמֵּד, *to teach,* from ‎לָמַד, *to learn.*

Pual.—This is the Pass. of Piel in its various senses.

Hiphil.—The characteristic of this conjugation is the prefix ‎ה and the insertion of ‎־ִי in the last syllable, which is in the 1st and 2d pers. preterite changed into ‎־ַ. It is the causative of Kal.

Hophal.—This is the passive of Hiphil and has the same characteristics.

Hithpaël.—The characteristic of this conjugation is ‎הִת, and its inflexion is the same as Piel, to which the ‎הִת is prefixed. When the verb begins with ‎ס or ‎שׁ the ‎ת is transposed with it, thus ‎הִתְשַׁמֵּר becomes ‎הִשְׁתַּמֵּר ; when it begins with ‎צ, the ‎ת is both transposed and changed into ‎ט ; thus ‎הִתְצַדֵּק becomes ‎הִצְטַדֵּק ; and when it begins with ‎ד or ‎ט, ‎ת is assimilated into them. Hithpaël is properly the reflexive of Piel, but it frequently means to make or show one's self to be whatever the verb expresses.

Irregular or Weak Verbs.—Those verbs are so called which contain in their stems one or more of the weak letters, viz. the gutturals, ‎א, ‎ה, ‎ח, ‎ע, ‎ר, the quiescents, ‎י, ‎ו, or ‎נ. As ‎פָּעַל, *to do,* was the example of conjugation given by the old grammarians, the first letter of any verb was called its *Pe,* the second its *Ayin,* and the third its *Lamedh,* and it is so accordingly that irregular verbs are named. Thus such a verb with a ‎נ in the first place is called a *Pe nun* verb, one with ‎ו in the second place is called an *Ayin Vav* verb and one with an ‎ע in the third place is called a *Lamedh Guttural* verb.

Verbs Guttural.—A verb is called a guttural if one of its radicals is a guttural, and of these there are three classes, according as the guttural is in the place of ‎פ, ‎ע, or ‎ל, of ‎פָּעַל, so that there are ‎פ gutturals, ‎ע gutturals, and ‎ל gutturals.

‎פ *Gutturals.*—To this class belongs such a verb as ‎עָמַד, *to stand.* These verbs take a compound instead of a simple sheva, as ‎עֲמֹד, and the preformatives generally take a vowel with an *a* sound, such as ‎־ַ or ‎־ֶ.

‎ע *Gutturals.*—To this class belongs such a verb as ‎צָעַק, *to cry out.* Here, too, the guttural always takes the compound sheva ‎־ַ, the preceding vowel conforming thereto, but usually lengthened, seeing the Daghesh forte is inadmissible.

‎ל *Gutturals.*—To this class belongs the verb ‎שָׁמַע, *to hear.* Here also the guttural takes an *a* sound before it, and a furtive pathach if it is preceded by a long vowel, as ‎שָׁמֹעַ.

Besides Guttural verbs there are also Quiescent verbs and Imperfect. Of Quiescents there are seven classes, according as the Pe letter is א, י, or ו, the Ayin י or ו, and Lamedh, א or ה. Under Imperfect verbs are included those whose first radical is נ, some whose first is י, and those whose second and third are alike. But for an account of these the reader is referred to the Hebrew Grammar prefixed to "The Hebrew Student's Manual." [1]

The Particles.—Under this head the Hebrew Grammar includes all words serving as adverbs, prepositions, conjunctions, and interjections; and, with the exception of a few primitives, and a few from verbs and pronouns, they are mostly borrowed or derived from nouns in the construct state, the word following being often dependent on them. They are often so abbreviated that they cannot stand alone, but require the support of some noun or pronoun to which they are attached as prefix or affix.

Adverbs of the primitive class are לֹא, *not;* שָׁם, *there;* אָז, *then.*

Of the derivatives some are nouns with prepositions, as בִּמְאֹד, *very* (lit. *with might*); כְּאֶחָד, *together* (lit. *as one*); and some nouns without prepositions, as מְאֹד, *very, greatly* (lit. *might*); יַחַד, *together* (lit. *union*); עוֹד, *again, yet* (lit. *repetition*). Adjectives, as כֵּן, *so* (lit. *straight*) are also so used, and pronouns, as זֶה, *here* (lit. *this*). Some are formed by adding ־ָם to nouns, as אָמְנָם, *truly,* and some are shortened forms of longer words as אַךְ, *only,* and הֲ, the interrogative particle *e.g.* in הֲלֹא, *is it not?*

Some adverbs involve a verbal idea, as יֵשׁ, *there is,* and אַיִן* (lit. *non-existence,* cons. state אֵין), *there is not.* These take pronominal suffixes like verbs, as אֵינֶנִּי, *I am not,* lit. *there is not I.*

Prepositions.—Most of these are nouns in the construct state, as אַחַר, *behind, after* (lit. *hinder part*); עַד, *until* (lit. *duration*), or nouns in the construct state with prefixes, as לִפְנֵי, *before* (lit. *in the face of*); לְמַעַן, *on account of* (lit. *for the purpose*). Besides the prepositional prefixes already given under the Noun, it will suffice to mention here as similarly construed, אֵת and עִם, *with;* אֶל, *unto;* and כְּמוֹ, *like.* With a pronoun attached אֵת becomes אֵת, as אִתִּי, *with me;* עִם becomes עַם, as עַמִּי, *with me;* אֶל becomes אֵל, as אֵלַי, *to me;* an כְּמוֹ becomes כְּמוֹ, as כָּמוֹנִי, *like me.*

---

[1] An admirable compendium, including Reading Lessons and a Hebrew-English Lexicon, for the further study of the language, published by Bagster, London.

Conjunctions.—The principal of these are—אֲשֶׁר, כִּי, *that, because;* אַל, בַּל, *that not;* בְּמֶרֶם, *before that;* אַף, גַּם, *also;* אִם, *if,* and עַל, *because.* But the conjunction most frequently in use is the inseparable וֹ (*and*), which takes the form of וּ before a sheva, as also before ב, מ, פ, and becomes Kamets before the accented syllable.

Interjections.—Some of these are expressions of mere natural sounds, as אֲהָהּ, אָהּ, *ah!* הוֹי, *ho!* הֶאָח, *aha!* The most, however, are from other parts of speech, as הֵן, הִנֵּה, *behold! lo!* הָבָה, *come!* אָנָּא, *pray!*

The Article.—The article generally accompanies a noun when the reference is definite, and is omitted when it is indefinite. It is used with the name of a class when all the class is meant, with a designation of eminence applied to an individual, with the names of mountains, rivers, and towns, and with appellatives, such as river, when the reference is to a definite member of the class. It is omitted before a noun in the construct state, as being rendered definite already by the genitive or pronominal suffix following; but when the noun in the construct state with its genitive denotes one compound idea, as "the men-of-war," which it is needful to render definite, the article is prefixed to the genitive. If the noun is definite, the adj. or demons. pronoun belonging to it must have the article also. Thus "the great city" is in Hebrew "the city the great;" "that place," "the place the that;" "thy strong hand," "thy hand the strong." It stands after כֹּל, *all, the whole.*

The Pronouns.—*Personal.*—Personal pronouns are always used in the nom. case, except when, for emphasis, they are in apposition with an oblique case, as in Gen. xxvii. 34: "Bless me, even me.' The suffix pronouns generally represent the accusative, though they sometimes also represent the dative; when in the acc. they have sometimes אֵת prefixed to them; when a compound idea is expressed by a noun in the construct state, followed by another in the genitive, the suffix pronoun is attached to the latter, as הַר קָדְשִׁי, *mountain of my holiness* for *my holy hill.* Sometimes the pronoun is not of the same gender as the noun to which it refers. *Demonstrative.*—These are sometimes used for relatives, and the pronoun of the 3d person הוּא is sometimes included among them in the sense of *that,* in which sense it should take the art. if its substantive has it. Thus "that man" in Hebrew is "the man the that." The *Interrogative* מִי may be used for things when persons are implied, for the plur. as well as the sing., and the possessive as well as the nominative, as בַּת מִי, "daughter of whom" for "whose daughter." It is also used indefinitely for *anyone,* as מָה (properly *what?*) is for *anything.* The *Relative* אֲשֶׁר gives a relative force to other parts of speech, such as adverbs of place and pronouns, thus: in connection with it שָׁם, there= where; לֹ, to him=to whom; and בֹּ, therein= wherein. It is sometimes omitted, as in English; as its antecedent also is when that happens to be a personal pronoun. *Distributive.—Every,* when it refers to persons, is expressed by אִישׁ (*man*), sometimes repeated; and when it refers to persons or things, by כֹּל (*all*), or by reduplication of the noun, as "*by morning, by morning,*" for "*every morning.*" *Indefinite.—Any one* is expressed by אָדָם or אִישׁ (*man*), and *any thing* by כָּל־דָּבָר.

The Noun: 1. *Its adjectival use.*—Substantives are extensively used in Hebrew for adjectives. Thus, for *silver vessels* the Hebrew has *vessels of silver,* for *holy mountain* it has *mountain of holiness.* Sometimes the qualifying substantive is in the construct state, instead of the dependent; thus for *thy choice valleys* we have *the choice of thy valleys.* Many adjectives signifying attribute or habit are expressed in Hebrew by a circumlocution, through the use of such words as אִישׁ, *man;* בַּעַל, *master;* בֵּן, *son;* and בַּת, *daughter;* as בֶּן־חַיִל, *son of valour,* for *valiant.* בַּעַל שֵׂעָר, *master of hair,* for *hairy.* 2. *Number.—*..ames of materials, liquids, metals, &c., have no plural, and some retain the form of the singular, though the sense is plural, as בָּקָר, *oxen,* a whole class being denoted. Many words are plural in Hebrew which are singular in other languages, such as the words for *life, youth, old age, heaven, height,* &c., and especially those expressing the ideas of God or Lord. The word אֱלֹהִים, *God,* though plural, commonly takes verbs and adjective words in the singular. Plurality, as well as distribution (see *Distributive Pronoun*), is frequently expressed by the repetition of the noun. 3. *The construct state.*—Sometimes we meet with a succession of nouns, all of which are in the construct state, except the last. When the word in the construct state denotes an action, such as violence, the dependent noun may be either the subject or the object of the action. The construct state is sometimes used when the word following is not in a dependent position like a genitive, but has some preposition attached, such as לֹ or בֹּ, or a relative pronoun with a preposition understood. 4. *Cases.*—While the genitive case of a noun is represented by being dependent on another in the construct state, the dative is expressed by לֹ (*to*), the accusative often by אֶת, and the ablative by מִן (*from*), בֹּ (*in*), or עִם (*with*). The accusative is sometimes used to denote the object to a verb, and sometimes adverbially.

Adjectives.—The adjective generally goes after the noun in Hebrew, and agrees with it in gender and number, except when it is dual, in which case the adjective is plural. When the noun is definite, the adjective takes the article. An adjective used predicatively often stands before the noun; it is undeclined, and has no article. An adjective in Hebrew may be accompanied by a substantive to limit its application, as *sorrowful in spirit,* in which case the adjective is in the construct state. Some few adjectives, as expressing some characteristic quality, are used for proper nouns, as אַבִּיר, *Mighty,* for *God;* לְבָנָה, *pale,* for *moon* (see Noun—*Its adjectival use*). *Degrees of comparison.*—The comparative is expressed by מִן between the adjective and the thing compared. Thus "sweeter than honey" is expressed by "sweet away from (*i.e.* in comparison with) honey," and "taller than any of the people" by "tall away from all the people." The superlative is expressed by the positive with the article, as הַקָּטֹן, *the small,* i.e., *the least,* and by such a construction as "holy of holies."

Numerals.—Numerals from 2 to 10 are construed with nouns in three different ways—in the construct state before the noun, in apposition before it, and in apposition after it. These almost always take the plural, but those from 20 to 90 take the noun in the singular when they precede it, and in the plural when they follow it.

The Verb—*The Tenses.*—As there are at the most only two tenses in Hebrew—a Preterite, and a Future—they are necessarily used to express various time relations. *a. The Preterite.*—This is used not only to express absolutely past time, including the pluperfect, but also both present and future—the present when the action or state is permanent or habitual, and the future in protestations or promises viewed as fixed and certain of fulfilment, as also when it is connected with a preceding future by וֹ. It has even the force of an imperative when an imperative precedes. *b. The Future.*—The future, when used simply, expresses not only future time, but also the present, in connection with general truths or what is abiding or customary; and the past with particles of time, such as אָז, *then,* when the action is continued. It is also used for the subjunctive after particles, such as *that, that not;* for the optative, the negative imperative, and occasionally the potential mood expressed by *may* or *can.* By means of *Vav conversive,* the future is so connected with what precedes that the time becomes that of the general narration. Its simplest use is to continue a narration, and so strongly is the idea of past time impressed upon the form that a historical narration may even commence with a converted future. The fut. with וֹ strongly marks the consecution of events, so that after *because* it is equal to *therefore* (see "Hebrew Manual," p. 105).

The Moods. — The *Imperative* not only commands, but also entreats and permits. When one imperative succeeds another, coupled by וְ, a strong promise is implied, as in "Do this and live." The *Infinitive Absolute* is used as an accusative after a verb, as an adverb along with a finite mood to give emphasis to it, as "charging he charged," for "he straitly charged," and sometimes for a finite verb. The *Infinitive Construct* is used as a verbal substantive, and may stand as the subject of a sentence, in the gen. after a noun or preposition, or as the accusative after a verb. As in the construct state it may have a noun or pronoun dependent on it. The *Participle* expresses generally present time, though sometimes also past and future; thus נֹפֵל not only means "falling" but "having fallen," "about to fall." It may take the place of the predicate like a finite verb, and represent past and future as well as present. The passive participles may have the force of the Latin participle in *dus*, like metuendus, *to be feared.* An active participle may govern the acc. like a verb, or the gen. like a noun.

Government of Verbs.—Most transitives take an acc. after them, and many which in other languages are intransitive, as if the preposition expressed in these languages were implied in the Hebrew instances. Verbs of this kind are such as those of clothing or unclothing, fulness or want, dwelling, and coming or going. Verbs in Hiphil, as also in Piel, when used causatively, take two accusatives in the case in which Kal takes one, as even verbs in Kal do with a causative meaning. The *Passive Voice.*—The agent after the passive most frequently takes the preposition לְ, sometimes מִן and sometimes בְ, while the instrument is found expressed by a noun put absolutely.

Subject and Predicate.—The verb *to be* as connecting subject and predicate is usually omitted. The predicate, whether verb, substantive, adjective, or pronoun, agrees with the subject in gender and number. From this rule, however, there are numerous exceptions, of which the following may be noticed: collectives commonly take the plural; plurals denoting animals or things often take fem. sing.; the predicate when it stands at the beginning of a sentence is generally in mas. sing.; when the subject has a dependent gen. the verb sometimes conforms to the latter.

Particles.—Of these there is room to say little. *Adverbs.*—These qualify sentences and even words, like adjectives. When repeated they denote intensity and continued accession. Two negatives do not destroy one another, and one at the beginning negatives all the succeeding clauses coupled by וְ, *and. Prepositions.*—A preposition often affects a succession of words coupled by וְ. It is sometimes omitted, especially בְ. *Conjunctions.* —Of these וְ is the chief, and it is used as expressing various links of connexion, such e.g. as is indicated by *even, therefore,* and *because.*

Note.—For further study of Hebrew the student is recommended to the "Hebrew Student's Manual," which contains a Grammar, Lexicon, Reading Lessons, and an Article on Pronunciation; "The Analytical Hebrew Lexicon;" "Gesenius' Hebrew Grammar;" and "Gesenius' Hebrew Lexicon," all published by Messrs. Bagster.

245

GENERAL INDEX